SENTENCING AND PUNISHMENT

SENTENCING AND PUNISHMENT

The Quest for Justice

Fourth Edition

SUSAN EASTON

AND

CHRISTINE PIPER

OXFORD

UNIVERSITY PRESS

OXFORD

UNIVERSITY PRESS

Great Clarendon Street, Oxford, OX2 6DP,
United Kingdom

Oxford University Press is a department of the University of Oxford.
It furthers the University's objective of excellence in research, scholarship,
and education by publishing worldwide. Oxford is a registered trade mark of
Oxford University Press in the UK and in certain other countries

First edition 2005
Second edition 2008
Third edition 2012

Impression: 1

Published in the United States of America by Oxford University Press
198 Madison Avenue, New York, NY 10016, United States of America

British Library Cataloguing in Publication Data
Data available

Library of Congress Control Number: 2016940838

ISBN 978–0–19–874482–5

Printed in Great Britain by
Bell & Bain Ltd, Glasgow

Outline Contents

Detailed Contents

Part A Sentencing Principles, Policies and Issues

Part B Punishing Offenders

Preface

The paintings on the cover of this and previous editions are reflective of issues to which we wish to draw attention. The message we wanted to convey when we used Vincent van Gogh's famous picture *The Round of Prisoners* on the cover of the second edition was that the 'warehousing' of offenders without adequate rehabilitation is as pointless as prisoners walking aimlessly in a circle in the exercise yard at Newgate Prison. The cover of the third edition was of a prison hulk and prisoners at work in Woolwich in 1777 and highlighted the problem of prison overcrowding at a time of prison expansion, the difficulty of providing constructive activities for prisoners in that context, and the potential contribution of prison labour to rehabilitation. We are, therefore, pleased that more attention is now being paid to the issues of work, education, and rehabilitation in prison.

For the cover of this edition we have selected an abstract, symbolic work by Paul Klee, *Rose Garden*. We thought the representation of castles, triangles, and roses and the use of bold colours epitomised several themes in this edition of our book. The castle/fortress, a place of confinement, represented in the painting with variations of the patterns of the building blocks, reflects the diversity of the population being punished. The need for penal policy and practice development to take account of the different backgrounds and experiences of those whom the state punishes, especially prisoners—both adults and children—is a theme in several chapters of this book. At the same time, Klee's use of strong colours and geometric shapes, together with the imagery of the garden and the motif of the roses, suggest more positive themes and the potential for change and development. Likewise, the use of triangles which draw the eye upwards can perhaps be seen as a metaphor for enlightenment, with its connotations of transformation and greater understanding or clarification. We hope that during the lifetime of this edition there will be renewed emphasis on the potential of prison to bring about change, rather than simply to contain or confine, and that the initiatives to transform community punishment do lead to more offender rehabilitation and reintegration.

This edition has involved substantial rewriting, as we note in 'New to this Edition'. For example, it covers the revised regime for sentencing the dangerous offender, noting parallels with earlier developments, but drawing attention to the latest 'danger'—those who commit terrorist offences. In Chapters 6 and 7 we bring together diverse material to shed light on new and old issues. In Chapter 6 we consider the extent to which restorative justice, principles of child welfare, and being mentally disordered do lead to approaches which are alternatives to punishment; in Chapter 7 we bring together material relating to both the offender and the victim in relation to the impact of the crime and/or the punishment on both. In several chapters, this edition stresses the continuing and important influence of human rights law and jurisprudence to influence sentencing and punishment in positive ways, but also reveals the tensions and limits, notably in Chapter 8 where we consider prisoners' voting rights and in Chapter 11 where we consider the conditions for minors in detention.

As in the previous editions, we have had to make difficult choices as to what to include and what to delete. Much has had to be omitted but we have referred readers in this book and in the Online Resource Centre pages to sources of further information and discussion.

We have taught and researched together for many years and are fortunate in being able to bring to bear on our material a variety of approaches. When we planned this book 12 years ago the structure was guided by our commitment to bringing together penal theory, penal policy, and sentencing law and practice. We continue to synthesise these elements—rather than addressing them separately—in this fourth edition, because without an overview of how policy develops and without a knowledge of the justifications for punishment it is not possible to evaluate adequately the concept of justice as it operates in sentencing and punishment. Our overarching concern in this edition is still to explore ideas on what a just system of sentencing and punishment should look like. Our subtitle—'The Quest for Justice'—may, as we admitted in the Preface to the last edition, evoke unwanted images from cinema blockbusters, but how we make sentencing decisions and how we punish offenders affects real lives, real families, and real communities. So we have emphasised the importance of keeping in mind the purposes of punishment and the need to ensure that punishment is just as well as cost-effective.

We began the first edition of this book with the following statement: 'Sentencing and punishment are currently high profile policy issues: proposals for new procedures, criteria and punishments make headline news and generate debate at all levels of public and social life. This policy area is also complex and volatile: legislative change is frequent and recurring, and issues of criminal justice practice and administration are continually in the public domain.' Unfortunately for us, as authors, these points are still relevant, but we have endeavoured to ensure that the law and policy are up to date at 30 November 2015.

We would like to thank the editorial staff, particularly Joanna Ramsay and Emily Spicer, as well as the production staff and the cover design team at Oxford University Press for their support. We have also benefited from the comments of reviewers and readers of the third edition. As always, we would also like to thank our families for their forbearance during the period we have been working on this book, but at least this time Christmas is not in jeopardy.

Susan Easton
Christine Piper
November 2015

New to this edition

- Highlights throughout the book, but particularly in Chapter 1, the changes and continuities in penal and sentencing policy over the last two decades, with a focus on the previous Coalition government and the current Conservative government.
- Includes more discussion of sentencing guidelines and their approach.
- Takes account of the impact of the relevant sentencing provisions in force since the last edition, notably in the Legal Aid, Sentencing and Punishment of Offenders Act 2012, the Crime and Courts Act 2013, the Anti-social Behaviour, Crime and Policing Act 2014, the Offender Rehabilitation Act 2014, the Criminal Justice and Courts Act 2015 and the Serious Crime Act 2015.
- Reviews the continuing influence of human rights law and jurisprudence on sentencing and punishment and the tensions which have arisen from this.
- Has two new chapters—'Instead of punishment?' and 'Impact on victims and offenders'—to bring together different, yet linked, areas of sentencing law and practice in order to provide new perspectives.
- Has restructured chapters on community punishment and young offenders in order to focus on recent developments, including the impact of cuts in spending on the provision of services, the privatisation of the delivery of community penalties and the 'rehabilitation revolution' in Chapter 10 and, in Chapter 11, the decreased use of custody but the continuance of aspects of detention which are of grave concern.
- Includes more material on the impact of the Equality Act 2010 on the treatment of different groups within the prison population.
- Includes case studies—often a sentencing scenario—and discussion questions at the end of each chapter. Guidance is given in the Online Resource Centre.

Acknowledgements

Grateful acknowledgement is made to all the authors and publishers of copyright material that appears in this book, and in particular to the following for permission to reprint material from the sources indicated:

Extracts from Crown Copyright material are reproduced under Class Licence Number C01P000148 with the permission of the Controller of HMSO and the Queen's Printer for Scotland.

Council of Europe for Table 1.3 'Breakdown (in percentages) of persons serving CSM or being under probation (STOCK) on 31 December 2013' in Aebi, M. and Chopin, J., *Council of Europe Annual Penal Statistics—SPACE II Survey Persons serving Non-Custodial Sanctions and Measures in 2013*, PC-CP (2014) 12, Council of Europe. © Council of Europe.

Mennonite Central Committee for Appendix: 'Paradigms of Justice Old and New' in Zehr, H., 'Retributive Justice, Restorative Justice', *New Perspectives in Crime and Justice*, Vol 4 (MCC Office of Crime & Justice, 1985).

NACRO for Chart: 'Sentences under section 91 (1980–2005)' in *Youth Crime Briefing: Grave Crimes, Mode of Trial and Long Term Detention* (NACRO 2007).

Prison Reform Trust for Figure 1, 'Total under 18s in custody 2000–1 to 2010–11 against DTO, remand and long sentences 2005–6 to 2010–11', in Allen, R., *Last Resort? Exploring the Reduction in Child Imprisonment 2008–11* (Prison Reform Trust, 2011) and Table 2.1. 'Type of custodial sentence received' in Jacobson, J., Bhardwa, B., Gyateng, T., Hunter, G. and Hough, M., *Punishing Disadvantage, A Profile of Children in Custody* (Prison Reform Trust, 2010).

Every effort has been made to trace and contact copyright holders prior to going to press, but if notified, the publisher will undertake to rectify any errors or omissions at the earliest opportunity.

Glossary

Key terms included within the Glossary are highlighted in **bold** at the first mention in a chapter to emphasise their importance in this book.

Anchoring point the level at which punishment is set.

Attorney General the principal law officer of the Crown who is responsible for the Crown Prosecution Service.

Benchmarking in the prison context refers to identifying the most efficient ways of working and then applying them across the prison estate, with separate benchmarks for each type of prison and prisoner.

Bifurcation, bifurcationary in relation to youth justice denote a two-pronged policy whereby the majority of offenders are diverted from prosecution and the minority are prosecuted and punished.

Cardinal proportionality non-relative proportionality where the overall level of punishment is addressed.

Censure the process of public denunciation and reproof of an offender's criminal behaviour.

Contestability the opening up of the market to new providers of goods and services, for example from the voluntary sector as well as the private sector.

Culpability blameworthiness in relation to criminal wrongdoing.

Defendant the person or company who is charged with a crime in a criminal prosecution or the party sued in a civil lawsuit.

Deterrence using punishment to deter the general public from offending (general deterrence) or to deter offenders from reoffending (special or individual deterrence).

Discretion the power of the sentencer or other official to make a choice of processes or outcomes available.

Doli incapax a Latin phrase meaning 'incapable of wrong'. Currently this refers to children under ten years of age in English law.

Early release means release from the custodial part of a prison sentence before the end of the term specified by the court for the whole sentence.

Felony formerly (until 1967) an offence more serious than a misdemeanour.

Fixed penalty a financial penalty which can be imposed by the police and other specified bodies for a range of offences.

Governance has different meanings in different contexts. Refers generally to the exercise of power more widely than that covered by the term 'government'.

Incapacitation preventing reoffending by removing offenders from society through the death penalty, imprisonment, or other means.

Indeterminate sentence a prison sentence which does not have a fixed length, although a minimum term to be served in custody is specified by the court.

Indictable offence an offence that may be tried on indictment, that is, by jury in the Crown Court. Some indictable offences are triable either way.

Just deserts the term used to refer to punishment calculated in relation to the culpability of the offender. It is an outcome justified on retributivist principles.

Less eligibility the principle, developed originally in relation to the Poor Law, that conditions inside prison must be worse than outside prison for the deterrent effect to operate.

Mentally disordered offender the term used to refer to offenders who have been categorised as such under s. 1 of the Mental Health Act 1983.

Misdemeanour formerly (before 1967) any of the less serious offences.

Moral panic a term used to denote a theory developed to explain the way an incident triggers a generalised and disproportionate public concern about a social issue or penal policy.

New Managerialism using strategies and techniques from the private sector in the management of punishment in the public sector, focusing on the most efficient use of resources, for example, using Key Performance Targets, Key Performance Indicators, and league tables.

New Penology an approach which is concerned with risk management, using actuarial data to predict and manage risk, and which focuses on categories of offenders rather than individuals.

Normalisation in the context of imprisonment, using the same standards in prison which are applied to the lives of offenders in the community as far as possible, within the constraints required by imprisonment, so that prisoners are able to lead as normal lives as possible apart from their loss of liberty.

OASys the system used by probation and prison services for assessing the risks and needs of an offender.

Ordinal proportionality an amount of punishment which is proportionate to culpability in terms of parity between offenders committing offences of similar gravity, and such that the relative severity of punishment reflects the seriousness-ranking of offences.

Outsourcing the management technique of tendering part of an organisation's work or services to an external provider.

Paramountcy principle the legal principle that the welfare of the child—the best interests of the child—shall be paramount, the determining factor, in the making of decisions about the child's upbringing.

Parsimony principle using the most economical means of punishment, to impose the least severe punishment necessary to achieve the objective of crime reduction.

Populist punitiveness the increased punitiveness of governments to attract public support.

Prisonisation the forms of adaptation of individuals and groups to prison life.

Privatisation the transfer of state functions or services to the private sector.

Protective sentencing sentencing with the aim of reducing the likelihood that the offender will cause harm to the public by offending in the future. The form such public protection takes may be incapacitation through imprisonment.

Prudential disincentive a penalty which is designed to deter an individual from offending.

Quantum the amount of money awarded as compensation or imposed as punishment.

Racism exclusionary practices based on assumptions about racial hierarchies, which see the qualities of social groups as fixed.

Rehabilitative ideal using treatment and training in custody or in the community to rehabilitate individuals so that they can contribute to society.

Restorative justice an approach to crime and disorder which focuses on the restoration of harmony between the victim, the offender, and the community.

Retributivism the theory of punishment which links punishment to the desert of the individual and which matches the severity of the punishment to the seriousness of the crime.

Ring-fencing specifying a proportion of a budget which can be used only for particular purposes.

Sentencing Guideline the guidance issued by the Sentencing Council (and the previous Sentencing Guidelines Council) in the form of Definitive Guidelines for use by all criminal courts.

Summary offences offences that can only be tried before magistrates. Most minor offences are summary offences.

Three strikes laws mandatory minimum sentencing schemes in the United States aimed at repeat offenders where the third sentence mandates 25 years to life in prison.

Utilitarian theories of punishment the use of punishment to reduce or prevent crime through deterrence, incapacitation, and rehabilitation.

Utilitarianism a philosophical approach which sees individuals as motivated by the pursuit of pleasure and avoidance of pain and uses this to devise policies which maximise the greatest happiness of the greatest number.

Welfare principles the principles which inform or direct decision-making by the courts or public bodies in relation to the upbringing of children and young people under 18 years of age. The **paramountcy principle** is one such principle.

Youth offending teams (YOTs) are the inter-agency bodies set up by local authorities as a result of s. 39 of the Crime and Disorder Act 1998 and have a variety of functions.

Table of Statutes

Table of Cases

Table of European Legislation

Table of International Treaties and Conventions

PART A

Sentencing Principles, Policies and Issues

SUMMARY

In this first part of *Sentencing and Punishment* we consider a range of issues relating to the principles which govern the law and practice of sentencing in England and Wales. We also review the development of policies in regard to sentencing and punishment. So Chapter 1 focuses on the various influences on penal and sentencing policy and summarises recent policy developments. Chapters 2 and 3 cover the retributivist justification for punishment, the ways in which sentencing discretion is structured, and the resulting sentencing framework. Chapters 4 and 5 focus on the utilitarian justifications of deterrence and incapacitation respectively, covering also the relevant sentencing law and policy, notably in relation to dangerous offenders in Chapter 5. Chapters 6 and 7 bring together different yet linked areas of sentencing law and practice. Chapter 6 reviews those areas of law and practice which might be viewed as non-punitive: the diversion of young offenders from the courts, the treatment orders for the mentally ill offender, and the use of restorative justice processes. Chapter 7 focuses on different aspects of the impact of the crime and sentence on the offender and the victim, covering issues such as the available court-based remedies for the victim and the role of personal mitigation in sentencing.

PART 2
Sentencing Principles, Policies and Issues

SUMMARY

1

Developing penal policy

SUMMARY

This chapter focuses on key questions in penal policy including justice, risk, and human rights. It also considers the principal factors which shape the development of penal policy, notably political imperatives, economic influences, and penological and criminological principles, as well as public opinion and the media, which have become much more influential since the early 1990s. We discuss recent penal policy developments to highlight significant trends and problems. We conclude the chapter by focusing on the **governance** of sex offenders and providing a case study and discussion questions for reflection on the issues.

1.1 Key issues

1.1.1 Our approach

The subtitle of this book is 'The Quest for Justice' and this will be a recurring theme again in this fourth edition. But 'justice' is a taken-for-granted word and symbols of justice—the even-handed figure with the scales, the 'avenging angel' of Miss Marple in Agatha Christie's *Nemesis*, the wise Judge Solomon—suggest justice is meted out above the everyday ambiguities and complexities of life. Yet in practice justice is inextricably linked with money, particularly now with austerity budgets and value-for-money contracts, and other variables which influence what is deemed to be justice are not independent and can be influenced by a variety of factors. For example, the selection of agreed justifying principles or decisions as to what counts as serious or dangerous are problematic processes contingent on time and place.

Our approach, then, is to identify what counts as 'justice' in the context of sentencing and punishment, and why. We will examine the ways in which Parliament, judges, and magistrates and criminal justice professionals seek to justify, impose, and implement policies which convey particular answers to these fundamental questions about sentencing and punishment. So we are not concerned only with what 'the law' says about sentencing and punishment, but with why the law has developed and whether it can be justified on the philosophical principles underpinning punishment. We are also concerned with what happens when the sentencing outcomes are put into practice: what is the experience of punishment like, what issues do these various penalties raise, do they achieve their intended results?

To understand how the state punishes, we will consider the relevant sentencing law, the policy guidelines, professional guidance, including national standards, and what we know about their implementation. Our interest lies not simply in 'how much' punishment, but also in wider questions on the range and types of punishment. In scrutinising why we punish we will discuss the 'answers' in two ways: first by analysing the political, policy, and pragmatic reasons and second by focusing on penology—the study of the reasons and justifications underpinning the practice of state punishment. These two questions, the how and why, are linked. The policy reasons or penological justifications for state punishment may determine how the offender is treated. For this reason, we will integrate discussion of policy and theory with analysis of sentencing law or punishment practice.

This chapter begins this project by reviewing key issues and concepts in penal policy and the major factors which influence its development. Chapter 1 will also look at the emergence of risk-based and rights-based penologies and will explore some of the issues this raises in relation to recent sex offender legislation. A case study exercise is provided at the end of the chapter, the aim of which is to encourage reflection on the practical outcomes which flow from adherence to one or other justification. Chapter 1 will look only briefly at penological theories; Chapters 2 and 3 will consider in more detail one of the classical justifications for punishment, **retributivism**, while Chapters 4, 5, and 10 will focus on **deterrence**, risk management, and **rehabilitation**, which reflect the other main justification of punishment, namely **utilitarianism**. Chapter 6 will review **restorative justice**.

The first key issue we discuss—in section 1.1.2—is one which underpins all the discussions in this book, namely punishment itself. This is not a straightforward concept and so we first need to consider what is meant by punishment.

1.1.2 **What is punishment?**

Punishment may, or will, involve pain or suffering but it can be distinguished from other forms of suffering, such as a painful treatment for a medical condition, where the harm is not an expression of moral condemnation, and not a response to our misdeeds. Punishment rests on moral reasons, the expression of moral condemnation, in response to rule infringements. Indeed, Feinberg (1994) refers to **censure** or condemnation as the defining feature of punishment. What distinguishes punishment, says Feinberg, is its expressive function: 'punishment is a conventional device for the expression of attitudes of resentment and indignation . . . Punishment, in short, has a *symbolic significance* largely missing from other kinds of penalties' (Feinberg 1994: 73). So, for example, a penalty in football is not comparable to imprisonment in terms of public reprobation. Punishment is 'a symbolic way of getting back at the criminal, of expressing a kind of vindictive resentment' (ibid: 76). Condemnation or denunciation, he says, conjoins resentment and reprobation.

The criminal law distinguishes between regulating and punitive statutes, often imposing strict liability in the former case. But in practice the line between regulation and punishment may not be so clear-cut, which can cause problems. For example, in the United States there are constitutional safeguards for those facing punishment which are not available if the measure is construed as a regulatory activity. So if a repressive act is defined as non-punitive, then the individual will be in a worse position. Similarly, in European Convention jurisprudence there are arguments about what constitutes punishment in relation to Article 7 of the European Convention on Human Rights. In *Gough v Chief Constable of Derbyshire* (2001), for example, the court held that a football banning order was not a penalty for the purposes of Article 7. Likewise, the European Commission of Human Rights held that the sex offenders' registration scheme did not constitute a penalty in *Ibbotson v UK* (1999). A similar approach was taken by the House of Lords in relation to anti-social behaviour orders (ASBOs) in *R (McCann)* [2003], where their Lordships held that an application for an ASBO was a civil and not a criminal matter as they are designed to prevent behaviour rather than to punish, do not appear on criminal records, and do not immediately entail imprisonment. Similarly, serious crime prevention orders imposed under the terms of the Serious Crime Act 2007 which may impose prohibitions, restrictions, or other requirements, as civil orders, are deemed not to be punitive and therefore do not breach the prohibition on retrospective punishment in Article 7.

A key feature of punishment is that it rests on a moral foundation, expressing a moral judgement. It is reflective and based on reasons. A further distinguishing feature of punishment is that it stems from an authoritative source, usually the state. Suffering consequent upon misdeeds is not punishment unless those who inflict it have authority over the offender. If we imagine that a murderer chased by the police crashes his car and dies before he can be tried, he has not suffered punishment but escaped it, even if the outcome is more severe than that which might have been afforded by the criminal justice system. A person participating in an illegal cockfight in California died in 2011 when he was stabbed by a rooster with a blade attached to its leg, and in a similar incident in India a person had his throat cut by a bladed cockerel. In Indonesia in 2011 a man who went on holiday and left his dogs for 14 days without food or water was eaten by them on his return. We may conceive of this misfortune as 'God's punishment', but we are still conceiving of punishment as derived from a higher power.

Although our focus in this book will be on state punishment, of course punishment may also be informal in so far as it is imposed outside the formal criminal justice system. Informal justice developed as an alternative to state-centred methods of dispute resolution as the parties sought to recapture conflicts from professionals (see Christie 1977, 2010; Abel 1982; Matthews 1988; and Chapter 6). An extreme form of informal justice would be vigilantism, and state punishment is usually seen as a necessary means of avoiding the excesses of unrestrained popular justice, by satisfying the public's demands for punishment and preventing vigilantism. In the UK punishment is also, as we shall see, increasingly outsourced to agencies independent of the state.

1.1.3 Understanding penal policy

The question of why some acts are criminalised and not others, and why society deals harshly with some wrongdoings but lightly with others, is much debated in criminology. But when we consider this in relation to penal policy, a fundamental issue is why punishment is seen as an appropriate response to a specific event or mode of behaviour. This entails asking three questions:

- First: what particular response is made and why?
- Second: if the response is penal, which particular penal option is selected?
- Third: what is the particular level of penal response?

These three dimensions of penal policy—what to punish, how to punish, and how much to punish—will shape policy outcomes, and while this book will focus principally on the last two questions, the first is still important as it sets the scene for the latter two elements.

In looking at the first question, we might ask why the response is punitive, rather than taking some other form, such as social assistance or a medical response. The offender might be seen as a wicked person who should be punished, or as a sick person requiring treatment, or as an inadequate individual whose criminality is the result of social deprivation and who needs social welfare support to address that problem, as well as appropriate crime-prevention strategies. So, in some societies, such as the former Soviet Union and modern China and Uzbekistan, political dissidence may be met with a medical response, using incarceration through 'judicial psychiatry' to detain dissidents in a psychiatric hospital.[1]

---

[1] http://www.hrw.org/en/news/2005/09/02/uzbekistan-dissident-forced-psychiatric-detention.

Drug therapies such as Ritalin may also be used to control the unruly behaviour of children and these are widely used in the United States and the UK. Experiments on the effect of vitamin supplements have also been conducted on young offenders at Aylesbury Young Offenders' Institution in England, with positive results on behaviour in that the group receiving vitamins committed fewer disciplinary offences than the group given placebos (Gesch *et al.* 2002; see also Benton 2007). The developing science of neurocriminology also draws on research on neurodevelopment to understand and treat anti-social behaviour (Ross and Hilborn 2007) and violence (Raine 2013). The potential and problems of neuroscience are highlighted by Walsh (2011) in relation to youth justice and by Glenn and Raine (2014).

So the punitive response is only one of several possibilities and each response will rest on a particular model of human behaviour. In practice we may find a combination of policies and strategies, depending on the type of offence and offender and on the political climate. Political pressures may also shift the reaction to crime and disorder from a penal response to a military response. Examples of this approach would be the use of troops to deal with sectarian conflict and disorder in Northern Ireland and in response to strikes in the UK, and of course, in more recent years, military responses have dominated the fight by the United States against terrorist-related crime.

However, it is conceivable that, in other contexts, pressures on governments might engender a move away from penal and punitive responses to a welfarist response, seeking to address problems in communities by supporting disadvantaged groups and promoting social inclusion. So we may find a variety of strategies depending in part on pressures on governments. In France transformational social therapy has been used to address disorder and riots in the *banlieues*, although with limited success (see Jobard 2009). So when considering the reasons why some harm-generating activities are controlled by criminal law and sanctions and others are not, economic factors may be significant (see Bowles *et al.* 2008).

Secondly, in terms of the particular type of response made through penal policy, a number of options may be available, from educational programmes, such as driver education or anger management, through to extreme punishments used in other societies, such as amputation, castration, and execution. Thirdly, in reviewing penal policy, we should consider the level of response via penal policy, in other words, how long is the sentence of imprisonment, how heavy is the fine, and how firmly is the response enforced.

1.1.4 Equality, fairness, and justice

Understanding penal policy also requires a focus on equality and fairness, particularly if some groups are selected for harsher punishment or if apparently neutral policies have differential impact. The concern with equality of impact in the late 1980s and the 1990s focused on disparities in sentencing, as well as on direct and indirect discrimination. This was also reflected in changes in the criminal law itself; for example, the Criminal Justice Act (CJA) 1991 made racial motivation an aggravating factor in assaults, and s. 95 of the same Act imposed a duty on the Secretary of State to publish information considered expedient to enable those involved in the administration of criminal justice to avoid discriminating against any person on the ground of race, sex, or any other improper ground (see Chapter 9). The Equality Act 2010 imposes on public bodies, including prisons, a duty to eliminate discrimination and to promote equality, and broadens the range of protected characteristics (see Chapter 9, section 9.1.1).

The principle of equality has also entered penal policy debates on the impact of apparently equal punishments imposed on individuals who are not equal. Examples of potentially unjust punishments would include fines which are unrelated to means, or punishments which impact adversely on people with particular medical conditions, for example those offenders who are mentally disordered (see Chapter 6, section 6.4). Policies may also indirectly discriminate against certain groups, such as women with children, or directly discriminate if there are problems of bias in the imposition of punishment (see Chapter 9).

Of course the notion of justice is not clear-cut: like 'rights', justice is a slippery concept which has been used by both right and left to embody aspirations and to legitimise policies. Justice was stressed by the Woolf Report (Woolf and Tumim 1991) as one of the key principles which should govern the treatment of prisoners (see Chapter 8). A sense of injustice, it argued, was an important contributory factor in the prison riots of 1990. 'Justice' was also a key strand of New Labour penal policy, expressed in the White Paper *Justice for All* (Home Office 2002c), which said the government's aim was to 'narrow the justice gap', by which it meant reducing the gap between the number of crimes reported to the police and the number of offenders brought to justice. *Rebalancing the Criminal Justice System in Favour of the Law-Abiding Majority* (Home Office 2006a) stressed that people want to see the system 'delivering justice—with fairer sentencing and fewer occasions when the system seems to let the offender off the hook' (ibid: para 2.2). The Home Office has described its role as 'supporting the efficient and effective delivery of justice' (Home Office 2008: 2).

The House of Commons Justice Committee (2010) in its report *Cutting Crime: The Case for Justice Reinvestment* emphasised the value of using 'justice reinvestment' approaches, that is, channelling resources on a geographically targeted basis to reduce the crime which brings people into the criminal justice system. Justice reinvestment was an idea developed in the United States by the George Soros Open Society Institute and refers to the aim of reducing the funds expended on imprisonment and redirecting some of those funds to the communities adversely affected by high levels of incarceration (see also Allen and Stern 2007; Allen 2014). In the UK incentives have been used in youth justice, for example, to encourage greater use of interventions to reduce the use of youth custody for 10–17-year-olds (see Wong *et al.* 2015). The Coalition government also argued for more efficient and effective justice for communities and 'giving communities better information about how justice is delivered, making services more responsive and accountable to the public' (Ministry of Justice 2010a: para 46).

Justice embodies notions of fairness to all members of the community, including victims and offenders, and striking a balance between their competing interests is the cornerstone of current criminal justice policy. But it also assumes a consensus on what constitutes justice, and achieving justice in terms of improving conviction rates, for example, may create injustice for particular individuals or groups. What is construed as fair treatment means different things in different theories of social justice,[2] but its construction also depends on how punishment is rationalised in the different theories of punishment which moral philosophers, penologists, and criminologists have developed, notably the classical theories of retributivism and utilitarianism. By retributivism is meant the approach which links punishment according to the desert or **culpability** of the individual and which matches the severity of the punishment to the seriousness of the crime and the culpability of the offender. By utilitarianism is meant the approach which sees individuals as motivated by the pursuit of pleasure and avoidance of pain and uses this to devise social and penal policies to promote the greatest happiness of

---

[2] For discussions of notions of justice see, for example, the following texts: Campbell (2010) and Rawls (1971) for a liberal concept of justice; for discussion of feminist concepts of justice see Rhode (1989), Heidensohn (2006), and Satz and Reich (2009). For an individualist approach, see Nozick (1974) and for a range of perspectives on justice see Knight and Stemplowska (eds) 2014.

the greatest number. Punishment, on this approach, is used to prevent offending and reoffending through deterrence, **incapacitation**, and rehabilitation.

Consequently, determining what constitutes the justice of a particular punishment requires a decision on the theory of punishment to be deployed: just punishment from a retributivist standpoint might seem unjust from a utilitarian perspective and vice versa. As we shall see later, preventive detention may be justifiable if the interests of the wider society are given priority over individual rights, but this raises problems for retributivism. Utilitarians and desert theorists also differ on the role that past convictions should play in determining the punishment for a current offence.

The dominant concept of justice may be only one of a number of key factors to consider in identifying the influences on modern penal policies: others might be ideologies, such as laissez-faire liberalism, which is essentially individualistic and construes society as a collection of egoistic individuals in which the state's role in economic and other spheres is minimal, and communitarianism, its opposite, which focuses on interdependence between citizens within the social framework, mutual obligations, trust, and group loyalty (Etzioni 1993, 2003, 2014). Other influences on penal policy which may be significant are political and economic factors and the role of public opinion. So a recurring theme in the following discussions will be the justice and injustice of punishment in the political and economic context in which decisions are made and policies formulated.

1.1.5 **Human rights**

Human rights have implications for both the theory and practice of punishment in justifying specific punishments, in assessing the justice of punishments, and in improving standards in penal institutions. Human rights instruments are, then, a key mechanism for achieving just punishment and rights are themselves an important element of many theories of punishment. For example, natural rights are a significant dimension of retributivist theory, which recognises the right of the offender to be treated with respect as an autonomous human being. Rights have therefore provided a launch pad to criticise the UK penal system which has been strongly influenced by utilitarianism, an approach which has been criticised for its failure to acknowledge the rights of the offender and for sacrificing the individual's rights for the wider public interest (see Chapter 4, section 4.4.3). Rights also have implications for issues such as the interviewing and detention of suspects before trial, the treatment of remand prisoners and the granting of bail, the defendant's right to a fair trial, the right to be presumed innocent, the treatment of witnesses, preventive detention, the right to be released when one's sentence is served, and the right not to be subject to unfair or discriminatory treatment. These principles may act as a control on judicial **discretion** and inhibit disparities in sentencing. Rights also extend to victims of crime and help shape policy on their role in the criminal process, and on their entitlement to redress. These issues will be considered further in subsequent chapters in relation to the principal justifications of punishment and to sentencing policy and practice.

Rights also have an important function in protecting prisoners from the excessive zeal of their keepers and, if prisoners retain fundamental rights as human beings while serving their sentences, this will help to ensure that they are treated with dignity (Easton 2011a, 2013, forthcoming). A system of punishment which respects human rights will have more legitimacy than one which rides roughshod over them, particularly as utilitarian arguments have failed to protect prisoners. Rights are therefore crucial to penal theory and practice and, while rights may be limited when rights are infringed, the state's justifications for doing so need to be interrogated. A rights standpoint is an important critical tool for assessing systems of punishment, providing a check on powerful regimes and on **populist punitiveness**. The term 'populist punitiveness', coined by Bottoms (1995), refers to the increased punitiveness of governments which they believe will appeal to the public and which has been used to justify increases in sentence severity.

For penal reformers, rights are seen as a way of achieving reform, although not all radical reformers share a commitment to a rights approach. Some Marxist theorists of law, who believe the rule of law may mask social injustice, are suspicious of rights because they are essentially individualist rather than collectivist, abstracting the individual from the historical and social context, and because they fail to deliver substantive justice (Easton 2008a; Boyd 2009).

There are, of course, problems in defining rights in jurisprudence. There is a huge body of literature with disagreement over what rights mean and what they entail, what should be included within their scope, and who possesses them. For Dworkin (1977), the right to equal concern and respect is paramount, while others have broadened their concern to include social rights and positive rights (Marshall 1950; Titmuss 1968; Búrca and de Witte 2005; Fredman 2008), and some see rights as a means of satisfying human needs (Campbell 1983). But they share a conception of fundamental rights as existing beyond positive law, that is, formal, black letter law in cases and statutes. Rights are entrenched and occupy a privileged position, protecting the individual from the state and protecting the weakest individuals from the majority. For Dworkin (1977, 1986, 2011), rights trump utility and, while rights may be limited if they conflict with competing rights, the circumstances in which this may occur are carefully drawn and more narrowly defined than on classical utilitarian models. Rights theorists argue that rights apply to all equally: even the worst offenders, such as war criminals, have procedural rights, for example, to take part in their trial and, when convicted, to non-degrading punishment. Because rights are universal they have a crucial role to play in the practice of punishment and apply to all offenders and ex-offenders: the mark of a civilised society is to respect the rights of all (see Easton 2009, 2011a). Due process rights have therefore been strongly protected in international criminal courts and tribunals prosecuting those accused of crimes against humanity (Fairlie 2013).

Rights have implications across the criminal justice system and at all stages of the criminal justice process,[3] but we will be particularly concerned with the impact of a rights jurisprudence on the experience of custody. Due process and substantive rights have implications for the treatment of prisoners. For example, prisoners can achieve fairer treatment in the context of disciplinary procedures and decision-making over issues such as segregation and transfers, but also in terms of substantive rights to food, exercise, and time unlocked (Easton 2011a). The European Convention on Human Rights had a considerable impact in improving prisoners' lives in the UK long before the Human Rights Act 1998 was passed. Following key decisions the UK has had to change secondary legislation, including the Prison Rules as well as Prison Service Orders, to comply with the European Court of Human Rights' judgments. However, while English judges have usually in the past followed the recommendations of the Strasbourg Court, in recent years they have been more willing to challenge the Court's findings and have entered into a dialogue with the Court. These issues will be considered in relation to imprisonment and prison policy in the UK in Chapter 8, section 8.6.

It has also meant that human rights compliance has itself become a risk for prison management, involving both organisational risks of intervention in prison management and

---

[3] For further discussion of the impact of rights across earlier stages of the criminal justice process, see Weber *et al.* 2014.

financial risks for the public as compensation may be paid to prisoners who succeed in establishing rights violations (Whitty 2011; Easton 2011a).

The jurisprudence of the European Court of Human Rights has remained an important influence on sentencing and penal policy. It has led to significant changes, for example, in the treatment of offenders in prison, with increasing weight being placed on the prisoner's right to life, his right to non-degrading treatment and punishment, and his procedural rights, and the move towards treating the prisoner as a citizen with rights and duties.

Rights have been given effect in a number of areas of prison life and it seems that future litigation on prison life will continue to be framed within the rights discourse of the European Convention. As we shall see, rights have been a significant influence on both the theory and practice of punishment in recent years and continue to provide a means of raising standards in the criminal justice process, particularly within the context of custody, and to provide a counter to demands for penal austerity.

However, since the third edition of the book, we have seen further criticism of the Human Rights Act 1998, and clashes between the Strasbourg Court and the UK government on the questions of whether prisoners should be given the vote, on the weight given to the right to family life in deportation decisions, and on the legitimacy of whole-life sentences. An independent Commission was set up to investigate the creation of a UK Bill of Rights and to advise on reform of the Strasbourg Court. Its report published at the end of 2012 recommended a UK Bill of Rights, albeit one which builds on the European Convention (Commission on a Bill of Rights 2012). We have also seen differences between the domestic courts and the Strasbourg Court, which have highlighted the contrast between common law and civil systems of law. Mindful of these criticisms, the Court has been more willing to allow states a margin of appreciation in implementing systems of sentencing and punishment. However, the Conservative party has indicated its willingness to withdraw from the Convention if its concerns are not fully addressed and the power of the Strasbourg Court's judgments is not reduced, and made clear its position in *Protecting Human Rights in the UK* in 2014 and in its election materials (Conservative Party 2014; Conservative Party 2015).

1.2 Key influences

What is seen as an appropriate response to crime—the type and level of response—may reflect political and ideological principles. Ideologies are chains of interrelated ideas, the principles underpinning penal policies. For example, laissez-faire liberal ideology, which was in the ascendant during the Thatcher period, has had an enduring resonance and is reflected in **New Managerialist** approaches to the criminal justice system, including the **privatisation** of prisons and the Probation Service and a concern with efficiency and economy of punishment. The role of New Right ideologies was revived by the 2010 Coalition government with a strong commitment to involvement of the private sector in the delivery of punishment and rehabilitation (Ministry of Justice 2010a, 2011a), a commitment continued by the Conservative government after the General Election in 2015. In contrast, welfarist ideologies have declined since the 1980s, although New Labour tried to chart a path, or 'Third Way', between them (see Giddens 1998, 2000).

1.2.1 Political imperatives

Debates on law and order and their corollary, crime and punishment, have dominated British politics since the 1970s. Moreover, in a deeper sense the crime question is inherently political in that questions of crime, law, and order raise fundamental questions about the relationship between the state and the citizen and the problem of how society can be held together in the face of internal social divisions and the fragmentation of individuals' self-interest,[4] as well as issues regarding how far the state may intervene to protect citizens from each other and from external threats. The political demand for social order has been seen as a key element in increases in incarceration (see de Koster *et al.* 2008). Failure to deal with law and order can be very damaging to governments, as illustrated by the riots in London and other UK cities in the summer of 2011, when the Coalition government was criticised for its failure to keep the streets safe and for the time taken to restore order.

Simon (2007) has argued that in the United States the war on crime has become a key element of governance, facilitated new forms of governance, and generated the growth of legislation to address the problem. Similar processes can be seen in the UK, with a substantial increase in legislation on crime and punishment since the 1990s.

The political dimension raises questions about power, including how much power a government has to implement policy. With a large majority in the House of Commons when it first came to power in 1997, the New Labour administration was in a strong position to enact its legislative programme, although it subsequently met opposition from the House of Lords on issues such as fox hunting and jury trial. The 2010 Coalition government was in a much weaker position, as the support of the Liberal Democrats was needed by the Conservatives even to form a government. During the Coalition government, this led to problems in achieving legislation which was satisfactory to either party. The current Conservative government has also found itself in a weak position, with opposition from the substantial number of Scottish Nationalists in tandem with other opposition groups as well as criticism from the House of Lords on key policies. But nonetheless, there is some consensus between the main political parties on law and order policies, and it is unlikely that a party would adopt a 'soft' policy on crime because of the perception that public opinion would be hostile (see section 1.2.3).

This is very clear in the debate over prisoners' right to vote, where all governments since 2005 have been reluctant to amend the law despite continuing pressure from the Strasbourg Court, for reasons of political expediency. It is also evident in the 2010 Coalition government's decision to abandon a proposed increase in the sentence discount for a guilty plea because of public hostility to the proposal. When the government indicated it was considering a reduction of 50 per cent for guilty pleas for offenders in *Breaking the Cycle* (Ministry of Justice 2010a), this met with outrage from the press, the public, and senior judges as well as many Conservative party members, who thought it would be too lenient and undermine public confidence in sentencing. Concern was intensified when the Justice Secretary Kenneth Clarke in a radio interview defended the reduction for rapists, suggesting that some rape cases were more serious than others. The proposal was abandoned in June 2011.

The furore over sentence discounts also highlights the difficulties facing the government when the political need to pursue policies and practices deemed by the public as legitimate conflicts with economic imperatives. Which priority 'wins' may depend on whether the policy would be implemented early or late in the government's term of office. Public opinion is a crucial pressure on the government at election time as parties try to capture floating voters, but may also be a significant force between elections at party conferences and in the constituencies. In the UK, Home Secretaries have been heckled at party conferences if

---

[4] This problem lies at the heart of social contract theory: see T. Hobbes' *Leviathan* (1651) and J.-J. Rousseau's *The Social Contract* (1743).

perceived to be weak on law and order, and crime has been a recurring key election issue and highlighted in party manifestos.

So political expediency may lead to the decision that it is not worth implementing an unpopular policy even if it saves money, or, conversely, a popular policy may be implemented despite imposing huge financial costs. An example of the latter would be the strong commitment of successive governments over the past 25 years to longer sentences and increased use of custody, resulting in expansion of the prison system—very expensive policies, but designed to show to the public that concerns on crime were being taken seriously.

On the other hand, a government may negotiate these conflicts by trying to formulate policies which appear to protect the public while reducing costs: an example would be risk management, which can reduce costs by focusing on those offences posing the highest risk of serious harm to the public. Certainly, since 1990 the key policy aim of public protection has been reflected in a series of measures including the 'longer than commensurate' sentence, the sentence of imprisonment for public protection (IPP), extended sentences, and the establishment of Multi-Agency Public Protection Arrangements (MAPPAs). There is a legal requirement on the police, Probation, and Prison Service in each of the police force areas of England and Wales to establish arrangements to assess and manage risks posed by sexual and violent offenders, to review and monitor these arrangements, and to publish annual reports.[5]

A government may find it is unable to relinquish a policy because it is so popular. For example, in the United States it may be politically damaging to retreat from the death penalty, when a large majority of the population support it and candidates try to exceed each other in their zealous commitment to it. Governor George Ryan of Illinois waited until he was retiring from office in January 2003 before commuting the death sentence for all 167 prisoners on Death Row in the state at that time. Yet, while the actions of governments can legitimise punitiveness by endorsing punitive policies including the death penalty, support for the penalty correlates with a wide range of variables (Unnever 2010). Local democratic political traditions may also play a key role, as Garland (2010) notes, as the structure of the American polity 'makes it difficult to abolish the death penalty in the face of majority public opinion and deprives governing elites of the opportunity for top-down, counter-majoritarian reform' (ibid: 310). The levels of public punitiveness and support for penal expansion in the United States also vary from state to state depending on local and state level institutional structures, as Barker (2009) illustrates in her study of divergent penal policies in California, Washington, and New York. As she argues,

> [T]he apparent link between public participation, punitiveness, and rough justice is not only historically contingent but dependent on specific state structures and patterns of civic engagement, patterns that tend to vary within the United States and across liberal democracies. Public vengeance depends on certain political institutions and collective agency to give it a legal and political expression.

> (Barker 2009: 11–12)

The structure of the polity may also be important in the UK, as Lacey (2008) has argued: neo-liberal market economies with first-past-the-post systems are more favourable to exclusionary penal policies and expanding prison populations than systems based on proportional representation, and issues of penal policy should be depoliticised to address the problem of prison expansion.

---

[5] For reviews and discussion of the work of MAPPAs, see Wood and Kemshall (2007), Ministry of Justice (2010f) and Ministry of Justice (2015e).

Powerful interest groups may also affect policy regardless of which government is in power, and in the UK the Police Federation and victim movements exert a strong influence, competing with those working with offenders such as NACRO and the Prison Reform Trust. The view that the balance has swung too far in favour of the defendant and away from victims and communities has been strongly expressed in recent policy documents (Ministry of Justice 2010a, 2011a). In that context the relative power of groups representing the public may be an important factor in policy initiatives.

One particular policy technique is that of diverting attention by blaming individuals for crime or demonising particular groups such as sex offenders (see section 1.6) in order to defuse hostility to the government over crime and disorder. There are also examples from the recent past of how dysfunctional and anti-social and fatherless families, and youths and truants, have been selected as criminogenic categories (see Day Sclater and Piper 2000). Professional failures, for example of social workers and teachers, have also been highlighted for criticism.

1.2.2 **The costs of punishment**

Penal policy can be seen as the result of a negotiation between the desire to sanction a moral code and the problem of limited resources to do so. Economic factors may be much more influential than penological theories and there may be conflicts between the Treasury and the Ministry of Justice over penal policy. The option which may best satisfy the public, namely imprisonment, is also the most expensive in terms of staffing and capital costs. The view that 'prison works', famously expounded by Michael Howard, the former Conservative Home Secretary, is very costly to implement. So a society has to negotiate both the amount of censure and the amount of punishment it can afford to incorporate into its penal policy. Some popular policies have proved massively expensive, as in the case of the **'three strikes'** legislation found in many states in the United States, including California and Washington. These are mandatory minimum sentencing schemes aimed at repeat offenders, where the third sentence mandates 25 years to life in prison. In California, however, the courts have ordered a reduction in the prison population because of concerns over the impact of over-crowding on prisoners' health (see Chapter 5, section 5.2.3).

Crime and punishment are costly in financial terms, to individuals who pay increased insurance premiums and to the public whose funds are used to finance law enforcement and punishment. As this is a substantial economic burden, inevitably costs are a signifi-cant influence on penal policy. Financial concerns have become increasingly important since the early 1990s, not just because of the ascendancy of New Right ideologies, but because increased punitiveness has been reflected in prison expansion which has led to substantial cost increases. Dobson (2010) has highlighted the heavy reliance on the use of custody, which is the most expensive penal option, during the Blair administration, and the accompanying economic and social costs. Since then the adult prison population has reached record levels.

These economic pressures are even more important now in the current economic cli-mate, and cost-effectiveness is a crucial consideration in current penal policy. So govern-ments must respond to the public's demand to reduce crime and to make society safe, while reducing economic burdens on the public purse. One way of negotiating this conflict has been to represent fines and community penalties as punitive in order to win public sup-port for them. Value for money, the allocation of scarce resources in the most efficient way, has also become an increasingly important criterion for evaluating penal policy. The Halliday Report (2001), for example, emphasised assessment of the costs and benefits of specific measures. Although its origins were in New Right theory, the quest for economic efficiency was adopted by both the Labour government and the Coalition government, with its Conservative majority. All public sector institutions and agencies have to justify their spending by transparent and comparable measurable results.

The focus on value for money is a key feature of the New Managerialist approach, reflected in the New Public Management. This approach applies methods from the private sector to the public sector, incorporating a concern with the efficient use of resources, the use of Key Performance Indicators, transparency, a move towards performance-related pay, and a stress on competition and **contestability**, that is, opening up the market to new providers of goods and services in the context of imprisonment and community penalties. We refer to this approach in various chapters of the book because it has been applied vigorously to the National Probation Service, the Police Service, the Prison Service, and the youth justice system.

Further measures to cut costs include a policy of privatisation of entire prisons or selected services within prisons or in the context of community punishment, making greater use of voluntary organisations where appropriate, and linking payments to private companies involved in rehabilitation to their results in cutting reoffending (see Chapter 10, section 10.6). This expansion of cooperation with the private and voluntary sectors has been described as the New Public Governance (Osborne 2009).

When deciding *what to punish*, some offences may be seen as uneconomic to punish, such as minor infringements or minor drugs offences which may exist on the statute book but not be enforced. Other offences, such as counterfeiting of bank notes, may need strong sanctions because they will destabilise the economy. Although the criminal law incorporates a moral code, that is, value judgements about expectations of behaviour, there will always be grey areas, particularly in relation to issues such as sexual behaviour and recreational drug use. In terms of *how to punish*, clearly a community sentence is cheaper than a custodial sentence, and supporters of the death penalty may argue that it is cheaper than life imprisonment, but if the collateral costs of appeals and reviews are included within the calculation, as well as the additional expense of long periods spent on Death Row, the costs per execution will be substantial and may exceed the costs of life imprisonment without parole. For this reason, in the United States several states have recently conducted audits of the costs of seeking execution. Out-of-court disposals will also be cheaper than court-imposed penalties but raise issues of accountability and deterrence.

In terms of *how much to punish*, a heavier sentence is more expensive than a lighter sentence, although it may offer more opportunities for rehabilitation which might, in the long term, cut the costs of crime. So when we talk of the 'prison crisis', it is not only a question of physical conditions or overcrowding or disorder but also a fiscal crisis, with the burden of prison building falling on taxpayers, diverting funds from other essential public services. As it is a labour-intensive mode of punishment, the largest running cost of imprisonment is labour, although prison officers are not highly paid. The costs of imprisonment increased substantially from 1990, when the prison population was 45,636, to 2010, when the population reached 85,000. It rose further to over 88,000 by the end of 2011 and now stands at over 85,000. However, operating costs fell by 13 per cent per prison place and 12 per cent per prison in the periods 2009/10 and 2013/14 (NOMS 2015c: 20). The National Offender Management Service (NOMS) is committed to further reductions in the face of reduced budgets. The cost per prison place in 2012/13 was £36,808 and the cost per prisoner £34,766 (NOMS 2015c: 35).

The number of prisons has been reduced as some have merged while others have closed, and the move is towards fewer but larger prisons. But whether continuing high levels of imprisonment are still viable in the current economic situation is questionable and, as Fox and Albertson (2010) argue, more economically efficient alternatives need to be explored.

In addition to running costs, there are capital costs of building prisons and indirect costs, such as welfare support for dependants affected by the imprisonment of the bread-winner, and costs to the national economy with the loss of productive labour and associated revenues, as well as social costs with the impact of imprisonment if future integration of offenders. There will also be an impact on the local economy if large numbers of individuals are incarcerated (see Clear 2007).

Research by Grimshaw *et al.* (2010a) for the Centre for Crime and Justice Studies found that by 2010 spending on the prison and probation system in England and Wales had grown by 36 per cent in real terms since 2004. This increase occurred despite major reorganisation designed to cut costs. Spending on the National Offender Management Service, which includes costs of prison and probation, increased in real terms from £3.6 billion in 2004/5 to £4.9 billion in 2008/9, but by 2014/15 it had been reduced to £3.7 billion (NOMS 2015a: 31). Obviously the increase in the size of the prison population was significant but the costs of building and staffing prisons had also increased. In addition, the economic costs of processing offenders at the earlier stages are significant, as Grimshaw *et al.* (2010b) found in their review of the levels of expenditure in the Crown Court and the magistrates' courts in the period 1999–2009. The costs of punishment may have reduced but still remain substantial. The Conservative government indicated in November 2015 that it will invest £1.3 billion in the prison estate over the next five years to make it more efficient and effective in supporting rehabilitation (HM Treasury 2015: 2.144).

1.2.3 Public opinion and the role of the media

Public opinion is clearly a key variable in shaping the response to crime and disorder. Indeed, many would argue that public opinion on law and order has been the major influence on penal policy and particularly on levels of punishment since the 1990s. Public opinion may be expressed through electoral choice, public opinion polls, focus groups, or sometimes by direct pressure on sentencers. Judges regularly receive letters from disgruntled members of the public complaining about sentences, mostly because these are seen as too short. Although many members of the public complain that judges and magistrates are out of touch with what the public want, this perception of judges has been challenged by recent empirical research on the judiciary (Darbyshire 2011). Magistrates who undertake the bulk of sentencing see themselves as dispensing popular justice, as representatives of the public, and believe that they should respond to public opinion.

Public opinion can be orchestrated to win support for policies, and public opinion and **moral panics** about particular crimes can be fanned by the media. Since the late 1980s, the public mood in Britain has been more favourable to punishment as the main response to criminal behaviour. The Conservative, Labour, and Coalition governments have all responded to and, arguably, encouraged the punitiveness of the public.

Public opinion is important in the sense that, for a criminal justice system to be effective, it must have legitimacy in the eyes of the public, but this creates a conflict for professionals in a number of areas of the criminal justice system. Agencies such as the police have to be accountable to the public yet may feel frustrated by the conflicting pressures to control crime while following rules and procedures designed to safeguard civil liberties. This conflict is reflected in efforts to strike a balance between civil liberties and crime control in the Police and Criminal Evidence Act (PACE) 1984 and in the Report of the Royal Commission on Criminal Procedure (RCCP 1981) which preceded it, and was recognised by the Royal Commission on Criminal Justice in its Report (RCCJ 1993) and in recent debates over the impact of the Human Rights Act. It may be difficult to retain public support when the avowed aims of penal institutions and the criminal justice system are not fulfilled, if crime increases, or if the defendant is seen to be privileged over the victim or the system of punishment seems to be ineffective in reducing reoffending.

The populist punitiveness of governments is problematic because it reinforces the view that crime can be controlled through punishment and leads to problems when harsher punishment does not succeed in controlling crime, as Brownlee noted about earlier policies (1998a). Once a government pursues the punitive route it may find that the public is never satisfied and that the demand for punishment exceeds the supply of punishment. Moreover, by reacting strongly to the perceived public concerns over crime, governments may increase the public's punitiveness and, as Tonry (2010) argues, the punitiveness of governments may increase the public's fear of crime. He illustrates this with reference to the focus of the Blair government on anti-social behaviour culminating in the introduction of ASBOs. This, Tonry claims, actually increased public concern about anti-social behaviour and undermined confidence in the ability of the criminal justice system to deal with it: 'high levels of fear are at least in part a consequence of the Labour government's unceasing and highly visible preoccupation with crime and antisocial behaviour' (2010: 403). He points out that in Canada and the United States fear of crime has fallen as crime rates have fallen since 1996, while in England fear of crime has persisted despite similar falls.

In any case, it is arguable that measures to control crime will not work without attacking deeper social causes and hence the problem of social exclusion needs to be addressed (Byrne 2005; Taket *et al.* 2009, Silver 2015). This itself may be problematic as the relation between penal policy and social policy is complex. As the welfare state has contracted, the penal system has to some extent taken over its role. There also appears to be a strong positive correlation between punitive penal attitudes and hostility to welfare spending both here and in the United States (Rubin 2011; Garland 2001b; see also the discussion in Chapter 5, section 5.2.3).

Key governmental concerns

Key concerns for governments are to promote public confidence in the criminal justice system, to stress the need to evaluate the cost-effectiveness of different sentences, to achieve more consistency in sentencing, and to introduce stronger punishments for repeat offenders. Section 80 of the Crime and Disorder Act (CDA) 1998 required the Court of Appeal to consider producing sentencing guidelines where there were none, and to review existing guidelines, and this initiative was taken further with the establishment of the Sentencing Advisory Panel and the Sentencing Guidelines Council, later replaced by the Sentencing Council (see Chapter 2). This may lead to conflicts with, and splits within, the judiciary over the desirability of custodial sentences in some cases. Research also suggests that further guidance to magistrates may not be sufficient to reduce continuing variations in sentencing practice (Tarling 2006). This was an issue raised in relation to sentencing following the riots in the summer of 2011, where there was some indication of inconsistency between courts but also some indications of harsher sentences than would normally be given for those involved in the riots and a higher imprisonment rate for offences committed in the context of the riots.

Negotiating public opinion may be particularly hazardous for the government when it is difficult to gauge or identify the public's opinion on issues of crime and punishment (see Roberts and Hough 2005b; Hough and Roberts 2005; Roberts *et al.* 2009). Public opinion cannot be inferred just from the headlines of the popular press, for the media may shape public opinion as well as simply reflect it. Most of our knowledge of public opinion comes from victimisation studies such as the Crime Survey for England and Wales, formerly known as the British Crime Survey, and similar social scientific research. Identifying attitudes to sentencing may also be problematic in so far as reports of attitudes to sentencing may reflect the methodologies used, as Hutton (2005) has argued. If more information is given in the scenarios presented to respondents, then a more lenient response may be elicited. The Crime Survey research has confirmed a high level of fear of crime in the UK, although this does not necessarily correlate with the actual risk of victimisation. The public also wants strong penalties for violent crimes, but may be willing to accept the decreased use of imprisonment for some crimes and does not object to community punishment for lesser crimes.

Public opinion does impact on legislation but while it may reflect genuinely deeply felt anxieties, it might also be based on inaccurate views and information. Underpinning the apparent public desire for tougher criminal justice policies is a mistaken public belief that offending is on the increase, even though crime fell from 1995 to 2004/5 and continued to decline during the next decade, although less sharply and with some fluctuations between years and with variations between offences (see ONS 2015, ONS 2016). However, police recorded crime for the year ending September 2015 showed a 6 per cent increase from the previous year and the number of rapes and other sexual offences reached the highest level recorded by the police since 2002/3. But this may reflect a greater willingness to report these crimes as well as improvements to the quality of recording. There were also increases in violence against the person, although these were in the violence without injury subgroup, and increases in offences involving knives (see ONS 2016: 8). Homicides also increased. Since 2009 the Crime Survey has extended its coverage to include crimes against children aged 10–15.

The views and attitudes of the public

Research using data from the Crime Survey, formerly referred to as the British Crime Survey, suggests that the British public are not necessarily excessively punitive but are often ill-informed about sentencing and unaware of the increased use of imprisonment in recent years; however, once aware of the levels of sentencing, they are more willing to accept them (Hough and Roberts 1998; Mattinson and Mirrlees-Black 2000). The public tend to overestimate crime levels, particularly for violent crime, and underestimate the severity of the criminal justice system in dealing with crime, particularly for serious offences. Yet, while they want custodial sentences for persistent offenders, the public do not necessarily support more prison building but are willing to use other forms of punishment, including restorative justice. Mattinson and Mirrlees-Black (2000) found that when the respondents were given a sentencing exercise to undertake, they were more lenient than the sentencing guidelines, and there was no evidence that being a recent victim increased the punitiveness of their sentencing. Indeed, the victim may prefer redress or compensation (see Kelly and Erez 1997).

A review of data from the 2007/8 British Crime Survey, however, found that public confidence in the ability of the criminal justice system to bring offenders to justice and reduce crime had increased in 2007/8 compared to earlier years (Smith 2010). Women were more confident than men and younger people more confident than older people. Those who had been victims of crime in the last year were less confident, as were those who thought there were high levels of anti-social behaviour in their local areas. Data from the 2010/11 BCS found that in terms of perception 60 per cent of people thought crime had risen in the country as a whole, compared to 66 per cent in 2009/10 (Chaplin *et al.* 2011). However, the number who thought crime had risen in their local area was only 28 per cent in 2010/11 compared to 55 per cent in 1996. Crime maps giving information on crimes in the local area have been available to the public since January 2011. Public confidence in the criminal justice system also increased from 59 per cent in 2009/10 to 61 per cent in 2010/11.

Research on punitive attitudes has found positive correlations with age, gender, and educational achievement, so older people are more likely to be punitive than younger people, men more than women, and those with low levels of education more than those with higher levels of education. Demker *et al.* (2008) found a correlation between punitiveness and tabloid newspaper consumption in Sweden. Research on possible links between race, religion, and fear of crime has found mixed results. However, research on victimisation suggests that differential experience of victimisation does not necessarily increase punitiveness (see King and Maruna 2009). Those who fear crime are more likely to be punitive, but victims of crime are no more punitive than others. Anger has also been found to be a significant predictor of support for punitive penal policies (Johnson 2009). Punitiveness may also reflect what has been described as 'ontological insecurity', that is, more general anxieties about social changes and feelings of helplessness (see Giddens 1990; van Marle and Maruna 2010). An Australian study using jurors in actual cases to explore public opinion on sentencing found a contrast between punitiveness in relation to general perceptions of leniency and a more merciful approach in relation to individual cases (Warner and Davis 2012).

A review of Australian and international research on attitudes towards sentencing and punishment, by Gelb (2008) for the Sentencing Advisory Council, found that when the public consider sentencing in the abstract, they often believe that sentences are too lenient, but when given further information about the crime or the offender, their level of punitiveness declines considerably. This review of research found that people have little confidence in the courts because they believe sentences are too lenient. But people have little accurate knowledge of crime and the criminal justice system, with the media being the primary source of information on crime and justice issues.

Similar findings have been found in relation to attitudes towards sentencing for murder. In their report, *Public Opinion and Sentencing for Murder: An Empirical Investigation of Public Knowledge and Attitudes in England and Wales*, Mitchell and Roberts (2010) found that public support for a mandatory sentence of life imprisonment for murder is more limited than had previously been supposed. However, the level of public support increased for more serious cases of murder. The respondents also underestimated the amount of time murderers spend in prison before being released on licence. The majority of respondents also believed that the murder rate had remained the same or had increased over the past ten years, when it had actually begun to decline. The Report highlighted the need to increase awareness of the public of sentencing to improve public confidence as well as the problems with a mandatory life sentence (see also Mitchell and Roberts 2012).

An Australian study of jurors' views on sentencing by Warner and David (2012) found that while respondents' general opinion of current sentencing practice was that sentences were too lenient, when informed of actual sentences given by judges in specific cases the majority thought they were appropriate. Their research confirms earlier findings which suggest that the gap between the public and judicial punitiveness is less striking than often supposed and that giving more information to the public decreases punitiveness. There was also greater dissatisfaction with sentencing for violent and sexual offences than property offences. At the general level, they found that the public response to polls appears to be based on the stereotypes of offenders portrayed in the media and popular culture as mad or bad. But when presented with a particular case, respondents are more likely to give more weight to situational and environmental factors and focus less on individual culpability. The study also demonstrates the value of using studies of jurors to complement public opinion surveys.

The urban riots in the UK in the summer of 2011 also brought sentencing and justifications for punishment into the public arena. Following the riots, custody rates and sentence length increased for offences committed during the disorder and committing an offence in the context of social disorder was treated as an aggravating factor. In particular, some first-time offenders were given relatively severe custodial sentences for thefts of small value items and despite guilty pleas. Although some of these sentences were reduced subsequently on appeal, they raised questions about the purposes of sentencing and the problems of exemplary sentencing, not least the inconsistency between the treatment of offenders in the riots and those committing similar crimes in other contexts. The punishment of rioters also reflected political pressures on sentencers from the government and the media to deal firmly with the perpetrators. It seemed that desert principles were being sacrificed on the altar of public opinion for benefits which were difficult to identify. It also meant that the prison population was swollen further, reaching record levels in the autumn of 2011.[6]

Roberts and Hough (2013) examined public attitudes to the sentencing offences associated with the 2011 rioting. Their findings were based on a nationally representative survey of adults. The study compared sentencing preferences for actual offences committed during the riots with preferences for similar offences committed under normal circumstances. While the riot subsample generally 'sentenced' more severely than the non-riot subsample, they sentenced much less severely than the courts. The majority also thought that a non-custodial sentence with a reparative element was an acceptable alternative to custody. 'These trends suggest an unusual divergence of perspectives between the community and the courts: although the public are generally critical of the courts for leniency, with respect to non-violent offending during the riots, the latter appear more punitive' (Roberts and Hough 2013: 234).

A key objective of governments is to reduce crime and fear of crime and thereby to promote confidence in the rule of law. For sentencing to have legitimacy, sentencers should include factors which the public see as relevant. But the public's views on sentencing come in part from the media, which tends to focus on erratic sentencing rather than dull sensible sentencing, and on grisly violent crimes rather than routine everyday crimes. American and English crime and police television series tend to concentrate primarily on violent crime rather than crimes like 'twocking' (taking a vehicle without the owner's consent) and theft, even though such crimes are numerically far more significant.[7] The press have also highlighted those cases where dangerous offenders have been released without appropriate supervision and have reoffended, which heightens public anxieties.[8] Clearly, the public needs more accurate information on sentencing, and the Sentencing Council has published more information since its inception.

Case study: prisoners' voting rights

McNulty et al. (2014) considered the role of the media in shaping the debate on prisoners' voting rights. They argued that the argument over prisoners' right to vote constituted a turning point for political and media discussions in the UK on human rights law and the roles of the UK Parliament and European institutions. They undertook a content analysis of national newspapers in the run-up to and the aftermath of the parliamentary debate on the question in February 2011. They also undertook an audience reception study to assess how that coverage had been received. Their findings indicate that the 'interplay between

---

[6] See http://blog.oup.com/2011/08/sentencing-the-rioters/ and http://blog.oup.com/2011/09/tough-sentencing/.

[7] See Moore (2014) for further discussion on how the media deal with crime stories.

[8] For example, Anthony Rice was convicted of murdering Naomi Bryant in 2005 while released on licence. A subsequent report was very critical of cumulative failings which meant that the risk of harm was not properly assessed or dealt with (HM Inspectorate of Probation 2006a).

politicians and the media is both complex and dynamic' (McNulty *et al.* 2014: 365). As they note, the media coverage was heavily skewed towards opposition, with 27 supporting quotes for prisoners' votes compared with 125 quotes opposing it. The arguments were framed in terms of the threat to parliamentary sovereignty and the interference from foreign judges and used as a vehicle for a Euro-sceptic approach. Prisoners' votes became 'symbolic of attitudes towards Europe' and also created the wrong impression that the Strasbourg Court is part of the European Union. Consequently, the focus of the debate shifted to the relationship between the UK and Europe rather than the substantive arguments for or against voting rights (ibid: 368). Ethical arguments in favour of re-enfranchisement were given very little attention, and even when aired, the political obstacles to changing the law were stressed.

The majority of members of focus groups were also unsympathetic to prisoners' rights including the right to vote and seemed to be 'strongly influenced by the way the issue was presented in large sections of the press' (ibid: 372). Similarly Gies (2014) examines the media construction of human rights and its hostility to human rights generally and to the Human Rights Act in particular, which has frequently been depicted as the 'villain's charter' and is almost 'a term of abuse in some media circles' (Gies 2014: 3). So discussion of human rights in the UK, she argues, has been shaped by intermediaries in the press and a variety of communicators. The hostility of the press may also reflect the constraints on its actions following the increasing recognition of the right to privacy facilitated by the HRA (see Wacks 2013).

Any reductionist policy has to address the issue of communicating to the public the effectiveness of alternatives to custody, the economic and social costs of custody, and also the actual levels of sentencing in cases of serious offences to assuage public concerns and to enhance confidence in the sentencing system. These issues have been addressed in key policy documents including the Carter Report (Carter 2003), the Consultation Paper *Making Sentencing Clearer* (Home Secretary *et al.* 2006), *Rebalancing the Criminal Justice System* (Home Office 2006a), *Breaking the Cycle* (Ministry of Justice 2010a), and *Transforming Rehabilitation* (Ministry of Justice 2013a).

1.2.4 Policy effects: prison expansion

The prison population has increased since 1993 for a number of reasons, including the actual number of cases going through the courts and the increase in the custody rate, that is, the proportion of the total number sentenced who received a custodial sentence. The number of cases processed was affected by demographic factors, namely an increase in numbers in the crime-prone age groups, and by the impact of drug-related crime. The custody rate in the Crown Court rose in the period 1992–2005 from 44 to 60 per cent (Home Office 2007a: 14), and the average custodial sentence length (ACSL) for adults in the Crown Court increased from 20.8 in 1995 to 25.9 months in 2005 (ibid). Imprisoning offenders who in the past would have received community punishment and giving longer sentences to those who would previously have gone to prison have added to the prison population.

There has been an increase in the numbers of prisoners defined as 'serious' and as presenting a risk to the public. The introduction by the Criminal Justice Act (CJA) 2003 of the sentence of imprisonment for public protection (IPP) also inflated the prison population and although this sentence was abolished by the Legal Aid and Sentencing and Punishment of Offenders Act 2012, many IPP-sentenced prisoners still remain in prison. Also, some offences now carry longer sentences as a result of changes in sentencing law and guidance. For example, Schedule 28 to the CJA 2003 raised the maximum penalties for drug-related offences, in some cases from 5 to 14 years. In 1995 the prison population passed 50,000 for the first time (Home Office 1996b); by 2002 it had passed the 70,000 total and has continued to increase, with slight fluctuations since then, reaching 85,000 in 2010. By the end of December 2011 it was over 87,000. The increase in 2011 was partly attributed to the impact of sentences for participation in the riots which took place in summer 2011. Since then it has fallen but still remains high, and by the end of November 2015 it was 85,982. Although it is difficult to make firm predictions because of the number of variables involved, including sentencing guidelines, it seems very unlikely that the current high levels of the prison population will decrease significantly in the near future. Projected prison population figures for the next few years remain high (see Chapter 8, section 8.2.2).

A review of the prison population for the period 1993–2012 by the Ministry of Justice examined trends in the prison population and considered the reasons for the substantial increase in the size of the prison population in this period (Ministry of Justice 2013b). Tougher sentencing and enforcement outcomes and a change in the offence groups coming before the courts were significant factors. Legislative and policy changes are also cited, including mandatory minimum sentences for some offences and new sentences for public protection as well as changes to requirements for failing to comply with licence conditions or breach of non-custodial sentences. In addition the cases coming before the courts became more serious, with three groups—violence against the person, drug offences, and sexual offences—having the most significant impact on the increase in the prison population. However, the Report notes that some recent legislative and policy changes may have been expected to reduce the prison population.

The expansion of the prison population may be affected by legislative changes and increases in crime detection, as well as strengthening enforcement of breach proceedings and more offenders being 'recalled to prison for breaking the condition of their licence' (Da Silva et al. 2007: 4). The expansion also arose during a period in which more emphasis was placed on retributivism yet, as we shall see in Chapter 3, in some other societies retributivist-based sentencing systems have prevented excessive punishment.

A number of explanations have been given for the increased use of custody since 2000, including the continuing influence of punitive public opinion on penal policy. More weight has been given to persistence and seriousness in offending (see Chapter 3, section 3.2) and more emphasis has been placed on protecting the public from violent offenders and sexual offenders, reflected in an increase in the number of prisoners serving indeterminate sentences. There is also a much wider range of orders, both civil and criminal, breaches of which are punishable by imprisonment and which have increased the numbers in custody.

The combination of these factors means that more pressure is exerted on the prison population and that more offenders are returning to prison following a period in the community. The implications of this expansion on the prison regime and the problems generated by overcrowding will be considered in Chapter 8. The expansion has meant that police cells and even court room cells have been used to house prisoners when necessary and a prison ship, HMP Weare, was also used for a period from the late 1990s until 2005.

The UK now has the highest incarceration rate within Western Europe, at 149 per 100,000 of population in 2015, compared with 76 in Germany and 75 in the Netherlands and Sweden (International Centre for Prison Studies 2015). This is surprising in so far as the UK has a far wider range of non-custodial options than most other Western European societies. Sentencing levels are also higher in the UK than in some other European societies, as evidenced, for example, by a comparative study of sentencing of burglars in England and Wales and Finland (see Davis et al. 2004). Increases in imprisonment rates are often seen as a reflection of public punitiveness but the rates themselves do not give us information on sentence length, which may also be significant (Frost 2008).

These rising figures for incarceration in the UK were fuelled by increases in both short and long prison sentences in the 1990s but the expansion of custody cannot be attributed solely to sentencers: the sentencing framework within which they operate is potentially more punitive and the guidance is more prescriptive (see Piper and Easton 2006/7). The implications of these specific changes in sentencing law will be considered in Chapters 3 and 5.

The House of Commons Justice Committee (2010), in its report *Cutting Crime: The Case for Justice Reinvestment*, referred to the need to address the root causes of expansion, rather than simply focusing on providing more prison places. The causes, it said, include 'a toxic cocktail of sensationalised or inaccurate reporting of difficult cases by the media; relatively punitive overall public opinion (compared to much of the EU); a self-defeating over-politicisation of criminal justice policy since the late 1980s, and the responsiveness to all these factors of the sentencing framework and sentencers' (ibid: 5). The Commission on English Prisons Today (2009), in its report, also argued for a reduction in prison numbers, the closure of some prisons, and greater use of community responses, as well as more investment in communities.

The problem is how to 'sell' to the public a reductionist policy, that is, one committed to the aim of reducing the use and extent of imprisonment. A modest decarceration programme or expanded use of alternatives needs to take seriously the public's fears of crime and to contest the public view of the courts as 'soft'. To do this the public need accurate information about crime levels and sentencing decisions and policies. For this purpose, Halliday (2001) proposed putting sentencing guidelines online for the public to access, and this was implemented. The public also have to be convinced that alternatives to custody will be effective and to be aware that the greater use of imprisonment may not substantially affect crime rates. For example, it is estimated that when the crime rate for violent crime fell in the United States in the 1990s, the large increase in incarceration accounted for only 25 per cent of the fall (see Spelman 2000; King, Mauer, and Young 2005). Obviously the relationship between crime and punishment is complex and it may be difficult to isolate the causal effect of an increase in imprisonment.

As we have seen, the public may be less punitive than sentencers, and the public is also selectively punitive. Roberts *et al.* (2008) report findings from empirical research on public attitudes towards the sentencing of culpable driving offences resulting in death. With the exception of one offence, they found greater tolerance of current sentencing practice than is commonly supposed. The public tend to underestimate sentences given and, when asked to give their own sentence for a particular case, suggested sentences similar to or more lenient than the Sentencing Advisory Panel's proposals.

Hough *et al.* (2003) argue that it is necessary to widen the awareness of those who sentence as well as the public, particularly in relation to the advantages of using non-custodial penalties, including fines. But changes in sentencing law and practice and changing public attitudes to crime and punishment will not succeed in reducing prison numbers without the political will and commitment to a reductionist policy. The relationship between political and economic factors is therefore complex, fluid, and indeterminate. While they may sometimes bolster each other, they may also conflict.

Reducing the use of custodial penalties has been a consistent policy imperative, but this goal is difficult to achieve when governments seek to be seen as tough on crime (see Hough *et al.* 2003; Sparks and Taylor 2001/2). However, in the face of mounting pressure on the prison system, the highest levels of the prison population on record, and the associated costs of incarceration, governments have been encouraged to explore possible reductionist policies, as we have seen, even if only in relation to specific offender groups, such as women. While some prisons have been closed and others have merged, this has been primarily cost-driven, to save money, rather than a wholesale commitment to reductionism.

This shift reflects the view that prison may not 'work' for all groups, and that, in some cases, alternatives may need to be considered for offenders convicted of non-violent offences. Ways of enhancing community punishments to make them more onerous and more acceptable to sentencers and the public have also been sought. The changes to the bail provisions to reduce the numbers remanded in custody were also primarily cost-driven.

These reductionist trends lie uneasily alongside the commitment to 'rebalance the criminal justice system' in favour of the law-abiding majority by dealing robustly with crime and anti-social behaviour, and by the restructuring of prisons to ensure efficient use of resources when dealing with the high volume of offenders. Section 27 of the Criminal Justice and Courts Act (CJCA) 2015 extends the application of the whole-life sentence to cases concerning the murder of a police officer or prison officer in the course of his or her duty. The Act also imposes further limits on the release of dangerous offenders.

1.3 The influence of theory on penal law and practice

1.3.1 Principles from criminology and penology

Penological principles also shape the development of penal policies. These principles are the justifications of punishment and include retribution, deterrence, rehabilitation, public protection, and, more recently, the restoration of social harmony, which will be discussed in Chapters 2–6 and 10. Together they constitute the store of knowledge regarding what is, theoretically, the best response in dealing with offenders. Because theorists from opposing traditions may agree that punishment is necessary, but differ in their views of what is the best response, the type of punishment may depend on which theory—which purpose of punishment—is implicit or explicit in policy. It may also depend on which philosophical ideas underpin the chosen punishment, for example whether individuals are seen as autonomous or possessing free will, or whether their actions are viewed as determined by the surrounding environment or genetic make-up.

Retributivism punishes according to **just deserts**, which assumes a free choice by a rational person who chooses how to act, while a utilitarian approach may use rewards and punishments to channel behaviour into desirable ends and aims to adjust the social context to change the individual's behaviour, using treatments and therapies to rehabilitate the offender. Compared to political and economic factors, the influence of penology and criminology is limited. However, the economic climate may favour the rise of a particular justification of punishment and particular criminological theories may also be appropriated by governments to legitimise a particular policy. For example, 'left realist' criminology, which developed in the 1980s, was used subsequently to legitimise strong law and order policies and to justify increased punitiveness in the interests of public protection. This theory takes crime seriously, while linking crime to class inequality, and focuses on both crime and the social reaction to crime (see Lea and Young 1984). It recognises crime as a serious social problem, in particular for working-class communities, and demands action accordingly.

Another perspective which has strongly influenced penal policy since 1990 is the so-called **New Penology**, although it is now over 25 years old. It draws on 'New' Managerialist and actuarial techniques to manage the risk of offending and reoffending, and is now well established as a theory and practice of punishment (see Feeley and Simon 1992; Simon 1998). This approach, also referred to as actuarial justice, uses technology and statistical calculations to enhance the risk management of high-risk groups. Crime is seen as normal, and the best one can hope for is to control crime and risk through actuarial policies and technocratic forms of knowledge, internally generated by the penal system (Feeley and Simon 1992; Simon 1998, Simon and Feeley 2003; see also Wills and Mastrofski 2012). This approach focuses on categories of potential and actual offenders rather than on individuals, and on managerial aims rather than the rehabilitation of the offender. Risk—the core concept of the New Penology—is no longer calculated on personal knowledge of particular individuals or by in-depth clinical judgements but is seen as distributed unevenly across categories of offenders (see Chapter 5). Prison would be reserved for the highest risk categories and actuarial justice provides a means of selecting the target population.

The New Penology has been a significant recent influence on penal policy both here and in the United States but it is also a policy approach. It is clear that concern with risk management has diffused through the key agencies of the criminal justice system, including the Prison Service and the Probation Service, and has been a significant feature of public concern, particularly in relation to dangerous offenders. It has met with some resistance from probation officers at the point of working with clients, while being well established at the central level of policy-making and at the Home Office and Ministry of Justice (see Deering 2011). Managing risk in the community and on release from a custodial sentence has been a major challenge for criminal justice professionals and this has been increasingly seen as a joint enterprise involving cooperation between agencies, as we shall see, in relation to sex offenders and dangerous offenders.

1.3.2 Classical theories of punishment

The principal justifications of punishment are closely associated with distinct philosophical traditions or schools. Both retributivist and utilitarian theories have a long history. Retributivism was influential in late eighteenth- and early nineteenth-century philosophy, and was revived in the 1970s and 1980s in the UK and the United States (see Chapter 2). It is strongly associated with the German idealist tradition, particularly the work of Kant and Hegel, which focuses on the role of ideas in the construction of reality and sees reality as mediated through consciousness. The rival tradition is utilitarianism, which includes the justifications of deterrence, social protection or incapacitation, and rehabilitation, associated with the English philosophers Bentham (1789) and Mill (1861) but also derived from the work of Beccaria (1767).

Retributivist and utilitarian theorists both accept that punishment may be justly inflicted, but differ in their views of what constitutes the justice of a particular punishment. Both seek to limit the use of discretion in sentencing in favour of a more rigorous principled approach and both address the issue of proportionality, but from quite different standpoints. Consequently both see a link between punishment and the seriousness of the offence by upholding the idea that custody should be reserved for the most serious offences. However, the utilitarian does so because it is hoped this will prevent the commission in the future of those offences which are most harmful to the public. So it is important to find the optimal level of punishment, to prevent offenders from reoffending, to deter the general public, and to protect the public from future offending by incapacitating individuals who threaten society. So there is scope on this theory for preventive sentencing. However, the aim in devising punishments is to prevent future offending at minimal expense, so utilitarians would not favour excessive or harsh punishment unless there are clear social benefits which result from that punishment. Punishment can also be used to rehabilitate the offender so that he can make a useful contribution within the prison community and on his return to the wider society.

Neither approach can be seen as purely theoretical as each has had a strong impact on penal policy. What is interesting is that although these theories are strongly opposed to each other in certain key assumptions, in practice they may both be incorporated in the same piece of legislation. The main provisions of the CJA 1991, for example, were based on a version of retributivist philosophy, but parts of that Act and subsequent legislation reflect utilitarian principles. So s. 142(1) of the CJA 2003, despite the continuance elsewhere in that Act of retributivist criteria for the use of different levels of sentence (see Chapter 3), imposes a varied—and potentially inconsistent—list of five 'purposes of sentencing' to which the courts must 'have regard': the punishment of offenders, the reduction of crime (including its reduction by deterrence), the reform and rehabilitation of offenders, the protection of the public, and the making of reparation by offenders to persons affected by their offences. Individuals may also hold, for example, strongly retributivist views on violent crimes but take a more utilitarian approach in relation to lesser offences.

On the retributivist approach, just deserts equates to determining a sentence which is proportional to culpability so that offenders receive what they deserve for what they have done. There is no concern with the future effects of the sentence; the concern is rather with a just response to wrongdoing. On retributivist theory, justice demands that the perpetrator of the offence suffers punishment, regardless of the effects the individual's suffering may have on himself or others. Justice is served only if the offender is made to suffer. In completing the term of punishment, the offender pays and cancels his debt to society. Chapters 2 and 4 will explore in more detail the foundational writings of the retributivist and utilitarian approaches and the problems they raise, and we have provided at the end of this chapter an exercise which you might wish to do. It makes very clear the difference that the application of principles makes to sentencing outcomes. Next, however, we will focus on just deserts.

1.3.3 **The influence of 'just deserts'**

One major influence on penal and sentencing policy has been a particular retributivist idea of 'just deserts'. Prior to 1991 its influence was not clear but the CJA 1991 imposed a new constraint on the courts' discretion—that of a presumptive sentencing rationale. In the 1990 White Paper *Crime, Justice and Protecting the Public*, the UK government had announced its intention to establish 'a new and more coherent statutory framework for sentencing' (Home Office 1990a: para 1.5): 'The aim of the government's proposals is better justice through a more consistent approach to sentencing so that convicted criminals get their "just deserts". The severity of the sentence of the court should be directly related to the seriousness of the offence' (ibid: para 1.6).

A general aim of sentencing on retributivist principles was not, however, invented in 1991. The Streatfeild Committee in 1961 said that 'sentencing used to be a comparatively simple matter. The primary objective was to fix a sentence proportionate to the offender's culpability', the assumption being that practice had diversified with the increased use of rehabilitative, community-based measures so that sentencers could freely choose to sentence on one or more principles. There had emerged a 'tariff system' under which sentencers could use a normal range of sentences and choose what was proportionate to a particular level of offence gravity (see Cross 1981: 167–73) but they could also choose a sentence based on the needs of the offender (see Henham 1995: 221–2).

The significance of the provisions in the CJA 1991 was, then, that they statutorily imposed on judges and magistrates 'just deserts' as the presumptive rationale. The 1991 Act imposed levels of seriousness as 'hurdles' to the use of two of the three main levels of punishment. Consequently, the sentencing decision-making process had to focus first on basic elements of a just deserts approach—the calculation of seriousness and the consideration of a sentence proportionate to it (see Chapter 2). This is not to say that all sentencing provisions in the 1990s were consistent with this rationale, given the existence of the provisions in the 1991 Act justifying custodial sentences on the basis of protecting the public, and the form of cumulative mandatory sentences added by the Crime (Sentences) Act 1997 (see Chapter 2, section 2.2.5) which were explicitly excluded from the just deserts approach (Powers of Criminal Courts (Sentencing) Act 2000, ss. 34(b), 79(1)(b), and 127).

This basic question of sentencing rationale—with its long history in classical theory—still remains high on the policy agenda and as a subject of academic critique. In particular, the recent changes have raised the fundamental question 'why punish?' Justifications are central to sentencing and they are also central to the legitimacy of policy. If sentencing policies are to be justifiable to the electorate they must be capable of being supported by reasons, to justify the actions, or failure to act, of sentencers and the costs of punishment imposed on society. As we have already noted, the CJA 2003 provides five punishment aims to be considered by sentencers. But Dingwall (2008) argues that notions of desert remain pervasive throughout sentencing law, policy, and sentencing guidelines.

1.4. Sentencing and punishment: the penal policy context

1.4.1 Policy trends

We can identify a number of important trends in penal policy in England and Wales since the Second World War, a major thread being the changing fortunes of the **rehabilitative ideal** with its optimism that the offender could be reformed. As we shall see in Chapter 10, the rehabilitative ideal was reflected in the development of community penalties to operate as alternatives to custody and a new option—the community service order—was introduced in England and Wales in 1972. However, the increase in crime and evidence of recidivism in the 1970s and early 1980s cast doubt on the validity of the treatment and rehabilitation approaches and their use declined in the 1980s and 1990s. Yet, the rehabilitative ideal has in recent years received support again, albeit prompted primarily by pragmatic cost considerations. It survives in the Probation Service and in offending behaviour programmes and has remained a major influence on penal policies in some other European societies, including the Netherlands (see Boone and Moerings 2007). The Coalition government was also committed to a *Transforming Rehabilitation* agenda, including a 'rehabilitation revolution', in the way offenders are managed in the community, involving private and voluntary service providers and payment by results (Ministry of Justice 2013a).

The end of the twentieth century was, nevertheless, marked by an increased use of punishment and incapacitation, with both the Conservative and Labour administrations tending to focus on punishment rather than crime. The endorsement in the CJA 1991 of just deserts as the primary principle of sentencing focused sentencing on proportionate punishment rather than treatment or deterrence per se. The increased concern with incapacitation became evident in the electronic monitoring and curfew provisions introduced by the CDA 1998[9] and through prison expansion, while a trend of making alternatives to custody more punitive—or at least to appear so—developed. Policies in the 1990s also showed

---

[9] Now consolidated in ss. 37 and 38 of the Powers of Criminal Courts (Sentencing) Act 2000; see also CJA 2003, ss. 204 and 215.

an increased concern with the safety, rights, and needs of victims, and a commitment to speed up the criminal justice process, so as to shorten the period between arrest and trial. The CDA 1998 introduced new penalties for young offenders and new measures such as curfews, ASBOs, and Sex Offender Orders, and a wide range of new criminal offences was created by the Sexual Offences Act (SOA) 2003.

Since 1990 concern with value for money has loomed large and this has encouraged the introduction of privatisation and New Managerialism within the residual state sector in all areas of the criminal justice system. At the same time there have been substantial improvements in the physical conditions and quality of life in prisons (see Chapter 8, section 8.3) and, with the incorporation of the European Convention on Human Rights into UK law in 1998, human rights issues have also assumed increasing significance in prison policy (see Chapter 8, section 8.6).

Trends which have continued since the publication of the third edition of this book are the declining influence of 'traditional' penal measures and the increasing use of civil or 'voluntary' measures in the repertoire of new tools for controlling anti-social behaviour. We have also seen a trend towards the greater use of fixed penalty notices—those fines which are outside sentencing courts and imposed administratively, not judicially. Although it is difficult to calculate the full extent of this, it is clear that this is seen as a way of avoiding the high cost of court processing. It does, however, raise serious questions of accountability, proportionality, and impact (Easton and Piper 2013). It is not an issue that will raise serious public concerns because generally such penalties mean that an offender is dealt with more leniently and quickly and are not, therefore, a matter for individual complaint unless the system is seen as too automatic and allowing insufficient space for putting forward a defence. In addition, with the increase in the number of civil orders for which the police can apply, the role of the police in punishing offenders has increased, with a corresponding decrease in the role of the sentencing court.

Another trend has been that towards a greater quantity and increased specificity of sentencing guidance. The Coroners and Justice Act 2009 set up a Sentencing Council with a wider remit and greater statutory definition of its functions than its predecessors. That Council has developed publicity materials, conducted consultations, and drafted new guidelines which have received more attention in the academic literature. The government's desire for efficiency and effectiveness has led to greater central control of those who deliver sentences as well as the agents of community punishment. The Sentencing Council includes judicial and non-judicial members (Schedule 15 to the Coroners and Justice Act 2009). While the judicial members are in the majority, the actions of the Council are themselves more constrained by the very detailed instructions regarding the making of guidelines set out by Parliament in the Coroners and Justice Act 2009.

There is also a greater emphasis on the sentencing stage in that the sentencer now has available a greater range of ancillary orders which can be imposed with a sentence, including the Sexual Harm Prevention Order. We now have a plethora of civil orders relating to a wider range of offences and offenders, including violent offenders, which encroach on freedom of movement. The courts are also being empowered to add more controlling types of requirements to community sentences and supervision on licence. For example, section 72 of the Legal Aid, Sentencing and Punishment of Offenders Act 2012 added a foreign travel prohibition requirement to the many options for individualised community orders. The effect of these changes has also had implications for the prison population as, in some cases, breaches of those orders have led to custodial sentences.

In the following sections we will consider the key policy documents since 2000 in more detail, flagging up the main influences on their content.

1.4.2 Key policy documents 2000–2004

Since 2000 there have been several major policy documents on sentencing and punishment which provide evidence of the continuing importance in policy of the factors outlined in the previous section. First, the White Paper, *Criminal Justice: The Way Ahead*, published in February 2001, affirmed the government's commitment to funding another 2,660 prison places and committed an extra £689 million for the Prison Service over the following three years, £21 million of which was to be used to prevent reoffending. The White Paper aimed to reduce both crime and fear of crime, and so also reduce the social and economic costs of crime.

Similarly, the Halliday Report, *Making Punishments Work*, published in July 2001, referred to the need to increase public confidence and reduce crime. It advocated more research on the costs and benefits of particular sentences and proposed a duty on the Secretary of State to disseminate information about the effectiveness of sentencing as well as its costs. The Report argued that the aims of sentencing should cover crime reduction, reparation, and punishment and set out what was needed to achieve these aims: to clarify what is effective, particularly in relation to short sentences, to produce clear guidelines to achieve sentence consistency, and to ensure that previous convictions are reflected in sentence severity. Both these policy documents also reflect the rise of actuarial justice, while the need to improve public confidence in sentencing was stressed by the Auld Review of the Criminal Courts published in 2001 which included recommendations on sentencing, including advance indication of sentencing for defendants pleading guilty (para 114) and the codification of the law of sentencing (para 198).

In response to the Halliday and Auld Reports the Labour government issued a White Paper, *Justice for All*, which stressed the need to 'rebalance the system in favour of victims, witnesses and communities', to give paramount importance to protecting the public, to restore public confidence in the criminal justice system, and to improve the coherence of the system by closer integration of the police, prosecution, courts, and Probation Service (Home Office 2002c). It proposed to set out the principles of sentencing in legislation and proposed a Sentencing Guidelines Council to formulate consistent guidelines. Many of the proposals in *Criminal Justice: The Way Ahead* and *Justice for All* were enacted in the CJA 2003, which incorporated wide-ranging provisions on evidence, procedure, and sentencing, including amending the law on double jeopardy, increasing the time limits for detention under PACE, removing the right to jury trial in complex fraud cases, and reforming the rules on the disclosure of evidence, bad character, and hearsay evidence. The Act introduced a new generic community punishment with a wide range of components (see Chapter 10, section 10.3) and the sentence of imprisonment for public protection (IPP), later repealed by LASPO 2012. The 2003 Act also created the Sentencing Guidelines Council (see Chapter 2, section 2.3.2). The aim of the CJA 2003, in line with *Justice for All*, was to rebalance the criminal justice system, and this implied increasing the rights of victims, even if this meant fewer rights for defendants.

1.4.3 Policy documents 2004–2009

After 2004 the focus on 'rebalancing the criminal justice in favour of the law-abiding majority' and on protecting the public from dangerous offenders and from a range of anti-social behaviours, and particularly from unruly young offenders, persisted. The policy paper *Rebalancing the Criminal Justice System in Favour of the Law-Abiding Majority* (Home Office 2006a) made clear the aim was to enhance public confidence in the fairness of the system, as 80 per cent of the public believed the criminal justice system was fair to the offender but only 36 per cent thought it met the needs of victims (ibid: para 1.20). It recommended a range of measures to assist victims and witnesses and stressed that this rebalancing programme would be supported by stronger enforcement. At the same time it advocated pursuing the use of restorative justice methods and outcomes for juvenile and adult offenders (see Chapter 6, section 6.2).

The Consultation Paper *Making Sentencing Clearer* (Home Secretary *et al.* 2006) was also intended to be part of the rebalancing process. Its aim was to make sentencing clearer for all parties involved—victims, witnesses, and defendants—and to give judges more discretion and flexibility in reducing the sentence discounts for a guilty plea. It also proposed greater use of fines, stronger community sentences as an alternative to custody, and better protection from dangerous offenders through the use of indeterminate sentences.

The Criminal Justice and Immigration Act (CJIA) 2008 amended relevant sections of the CJA 2003, 'clarified' the principles of sentencing for offenders under 18, added further requirements for use with ASBOs, and introduced youth rehabilitation orders (YROs) which are intended to give more flexibility to the court as the court can incorporate several requirements. It gave sentencers greater discretion, particularly on whether to impose a sentence of imprisonment for public protection (IPP) and extended sentences.

The Coroners and Justice Act 2009 contained provisions setting up the new Sentencing Council for England and Wales, with a wide range of duties, including the preparation of sentencing guidelines and assessing the impact of policy and legislative proposals (see Chapter 2, section 2.4.4).

There were also a number of organisational changes during this period, including the establishment of the NOMS, which took over responsibility for the overall management of offenders. Its aim is to protect the public and reduce reoffending by delivering punishment and supporting rehabilitation. A major organisational change was the creation of the Ministry of Justice in 2007, which took over responsibility for prisons, probation, and sentencing from the Home Office. The NOMS and the Prison and Probation Services are now the responsibility of the Secretary of State for Justice and the Ministry of Justice.

The reforms initiated during the last few years of the Labour administration were met with some criticism. The pace of change and the volume of legislation added to the burdens on practitioners working with the criminal justice system. There were also concerns that the balance had swung too far in favour of the state, with an increasing range of controls over individuals' movements, based on the prospect of future rather than past offences, which led to extensive criticisms of the government (see Liberty 2006, 2007).

1.4.4 **Policy documents 2010–2015**

During the 2010 General Election campaign the need to be tough on crime was stressed by all the main parties. Following the General Election, the new Coalition government made clear that it would be placing reform of the delivery of punishment at the forefront of its programme. In May 2010 the Justice Secretary Ken Clarke announced that he wished to make greater use of community punishments with greater involvement from the voluntary and private sector (Clarke 2010). He also said he did not believe that prison expansion had led to a fall in crime. The Green Paper *Breaking the Cycle: Effective Punishment, Rehabilitation and Sentencing of Offenders* published in December 2010 set out the Coalition government's proposed reforms (Ministry of Justice 2010a).

The focus was on effective rehabilitation and the Paper emphasised the importance of the accountability of service providers so that they are paid according to the results they achieve. Providers from all sectors, including private, voluntary, and community, will be given freedom to introduce innovative programmes to achieve results and will be paid

according to the outcomes. One payment would be made for meeting statutory requirements and ensuring compliance with the sentence. A further payment which depends on
the result the provider delivers in reducing reoffending will then be made. Pilot schemes
of support for prisoners serving short sentences at Doncaster and Peterborough did show
a fall in reconviction rates measured within a 12-month period from release, at Doncaster
by 5.7 per cent and at Peterborough by 8.4 per cent (Ministry of Justice 2014a). The aim of
the proposed reforms was to promote competition, increase cost-effectiveness, and involve
local groups and organisations in these efforts to promotion rehabilitation.

There was also a declared commitment to expanding work for prisoners, increasing
reparation from prisoners to their victims, and reducing the number of IPP prisoners. The
number of remand prisoners would be also be reduced through reforming the Bail Act, and
new provisions making it harder to refuse bail where the offender was unlikely to receive
a custodial sentence were introduced by LASPO 2012. Community penalties were also to
be made more intensive and curfew orders were to be extended. Payment by results was
also to be used in community penalties and these issues were highlighted in *Transforming
Rehabilitation* (Ministry of Justice 2013a). Greater use was to be made of out-of-court disposals and of restorative justice.

The aim as stated in *Breaking the Cycle* was to make the sentencing process more transparent and easier for the public to understand and for sentencers to use, and to review the
sentence of imprisonment for public protection (IPP). The Green Paper also indicated that
the discount for a guilty plea might be increased to 50 per cent but, as noted earlier, this was
jettisoned in the face of considerable opposition (see Chapter 3, section 3.3.3).

The government published its response to the consultation on the proposals in the Green
Paper in June 2011, when it reaffirmed the importance of prison as a place of work and
announced a review of sentencing for serious sex offenders and violent offenders, including replacement of the IPP with a determinate sentencing framework (Ministry of Justice
2011a). It also referred to greater use of compensation orders and of restorative justice. It
also published consultation papers—*Punishment and Reform: Effective Probation Services*
and *Punishment and Reform: Effective Community Sentences*—which discussed further the
proposed strategy outlined in *Breaking the Cycle* (Ministry of Justice 2012a, 2012b).

Many of the proposals in *Breaking the Cycle* and the government's *Response* were contained in the Legal Aid, Sentencing and Punishment of Offenders Act (LASPO) 2012. It
required the courts to consider making compensation orders where victims have suffered
harm or loss; reduced the detailed requirements on courts when they give reasons for a sentence; and allowed courts to suspend sentences of up to two years rather than 12 months.
It also introduced new powers to allow curfews to be imposed for more hours in the day
and for up to 12 months rather than the previous six months and changed the law on bail
and remand, to reduce the number of those who are unnecessarily remanded into custody.
Under the new 'no real prospect' test, people should be released on bail if they are unlikely
to receive a custodial sentence. In addition the Secretary of State was given new powers to
make prison rules about prisoners' employment, pay, and deductions from their pay. The
intention of these provisions is that prisoners should make payments which would support victims of crime. It also allows for foreign national prisoners serving indeterminate
sentences to be deported when their tariff expires. The Prisoners' Earnings Act was also
activated by LASPO 2012 (see Chapter 8, section 8.3.3), which also repealed the custody
plus and intermittent custody provisions in the CJA 2003 (see Chapter 10, section 10.4.2).

Since 2010 there have been more closures and mergers of prisons, which have meant
more prisoners are held in larger prisons. The Coalition government also continued its privatisation policy and extended it to the Probation Service. At the same time it maintained
its resistance to granting prisoners' rights, despite pressure from the Strasbourg Court.

The government set out its competition strategy for offender services which elaborates on the plans for increased involvement of the private and voluntary sectors in the rehabilitation process and the creation of a market in the provision of offender management and rehabilitation (Ministry of Justice 2011e). The assumption was that competition and increased flexibility for the 'winners' would lead to more cost-effective and more successful programmes to rehabilitate offenders. The policy was further elaborated in *Transforming Rehabilitation*, where the aim was to reduce reoffending rates and to open up the market to a wide range of providers by providing support and services 'through the prison gate' for offenders released from short custodial sentences of less than 12 months, engaging with the prisoner before their release and then maintaining support. This group of prisoners was selected because of their high reconviction rates. These providers would be paid in full only when reconviction rates were reduced.

The increasing centralisation of punishment in terms of fiscal controls and policies governing the day-to-day work conducted in prisons, and in the Probation Service the increasing control of discretion to implement central policies, have raised problems for delivery of services to specific groups of offenders. The greater use of voluntary bodies and community involvement and devolution to the private sector reflected the Coalition government's commitment to its rehabilitation revolution, but the success of those changes has been limited by the expanding prison population and the availability of funding to voluntary groups. The greater use of management tools such as monitoring, standardisation, rigid line management, and budget control may erode the scope for professional expertise and make it harder to achieve justice on an individual basis.

1.4.5 Future directions 2015–2020

Concern over terrorism and insecurity has continued to increase with the rise in the number of terrorist attacks within Europe and with evidence of the involvement of UK nationals in the kidnapping and beheading of hostages in Syria and Iraq. Attention has also focused on the prison itself as a source of extremism and this is likely to continue to be an important area of research and policy in the near future. Under the current Conservative government, privatisation will also remain an important element of penal policy and be a key ingredient of the provision of punishment and rehabilitation programmes. The involvement of the voluntary sector is also likely to continue. Although there will be investment in building new prisons over the next five years, reductions in budgets for offender management are likely to affect the provision of services. The government has said it will build nine new modern prisons, five of which will open during the current Parliament. Older, less efficient prisons will be sold off and the land they occupy released for housing (HM Treasury 2015).

Initial statements from the new Justice Secretary, Michael Gove, suggested a renewed focus on the rehabilitative functions of prisons and renewed interest in the role of education in prisons, as well as further streamlining of the prison estate and greater powers for prison governors (Gove 2015a). In a speech to the Howard League Annual General Meeting, he acknowledged the need to cut prison numbers but stressed this would be best achieved through effective rehabilitation to prevent reoffending; he also indicated the possibility of sentencing reform (2015b). The specific needs of women offenders will also be given more attention by the Prison Service and probation providers (see House of Commons Justice Committee 2015b: Appendix). The Conservative government has also stressed its intention to retain the voting ban on prisoners, despite the recommendations of a Parliamentary Committee, even if it means withdrawing from the European Convention. Issues relating to sentencing and punishment are likely to continue to feature in the attack on human rights during the lifetime of the current government. These issues will be considered further in Chapters 8 and 9.

1.5. Conclusion: reflecting on the issues

1.5.1 A more complex criminal justice system

We have identified a number of key influences on penal policy. Recurring themes are removing inconsistency in sentencing, targeting persistent offending, and improving cooperation between different agencies. There has also been a move towards the aim of a centralised criminal justice system by unifying the separate probation services into a National Probation Service for England and Wales under provisions in the Criminal Justice and Court Services Act 2000, and by conjoining the Prison and Probation Services into NOMS in 2004.

Over the past decade we have seen major changes in the administration of criminal justice, with the breaking up of the Home Office; the creation of the Ministry of Justice and the transfer to it of key areas of criminal justice policy and management, including offender management; the arrival and departure of several Home Secretaries; and the election—albeit by default—of a Coalition government, for the first time since the 1940s.

We have also seen the continuing rise of the market in recent years, with contestability extended to a wider range of criminal justice functions including community punishment. The role and status of the Probation Service have also changed: it is now a national body, under direct central control and subject to National Standards and the detailed statutory provisions of the CJA 2003. It also became part of the larger National Offender Management Service in a merger with the Prison Service and NOMS itself has been restructured. The Probation Service has been stripped of responsibility for large areas of work as responsibility for low- and medium-risk offenders has been transferred to the private and voluntary sectors (see Chapter 10, section 10.6). However, the Probation Service remains responsible for ensuring that other providers effectively manage the risk of harm to the public, as well as retaining direct responsibility for managing high-risk offenders. The Serious Organised Crime Agency was also closed in October 2013 and replaced by the National Crime Agency, created by the Crime and Courts Act 2013, to fight serious and organised crime. Sentencing procedures are also now being reviewed by the Law Commission.

So the criminal justice landscape is much more complex than a decade ago, and this is likely to increase with proposals to make greater use of the voluntary sector in the provision of rehabilitation.

Some of the issues which we have discussed in relation to the formulation of penal policy will now be considered by focusing on the governance of sex offenders in England and Wales, because this raises concerns about the protection of the public, the impact of populist punitiveness, just deserts, human rights, and the influence of risk management and actuarial justice. We then offer a case study which invites you to think about these influences in relation to a specific penal policy.

1.5.2 The governance of sex offenders: an example of policy formation

A number of measures aimed at improving the control, detention, and arrest of sex offenders were introduced in the UK in the late 1990s. They included the registration scheme established by the Sex Offenders Act 1997 and Sex Offender Orders created by the CDA 1998, a life sentence for a second serious sexual offence in the Crime (Sentences) Act 1997, and legislation dealing with stalkers in the Protection from Harassment Act 1997. New measures to deal with sex tourism were introduced in Part II of the Sex Offenders Act 1997, as amended by para 4 of Schedule 5 to the Criminal Justice and Court Services Act 2000, as well as measures to prevent the improper use of evidence relating to sexual offences in the Sexual Offences (Protected Material) Act 1997. Special measures to assist complainants of sexual offences were introduced by the Youth Justice and Criminal Evidence Act 1999. Monitoring of persons working with children was strengthened by the Protection of Children Act 1999 and the Criminal Justice and Court Services Act 2000 and by the establishment of the Criminal Records Bureau. The Protection of Freedoms Act 2012 established a new organisation with responsibilities for vetting the criminal records of potential employees working with vulnerable groups, including children: the Disclosure and Barring Service, which replaced and combined the functions of the Independent Safeguarding Authority and Criminal Records Bureau.

In addition, penalties for possession of indecent photographs of children were increased and the regime for inspecting residential homes was improved. Cooperation between agencies to manage the risk posed by sexual and serious offenders in the community was formalised and given a statutory basis in the Criminal Justice and Court Services Act 2000, re-enacted by the CJA 2003. The SOA 2003 changed the law relating to the issue of consent in rape cases and included provisions on sexual offences against children, abuse of a position of trust, abuse of children through prostitution and pornography, and introduced new civil preventive orders designed to protect children. A new offence of possession of extreme pornography was also created by s. 63 of the CJIA 2008 and extended to include images of rape and assault by penetration by s. 37 of the CJCA 2015 (see also Easton 2011b).

New measures to control the movements of sex offenders were also introduced in the late 1990s. The Sex Offenders Act 1997 provided for the creation of a register recording all persons convicted of or cautioned for a sexual offence. Part I imposed a requirement for convicted and cautioned sex offenders to notify the police of their name and address and inform them of any changes of residence, including holidays. How long the individual stayed subject to the notification requirements depended on the length of the sentence imposed for the offence. These notification requirements are now found in the Sexual Offences Act 2003.

The CDA 1998 introduced the Sex Offender Order, a civil order which prohibited the offender from engaging in conduct such as loitering near a school. The Chief Officer of Police could apply for an order if a person who is a convicted or cautioned sex offender had acted, since his conviction or caution, in such a way as to give reasonable cause to believe that an order under the section was necessary to protect the public from serious harm. The Sex Offender Order was then replaced by the Sexual Offences Prevention Order (SOPO) in the SOA 2003.

The SOPO was a civil order whose aim was to protect the public from serious sexual harm, although, as before, its breach constitutes a criminal offence, punishable on conviction by a maximum of five years' imprisonment. The SOA 2003 also introduced foreign travel orders which enabled the magistrates' court to restrict the travel of those convicted in the UK or abroad of sexual offences against a child under 16, if the court was satisfied that the defendant's behaviour since the relevant conviction made this necessary in order to protect children from serious sexual harm from the defendant. The orders could prevent travel to a specified country or travelling to anywhere in the world. The 2003 Act also introduced a new 'Risk of Sexual Harm Order'. This was more extensive, in so far as it was not necessary for the defendant to have been convicted of an offence; only that on at least two previous occasions, the defendant had engaged in two acts of a sexual nature which made it necessary to grant such an order. The order could prohibit the offender from doing anything described in the order which is necessary to protect the child or children from harm from the defendant.

A new regime was introduced by s. 113 of the Anti-social Behaviour, Crime and Policing Act 2014, which amended the 2003 Act, as the above orders were abolished and replaced by two new orders in England and Wales. The Sexual Harm Prevention Order (SHPO) applies to a wide range of sexual offences defined in Schedules 3 and 5 to the Act. An order may be granted if the court is persuaded that the defendant's behaviour subsequent to the first relevant conviction makes the order necessary to protect the public or any particular members of the public from sexual harm from the defendant. It may prohibit the offender from carrying out any activities described in the order and can include a ban on foreign travel. The offender will also be subject to the notification requirements in the 2003 Sex Offenders Act for the duration of the order if he is not already a registered sex offender. The order will last for a minimum of five years.

The order also brings the offender within the remit of the Multi-Agency Public Protection Panel arrangements. There is a legal requirement on the police, and the Probation and Prison Services, to organise arrangements to assess and manage the risks presented by violent and sexual offenders, to monitor these arrangements, and to furnish annual reports.

The new Sexual Risk Order (SRO) replaces the Risk of Sexual Harm Order. The court can grant the order if it believes that an order is necessary to protect the public or a particular member of the public from harm from the defendant or to protect a child or vulnerable adult from outside the UK. The court can grant such an order if it is satisfied that the defendant has committed one act of a sexual nature as a result of which it is necessary to make such an order. Under the RSHO two acts were necessary. The SRO can include prevention of foreign travel to specified countries. Breach of the order will mean the defendant becomes subject to the notification requirements. It is not necessary for the defendant to have been convicted. In relation to both SHPOs and SROs interim orders can be granted and the defendant can appeal against the making of the order.

Although these are also civil orders, their breach constitutes a criminal offence punishable by a maximum of five years' imprisonment. Each of the orders in the Act is essentially based on an assessment of the risk of future offending and, as such, raises problems of prediction and justification, which will be discussed further in Chapter 5.

Sex offenders have now been absorbed into the discourse of risk management, and surveillance has extended beyond the prison into ordinary life. Risk assessment is part of this process of transcarceration and the move towards ever greater surveillance and acquisition of knowledge, charted by Foucault (1977) and Beck (1992), has found expression in the new legislation. There is now less public tolerance of sex offenders in the UK, less sympathy for medical models of individual pathology, and greater willingness to see sex offenders as bad rather than mad, to be removed from the community rather than being changed or cured through treatment. The dominant model in therapeutic programmes is the cognitive-behavioural model, which accepts that it is more productive to focus on the development of reasoning skills and new ways of thinking rather than to search for the underlying causes of deviant behaviour, which may be too time-consuming and ultimately unattainable. The issues of risk assessment of sexual offenders, as well as the efficacy of current policies and methods of treatment, are assessed by Harrison (2011), who considers the ways of addressing gaps within the system and improving the treatment of serious sexual and violent offenders, while Reeves (2013) considers the impact of the prevailing discourse on sex offenders on their experiences of life in a probation-approved hostel. Within prison sex offenders are themselves at risk from other prisoners, and Ievins and Crewe (2015) consider the way they negotiate their stigmatisation and moral exclusion.

Attempts to categorise levels of risk of sex offenders for the purposes of the registration scheme may be problematic, as the criteria for registration are unwieldy and do not distinguish between them in terms of individual risk but, rather, impose a period of registration based on sentence length. The penalties imposed for breaches of the orders have also been variable (see Shute 2004a).

The UK government's focus on risk management in response to the public's punitiveness has also raised problems as it has come into conflict with the protection of human rights. For example, the UK courts have already issued a declaration of incompatibility over the imposition of lifelong notification requirements for offenders sentenced to over 30 months, without any provision for review. In *R (on the application of F and Angus Aubrey Thompson) v Secretary of State for the Home Department* (2010), the Supreme Court has ruled that the absence of a review is disproportionate and breaches Article 8 of the European Convention on Human Rights. The court ruled that there must be an opportunity for the offender to show that indefinite notification is no longer necessary. In this case one of the appellants had committed the offence as a child. In response to this decision, the government drafted a Remedial Order, setting out a review mechanism, and is awaiting comments on this consultation. It has also undertaken a consultation on strengthening the notification requirements, for example with new provisions for those of no fixed abode.

However, for some sections of the public the measures to control sex offenders that are currently available are insufficiently punitive and should be supplemented by full disclosure and preventive detention. A limited step towards disclosure was made by setting up public disclosure pilot schemes in 2008 in Hampshire, Warwickshire, Cambridgeshire, and Cleveland police force areas. These schemes permitted parents, guardians, or carers to check with the police if a person with access to their children had convictions for child sex offences. The Child Sex Offender Disclosure Scheme was subsequently extended to all police forces in England and Wales in 2010/11. The One Year Disclosure Pilots were reviewed by Kemshall and Wood (2010), who found a lower number of applications than expected, no evidence of serious breaches of confidentiality, and no changes in compliance of offenders with registration and probation supervision. A new Domestic Violence Disclosure Scheme, known as Clare's Law—after Clare Wood, who was murdered by her ex-boyfriend—was also introduced in 2014 and allows the police to disclose information on request regarding a partner's previous history of violence or domestic violence.

The move towards restricting the movement of sex offenders reflects a wider use of civil orders to reinforce the criminal law, while avoiding Article 7 Convention challenges as retrospective penalties. As well as the range of measures directed against sex offenders, we have seen in recent years increased use of ASBOs, originally introduced by the Crime and Disorder Act 1998 and replaced by the injunction to prevent nuisance and disorder and the criminal behaviour orders in the Anti-social Behaviour, Crime and Policing Act 2014. Section 1 of the Serious Crime Act 2007 introduced another order, the serious crime prevention order, which is similar in some respects to the SHPO and ASBO, and which aims to exert control over the movements and assets of those involved in serious crime. Although creating civil orders, these provisions create new criminal offences of failing to comply with these orders, which attract criminal penalties. The aim is to protect the public by preventing, restricting, and disrupting involvement in serious crime. In addition, the courts have powers to impose extensive controls on individuals' movements under anti-terrorist legislation and to impose travel restriction orders in relation to serious cases of drug trafficking.

We also now have Violent Offender Orders (s. 98) introduced by the CJIA 2008. The aim of the Violent Offender Order is to protect the public from serious harm by imposing further restrictions on violent offenders. However, it is likely that if the terms imposed are too restrictive the move towards increasing controls may raise future Convention challenges and arguments over whether they constitute retrospective punishments. Collectively we can see a shift towards controls within the community intended to protect the public by preventing possible future offending, which, as we shall see in Chapters 2 and 3, raises problems for retributivism. We also find increasing emphasis on prisoners' rights under the European Convention on Human Rights, with Convention challenges being brought in both the domestic courts and the Strasbourg Court (see Chapter 8, section 8.6).

1.5.3 **Case study: JD**

JD, aged 40, has a history of sexual offences against young children over the past 15 years, for which he is currently serving a custodial sentence. His favoured methods of gaining access to children include watching them in the school playground, following them home, approaching children in amusement arcades, and befriending children playing on the seafront.

His last conviction was in 2010 and he is shortly to be released. On his release he plans to move back to his former home town of Brighton, where he has many friends, and hopes to find employment in the area. He also has a new girlfriend, whom he met on an Internet dating site, and hopes to move in with her and her young family. The police are concerned that he remains a threat to young children.

1. Consider what can be done to protect young children living in the area from this person.

   In considering your options, select from the range of measures now available to monitor the movements of offenders released into the community and ways of restricting their movements.

2. Do the measures you identify respect the offender's human rights?

3. Are you satisfied that the measures you have discussed are adequate to protect children in the local area? If not, what further measures might be introduced and what problems might they raise?

online resource centre

Guidance on approaching these questions is given in the Online Resource Centre, where you will also find references to texts and cases which you might find useful.

1.5.4 **Questions for discussion**

Consider the influence of the following factors on the introduction of the raft of new measures to deal with sex offenders in and since the 1990s.

(a) Political factors.

(b) Economic factors.

(c) Public opinion.

(d) Penological theories.

2

Structuring sentencing

SUMMARY

A sentencing system in which there were no controls on how the judge or magistrate came to a decision on sentence would not be a principled system and could lead to injustice in individual cases. This chapter examines the ways in which sentencing discretion is constrained, not only through law and guidance but also through the use of a justificatory principle as a constraint. In particular it reviews the development of new forms of sentencing guidance, notably the definitive guidelines produced by the Sentencing Council, and discusses in detail the importance of a retributivist rationale.

2.1 Justice and discretion

2.1.1 Who decides what is 'fair'?

Judges, magistrates, politicians, and the public want sentencing to be 'fair'. They do not want to see offenders getting different punishments for the same offence; they want punishments not to be too severe or too lenient but 'just right'. This is a tall order, and one which goes to the core of sentencing and the extent to which the discretion of the courts needs to be limited to achieve the 'just right' outcome. In other words: how far should the government or bodies set up by Parliament be able to control the individual sentencer in this search for fairness and justice?

Since we wrote the first edition of this text in 2005 we have seen a significant change in the amount and type of guidance for sentencing courts. In the twenty-first century there has been what Ashworth has referred to as a 'struggle for supremacy in sentencing' (2013: 15). The result was that, despite opposition from the judiciary and magistracy, the Sentencing Advisory Panel set up in 1998 was joined by the Sentencing Guidelines Council, and then both were replaced by the Sentencing Council. Arguably, the freedom of the judge or magistrate to choose a particular sentence has been reduced over the past two decades by these changes such that judicial discretion has been restricted. In contrast, for most of the twentieth century, sentencers had considerable freedom to choose a penalty. Ashworth and Roberts argue that the change has been driven not only by the desire for greater consistency at the sentencing stage but also by 'the need to achieve greater accuracy in projections of the number of prisoners' (Ashworth and Roberts 2013: 1). Other objectives have been noted: guidelines 'provide a more sophisticated range of mechanisms' through which Parliament can influence sentencing practice and they increase transparency in sentencing policy and practice (Young and King 2013: 203–5).

It is of course axiomatic that a principled structure for sentencing entails constraining the sentencer: the proper control and exercise of judicial discretion is crucial in the quest for justice in sentencing. However, what is construed as fair or just depends on changing ideas of social justice and on the theoretical approach which is taken to understanding the notion of punishment itself. There is consensus only in the belief that it would be unjust if an agency or individual could use its power to impose and implement whatever punishment it wished to impose, so justice in sentencing requires at the very least that the discretion of those individuals who undertake the sentencing of convicted criminals is checked by a set of principles or a framework of rules. But, as Ashworth asks in relation to sentencing guidelines, 'how tightly should they bind?' (2013: 30). Further, in a democracy, sentencing may not be perceived as just if those rules and principles are not acceptable to the electorate.

The discretion continuum

If we consider discretion to be operating on a continuum, from complete to no discretion, available to those who must make sentencing decisions in individual cases, it can be argued that outcomes at both ends are unjust. At one extreme, sentencing is unjust because there are no constraints whatsoever on the sentencer, who can then make decisions, if he or she so wishes, based on personal prejudices and whims. Since K. C. Davis published *Discretionary Justice* in 1969 a strand of academic thinking has regarded discretion, as he did, as the major source of injustice and something to be confined and structured (see, for example, Hawkins 1992: 16–17). At the other end of the spectrum is the sentencer who has no discretion whatsoever because the rules and principles are so tightly drawn, with all potential factors accounted for, that the sentencer is simply the technician who feeds in the data and reads off the answer, in this case the sentence. This too might be viewed as potentially unjust in that it could not take account of any individual circumstances that had not been foreseen when the rules were drawn up.

The logical conclusion is that justice is to be found between the two ends of this discretion spectrum, but this still leaves a wide scope for a variety of approaches to limiting total discretion in sentencing. And, as Gelsthorpe and Padfield have argued, discretion is one of the most contentious concepts in criminal justice:

> Indeed it is the day-to-day discretionary action of police officers, prosecutors, defence lawyers, judges, psychiatrists, prison, probation and immigration officers, among others, which are the 'stuff of justice' and which make for justice or injustice.

> (Gelsthorpe and Padfield 2003: 1)

That is why we are focusing on this issue first: the second half of this chapter will concentrate on fundamental principles and how they can be, and are, used to constrain discretion.

We will examine in detail the classical retributivist justifications for punishment, with a focus on Kant and Hegel, because those justifications have been, and still are, very important in structuring sentencing discretion. They determine what should be the first, and so most influential, questions that the judge or magistrate addresses in the process leading to a sentencing decision. The notion of 'just deserts', that the punishment is what the offender deserves and that it is proportional to the offence, is the term currently used to sum up a retributivist approach to sentencing and so we will also analyse contemporary thinking on just deserts. In Chapter 3 we will examine in detail the ways, and the extent to which, this approach has been incorporated in English sentencing law.

One reason why constraints are placed on the sentencer by the state is, then, to respond to the notion that totally unconstrained discretion is inherently unjust: 'In a liberal state, law is to be applied consistently, openly, and dispassionately; rules are regarded as the most appropriate means to these ends. Discretion represents the opposite; it is subjective justice where rules are formal justice' (Hawkins 1992: 150). The expectation is that the rule of law will be upheld because the citizen must have confidence in the law and institutions of the state. 'Discretionary decision-making is condemned as a cavalier disregard for this imperative' and threatens to undermine the 'moral' allegiance of the citizen to the criminal justice system (Salter and Twist 2007).

Constitutional issues

Consequently, in democratic states neither the professional nor the lay judge can do just what they might want to do when sentencing. There are rules that, to a greater or lesser extent, guide them in the exercise of their discretion. Having said that, the discretion of the sentencing judge, established in the course of the eighteenth century, has been described as 'the central principle of the English sentencing system' (Thomas 2002: 473) and changes threatening to constrain that discretion still provoke debate as to the right balance between democratic control and judicial independence. As noted, 'The first decade of the twenty-first century saw further conflicts in what may be termed the politics of sentencing' (Ashworth 2013: 15). For example, the House of Commons Justice Committee revisited the issues when discussing the role of the newly created Sentencing Council. Its Report (Justice Committee, 2009: para 24) included the statement of the Rt Hon Lord Judge, Lord Chief Justice, that '[t]he point about the judicial discretion is that a judge is trying to do justice in the individual case'.[1] The Council for HM Circuit Judges also expressed their fear that 'executive or legislative encroachment would put the separation of powers at risk undermining the Constitution'.[2] Yet democratic legitimacy requires that Parliament has a role in determining the sentencing framework.

How far rules should constrain the sentencer is, then, a matter of debate. As we shall see in section 2.2, in the UK we have the paradoxical situation where judges and magistrates have, historically, been provided with an increasingly wide choice of available penalties, while, at the same time, the trend has been to circumscribe their discretion. In section 2.1.2 we consider the arguments in favour of the trend towards more constraining guidelines.

2.1.2 **Discretion as 'bad'**

This idea that discretion is the opposite of formal justice, arising from debates around the concept of 'the rule of law' (Dicey 1885), has led to a raft of criticisms of a wide discretion for sentencers. One of the most compelling, already noted, is that it leads to inconsistency of sentencing in which similar cases may not be treated similarly. Indeed, parliamentary anxiety about the differential treatment of persistent but minor offenders was one of the factors leading to the creation of the Court of Criminal Appeal in 1907 (see Thomas 2002: 474, 484–5).

By the end of the twentieth century a major concern arising from research results was that there appear to be geographic variations in custodial sentencing in England and Wales. For example, in 2000 the custody rate in magistrates' courts varied from 0.8 per cent in Elbes (Lincolnshire) to 23.4 per cent in Luton and South Bedfordshire,[3] while research on environmental prosecutions in 1999–2003 (primarily on offences relating to pollution and wildlife) also found that the average length of a custodial sentence varied

---

[1] Oral Evidence taken before the Justice Committee on Sentencing Guidelines, 22 January 2008, HC (2007/8) 279-i.

[2] Council of HM Circuit Judges Response to the Sentencing Commission Working Group Consultation, 30 May 2008.

[3] The annually published *Criminal Statistics* web link provides a variety of supplementary tables as well as the national statistics. See the Online Resource Centre.

considerably—from two months in Wales to nearly 18 months in the eastern region, with the highest average fine of nearly £5,000 to be found in the London region and the lowest, at under £2,000, in the eastern region and Wales (Dupont and Zakkour 2003: 12, 17). Home Office research on the period 2003 to 2006 similarly showed that average custodial sentence lengths and the use of life and indeterminate sentences for public protection varied significantly across the 42 Criminal Justice Areas in England and Wales. Again the research found that differences in sentencing practice could not be explained solely in terms of the characteristics of the cases or of the offenders coming before the courts (Mason *et al.* 2007).

The concern is that the exercise of discretion is not being limited to the 'relevant idiosyncrasies' of a case (Feldman 1992: 172–5). While it is not necessarily easy to establish what counts as relevant, this must be done or, as Ashworth put it, the notion of disparity 'might be used as a basis for criticising our sentencing system for not treating all red-haired offenders in the same way' (Ashworth 1987: 24). Further, when apparent disparities have been found, the counterargument expressed is that 'no two cases are the same' or that research has not identified the crucial differences. On the other hand, as Hood noted some time ago, 'magistrates and judges . . . place particular value upon their experience in sentencing. Now, if this experience is to be of value, then all cases cannot be unique, they must be comparable in some respects' (1962: 16). Yet whether studies focus on geography, race, gender, or class, whether 'real' disparity is proved, or whether there is only a perception that sentencing is inconsistent, the policy concern is the same—that the legitimacy of the sentencing process may be undermined in the eyes of the public.

What is of particular concern is whether discretion allows 'space' for discrimination—personal or institutional—to occur. Again the focus of research has often been the custodial sentence and, notably, the fact that particular ethnic minorities are over-represented in prison (see Chapter 9). Criminologists have focused on disentangling whether or not this discrepancy is the result of direct or indirect racial discrimination (see Bowling and Phillips 2002: chapter 7). Research has also investigated whether personal, class, or gender aspects of the defendant's behaviour influence the sentencer. For example, Hedderman's research suggested that 'women may receive more lenient sentences than men because they are more nervous and act more respectfully and deferentially to the Bench' (1990: 36).

Wide discretion is also criticised as diminishing the possibility of accurately predicting sentence outcome: sanctions cannot give a clear deterrent message to past or potential offenders, and solicitors and barristers are unable to advise their clients effectively. Further, if judges or magistrates tend to sentence at the top end of what is legally permissible, 'over-sentencing' occurs and resource issues arise. As previously noted, too wide a sentencing discretion has implications for governments wishing to introduce new sentencing policies.

The rules to achieve sentencing goals—the techniques and tools by which sentencing discretion is 'structured'—can take many forms, not just the Sentencing Council guidelines to which we have so far referred. The more obvious ones are the rules relating to the availability and choice of punishments, and to the maximum and minimum amounts of punishment allowed in a particular jurisdiction. They might also be financial or administrative constraints. What has become increasingly important is the constraint of an imposed justificatory principle, and we examine that in sections 2.4–2.6.

2.1.3 Criticism: discretion is 'good'

Not all academic analysis has concurred with the idea that discretion is inherently 'bad', that inconsistency is caused by individual behaviour, or that discretion needs to be rule-guided. Writing in the context of prosecutorial discretion in the Health and Safety Inspectorate,

Hawkins has argued that '[s]ystems of formal rules, for all their appearance of precision and specificity, work in only imprecise ways. Indeed, precision and consistent practice are not necessarily assisted by the drafting of ever more elaborate schemes of rules' (2002: 424).

The use of the tool of mandatory sentences (see section 2.2.5) to achieve policy outcomes has received particular criticism on the basis that constraints on the exercise of judicial discretion have gone too far towards the other end of the spectrum. The main arguments in favour of some or more sentencing discretion are the following:

1. Reduced discretion results in a decreased possibility that justice can be tailored to the specific circumstances of a case or individual. This might itself lead to injustice.

2. Research on practice in jurisdictions which have had mandatory sentencing for some time would suggest that its stated utilitarian aims cannot be delivered. Tonry, in a chapter summarising what is known about the effectiveness of mandatory sentences, begins: 'the greatest gap between knowledge and policy in American sentencing concerns mandatory penalties' (Tonry 1996: 134). The conclusion is that selective incapacitation has little deterrent or protective function in practice (see the discussion in Chapters 4 and 5).

3. Judges and other legal professionals may seek ways to circumvent mandatory provisions. Discretion elsewhere in the criminal justice process could become the site for increased professional activity to 'negotiate justice' for clients in order that the mandatory sentence might be avoided (Tonry 1996: 148–54). The image used to illustrate this is that of a hosepipe in which the pressure of water must burst out somewhere if all the 'holes' of discretion are blocked. An example given of this 'hydraulic effect' is plea bargaining: lawyers would negotiate a lower charge in return for a guilty plea to avoid a charge which could lead to a severe mandatory sentence. Judges too might engage in adaptive behaviour and attempt to circumvent sentencing guidelines to avoid doing what they believed would amount to an injustice (Tonry 1996: 150–1, 169–73; see also Ashworth 1998a: 235).

4. The lack of discretion at the sentencing stage could encourage more 'not guilty' pleas. The accused might consider that more is at stake if the likely penalty is severe and so choose to risk a trial. This would increase the workload of courts and add to the financial cost. Research by the US Sentencing Commission, *Mandatory Minimum Penalties in the Federal Criminal Justice System*, did find significantly higher than normal trial rates where the offence concerned mandatory sentences (Tonry 1996: 150; see also Henham 1997: 273).

5. The insertion of specific sentences into an otherwise discretion-based sentencing system will skew the 'tariff' which in practice determines a scale of severity-related punishments.

6. The lack of discretion may lead to constitutional or human rights violations.

Yet these arguments may have little policy force because there are, as we have seen, political imperatives and symbolic goals which may outweigh the money 'wasted' or even the likelihood of a rights challenge. Mandatory sentences have given clear messages to the electorate that Parliament is ensuring that sentencers will be sufficiently tough to protect them.

2.1.4 Sentencing choices: contradictory trends

We saw in Chapter 1 that there are a variety of complex influences accounting for the changes in penal policy in the 1990s and the early years of the twenty-first century. Here we wish to review the longer-term trend towards widening the choice of penalties while narrowing the discretion to choose. This development has not been a steady incremental process but has occurred as periodic responses to particular sets of problems perceived at that time.

Garland argues that 1895–1914 was the crucial period in the history of modern penality, with the number of sanctions almost doubling in this period (1985: 19). Legislation, including the Prison Act 1898, the Probation of Offenders Act 1907, and the Prevention of Crime Act 1908, added probation orders, Borstal training, preventive detention, and detention of those whom we would now call mentally disordered offenders. The impetus was a general social, economic, and political anxiety about the 'underclass' and a belief that a mixture of penal and social welfare reforms could 'solve' the problems (Garland 1985: 244–52).

The next period of change was between 1945 and 1973, when two 'bursts' of sentencing legislation took place. The legislation passed immediately after the Second World War and that in the late 1960s and early 1970s evidenced a renewed focus on the offender and the development of rehabilitative and community-based penalties. The Criminal Justice Act of 1948 made the use of fines more widely available and introduced new sentences with a focus on the offender. In 1965 another spate of legislation saw the abolition (for most purposes) of the death penalty, and the addition of suspended prison sentences (Criminal Justice Act 1967), absolute and conditional discharges (Powers of Criminal Courts Act 1973), community service orders, and compensation orders (Criminal Justice Act 1972). The social and political contexts for both these periods were ones of social and economic optimism when there was a strong belief in the power of science, including social work, to solve the problem of crime.

Those contexts contrast with the period 1982–91, when there was a less favourable economic climate and the New Right approach developed as a political response. The welfarist solutions favoured since the 1940s gave way to a focus on legal justice, individual responsibility, and encouragement of the 'privatisation' of penal provision. For sentencers it meant a greater focus on offender culpability, evidenced in the establishment of 'just deserts' as the main sentencing rationale. It also entailed more punishment for those who were not behaving as responsible citizens, evidenced in increases in maximum terms of imprisonment and the greater availability of restrictive conditions for supervision and probation orders. On the other hand, increasing expenditure on prisons led to reduced judicial discretion by the imposition of statutory criteria to limit the use of custodial penalties, first for minors in the Criminal Justice Acts of 1982 and 1988 and then for all offenders in the Criminal Justice Act (CJA) 1991.

During this period the growing perception that communities were disintegrating, paradoxically, also fed into a policy interest in punishment in and by the community (see Chapter 10) evidenced in the CJA 1991. In addition, new provisions to make it easier for the courts to confiscate the proceeds of crime were introduced (see Chapter 7, section 7.2).

The period since 1993 is more difficult to summarise. On the one hand, the new penological thinking and the development of the public's punitiveness encouraged 'tougher' sentencing with a reduced discretion in relation to offenders perceived to be dangerous, particularly in relation to the new sentences introduced by the Criminal Justice Act (CJA) 2003, until they were amended by the Criminal Justice and Immigration Act (CJIA) 2008 (see Chapters 1 and 5). Several Acts increased the statutory maxima for custodial sentences for various offences; the Crime (Sentences) Act 1997 introduced automatic life (repealed in 2003) and mandatory minimum custodial sentences. The Criminal Justice Act 1993 apparently allowed the courts to give more weight to previous offending and the CJA 2003 consolidated this approach. On the other hand, there has been a greater focus on community sentences and restorative justice with a corresponding wider range of options for the courts: the Crime and Disorder Act (CDA) 1998 introduced, inter alia, new youth court orders and extended post-custody supervision; the CJIA 2008 introduced the new youth rehabilitation order (YRO); and the Legal Aid, Sentencing and Punishment of Offenders Act (LASPO) 2012 widened the use of referral orders.

Sentencing legislation was consolidated in the Powers of Criminal Courts (Sentencing) Act (PCCSA) 2000 but most of the sentencing provisions were quickly superseded. The CJA 2003 introduced new custodial and community sentences and a revised sentencing framework for their use. The Domestic Violence, Crime and Victims Act 2004 signified the increasing policy emphasis on victims while the CJIA 2008, inter alia, introduced YROs and Violent Offender Orders. LASPO 2012 significantly altered the sentences for dangerous offenders (see Chapter 5) and also allowed courts to suspend sentences of up to two years rather than 12 months. (See Chapter 1, section 1.4.4 for more information about sentencing policy changes in the period 2010–2015.)

In the period since 1993, legislation to structure sentencing has evidenced 'traditional' constraints, such as the availability of penalties and restrictions on their use, but also new ways of constraining sentencing discretion, notably statutory 'hurdles' to the imposition of certain penalties. This period has also witnessed very significant developments in relation to the bodies providing guidance to sentencers. These will be considered in sections 2.2 and 2.3.

2.2 Constraining the sentencer

2.2.1 The availability and use of penalties

Perhaps the most obvious point to make is that judges and magistrates can only impose a penalty which is legally available in the jurisdiction. The current range of penalties contrasts with early sentencing law when there were only three options: 'The penalty for **felony** was death; the penalty for a **misdemeanour** was unlimited imprisonment or an unlimited fine' (Thomas 2002: 473). Even in 1905 the only available penalties for use in England and Wales for offenders aged over 17 were still death, imprisonment, penal servitude, fines, and common law binding-over powers (including supervision by the Police Court Mission after the Probation of Offenders Act 1887). A century later, after the implementation of the CJA 2003, the following penalties were available to the court:

- imprisonment/detention, suspended sentence;
- community orders—with a list of requirements from which the sentencer can choose;
- various ancillary orders including the compensation order;[4]
- fine;
- discharge.

Judges and magistrates are also constrained with respect to the amount of punishment they can order. There are restrictions on the upper 'amount' of sentence that can be legally imposed—the maximum laid down in legislation—whether it be in terms of sentence length for custodial and community penalties or for the amount of a financial penalty. For example, many of the more serious offences, such as domestic burglary, supplying a Class B drug, and racially aggravated criminal damage, carry a statutory maximum of 14 years' imprisonment. These maxima are changed by Parliament in response to public perceptions of seriousness. For example, Schedule 28 to the CJA 2003 raised to 14 years the maximum for other specified drug-related offences.

---

[4] These are dealt with more fully in Chapter 7, section 7.2.

Taken as a whole, maximum penalties do not necessarily constitute a well-thought-out and coherent system. As a report of the Advisory Council on the Penal System stated nearly 40 years ago, 'on looking into the history of maximum penalties of imprisonment in this country, we discovered that they have grown up largely as a result of historical accident' (1978: para 14). There are also political and pragmatic considerations which override rationality. Neither should the maximum penalty be seen as the 'normal' top end of the sentencing options: courts established their own 'normal range' of penalties and the new bodies charged with producing guidelines have also largely used this approach (see Chapter 3).

Not all of these penalties are available for all sentencers or for all offenders. There are several different sorts of limit which apply, in addition to the statutory maxima.

Limits on sentencing powers of magistrates' courts

Cases are allocated for trial and sentencing to one or other of the two levels of courts in England and Wales (see, generally, Sanders *et al.* 2010: chapters 9 and 10) and for most offences minors must be allocated to the youth court. The lower courts—the magistrates' and youth courts—are more restricted in their sentencing powers than the Crown Court. So, to use domestic burglary as an example, the magistrates' court cannot impose the maximum sentence of 14 years because the statutory maximum custodial sentence available to the magistrates' court is six months.[5] Magistrates are also subject to a minimum term of five days when imposing a custodial sentence (Magistrates' Courts Act 1980, s. 132).

Age categories

Certain penalties may not be available for children and young people or for adults. For example, reparation orders are currently available only for those under 18 years of age (PCCSA 2000, s. 73), although reparation may be part of an activity requirement in a community order for any offender (CJA 2003, s. 201(2)). There are also extra restrictions on using custodial penalties for minors (see Chapter 11).

2.2.2 Financial and organisational factors

There are important extra-legal factors which influence either the amount of discretion the sentencing courts can exercise or the outcome post-sentencing.

Allocation of resources

In relation to both community and custodial sentences, funding is a major influence on practice. The setting and **ring-fencing** of budgets for the National Probation Service (NPS) and the **outsourcing** of services affects the content and availability of community penalties and the custodial experience. This could lead to gender differences in sentencing if, for example, resources did not permit the establishment of community punishment schemes suitable for women, particularly those with young children. It can also lead to a different range of options for sentencers if, for example, a particular community rehabilitation company has not commissioned specific rehabilitation programmes.

Administrative and executive powers

Traditionally the Home Secretary and also bodies such as the Parole Board have had powers which can affect the length of custodial sentences served. In recent years the

---

[5] The CJA 2003, s. 154(1) would have raised this maximum to 12 months but the provision was never implemented: the LAS&PO Bill 2011 originally proposed to repeal this section but that was dropped. Note that consecutive terms of imprisonment are allowed by the Magistrates' Courts Act 1980, s. 133.

influence of the European Convention on Human Rights has affected the operation of these powers and proved to be a constraint on their use (see, for example, Chapter 8 in regard to prison procedures and conditions and Chapter 11 for issues relating to minors).

Guidance and training

The guidance from the Sentencing Council and its predecessor bodies will be dealt with in section 2.3, but here we note that the Home Office, in particular, has been involved for some time in developing and circulating guidance generally on policy and professional practice. For example, 30 years ago the Home Office sent a copy of an interim report, *The Length of Prison Sentences*, to every judge and bench of magistrates. The message of that report was that prison should be used as little as possible: 'the general rule which we advocate . . . is to stop at the point where a sentence has been decided upon and consider whether a shorter one would do just as well' (Advisory Council on the Penal System 1977). More recent examples are the National Standards in regard to the aims and best practice of the Probation Service and Youth Justice Services.

It has been accepted since at least the report of the Streatfeild Committee in 1961 that judges require training in the principles and approaches desired by Parliament and laid down in guidance. The Final Report of the Bridges Committee in 1978 had, however, been forced to replace the word 'training' used in the interim report with 'studies' because of judicial hostility to what was seen as a threat to judicial independence (see Ashworth 1983). The function of judicial training was for many years undertaken in England and Wales by the Judicial Studies Board (JSB), which after 1985 also had responsibilities for training stipendiary magistrates, now district judges, and had an advisory role in the training of lay magistrates. Since April 2011, when the JSB and Tribunals Judicial Training Group merged, these functions have been carried out by the Judicial College.[6]

Other factors

The background to many of these constraints is the contentious issue of the relationship between public opinion, the media, and sentencing policy. As Chapter 1 pointed out, the nature of the relationship is problematic, given the public's misconceptions about sentencing and the difficulty of researching either public opinion or its influence on those who decide policy or who sentence (see, for example, Roberts *et al.* 2008 in relation to offences involving death by driving, and Hough *et al.* 2009 re sentencing principles). Equally problematic is the potentially influential new constraint, that of the victim's assessment of the seriousness of the offending against him. (For details of the new procedures for gaining the views of victims, see Chapter 7, section 7.1.3.)

2.2.3 **The policy context for new constraints**

An increasing concern of governments in the 1990s was to enhance the legitimacy of the sentencing system, if necessary in ways that conflicted with the need to save money. The Halliday Report made this important statement—echoing our discussion about justice and discretion—on the first page of its report:

> At its roots, sentencing contributes to good order in society. It does so by visibly upholding society's norms and standards; dealing appropriately with those who breach them; and

---

[6] See https://www.judiciary.gov.uk/about-the-judiciary/training-support/judicial-college/.

enabling the public to have confidence in its outcomes. The public, as a result, can legitimately be expected to uphold and observe the law, and not to take it into their own hands. To achieve this there must be confidence in the justice of the outcomes, as well as in their effectiveness.

(2001: para 1.3)

Policy based on these concerns encouraged a reduction in the use of custody for the 'normal' offender while allowing its continued or greater use for particular classes of offender where other policy imperatives, notably the need to restore confidence in the criminal justice system, were deemed politically expedient. This is a **bifurcationary**, or two-pronged, policy to achieve conflicting policy aims by allocating each aim to different sets of offenders. *Justice for All* said that 'prison must be reserved for serious, dangerous and seriously persistent offenders and those who have failed to respond to community punishment' (Home Office 2002c: 17) and Lord Falconer explained, 'in other cases, public protection can best be achieved effectively through rigorous community sentences' (Home Office 2002b).

Government concern with public confidence in the criminal justice system has also led to a policy concern with the principles and theories which might be used to justify current practice and proposed changes. The 1970s and 1980s witnessed a reaction against rehabilitative approaches and a renewed focus on seriousness; the 1990s saw the priority given to seriousness diminishing and new ideas about restorative sentencing becoming more influential (see Chapter 6), with discredited ideas about rehabilitation themselves being rehabilitated under a 'what works?' policy focus (see Chapter 10), and concern with risk and public protection (see Chapter 5).

There were also four developments in the 1990s to help structure sentencing discretion in line with policy aims. These were the incorporation in legislation of new 'hurdles' for the imposition of custodial and community sentences, the introduction of new mandatory sentences, the prioritisation of a sentencing rationale, and the establishment of new bodies to produce guidance on sentencing policy.

2.2.4 **Imposing hurdles**

The CJA 1991 introduced a provision whereby custodial and community sentences could be imposed only if the offence reached a particular level of seriousness so that the statutory hurdle could be surmounted. This technique is not strictly an invention of the 1990s as it had similarities to the first-time offender provision in the PCCA 1973 and provisions for juveniles and young adults in the Criminal Justice Act 1982. That Act had stated that custody could be imposed only if at least one of the following criteria applied: an unwillingness on the part of the offender to respond to non-custodial penalties, that custody was necessary to protect the public, and that the offence was so serious that only custody could be justified. Their policy import was not immediately understood by the judiciary or magistracy (Burney 1985; Reynolds 1985) but Court of Appeal judgments and pressure from the Parliamentary All-Party Penal Affairs Group led to amendments made by the Criminal Justice Act 1988 to strengthen the constraint (Dunbar and Langton 1998: 73–8).

At least partly because of those provisions, the custodial rate for minors had decreased in the 1980s, and that fact was a major influence on the genesis of the CJA 1991 (see Dunbar and Langton 1998: chapter 8). Section 1 borrowed the 'so serious that only' custody could be justified and the 'only such a sentence would be adequate to protect the public' criteria from the 1982 Act to apply to the imposition of custody for all offenders. Similarly, community penalties could only be imposed if they were 'serious enough' for such punishments and a fine had to reflect the seriousness of the offence. These were re-enacted in the PCCSA

2000 (ss. 35, 79–80, and 128) and, with minor amendments, in the CJA 2003 (ss. 148, 152, and 164). In regard to community sentences for adults and minors, s. 10 of the CJIA 2008 inserts a new s. 148(5) into the CJA 2003 to give the court discretion not to impose such a sentence even if the hurdle has been surmounted. These provisions will be dealt with in more detail in Chapters 3 and 10.

2.2.5 **Using mandatory sentences**

Parliamentary 'encouragement' of the use of particular penalties by sentencers was not unique to the 1990s (see Tonry 1996: 142–59). In addition to the mandatory sentence of life imprisonment for murder, there were already presumptive sentences which sentencers have to impose unless the facts of the case fall within defined exceptions. An example is mandatory disqualification for drunken driving unless 'special reasons' prevail, and mandatory activation of a suspended sentence unless it would be 'unjust to do so'.

However, the passing of ss. 1–4 of the Crime (Sentences) Act 1997, re-enacted—with the omission of the original s. 1—as ss. 109–111 of the PCCSA 2000, signalled the introduction into English sentencing law of a more intrusive tool being used in other jurisdictions, notably the 'three strikes and you're out' legislation of several of the states in the United States. Sections 110–111, in force from 1997 and 1999 respectively, limit judicial discretion when there is repeat offending in regard to specified offences. Section 110 relates to Class A drugs offences (see Drug Trafficking Act 1994) and imposes a minimum sentence of seven years on conviction for a third offence. Section 111 similarly imposes a minimum sentence of three years for a third domestic burglary.[7] Since then other firearms and knife offences have been subject to the imposition of this type of sentence—see Chapter 5, section 5.3.3—and the new s. 224A inserted by LASPO 2012 into the CJA 2003 has introduced a life sentence which is mandatory for a second listed offence if the offender fulfils the conditions.

The 1997 legislation was preceded by a White Paper (Home Office 1996a) and accompanied by ministerial comment, notably Home Secretary Michael Howard's dictum in his speech in October 1993 that 'prison works'. These put forward various policy arguments to support the enacting of these sections, all essentially specific arguments against the existence of a wide sentencing discretion to ensure that sentencing achieves the desired policy ends of protection of the public through containment, deterrence through certainty of punishment, and protection of the public by incorporating discretionary release on criteria of risk.

How mandatory such provisions are in practice, and so how far sentencing discretion is curtailed, depends on how widely drafted is what Ashworth refers to as the 'escape clause'. He argues that in relation to the drug and burglary provisions the escape clause, allowing the courts not to impose the mandatory sentence if 'unjust in all the circumstances', is a wide one; not so the 'exceptional circumstances' of the repealed automatic life sentence provision (1998a: 234–5). The Human Rights Act 1998 proved more effective in significantly reducing the constraint imposed on judges by the latter provision (see the case of *Offen*) which was subsequently repealed.

The sentencing framework for 'dangerous offenders' set up by the CJA 2003 instead introduced a new, but now repealed, indeterminate sentence for public protection (IPP) (see Chapter 5, section 5.4.1). The IPP led to widespread concern amongst sentencers, campaigning groups, and academics that reduced discretion was causing more injustice

---

[7] Until repealed, s. 109 mandated the imposition of an automatic life sentence on conviction for a second sexual or violent offence as listed in s. 109.

to offenders than the provision it replaced. The government changed the criteria for its imposition by the CJIA 2008 such that judicial discretion was reintroduced but LASPO 2012 removed the IPP sentence from the statute book for offenders convicted after 3 December 2012.

2.2.6 **Guideline judgments**

In a sense these are 'new' constraints because they were not developed until the 1970s and 1980s and because they are an early precursor to the guidelines now produced by the Sentencing Council (see section 2.3). Two Lord Chief Justices, Lawton LJ and Lane LJ, had developed more structured guidance through designated appellate judgments referred to as guideline judgments (see Ashworth 1984; Ashworth and Roberts 2013). Such judgments considered sentencing for a whole category of offences or particular sentencing factors, rather than one individual and individualised case. They also gave indications of the 'proper range' of sentences and the interpretation of sentencing legislation, and listed particular factors as legitimately aggravating or mitigating the seriousness of the offending and the level of the punishment.

Guideline judgments were also used to endorse a particular principle (possibly with a limited life) such as the 'clang of the prison gates' principle in the early 1980s to justify short prison sentences on first offenders, particularly if of good character, 'who it was thought would be severely affected by any experience of imprisonment, however short' (Henham 1995: 219; see *Upton* 1980). In *Bibi* (1980) the Court of Appeal stated that prison overcrowding should be a relevant sentencing factor in specified situations, and this was reiterated in *Kefford* (2002) by Taylor LJ when he said that 'the courts must accept the realities of the situation' and, where appropriate, should use community penalties or fines instead of (short) prison sentences.[8]

Another principle established by Court of Appeal guidance in the 1980s is now enshrined in legislation. Enacted as the CJA 1991, s. 28(2)(b), now CJA 2003, s. 166(3)(b), is the 'totality principle': that the aggregate of consecutive sentences should not be out of proportion to the overall seriousness of the offending and so the court can legitimately mitigate the sentence of a multiple offender (see Henham 1995: 220; Ashworth 2010: 270–7).

Court of Appeal guidance is clearly very limited in scope. Only convicted offenders and, since the Criminal Justice Act 1988, the **Attorney General** can appeal against a sentence. The offender is unlikely to appeal if his penalty is at the lower end of the sentencing portfolio and the Attorney General[9] refers only those cases where it appears that the sentence is 'unduly lenient' (s. 36(1)). While the range of issues and penalties on which the court commented widened after 1988, the result was still very patchy guidance (see Ashworth 1984: 522–3; Henham 1995: 218).

It was further argued specifically in relation to the lower courts that 'there is scant authority to assist magistrates in their sentencing jurisdiction', appellate guidance from the Crown Court being 'generally cursory' and the Divisional Court interfering with outcome only exceptionally (Wasik and Turner 1992: 345). Instead the Magistrates' Association produced its own guidance which posed questions in relation to seriousness, indicated a guideline starting point, and gave examples of potentially relevant mitigating and aggravating factors. These guidelines have since been overseen and published by the new sentencing bodies: the Sentencing Advisory Panel published a new definitive version in 2008,

---

[8] See Chapter 3 for examples of offence-based and custody threshold guidance.
[9] See, for information on the role and holders of this post, http://www.nationmaster.com/encyclopedia/Attorney-General-for-England-and-Wales.

which was updated by the Sentencing Guidelines Council, and is now to be found on the Sentencing Council website.

2.3 The development of guidelines

This development—the constraint of discretion by the use of guidelines and by specific, statutory duties to comply—is significantly different from the traditional constraints reviewed in section 2.2. Traditionally guidance was purely judicial through Court of Appeal decisions, but since 1998 guidance has been issued by new bodies specifically set up to do so.

2.3.1 The Sentencing Advisory Panel

Given the criticisms of appellate guidance that we reviewed in section 2.2.5, but also aware that the judiciary was protective of its sentencing discretion, the Labour government introduced a compromise solution. Sections 80–81 of the CDA 1998 established a Sentencing Advisory Panel (SAP) with the function of making proposals for new guidelines which the Court of Appeal could issue when a suitable case to do so came before the court. The SAP's first Chair was Professor Martin Wasik and the Panel's 14 members included Professors of Law (Andrew Ashworth), Ethnic Health (Lord Chan), and Social Policy (Frances Heidensohn), together with members of the judiciary, Crown Prosecution Service, Department for Education and Skills, Parole Board, and Probation Service.

Within the first two years the Panel's advice on the importation of drugs, racially aggravated offences, and handling stolen goods—backed up by consultation and research—were accepted and incorporated in appellate guidelines. In 2002/3 its advice to the Court of Appeal covered offences involving child pornography, alcohol and tobacco smuggling, rape, and the offence of causing death by dangerous driving (Sentencing Advisory Panel 2003: 1). The obvious value of the reasoned and researched advice given by the SAP, together with an acknowledgement that not all advice could easily and quickly be incorporated in guidelines, led to the establishment of another statutory body—the Sentencing Guidelines Council (SGC) (see section 2.3.3)—to take further the process of providing systematic guidance to the courts.

The role of the SAP then became to advise the SGC and in its first year in the new role it proposed that the SGC should issue guidance on street robbery or mugging, robberies of small businesses, and less sophisticated commercial robberies; published consultation papers on domestic violence and sexual offences; and issued advice on the new sentencing framework introduced by the CJA 2003. The SAP continued to produce useful advice based on research and consultation until its demise in 2010.

2.3.2 The Sentencing Guidelines Council

The establishment of the SGC by s. 167 of the CJA 2003 was a very significant change in the production of sentencing guidance. Although it had judicial and lay members and was chaired by the Lord Chief Justice, it, in effect, took over the Court of Appeal's responsibility for issuing guidelines because of its statutory duty to publish guidelines and consult with the government. Importantly, the Secretary of State could order the Council to review or produce particular guidelines (s. 170(2) and (3)) and the Act imposed the aim on the SGC of having regard to 'the need to promote consistency in sentencing' (s. 170(5)). This aim had been prioritised by the White Paper preceding the CJA 2003 'to end the unacceptable variations in sentencing' (Home Office 2002c: Executive Summary, 8). Ashworth queried in 2003 whether comprehensive guidance could be produced by the new bodies 'with a part-time panel, an SGC that meets once every few months, and only a modest administrative support' (2003: 9), but the output nevertheless led to criticism from the judiciary that its discretion had been unduly restricted, notably in relation to the discount for a guilty plea, setting the minimum term in a life sentence, and imposing the indeterminate sentences introduced by the CJA 2003.

The SGC produced consultation papers as well as guidelines, often on the same day as the SAP published its advice on the subject. Its first guideline at the end of 2004 was *Overarching Principles: Seriousness* (Sentencing Guidelines Council 2004a), followed by *New Sentences: Criminal Justice Act 2003* (2004c), while those published in its last three years of operation include its definitive guidelines on the reduction in sentence for a guilty plea (2007a), the Sexual Offences Act 2003 (2007c), assault on adults and children (2008a, 2008b), sentencing youths (2009b), and corporate manslaughter and health and safety offences which cause death (2010).

The level of compulsion to which the sentencer is subjected is a matter to which we will return. The previous duty is to be found in s. 172 of the CJA 2003, which required judges and magistrates to 'have regard' to the guidance issued. In *R v Oosthuizen* (2005) Rose LJ emphasised this duty but quoted the statement of Lord Woolf CJ in *Last* (2005) that 'have regard to' did not mean a guideline had to be followed, and also the statement of Judge LJ in *Peters* (2005) that they 'are guidelines: no more, no less': 'It does not necessarily follow that in every case a guideline will be followed.'

2.3.3 **The Sentencing Council**

The government wished to take further the question of guidance production and the judicial duty to follow it. Lord Carter's *Review of Prisons: Securing the Future: Proposals for the Efficient and Sustainable Use of Custody in England and Wales* (2007) had proposed that a permanent Sentencing Commission should be developed, with judicial leadership. In line with his proposals a working group was set up under the chairmanship of Lord Justice Gage and made up of 15 members including lawyers, academics, judges, and criminal justice professionals. The group received 229 responses to its consultation document (Sentencing Commission Working Group, 2008a), including 203 from the judiciary (Sentencing Commission Working Group, 2008b: 2). The group reported that '[t]here was a widespread belief amongst judicial respondents that a structured sentencing system would mean resources would be prioritised over the justness of an individual sentence' and that '[m]any judges felt that sentencing was "an art not a science" and was not amenable to prescriptive guidelines' (ibid: 3). Many responses were detailed (for example, Hough and Jacobson 2008), some very critical of the kind of sentencing commission to be found in parts of the United States which imposed rigid structures on sentencers.

In the event, the recommendation in its final report (Sentencing Commission Working Group, 2008c)[10] was the creation of an enhanced SGC combining the SGC and the Sentencing Advisory Panel into one body to be called the 'Sentencing Council'. It also proposed additional duties on the new Council. The government subsequently published the Coroners and Justice Bill; in response, the House of Commons Justice Committee warned against undue haste in formulating and implementing these proposals (HC 185 Session

---

[10] Now accessible at http://webarchive.nationalarchives.gov.uk and http://www.justice.gov.uk/publications/sentencing-commission.htm.

2008/9: para 32) and was concerned that there should be more clarity as regards the procedure for parliamentary scrutiny of new definitive guidelines (ibid: para 33).

Functions

Nevertheless, the Coroners and Justice Act received Royal Assent in 2009 and mandated the establishment of a Sentencing Council with specified functions (ss. 118–136). This new body for England and Wales began work in April 2010, replacing the SGC and SAP. Its website states that the Council has responsibility for:

- developing sentencing guidelines and monitoring their use;
- assessing the impact of guidelines on sentencing practice. It may also be required to consider the impact of policy and legislative proposals relating to sentencing, when requested by the Government; and
- promoting awareness amongst the public regarding the realities of sentencing and publishing information regarding sentencing practice in Magistrates' and the Crown Court.

In addition to the functions above, the Council must:

- consider the impact of sentencing decisions on victims;
- monitor the application of the guidelines, better to predict the effect of them; and
- play a greater part in promoting understanding of, and increasing public confidence in, sentencing and the criminal justice system.

(Sentencing Guidelines Council, https://www.sentencingcouncil.org.uk/about-us/)

Guideline formats

The Council has already initiated consultations and research on sentencing a very wide range of offences, many resulting in new guidelines. Recent Definitive Guidelines include *Environmental Offences* (2014b), *Sexual Offences* (2014c), *Theft Offences* (2015a), and *Health and Safety Offences, Corporate Manslaughter and Food Safety and Hygiene Offences* (2015b). Various formats for guidelines were tried in the early days of the SGC and the Sentencing Council but there is now a standard two-step format in the guidelines for establishing and adjusting the starting point for a sentence, together with subsequent steps which include the reduction for a guilty plea and the imposition of ancillary orders. We will consider these steps in more detail in Chapter 3, sections 3.2 and 3.3.

Departure test

In its final report the Sentencing Commission Working Group dealt with what it referred to as the 'departure test' (2008c: 25–6), meaning the criterion by which the sentence can justify departing from the duty to implement the relevant guidance. As previously noted, the CJA 2003 required courts to 'have regard to' guidelines but the Working Party proposed a more stringent duty. The Coroners and Justice Act 2009, s. 125 replaced the previous provision with the following:

Every court—
(a) must, in sentencing an offender, follow any sentencing guidelines which are relevant to the offender's case, and
(b) must, in exercising any other function relating to the sentencing of offenders, follow any sentencing guidelines which are relevant to the exercise of the function

unless the court is satisfied that it would be contrary to the interests of justice to do so.

In 1992 the Council of Ministers of the Council of Europe issued Recommendation No. R (92) 17 on 'Consistency of Sentencing', which declared approved principles and suggested techniques for enhancing consistency. Whether these constraints and guidance amount to a principled structuring of sentencing such that there is consistency of sentencing in the UK is not yet clear. However, the new mandatory requirement in regard to following guidelines (see Roberts 2011a) and the duty to explain the sentence in detail amount to 'significant steps in the direction of transparency' (Ashworth 2010: 372) and can only aid consistency. The work of the Sentencing Council will, therefore, enhance uniformity of sentencing, but only if it is not undermined by other changes which might produce the opposite effects. This uncertainty of policy outcome—because of the diverse and sometimes divergent policies being introduced—is an issue which will run through many chapters in this book.

2.4 Retributivist rationales

2.4.1 The concept of the individual and the state

In Chapter 1 we noted the importance of penological principles, particularly retributivist principles, in English sentencing frameworks, notably since the implementation of the CJA 1991 (see Chapter 1, section 1.4.3). It is this imposition of a particular sentencing rationale which is the third major constraint—after traditional constraints and the newer definitive guidelines—on sentencing discretion.

On the retributivist theory a wrong action should be met by a sanction appropriate to the action and deserved by the offender, so it is argued that: (i) punishment should be given in response to its being deserved; (ii) the penalty should be appropriate to the wrong action; and (iii) the consequences of punishment are irrelevant. The quest for justice is the underlying rationale of retributivism: justice is satisfied if the guilty are punished according to desert and in proportion to the gravity of the offence. An unjust punishment would include an excessive or inappropriate punishment, one which fails to respect the dignity of the offender, and one imposed for external reasons unrelated to desert. Retributivist or desert theory is therefore more protective of individuals' rights than the utilitarian approach which focuses on deterrence and rehabilitation.

Retributivist philosophy depends on a particular view of human beings. For Kant the model of the individual is of a rational agent for whom law functions as an imperative, not coercively but because the individual recognises that law imposes duties and obligations (Kant 1796–7). Moreover, the inherent autonomy of each person requires that all individuals, including offenders, should be accorded dignity and treated with respect.

An act which reduces the capacity to act rationally and autonomously would violate human dignity for Kant. Any act which shortens or ends the lives of others is morally wrong, because life has an intrinsic value. Modern examples would be using prisoners, without their consent, to test drugs in order to provide benefits for the wider population. For utilitarians such experiments might be justified if they maximise utility; an individual's welfare could be sacrificed if by doing so it maximises the welfare of others. No rational or autonomous creature should be treated as a mere means for the enjoyment or happiness of others. On Kant's theory, we may choose to sacrifice our lives for others, but others should not use our lives or bodies as a means to pursue their goals.

Similarly, Hegel, who was well versed in the philosophical foundations of utilitarianism through the writings of Hume and others, rejected the utilitarian view of the individual as seeking the satisfaction of desires, the pursuit of pleasure and happiness (see Walton 1983; Hinchman 1991). Hegel distinguishes men from animals, who are governed by impulses, desires, and inclinations (Hegel 1832: addition 10). He is critical of those who base their theories of punishment on threats and coercion, because, he says, this 'is to treat a man like a dog instead of with the respect and freedom due to him as a man' (ibid: addition 62). He also rejected the utilitarians' focus on psychological explanations of human behaviour which reduce social processes to the aggregated behaviour of individuals. Instead, Hegel argues strongly for an understanding of the individual through his social relations, and in doing so paved the way for a new approach later to be developed by Marx and Marxist sociologists.

The utilitarian notion of drawing up a balance sheet when deciding on moral choices was seen by Hegel as absurd and self-defeating. Both Kant and Hegel see a good action as one undertaken for its own sake, because it is morally right (see Hinchman 1991), rather than because it offers extrinsic rewards.

Retributivist philosophy also depends on a particular view of the state. In contrast to the social contract theorists, Kant does not see the well-being of a state as lying in the welfare of its citizens or their happiness, but rather '[b]y the well-being of a state is understood, instead, that condition in which its constitution conforms most fully to principles of Right; it is that condition which reason, *by a categorical imperative*, makes it obligatory for us to strive after' (Kant 1796–7: 129). Kant's conception of the relationship between the state and its citizens allows no right to rebellion or revolution; indeed, he thinks this would constitute high treason, which should be punishable by the death penalty (ibid: 131). He is strongly opposed to the execution of the sovereign even in a defective state; instead, reform should come from the sovereign. Hegel also rejects the conception of the state as a contract. The social contract model construes the state as an instrument to protect the life and property of individual citizens rather than as constituting ethical life. These ideas on the nature of the state and the individual shape the theories of punishment developed by Kant and Hegel.

2.4.2 **Kantian retributivism**

Punishment is considered by Kant in the context of his analysis of right in *The Metaphysics of Morals* published in 1796–7. 'The *right to punish* is the right a ruler has against a subject to inflict pain upon him because of his having committed a crime' (Kant 1796–7: 140). Kant stresses that '*Punishment by a court* . . . can never be inflicted merely as a means to promote some other good for the criminal himself or for civil society. It must always be inflicted upon him only *because he has committed a crime*. For a man can never be treated merely as a means to the purposes of another' (Kant 1796–7: 140).

Kant's theory of punishment rests on coherent ethical principles, which recognise the autonomy and rationality of individuals and their capacity to make choices and take responsibility for their actions, and to act on the basis of reason and principles rather than 'passions'.[11] If justice is sacrificed, for example, by withholding punishment, the quality of life of the community is undermined. For example, the execution of a prisoner might be waived if he agrees to dangerous medical experiments being conducted upon him which might generate knowledge of benefit to the community as a whole. This strategy might be justifiable on utilitarian theory, but would be rejected by retributivists, including Kant, as incompatible with the principle of justice.

The form of punishment and **quantum** of punishment, argues Kant, must be based on the principle of equality, so the 'undeserved evil' the criminal inflicts on the victim is matched by a similar amount on himself. He argues that 'only the *law of retribution* (*ius talionis*) . . . can specify definitely the quality and the quantity of punishment; all other

---

[11] For further discussion of Kant's ethical theory see Timmermann (ed) 2013 and Sensen (ed) (2015).

principles are fluctuating and unsuited for a sentence of pure and strict justice because extraneous considerations are mixed into them' (ibid: 141). To base a decision on whether to punish, how to punish, and how much to punish on extraneous considerations, such as which measures are most effective in eliminating crime, cannot generate a just sentence (ibid: 168).

Kant's focus is on the moral foundation of punishment, rather than what is useful for society or best for the criminal justice system. He contrasts his approach—which offers punitive justice grounded in ethics—with mere punitive prudence. Central to punitive justice is the principle of proportionality. The term Kant uses is *Gleiches mit Gleichem*, usually translated as 'like for like', or measure for measure, which suggests both quantitative and qualitative matching in terms of the amount of pain and type of punishment. He accepts that it may be difficult to find appropriate punishment for some crimes while in others, such as the death penalty for murder and castration for rape, it may be more clear-cut. Someone who steals should be reduced to the status of a slave through convict or prison labour, he argues, while the person convicted of bestiality should be expelled from civil society because he has shown himself unworthy of membership of it. But the murderer must be executed, says Kant, as no other sentence is sufficient to satisfy the demands of justice and a life sentence is inadequate: 'There is no *similarity* between life, however wretched it may be, and death, hence no likeness between the crime and the retribution unless death is judicially carried out upon the wrongdoer, although it must still be freed from any mistreatment that could make the humanity in the person suffering it into something abominable' (ibid: 142).

He gives the example of a civil society, of a people inhabiting an island, who decide to disperse and go their separate ways. In such circumstances, he says, 'the last murderer remaining in prison would first have to be executed, so that each has done to him what his deeds deserve . . .'. If the crimes go unpunished, he argues, the community that withholds punishment will be collaborating in the public violation of justice. Similarly, the right of the sovereign to grant clemency to the criminal by granting lesser punishment or no punishment at all is criticised by Kant, for failure to punish is the greatest wrong against his subjects and should be used only if the wrong is done to himself and to use it would not endanger the security of the people.

Kant sees the death penalty as appropriate for murder, accomplices to murder, and crimes against the state. If a court gave sentenced prisoners a choice between death or convict labour, the man of honour, he says, would choose death while the scoundrel would choose convict labour. For Kant the consequences of punishment are irrelevant: the sole issue is the guilt of the individual. It follows that the innocent person should never be punished, even if it to do so would offer clear social benefits. Where punishment is deserved, then the level of punishment should be appropriate to the seriousness of the offence. In focusing solely upon desert Kant is trying to offer a rational and objective standard of punishment which recognises the autonomy of individuals and prevents arbitrariness and bias from influencing outcomes. In this sense his approach may be seen as countering the subjectivity of discretion. It also means that retribution must be imposed by a properly constituted court rather than through private acts of vengeance.

2.4.3 Hegel: the 'right' to punishment

Hegel's theory of punishment is found in Part One of *The Philosophy of Right* (Hegel 1832) in his discussion of abstract right, written in 1820 as part of his analysis of the development of the ethical life of the state. Hegel argues that abstract right is the first stage in the development of the concept of freedom and stresses that right is restored by annulling the crime (Hegel 1832: para 99). He is critical of the view of punishment merely as 'a preventive, a deterrent, a threat, as reformative' rather than focusing on the 'righting of wrong'. Hegel accepts that deterrence and reformation have their place and are worthy of examination particularly when considering modes of punishment, but the key element for Hegel is that those who deserve punishment should receive appropriate punishment. 'The injury [the penalty] which falls on the criminal is not merely *implicitly* just, it is an embodiment of his freedom, his right . . . it is also a right *established* within the criminal himself, i.e. in his objectively embodied will, in his action' (ibid: para 100). The reason, says Hegel, is that his action is that of a rational being; the crime is of the 'individual's volition' for which he is responsible.[12] In that sense, 'punishment is regarded as containing the criminal's right and hence by being punished he is honoured as a rational being' (ibid: para 100). It follows that '[h]e does not receive this due of honour unless the concept and measure of his punishment are derived from his own act. Still less does he receive it if he is treated either as a harmful animal who has to be made harmless, or with a view to deterring and reforming him' (ibid: para 100).

In Hegel's remarks we find the essence of the retributivist theory of punishment: the presumed rationality of the criminal, the imposition of punishment only if the individual is guilty, the exclusion of social consequences from the prime purpose of punishment, and the view that punishment annuls the crime. By punishing the criminal we acknowledge him as a rational individual, rather than treating him like a mad dog, as dangerous and requiring constraint. The criminal, he says, 'gives his consent already by his very act' (Hegel 1832: addition 63).

2.4.4 Punishment as the annulment of crime

'The annulment of the crime is retribution', says Hegel, and its negation. 'Crime . . . contains its negation in itself and this negation is manifested as punishment' (Hegel 1832: para 101). This might also include an element of reparation, or restoration, as the community is being returned to how it was before the crime occurred. Of course, for Hegel, crime is not simply an offence against the individual, but against the law itself, and hence infringement requires a social response in the form of state punishment. Even without an individual victim, crime deserves punishment.

There is a 'necessary connexion between crime and punishment', argues Hegel (ibid: para 101). He acknowledges the absurdity of a literal notion of equality of punishment, of an eye for an eye or a tooth for a tooth, and the problem of what happens if the perpetrator has no teeth or only one eye, but stresses that the concept of retribution 'has nothing to do with this absurdity' (ibid: para 101). Rather, he says, the notion of equality means focusing on the deserts of the criminal and to offer a punishment comparable in value. 'Injustice is done at once if there is one lash too many, or one dollar or one cent, one week in prison or one day, too many or too few' (ibid: para 214).

Hegel acknowledges that 'The annulling of crime . . . is principally revenge, which is just in its content in so far as it is retributive' (ibid: para 102). But his concept of justice is of justice 'freed from subjective interest' (ibid: para 103). Justice demands equal respect for all, including the offender. Hegel, like Kant, argues that punishment must be administered through a proper criminal justice system rather than informally, and applied only to blameworthy individuals in contrast to the arbitrariness of vigilantism. Hegel's concept of punishment applies to a rational ethical state where obedience is based on duty and reason rather than crude coercion. He also notes that harsh punishments are not necessarily

---

[12] For further discussion of Hegel's notion of responsibility see Alznauer (2015).

unjust. This will depend on the prevailing conditions, and criminal codes will change through time to reflect this.

Desert is the primary justification of punishment for Hegel. However, this does not mean that reformation, reparation, and deterrence have no place in a system of punishment. By applying retributivist punishment we may find that a side effect is reform and education of the criminal. But deterrence from committing future crimes for Hegel is a result of punishment, rather than operating as a threat, or as its prime purpose (see Harvey 1984). The threat of punishment and the sanctions of criminal law do not coerce men into obeying the law; rather, criminal law and institutions are a framework within which men become morally good (Nicholson 1982). This would also be consistent with his dynamic model of the development of ethical life, to the point where the state develops sufficiently so that individuals understand fully the rational foundation of laws. Moreover, while punishment may have elements of reparation and restitution it cannot be reduced to them, so we cannot conceptualise crimes in the same way as civil offences.

Hegel elucidates the philosophical principles justifying punishment rather than offering a tariff of particular punishments for specific crimes. So his discussion of the death penalty, for example, is incidental to his theory of punishment. However, Hegel does accept that the death penalty is appropriate for murder when the only punishment can be the taking away of a second life, but acknowledges that in other types of crime it will be hard to find an equivalent requital (Hegel 1832: addition 64; see also Hetherington 1996; Heyman 1996). The executioner has both a right and a duty to apply the punishment. By the time Hegel was writing, capital punishment had become rarer, which, he argues, is appropriate for such an extreme punishment. Hegel argued that campaigns for its abolition were useful because, although they did not succeed, they forced a reconsideration of which crimes should receive this punishment (ibid: addition 63).

2.5 Questions raised by the classical retributivist model

2.5.1 Just punishment or injustice?

The merit of the classical retributivist model is that it seeks to remove arbitrariness and bias from punishment. However, the idea that punishment must be imposed regardless of any positive outcomes, simply for the sake of it, could be seen as cruel, pointless, and unjust. Does harming others as an end in itself restore the balance of justice? If the retributivist tempers this by saying that we may sometimes take account of consequences such as deterrence, but desert is the primary justification, then this weakens the basis of the theory. Tonry (1993) argues that proportionality conflicts with parsimony, and the reduction of suffering, because theorists of proportionality will always favour imposing what the offender deserves and treating similar offenders equally, rather than using the most economical means of punishment: imposing the least severe punishment to meet social goals and minimising suffering. Rubin (2003) argues that there is a danger in focusing on retribution as it may be achieved by any means and this opens the door to inhumanity in punishment, in terms of the amount of punishment and the modes of punishment. He contends that in a climate of punitiveness and penal expansion a focus on rehabilitation rather than retribution is better able to raise standards of decency and humanity in punishment and to protect the prisoner from abuse, as retributivism gives no guidance on how the offender should be treated within prison.

However, as we shall see, modern retributivists such as von Hirsch argue that proportionality provides a restraint on unlimited punishment and may in practice mean a less severe sentence than that demanded by rival theories. The principle has also been used to challenge excessive sentences imposed under 'three strikes' legislation in the United States. It may also have implications for the treatment of prisoners, for example in terms of the penalties imposed on prisoners for offences against prison discipline.

There is also the problem of to whom the debt is paid, whether it is the victim or society as a whole. But how does society as a whole benefit from the suffering of a criminal unless it is through the deterrent effect or the ultimate rehabilitation of the offender? It is therefore hard to avoid referring to consequences and thereby lapsing into utilitarianism.

The assumption of individual responsibility and autonomy is also disputed by those moral philosophers who see social, psychological, or socio-biological constraints on action as more important than free will. As the social sciences have progressed since the early nineteenth century, it is now recognised that human behaviour is more complex and the development of the individual may be shaped by a range of environmental factors, family dynamics, and other influences.

2.5.2 Equivalence and proportionality

The notion of equivalence—that the punishment should equate with the severity of the crime—is also problematic. Kant advocates a catalogue of qualitative and quantitative punishments, but it may not be so clear-cut and such a system would be difficult to administer in practice. Even in the case of murder, there may be problems in executing punishments for different types of murder or where an offender has committed multiple murders. There may also be problems in relation to the determination of culpability and the appropriate sentence in cases of involuntary manslaughter at the top end of the seriousness scale (Mitchell and Mackay 2011). When we look at sentencing practice, we find a range of mitigating and aggravating factors to consider when deciding the appropriate punishment (see Chapter 3). This is already a very complex process and, if a Kantian model were superimposed, this would mean that there would be insufficient punishments to fit all cases. Feinberg (1994) is critical of those retributivists who try to match the pain exactly to the crime. As well as the problem of measurement, there is also the effect on the defendant's innocent family to consider. He argues that it is social disapproval and its expression which should fit the crime rather than the quantity of pain.

A modern example reported by Amnesty International[13] is of a court in Tabuk, Saudi Arabia, which had approached several hospitals to see if it was possible to cut a prisoner's spinal cord in order to carry out the punishment requested by the injured victim who had been paralysed by the offender in the course of the crime. This was widely condemned as torture, inhuman and degrading punishment, and a gross violation of medical ethics. Past forms of 'qualitative proportionality' and retribution used in the Saudi criminal justice system have included eye gouging and tooth extraction. Similarly, in Iran a court sentenced an offender, Majid Movahedi, to blinding with acid drops, after he was convicted of blinding and disfiguring his victim, Ameneh Bahrami, by throwing acid at her, on the principle of strict equivalence in Islamic law. The sentence requested by the victim was due to be carried out in May 2011 in the presence of medical specialists, but the victim in the end pardoned her attacker.

A severe punishment may well affect innocent third parties vicariously, as international human rights law has recognised, for example in Article 6(5) of the International Covenant

---

[13] http://www.amnesty.org.au/news/comments/23567, 27 August 2010, accessed 28 May 2011.

on Civil and Political Rights (ICCPR) which states that sentence of death shall not be carried out upon pregnant women.

Notwithstanding these examples of extreme punishment, it has been argued that proportionality can act as a restraint on punishment. Fish (2008) reviews the history of *lex talionis* and argues that it constituted a turning point in the history of punishment in giving justice by punishing in relation to desert and in proportion to the wrong rather than arbitrarily. Moreover, the principle of proportionality offered a restraint on punishment. He claims that proportionality should not be viewed as demanding a literal 'mirror' punishment or as sanctioning state cruelty, but rather as demanding a measured and appropriate level of punishment for the offender's conduct. So in the case of the Saudi blogger, Raif Badawi—who was sentenced in 2014 to 1,000 lashes in public and ten years' imprisonment and given a one million Saudi Riyal fine (equivalent to over 250,000 US dollars) and a travel ban for ten years after his prison sentence, for insulting Islam through electronic means by creating and managing an online forum which advocated a separation of state and religion—the punishment was disproportionate, inhuman, and degrading and widely condemned by the international community (Badawi 2015). The sentence was upheld by the Saudi Supreme Court in June 2015. Badawi was given 50 lashes in 2015 but the resulting injuries were so severe that further floggings had to be postponed.

Classical retributivism does seem to fit our moral intuitions, that it is intrinsically right that the wrongdoer should suffer, but there may be dangers in relying on intuitions, particularly in the theory and practice of punishment. Human feelings can be capricious and inconsistent as we may forgive some acts but not others.

Walker (1991) is critical of what he sees as fundamental weaknesses of retributivism. He argues that Hegel does not establish why annulment should take the form of a sentence rather than another response and it is not clear why Kant's 'last murderer' should be dealt with punitively rather than in some other way, such as persuading the individual to repent. Retributivism, he argues, does not explain why there should be a moral obligation to inflict the just desert on the offender. Exact commensurability is unattainable so the best the retributivist can offer is proportionality, but this, he says, 'is a ladder with rungs that are both sliding and elastic' (ibid: 138).

Walker (1991) also highlights the problems for retributivists in dealing with repentance, remorse, and mercy: it is unclear whether they play a mitigating role in retributivism. Most retributivists exclude them from consideration, but where they do take account of them, this would appear to conflict with the principle of proportionality. However, Maslen (2015) explores the theoretical justifications for allowing a role for remorse within a retributivist sentencing framework and notes that remorse is accepted as a mitigating factor within many sentencing regimes. The courts may also take account of a range of other factors, including age and special hardship, which will be considered in Chapter 7, section 7.4.

2.6 Modern retributivism

2.6.1 The revival of desert theory

Given these criticisms of classical retributivism, one might reasonably have expected it to be of historical significance only. For many years, as we shall see in Chapter 4, the other main philosophy of punishment—utilitarianism—was seen as more 'modern' and 'humane'. However, utilitarianism itself was heavily criticised from the 1970s in several jurisdictions. In particular, criticism focused in the United States on the increased use of indeterminate and extended sentences for dangerous offenders, selective incapacitation, and the apparently unrestrained use of state punishment. In the UK and the United States criticism also focused on the 'inequities' and ineffectiveness of rehabilitation, and on wide judicial discretion. While retributivist thinking has always been present in English sentencing policy and practice, the proponents of such an approach came to believe that a rejigged version was essential if 'justice' as a specific aim of punishment—rather than as the yardstick for judging any penal aim—was to become more influential in practice.

A leading advocate for modern retributivist theory in the 1970s was von Hirsch, who argued that fairness and justice should be the key elements of a coherent penal theory. In *Doing Justice* (1976), he maintained that the aim of the penal system should, then, be to 'do justice' rather than to maximise utility. Justice—as in classical retributivism—was defined as giving offenders punishments in proportion to their crimes and, in doing so, recognising them as moral agents possessing autonomy. However, he proposed that penalties should be anchored at a lower level to counter the belief that retributivism leads to harsh sentencing. So, in contrast to the classical retributivists, von Hirsch argued for a maximum incarceration of three years for serious offences and five years for some homicides.

However, theorists have since alerted us to the fact that, depending on the political climate, the adoption of retributivist principles can lead to unintended outcomes. Tonry, for example, has pointed out that 'just deserts' principles do not automatically guarantee the sort of penal system many theorists were hoping for. The pressure for more structuring of what retributivist theorists saw as too wide a judicial discretion, and the focusing only on the offending, can still justify the increased use of higher levels of determinate sentencing. Further, the imposition of rigid guideline systems in the United States is, for Tonry, evidence that 'just deserts has backfired' (Tonry 1996: 13). Yet the 'politicisation' of sentencing and punishment that we discussed in Chapter 1 means, in policy terms, that 'sentencing matters . . . more than ever before' (ibid: 1) and proponents of retributivist justifications have been continually prompted to rethink and refine their theories. For example, Morris and Tonry have re-conceptualised proportionality and parsimony, and von Hirsch has focused on censure. The next sections will look in more detail at some of these principles.

2.6.2 **The 'why' of punishment: censure**

In *Censure and Sanctions* (1993), von Hirsch describes punishment as the expression of blame—the censure which the criminal deserves. For von Hirsch censure is the prime aim of punishment: 'public reproof' is intended to ensure that the individual recognises his own blameworthiness. If punishment is to achieve this, the degree of censure should be reflected in the severity of punishment and so proportionality is still crucial. A censure-based justification makes sense to most people, as in everyday life we make moral judgements about others and blame each other for transgressions. If a person behaves badly—in morally reprehensible ways—others judge him adversely. Censure consists of the expression of that judgement combined with the accompanying sentiment of disapproval. In censuring the individual, we again recognise him as a moral agent, a person capable of choices and worthy of respect, whose dignity is respected. An animal in contrast would not be affected by censure. A dog about to steal another dog's bowl of food will be unmoved by appeals to the moral wrongness of such an act, although he may retreat if met by a growl.

In von Hirsch's reworking of retributivism, censure is addressed not just to the offender but also to the victim and others in society:

1. *The victim*: it acknowledges that the victim's hurt occurred through the fault of the perpetrator.

2. *The perpetrator of the act*: it gives the message that he has harmed someone, he is responsible and society disapproves of what he has done, and that a moral response is expected of him, namely some acknowledgement of his wrongdoing. Even if he is indifferent, he should be made to feel that others do not treat his actions so lightly but it is up to him as a moral agent how he responds.

3. *Third parties*: it gives them a good reason to avoid such conduct, not to avoid the pains of punishment as a utilitarian would argue, but, rather, because they recognise the action as morally wrong.

Censure is given formal expression in the criminal law. Blaming is the central feature of criminal law, in contrast to civil law, which offers recovery and compensation for losses. The censure embodied in the sanctions of criminal law conveys that certain types of conduct are wrong and variations in consequences reflect the degree of censure.

The moral agent is thus given grounds for avoiding proscribed actions, but this appeal to the individual's moral sense of the wrongfulness of the criminal act is backed up by a 'prudential disincentive'. Censure relies on the individual's sense of moral culpability but, because people are fallible and may be tempted to act badly, they need a further reason to resist that temptation, says von Hirsch—namely, a criminal sanction. But this supplements rather than replaces the moral basis of obedience to law. A person who accepts that he should not offend and recognises that he may be tempted can see the sanction as an aid to carry out what he sees as the proper course of conduct. The 'blaming' function has primacy, the prudential disincentive function has only a secondary role, and the level of punishment should not be set too high or fear will displace the moral response. Von Hirsch and Ashworth (2005) emphasise that the justification of punishment needs to rest primarily on a normative non-consequential retributive theory, namely penal censure, but there is a complementary, albeit secondary, 'preventive' role for punishment, in preventing crime.

2.6.3 The mode of punishment: respect for human dignity

For von Hirsch a degrading or humiliating or intrusive punishment would be unacceptable, because the offender must still be recognised as a human being and treated with respect (von Hirsch 1993). So his theory would preclude torture, routine solitary confinement, verbal abuse such as used in boot camps, and degrading rituals. It would also preclude compulsory 'attitudinising', such as forcing the offender to accept views he does not freely choose, for example on the use of drugs, or wearing self-accusing labels which identify him to others as an offender. So modern retributivists have been very critical of harsh penal policies.

Tonry, for example, has castigated politicians for not giving sufficient policy weight to the harmful effects of punishment on people's lives. He refers to the comment made by Trotsky in relation to the suffering that the 1917 Russian Revolution imposed—that omelettes cannot be made without breaking eggs—and argues that 'many of the more cynical recent proponents of harsh crime control policies have apparently decided that elections cannot be won without breaking people' (1996: 194).

For modern retributivists, then, punishment must be administered in ways consistent with human dignity, so compulsory searches of the offender or constant surveillance at home would be inconsistent, although electronic tagging is acceptable. Solitary confinement should be used only if there is an immediate threat to the offender or others. Third parties such as the offender's family should not be affected by a penal sanction any more than is necessary. The rights of offenders' families have been given increasing recognition in international human rights law as illustrated by the European Court of Human Rights' decision in *Dickson v UK* (2007), where a prisoner and his wife succeeded in establishing that the denial of access to artificial insemination breached their right to family life under Article 8 of the Convention.

2.6.4 **The amount of punishment: ordinal proportionality**

Von Hirsch is also hostile to individualised or personalised sentences because of the dangers of caprice and inconsistency. The aim should be to standardise punishment by focusing on objective criteria of the degree of blameworthiness and harm caused by the perpetrator. Looking at how much to punish, we need to focus again on proportionality, as von Hirsch's censure-based justification for punishment is necessarily linked to that principle. If punishment conveys blame then it is logical that the quantum of punishment should bear a reasonable relation to the degree of blameworthiness of the individual's conduct. He argues that the proportionality principle fits our intuitions: a child would express a sense of injustice if punished excessively for a minor misdemeanour. So the case for proportionality for von Hirsch rests on three arguments:

1. The severity of the sanction expresses the degree of censure: the harshness of treatment reflects the disapprobation.

2. The state's sanctions against the proscribed conduct should take a punitive form, and impose deprivations in a way that expresses blame or censure.

3. The punitive sanction should reflect the seriousness of the conduct and this is important for fairness and consistency.

The appropriate penalty will be determined by the seriousness of the crime, in terms of the harm caused, that is, the impact on the victim's quality of life and standard of living including economic and non-economic interests, and the extent of the offender's culpability (see also the discussion in Chapter 3, section 3.2.2). The severity of the sanction will be measured by how far it affects the material interests and living standards of the offender.

Von Hirsch discusses the distinction between two types of proportionality, **ordinal** and **cardinal proportionality**. Ordinal or relative proportionality consists of three elements: the first element is parity, which means that persons convicted of crimes of similar gravity should receive punishments of comparable severity. This does not mean that there must be identical punishments for all people who commit particular offences, because of course there may be degrees of culpability, but once they are established, offences of comparable seriousness should receive punishments of the same degree of onerousness. Desert theories encompass some modifications to sentencing for aggravated harms and mitigation to allow for degrees in culpability (von Hirsch 1986; Tonry 1996; von Hirsch and Ashworth 2005) but of course these are still linked to, and proportional to, what the individual deserves for the current offence, rather than reflecting external factors.

The second element is rank-ordering, which means that, when people are convicted of crimes of differing gravity, then punishments should be graded. Punishments should be ordered on a penalty scale, so their relative severity reflects the seriousness-ranking of the offence. The third element is spacing. If we imagine three crimes, A, B, and C, and A is considerably more serious than B, but B is only slightly more serious than C, then, says von Hirsch, there should be a larger space between the penalties for A and B than between B and C. However, as he points out, we could theoretically have a system which satisfies all the requirements of ordinal proportionality, parity, rank-ordering, and spacing, yet is very unfair because it starts with a prison sentence, say of ten years for a minor offence, and progresses to torture and death. We need then to look separately at the important issues of cardinal or non-relative proportionality and parsimony.

2.6.5 **Cardinal proportionality and reductionist penal policies**

Before we can determine the relative punishments for different crimes we need an appropriate **anchoring point** for penalty scales. Von Hirsch challenges the popular view of retributivists as 'bloodthirsty' by arguing that desert theory is capable of finding an anchoring point which may be set relatively low. A huge increase in punishment for a relatively minor offence could be justified on utilitarian grounds if it was effective in eliminating a particular crime or in responding to public concerns. It cannot be justified on retributivist grounds because the degree of punishment exceeds the blameworthiness. Proportionality, then, can constitute a restraint on excessive punishment. Furthermore, some other non-condemnatory measures, for example, a form of civil quarantine for dangerous offenders which could also be justified on utilitarian arguments, would conflict with desert-based retributivist principles. This is because it would be based on future rather than past crimes and would fail to recognise individuals as moral agents with the capacity to choose to avoid future criminal actions.

Consequently, von Hirsch rules out the use of the death penalty as an inhumane and degrading punishment and favours relatively low levels of incarceration, with a longer prison sentence for the most serious and a fine for lesser offences. But von Hirsch argues that a sentence of three years would still constitute a prudential disincentive so that we could reduce levels of punishment without displacing the censuring message. What his theory does not justify is using the state's resources—its penal capacity—as a starting point: this is unprincipled and would lead to differences between states with different capacities.

Von Hirsch favours using the least severe penalty while seeking to impose the appropriate degree of censure. At first sight this might seem akin to the utilitarian notion of parsimony advocated by Bentham and others, which entails using the least severe penalty necessary to deter the criminal, thereby minimising the public costs of punishment. However, the issue for desert theorists is whether desert can be satisfied by setting a lower anchoring point rather than whether costs can be saved (von Hirsch 1986).

Morris (1974) incorporated this idea into a theory of 'limiting retributivism', a hybrid theory, incorporating elements of both retributivism and crime prevention. The argument is that desert can be applied in a parsimonious way because the aims of retributivist theory can be met with a lower anchoring point (von Hirsch 1986). At higher levels of seriousness proportionality prevails, which prevents harsh, excessive, or aggravated punishments which might otherwise be justified on predictive or rehabilitative grounds. But within the parameters set by proportionality the sentencer should be able to impose the least severe sentence consistent with the aims of sentencing. At lower levels there is more scope for flexible parsimonious sentencing.

Against these arguments, utilitarians would say that, if penalties are set too low, the fear of punishment will be undermined. However, as the available research suggests that changing levels of punishment have little effect on crime rates (Cohen 1978; Tarling 1979; Spelman 2000; Carter 2003; King *et al.* 2005), then, argues von Hirsch, the arguments against reducing penalty levels are unconvincing and a reductionist policy is at least worth considering. Moreover, the criterion of success for desert theory, he argues, is not whether it reduces crime, but whether the penal response is scaled to the gravity of the crime. It should therefore be able to resist pressures to increase sentences when crime rises or to selectively incapacitate offenders of particular public concern. It also provides a counterweight to the demands for preventive justice which, as Ashworth and Zedner (2014) argue, has assumed increasing importance in recent years in the climate of insecurity. Tonry has also argued that sentencing law and guidance should 'establish a presumption that, within the range of sanctions set out in applicable guidelines, judges should incorporate the least punitive and intrusive appropriate penalties' (1996: 194).

The exercise of scaling a penal response to seriousness raises another difficult issue: should the punishment, or the impact of the punishment on the offender in question, be proportionate to the seriousness of the offending? In the next chapter we will apply the first approach—where a fixed amount of punishment proportionate to a particular amount of seriousness is imposed. In Chapter 7, section 7.3 we will examine the second approach, where just deserts theory operates in relation to the impact of punishment.

2.6.6 **Policy implications**

Von Hirsch acknowledges that his reasoning—that the best way to resist expansionism is to provide a rational way of anchoring penalties and that desert theory is better able to do this than the alternatives of deterrence and incapacitation—may not be politically attractive for governments. If there are public pressures for law and order, policy will include increased penalties, and penal theory on its own will be unable to prevent it. As we have seen, in this chapter and in Chapter 1, this is precisely what has happened in both the UK and the United States since the 1990s when populist punitiveness has prevailed. As von Hirsch observes, 'A jurisdiction's traditions in punishment, its politics, and its public's degree of fear of crime and criminals probably will affect leniency or severity more than any choice of sentencing theory' (von Hirsch 1986: 169). However, as Chapter 1 also noted, the financial cost of the growing prison population is also a political issue. As we saw, one of the aims in the Coalition government's Green Paper, *Breaking the Cycle: Effective Punishment, Rehabilitation and Sentencing of Offenders* (Ministry of Justice 2010a), was to reduce the numbers in prison and to provide more effective punishment by focusing on payment by results to providers in the punishment process.

Modern retributivism, with its arguments in favour of parsimony and just deserts, may justify fewer and shorter prison sentences and a less expensive penal policy. But it may also improve the conditions of those held in custody. It has been argued by Lippke, for example, that a modern retributivist approach can provide the basis for minimally restrictive and humane imprisonment rather than extreme or harsh conditions of confinement, by providing constraints on punishment. Retributivism, he argues 'sets exacting requirements for liability to punishment and entails substantial constraints on how it is carried out' (Lippke 2007: 265). On this approach the prisoner clearly remains a citizen during his period of incarceration, retaining the fundamental rights of the citizen, including the right to vote, enshrined in human rights law (see Chapter 8, section 8.6). The implications of this will be discussed in further detail in Chapter 8 (see also Easton 2011a, 2013).

The merit of von Hirsch's principled approach is that it sets limits to punishment in a coherent way. The principle of proportionality can be applied to a range of punishments, offering a way of assessing the burdens of sanctions, and stressing the need for equivalence of penal bite. So, a government with an economic imperative to solve the prison crisis can endorse the application of desert theory to justify increasingly restrictive community penalties as a legitimate punishment which affects the material interests and lifestyle of the offender. Further, a retributivist focus on individual moral culpability buttresses a political ideology stressing the responsibility of the citizen. This focus on the mode of punishment and ordinal proportionality in modern retributivism has been contrasted with the 'vengeful retributivism' of *lex talionis* in which the primary focus is on the harm done to the victim and satisfying the victim by imposing comparable harm on the offender (see Robinson 2008; Thorburn 2012).

Modern retributivism, therefore, seemed to provide a solution to a range of legal, moral, political, and economic issues. In England and Wales the response was in the form of the Criminal Justice Act 1991. Although it has been superseded by more recent legislation, the just deserts legacy of that Act is still vitally important in English sentencing, and current law and practice cannot be properly understood without an understanding of the sentencing framework it introduced. Dingwall (2008) argues that the CJA 2003 preserved the key concepts of retributivism although it may have reduced the role of desert by requiring sentencers to take into account a range of purposes of sentencing, including punishment, reparation, crime reduction, public protection, and reform and rehabilitation. However, desert still has a key role in the sentencing of adult offenders in so far as the sentence has to be proportionate to the seriousness of the offence and, Dingwall argues, the sentencing guidelines have also retained a central role for desert. There is, however, debate not just as to whether modern retributivist principles are still central to the English sentencing system but also as to whether that is a good or a bad thing. Chapter 3, therefore, will evaluate the detail of sentencing law, guidance, and practice since 1991, with a focus on its retributivist elements.

However, we have not reviewed the increasingly important rights framework within which English law now operates: section 2.7 will remedy that deficit by asking whether rights can be, and have been, used to control sentencing discretion and, in particular, the use of the death penalty in other jurisdictions.

2.7 Rights as a constraint on sentencing

2.7.1 Rights theory

Recent developments in rights theory provide justifications for limiting excessive punishment which are independent of penological thinking, although retributivists are usually strongly committed to rights. However, one may find appeals to rights without a commitment to retributivism, notably in civil libertarian critiques of capital punishment. For example, Amnesty International's critique of the death penalty construes the use of the death penalty as ultimately a human rights issue (see section 2.7.2). Rights-based critiques also extend to corporal and custodial forms of punishment. Article 3 of the European Convention, based on Article 5 of the UN Declaration of Human Rights, states that no one should be subjected to torture or to cruel, inhuman, or degrading treatment or punishment. Moreover the right is absolute, allowing no derogations in time of war or public emergency. Even when a punishment is deserved and even if a deterrent effect could be established, an extreme punishment would be precluded if it constituted inhuman or degrading treatment. For example, corporal punishment in the Isle of Man was seen as degrading in *Tyrer v UK* (1979–80). Article 3 is relevant to extreme punishments but conditions in prison may have to be quite harsh to constitute a breach (see Chapter 8).

While UK lawyers in the past were wary of rights, a rights culture is now well established. A rights-based system of punishment will achieve legitimacy for a system of punishment and the use of international standards will be a key restraint on punishment systems and an antidote to discretion. While claims within the UK usually rely on the European Convention, other rights instruments have been invoked worldwide, including the UN Convention against Torture and the ICCPR. The right not to be subjected to a disproportionate punishment is also being given more weight in international human rights instruments (see van Zyl Smit and Ashworth 2004), while the Strasbourg Court has also become increasingly critical of the use of whole-life sentences. Its evolving jurisprudence has highlighted the need for continued detention to be justified through regular reviews, which has brought it into conflict with the domestic courts (see Ashworth 2014; *Vinter and others v UK* (2014); *Hutchinson v UK* (2015) and Chapter 5). However, whether an individual should be released following review will depend on the assessment of dangerousness.

2.7.2 **The death penalty in the United States—a case study**

The US Supreme Court has justified the use of the death penalty in retributivist language, as the appropriate penalty for the most serious crimes (Garland 2010: 56). However, a strong retributivist argument for *abolition* of the death penalty is given by Markel (2005), who defends Governor Ryan's 2003 commutation of all the sentences of prisoners on Death Row in Illinois. Markel's critique of capital punishment is based on the importance of dignity in punishment, concerns over the reliability and accuracy of the criminal justice system in the face of evidence of errors in the sentencing of Death Row prisoners, and the problem of arbitrariness in the imposition of the penalty and its implications for equality in sentencing. The focus on human rights values has also been influential in shaping campaigns against the death penalty in China, as Miao (2013) notes.

From a rights perspective, abolitionists argue that the inalienable right to life is violated by the death penalty, the manner in which the punishment is carried out is inhuman and degrading and shows no respect for human dignity, and the punishment cannot be justified on the grounds of self-defence because it is not undertaken in response to an immediate threat to life.

In the Universal Declaration of Human Rights in 1948 each person has the right to life (Article 3) and no person shall be subject to torture or to cruel, inhuman, or degrading treatment or punishment (Article 5). Capital punishment is premeditated killing when other means are available. It is cruel treatment because it is a physical and mental attack on a helpless person. It raises the question whether there is a meaningful difference between, for example, hanging as a form of torture and hanging as a form of execution. Shooting or electrocuting a helpless person would also be seen as torture, so critics argue: it does not make any difference that the state is carrying out that punishment.

United Nations policy

UN policy now favours abolition, reflected in Article 6 of the ICCPR, which protects the right to life. It states that in countries which have not abolished the death penalty, the sentence may be imposed only for the most serious crimes and then not on persons below the age of 18 or on pregnant women, but stresses that nothing in Article 6 shall be invoked to delay or to prevent the abolition of capital punishment by any state parties to the Covenant. In December 2008 the majority of states in the UN voted in favour of a Resolution calling for a moratorium on the use of the death penalty with a view to abolition. The Resolution gained more support each time it was reconsidered, in November 2010, in 2012, and most recently in 2014, when 117 of the 193 UN member states supported it (UNGA Res 69/186, adopted 18 December 2014).

International human rights law is becoming more important in the debate, as illustrated by, for example, the cases of *Lagrand (Germany v United States)* (2001), *Avena and other Mexican Nationals (Mexico v United States)* (2004), and *LJR v Australia* (2008) where the treatment of prisoners is reviewed.

On the rights-based argument, the death penalty is wrong even if we can show that it meets a social need such as crime control, prevention of homicides, or providing assistance to efforts to combat drug trafficking. The whole point of the right is that it should not be jettisoned whenever the public interest or welfare seem threatened. Similarly, the use of torture could not be justified even in the most challenging circumstances, including terrorist attacks, as the European Court of Human Rights emphasised in *A and others v UK* (2009). On the Dworkinian model, rights should trump utility and rights have a privileged position, usurping the principles of desert and proportionality (Dworkin 1977, 2011). Rights apply to all and even the worst offenders who have committed terrible crimes retain these rights. So rights have implications for punishment at all levels, from the use of non-custodial options, including electronic tagging, to prison and the death penalty (see Chapter 8, section 8.6).

European Convention on Human Rights

Under the European Convention on Human Rights, Article 2 protects the right to life, but Article 2(1) explicitly states that '[n]o one shall be deprived of his life intentionally save in execution of a sentence of the court, following his conviction from a crime for which the penalty is provided by law'. So here the Convention is not as progressive as the ICCPR. However, the Sixth Protocol to the European Convention expresses commitment to abolition and not allowing any executions in the interim period. The Protocol has been ratified by all member states of the Council of Europe except Russia, who has signed but not yet ratified it. Russia has not carried out any executions since 1996 and the last execution in the Chechen Republic was in 1999. Russia's moratorium on executions was extended in 2009 and it remains de facto abolitionist despite demands for its restoration for crimes involving terrorism and murder. Belarus, which is not a member of the Council of Europe, retains and carries out the penalty and this has constituted a major obstacle to its membership. In Belarus there were three executions in 2014 and a death sentence was imposed on a defendant in March 2015.

Protocol 13 to the Convention adopted by the Committee of Ministers of the Council of Europe in February 2002 abolishes the death penalty in all circumstances, including times of war or public emergency. It has now been ratified by most member states and came into force on 1 July 2003. Some of the Convention issues were considered in the case of *Ocalan v Turkey* in 2003. In this case, the leader of the Kurdish Workers Party (PKK) was given a death sentence, later commuted to imprisonment. Here the European Court found that there was a breach of Article 5(4) because Ocalan had been unable to challenge the legality of his detention pre-trial and a breach of Article 6 because he had not been tried by an impartial tribunal. Article 3 was also breached because the death penalty had been imposed following an unfair trial, wrongfully subjecting Ocalan to the fear that he would be executed. The courts also took account of the fact that member states had now rejected the death penalty in deciding that in this particular case the death sentence amounted to inhuman treatment.

However, the status of the death penalty has arisen in relation to extradition cases to the United States and raises the issue of whether the penalty is a cruel, inhuman, and degrading punishment and therefore prohibited by Article 3. In *Soering v UK* (1989), a case concerning the extradition of a prisoner to the United States to face the death penalty, the Strasbourg Court said the circumstances in which the death penalty was administered could amount to inhuman and degrading treatment, although the death penalty per se was not inhuman and degrading. Here the circumstances were that the applicant was likely to be on Death Row for years and there were also mitigating circumstances in that case. After *Soering* there was an understanding that defendants would not be extradited to the United States from Europe if they would receive the death penalty but will be dealt with by other means, and this informal agreement has now been formalised. In 2003 a new UK–US Extradition Treaty stated that the executive authority may refuse extradition unless the requesting state provides an assurance that the death penalty will not be imposed, or, if imposed, will not be carried out. Similar provisions were included in the EU–US Extradition Treaty in 2009.

The issue has also been considered by the Strasbourg Court in relation to extradition to Iraq. In *Al-Saadoon and Mufdhi v UK* (2010) the Court said that the right, under Article 3 of Protocol No. 13, not to be subjected to the death penalty ranks as a fundamental right comparable to other rights under the Convention. Since the drafting of the Convention, the passing of Protocols 6 and 13 effectively amounts to a prohibition of the death penalty. This justifies the duty not to expel or extradite a person when he runs a serious risk of receiving the penalty. But the UK government breached Article 3 of Protocol 13 by failing to negotiate to prevent that risk.

The Eighth Amendment

Within the United States, rights-based constitutional challenges to the penalty have repeatedly been brought under the Eighth Amendment prohibition on cruel and unusual punishment. These led to a temporary moratorium on its use in the 1970s in *Furman v Georgia* (1972), and a narrowing of the application of the penalty to offenders with learning difficulties in *Atkins v Virginia* (2002) and offenders under 18 in *Roper v Simmonds* (2005). Both the Eighth and Fourteenth Amendments forbid execution of individuals with intellectual disability. This issue was revisited more recently in *Hall v Florida* 752 US (2014), which discussed the constitutionality of using an IQ score test as conclusive evidence of intellectual capacity. Here the defendant had an IQ test score of 71, but the relevant Florida state required a test score of 70 before allowing the accused to present any additional disability evidence. The US Supreme Court decided that current thinking does not regard using this strict cut-off point as proper or humane (see also Sarma 2015).

The methods of execution have also been challenged. In *State v Mata* (2008) the Nebraska Supreme Court ruled that the use of the electric chair did violate the constitutional prohibition on cruel and unusual punishment. The evidence showed that electrocution does inflict intense pain and suffering on the prisoner (see also Denver *et al.* 2008; Mills 2009). At that time Nebraska was the only state still using that mode of execution. However in *Baze v Rees* (2008) the majority of the United States Supreme Court decided that the use of the lethal injection does not breach the Eighth Amendment prohibition on cruel and unusual punishment. For capital punishment to be constitutional it must not create or involve a risk of unnecessary or gratuitous suffering, and the method of execution used in Kentucky did not create such a risk. This decision paved the way for the resumption of executions, as most states had halted executions while awaiting the outcome of this case.

However, recently this method has also been problematic as a shortage of drugs needed for execution by lethal injection has made it difficult to administer the punishment and executions have been delayed in some states. Some US drugs companies do not want their drugs used in executions and the European Union has banned exports of the relevant drugs used for this purpose. The quest for alternative drugs has resulted in more so-called 'botched executions', although problems did exist before the drugs shortage and approved drugs may cause problems if not used properly. Sarat (2014), in his recent study of executions, argues that almost 7 per cent of all lethal injection executions have been visibly botched. Concerns intensified when Clayton Lockett died of a massive heart attack 40 minutes after the administration of a new lethal injection protocol in Oklahoma in April 2014.

Some states have now authorised alternative methods of execution. In Oklahoma in March 2015 the Governor signed legislation allowing the state to use a firing squad if drugs for lethal injection are unavailable. The following month the Oklahoma legislature passed a bill authorising the use of lethal nitrogen gas as an alternative method of execution if drugs are unavailable, and this was also signed by the Governor. The use of firing squads is also permitted in Utah in such circumstances. The shortage of thiopental has also increased demands for a return to the electric chair, although clearly these rival methods are also open to rights challenges. However, a further challenge to the use of the lethal injections in Oklahoma in the Supreme Court in 2015 in the case of *Glossip v Gross* No. 14-79655 did not succeed. This case concerned the use of the drug midazolam, which was also used in the Lockett execution. In affirming the decision of the lower court, the Supreme Court noted that the petitioners had failed to identify a known and alternative method of execution which entailed a lesser risk of pain which was necessary to succeed in an Eighth Amendment method of execution challenge. The petitioners also failed to establish that Oklahoma's use of a massive dose of midazolam as part of its execution protocol entailed a substantial risk of severe pain.

Rights-based arguments have therefore been a key means of challenging extreme punishments, although abolition has not yet been achieved in the United States. While the use of the lethal injection has survived the above challenges, the scope of the penalty has been limited.

2.8 Reflecting on the issues

2.8.1 Questions for discussion

Read the comments below and then consider the questions posed under 'Tasks'.

This chapter has examined the traditional and the more recent tools for structuring the discretion of those who sentence. In England and Wales the judges have sometimes resisted the new constraints, on the basis that a wider discretion gives them the power to do justice in individual cases. On the other hand, public and policy pressure has more usually been in favour of constraining judicial independence on the assumption that this would reduce the injustice of inconsistency and achieve particular policy objectives.

Most of these statements and assumptions cannot be tested empirically in any way that will give closure to the debate about sentencing discretion. While there is evidence that the provisions of the CJA 1991—after an initial decrease—did not reduce the use of custody and that there was an increase from 1993 onwards, there is not necessarily a clear link. Several possible explanations have been suggested: that the amendments made to the Act in 1993 reintroduced discretion in relation to previous offending and associated offences (see Chapter 3), that community penalties lacked legitimacy and were under-resourced, that later legislation provided too many exceptions to the restriction on the use of custody, and that popular and government punitiveness influenced judicial thinking. Some of these factors involve judicial discretion, others do not; although the Halliday Report (2001) implicitly blamed the sentencer when arguing that the system was not 'working' in line with policy objectives, that seriousness is not measured 'properly', and that there should be a 'limited' retributivism.

Task:

1. What evidence would you need to demonstrate the effectiveness of guidelines in constraining discretion?

2. In the light of our comments above, do you think that the guidelines issued since 2011 are effectively constraining discretion? Why/why not?

You might find the following helpful:

Padfield, N. (2013) 'Exploring the Success of Sentencing Guidelines' in Ashworth, A. and Roberts, J. (eds) *Sentencing Guidelines, Exploring the English Model*. Oxford, Oxford University Press.

Roberts, J. (2013) 'Complying with Sentencing Guidelines: Latest Findings from the Crown Court Sentencing Survey' in Ashworth, A. and Roberts, J. (eds) *Sentencing Guidelines, Exploring the English Model*. Oxford, Oxford University Press.

Sentencing Council (2015a) *Theft Offences, Definitive Guideline*. London, Sentencing Council (an example of a recent guideline)

Sentencing Council (2015c) *Crown Court Sentencing Survey, Annual Publication January to December 2014 England and Wales*. London, Sentencing Council.

2.8.2 **Case study**

Imagine that you know no sentencing law and guidance and that you have complete discretion to sentence how you like. What would you do with Arti and Burt in the following scenario?

The following are the agreed facts of your 'case':

Arti, a 20-year-old, and his friend, Burt, aged 17, came back to Arti's family home one evening feeling upset and angry because their twin-sister girlfriends had just ditched them. Arti took his grandad's radio—of great sentimental significance to his grandad because it had been a present from a dying friend—couldn't find the right wavelength, and smashed the radio. Burt insulted and swore at Arti's grandad.

Burt and Arti then decided to take a motorbike from the neighbour's yard (without asking him) and, taking turns, drove the motorbike round the town. (Arti had apparently done this twice before.) They then abandoned the motorbike. While they were gone, Arti's grandad had a stroke and died two hours later.

Task:

You should justify an outcome (a 'sentence') separately for Arti and Burt in relation to what each has done. However, you should do this twice using the following information and then compare your conclusions.

1. Decide you will punish Arti and Burt in a way which seems to you *what they deserve* for what they have done. State what factors of the case you took into account and decide whether your answer would be any different if you had been aware that insulting or harming grandparents was viewed as *a very serious matter* in their community?

2. Decide *what you think* will be the most *effective* outcome for everyone concerned. State the purpose of your decision and what factors you took into account.

If your answers to 1 and 2 are different, that is probably because you were applying different principles or rationales in each one. The first approach asks you to sentence on retributivist principles; the second allows you to choose a utilitarian or even a restorative principle and objective.

online resource centre

See the Online Resource Centre for ideas and further reading around the issues raised by this 'case'.

3

Determining 'just deserts'

SUMMARY

Seriousness and proportionality are key concepts in the 'just deserts' approach to sentencing which was endorsed by the Criminal Justice Act 1991. This chapter analyses the extent to which this framework with its retributivist principles has been undermined by subsequent changes in legislation, notably the Criminal Justice Act 2003, and by amendments to that Act. It examines law and guidance on constructing seriousness, particularly in relation to harm and culpability, and on determining a commensurate sentence. It illustrates issues by using examples from recent guidelines and focuses discussion on custodial sentencing. Finally it discusses criticisms of modern retributivism.

3.1 A retributivist sentencing framework?

3.1.1 'The accepted account'

As we saw in Chapter 2, the 'just deserts' approach was developed by modern retributivists to address some of the criticisms made of classical versions of retributivism. For England and Wales, it is the Criminal Justice Act (CJA) 1991—'The first systematic effort at sentencing guidance in England and Wales' (von Hirsch 2011: xiii)—which has been viewed as the piece of legislation most infused with a just deserts approach. Von Hirsch argues that the Act provided norms 'aimed at helping to establish gradations of sentence for various crimes, based chiefly on offence-seriousness' (2011: xiii). *Crime, Justice and Protecting the Public*, which had set out the thinking leading to the CJA 1991, proposed that just deserts should be the primary criterion for sentencing and incorporated in statute for the first time (Home Office 1990a: para 1.6). Elements of the utilitarian concern with social consequences were reflected in the proposed aim of crime reduction (para 1.7) but deterrence was explicitly criticised as being an unrealistic aim (para 2.8). Its concept of a bifurcated approach—whereby most offenders are sentenced on the principles of just deserts and parsimony, while a minority receive sentences for public protection longer than justified on retributivist principles—still underpins policy.

Both the CJA 1991 and the later CJA 2003 have been criticised for setting up unworkable hybrid sentencing frameworks (see Ashworth 2000: 84; Ashworth and Player 2005; Koffman 2006) but the provisions of the CJA 1991 made clear that the main sentencing decision was to assess just deserts and other considerations, such as rehabilitation, came into play only in the choice of a community sentence. The risk-based sentences were aimed at, and used for, only a small subgroup of offenders[1] and the other exceptions, such as compensation orders and the options for dealing with **mentally disordered offenders**, are not incompatible with the basic retributivist rationale (see Chapters 6 and 7).

As enacted, then, the CJA 1991 had characteristics which are familiar in current law:

- a presumptive rationale—just deserts—with a focus on a sentence proportionate to the seriousness of the offence in question (not offending history);

- sentences to be treated as punishments which could be theorised in terms of deprivation of liberty (probation previously had not been so theorised);

- statutory hurdles for passing custodial and community sentences so that parsimony in sentencing could be encouraged. In effect it meant the sentencer 'must justify each upward step in the "sentencing pyramid" in accordance with the seriousness of the offence' (Wasik and von Hirsch 1994: 409).

The introduction for the first time in 1991 of the statutory 'seriousness' thresholds as well as the commensurability principle clearly flagged up the principles of modern retributivism outlined in Chapter 2. More contentiously, those provisions which downgraded the effect of previous convictions and reformed the process of deciding on the amount of a fine could also be viewed as reflecting retributivist principles.

However, Dingwall and Hillier state that 'The accepted account is that the Criminal Justice Act 1993 was the first incremental step in a process which reduced the importance of retribution in the sentencing process' (2015: 44; see also Koffman 2006). Certainly, the Halliday Report, when proposing the new framework which was incorporated in the Criminal Justice Act (CJA) 2003, claimed that the just deserts approach had 'failed to take root' in sentencing courts (2001: para 1.34) and it is now argued that the current sentencing framework cannot be viewed as one which acts as a constraint on discretion by mandating a clear 'just deserts' approach. According to Lacey and Pickard, 'punitive rationales have in practice continued to be shaped by consequentialist considerations such as incapacitation and deterrence, with consequentialist and retributive considerations often blurred not only in public debate and political discourse but also in sentencing practice' (2015: 217). This chapter hopes to shed light on the reasons for these divergent viewpoints.

At the time of writing, the most recent pieces of legislation with sentencing provisions are the Criminal Justice and Immigration Act (CJIA) 2008, the Coroners and Justice Act 2009, the Legal Aid, Sentencing and Punishment of Offenders Act (LASPO) 2012, the Crime and Courts Act 2013, the Serious Crime Act 2015, and the Criminal Justice and Courts Act 2015. However, in so far as they have affected the sentencing framework for adults[2] they have nearly all done so by amending the CJA 2003 (or statutes governing ancillary orders) and so that is still the main source of sentencing law. This chapter will start, then, by summarising the retributivist provisions of the 2003 Act before examining relevant aspects of legislation passed in, and since, both 1991 and 2003 in order to assess the extent to which the just deserts principles underpinning the 1991 Act have—or have not—been diluted.

---

[1] Although we shall see in Chapter 5 that for a period after 2003 far too many offenders were given an **indeterminate sentence** because of the mandatory nature of new provisions before they were amended in 2008 and the IPP sentence repealed in 2012.

[2] But see Chapters 6 and 11 for current law regarding minors.

3.1.2 **The Criminal Justice Act 2003**

The Halliday Report in 2001 had robustly criticised the framework set up in 1991. It made, inter alia, the following arguments for change:

1. The 1991 (as amended) sentencing framework has 'a narrow sense of purpose' and is a 'less than complete guide to the selection of the most suitable sentence in an individual case' (para 1.9). Sentencers are not encouraged to consider reparation or crime reduction.

2. The framework has too much discretion which has led to inconsistency of sentencing: sentencers have insufficient guidance on the measurement of seriousness (para 1.9) and greater clarity is required to aid sentencers (para 1.44).

3. The framework has 'a muddled approach to persistent offenders' (para 1.11). The persistence of offending—the issue of criminal history and recidivism as a factor in the process of determining sentence—is one of the Halliday Report's main reasons for advocating change.

However, the Report was not without its critics. Hudson argued that it offered 'a pick and mix of almost every criminal justice idea of the last few years—public protection through incapacitative incarceration; reparation and restoration; curfews and electronic monitoring; treatments and controls' (Hudson 2001/2: 17); Baker and Clarkson (2002) argued that the higher importance attached to risk assessment and rehabilitation in deciding on a sentence could increase disparity. In the event the 2003 Act responded to some but not all of the criticisms and the framework set up by the Act is still, we argue, basically retributivist.

To start with, the calculation of seriousness and of a proportionate sentence is still very important in current English sentencing law. Section 143(1) of the CJA 2003 gives guidance on determining the seriousness of an offence which, in effect, summarises the approach of the courts before the 2003 Act: that both the offender's culpability in committing the offence and any harm caused (or intended to be caused) by the offence must be considered as part of the assessment. An indication of the importance of seriousness in the 2003 Act is the fact that one of the earliest guidelines produced by the (then) Sentencing Guidelines Council (SGC) concerned the process of calculating seriousness (Sentencing Guidelines Council 2004a). More recently, Parliament in 2009 mandated the matters to which the Sentencing Council must 'have regard' when producing guidelines: they focus on culpability, harm, and factors which affect the seriousness of the offence.[3]

Further, s. 153(2) of the CJA 2003 restates a long-standing principle that not only should the sentence be proportionate to the level of seriousness, but it should also be 'for the shortest term' that is commensurate with seriousness. Both these aspects are features of modern retributivism, as are the 'hurdles' for the imposition of custodial and community penalties. Section 152(2) states that '[t]he court must not pass a custodial sentence unless it is of the opinion that the offence, or the combination of the offence and one or more offences associated with it, was so serious that neither a fine nor a community sentence can be justified for the offence'.[4] In practice, how high this hurdle is construed may depend on how low guidance sets the 'anchoring points' (see Chapter 2, section 2.6.5). However, s. 166(2) states that s. 152(2) 'does not prevent a court . . . from passing a community sentence even though it is of the opinion that the offence, or one or more offences associated with it, was so serious that a community sentence could not normally be justified for the offence'. Sentencers have

---

[3] Coroners and Justice Act 2009, s. 121.
[4] Legislation 2012–15 has, however, lengthened the list of exceptions to this: see s. 152(1A).

a discretion, therefore, to take account of mitigation or mental disorder and impose a non-custodial sentence even if the custody threshold is met.

The CJA 2003 also includes, in s. 148(1), a statutory criterion for the imposition of a community penalty: the offending must be 'serious enough to warrant such a sentence'. Section 148(5)[5] similarly gives the court discretion to take into account any factors which would justify a lesser sentence. The as yet not in force s. 151 would allow the court to make a community order even when the offending is not 'serious enough' if on three or more previous occasions when convicted of an offence the offender has received (only) a fine as a penalty, provided that it 'would be in the interests of justice'.[6] Section 151(3) specifies the factors which would have to be considered in making this judgement: the nature of previous convictions, their relevance to the current offence, and the time which has elapsed. As we shall see in section 3.2.4, using persistence of offending to justify what would otherwise be a disproportionate sentence does not fit easily into retributivism. However, the CJIA 2008 inserted a new s. 150A in the 2003 Act which confines the use of community orders to imprisonable offences, which may limit the effect of this provision.

In section 3.2 we will look at other elements of the current sentencing framework which are predicated on a just deserts approach, notably the determination and application of factors which mitigate and aggravate seriousness. It is true that the generic community order with specified components (see Chapter 10, section 10.3) requires the court to assess which requirement is most 'suitable' for the offender. This secondary decision can be decided on the basis of aims alien to retributivism, for example, the utilitarian aim of rehabilitation or the restorative aim of reparation, but the restrictions on liberty that the order imposes are retributivist in nature: they must be commensurate with seriousness (s. 148(2)).

The fine must also reflect the seriousness of the offending (s. 164(2)) and the financial circumstances of the offender can reduce or increase the amount of the fine (s. 164(4)).[7] Further, nearly all the guidelines issued by the SGC and the Sentencing Council provide an increasingly structured approach which is concerned almost entirely with determining seriousness and proportionality. The exceptions are in relation to the 'dangerous' offender and to requirements of a reparative nature (which we will deal with in Chapters 5 and 6) but these exceptions prove the rule: the current sentencing framework, despite amendments and additions, is that of just deserts. However, there are now aspects of the sentencing framework which, arguably, are not as strongly retributivist as those introduced by the CJA 1991, and section 3.1.3 will review them.

3.1.3 The development of the sentencing framework

The provisions of the CJA 1991 were re-enacted in the Powers of Criminal Courts (Sentencing) Act (PCCSA) 2000 but there had already been amendments to the original wording. Three aspects of the CJA 1991 as passed particularly 'upset' influential sections of public and professional opinion (see Worrall 1997: chapter 3): the new system of unit fines (see Chapter 10, section 10.2.2), the sentencing focus on the offence in question and only 'one other' associated offence (which reduced the total amount of seriousness to be considered), and the assumed prohibition on sentencers taking past convictions into account when assessing seriousness. In particular the tabloid press and the Magistrates' Association

---

[5] Inserted by the CJIA 2008, s. 10 and in force since 2008.

[6] This replaced the Powers of Criminal Courts (Sentencing) Act (PCCSA) 2000, s. 59, a similarly problematic provision allowing discretion if fines had previously been unpaid.

[7] The Crown Court is specifically empowered by s. 163 to fine an offender convicted on indictment instead of, or in addition to, any other penalty.

fiercely criticised unit fines and the government hastily amended these provisions by ss. 65–66 of the Criminal Justice Act (CJA) 1993. Section 18 of the CJA 1991 was replaced by provisions returning the sentencing law for fines to something akin to the pre-1991 situation. Nevertheless, a just deserts approach was retained by the new subsection 18(2). 'The amount of the fine fixed by the court shall be such as . . . reflects the seriousness of the offence.' Sections 1 and 2 of the CJA 1991 (relating to custody) and s. 6 (relating to community penalties) were also amended to allow the courts to consider 'one or more' associated offences.

The third problem provision, s. 29, dealt with those factors which could aggravate the seriousness of the offence in question. The wording of the section as passed in 1991 was that an offence 'shall not be regarded as more serious' (s. 29(1)) because of the persistence of offending or the 'failure to respond' to previous (community) penalties. The amendments made to this section by the CJA 1993 made clear that the court could take these two factors into account when calculating the seriousness of the offending.[8] These changes could be seen to be taking some focus away from the instant offence which is the focus of a retributivist justification for punishment.

The 1993 amendments to s. 29—re-enacted as PCCSA 2000 s. 151(2), now CJA 2003 s. 143(3)—also added 'offending on bail' as a factor that courts *must* take into account. This can be justified as increasing the seriousness of the offending because the culpability is greater: the offender was on note not to reoffend. Since then, further mandated aggravating factors have been added: offending that is motivated by religion or race, and where the offender was motivated by or showed hostility based on the sexual orientation, disability, or transgender identity of the victim.[9] These factors also go to culpability.

In the decade after 1993 other new provisions were more problematic in relation to the retributivist basis of the sentencing framework. The Crime (Sentences) Act 1997, as we saw in Chapter 2 (section 2.2.5), introduced automatic life and mandatory minimum sentences which could lead to a higher penalty than justified by proportionality. The CJA 2003 also introduced new indeterminate and preventative sentences—amended by the CJIA 2008 and repealed or amended by LASPO 2012—which sentenced partly or wholly on risk of future offending. These longer sentences are justified on utilitarian, not retributivist, principles and will be dealt with in Chapter 5.

Changes have also been made by the CJIA 2008 and LASPO 2012 to the disposals for young offenders (see Chapter 11, section 11.3) but, arguably, none of these changes alters in any significant way the retributivist framework for sentencing the 'non-dangerous' offender. The framework set up by the 1991 Act is, then, still recognisable in current law and guidance, and Table 3.1 sets out that framework as a series of crucial questions in the order they were introduced in the 1991 Act. This may not be the most logical order but it shows the extent to which the components of the 1991 Act remain and where they can now be found in legislation. The italics draw attention to the desert-based hurdles to the use of a category of punishment and the underlined words refer to amendments by the CJA 1993. Bold type is used to indicate the three main levels of punishment (custody, community, and financial). The section numbers are given for both the CJA 1991 and their re-enactment in the PCCSA 2000. Where there is a directly comparable provision the section number in the CJA 2003 (as amended, if relevant) is also given.

---

[8] Because this issue of persistence has been so important a policy issue in relation to both the CJA 2003 and the CJA 1991, we will discuss it in more detail in section 3.2.4.

[9] By the Crime and Disorder Act 1998, the Anti-Terrorism, Crime and Security Act 2001, the CJA 2003, and LASPO 2012 respectively, the first two provisions having been re-enacted in the PCCSA 2000 s. 153 before all these provisions were consolidated in the CJA 2003 ss. 145–146.

Table 3.1 The sentencing framework in legislation

Decision stage	CJA 91 ss.	PCCSA ss.	CJA 2003 ss.	Question	Outcome
1.	1	79	152(1)	Is the offence one that is punishable by custody?	If NO go to 4. If YES go to 2.
2.	1(2)(a)	79(2)(a)	152(2)	Is the offence (+ one or more other/s) so serious that only custody* is justified?	If NO go to 3. If Yes:
	3(3)(a)	81	156	What information must or may the court take into account?	and
	2(2)(a)	80(2)(a)	153(2)	What sentence length is 'commensurate with the seriousness of the offence' (or the combination of that offence + one or more associated offences)?	Consider whether stage 3 applies. If not SENTENCE
3.	1(2)(b)	79(2)(b)	224	Is the offence of a violent or sexual nature? (now a 'specified offence')	If NO go to 4. If YES:
	3(3)(a) & (b)	81	[229]	What information must or may the court take into account about the offending or offender? [now to assess risk]	and
	1(2)(b)	79(2)(b)	[225–8**]	Would only a custodial sentence be adequate to protect the public from serious harm?	If NO go to 4. If Yes:
	2(2)(b)	80(2)(b		Originally: what longer term than one commensurate with the offence seriousness is necessary? Now: decide whether any of the sentences in CJA 2003 ss. 224A–228 can/should be used.	SENTENCE
4.	6(1)	35(1)	148(1)	Is the offence (+ one or more others) serious enough to warrant a community sentence?	If NO go to 5. If Yes:
	6(2)(a)	35(3)(a)	148(2)(a)	What orders are most suitable for the offender?	and
	7(2)	36(1)	156(2)	What information is there about the offender and shall we take it into account?	and

(Continued)

Table 3.1 Continued

Decision stage	CJA 91 ss.	PCCSA ss.	CJA 2003 ss.	Question	Outcome
	7(1)	36(2)	156(1)	What information is there about the circumstances of the offence?	and
	6(2)(b)	35(3)(b)	148(2)(b)	What amount of restriction on liberty in the orders is commensurate with the seriousness of the offence (and any others)?	SENTENCE
5. Fines	18(2)	See below		What number of units is commensurate with the seriousness of the offending? What is the offender's disposable weekly income? Calculate the value of the fine.	SENTENCE

* Now 'so serious that neither a fine alone nor a community sentence' can be justified.
** These provisions were in 2003, 2008, and 2012. Since 2003 there has been the possibility of an indeterminate or extended, rather than 'longer than normal', sentence: see Chapter 5 for a review of dangerous offender provisions in the CJA 2003.

Note: the original s. 18 was totally replaced with:
s. 18(1) [128(1)] What are the financial circumstances of the offender?
s. 18(3) [128(3)] What information is there about the circumstances of the case, including the financial circumstances of the offender? and
s. 18(2) [128(2)] What fine 'reflects the seriousness of the offence'?
s. 18(5) [128(4)] Should the financial circumstances of the offender increase or reduce the fine?

See Chapter 10, section 10.2 for a discussion of the fines sentencing framework in the CJA 2003, which largely re-enacts previous provisions.

3.1.4 **A focus on custodial sentences**

Although we mention financial and community penalties in this chapter, we deal with financial and community penalties in Chapter 10, while the bulk of the examples in sections 3.2 and 3.3 of this chapter are taken from custodial sentencing. Before we move to further discussion of just deserts we will, therefore, summarise the current options for sentencers in relation to custody.

The 'standard' custodial sentence—which is the result of an assessment of seriousness and proportionality concluding that the criterion for custody is met—is a determinate sentence: the judge specifies exactly how long it will be. Assuming guidance is followed, that length is subject only to the maximum sentence set in law for each offence and the maximum allowed in a magistrates' or youth court (see Chapter 2).[10]

A rejigged suspended (custodial) sentence was introduced in the CJA 2003 such that requirements can be placed on the offender, as in community sentences. Suspended

---

[10] However, there is a minimum sentence of five days in a magistrates' court.

sentences can be used for any term of imprisonment from 14 days to two years. See Chapter 10, section 10.4.1 for further details.

There is one mandatory life sentence in English law, which is the sentence for an offender found guilty of murder. The judge sets a minimum term—based on the guidance set out in Schedule 21 to the CJA 2003—to be served before the offender can be considered for release. There are also custodial sentences to be used with offenders who are deemed to be a risk such that the public need protection for longer or indeterminate periods. Over the period 1991 to the present there have been many attempts to produce workable, effective, and rights-compliant versions of such special custodial sentencing provisions. For the current law see Chapter 5.

In addition there are the (mandatory) minimum sentences (see Chapter 2, section 2.2.5) in relation to Class A drug trafficking, domestic burglary, certain firearms offences, and the offence of using someone to mind a weapon.

3.2 Calculating seriousness

3.2.1 The approach of the guidelines

This chapter is focusing on the retributivist concepts of seriousness and proportionality and this section will review the ways in which the seriousness of the offending is evaluated. However, while a book may proceed chapter by chapter and deal with separate points in turn, sentencing in practice is not like that. The different issues are intertwined and, when faced with a real case, or a problem question, an overall view of the process and possibilities is necessary before decisions can be made about what law and issues are going to be relevant. We will, therefore, summarise the general approach of the guidelines and also provide our own sentencing 'checklist' to help you see how the various components of the process of deciding on a sentence fit together.

Format of Sentencing Council guidelines

As we mentioned in Chapter 2 (section 2.3.3), the approach of the offence-based guidelines since the establishment of the Sentencing Council has been to outline a series of 'steps' with a crucial first two steps. Step 1 is to determine the offence category and Step 2 is 'shaping the provisional sentence' (see Ashworth and Roberts 2013: 6-9). For example, the *Burglary Offences Definitive Guideline* (Sentencing Council: 2011b), in relation to the offence of aggravated burglary, gives as Step 1 in the assessment of seriousness the need to place the facts of the offending in one of the following three categories: category 1 which is 'greater harm and higher culpability', category 2 which is 'greater harm and lower culpability or lesser harm and higher culpability', and category 3 which is 'lesser harm and lower culpability'. Then 'The court should determine culpability and harm caused or intended, by reference only to the factors below, which comprise the principal factual elements of the offence' (2011b: 4). Lists of factors indicating greater harm or higher culpability are then provided. Ashworth and Roberts refer to their 'primordial status' because the determination of the category range 'is the step which will have the greatest influence on severity of sentence' (2013: 6). Yet, as the Burglary Guideline states at Step 1: 'Where an offence does not fall squarely into a category, individual factors may require a degree of weighting before making an overall assessment and determining the appropriate offence category' (Sentencing Council 2011b: 4) and there is no guidance on that weighting.

Step 2 'requires the court to "fine tune" the calibration of harm and culpability (Ashworth and Roberts 2013: 7). Again there are lists of factors—in this case, according to the guideline, the list is a 'non-exhaustive list of additional factual elements providing the context of the offence and factors relating to the offender' (Sentencing Council 2011b: 5). The court should then consider further adjustment within the category range for features which aggravate or mitigate seriousness or take into account personal mitigation. Step 2 of the Health and Safety Guideline is somewhat different in that, using the tables on subsequent pages, 'the court is required to focus on the organisation's annual turnover or equivalent to reach a starting point for a fine' (Sentencing Council 2015b: 6).

If the offence in question could receive a non-custodial or a custodial sentence then, at Step 2, some guidelines have drawn attention to the statutory thresholds. For example, in the Dangerous Dogs Guideline applicable before 1 July 2016 (re Dangerous Dogs Act 1991 ss. 3(1)) and 3(3)(a)), it says:

> When sentencing category 1 or 2 offences, the court should also consider the custody threshold as follows:
>
> - has the custody threshold been passed?
> - if so, is it unavoidable that a custodial sentence be imposed?
> - if so, can that sentence be suspended?
> - When sentencing category 2 offences, the court should also consider the community order threshold as follows:
> - has the community order threshold been passed?
>
> (Sentencing Council 2012b: 5; see also Sentencing Council 2014c: 15)

Steps 1 and 2 usually allow a provisional sentence to be determined and the steps from 3 onwards include reductions for assisting the authorities and/or for a guilty plea, compensation and ancillary orders, the totality principle, giving reasons for sentence, and consideration of remand time. In the Dangerous Dogs Guideline, for example, the ancillary orders include 'Disqualification from having custody of a dog' and a 'destruction order'.

The number and order of steps varies slightly, however, depending on the extra stages that are available for some offences. For example if, as in the Assault Guideline, the dangerousness provisions in the CJA 2003 are relevant to the offence in question then there is an additional step. So, in the Burglary Guideline 'Credit for a guilty plea is taken into consideration only at step four in the decision making process, after the appropriate sentence has been identified' (Sentencing Council 2011b: 2); in the Health and Safety Guideline it is at Step 6.

Other guidelines have additional or substituted steps because of specific factors relevant to the offence. At the time of writing, the latest guideline is the *Health and Safety Offences, Corporate Manslaughter and Food Safety and Hygiene Offences Definitive Guideline* (Sentencing Council 2015b; see Online Resource Centre for details of later guidelines). For the first group of Health and Safety offences where the offender is an organisation, Step 3 is 'Check whether the proposed fine based on turnover is proportionate to the overall means of the offender' and Step 4 is 'Consider other factors that may warrant adjustment of the proposed fine.' This is because the penalty can only be a financial one with an unlimited maximum and an 'offence range' of fines from £50 to £10 million. There are exceptions to the 'normal' stages 1 and 2. The Environmental Offences Guideline in relation to the offences committed by organisations has 'Compensation' at stage 1 and 'Confiscation' at stage 2 (Sentencing Council 2014b: 4). Steps 3 and 4 are then as for stages 1 and 2 of most guidelines. That guideline consequently has 12 steps.

In addition to these offence-focused guidelines there are generic ones: notably on seriousness (Sentencing Guidelines Council 2004a), on reduction in sentence for a guilty plea (Sentencing Guidelines Council 2007a), on dangerous offenders (Sentencing Guidelines Council 2007b), and on sentencing youths (Sentencing Guidelines Council 2009b). Also there are SGC guidelines which are still current, for example 'Causing death by driving' (Sentencing Guidelines Council 2008c), but which have different formats from the ones just described. Like most of the earlier guidelines the guidance was set out in a more narrative way, without tables and clear steps, but, nevertheless, covered similar components in relation to harm, culpability, and factors aggravating or mitigating seriousness.

Checklist

The guidelines give very detailed guidance. It is, consequently, sometimes difficult to get an overview of the whole process. The checklist below is intended to supplement your understanding and provide a tool to help you deal with sentencing scenarios. Some of the elements on this checklist will be dealt with in more detail later in this text and so you are not expected to understand their import at this stage. While—to a greater or lesser extent—the just deserts approach to sentencing is the 'normal' sentencing framework, steps 1–3 in the checklist remind you that there are exceptions to that approach, triggered when the selective incapacitation or extended supervision provisions apply and when the offender is mentally disordered. They will be dealt with elsewhere (see Chapters 5 and 6).

Checklist

In light of the facts of the case in question:

1. Is the offender mentally disordered? Consider the provisions of the Mental Health Act 1983 and any other relevant legislation.

2. Are any of the minimum sentences relevant (particularly PCCSA 2000, ss. 110–111, and some firearms offences)? Is the sentence fixed by law (murder)? Are the sentences for public protection applicable (particularly CJA 2003, ss. 224A–228)?

3. Is the case to be dealt with in terms of proportionality/seriousness/just deserts? What statutory provisions are (most) relevant?

4. What is the statutory maximum penalty? If being dealt with in the magistrates' court, what is the maximum that can be imposed?

5. Is there an offence-based guideline for this offence issued by the Sentencing Guidelines Council or Sentencing Council? If not, is there an appellate guideline judgment? If relevant, what do the *Magistrates' Court Sentencing Guidelines* say?

6. What guidance is given on assessing relative levels of culpability and harm in calculating seriousness? Are there relevant general guidelines (e.g. on seriousness or dangerousness)? Which (other) factors from case law or guidance on mitigation or aggravation are relevant? Which statutory factors must be taken into account to aggravate (or mitigate) severity?

7. Can you now decide what is the 'normal range' or 'starting point' for sentencing this offence or subcategory of the offence?

8. Is there any recent guidance which is pertinent to deciding whether the facts of the case fulfil the seriousness criteria for imposing custodial or community penalties? Can you now fix a sentence before proceeding further?

9. (a) For a community sentence: do any facts of the case suggest particular requirements/penalties are appropriate?

   (b) For a custodial sentence: is the sentence length as short as is necessary for the penal purpose?

---

10. Are there any personal mitigating factors? Should they be taken into account?

11. Is there a sentence discount for a guilty plea? If so, how much?

12. What compensation order should be imposed? If not, why not? What victim's surcharge should be imposed? Is a confiscation order, or any other ancillary order, relevant?[11]

13. Given the answers to 9–11, what sentence should now be imposed?[12]

14. Are there any other powers that should be exercised for the purpose of protecting the public from harm from the offender?

3.2.2 **Culpability and harm**

Section 143(1) of the 2003 Act and also subsequent guidelines have increasingly made clear the importance of focusing on the two elements which comprise seriousness: culpability and harm. We have noted in section 3.2.1 the approach of guidelines to this. However, while providing useful, detailed, and necessary guidance, such an approach hides the fact that it is very problematic to make such judgements about culpability and harm or, indeed, to clearly separate culpability from harm. Such an exercise—and the rest of the process of finding a proportionate outcome for the offending in question—entails having answers to the following difficult questions:

1. What factors can legitimately make something more or less serious? Should previous offending be considered in this process?

2. How do you decide what sentence is proportionate to any amount of seriousness? In particular, where should the anchoring point be and so where, for example, should the custody level be set?

Guidelines have sought to address these questions.

If we focus on the first question, we need to note that there are two very different types of judgement in assessing seriousness. First, there is a normative judgement about wrongfulness. With the exception of murder, different individuals, communities, and nations may have very different ideas about what counts as most or least serious. In the sentencing exercise provided at the end of Chapter 2, for example, our law students might or might not think that the harm done (theft of a motorbike and radio, and verbal insults) was serious, depending on the importance of such in their peer group or country; they might or might not take into account the feelings of, and effect on, the victim of the offences; and they might or might not feel culpability had been affected by an incident in the offenders' love lives.

You might want to consider the following actions. To what extent do you think each is worthy of blame? Which shows the greatest/least/no culpability? Which shows the greatest/least/no harm? Do your answers make it easy to put them in order of seriousness?

- Copying passages of a book into an essay without providing a footnote/reference.
- Parking in a space allocated to the disabled.
- Taking the last chocolate biscuit.

[11] Compensation and confiscation orders are dealt with in Chapter 6.
[12] Compensation and other ancillary and preventative orders would usually be decided after sentence but, as we shall see in Chapter 7, a compensation order can be made instead of a fine.

- Filling in a claim form when you haven't had an accident.
- Not handing in to lost property a wallet found on campus.

Our students found this surprisingly difficult. Academic writers would sympathise. For example, Greenfield and Paoli (2013) focused on evaluating criminal harms and exposed the complexities in doing so, while Simons (2012) discussed culpability via a focus on strict liability offences and also raised difficult questions.

Culpability

In an early analysis of the issues Cross, drawing on judicial comments and practice, suggested that four factors affect how the courts calculate seriousness as well as the factor of harm done: wickedness, social disapproval, social danger, and social alarm (1981: 178–82).

1. *The 'evilness' of the perpetrator.* This focus on degrees of wickedness is perhaps the most difficult, depending as it does on normative judgements and underlying moral codes. In the fragmented modern society there may be little consensus as to what actions are most blameworthy and, further, its focus on the mental state of the offender raises difficult questions as to intention, provocation, malice, and excuses.

2. *Social disapproval.* This is an equally slippery concept, again depending on society's values. The strength of public denunciation of an offence (within its offence category) is often strongly influenced by the age or sex of the victim: babies or children as victims generally attract more social disapproval and so the offending is construed as more serious. There might also be more social disapproval of an offender if he has committed the offence before.

3. *Social danger or social alarm.* The clearest example of this factor might now be terrorist-related offences: the degree of extreme social anxiety about global terrorism feeds into a heightening of perceptions of the severity of offences such as possession of a firearm or counterfeiting documents. Cross's example of social alarm upgrading seriousness is that of the person illegally entering a residential property—as opposed to commercial property—where the same amount of damage or theft causes a greater alarm.

In providing early guidance on 'seriousness' the SGC approached the issue of culpability by focusing on the 'amount' of intention and identifying four 'levels' for sentencing purposes:

Where the offender—

(iv) has the *intention* to cause harm, with the highest culpability when an offence is planned. The worse the harm intended, the greater the seriousness.

(v) is *reckless* as to whether harm is caused, that is, where the offender appreciates at least some harm would be caused but proceeds giving no thought to the consequences even though the extent of the risk would be obvious to most people.

(vi) has *knowledge* of the specific risks entailed by his actions even though he does not intend to cause the harm that results.

(vii) is guilty of *negligence*.

(Sentencing Guidelines Council 2004a: para 1.7)

Harm

The second element of gravity is the factual judgement on the amount of harm caused by the offending. On the face of it, this is a much easier judgement because 'harm' appears as an objective, value-free concept. Arguably this is so if we are talking about theft, where the offence is the deprivation of an amount of money or property whose value is easy to calculate. But, as we saw with the sentencing problem at the end of Chapter 2, the value to the victim may be 'sentimental' because, say, of the giver of the gift stolen, or the offence might be assault where the monetary value to be placed on the injury depends not only on the permanence or otherwise of the harm but also on the context of the victim's life. A scar on the face is, arguably, much more serious if the victim is a model whose living depends on facial perfection, and a jaw injury might take away the pleasure of playing in a brass band, but this raises further questions. Should the loss to a particular individual be part of the calculation of harm or should the offender be punished proportionately to the harm an 'average' victim would have suffered from his offending? How do you put a price, not only on potential loss of earnings, but on the more difficult issue of loss of pleasure, whether caused by the loss of a hobby or of one of the five senses?

One can take a broad interpretation, as did the SGC when referring to the statutory provision as 'widely drafted', so that harm 'encompasses those offences where harm is caused but also those where neither individuals nor the community suffer harm but a risk of harm is present' (Sentencing Guidelines Council 2004a: para 1.8). The Seriousness Guideline also provides a list of 'factors indicating a more than usually serious degree of harm' which includes 'multiple victims', 'an especially serious physical or psychological effect on the victim, even if unintended', 'a sustained assault or repeated assaults on the same victim', and offending committed in the presence of friends or relatives (Sentencing Guidelines Council 2004a: para 1.23).

There is a further difficulty: the relationship between these two levels of judgement—the normative (culpability) and the 'factual' (harm)—is also problematic: how do you reconcile different amounts of 'wrongfulness' and damage? As the guidance notes:

> Assessing seriousness is a difficult task, particularly where there is an imbalance between culpability and harm:
>
> - sometimes the harm that actually results is greater than the harm intended by the offender;
> - in other circumstances, the offender's culpability may be at a higher level than the harm resulting from the offence.
>
> (Sentencing Guidelines Council 2004a: para 1.16)

Yet these difficult issues are unavoidable in the calculation of proportionality. As noted in Chapter 2's examination of retributivist principles, ordinal proportionality concerns the question of how offences should be punished, relative to each other, on the basis of the seriousness of the offending; cardinal proportionality concerns the choice of the level of severity to anchor the ranked penalties. Empirical research suggests that there is some consensus on the seriousness-ranking of the most serious crimes, such as murder and rape, but that even in this element of ordinal ranking there was not complete consistency, with, for example, social workers and prison staff ranking actual bodily harm higher than other groups (Cavadino and Wiles 1994: 490–3; see also Rossi et al. 1974). There appears to be less agreement about where to 'anchor' the penalty scale: responses to hypothetical cases by practitioners produced statistically significant differences between criminal justice agencies as to the level of seriousness deemed necessary to justify custody (Cavadino and Wiles 1994: 493–8; see also, for reference to other surveys and interpretation problems, Ashworth 2010: 106–8).

3.2.3 **Aggravation of seriousness**

> If mitigating and aggravating factors had only a minimal impact on sentencing it might be reasonable to leave the matter to judicial discretion. However, these factors can exert a powerful influence over sentence outcomes.
>
> (Roberts 2011b: 3)

The selection and legitimation of factors which may mitigate or aggravate seriousness are a crucial issue in sentencing. As Lord Bingham CJ noted, 'the seriousness of the offence can vary almost infinitely from case to case', and so 'whether a custodial sentence is required, and if so the length of such sentence, is heavily dependent on the aggravating and mitigating features' (*Brewster*, 1998 at 225–6). A similar approach was taken in *Howells* (1998) and is now taken in the Sentencing Council guidelines. In all the recent guidelines lists are given of factors which can aggravate—increase—or mitigate—decrease—the seriousness of the offending in question, and applying those factors is crucial, as Roberts points out, in calculating seriousness. Recent findings from the Crown Court Survey would endorse this.

> *How likely is an offender to have aggravating or mitigating factors that influence their sentence, and if they do, how many do they usually have?*
>
> - The presence of **aggravation** was most likely for robbery offences and least likely for drug offences. In general, aggravating factors were used on their own rather than in combination with other aggravating factors. The exceptions to this were driving offences, which were more likely to have either one or two factors and robbery offences, which were more likely to have four or more aggravating factors).
>
> - **Mitigating factors**, on the other hand, were most likely for offences causing death and least likely for burglary offences.
>
> - Across all offence types, when mitigating factors were present, it was most likely to be for just a single factor.
>
> (Sentencing Council 2014d: 23, Summary Box 4.1)

Of the many factors which can aggravate seriousness, some are offence-based, others are more general, some are set out in statute, and others can be found in relevant guidelines or appellate guidance. We will review first those which Parliament has decided must be considered.

Aggravating factors in statute

Section 156(1) of the CJA 2003, replicating previous provisions (see Table 3.1), requires courts, when deciding whether the seriousness of the offence in question merits a community or custodial sentence, to 'take into account all such information as is available to it about the circumstances of the offence . . . including any aggravating or mitigating factors'. However, Ashworth questions whether all the aggravating factors allowed by legislation and guidance can be theorised in relation to culpability or harm and so fitted into proportionality theory because 'courts have often adopted the terminology of deterrence' (2010: 166; see also Roberts 2008a).

Statutory aggravations have become increasingly important in the past decade or so and we set out the sections and their history in Table 3.2, which takes the same format as Table 3.1 in section 3.1.3.

Table 3.2 Statutory mitigation and aggravation of seriousness

Whatever sentencing framework is being used to decide on a sentence the court must consider whether statutory factors apply—either to set a determinate sentence or to set the minimum period of an indeterminate sentence.

CJA 1991	PCCSA	CJA 2003	Question
29(1)–(4)	151	143(2), (3)	Has aggravation of offence seriousness been done where 'allowed'/'suitable' (previous convictions, failure to respond to previous sentences,[13] whether offence committed on bail)?
N/A	152	144	Can there be a reduction in sentence for a guilty plea? How much?
N/A	153	145	Was there racial or religious aggravation? If so this must increase the seriousness.
N/A	N/A	146	Was there aggravation related to disability, sexual orientation, or transgender identity of the victim? If so this must increase the seriousness.

Of supreme importance is s. 143(2) of the CJA 2003, which replaces the provision enacted in 1993 and mandates aggravation for relevant previous convictions: this will be dealt with separately in the next section. Linked to this is the practice of asking the sentencer to 'take into consideration' offences with which the offender has not been charged (TICs): see Sentencing Council (2012c) for the relevant guideline. This practice benefits both the offender and the criminal justice system although there are circumstances when this is not appropriate (see guidance issued by the Crown Prosecution Service[14]).

Offences committed on bail

The amendments made by the CJA 1993 increased seriousness if the offender had failed to respond to previous penalties and if the offence was committed while the offender was on bail (whether or not that bail related to an offence for which the offender was ultimately convicted and imprisoned). 'Failure to respond' was one of the three justifications for imposing custody on young offenders in the Criminal Justice Act 1982. It was not incorporated in the criteria extended to all offenders by the CJA 1991 s. 1 and was prohibited as an aggravating factor in the original s. 29, but the PCCSA 2000 re-enacted the failure to respond aggravation. In a further twist, the CJA 2003 repealed this provision (Schedule 37, Part 7) but re-enacted aggravation for offences on bail (see Table 3.2).

Racially motivated offences

In 1998 the Crime and Disorder Act (CDA) added motivation by racial hostility as a new statutory aggravation. This had already been established by case law, notably *Craney and Corbett* (1996), and ss. 29–32 of the CDA 1998 mandated an increase in offence seriousness for specified offences by increasing the statutory maximum, as well as imposing a duty to increase seriousness in relation to any other offence in s. 82. The Sentencing Advisory Panel (SAP) (2000) issued guidance on the amount of sentence enhancement to be imposed and suggested 40–70 per cent for fines, community, and custodial sentences unless this pushed

---

[13] This is no longer a statutory aggravation.
[14] See: http://www.cps.gov.uk/legal/l_to_o/offences_to_be_taken_into_consideration_guidance_(tics)_/.

the sentence over a threshold. In *Kelly and Donnelly* (2001) the Court of Appeal adopted the SAP's list of factors to be used to scale gravity, but rejected formal percentage enhancements (see Ashworth 2010: 160).

Religion, disability, sexual orientation, and transgender identity

The Anti-Terrorism and Security Act 2001 amended the legislation to add 'religiously aggravated offences', now to be found in the CJA 2003, s. 145, while s. 146 of that Act added similar provisions to mandate an increase in sentences for aggravation related to disability or sexual orientation (see Table 3.2). Most recently LASPO 2012 added transgender identity.

These statutory aggravations can be found on the list of 'factors indicating higher culpability' in the guidance on seriousness (Sentencing Guidelines Council 2004a: para 1.22). Note also that the guidance in the CJA 2003 about minimum terms to be served by those convicted of murder gives a starting point of 30 years for murders motivated by race, religion, or sexual orientation (Schedule 21, para 5(2)(g)).

Guidance on aggravation

Much more difficult to summarise is the appellate and Sentencing Guidelines Council/ Sentencing Council (SGC/SC) guidance about other factors which should or should not legitimately aggravate seriousness and the extent to which that should be done. In the guideline on seriousness there is a long list—without detail—at para 1.22 of a range of factors which can aggravate (Sentencing Guidelines Council 2004a). There are now many detailed offence-based guidelines which include lists of factors and the more recent guidelines, as we have noted in section 3.2.1, divide this exercise into two steps. Referring to s. 125(3)–(4) of the Coroners and Justice Act 2009, the Assault Guideline, for example, first of all specifies offence ranges—the range of sentences appropriate for each type of offence.

> Within each offence, the Council has specified three categories which reflect varying degrees of seriousness. The offence range is split into *category ranges*—sentences appropriate for each level of seriousness. The Council has also identified a starting point within each category. . . . Once the starting point is established the court should consider further aggravating and mitigating factors . . .
>
> (Sentencing Council, 2011a: 2)

The division into a first stage where there are lists of factors indicating greater harm or higher culpability allows for an immediate categorisation into different sentencing ranges, but it is somewhat problematic in the selection of factors for these lists and the subsequent lists of factors increasing or decreasing seriousness. So, for example, in this Assault Guideline the non-statutory factors indicating greater harm in relation to the offence of grievous bodily harm include 'victim is particularly vulnerable because of personal circumstances' (ibid: 4), while in Step 2 the location and timing of the offence as well as 'gratuitous degradation of victim' are amongst the aggravating factors (ibid: 5).

For particular offences and offence categories there is also the useful *Guideline Judgments Case Compendium*, first issued by the SGC in 2005 to summarise appellate guidance and updated several times since. It is, however, the growing body of ever more detailed guidance being produced by the Sentencing Council which is most important. This book cannot seek to address aggravating factors comprehensively or in detail. We will simply discuss selected topics which have consistently been upheld as influential, or have been of recent interest.

Breach of trust

The Court of Appeal and now the guidelines have consistently condemned offending which involves a breach of trust, and research suggests that abuse of trust, together with premeditation, are the two factors most likely to tip the balance in favour of a custodial sentence (Flood-Page and Mackie 1998: 11). However, Flood-Page and Mackie found that in the Crown Court over half of breach of trust theft cases did not result in a custodial sentence because of balancing mitigating factors (1998: 85). Nevertheless, the new theft offences guidelines, including theft in breach of trust (which carries a maximum penalty of seven years), put into the highest category of culpability the offences evidencing 'Breach of a high degree of trust or responsibility' (Sentencing Council 2015a: 4). When read off against levels 1–3 of harm the starting point ranges from 3.5 years to 1 year in custody. Only at the lowest level of harmfulness—category 4—is a high-level community order the starting point.

The consequences to the victim

The effect of the crime on the victim has gained a higher profile as an aggravating factor. Indeed, legislation has stated that in producing guidelines the Sentencing Council must have regard to several matters including 'the impact of sentencing decisions on victims of offences'.[15] In the context of the (previous) burglary guidelines in *R v McInerney, R v Keating* (2002), Lord Woolf CJ, at the beginning of his *Statement in response to inaccurate comments on the guidelines issued by the Court of Appeal as to the sentencing of domestic burglars* (14 January 2003), noted that the court had endorsed the principle that 'the consequences to the victim should always be of the greatest significance in determining the appropriate punishment' (para 3).[16] SGC guidelines on seriousness endorse old age or youth, disability, and the nature of a victim's job as potential forms of vulnerability (Sentencing Guidelines Council 2004a: para 1.17).

The guideline for sentencing when the offence involves domestic violence also upgraded the focus on the victim. It states that 'offences committed in a domestic context should be regarded as being no less serious than offences committed in a non-domestic context' and then lists various factors arising from the nature of the offender–victim relationship which make the victim more vulnerable and so the offending more serious (Sentencing Guidelines Council 2006: 3–4).

Other forms of vulnerability in the victim have been taken to aggravate. In another reference by the Attorney General (*No. 45 of 2000*) reported in 2001, the victim of robbery and false imprisonment was a doctor, seen by the court as a highly vulnerable member of the community when making a house call late at night in unfamiliar surroundings. The judgment stated that courts had a duty to deter the commission of offences against such victims. Such ideas can also be seen in recent guidance. In the Assault Guideline the 'factors increasing seriousness' in relation to the offence of assault occasioning actual bodily harm include the following: ongoing effect upon the victim; offence committed against those working in the public sector or providing a service to the public; presence of others including relatives, especially the children or partner of the victim; in domestic violence cases, victim forced to leave their home (Sentencing Council 2011a: 13).

Other factors

The seriousness of the harm done aggravates all offences but there are a number of other factors which crop up in many guidelines: for example, premeditation and planning, a professional or group operation, and unnecessary violence. Prevalence of the offending

---

[15] Coroners and Justice Act 2009, s. 120(11)(c).   [16] See also the *Case Compendium* (SGC 2005: 72).

might also be added, as *Cunningham* (1993) did not rule this out after the implementation of the CJA 1991 and, regrettably, neither did the SGC: 'There may be exceptional local circumstances that arise which may lead a court to decide that prevalence should influence sentencing levels. The pivotal issue in such cases will be the harm being caused to the community' (Sentencing Guidelines Council 2004a: para 1.39). That wording has also been replicated in Sentencing Council guidelines: see, for example, the Theft Guideline (2015a: 5).

Two offence categories which raise particular issues about aggravation will be discussed in more detail: causing death by dangerous driving and smuggling.

Causing death by dangerous driving

Causing death by dangerous driving is a particularly difficult offence on which to sentence because the two ingredients of seriousness—the culpability of the offender and the harm done (CJA 2003, s. 143(1))—may not point in the same direction. The death—the most serious of harms—was not intended and so the calculation of culpability is relatively low in relation to the total of harm caused. 'Unintended consequences' have in effect downgraded the factor of harm done in relation to this offence and the calculation of seriousness is, rather, made in relation to the dangerousness of, and risk posed by, the offender's driving.

Cooksley and others (2003) incorporated advice from the SAP on sentencing for the offence of causing death by dangerous driving (and also careless driving while under the influence of drink or drugs). As Wasik pointed out in the Preface to the SAP's advice, and as quoted by Lord Woolf CJ in his judgment, '[u]nderstandably, this often leads to calls from the victims' families, and from the wider community, for tough sentencing' (*Cooksley and others* (2003) at para 1). The court endorsed the view of the SAP that 'briefly dozing at the wheel' should no longer be viewed as indicating a less serious offence (ibid), and that dangerous driving resulting in death should attract a higher sentence than that which does not, the impact on the family being a matter the courts can legitimately take into account (ibid: para 11). The court endorsed the 16 aggravating factors suggested by the SAP and listed them (ibid: para 15), before discussing sentence length in four bands: no aggravating circumstances, intermediate culpability, higher culpability, most serious culpability. The lowest starting point would be 12–18 months even on a plea of guilty, the highest six years or more. The aggravating factors likely to place the case in the 8–10-year category might be a combination of multiple deaths, excessive speed, excessive alcohol, and seeking to avoid responsibility (ibid: para 31).

This tougher approach was upheld in *Emery* (2003) where the driver had fallen asleep at the wheel. He had subsequently been diagnosed as suffering from obstructive sleep apnoea, a diagnosis which he contended he had not been told of seven years earlier when he had undergone nose surgery after falling asleep at the wheel of his vehicle on two occasions. Nevertheless, the Court of Appeal endorsed the comments of the trial judge that he had been 'grossly inattentive' of his sleep problems[17] and upheld the sentence of two years' imprisonment.

The consultation guideline on *Causing Death by Driving* (Sentencing Guidelines Council 2008c) listed five factors 'that may be regarded as determinants of offence seriousness': 'awareness of risk, effect of alcohol or drugs, inappropriate speed of vehicle, seriously culpable behaviour of [the] offender and failing to have proper regard to vulnerable road users' (ibid: 4). The definitive guideline published in 2008 states, for example, that the starting points for the offence of causing death by careless or inconsiderate driving should be 15 months' imprisonment, 36 weeks' imprisonment, or a community sentence depending

---

[17] Note that an aggravating factor (g) in *Cooksley* is 'driving while knowingly suffering from a medical condition which significantly impairs the offender's driving skills' (at para 15).

on the level of seriousness, and lists appropriate aggravating factors such as 'serious injury to one or more persons in addition to the death(s)' and 'irresponsible behaviour, such as failing to stop or falsely claiming that one of the victims was responsible for the collision' (Sentencing Guidelines Council 2008e).

Smuggling

The SAP issued advice on the fraudulent evasion of excise duty on importing tobacco and alcohol in July 2003. The same month, in *Czyzewski* (2003), the Court of Appeal stated that such an offence is aggravated if a **defendant** (i) played an organisational role; (ii) made repeated imports particularly after receiving warnings; (iii) was a professional smuggler; (iv) used a legitimate business as a front; (v) abused a position of privilege; (vi) used children or vulnerable adults; (vii) threatened violence; (viii) dealt in goods with an additional health risk because of possible contamination; or (ix) disposed of goods to underage purchasers. These factors were in line with the SAP's recommendations and the first Fraud Offences Guideline noted the *Czyzewski* case as relevant to the aggravating factors listed in regard to revenue fraud against HM Revenue and Customs (Sentencing Guidelines Council 2009a: 28, n 45). In 2014 the Sentencing Council issued a new *Fraud, Bribery and Money Laundering Offences* Guideline which for revenue fraud lists similar factors, though they are now incorporated in the two-step format and more factors are given, for example, 'Blame wrongly placed on others' and 'Number of false declarations' (2014a: 24).

It is worth noting that the aggravating factors of abuse of trust, the vulnerability and suffering of the victim, and premeditation, together with concealment of the body and the use of threats, are now listed in para 10 of Schedule 21 to the CJA 2003 to assist the court in its determination of the minimum term of a mandatory life sentence for murder.

3.2.4 **Persistence as the problem**

The issue of whether and how to sentence in relation to persistence is a very important but very difficult and long-standing sentencing problem (see Flaherty 2006/7; Roberts, 2008b; see also Home Office 2010 in relation to the findings from the Prolific and Other Priority Offenders cohort). Of the three possible responses—flat-rate sentencing, 'progressive loss of mitigation', and cumulative sentencing—only the first takes no notice of previous record, while the second and third responses do consider previous offending but conceptualise the importance differently. This reflects the fact that modern retributivists have been divided in their approach to persistence—the relevance of past offending and good character—as a sentencing factor. In utilitarian theory the focus on past offending would be relevant to the calculation of future risks, but in retributivism its role is different.

Justifications

Von Hirsch allows previous convictions as the only exception to the principle that offences of comparable seriousness should receive a punishment with the same degree of severity (von Hirsch 1986, 1993). If an offence is committed for the first time it might be successfully argued in mitigation that the action is out of character and so there is, in effect, a penalty discount for first offenders, but with each repeated offence this argument will be less plausible. The offender is still being censured for the current act, but censure may be reduced because we acknowledge that it was the first time the person had succumbed to the temptation to act badly and they had resisted it before. But while a 'discount' may be appropriate here, von Hirsch emphasises that there must not be a large differential between punishments for first offenders and recidivists: 'afirst offender should receive less punishment than a recidivist, but . . . this punishment differential should only be a modest one' (1986: 90).

For von Hirsch there would be a limit on how far previous convictions would increase the severity of the sentence, and the upper limit would very likely be lower than permitted on utilitarian models (von Hirsch 1986). He acknowledges that past criminal record has implications for desert for the current offence, so he argues for 'primary but not exclusive emphasis on the current offence' (ibid: 78). Other desert theorists, such as Fletcher (1982), would see a focus on previous offending as incompatible with just deserts principles. He argues that previous convictions do not affect desert for the current offence, and should not influence the sentence, as the offender has already been punished for past convictions.

If the offender persists, he would lose what von Hirsch calls his first offender discount and this would be done progressively. However, once that discount had been used up, he would receive the full amount of punishment, but no more than this. The alternative of continually increasing punishment for recidivism would lead to the situation where relatively minor offences could incur harsh punishments. The primary concern on von Hirsch's approach is still with the current offence and the size of the differential between the two punishments should be kept 'within proper bounds' (von Hirsch 1986: 91).

However, the efforts of retributivist theory to provide a rational basis for dealing with multiple offences through a 'ceiling' on punishment are criticised by Ryberg (2005), who argues that this approach is both theoretically flawed and unable to provide a practical basis for sentencing.

In cumulative sentencing the sentence increases on each subsequent conviction. If represented graphically, cumulative sentencing is seen as a straight upward line to the 'normal' penalty and beyond to the statutory maximum; progressive loss of mitigation is a line with an upward slope but it then reaches a plateau at the normal ceiling for the offence (Wasik and von Hirsch 1994: 410). Flat-rate sentencing would take no account of previous convictions whatsoever. Figure 3.1 illustrates this in graph form.

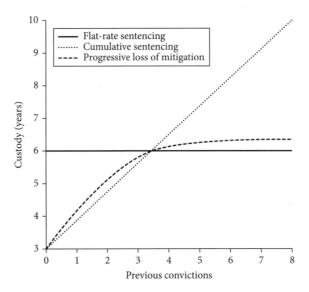

Figure 3.1 Persistence

The graph assumes:

- the maximum penalty for this offence is ten years;
- the normal range is five to seven years and the court uses six years as the norm every time;
- previous convictions are all for offences of a similar gravity;
- the court starts with a three-year sentence for this offence if there are no previous convictions;
- where progressive loss of mitigation operates, the loss for the first offence is greater than for subsequent offences.

The legislation

Arguably, the progressive loss of mitigation approach was endorsed by the Court of Appeal prior to 1991 (Wasik and von Hirsch 1994: 411), but, as passed, s. 29 of the CJA 1991 stated that an offence was not to be regarded as more serious 'by reason of any previous convictions of the offender'. It was not clear whether that implied the loss of mitigation approach or simply stated that previous convictions did not aggravate seriousness unless special culpability was disclosed by the record. However, the CJA 1993 repealed the whole of s. 29 and substituted a new section.

The amended subs. 29(1) stated: 'In considering the seriousness of any offence, the court may take into account any previous convictions of the offender', wording which Henham warned could 'lead to an increase in cases where individuals are sentenced "on their record"' (1995: 223). However, Wasik and von Hirsch (1994) argued that this did not give the sentencer 'unfettered discretion' in dealing with previous convictions. They refer to Hansard, which seems to suggest that the government wanted only to return to (or make clearer) the pre-1991 approach, not to allow a system of cumulative sentencing (1994: 412–13).

Their arguments do of course raise the question as to what the courts were doing in practice. Roberts (2002) cites statistics given in the Halliday Report (2001: Appendix 3, Table 1) which showed that the probability of being given a custodial sentence increased in direct relationship to the number of previous convictions. He argues that this suggests there was already 'a robust recidivist premium' by 2000 (Roberts 2002: 430). Others argued that the changes in 1993 were a 'remarkable *volte face*' (Henham 1995: 223).

Nevertheless, the CJA 2003 enhanced the role of past record. Halliday had argued that 'clarification needs to be based on a clear presumption that sentencing severity should increase as a consequence of sufficiently recent and relevant convictions' (2001: para 2.7). The CJA 2003 incorporates this intention in s. 143(2):

> In considering the seriousness of an offence . . . committed by an offender who has one or more previous convictions, the court must treat each previous conviction as an aggravating factor if . . . the court considers that it can reasonably be so treated having regard, in particular to—
>
> (a) the nature of the offence to which the conviction relates and its relevance to the current offence, and
>
> (b) the time that has elapsed since the conviction.

The effect of s. 143 on sentencing practice depends, notwithstanding its mandatory force, on how the courts exercise the discretion not to consider each previous conviction as an aggravating factor. As in case law on this issue, the discretion focuses on the reasonableness of so doing where the nature of the offence may be very different from the current offence, may be relatively trivial, and may have taken place many years previously. There is scope here for sentencers to interpret it in a way which is not significantly different from the progressive loss of mitigation doctrine.

Previous convictions are, of course, listed in the Definitive Guidelines as aggravating factors that must be considered. For example, in the 'Dangerous Dogs' Guideline 'previous convictions' increase seriousness and 'No previous convictions or no relevant/recent convictions' is one of the factors which can mitigate seriousness (Sentencing Council 2016: 9).

However, as Roberts and Pina-Sánchez note, the Sentencing Council changed the approach of the SGC guidelines to previous convictions such that they are now dealt with at Step 2, and this may have affected practice: 'One possibility is that the new format would constrain the inflationary effect of previous convictions on custody rates...Step Two factors affect only the location of the sentence *within* the guideline's category range of sentence' (2014: 580). However, they go on to say: 'Against this view it may be noted that the guideline permits courts to move out of the identified category range in the event that the Step Two factors (including prior convictions) justify so doing' (2014: 580). Nevertheless, their analysis of data from the Crown Court Sentencing Survey and the Ministry of Justice leads Roberts and Pina-Sánchez to conclude that 'For offenders in the more serious criminal history categories, courts are moderating the increase in severity to ensure that previous convictions do not overwhelm the seriousness of the current offence' (2014: 587–8).

Be that as it may, previous convictions do make a difference when an offender is on the 'in–out' line:

> Where an offender does have recent and relevant previous convictions, that offender is more likely to be sentenced to immediate custody, with this likelihood increasing as the number of previous convictions increases. . . . In general, where an offender already had at least one recent and relevant previous conviction, any further ones taken into account by the judge had less of an impact on the likelihood of being sent to immediate custody.
>
> (Sentencing Council 2014d: 4)

As is clear from Figure 3.2, the custody rate for several offences does increase in line with the increase in the number of previous offences. On the face, there appears to be at least some cumulative sentencing in practice.

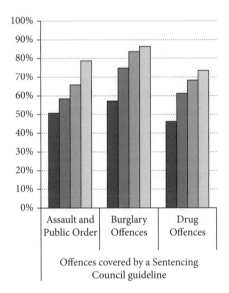

The custody rate is down the LH side

dark blocks = 0 previous convictions, lightest blocks = 10+ convictions

Figure 3.2 Number of previous convictions taken into account, by offence type and custody rate, Crown Court, 2013

Source: Sentencing Council 2014d: taken from Figure 4

3.2.5 **Mitigation of seriousness**

The court must also consider mitigating factors relating to the offence when assessing seriousness, but has discretion to assign a weight to such factors and to balance them against the weight of aggravating factors. Again, *Overarching Principles: Seriousness* (Sentencing Guidelines Council 2004a) lists appropriate general mitigating factors and offence-based guidelines provide examples of relevant mitigation. As Ashworth points out, however, mitigating factors comprise a 'much more heterogeneous collection' (2005: 160). Some factors amount to the absence of aggravation: less offender culpability, lack of premeditation/impulsiveness, a lone/amateur operation, lack of violence or intimidation, and no previous criminal record. Others focus on the relative lack of harm done. There are also mitigating factors relating to culpability which are in effect criminal defences, not used or not successful in the pre-conviction process, but which have a long history as 'excuses' at the sentencing stage. These are necessity, duress, mistake of law, and provocation,[18] to which can be added entrapment,[19] all justified on the grounds that offending with these motivations or in these contexts entails less wickedness (Wasik 1983). More generally, exceptional stress or emotional pressure are potential mitigations of seriousness, as, for example, when someone steals to provide for a dying relative (Ashworth 2000: 140).

Court of Appeal cases and SGC/SC guidelines lay down a wide range of mitigating factors relating to particular offences. For example, the two mitigating factors discussed in the Domestic Violence Guideline are 'positive good character' and provocation (Sentencing Guidelines Council 2006: 5–6), while the mitigating factors listed in relation to setting the minimum period for murder (CJA 2003 Schedule 21: para 11) include an intention to cause serious bodily harm rather than to kill, lack of premeditation, and a belief by the offender that the murder was an act of mercy.

There is little guidance on how to balance mitigating and aggravating factors and so it would be easy for disparity to occur. Further, where the offence is very serious or where the courts wish to give a particular message, notably a deterrent one, mitigating factors relating to the offence or the offender may have little or no effect (Piper 2007). An example could be taken from *Cooksley* (2002), discussed earlier in this section, where Lord Woolf CJ said: 'it is important for the courts to drive home the message as to the dangers that can result from dangerous driving on the road . . . drivers must know that . . . no matter what the mitigating circumstances, normally only a custodial sentence will be imposed' (para 11).

3.3 Establishing proportionality

Lacey and Pickard have recently argued that 'it is widely acknowledged that, in countries such as the UK and, particularly, the USA, the aspiration of many proponents of the retributive revival to place clear limits on punishment by ensuring proportionality has not been fulfilled' (2015: 217). In this section we will review the main components of the process of establishing what amounts to a proportionate punishment, revealing the various problematic elements.

---

[18] The correlative 'excuse' to the insanity defence will not be dealt with here: the treatment of mentally disordered offenders will be examined in Chapter 6 (section 6.4).

[19] Case law has established this is not a defence in English law: see Ashworth (2000: 140) for cases.

3.3.1 **The seriousness thresholds**

The CJA 2003 re-enacted the 'so serious that' and 'serious enough' criteria for imposing custodial and community sentences, respectively, and the SGC published guidance on seriousness in 2004. However, how the appellate courts construed key concepts in the CJA 1991 continues to have an influence on interpretation of the CJA 2003 and so the cases to be discussed are not simply of historical interest.

In 1997 Ashworth and von Hirsch wrote an important article entitled 'Recognising Elephants: The Problem of the Custody Threshold'. This intriguing title referred to a test set out by Lawton LJ before the CJA 1991 in relation to the very similar 'so serious that only' hurdle for custody of young offenders in the Criminal Justice Act 1982. The conclusions of the article were based on more than 50 reported Court of Appeal cases ruling on the custody criterion in the CJA 1991, the first of which was *Cox* (1993). In that case, Lord Taylor CJ retained Lord Justice Lawton's test of the 'right thinking members of the public' laid down in *Bradbourne* (1985 at 183), whereby a custodial sentence was justified if such right-thinking people, 'knowing all the facts', would 'feel that justice had not been done by the passing of any sentence other than a custodial one'. Lawton LJ said that he was confident that 'courts can recognise an elephant when they see one, but may not find it necessary to define it'. Ashworth and von Hirsch concluded that this purportedly 'common-sense' test of the 'right-thinking' person was 'conceptually flawed and empirically unsupported' (1997: 189) and Lord Bingham CJ endorsed those criticisms in *Howells and related appeals* (1999 at 53):

> There is no bright line which separates offences which are so serious that only a custodial sentence can be justified from offences which are not so serious as to require the passing of a custodial sentence. But it cannot be said that the 'right-thinking' members of the public test is very helpful, since the sentencing court has no means of ascertaining the views of right-thinking members of the public and inevitably attributes to such right-thinking members its own views. So, when applying this test, the sentencing court is doing little more than reflecting its own opinion whether justice would or would not be done and be seen to be done by the passing of a non-custodial sentence.

The Court of Appeal found itself, however, unable to substitute a new test (ibid) and its approach, and that of the SGC (2004a), was to focus on the custody/community penalty dividing line, and to specify the mitigating and aggravating factors which would or would not tip the case over the custody seriousness threshold. Lord Bingham CJ first listed five factors for courts 'ordinarily' to take into account: an admission of guilt, self-motivated and proven determination to address the causes of offending if 'fuelled by addiction', youth and immaturity, whether the offender was of previous good character, and whether the offender had previously been sentenced to custody (at 53–4). The court then dealt separately with *Howells* and each of the other related appeals, discussing these factors and others such as premeditation, the use or threat of violence, the time of day, provocation, and the harm caused. SGC guidance included these factors in more accessible, simplified lists (2004a).

The case of *Mills* (2002), dealing with offences of dishonesty, also discussed factors that should be considered when the offence is one that often receives a custodial sentence but the circumstances of the particular case reveal mitigating factors. Significantly it stated that, as well as asking whether prison is necessary, 'the sentencing judge also had to take into account the reality of sentencing policy' and, in particular, three factors: the inability of the prison service to achieve anything positive in the way of rehabilitation during a short sentence (at 331), the effect on children if a single mother is imprisoned, and, specifically in relation to female prisoners, the fact that she might be allocated to a prison far from her home and children (at 332; also see Chapter 7, section 7.4.5).

Shortly after the implementation of the 1991 Act the Court of Appeal dealt with another principle in applying the seriousness criteria. In *Cunningham* (1993) the court was asked to rule on whether deterrence could form part of the calculation of seriousness.

> Section 2(2) of the Act provided that a custodial sentence should be commensurate with the seriousness of the offence or offences for which it is passed. That provision did allow the sentencer to take into account the need for deterrence. The purposes of a custodial sentence were to punish and deter. The phrase 'commensurate with the seriousness of the offence' must mean commensurate with the punishment and deterrence which the offence required . . . The prevalence of an offence was a legitimate factor in determining the length of a custodial sentence. The seriousness of an offence was clearly affected by how many people it harmed and to what extent.
>
>   (Criminal Law Review 1990: 150)[20]

The above cases would suggest that the custody test established by the CJA 1991 was 'easily satisfied' because of its 'broad interpretation' (Thomas 1995: 146–7). The Seriousness Guideline issued after the 2003 Act specifically notes that 'the clear intention of the threshold test is to reserve prison as a punishment for the most serious offences' (Sentencing Guidelines Council 2004a: 8), but it too argues that 'it is impossible to determine definitively which features of a particular offence make it serious enough to merit a custodial sentence' and that 'it would not be feasible to provide a form of words or to devise any formula that would provide a general solution to the problem of where the custody threshold lies. Factors vary too widely between offences for this to be done' (ibid: 8, 9).[21] Considerable discretion was left to the sentencer, although the format of the more recent and very detailed guidelines restricts discretion at Step 2 where there are several categories within which custody is or is not within the category range of penalties. However, there are also many guidelines where, within many of the categories, an in–out decision will be needed: see for example the 'General Theft' Step 2 categories (Sentencing Council 2015a: 6).

3.3.2 **Mitigation relating to the offender**

There is also mitigation relating to the circumstances and character of the offender rather than to the seriousness of the offending. In effect they mitigate sentence once seriousness has been established, and s. 166(1) of the CJA 2003, reflecting previous practice, states that nothing in the crucial sentencing sections about the criteria for imposing the three levels of sentence 'prevents a court from mitigating an offender's sentence by taking into account any such matters as, in the opinion of the court, are relevant in the mitigation of sentence'. Further, s. 166(2) states that the court is not prevented from imposing a community rather than custodial sentence in the light of mitigating circumstances and s. 156(2) specifically gives the court discretion to take into account any information about the offender which is before it in deciding the type of community or youth rehabilitation order to impose. The CJIA 2008, s. 10 amended s. 148 of the CJA 2003 to provide similar judicial discretion in relation to community orders.

---

[20] For comments regarding prevalence by the SGC, see *Overarching Principles: Seriousness* (2004a: Section F; also note the references in '*Other Factors*' in section 3.2.5).

[21] For a discussion of factors which influenced the custodial decision in the sentencing of domestic violence offenders in New South Wales, Australia, see Ringland and Fitzgerald (2010).

Issues

There is very little guidance on the role of personal mitigation in the Guideline on 'Overarching Principles' (Sentencing Guidelines Council 2004a) and it is, arguably, confusing: 'One is left with the feeling that there is a rather unclear dividing line between the mitigating and aggravating factors listed and "personal mitigation"' (Shapland 2011: 63). Shapland also analyses the format of the guidelines for magistrates and comments that 'this is hardly in-depth guidance to offender mitigation' (2011: 65).

Despite this lack of detailed guidance, as Jacobson and Hough point out: 'Mitigation casts into sharp focus some fundamental issues about sentencing principles and judicial discretion. Is justice best served by sentencing the offence or the offender? What balance ought to be struck between the two?' (2007: 1). They note that 'few of our respondents made explicit the connection between particular sentencing rationales and particular forms of mitigation' (2007: 39) and one of their respondents, a judge, described sentencing as 'terrifying because it's a very subjective exercise' (2007: 48; see also Chapter 7, section 7.3.1)

Personal mitigation can be placed into three categories, relating to:

1. The good qualities of the offender.
2. The efficient and fair operation of the criminal justice system.
3. The impact of the sentence on the offender.

The last category of personal mitigation—the adverse or abnormal impact of the sentence on the offender—will not be dealt with here: see Chapter 7. In this chapter we will focus briefly on the first and second categories before dealing in some detail with the guilty plea, a form of personal mitigation justified as a 'reward' for those who help the system.

A 'good' offender

The offender or his or her lawyer has complete discretion to introduce whichever factors appear relevant in relation to the first category—where the personal characteristics and circumstances of the offender are considered. The sentencer has complete discretion to accept or reject the mitigation and may not take it into account where the offending is of a very serious nature. Where the court does reduce the sentence it can be justified on the basis that the criminal justice system should be administered as mercifully as possible.

The factors which may be considered by sentencers include the following: stress in life at the time of committing the offence (for example, extreme poverty or imminent childbirth), meritorious conduct (for example, making reparation for harm done), leading a law-abiding and stable life since the offence was committed (for example, finding employment or getting married), and the age of the offender (for example, if below 21 or of an advanced age). Moral credit has also sometimes been given for something unconnected with the offence, such as a 'good' war record, donation of a kidney, or starting a youth club (see Walker 1985: 50). In Ashworth's categorisation of 'extraneous factors'—those not directly relevant to culpability and harm—the latter examples would come under 'positive social contributions', inclusion of which is quite difficult to justify (Ashworth 2011: 27–9).

The effect of the sentence on others, notably children or employees, has sometimes been influential. This example is part of a group of mitigating factors which Ashworth refers to as 'collateral or consequential effects of the sentence on third parties', for which he says that 'the "best fit" reasoning is that the state's interest in imposing a proportionate sentence should be overridden by the interest of (innocent) third parties in not being disadvantaged by events over which they had no control' (Ashworth 2011: 32). Ashworth also provides as a separate category 'the pursuit of equality policies', for which he gives the examples of the differential effect of sentences on women and the significance of employment (Ashworth 2011: 29–30). These can be seen as part of the principle of equal impact, and we will discuss the influence of the impact of sentence on the offender's family and also the impact on the offender in Chapter 7 (section 7.3).

There is also the issue of remorse, which might be seen as irrelevant because it occurs after the offending in question. A recent book (Maslen 2015) has reviewed a range of justifications including the 'merciful compassion argument', which is also relevant to the impact of sentence factors. Maslen refers to a statement in the *Susan Tagg* (2011) case as an example of this judicial approach: 'there was no doubt that she had shown genuine and substantial remorse. It was possible to extend a degree of mercy to her, so that her sentence would be reduced to one of 12 months' imprisonment.' Maslen also deals with the 'changed person', reduced harm, 'already punished', and 'responsive censure' arguments which are relevant to particular offender scenarios.

Fair operation of the system

There are other circumstances which can mitigate sentence severity. They can be rationalised either as allowing the criminal justice system to be seen to be administered with as little injustice as possible, or as encouraging cost-efficient and effective criminal justice processes. The discount for a guilty plea is the obvious example of the latter and will be dealt with in section 3.3.3. The factor of assisting law enforcement clearly also falls into that category, with the position of informers being a good example. Mitigation—or not—on this basis has a long and varied history and the unfavourable publicity given to the effects of such mitigation in the 'supergrass' cases of the 1970s led to smaller sentence reductions, but *Sivan and others* (1988) and *A and B* (1999) confirmed there could be a reduction in sentence where assistance to the police is given before sentence. More recently, *R v P and Blackburn* (2007) has given detailed advice about the approach to sentencing where the assistance to the police relates to provisions in the Serious Organised Crime and Police Act 2005, ss. 73–75.

Mitigation relating to 'fairness' includes the approach taken to sentencing co-defendants and to multiple sentences. In relation to the former the sentence may be reduced in order that like cases may be seen to be treated alike. For the latter the court can impose concurrent sentences if the total punishment appears unjust and disproportionate. This 'totality principle' is now enshrined and the practice tends to be that consecutive sentences are imposed where the sentences are for unconnected offences,[22] but concurrent sentences where the offences are all part of the same offending incident (Walker 1999: 98–100). The Sentencing Council undertook a resource assessment on totality, TICs, and allocation (Sentencing Council 2011c) and issued guidance (Sentencing Council 2012c).

The issue of how to charge and sentence multiple offenders, whether they be offenders whose offending incident gives rise to a variety of charges or whether a prolonged period of offending behaviour produces a long list of similar offences, is, however, much more complicated than this, and the justifications are varied. Ashworth devotes a whole chapter to these issues (2015: chapter 8) and we would refer readers to this.

3.3.3 Discount for a guilty plea

Justified as giving credit to the offender for his contribution to the efficiency of the system by reducing the need for a trial, with its cost implications and its burdens on witnesses, the discount for a guilty plea can have a substantial effect on the level of sentence and is potentially available for all offenders. Guidance has made clear that 'the sentencer should now address

---

[22] See CJA 2003, s. 155 for powers of magistrates' courts.

separately the issue of remorse, together with any other mitigating features, before calculating the reduction for the guilty plea after all the matters noted above relating to the assessment of seriousness have been dealt with' (Sentencing Guidelines Council 2007a: para 2.4).

The CJA 2003, s. 144 replaced the PCCSA 2000, s. 152,[23] but the law is the same: where the offender has pleaded guilty the court must take into account the stage in the proceedings at which he indicated his plea of guilt and the circumstances in which it was given (s. 144(1)). As part of the 'duty to give reasons for sentences given' the court must now also explain whether a guilty plea has reduced the sentence (CJA 20013 s. 174(4), inserted by LASPO 2012 s. 64).

A particular difficulty has arisen in relation to those who are caught 'red-handed'. *Hussain* (2002) upheld the previous position in case law whereby particular circumstances, such as being caught red-handed, might justify the non-implementation of a discount. However, SGC guidance stated that it is in everyone's interest that those who are guilty of an offence indicate willingness to plead guilty at the earliest opportunity (2004b: Preface) and said that the normal sliding scale applied to those caught red-handed but that '[i]f the not guilty plea was entered and maintained for tactical reasons (such as to retain privileges while on remand), a late guilty plea should attract very little, if any, discount' (2004b: 5).

However, the 2004 guidance received criticism in relation to this issue amongst others and a consultation exercise was undertaken by the SAP, at the request of the SGC, in 2006. The key issues were:

- Does a maximum reduction of one-third properly balance the interests of justice and the encouragement of guilty pleas?
- Should there be an upper limit on the amount of the reduction?
- What further clarification of the 'first reasonable opportunity' for entering a guilty plea is necessary?
- To what degree, if any, should the fact that the prosecution case is overwhelming influence the level of reduction?

New guidance was issued in July 2007 (Sentencing Guidelines Council 2007a). It confirmed that the level of reduction 'should be a proportion of the total sentence imposed, with the proportion calculated by reference to the circumstances in which the guilty plea was indicated, in particular the stage in the proceedings' and that 'the greatest reduction will be given where the plea was indicated at the "first reasonable opportunity"' (ibid: para 4.1). The maximum discount remains at one-third with recommended reductions of one-quarter and one-tenth for pleas given at later stages of the process (see Figure 3.3).[24]

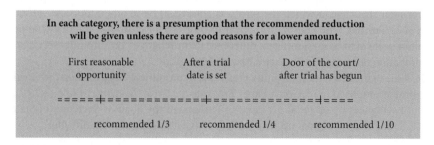

Figure 3.3 A sliding scale

Source: Sentencing Guidelines Council (2007a)

---

[23] First enacted as s. 48 of the Criminal Justice and Public Order Act 1994 and repealed 4 April 2005.

[24] SGC guidance specifically in regard to sentencing for murder sets a maximum discount of one-sixth.

The SGC agreed that some discretion should be introduced where the prosecution case is 'overwhelming' (Sentencing Guidelines Council 2007a: para 5.3) but did not accept the recommendation of the SAP to cap the effect of a reduction on very large fines. The guideline specifically noted that where the maximum penalty for the offence is thought to be too low, a sentencer cannot remedy perceived defects by refusal of the appropriate discount (ibid: para 5.6).

Until December 2012 the only statutory exceptions were in relation to mandatory minimum sentences for domestic burglary and Class A drugs offences. Amendments made by LASPO 2012 and the Criminal Justice and Courts Act 2015 have provided further restrictions. Mandatory sentences in relation to firearms are exempt, although new subsections 144(4) and (5) allow the courts to take a guilty plea into account if the offender is aged 16 or 17. In addition, since July 2015, in regard to the exempt provisions listed in s. 144(3) 'nothing in that provision prevents the court, after taking into account any matter referred to in subsection (1) of this section, from imposing any sentence which is not less than 80 per cent of that specified in that provision'.

Annex 1 to the SGC guideline provides further clarification of 'first reasonable opportunity' by listing examples which would count as such depending on the circumstances. So, 'the first reasonable opportunity may be the first time that a defendant appears before the court and has the opportunity to plead guilty' but the court 'may consider that it would be reasonable to have expected an indication of willingness even earlier, perhaps whilst under interview' (Sentencing Guidelines Council 2007a: 10). Subsequent case law further clarifies as follows:

> A plea of guilty at a plea and case management hearing will ordinarily not be significantly different from a plea notified shortly after it. Whatever the exact procedure in different courts for fixing trial windows or trial dates this is clearly the stage at which the Guideline contemplates a reduction of about a quarter.
>
>   By 'indicate plea of guilty' we mean to include the case where, either in the magistrates' court or at or soon after arrival in the Crown Court, the defendant through counsel or solicitors notifies the Crown that he would admit a lesser charge or invites discussion as to the appropriate charge, at any rate where the position taken up is a reasonable one.
>
> *Caley (David)* (2012: paras 19 and 20)[25]

The general approach of the SGC guideline follows the Magistrates' Association Guidelines before 2003, which suggested a discount of about one-third. However, various research projects and criminal statistics had indicated that reductions in practice varied between 22 per cent and 40 per cent (see Ashworth 2000: 145–7 for references and discussion). Research would also suggest that—at least in the mid-1990s—35 per cent of judges did not consider the stage at which the plea was entered to be of any importance (Henham 1999: 527). Further, while discounts appear to be given for custodial and financial penalties, there seemed to be no significant difference in the length of a community service order or a probation order (Flood-Page and Mackie 1998: 92).

The issue of the discount for a guilty plea came to prominence again when the Coalition government proposed in its Green Paper *Breaking the Cycle* (Ministry of Justice 2010a) to discount sentences by up to 50 per cent. In Parliament the Shadow Secretary of State for Justice, Sadiq Khan, summed up criticism of so high a discount for a guilty plea:

> I accept that a sentence discount represents a tension between the delivery of justice and the improving of efficiency in the legal system, but that tension can potentially bring benefits to victims who are spared the trauma of a long period in court. Up until now, the system has always sought certainty that the right balance is being struck. If the sentence reduction is

---

[25] For a comparison of sentence discounting in England and Scotland see Brown (2013).

too great, it threatens to undermine the principles of sentencing and public confidence in the system. Worse still, it may mean that justice is not being served.

(Hansard, 23 May 2011: Column 659)

The Sentencing Council, in its written response to the Green Paper, had also noted that 'in other common law jurisdictions the largest discount on offer is around a third, with some offering up to 35%' and that '[t]he Council has not identified any research to date that indicates that an increase in the level of the discount would be likely to increase the volume of early guilty pleas' (Sentencing Council 2010: 10).

Research sponsored by the Sentencing Council found that '[f]or the general public, there was weak support for higher levels of reductions beyond the current guideline range of up to 33% and a fifth (20%) felt that there should be no reduction at all' (Dawes *et al.* 2011: 4). The main factor determining whether or not offenders plead guilty was the likelihood of being found guilty at trial. The key 'tipping point' here was when offenders realised that the chances of their being found guilty were greater than those of being found not guilty. Weight of evidence and advice from solicitors/barristers were pivotal in offenders' assessments of whether they were likely to be found guilty and therefore crucial in determining when a guilty plea was entered (ibid: 5). The proposal to increase the discount was subsequently not included in the LASPO Bill.

3.3.4 **Not a mathematical exercise?**

We have dealt in turn with the most important aspects of the process of determining a proportionate sentence under retributivist principles. At one level this might be seen as a logical process which can be worked through in an entirely objective way and the suggested questions for dealing with the custody threshold in *Overarching Principles: Seriousness* appear unproblematic:

- Has the statutory threshold been passed?
- Is custody unavoidable?
- Can the sentence be suspended, (or be served intermittently)?
- What is the commensurate sentence?

(Sentencing Guidelines Council 2004a: para 1.33)

However, the third update to the *Case Compendium* sounded a cautionary note when summarising the *Martin* case.

R v Martin [2006] EWCA Crim 1035

- The sentencing decision does not represent a mathematical exercise, nor does it result from an arithmetical calculation.
- It is not the case that each element relevant to the sentencing decision has or should have ascribed to it some notional length of sentence so that, depending on whether the individual ingredient constitutes aggravating or mitigating material, the actual sentence should increase or reduce in accordance with that figure. The reality is that a sentencer must balance all the circumstances of the case in order to reach an appropriate sentence.

(Accessed at https://www.sentencingcouncil.org.uk/wp-content/uploads/Compendium_
update_three_Apr07.pdf)

We are well aware that just deserts sentencing leaves many difficult decisions about seriousness and proportionality to the judges and magistrates and that guidance on sentencing levels is not yet comprehensive. That the effect of mitigation can be so crucial in relation to the choice or length of a custodial sentence is an issue to which we will return in Chapter 7. The question of whether the difficulties still lie with retributivism itself will be examined next.

3.4 Critiques of modern retributivism

We have reviewed current sentencing practice within a predominantly just deserts framework and summarised the recent changes to that framework and criticisms of them. We will now examine more fundamental criticisms of just deserts as a primary rationale.

Criticism of retributivism has come from all shades of the political and theoretical spectrum and so we will, in this section, consider the current penological debates and also the critiques from Marxist perspectives.

3.4.1 The limits of just deserts

The approach of modern retributivism, based substantially on the work of von Hirsch, does not satisfy all critics of retributivism or resolve all the problems with the retributivist approach. There remains the issue of the extent to which proportionality as the primary purpose of sentencing should take priority over other factors in 'exceptional' cases. For example, should effectiveness and efficiency, or public safety, take priority over individual rights as in the case of dangerous offenders who need to be quarantined; or, with certain 'abhorrent' crimes, is it possible to find a commensurate sentence? The greatest difficulty in practice is how to find a mechanism and a consensus to calculate seriousness, to rank offences, mitigations, and aggravations, and to rank penalties in such a way that the key element of proportionality is clear and justly operationalised. However, the attempt to achieve clarity by producing accurate theoretical models of ordinal and cardinal proportionality could result in as many types of punishment as there are offenders, with different degrees of culpability, which would be impossible to administer.

As we have seen, the present system has been criticised for its complexity and incoherence. The problem is that, even if we take full account of desert and proportionality, we can still find some cases of lesser offences receiving much harsher sentences than serious offenders with mitigation, which has implications for the legitimacy of the system and public support. So it may be better, as Bagaric (2001) argues, to have fixed penalties, but this raises the sort of questions about the inflexibility of grid-type sentencing that prompted Tonry to rethink retributivism.

These difficulties with the key issue of proportionality in desert theory have prompted alternative approaches. Braithwaite and Pettit (1990) have developed an alternative theory, grounded in restorative justice (see Chapter 6, section 6.2). They distinguish their own model, which advocates instrumental shaming, from the penal censure of retributivism, because they seek to separate shaming from the degree of severity of sanctions. They also advocate reducing the level of punishment to the point at which crime starts to increase. Censure for them is essentially stigmatising and may be achieved by a variety of means, including adverse publicity.

Another issue is whether it is ever possible to make the justification for a retributivist approach sufficiently clear and logical for both popular understanding and political legitimacy. For example, it has been argued that von Hirsch's modified form of retributivism may be hard to justify without lapsing into consequentialism, which is a utilitarian rather than retributivist notion. So von Hirsch, Bagaric (2001) argues, never establishes why his censuring account of punishment is morally justifiable. Yet there are good consequentialist reasons to support von Hirsch's theory, such as his recognition of the secondary role of deterrence and the positive functions of blaming, and the beneficial social consequences of the acknowledgement of the victim's harm which may prevent vigilantism as well as satisfying the victim. Showing the third party that an action is wrong may ultimately prevent offending, another good consequence. As Bagaric observes, there is no point in blaming the offender if there are no beneficial effects.

Others have focused on the role of restitution rather than retributivism. Holmgren (2012), for example, argues for a key role of forgiveness in punishment. Although she shares with retributivists a respect for the moral agency of the offender and recognition of the harm to victims, she argues that her approach based on virtue ethics leads to a focus on restitution. We should forgive those who harm us but work through a process of addressing the wrong. The focus on the victim will be considered further in Chapter 7, sections 7.1 and 7.2.

Retributivism has also been criticised more generally as a conservative and repressive theory which can too easily lend legitimacy to punitive penal policies. The main elements of that critique are that the theory, by focusing only on desert, fails to acknowledge the implications of poverty and social inequality for offending behaviour, and that it is most strongly associated with reactionary regimes around the world—whether based on religious or secular principles—and is repressive in generating an escalation of punishment. Rubin (2003), for example, argues that embedding retribution within the Model Penal Code of the American Law Institute would have an adverse effect, leading to longer sentences. But these assumptions are problematic.

First, there is no automatic association between repressive regimes and retributivism. As von Hirsch and Ashworth (2005) emphasise, if we look around the world we find the most progressive regimes in Scandinavia have used proportionality and desert as principles of punishment rather than incapacitation or rehabilitation. In contrast the Stalinist penal regime, one of the most brutal in history, was based on an extreme form of 'social efficiency' rather than desert. Yet in Sweden there is a presumption against custody unless the offence is serious. Past convictions have a very small role there, being limited to the past three or four years. However, there has been increasing pressure in recent years to expand this role as the Swedish public has become more punitive, seeing sentences as too lenient (see Demker *et al.* 2008; Asp 2010). Nonetheless, the Swedish imprisonment rate remains substantially lower than the UK rate despite these pressures and the Nordic countries have resisted increasing public punitiveness (see Ugelvic and Dullum (eds) 2011; Pratt and Eriksson 2013).

Second, a concern with desert and proportionality may limit excessive punishment in its rejection of exemplary sentences, selective incapacitation, and preventive sentencing. Although it is true, as von Hirsch acknowledges, that incarceration increased in some states in the United States, such as California, which adopted a just deserts model in the mid-1970s, closer examination shows that the prison population was already increasing before the model was adopted. Furthermore, proportionality was not used in making the decision to impose custody, but only in determining the length of the sentence. Moreover, the impact of penal justifications is also shaped by local political structures and conditions, as Barker (2009) demonstrates, and in California the impact of populism on penal sanctioning was a key variable in its penal expansion from the mid-1990s.

Yet, as von Hirsch notes (1986), the Minnesota Sentencing Guidelines of the late 1970s and early 1980s, which were based on a modified desert principle, did lead to consistent sentencing. At the time they prevented the expansion of the prison population because they imprisoned those convicted of the most serious crimes, but imprisoned fewer convicted of lesser crimes, and were subject to safeguards to limit the size of the prison population. Moreover, as he points out, the Sentencing Commission in Minnesota did take account of prison capacity when drawing up the sentencing guidelines. Minnesota still has a lower imprisonment rate than states such as Texas whose sentencing guidelines give less weight to desert. It has also been argued by Lippke (2007) that retributivism, by limiting punishment to those who have committed serious harms to others and not sentencing simply to satisfy public opinion, can be an effective constraint on increased punitiveness. Furthermore, he argues, a penal system which recognises and does not crush offenders' capacities to lead autonomous lives will result in a more humane form of imprisonment. As we saw in Chapter 2, section 2.7, limiting excessive punishment can also be achieved by an appeal to human rights.

Henham (2012) has challenged retributivist approaches for offering little scope for victim participation in the criminal justice system and for failing to deliver sentencing outcomes which fit citizens' perception of justice. Retributivism's focus on free will, he argues, also does not take account of the extent to which communities may bear some responsibility for crime, so desert should be expanded to encompass social deserts. The failure of desert theory to address the underlying social problems of inequality, poverty, and injustice, which may be linked to offending, has also been raised by radical approaches.[26]

3.4.2 **Radical critiques of retributivism**

Marxist critiques of retributivist theory, for example, have used social scientific research to show the problems with individualist models and the links between marginalisation and criminality. However, this raises the question of whether it is the task of any penal theory to undertake the gargantuan task of solving problems of social inequality: certainly rival theories of punishment from utilitarian traditions or from restorative justice do not do so. But at the least one can say that desert theory is compatible with progressive social policies, as evidenced by those European jurisdictions—such as Sweden and Finland—which have primarily desert-based sentencing systems and progressive welfare and social programmes.

Radical critiques also raise the issue of whether we should focus on the social disadvantage of offenders when imposing punishments, and treat disadvantage as a mitigating factor. On desert theory the individual is still culpable even if this culpability is reduced by extreme poverty or economic distress. In any case, most crime falls far short of necessity in the sense used in the criminal law[27] and modern studies of wealth and poverty in the UK have focused on inequality and relative deprivation rather than absolute poverty (see Dorling *et al.* 2007). Even if deprivation is a factor in the circumstances surrounding the offence, this does not mean proportionality is no longer relevant, although reducing a sentence for a particular offender on social grounds would be unfair on the retributivist model. Moreover, if social and economic factors are given precedence over issues of desert, this may work to the disadvantage of economically and socially deprived offenders; for example, social and economic factors are already included in OASys (the Offender Assessment System), to predict the risks posed by offenders and to make decisions on their release and management.

Furthermore, one could argue that poor or disadvantaged offenders may be more strongly protected by desert theory than by rival theories. As von Hirsch (1993) argues, there is more scope for raising such issues in desert theory and poorer offenders would be better protected by lowering the anchoring points for penalties than by looking at

---

[26] Some of these problems in relation to social exclusion will be considered in Chapters 7 and 9.

[27] *Dudley and Stephens* (1884) 14 QBD 273. While Kant accepts the non-criminality of homicide from necessity and gives the example of the person who—in order to save his own life in a shipwreck—pushes another person, whose life is equally in danger, off a plank on which he has saved himself, this is far removed from the kinds of choice relevant to discussions of 'everyday' crime (Kant 1796–7). See also von Hirsch and Ashworth (2005).

individual disadvantage, which might encourage the disadvantaged offender to be seen as a higher risk, although this argument is unlikely to satisfy those who want compensation for disadvantage.

The problems which arise in taking account of the impact of punishment in an unequal society are further considered in Chapter 7, while the issues of inequality and discrimination will be considered in Chapter 9, in relation to the experience of imprisonment.

Marx himself said little on punishment and did not offer a theory or justification of punishment, but rather was concerned to contextualise punishment in its social, economic, and historical context. He did write a short article on 'Capital Punishment' (Marx 1853) in which he argued that it would be 'very difficult, if not altogether impossible, to establish any principle upon which the justice or expediency of capital punishment could be founded', while Engels said that how to punish criminals was a topic he left to his readers (Engels 1843). The implications of Marx's analysis for modern critiques of the death penalty are discussed by Bohm (2008).

However, Marx was more sympathetic to retributivism than to **utilitarian theories of punishment**. He was critical of the view that punishment may be ameliorating or intimidating, because of the absence of proof of the effectiveness of punishment in preventing crime, and he praised Kant's and Hegel's theory of punishment because it recognises human dignity and the rights of the person punished, treats the individual as 'a free and self-determined being', and focuses on rights and autonomy. But he argued that the retributivists' reification of free will fails to take account of the impact of social and economic pressures on the individual (Marx 1853)[28] and that German idealism abstracts the individual from society. What the idealists see as universal features of all societies are products of a specific mode of production and limited to specific strata. Given the incidence and recurrence of crime in nineteenth-century society, effort should be addressed to dealing with the underlying social system which generates crime, rather than focusing attention on refining systems of punishment.

Marx's relationship to retributivism is considered by Murphy (1973), who argues that, while Marx sees retributivism as the most defensible theory of punishment, the conditions in modern society render the theory inapplicable in most modern societies and rob those societies of their moral right to punish. The picture of individuals exercising free will and of autonomy and rationality fits uneasily with the reality of the alienation of modern capitalist society, which is crime-ridden, where individuals act out of greed and self-interest, and where society is marked by an absence of reciprocity, in contrast to the Hegelian state where there is a genuine community and where the rules are internalised. In our society, says Murphy, it is hard to see how the socially deprived benefit from membership or to construe individuals as acting freely when responding to severe social deprivation, but these issues are overlooked by the classical retributivists. However, the links between crime and deprivation have been explored by Marxist criminologists including Willem Bonger (1916).

Murphy argues that, if society were reconstructed to meet the Marxian ideal of a society where all individuals participate in relations of mutuality, then it would fit the retributivist model because there would be genuine autonomy of all individuals and in that case retributivist punishment would be justifiable, although, in any case, in such a society crime would be likely to decrease.[29]

---

[28] A similar argument is advanced by Marx and Engels in their critique of the Young Hegelians in *The Holy Family* (1845).

[29] The relationship between justice and the mode of production may itself be problematic within Marxian theory. See Wood (1972, 2004), McBride (1975), and Easton (2008a). But Marx argues in *The Holy Family* that in communism, 'under *humane* conditions punishment will *really* be nothing but the sentence passed by the culprit on himself' (1845: 179), which is closer to the Hegelian ethical idea.

The implications of social deprivation for retributivism will also be considered in the context of a discussion of equality of impact and impact mitigation in Chapter 7, section 7.3.

3.4.3 **Modern Marxian critiques**

Modern Marxists have been more concerned with processes of criminalisation than with punishment, although humanist Marxist social historians, including Thompson (1977) and Hay *et al.* (1975), have considered the historical development of modes of punishment, the legitimacy of punishment, the significance of the notion of the rule of law as an ideal and ideology, and the role of law in maintaining the hegemony of the ruling class. Critical legal scholars have subjected key concepts of liberal legalism, including rights and equality, to a rigorous critique. A historical materialist approach to punishment means understanding punishment historically, changing through time and shaped by the mode of production. On classical Marxist theory the specific form which punishment takes will reflect underlying economic conditions and the needs of the dominant class. In early capitalism, as the demand for labour increased in the new factory mode of production, imprisonment displaced capital punishment. Punishment does not simply reflect desert, as on a retributivist model, but is a means of social control. Punishment is also used to discipline the working class, in so far as conditions in prison are made worse than the poorest conditions in the labour market outside, to inculcate work discipline through the experience of imprisonment and, historically, to provide a source of labour through transportation to the United States, replacing slave labour after the abolition of slavery (see Rusche and Kirchheimer 1939). Rusche and Kirchheimer see the declining use of imprisonment in the early twentieth century as reflecting the shift towards disciplining the workforce within the production process, as new processes such as the assembly line developed. Structuralist Marxists such as Althusser (1971) considered the role of the penal system as part of the repressive state apparatus but also emphasised the ideological functions of law.

Using historical materialist methods, we can see that the levels and forms of punishment vary according to economic conditions in the sense that when labour is scarce, punishment is less severe and when labour is oversupplied, punishment becomes harsher. So in times of full employment, such as the 1960s, we see a liberalisation of punishment, a concern with reform and rehabilitation, and loss of support for capital punishment here and in the United States. But in times of recession fear of crime increases and incarceration rates increase.

The work of Loic Wacquant (2001a, 2001b, 2007, 2008a, 2012) has focused on the role of the prison as a way of absorbing surplus labour as changes in the forces of production have reduced demand for unskilled labour, while the marginalisation and demoralisation of the 'lumpenproletariat' has contributed to rising crime. Wacquant argues: 'What the state needs to fight is not the symptom, *criminal insecurity*, but the cause of urban disorder: namely, the *social insecurity* that the state itself has spawned by becoming the diligent handmaiden to the despotism of the market' (Wacquant 2008a: 118). He sees the carceral expansion in the US as resulting from the penalisation of poverty and changes in the economic, welfare, and justice functions of the state (Wacquant 2012; see also Squires and Lea (eds) 2012).

The political economy of punishment has also focused on the criminalisation of migrants. De Giorgi (2010, 2012) examines the use of incarceration as a strategy in the war against unauthorised migration in the context of a deregulated neo-liberal economy. The focus on 'crimmigration', the convergence of criminal law and immigration law, in the United States has also received increasing attention, so Garcia Hernandez (2014), for example, argues that immigration detention should be conceptualised as punishment. In the UK context, Bowling *et al.* (2014) have focused on the relationship between race and political economy in the context of the coercive state.

How useful are Marxian and critical approaches to punishment? Classical Marxism has been criticised for its economic reductionism and failure to offer concrete proposals for penal reform. Modern critical approaches have been criticised for their failure to generate radical changes in the penal system or criminal justice system generally. Even those modern theorists sympathetic to sociological models of punishment, such as Garland and Murphy, find Marxian theory of limited value in giving guidance to modern penal institutions and policies and, as we have argued, this was not a project of interest to Marx himself. But Marxist approaches highlight the inherent problems facing crime reductionist policies which fail to take account of criminogenic social and economic conditions. They also offer an alternative to liberal conceptions of state punishment. Although Hudson (1993) dismisses Marxism as a form of modernism whose time has gone, many of Marx's concepts, such as alienation, are still relevant to postmodern debates on crime and social exclusion (see Easton 2008b).

Placing punishment in its social, historical, and political context is part of Marx's legacy and is reflected in modern sociological perspectives on punishment. For example, Garland (1991) has considered the impact of economic and social factors on contemporary sentencing and, while cautious regarding monolithic explanations of complex behaviour, he appreciates that Marxian analyses transcend a narrow approach to penal theory and practice. There has also been some interest in developing communitarian approaches to punishment which recognise the primacy of social relations (see Lacey 2003 and Duff 2003b).

3.5 Reflecting on the issues

3.5.1 Case study

This sentencing exercise is about Tess, who was arrested, charged, and pleaded guilty to fraud by false representation under s. 2 of the Fraud Act 2006, for which the maximum penalty is ten years' imprisonment. The facts of the case, on which the Crown Court judge must pass sentence, are as follows:

Tess, a 21-year-old undergraduate, has been working part-time for the last two years as a care assistant at a Residential Home for the Elderly. In this capacity she persuaded six elderly residents to hand over £60 each to her, ostensibly to pay into a Christmas fund. This they all did one morning as arranged and she told them she would collect another instalment the following month. Tess used the money to pay her rent as she had large debts and could not rely on her father, whose business had just collapsed. She was seriously depressed and was attending counselling sessions.[30]

Tess's deception was discovered before the next instalment was due because one of the residents from whom she had obtained money asked the manager about the Christmas fund. Tess did not at first plead guilty, fearful that she would never obtain employment on graduating and believing the elderly residents were too ill and mentally confused to give evidence. In the event, a change of medication dramatically improved the physical and mental health of one of them. Consequently, Tess changed her plea to guilty before the trial.

In between the offending and trial, Tess graduated and was left a legacy of £3,000 by an aunt. After paying her debts she has £150 left. She was given a reprimand[31] at the age of 14 for shoplifting (under the Theft Act 1968, s. 1) and had one previous conviction, at the age

---

[30] You are not expected to use the provisions of the Mental Health Act 1983 in this exercise: these possibilities will not be dealt with until Chapter 6, section 6.4.

[31] Reprimands and warnings have been replaced by youth cautions: see Chapter 6, section 6.3. The court might view this as a previous conviction.

of 16, for burglary of a dwelling under s. 9 of the Theft Act 1968, for which she received a referral order. (She was not given detention in a young offender institution because of mitigation in relation to the death of her mother and a subsequent depressive illness.)

1. Sentence Tess, explaining and justifying your chosen sentencing framework and particular sentence.

2. Decide whether your sentence would be different if:

   (a) Tess had no previous convictions.

   (b) Tess defrauded the residents because they were all South Asians.

   (c) The current offence was committed while Tess was on bail awaiting trial for a drug offence—a charge of which she was subsequently acquitted.

   (d) Tess's current offence was burglary in a dwelling, not fraud.

You might find helpful the checklist provided in section 3.2.1, and also the relevant guidelines:

Sentencing Council (2011b) *Burglary Offences: Definitive Guideline*, London, Sentencing Council.

Sentencing Council (2014a) *Fraud, Bribery and Money Laundering Offences: Definitive Guideline*. London, Sentencing Council.

online
resource
centre

The Online Resource Centre will provide further guidance.

3.5.2 **The importance of seriousness: questions for discussion**

Policy debates in the past decade have been dominated by legislation and proposed changes in relation to the offender deemed to be a serious risk to the public, and also in relation to the effectiveness of community punishment. However, in law and in practice it is the issues of seriousness, proportionality, and just deserts principles which are the bread and butter of those who sentence and the determinants of outcome for most offenders. Sentencing guidelines are making this process ever more technical and detailed, but clearly within a retributivist framework. The riots in England in the summer of 2011 also revealed popular support for ensuring offenders received their just deserts as an aim of punishment, albeit that some calls were for a sentence which might be viewed as disproportionate. However, those riots also led to a focus on deterrence, a utilitarian aim, which we will consider in the next chapter.

We would also point out that issues regarding the victim, reparation, rehabilitation, and control are grafted on to this retributivist framework and we do not ignore the fact that another framework—for the dangerous—runs alongside it. In Chapters 5, 6, and 10 we will focus on these other issues.

Task:
How would you answer the following question?
Does the approach of the guidelines published since 2012 make sentencing too mechanical an exercise?

4

Utility and deterrence

SUMMARY

In this chapter we examine an approach which focuses on the consequences or outcomes of sentencing and punishment. The origins of this approach in the work of Beccaria and Bentham, and its modern expression in the work of writers such as Wilson and Kennedy, will be discussed. We will focus here on the specific outcome of deterrence, considering whether punishment is effective in reducing offending, reviewing the available research and the problems which arise in proving a deterrent effect. We will also consider some of the difficulties with this justification for punishment.

4.1 A focus on outcome

4.1.1 Recent trends

> Offences of this kind, carrying an offensive weapon or knife, have recently escalated. They are reaching epidemic proportions. . . . For the time being, whatever other considerations may arise in the individual case, sentencing courts must have in the forefront of their thinking that the sentences for this type of offence should focus on the reduction of crime, including its reduction by deterrence, and the protection of the public.
>
> (*Povey* 2008 at para 4)

These comments were made by Sir Igor Judge (then President, Queen's Bench Division) when the *Magistrates' Court Sentencing Guidelines* were revised in relation to knife crime; the (then) Sentencing Guidelines Council[1] drew attention to them in the accompanying note. The *Povey* case had not overruled the previous guideline case, *Celaire and Poulton* (2003), but had stated: 'Conditions now are much more grave than they were five and a half years ago and the guidance given in *Celaire and Poulton* should be applied with the current grave situation as we have endeavoured to explain it' (para 5). What was therefore justifying treating and punishing such offences as more serious than before was a focus on prevalence of the offending but also deterrence and protection of the public. In other words, the outcome of punishment was seen to be as much of a factor as providing just deserts.

The riots in England in the summer of 2011 also led to a renewed focus on deterrence by the public and the judiciary. The issue was whether and to what extent the context of offending should influence sentencing levels in terms of both retribution and deterrence. While some sentences led to successful appeals,[2] others did not and, in the appeals heard

---

[1] See http://sentencingcouncil.judiciary.gov.uk/docs/sentencing_guidelines_knife_crime.pdf.
[2] See, for example, Bowcott (2011).

in *R v Blackshaw and others* (2011), Lord Judge, Lord Chief Justice, endorsed deterrence as a justification:

> There is an overwhelming obligation on sentencing courts to do what they can to ensure the protection of the public . . . This is an imperative. It is not, of course, possible now, after the events, for the courts to protect the neighbourhoods which were ravaged in the riots or the people who were injured or suffered damage. Nevertheless, the imposition of severe sentences, intended to provide both punishment and deterrence, must follow . . . They must be punished accordingly, and the sentences should be designed to deter others from similar criminal activity.
>
> (*R v Blackshaw* at para 4)

To justify sentencing in terms of outcome in this way clearly contrasts with the retributivist, 'just deserts', sentencing framework discussed in Chapters 2 and 3, which is not primarily concerned with outcome or the consequences of the sentencing decision other than that of ensuring that justice has been done. Only when we discussed the *Cunningham* (1993) case did we note reasoning similar to that in the *Povey* case where prevalence justified a sentence which was, in effect, a deterrent one.

In 2010, Lord Justice Leveson, now President of the Queen's Bench Division, while giving evidence to the Justice Committee in relation to the revised sentencing guideline on assault, said: 'If there was no evidence that a particular sentence had a deterrent effect that would be relevant when we come to devise a sentencing guideline' (House of Commons Justice Committee 2011: Ev12, Q45). He then gave the example of sentences for 'mules'—people bringing drugs in from foreign countries—and said that the Sentencing Council would be gathering evidence to see whether current sentences did deter. It would appear, therefore, that guidelines, in setting offence categories of proportionate punishments, include deterrence in calculations of seriousness.

In policy documents deterrence is also often claimed as an aim, together with wider aims of reducing offending. In 2001 *Criminal Justice: The Way Ahead* argued that an effective, well-run criminal justice system must be, inter alia, 'effective at preventing offending and reoffending' (Home Office 2001a: para 4).[3] More specifically, that White Paper gave priority to the aims of reduction of offending and reparation to the victim: sentencing will pay 'more attention to sentence outcomes such as crime reduction and reparation' (Home Office 2001a: para 2.66). The Halliday Report made clear, however, that of the sentencing goals identified, 'reform and rehabilitation' (rather than incapacitation or deterrence: see 2001: paras 1.58–1.68) were their favoured methods of achieving crime reduction (ibid: para 1.69). *Making Sentencing Clearer* similarly stated that the government's sentencing aims were outcome-focused: 'The proposals in this document are . . . designed to ensure that the public are better protected from dangerous offenders' (Home Secretary *et al.* 2006: Foreword).

Some changes made by the Criminal Justice and Immigration Act 2008 also increased the focus on outcome of sentence. Arguably, the following provisions have a utilitarian element: sections 1 (youth rehabilitation order), 9 (sentencing aims for young offenders), and 98 (Violent Offender Orders). For example, by s. 102(1) the court can include in a Violent Offender Order prohibitions, restrictions, or conditions preventing the offender:

   (a) from going to any specified premises or any other specified place (whether at all, or at or between any specified time or times);

---

[3] These characteristics relate to the criminal justice system as a whole but Part 2 of the document makes it clear they also relate specifically to the sentencing stage.

(b) from attending any specified event;

(c) from having any, or any specified description of, contact with any specified individual.

This reveals a focus on incapacitation and regulation rather than a (purely) proportionate and retributivist response.

Although somewhat tangential, it is worth noting that the Crime and Courts Act 2013 includes a provision for the court to award exemplary damages under s. 34(6)(b) against the publisher of news-related material when the court is satisfied 'the conduct is such that the court should punish the defendant for it' and specifically states that the court 'may regard deterring the defendant and others from similar conduct as an object of punishment' (s. 35(5)).

The Halliday Report (2001) acknowledged but sidestepped the philosophical confusion caused by the imposition of outcome-based aims on a just deserts sentencing framework. It simply stated that '[o]pinions differ as to whether punishment is a goal in its own right or is, rather, a means of achieving the other two goals' (2001: paras 1.4 and 1.5). Neither did the Criminal Justice Act 2003 clarify the situation—rather the reverse—when it specified five purposes of sentencing:

(a) the punishment of offenders;

(b) the reduction of crime (including its reduction by deterrence);

(c) the reform and rehabilitation of offenders;

(d) the protection of the public;

(e) the making of reparation by offenders to persons affected by their offences.

   (Section 142(1))

While the first purpose is retributivist and the fifth restorative, the remaining three are utilitarian. Yet, theoretically speaking, if the justification is utilitarian, the issue of proportionality should either be downgraded or ignored; if the justification is retributivist, the sentence should be calculated solely on the basis of proportionality. So, as Dingwall and Hillier point out, deterrence is problematic as it 'is consistent with this aim that a more blameworthy offender who is less likely to offend in future receives a lesser sentence than a less blameworthy offender who, perhaps through no fault of his own, is more likely to reoffend' (Dingwall and Hillier 2015: 41).

The 'solution' introduced by the CJA 1991 was that there could be a 'secondary' focus on outcome. So, while the primary sentencing decision concerns just deserts, the specified amount of retributively imposed punishment could be used to achieve outcomes other than that of a sense of justice achieved through the application of retributivist principles. The CJA 2003, however, increased the focus on this second set of aims and so reinforced the utilitarian aspect of sentencing and punishment.

4.1.2 **Deterrence as a sentencing aim**

Aiming to reduce offending by deterring offenders or others from committing crimes in the future is only one outcome-based sentencing aim and, as we have seen, it is not one to which recent sentencing policy documents have generally given priority. It is also perhaps significant that a recent edited collection on English sentencing guidelines has only one reference to 'deterrence' in the index (Ashworth and Roberts 2013). However, there is a widespread assumption that the resulting punishment *will* deter the convicted offender from reoffending, or potential offenders from offending, and, as we have noted already, cases such as *Povey* (2008) and *Blackshaw and others* (2011), as well as the statement of Lord Justice Leveson (House of Commons Justice Committee 2011), are evidence that deterrence as an aim of punishment is still in the minds of sentencers and the Sentencing Council.

For example, in 2015 in *R v Brooke (Simon)* a sentence of 63 months for attempted robbery was upheld on appeal because the offender had intentionally targeted a vulnerable victim who suffered from cerebral palsy, and the psychological effects on the victim had been severe. The Appeal court specifically said that the judge had been entitled to conclude that the circumstances of the offending called for a deterrent sentence.

Forlin (2015), commenting on *R v Thames Water Utilities Ltd* (2015), points out that the Court of Appeal made it clear that fines for serious environmental offences by large corporations should rise and one factor was clearly deterrence. The judgment said that, in the 'worst cases', 'the objectives of punishment, deterrence and the removal of gain (for example by the decision of the management not to expend sufficient resources in modernisation and improvement) must be achieved by the level of penalty imposed' (at para 40 per Mitting, J).

The 'exemplary sentence', where the penalty is arguably higher than a strictly proportionate sentence, is justified in terms of general deterrence and, notably in relation to robbery or 'mugging', this rationale has been a long-standing sentencing feature (Ashworth 2010: 82). Guidance from the Sentencing Guidelines Council (SGC) allows prevalence to be taken into account in exceptional circumstances if justified in terms of greater harm caused (2004a: para 1.39). However, in *R v Oosthuizen* (2005), where the judge at first instance had decided to impose a deterrent sentence owing to the prevalence of robbery of handbags in the area because '[w]omen in Guildford were entitled to feel safe on the streets in broad daylight' (at para 9), the Court of Appeal stated that the deterrent element in a sentence must be supported by statistics about prevalence: 'even a judge with experience of that area should not assume that prevalence was more marked in that area than nationally' (at para 16). In *R v Hussain (Mohammed)* (2005), a custodial sentence of three years and seven months was given to Hussain for stealing postal votes: the aim of the sentence was to deter electoral fraud.

So we see deterrence linked with punishment and even with proportionality in a retributivist system of sentencing. This is evident in the phrase 'retribution and deterrence' or 'punishment and deterrence' used, commonly, by official guidance and by the courts in relation to the 'tariff' or minimum period of a mandatory or discretionary life sentence (see Chapter 5) or of detention during Her Majesty's pleasure for minors (see Chapter 11). For example, in the House of Lords, in *R v Lichniak, R v Pyrah* (2001), Lord Hutton noted that the young person is not detained indefinitely 'but rather is only detained for the tariff period sufficient to satisfy the requirements of retribution and deterrence in the circumstances of the particular case' (at para 29).[4] Mr Justice Silber also used the same phrase— 'retribution and general deterrence'—in relation to the minimum term to be served in *Gareth Wealleans* (2008 at para 10).

The inclusion of 'deterrence' in this phrase is usually not explained. In advice from the Sentencing Advisory Panel (SAP 2002) on minimum terms[5] in murder cases, for example, 'retribution and deterrence' was used in the introductory pages. However, the detailed justification for the proposed minimum terms was (only) in terms of seriousness (ibid: para 15 (*et seq.*)) and there was no discussion as to what would deter others: the 'public' are mentioned only in terms of risk to the public and of public confidence that the murderer is sufficiently punished.

---

[4] Unless there are 'elements of dangerousness and risk' to justify longer detention (*Stafford v United Kingdom*, Application No. 46295/99, 28 May 2002 at para 87): see Chapter 5.

[5] The SAP suggested that 'tariff' should be replaced with 'minimum term' for the sake of clarity (2002: para 2).

Deterrence is then the taken-for-granted outcome of punishment, and one which causes concern only if it is believed that a sentence would not be sufficiently tough to deter. So while it is currently neither a priority aim in sentencing law and policy, nor—at the level of individual deterrence—a clear factor in the delivery of punishment, deterrence is an outcome which is still of significance in judicial and policy thinking and one to which the public has great attachment. As we shall see, the theory and the delivery of deterrence are much more complicated than political and media pronouncements would suggest. Deterrence is also only one form of punishment outcome which can be justified on utilitarian grounds.

Other beneficial consequences of punishment would include incapacitation of the offender to protect the public and rehabilitation of the offender, and we will deal with these desired outcomes in Chapters 5 and 10 respectively. First, we will examine utilitarian theory before returning to a focus on deterrence.

4.1.3 **Utilitarianism: good or bad?**

Utilitarian philosophies of punishment have received a mixed response. Their apparent advantage over retributivist justifications is that they aim to reform or deter or prevent reoffending by focusing on costs and benefits, that is, the consequences of punishment. They seem to offer the prospect of a more efficient use of punitive resources. Further, a utilitarian theory of punishment has long been associated with reform of punishment—for example, in the work of its earliest 'modern' proponents, Beccaria and Bentham, in the eighteenth and early nineteenth centuries. Bentham argued penal institutions should be assessed against the yardstick of utility: if an institution fails to meet its stated purpose, then reforms are necessary. In the nineteenth and early twentieth centuries, utility was a major theoretical tool used to implement and defend reforms in the United States, the UK, and Europe. It focused public policy on the concrete effects of the penal system and considered the implications for human suffering and the broader social aims of deterrence, rehabilitation, and social protection.

On the other hand, utilitarian philosophies—or reductivist philosophies as they are sometimes called, because they aim to reduce offending—may justify harsher sentences than retributivist theory. For example, it may be seen as in the public good to give some offenders very harsh punishments to deter others, or long prison sentences to incapacitate them and so severely restrict their capacity to reoffend. Such sentences may undermine individual rights and appear unjust, as the needs of the state or the community are given more importance than the severity of the offending in question when the sentencing decision is made.

4.2 **Utilitarian justifications**

4.2.1 **Classical principles**

Utilitarian theories have their origins in the classical criminology of Beccaria and Bentham. Beccaria's *On Crimes and Punishments*, first published in English in 1767, was one of the first utilitarian theories of punishment and a key influence on Bentham. Like Bentham, Beccaria sees individuals as motivated by the pursuit of pleasure and the avoidance of pain and uses utility as a basis of social criticism. Laws should be assessed, he argues, 'from the point of view of whether they conduce to the greatest happiness shared among the greater number' (1767: 7). He saw the retributivism of his time as pointless, arbitrary, and excessively harsh. For Beccaria the aim of punishment is to prevent offenders from committing new harms and to deter others from doing so, rather than to punish just for the sake of it:

> [T]he purpose of punishment is not that of tormenting or afflicting any sentient creature, nor of undoing a crime already committed . . . The purpose, therefore, is nothing other than to prevent the offender from doing fresh harm to his fellows and to deter others from doing likewise . . . punishments and the means adopted for inflicting them should, consistent with proportionality, be so selected as to make the most efficacious and lasting impression on the minds of men with the least torment to the body of the condemned.
>
> (ibid: 31)

Beccaria includes the key utilitarian notions of deterrence and the optimal level of punishment, the minimum pain necessary to achieve the aims, but also refers to proportionality. Punishment should be enacted as swiftly as possible, and fit the nature of the crime—so non-violent thefts, for example, should be met with fines, violent thefts with a combination of corporal punishment and penal servitude, and social parasites should be banished.

He was also one of the first theorists to focus on the importance of certainty rather than severity: 'The certainty of even a mild punishment will make a bigger impression than the fear of a more awful one which is united to a hope of not being punished at all' (ibid: 63). If punishment is too severe, the offender may seek to evade it by committing further crime (ibid: 64). It is essential, he argues, that punishment 'should be public, speedy, necessary, the minimum possible in the given circumstances, proportionate to the crime, and determined by the law' (ibid: 113), rather than imposed through acts of vigilantism. The level of punishment should be as much as is necessary to prevent harm to society, to protect the public from the offences committed by individuals. Beccaria thought that, as society progressed, the severity of punishment would diminish. He was also very critical of the death penalty, and saw it as wasteful, of questionable deterrent value, and denying the community the person's future potential contributions.

It is, however, Bentham whose work has become synonymous with utilitarianism. Although the principle of utility had already been used by Beccaria, Hutcheson, and Priestley, Bentham is seen as the source of modern utilitarianism and a key voice of the English enlightenment. His work on *The Rationale of Punishment*, published in English in 1830, is seen as a major contribution to nineteenth-century debates on penal reform, but in fact was written much earlier, in the 1770s.

4.2.2 **Bentham's approach**

Bentham's *Introduction to the Principles of Morals and Legislation*, first published in 1789, aimed to promote the public interest and happiness through the use of reason. His philosophical approach is quite distinct from retributivism and expresses his aim to introduce rationality into all stages of the criminal justice system. For Bentham utility is the arbiter of law and morals. The principle of utility is 'that principle which approves or disapproves of every action whatsoever, according to the tendency which it appears to have to augment or diminish the happiness of the party whose interest is in question' (Bentham 1789: 12). Utility means the minimisation of pain and suffering and the maximisation of pleasure. 'Nature has placed mankind under the governance of two sovereign masters, *pain and pleasure*' (ibid: 11, emphasis in the original).

Utility is maximised when the result adds up to the greatest happiness of the greatest number. Bentham devised a felicific calculus, and argued that how we assess acts, choices, and ways of behaving is by calculating whether the sum of pleasures exceeds the pain. In calculating the costs and benefits we measure a number of factors: the intensity of pain and pleasure; its duration; the certainty or uncertainty of benefits accruing; the propinquity or nearness of the ensuing pleasure, that is, how quickly the pleasure will be generated; its fecundity, whether it will generate further pleasures or pain; its purity, whether or not it is likely to be followed by its opposite, pain, or pleasure; whether it is unmixed with painful consequences; and its extent, that is, the number of people affected by it.

By using these criteria, we can see if the sum total of pleasures outweighs the costs. Bentham says that the quest for pleasure and the avoidance of pain is the key to understanding human behaviour. We can build social policies on this assumption and use rewards and punishment to channel behaviour to maximise the greatest happiness of the greatest number.

Like all utilitarianism, Bentham's theory is consequentialist: the only matter for the evaluation of laws and policies is consequences in terms of the pain and pleasure resulting from the event, policy, or state of affairs. A good policy maximises the happiness of the majority, and utilitarianism is essentially a majoritarian approach.

When this theory is applied to punishment, then punishment is justified only by the good consequences which will result from it, so suffering should never be imposed unless it will prevent greater suffering, because all suffering is intrinsically bad as it causes pain: 'But all punishment is mischief: all punishment in itself is evil. Upon the principle of utility, if it ought at all to be admitted, it ought only to be admitted in as far as it promises to exclude some greater evil' (ibid: 158). Punishment should not be inflicted just because someone has done something wrong because that, considered on its own, will only increase the total amount of human suffering. But if by inflicting it we can prevent greater suffering, either by preventing the offender from doing further harm or by deterring others from doing the same thing, it is not only morally justified but morally necessary.

Punishment for Bentham cannot be justified merely as an act of retribution, but only by the fact that the harm done by punishing the offender is outweighed by the benefits. Given that punishment is a 'cost-expense' in terms of the suffering of the incarcerated and the cost to society of keeping them in prison, the aim should be to maximise income, that is the deterrent effect, at the least possible expense, using a cost–benefit model. Punishment should not be inflicted if it is groundless, inefficacious, unprofitable, or needless, argues Bentham. Some cases may turn out to be too unprofitable to punish at all because costs outweigh benefits—for example, trivial offences or victimless crimes, where the evil of punishment outweighs that of the original offence.

The aim of punishment is to prevent offences, to prevent worse offences, to minimise the 'mischief', and to prevent the mischief as cheaply as possible, to achieve the object with least possible expense (ibid: 165). Punishment may also satisfy the injured party and meet public concerns.

4.2.3 Frugality in punishment

Bentham argues that we should calculate the optimum level of punishment and, if effective deterrence could be achieved by a lesser sentence, then on utilitarian principles, it is a useless and needless expense to impose a higher sentence. Bentham was critical of the excessive and arbitrary punishments of his time, including the death penalty, which was often used for relatively minor offences. He wanted an external standard against which sentencing decisions might be judged, so ideally two sentencers armed with the same knowledge of the facts of a particular case would reach the same decision on the type and level of punishment.

For Bentham, punishment is not justified on the ground of being good for the individual as the individual can have no interest in being punished at all. Instead, what justifies punishment is what is good for society, sacrificing a few individuals for the greater good of others. Punishment deters others from engaging in certain acts, promotes the public good, and promotes greater happiness. The 'happiness' of the person punished is considered alongside that of others but if it is necessary to ensure the happiness of the majority, his happiness may be sacrificed.

Bentham is committed to the principle of frugality, or what we would now call parsimony, to use the most economical means of punishment, to impose the least severe punishment to meet the social objective. Frugality is achieved where no superfluous pain is imposed on the person punished. The amount of punishment should not be less than needed to outweigh the profit of the offence. If it is too little it will be inefficacious; if too much it will be needless. The optimal level of punishment will depend on the circumstances. Generally the greater the mischief of the offence, says Bentham, then the greater is the expense which it may be worth incurring in the administration of punishment, and punishment should be adjusted so that a person would favour a lesser rather than a greater offence.

This means that there should normally be gradations in severity of punishment to match the seriousness of the offence. Bentham says that there should be upper and lower limits on punishment to guide judges. So, there is room for proportionality in his theory of punishment because penalties will normally be linked to the gravity of the crime. However, proportionality is deployed on a basis quite different to retributivism, as it is determined by the need to deter the offender, rather than being based on desert, and is linked to crime prevention. Bentham argues that greater deterrence will be achieved by increasing the penalty as much as is necessary to prevent future crimes, rather than reflecting the degree of censure or blame. But deviations from the principle of proportionality, such as exemplary sentences, for example, may be justified in the public interest.

We should consider whether a less expensive means of punishment could achieve the same purpose and whether it is profitable to punish at all. In deciding on a mode of punishment we should take account of the aims, the principal ones being example, reformation, disablement, or what we would now call incapacitation, and compensation. However, Bentham acknowledges that achieving disablement may run counter to frugality, for example, when a disabled offender could still benefit others through future actions.

Bentham favours imprisonment because it is able to achieve fine gradations, and in the 1780s he designed a model prison completely based on utilitarian principles. Capital punishment in contrast is the most unfrugal method of punishment, he argued, as well as raising the problem of irreversibility in cases of error. Bentham's point is well made as 151 prisoners convicted and sentenced to death were released between 1973 and 2015, because they were subsequently acquitted, had the charges dropped by the prosecution, or received a pardon based on evidence of innocence (Death Penalty Information Center 2015). Using statistical analysis, Gross et al. (2015) estimate that 4.1 per cent of defendants on Death Row could be wrongfully convicted.

For Bentham, the system of law and punishment should be designed so that when people seem to follow their interests, they are led to do those things which result in the greatest happiness of the greatest number. Prolonged punishment of an infirm individual who is unlikely to reoffend, or to threaten society, would be hard to justify, while on a retributivist model, the offender's advancing years or state of health at the time of sentencing would be irrelevant; what is important is his culpability at the time of committing the offence. Bentham is usually seen as an act-utilitarian, in so far as he focuses on the immediate consequences of a particular course of action, and this is contrasted with rule-utilitarianism, in which one considers the effect of generalising that particular course of action as a general rule and then considering the consequences of such a rule.[6]

Utilitarians may favour leniency in applying the principle of parsimony, accepting in some cases a punishment which is less severe than retributivists favour, depending on the particular circumstances. Retributivists, on the other hand, favour the punishment that is appropriate, which may entail severity. But for the utilitarian it depends on the consequences and empirical facts of the particular case. So there may be situations where the utilitarian might demand a harsher punishment than a retributivist would contemplate, punishing disproportionately to the offence to achieve a positive outcome, for example, to allay public concerns. Utilitarians might also recommend punishment where a retributivist would say there should be none at all, as in the extreme case of punishing the innocent. It is for this reason that many find the utilitarian approach unacceptable.

4.2.4 **Contemporary utilitarianism**

Bentham's work has been a major influence on modern utilitarianism. Modern writers in this approach would include Wilson (1985), Andenaes (1974), van den Haag (1981), and Kennedy (2009). These theorists are primarily concerned with deterrence and incapacitation rather than rehabilitation. In contemporary utilitarianism, the consequences which justify punishment are:

1. General deterrence, that is deterring the general public from doing the act punished.

2. Special deterrence, that is deterring the person being punished.

3. Incapacitation, that is protecting the public by removing a dangerous person from society so he or she is unable to reoffend. This has been an increasingly important element of penal policy in recent years. It recognises that prison may not work in deterring offenders but it aims to protect society, by giving the public a temporary break from a persistent offender, or by removing dangerous offenders from society until they are no longer a threat, or, if necessary, incarcerating them permanently.

4. Rehabilitation, where a period in custody, or of supervision within the community, is used to rehabilitate an offender, so that in the future the person can contribute to society.

Although each of these consequences may be construed as utilitarian, they may conflict with each other. For example, as Simon (1995) observes, indeterminate sentencing, which is usually associated with a rehabilitative model, makes it harder for an individual to make rational calculations of the costs and benefits of criminal activities, while determinate sentences have been criticised for undermining both rehabilitation and incapacitation, because sentences cannot be individualised. So rehabilitation has been criticised by those who favour incapacitation and deterrence as well as from the retributivist standpoint.

Utilitarianism is also associated with the use of predictive or preventive sentencing to control future crime, in contrast to retributivism, which focuses on punishment for past crimes. In modern sentencing practice utilitarianism favours sentencing tailored to the individual, while retributivists support sentencing according to a tariff. Utilitarians use scientific knowledge to target resources effectively and counter limitless penal expansion, while retributivists argue that a desert-based theory which reserves prison for the most serious crimes limits expansion more effectively (see von Hirsch 1986). Moreover,

---

[6] For further discussion of rule and act utilitarianism, see Mill (1861) and Smart and Williams (1973).

utilitarianism may generate penal expansion through exemplary and predictive sentences, the most expensive penal option, although a strict application of the principle of parsimony should in some cases provide a brake on expansionism.

Utilitarianism has flourished in modern penal policy and practice because it focuses on future effects and seems more appropriate to the rational planning essential to a complex modern society. Utilitarianism, in effect if not name, is found in the Halliday Report (2001) and in the White Paper *Criminal Justice: The Way Ahead* (Home Office, 2001a). Similarly, in *Rebalancing the Criminal Justice System in Favour of the Law-Abiding Majority* (Home Office 2006a) the utilitarian approach is paramount; the key aims are cutting crime, reducing reoffending, and protecting the public. The stress is on meeting the needs of whole communities and giving more weight to the needs of the majority, including victims, and less to the offender, to protect the public from crime and to make the criminal justice system more efficient. Utilitarian considerations also underpin the current focus on the anti-social behaviour of deviant individuals and families which threatens the peaceful habitation of the majority.[7]

More attention is now being given to the risks of reoffending and measures to reduce reoffending. *Criminal Justice: The Way Ahead* (Home Office 2001a) further argued that sentencing should take more account of crime reduction, by considering the outcomes of sentences and what works for particular groups of offenders. It also emphasised that prisons need to focus more on preventing reoffending, such as preparing for work outside, as well as 'punishing'. The Labour government considered that the CJA 2003 had begun the process of putting more 'effective' sentencing and punishment in place but the 2006 White Paper, *Making Sentencing Clearer*, made clear that more work was needed to deal with prolific offenders including drug users (Home Secretary *et al.* 2006: para 1.19).

Utilitarianism also strongly underpinned the Coalition government's criminal justice policy, which was shaped by cost–benefit concerns. The Green Paper *Breaking the Cycle* (Ministry of Justice 2010a) focused on competition, promoting work opportunities and work discipline in prison, making prisons more cost-effective by using prisoners to contribute to prison services, and ensuring prisoners are in work rather than dependent on welfare when they leave custody, and reducing the financial burdens on the state. It also referred to the government's aims of reducing the costs of foreign national prisoners and cutting the number of remand prisoners, and increasing investment in drug, health, and alcohol services as part of the drive to cut reoffending. It also focused on payment by results to providers of rehabilitation services (Ministry of Justice 2011a: 7, 2014a). In *Transforming Rehabilitation* the emphasis was again on providing cost-effectiveness while transforming the way offenders are managed within the community, reducing reoffending through the use of incentives, protecting the public, and providing better value for money for taxpayers (Ministry of Justice (2013a). Pilots were initiated in Doncaster and Peterborough using financial incentives to motivate service providers to reduce reoffending and to maximise value for money (Ministry of Justice 2014a). These strategies seem likely to persist under the current Conservative government (see Chapter 1, section 1.4.5).

Similarly, in the United States the financial costs of prison expansion have led to greater attention on the effectiveness and efficiency of punishment, instead of focusing simply on retribution, which has been seen as contributing to that expansion. As Steen and Bandy argue (2007), these costs issues have encouraged increasing attention to the need to be 'smart on crime' and to target resources effectively, and this can stimulate penal reform.

---

[7] See also Chapter 11, section 11.1.2 for a discussion of the use of anti-social behaviour orders.

4.2.5 **Collateral issues**

We will concentrate, for the rest of this chapter, on the particular issues raised by deterrence. Incapacitation will be considered in Chapter 5 when we also focus on the discourse of risk and danger in penal policy because incapacitation—either in terms of custody or by using electronic means to control the activities of offenders in the community—has been the main tool for responding to the new concerns. Rehabilitation will be discussed in Chapter 10 when we focus on punishment in the community, as it is the Probation Service and the new community rehabilitation companies which will be at the forefront of offence- and drug-focused programmes to reduce reoffending. Offending behaviour programmes in custodial establishments will be considered in Chapter 8.

4.3 Deterrence

4.3.1 **Key concepts**

Penal institutions may combine individual and general deterrence: if conditions are harsh in prison it will deter the individual offender from reoffending and also warn those outside prison of the costs of committing a crime. For general deterrence to work, then, the public need to be aware of the probability of punishment, so perceptual deterrence must be enhanced. Bentham advocated using the principle of **less eligibility**, whereby the conditions in prison must be worse than those outside prison for the deterrent effect to operate on the individual or the general public.

Whether punishment does have a deterrent effect has been subject to debate and raises questions about how a deterrent effect may be measured or ascertained. Even if we accept the desirability in principle of using a particular mode of punishment or level of punishment to reduce crime rates, in practice we may have insufficient knowledge to ensure the success of a policy designed to deter. We also need to distinguish between primary deterrence, when a deterrent effect results from a punishment imposed on conduct previously unpunished, and marginal deterrence, changes in deterrence which result from an alteration in the level of punishment for actions already punishable. Most modern policy debates have been centred on increasing levels of punishment, rather than creating new criminal offences. Although the research so far has been most promising in linking effective deterrence to the certainty of punishment rather than the severity of punishment (see section 4.3.2), policy debates in the UK and the United States, as we saw in Chapter 1, have tended to focus on increasing the severity of punishment as a significant element of populist punitiveness.

So, even when there is a lack of evidence of a deterrent effect for a particular punishment and even when the economic costs are very high, it may be retained for political reasons, to satisfy public demands for high levels of punishment. The death penalty imposes substantial economic burdens in California and other retentionist states, but retains some public support, reflecting in some cases a belief in its deterrent effect. The 'three strikes' laws in California also imposed significant financial burdens, as they have contributed to the swelling prison population, with no compelling evidence of a deterrent effect (Domanick 2004; Barker 2009). However, the Three Strikes Reform Act of 2012 (Proposition 36), enacted in California, eliminated life sentences for those convicted of non-serious and non-violent crimes and introduced a procedure for those sentenced to life for a third minor crime to petition the court for a reduction sentence by showing they were not a risk to public safety. Over a thousand prisoners were released in the first eight months following implementation and the change is expected to lead to substantial cost reductions.

Deterrence theory was popular in the late 1970s and early 1980s in the work of writers such as J. Q. Wilson (1985) and E. van den Haag (1981), who argue that crime may be reduced through punishment. More recently the use of deterrence has been defended by Kennedy (2009), who focuses on deterrence as a process involving communication of risk of arrest and punishment to offenders.

On this approach, issues of desert are displaced to the outer limits of setting punishment scales. The emphasis in modern utilitarianism has been primarily on special deterrence rather than general deterrence, although the latter is still important. So Wilson is committed to the use of punishment to deter as well as to selectively incapacitate, and to using preventive detention when appropriate, strategies which would normally be prohibited on a retributivist model. In *Thinking about Crime*, he argued that deterrence does work in reducing crime and that it does so not simply by removing offenders from society (Wilson 1985). Wilson claims that there is sufficient evidence to justify the claim that the crime rate is influenced by the costs of crime and that we could reduce the crime rate by increasing the certainty of criminal sanctions. In terms of criminal justice policy, then, we should try to enhance the benefits of compliance while increasing the costs of crime. In assessing deterrence, argues Wilson, we need to calculate the amount of crime which can be prevented by increasing the certainty or the severity of punishments. He cites the example of Ehrlich's work on the death penalty, which calculated that for every murderer executed, eight murders were prevented (Ehrlich 1975).

For Wilson, crime is a rational enterprise and like other activities shaped by rewards and penalties, and, he argues, criminals make similar calculations to ordinary citizens: 'People are governed in their daily lives by rewards and penalties of every sort . . . To assert that "deterrence doesn't work" is tantamount to either denying the plainest facts of everyday life or claiming that would-be criminals are utterly different from the rest of us' (1985: 121). Even if criminals have a weaker conscience than others, they still take account of the costs and gains of crime and make rational choices. Profit maximisation and effort minimisation may also affect decisions regarding how and where a crime is undertaken, as Vandeviver *et al.* (2015) note in their study of burglary patterns and the selection of burglary targets. Deterrence theory is useful because it seems to fit our intuitions and because we act in ways consistent with it in everyday life, that is, we do engage in cost–benefit calculations. Research suggests that the certainty of sanctions is a major influence on this calculation.

4.3.2 **The certainty of punishment**

Despite methodological problems in devising appropriate experiments, there are some indications that the crime rate is influenced by the costs of crime, if detection, imprisonment, and punishment are certain. Wilson cites the work of Wolpin (1978), who examined changes in crime rates and changes in the chances of being arrested, convicted, and punished in the period 1894–1967 and found that 'changes in the probability of being punished seemed to cause changes in the crime rate' (Wilson 1985: 123).[8] Another example often cited is the experiment of Sherman and Berk (1983) in Minneapolis using different police strategies to deal with domestic violence. Those who were arrested were less likely to be reported to the police for subsequent assault than those receiving counselling or sent out of the house to calm down. Increasing police attention and intervention in domestic

---

[8] However, Wilson acknowledges that it may be difficult to draw a sharp distinction between rehabilitation and special deterrence, as both involve inducements and negative sanctions for non-compliance with therapy and both involve restrictions and coercion.

violence incidents in Killingbeck, West Yorkshire, in 1997 also led to a substantial reduction of reoffending (Hanmer *et al.* 1999).

There is evidence to suggest that, when certainty is removed, the crime rate increases:[9] for example, during the Melbourne police strike in 1923, mobs poured into the city and looting lasted for two days before order was restored. In Egypt in the spring of 2011, during the period of the uprising when the police force was weakened, crime increased. The initial absence of a strong police presence on the streets was also seen as a significant element in the continuing disorder in UK cities in the summer of 2011. In Britain, when the breathalyser was first introduced, there was a decline in road accident casualties (Ross 1973). If fear of detection does reduce crime, then an increased police presence may be more useful than increasing the severity of sentencing.

Kennedy (2009) cites the example of the successful elimination of overt drug markets in a US city, High Point, in North Carolina, where dealers were carefully identified and information on their activities accrued to a point where an arrest warrant could be issued. At that point dealers were called to a meeting and advised that if they continued they would be arrested, so the consequences were made very clear. Attention was also focused on strengthening community norms against dealing. The strategy succeeded, as the drugs market vanished and the nature of the community changed. Moreover, displacement of those activities did not occur. As Kennedy observes: 'it is what matters to offenders . . . that matters in deterrence. It means that if offenders do not know about the sanctions they face, those sanctions cannot matter' (ibid: 182).

Wilson argues evidence suggests that 'changes in the probability of being punished can lead to changes in behaviour' (Wilson 1985: 137). Even in crimes undertaken under the sway of emotions, rational calculations occur. He gives the example of the fact that the arrival of a police officer will often end a fight and that costs are still calculated at times of heightened emotions, so in a pub brawl one is likely to avoid hitting the toughest opponent, while arguing couples will avoid throwing the best china. Similarly, Kennedy (2009) points out that even psychopaths will avoid killing in front of the police and drunk drivers will drive more cautiously if they see a police car.

Wilson argues that we need to see people's deterrability as lying on a continuum. Some people have strong internal restraints on their behaviour and may also think how much they have to lose by being caught, but others may have few internal controls yet fear external constraints of imprisonment. Some have little fear and few internal constraints; others may wish to commit crimes because of their status within a criminal subculture. Some individuals, he argues—mostly young males—will lack strong internalised restraints on misconduct and greatly value a quick reward. Others may conform not simply because of the fear of formal sanctions but because of the belief that crime is morally wrong, while others will commit crime regardless of the risk, and others are 'only dimly aware that there are any risks' (Wilson 1985: 252). For some, informal sanctions such as the stigma of a criminal conviction and the shame of the criminal prosecution may be sufficient.

The results of some UK surveys reflect this complexity. A *Youth Lifestyles Survey* conducted in 1998/9 asked 12–30-year-olds what would stop them committing a number of crimes. Almost half (45–47 per cent) of respondents said they would not commit any of the specified offences because 'it was wrong'.[10] On the other hand, in a MORI *Youth Survey* in 2000, 45 per cent said that the main deterrent would be 'worry about how parents react', while 45 per cent also said that 'fear of being caught' would have the biggest effect. The

---

[9] For further discussion of the significance of certainty, see Blumstein *et al.* (1978), Beyleveld (1980), and Ross (1992).

[10] Details can be found at http://www.esds.ac.uk/findingData/snDescription.asp?sn=4345.

2004 survey, perhaps not surprisingly, found that '[y]oung people who commit the most offences are the least likely to think being caught will stop them from offending' (Youth Justice Board 2004a: 41).[11] Clearly the options open to respondents in their replies are crucial here but, just as important, we need to know more about the social context in which offending occurs and the impact of other influences on decision-making before we can adequately assess the research findings.

The issue of certainty of detection has been considered in the context of the use of closed-circuit TV cameras (CCTV) to deter crime, but the results have been variable. Gill and Spriggs (2005) conducted a study of the impact of cameras across 13 sites but found a decline in crime in only one case which could be attributed to their presence, namely vehicle crime in a car park. A review of the impact of CCTV by Welsh and Farrington also found that CCTV reduced crime only to a small degree, but was most effective in car parks (Welsh and Farrington 2002). However, cameras may, of course, still have value in providing evidence of crime, and technological tools are being increasingly used to deter car and other crime (see Lyon 2006). For example, the DVLA has developed a set of initiatives to deter car crime including a range of vehicle identity checks.[12] Research on offenders suggests that they are unconcerned about cameras, but those who have been caught through cameras see them as more of a threat. Civil libertarians have argued that the case for CCTV surveillance as a crime detection strategy has not yet been made out and have highlighted the dangers of breaches of the right to privacy and the need for greater regulation (see Crossman 2007; Mathiesen 2013). Furthermore, the use of surveillance technologies may also reflect political and social processes rather than the extent of the threat. As Coleman and McCahill (2010) note, far more effort and expense is expended on surveillance relating to benefit fraud than tax evasion, although the latter incurs greater economic losses to the public purse. Nonetheless, the use of surveillance technologies has increased on the assumption that they may deter and can increase public protection. A Code of Practice governing the use of surveillance cameras including CCTV, automatic number plate recognition, and other surveillance technologies came into force in 2013, under powers established in the Protection of Freedoms Act 2012 (Home Office 2013). While evidence of deterrence may be inconclusive, the cameras may assist in the detection of crime and provide evidence in support of prosecutions.

Deterrence theory has been criticised by those who reject the underlying rational choice approach to crime, while others argue that the empirical research is not encouraging and that crime rates and recidivism have increased despite deterrent sentencing, and some question the methodology used to 'prove' a deterrent effect.[13] Critics of deterrent penalties usually point to the high rate of recidivism as evidence of their failure to deter.

Instead of saying 'nothing works', we can say that deterrence may be intermittent and that some people may be temporarily undeterrable. Certainly the association of crime rates with the length of imprisonment is weak. Much of the research on deterrence is on the deterrent effect of the death penalty on homicides, but less is known on other offences, although homicide may be comparable to serious assaults. A person who is minded to consider the consequences before committing violence is more likely to focus on *whether* he is likely to go to prison rather than how long. Deterrence may also be effective in corporate contexts. Tombs and Whyte (2013), for example, argue that deterrence has been underused in corporate regulation particularly in relation to workplace safety, and that corporations

---

[11] See, for links to MORI *Youth Surveys*, http://www.yjb.gov.uk/publications/Scripts/prodView.asp?idProduct=187&eP.

[12] See http://www.direct.gov.uk/en/Motoring/VehicleCrime/index.htm.

[13] See, for example, Robinson and Darley 2004.

have the resources to gather information on which to make rational calculations regarding occupational safety.

Von Hirsch *et al.* (1999) reviewed research on deterrence from the 1970s to the late 1990s and found the research shows that deterrence does work and that recent studies continue to support the thesis that the certainty of punishment can affect decisions to offend. Increasing certainty of punishment, they conclude, can increase marginal deterrence. Changes in sentencing policies may also affect how a crime is committed rather than whether to commit it; for example, the decision to expedite a burglary to avoid staying at the crime scene. In the research drawn from England, the United States, and Western Europe, we do find a negative correlation between certainty of punishment and crime rates. The National Academy of Sciences Research Study (Blumstein *et al.* 1978) drew attention to the methodological problems of proving the effects of either incapacitation or deterrence on crime rates, but did find that deterrent sanctions influenced *some* individuals. But deterrence remains an important aim of sentencing both by the courts and in relation to on-the-spot fines. For example, deterrence is a key rationale behind the introduction of fixed penalties for careless driving (Easton and Piper 2013).

4.3.3 The severity and celerity of punishment

However, the evidence is much less convincing for a link between the *severity* of punishment—that is, how stringently the person is punished once caught, whether a custodial sentence is imposed, and its duration—and crime rates (von Hirsch *et al.* 1999). For example, research by Weatherburn and Moffatt (2011) into the specific deterrent effect of high fines on drink-driving offenders in New South Wales found no significant deterrent effect from higher fines. This was despite substantial variation in the fines imposed in the study sample by magistrates. They found that offenders had a low perceived risk of apprehension, which may in part reflect the number of times the driver has previously been stopped by the police after drinking and also how many times his past drink-driving has gone undetected. However, a study of driving under the influence cases in Washington found some evidence to suggest that severity of punishment reduced recidivism in both the short and the long term (Hansen 2014).

Furthermore, although perceptions of severity are important, changes in severity levels will be less visible and immediate than a stronger police presence and perceptions may not match the reality of sentencing. What evidence there is suggests that the length of imprisonment is less important than the certainty of imprisonment and increasing sentence length will not produce corresponding gains in deterrence. In the United States, we find falls in crime rates in states with and without harsher sentences.

The celerity of punishment also needs to be considered, that is, how quickly the punishment is delivered. Beccaria (1767) argued that punishment should be enacted as swiftly as possible to strengthen the association between the ideas of crime and punishment and that delay would weaken the link between the two ideas. Bentham also argued that in calculating the consequences of an action, the proximity of the punishment to the offence would be considered and weighed against the immediacy of the profit of the offence (Bentham 1789: 169). So, if the individual receives immediate gratification from the offence, this may well be more significant than the prospect of a distant punishment.

The importance of speedy justice was considered in the Coalition government's White Paper, *Swift and Sure Justice: The Government's Plans for Reform of the Criminal Justice System*, which emphasised that 'justice needs to be swift to be effective' (Ministry of Justice 2012c: 2). It set out plans to speed up the criminal justice process to ensure that offenders are punished more speedily and that courts dispense justice more quickly. It also noted that 'the prospect of being caught is a greater deterrent to criminals than the severity of the punishment' (ibid: para 9). The swiftness of punishment as well as cost reductions also account for governments' increased support for fixed penalty notices.

However, the celerity of punishment has been under-researched compared to certainty, although it has been discussed in relation to capital punishment, where there can be considerable lapses of time before the punishment is carried out, and in relation to penalties for drink-driving (see Ross 1992). But informing drug dealers that they would be arrested and punished on a specific date in the near future was effective in the High Point study (see Kennedy 2009). The delays in delivering the punishment have been seen by supporters of the death penalty as weakening its deterrent value. Jeffrey (1965) argues that it should be enacted immediately to be an effective deterrent. However, Bailey (1980) found no evidence that the speed of executions was significant.

The importance of celerity of punishment was also stressed by the former Director of Public Prosecutions as a factor in bringing the riots in England in the summer of 2011 to an end:

> For me it was the speed [of processing cases] that I think may have played some small part in bringing the situation back under control . . . I don't think they [rioters] would have thought: 'Oh well, am I going to get 12 months or 18 months? 'I don't think people gamble on the length of sentence, particularly. They gamble on: 'Am I going to get caught? Am I going to get sentenced and sent to prison?'
>
>   (http://www.guardian.co.uk/uk/2012/jul/03/riot-prosecutions-sentences-keir-starmer)

His conclusion accords with research over many years which suggests that the certainty of being caught and convicted, and possibly also the celerity of the pre-sentence process, are more significant factors in producing a deterrent effect than the severity of the sentence.

4.3.4 **The mode of punishment**

The role played by the actual nature of the penalty is less clear, although there are some positive examples. Replacing parking fines with wheel clamps in central London did lead to a substantial decline in illegal parking (see Walker 1991). We also know that disqualifications are more feared by drivers than fines (Department for Transport 2013). So the nature of the penalty may be a consideration (see also section 4.4.1). Fixed penalties for driving using a mobile phone did lead to a decrease in the proportion of drivers observed using hand-held phones (Walter 2010).

Reconviction rates have been used as a measure of the effectiveness of different types of punishment in deterring and/or rehabilitating offenders and research on reoffending is regularly conducted by the Home Office. A study of England and Wales in 1972 referred to by Walker (1991) found that reconviction rates for imprisoned offenders were better than for those with suspended sentences, which suggests that the experience of prison deters more than a mere threat. However, more recent studies have found little difference between prison and community punishments (see for example the discussion of the debate on prison versus community punishment in Hough *et al.* 2013).

Kershaw *et al.* studied the reconviction rates of offenders sentenced or discharged from prison in 1995. They found that 58 per cent of all sentenced prisoners discharged in 1995 were reconvicted of a standard list offence within two years (Kershaw *et al.* 1999). Standard list means all **indictable offences** and some of the more serious summary offences, such as indecent assault, child neglect, and assault on police officers, but it excludes most summary motoring offences. For offenders commencing community penalties, that is, what were in 1995 community service orders, probation orders, and combination orders, the reconviction rate was 56 per cent. So after taking into account all possible relevant factors, in this study there was no significant discernible difference between custodial and community penalties. The results of similar comparisons suggest little real difference in reconviction rates for earlier years: 44 per cent of offenders given a conditional discharge and 43 per cent of offenders fined for a standard list offence in 1995 were reconvicted for another such offence within two years, and there were lower rates for fines and discharges than for community penalties.

A study published by the Home Office in December 2005 supplied information on reoffending by adults, defined as those over 18 (Cuppleditch and Evans 2005). The reoffending rate of adults increased from 57.6 per cent in 2000 to 58.5 per cent in 2002. For the purposes of this research, reoffending means that the offender committed an offence within the two-year follow-up period and was convicted in court. The figures relate to those released from prison and those who commenced community penalties in the first quarter of 2002. A follow-up study was conducted in March 2007 for the Home Office by Cunliffe and Shepherd (2007). This showed that for 2004 the reoffending rate was 55.5 per cent. As not all of those who reoffend may be caught or convicted and some may reoffend beyond the two-year period, these figures may be underestimates of the true reoffending rate.

An analysis of the reconviction of prisoners based on a longitudinal survey, *Surveying Prisoner Crime Reduction*, was published in 2010 (Ministry of Justice 2010b). Data from the study on reoffending rates for adults discharged from custody or who started a court order under probation supervision between January and March and who were reconvicted at court within one year showed a reconviction rate of 40.1 per cent (Ministry of Justice 2010b). The reoffending rate for juveniles who received a reprimand or warning, left custody, or started a court order was 37.3 per cent. A comparison was made of short custodial sentences (less than 12 months) and court order commencements under probation supervision. This found that the latter were more effective than short custodial sentences in reducing one-year reoffending rates. Completion of a cognitive-behavioural programme, *Enhanced Thinking Skills*, also reduced the one-year reconviction rate.

Data on reoffending for the year ending December 2013 found that 26.5 per cent of offenders released from custody, or who had received a non-custodial conviction, caution, or reprimand, reoffended during a one year follow-up period (Ministry of Justice 2015a). This constituted an increase of 0.5 per cent compared to the previous year. For adult offenders the overall proven reoffending rate was 25.4 per cent, but for juvenile offenders it was 37.9 per cent. The proven reoffending rate for adult offenders released from custody was 45.8 per cent, a fall of 5.6 per cent since 2003. For adult offenders commencing court orders, that is, community sentences or suspended sentence orders, the proven reoffending rate was 34.3 per cent, a fall of 5.6 per cent since 2003 (ibid: 5). For juvenile offenders released from custody, the reoffending rate was 66.5 per cent, a fall of 8.4 per cent since 2003. For juvenile offenders given a reprimand, warning, or youth caution the reoffending rate was 29.7 per cent, an increase of 4.2 per cent since 2003 (ibid: 12).

4.3.5 **The type of offender**

A number of factors affect the propensity to reoffend, including age, sex, and previous criminal history. Some studies of recidivism have found that men are more likely to be reconvicted than women, teenagers are more likely to be reconvicted than older offenders, those with the greatest number of previous convictions are more likely to be reconvicted in future, and the unemployed are also more likely to be reconvicted than the employed (see Kershaw *et al.* 1999). Reoffending rates also vary with the type of offences. Research by Brunton-Smith and Hopkins (2013) using data from the *Surveying Prisoner Crime*

Reduction survey also found that previous reoffending was the most important factor in predicting reoffending. Those convicted of acquisitive crimes were more likely to reoffend than those sentenced for other crimes and insecure accommodation, employment need, and substance misuse were also good predictors of reoffending. Brunton-Smith and Hopkins also note that prisoners who received additional punishment in prison were more likely to reoffend, as were former truants and those who had served shorter sentences. Age was also significant, with each year of age associated with a 2 per cent reduction in reoffending.

The *Surveying Prisoner Crime Reduction* survey (Ministry of Justice 2010b) considered prisoners' early life experiences, accommodation, education and employment, substance use, and mental health needs. Data based on the sample of prisoners studied found that reconviction rates were higher for prisoners who reported seeing violence in the home as a child, and for those who had been expelled or excluded from school. Higher reconviction rates within one year were seen for 79 per cent of offenders who were homeless before entering custody. The survey confirmed that prisoners were less likely than the general population to have worked before entering custody and more likely to have been homeless. Of the sample, 81 per cent reported using drugs before entering prison. The highest reconviction rates were found in the sample for those who were poly-drug users in the four weeks before entering custody, that is, using Class A drugs with Class B and/or Class C drugs. Juveniles receiving a reprimand or warning had a higher proven offending rate than adult offenders receiving a caution. In all, 17 per cent of offenders said that they had been treated or counselled for a mental health or emotional problem in the year before their imprisonment.

In Kershaw's study burglars had much higher reconviction rates than sex offenders. Prisoners serving sentences for burglary, theft, and handling were most likely to be reconvicted within two years (Kershaw *et al.* 1999). The rates were 77 per cent for burglary and 69 per cent for theft and handling. The lowest rates, calculated as the percentage reconvicted within two years, were 18 per cent for sexual offences, 29 per cent for fraud and forgery, and 33 per cent for drug offences. Most of the prisoners were not reconvicted for the same offence, although they were more likely to be convicted if originally convicted for burglary or theft. The reconviction rate was higher for young male offenders than for adult males. Those originally convicted for homicide and released on licence have lower reconviction rates than other offenders, which has implications for the debate concerning the alleged uniquely deterrent effect of the death penalty. Although reconviction rates for women were lower than those for men in the 1990s, in 2002 reconviction rates for women in England and Wales reached the same level as those for men (Home Office 2003f). Older offenders tend to have lower reconviction rates than younger offenders; reconviction rates are lower for those serving longer sentences. The greater the number of previous convictions, the higher were the reconviction rates. So past criminal history is the most influential variable for prediction of any future offending, although controlling samples to take account of prior probabilities of reconviction may be difficult.

Of course we cannot know for sure whether some individuals did reoffend but simply did not get caught. We also cannot infer a causal connection from a correlation without further analysis of the intervening variables. However, given the contemporary concern with risk management, an actuarial approach to criminal justice could take these statistics at face value, without a full understanding of the underlying factors, and could concentrate resources on those offenders perceived to be most at risk of reoffending (see Chapter 5).

Gender is also an issue to consider, although gender differences in relation to deterrence have been under-researched. However, Corbett and Caramlau (2006) studied the deterrent effect of speed cameras and found significant differences between men and women on issues of driver safety: women drove more safely than men, were more safety-conscious, and were more positive regarding the value of speed cameras than men. Male drivers in the study were more likely to have been 'flashed' by cameras at least twice and were more likely to view them as a money-raising exercise than as a genuine contribution to road safety. Differences were also found between older and younger drivers, with the former being more safety-aware.

Deterrence theorists assume that people's attitude to lawbreaking is rational and calculating, that we obey the law to avoid the pain of punishment, but there may be a moral obligation independent of the fear of consequences, as retributivists would argue. Many of us think it is wrong to steal irrespective of the penalty, and this element has received little attention within deterrence theory. Moreover, for those who do comply, this may be based on normative factors rather than fear of punishment. From the standpoint of the state the aim should be to secure normative compliance, where individuals obey the law because they believe it is morally right to do so rather than because of the fear of detection or punishment. Jackson *et al.* (2012) stress the importance of legitimacy in compliance with the law, so the power of the police to enforce the law must be seen as justified to ensure compliance.

Moreover, rationality may not be universal and the development of reasoning skills is an important feature of offending behaviour programmes which use cognitive-behavioural models, which suggests that rationality can be developed. Cognitive-behavioural programmes have been used with some success with sex offenders (see Moster *et al.* 2008). We also do not know if offenders will favour short-term benefits against longer-term costs.

4.3.6 Methodological problems in proving deterrence: interpreting the evidence

The difficulty is how to test the deterrent effects of punishment. It may be unclear whether individuals were deterred by the unpleasant experience of a penalty, reformed because they now believe it is wrong to offend, or rehabilitated by being given useful employment. It is also unclear whether we should measure the deterrent effect of imprisonment simply by looking at those who have already been punished and returned to society, or at the population as a whole who may be tempted to commit a crime, that is, general deterrence. Those who have already committed a crime have shown themselves to be less deterrable than the rest of the population, because they have already risked punishment by committing the crime. Moreover, desistance from crime may be uneven—some may commit further offences less frequently, others may commit less serious offences—so desistance takes place gradually rather than abruptly, but this makes it harder to measure (see Kazemian *et al.* 2009; Shapland and Bottoms 2011). It may also be affected by wider structural changes which require social policy responses (see Farrall *et al.* 2010). Moreover, as Walker (1991) notes, many studies measure the objective probability of conviction when it is the subjective probability which is the most important influence on behaviour, as a low estimate of risk is usually associated with high frequency of offending and vice versa. So potential offenders may consider whether they are likely to get caught and the possible consequences.

The methodology is also crucial in determining the correct timescale if we try to ascertain the likelihood of future offending, or view offending retrospectively. If there is a long delay then the initial response to a change in sentencing levels may no longer operate, and if there is a short delay then it may be too early to consider whether the individual has been fully deterred. The deterrent effect of a change in punishment may also decline over time, a process known as deterrence decay, as perceptions of apprehension change—for example if individuals think they might have miscalculated the chances of being caught or overestimated the rigour of enforcement. Furthermore, studies of deterrence do not always distinguish sufficiently clearly between the issues of certainty and severity.

If we consider general deterrence, we find that some societies with relatively harsh systems of punishment, such as the United States, also have high crime rates, which are used to justify the high incarceration rates (see Garland 2001a). When crime rates do fall, it may be hard to link this with the degree of severity of punishment, but the fact of being punished may be more important than the precise level of punishment. Moreover, when we look at these statistics, we face the problem of isolating the precise causal effect of punishment from the numerous intervening variables and of distinguishing deterrent and incapacitating effects. If we find an increase in punishment severity and a fall in crime rates we could not immediately infer a causal relationship. We need to know whether the changes actually led potential offenders to refrain from crime, and clearly many factors may influence the final crime figures.

Official statistics are notoriously inaccurate as a true measure of crime; for example, figures on prison populations may be an inaccurate measure of criminal activity if not all offenders are caught and punished, and of course if this is well known it may undermine the deterrent effect of punishment. Prison numbers may fluctuate as a result of sentencing policies and guidelines as well as the range of factors considered in Chapter 1.

Even if the crime rate fell following an increase in punishment, we cannot be sure that this resulted from the punishment rather than from the numerous other factors which affect crime. If we find a group for whom a particular punishment does have a deterrent effect, it may be hard to generalise. Moreover, sanctions may affect behaviour without necessarily deterring; for example, sanctions against drugs use or arms dealing may lead users and arms dealers to become more secretive rather than giving up their habit or curtailing their trade.

Aggregated statistics may obscure local variations in law enforcement and local applications of sentencing policies. A comparative study of California, Washington, and New York by Barker (2009) showed that key differences in local political institutions and democratic traditions shape penal and social policies. Similarly, Garland examines the implications of local democratic traditions for the survival of the death penalty as 'it continues to be driven by local politics and populist politicians' (Garland 2010: 33). As he observes, 'In America . . . all politics are local and democracy can kill' (ibid: 310). Because power is devolved to the local level and individual politicians are accountable to the local populace, there is much more scope for majority public opinion to prevail on this issue.

Interpreting the relationship between punishment and crime using official statistics is difficult. We also need to control for other significant variables which might affect crime rates. If crime rates fall as the quantum of punishment increases, we cannot infer a causal effect; we need to know whether the increase affected the behaviour of offenders or whether other factors were operating, such as cultural factors or strong religious sanctions. We also know from the experience of some European states, such as the Netherlands, that less harsh sentencing policies and lower imprisonment rates do not necessarily lead to a sudden increase in crime rates.

The problem for utilitarian theory is to calculate the optimum level of punishment. If punishment is increased over time it may have diminishing returns, if individuals do not believe it will apply to them or think that they will not be caught. If an increase in punishment produces an immediate response in terms of crime reduction, this may not be sustained in the long term. So a punitive policy may prove uneconomic on the principle of parsimony, regardless of the issues of unfairness which would trouble retributivists. An increase in sentencing levels across the whole range of crimes may also weaken the gap between serious and less serious offences. An increase in punishment at the lower end of the scale may be unnecessary if it is excessive for those who would have been deterred by a lesser punishment and are unlikely to commit offences in any case. On the other hand, an increase at the higher end may have little effect on those strongly committed to criminal activity or with long criminal careers. Some of these issues have been addressed in relation to the death penalty.

4.3.7 **The death penalty**

In the UK the death penalty has not been available as a sentence since 1965. However, we are including a brief discussion here because research on whether the death penalty for murder has a unique deterrent effect has been an important element of the debate on deterrence. Empirical research in the 1950s and 1960s in the UK and other jurisdictions challenged its unique deterrent effect and brought into question the underlying assumptions of deterrence theory. However, deterrence theory revived in the late 1970s, and Ehrlich's work on the deterrent effect of capital punishment contributed to this revival (Ehrlich 1975). While it might be argued that the offence of homicide raises specific issues which make it hard to generalise research findings to many other offences, murder is not so dissimilar to other serious offences against the person.

Many defenders of the death penalty still argue that the death penalty has a uniquely deterrent effect in preventing future crime—particularly homicides and drug trafficking offences—thereby promoting public welfare, although evidence of this is inconclusive. Sarat (1976) argues that, if the public were fully informed about the absence of a unique deterrent effect, their attitudes would change. But public support for the penalty also may be based on retributivist grounds and on the belief that no other penalty can match the enormity of the crime or communicate public anxieties over law and order so powerfully.

The debate on deterrence has produced much empirical work, often conflicting in its findings, which is beset by difficult methodological problems, some of which have been discussed in this chapter. The body of work has been reviewed periodically and the empirical research suggests that the death penalty does not have a unique capacity to deter.

The Royal Commission on Capital Punishment's Report (1953) found that the evidence available at that time did not support the claim that abolition of capital punishment would lead to an increase in homicide rates, or that its reintroduction after abolition would lead to a fall in homicide rates. Reviews of research in the 1980s (Zimring and Hawkins 1986) and the 1990s (Bailey and Peterson 1997) also found no conclusive proof to support the claim that it had a greater deterrent effect than life imprisonment. There was no clear link established between the penalty and changes in crime rates. Given that the death penalty is given relatively rarely and the sentence is not always carried out, its deterrent potential may be limited. The US Supreme Court has also justified the penalty principally on retributivist grounds as an appropriate punishment and an expression of public censure for the most heinous crimes rather than because of its deterrent effect.

We can find abolitionist societies, such as Canada, where the homicide rate fell after the death penalty was abolished, in contrast to the UK where the homicide rate increased in the 1960s following abolition. However, the increase in the homicide rate was smaller than the increase for other violent offences which were not affected by abolition.

In the United States we can find variations in crime rates in states with and without the death penalty, which suggests that other variables may influence crime and homicide rates. Murder rates are lower in non-death penalty states than in states with the penalty and this gap has increased over the past ten years. In societies which have used the death penalty to control drug trafficking, such as Malaysia, drug trafficking has continued despite these penalties, which has led some to argue that measures such as surveillance, crop elimination in supplier states, and building up local economies may have more success in controlling the supply of drugs. Hood and Hoyle (2015) also conclude from their review of the evidence that it has not provided scientific proof to support the hypothesis that capital punishment, as practised in the US, deters murder more effectively than the alternative punishment of life imprisonment. A Committee on Deterrence and the Death Penalty was convened to review the available research in the United States in the 35 years since *Gregg v Georgia* (1976). The Committee concluded that 'the research to date is not informative about whether capital punishment decreases, increases, or has no effect on homicide rates' (Nagin and Pepper 2012: 2). It argued that the available evidence should not be used to inform judgements regarding the effects of the death penalty on homicide, noting that lack of evidence is not itself evidence for or against the claim of deterrence. Of course deterrence is only one of many factors which may inform judgements on whether the death penalty is good public policy.

There are several reasons why it is difficult to sustain the argument for the unique deterrent effect. First, the causes of crime are complex; punishment is only one factor in crime control and may be swamped by other factors which affect offending. It is difficult to draw any meaningful inferences from the figures from longitudinal studies before and after abolition, because of the difficulties of isolating the causal effect of abolition. But even if a correlation were found between the death penalty and high or low crime rates, this would not of itself establish a causal link. Donohue and Wolfers reviewed the available statistical evidence on the United States and found that 'the death penalty . . . is applied so rarely that the number of homicides it can plausibly have caused or deterred cannot be reliably disentangled from the large year to year changes in the homicide rate caused by other factors' (Donohue and Wolfers 2006: 791). Prisoners who are given capital sentences may find their sentence reversed through exoneration or through the appellate process, so the executions are carried out relatively rarely. In practice the majority of defendants sentenced to death serve life imprisonment instead. Societies moving towards abolition may use the penalty less frequently in the years leading up to abolition because of changing attitudes, which may make it difficult to accurately test the deterrence thesis. There is also the problem of determining the appropriate time span for comparison. The Royal Commission found some examples where societies experienced an increase in crime rates for a short period following abolition, but there was no long-term increase in crime. Cross-cultural comparative studies are difficult as one may be comparing societies with quite different cultures, legal systems, criminal procedures, and social problems.

Second, if many homicides are committed under the sway of emotions or psychological disturbances, or in a state of panic, or under the influence of alcohol or drugs, it is unlikely that offenders weigh up the consequences of their action and consider the outcome in a rational way. It may well be that many murderers do not make a meaningful decision to kill at all initially, let alone weigh up the penalties if caught. Of course some homicides are premeditated but even those who do calculate rationally may find the prospect of a long prison sentence as frightening as a quick death. Project criminals, that is, professional robbers who commit well-planned and organised crimes purely for financial gain, may be more calculating, but may still think the risk worth taking as they are unlikely to get caught precisely because the crime is highly planned. Examples of project crimes would be the Great Train Robbery in 1963, the Heathrow Brinks-Mat Robbery in 1983, and the Hatton Garden raid in 2015. Moreover, the certain and self-inflicted death of the perpetrator may already be an essential element of the modus operandi of some crimes, as in the case of the modern suicide bomber.

The Royal Commission did find an American case where a man drove his wife across the state line before killing her because there was no death penalty there, but not all homicides will be so calculating. In the case of premeditated terrorist or political crimes, the perpetrators may not be deterred if their motives are altruistic rather than individualistic. Thirdly, murderers as a group have relatively low rates of reoffending compared to other offenders, and good parole records. This might be used to support the claim that prison has a sufficient deterrent effect, or simply indicate that the nature of the crime is such that it is unlikely to be repeated. A study in New York of the period 1930–61 found that of 63 first-degree murderers released on parole, only one committed another crime (see Stanton 1969). Similar results have been found for other states and in later studies (see Marquart *et al.* 1989; Bedau 1997).

What we can say is that the death penalty may have a stronger deterrent effect than other methods of punishment on *some* people, but a negligible effect on others. Imprisonment may be sufficient to deter some potential murderers, but not others. Given that it is difficult to establish the uniquely deterrent effect, and in the absence of conclusive evidence, the utilitarian principle of parsimony would suggest that it would be better to use more humane methods of punishment if they can achieve the desired deterrent effect in a less painful way. However, the fact that the deterrent effects are inconclusive may not defeat the case for the death penalty. For example, van den Haag (1985) argues that, even if the deterrent effects of the penalty are uncertain and inconclusive, it is still better to risk the lives of convicted murderers than to risk the lives of innocent people who might be possible future victims. When outcomes are uncertain, he argues, future victims should be given more weight in our calculations than convicted murderers. From a utilitarian standpoint it may also make the majority of the public happier in reflecting their wishes. The penalty may also be defended on retributivist grounds, as we saw in Chapter 2, while Kramer (2011) defends the use of the penalty for the most horrific crimes, offering a free-standing justification independent of deterrence-based and retributivist arguments. However, those who oppose the penalty on human rights grounds, who see it as inhuman and degrading punishment, are unlikely to be persuaded by any evidence of its deterrent effect or beneficial social consequences (see Council of Europe, Parliamentary Assembly 2011).

4.4 Problems with the theory and practice of utilitarianism

4.4.1 Does deterrence work?

In view of these problems and the available empirical research, we cannot say that deterrence never works, but we can say that punishment may deter fewer offenders and potential offenders than we would like. Prison deters some offenders, provided that they are in deterrable states of mind. There is also some limited evidence that deterrence operates at the other end of the penalty scale. Research in the 1980s on 'regulatory offences'—where there is a breach of a regulation, generally an omission rather than a deliberate act of commission—such as road fund licence evasion or not declaring excess duty-free goods, suggested that people were deterred by having to go to court and receiving adverse publicity rather than by the size of the fine (Orton and Vennard 1988: 168). The exception was TV licence evasion, where 40 per cent of respondents regarded the size of the fine as a deterrent (ibid). However, the researchers pointed out that respondents gave their answers within the context of 'mostly mistaken' ideas about the likelihood of being caught and the maximum level of fine (ibid: 175–6).

In the context of custody, the 'pains' of imprisonment may affect different offenders differently. In a study of the subjective experiences of adolescent male offenders in Germany sent to prison for the first time, Windzio found that there was a deterrent effect from the deprivation of contact with people outside the prison, but this did not affect those without strong bonds, so prisoners will experience prison in different ways. He also found no deterrent effect from the fear of other prisoners, but rather found that 'the higher the fear of other inmates, the higher the rate of recidivism' (Windzio 2006: 341).

For deterrence to work, it is not essential that all individuals conform to Bentham's model of economic rationality, calmly calculating costs and benefits using the felicific calculus. The question is whether deterrence operates to a sufficient extent to influence enough people to make a difference to crime levels and make a deterrence-based policy justifiable. Some individuals may be acting under the impulse of emotions or mind-changing substances, or may simply have so little to lose that an increase in certainty or severity of punishment would have little effect. Von Hirsch (1999: 36) cites Farrington's (1997) work to show that impulsivity is a key characteristic of persistent offenders which raises problems when using deterrent strategies in such cases.

Moreover, increasing levels of punishment and drawing more individuals into the punitive net may have the effect of normalising punishment so that it is less stigmatising. Within criminal subcultures the experience of surviving harsh punishment may itself be a source of status within the group and imprisonment may become more tolerable over time as the individual develops adaptive strategies. This is discussed, for example, in Clemmer's work on the process of '**prisonisation**', which examines how different groups adapt to imprisonment (Clemmer 1940), and also in later studies by Toch (1976), Gravett (2003), and Crewe (2013).

Explaining why punishment fails to deter in some cases may mean we need to look at the social context of offending, drawing on the symbolic interactionist approach in criminology, to focus on the effects of labelling and the changing self-image. Moreover, incarceration may itself provide increased illegitimate opportunities to commit crimes, both inside prison and on release, in enabling offenders to make contact with each other. Punishment is only one factor in reoffending. Research using data from OASys, the Offender Assessment System, shows that offenders have on average four problems or 'criminogenic needs' which may contribute to their offending: for example, accommodation, unemployment, substance misuse, and low levels of educational achievement (see Harper and Chitty 2005). Many offenders have poor basic skills, which contribute to their poor employment histories, and these are the issues which need to be addressed in rehabilitation programmes in custody and in the community.

In testing the effects of specific policies we need to know whether potential offenders were aware of those changes, whether the changes affected their behaviour, and if so, what they perceived as possible outcomes and the significance of being punished within their social groups. Perceptual deterrence is under-researched but what we do know is that people's awareness of sentencing may be misinformed and unrealistic, as we saw in Chapter 1, section 1.2.3. If the public underestimate levels of punishment or the certainty of punishment then the deterrent effect of a change in policy will be weakened, so perceptual deterrence is crucial. Improving the public's understanding of sentencing policy and practice is an important feature of current penal policy and this may not only reduce the fear of crime, but also communicate the risks of committing crime to potential offenders. Most research on perceptions so far has been on whether fear of punishment will affect the decision to offend, rather than on whether a specific change in severity, certainty, or celerity of punishment will affect decision-making. Perceptions of severity and celerity should therefore also be considered at the subjective level. Hirtlenlenher et al. (2014) examined the interplay of perceptual deterrence and level of self-control in explaining differences in self-reported offending, using data from Austria, Belgium, and

Slovenia, and found that 'the impact of the perceived risk of apprehension on offending depends on the individual's level of self-control ... the deterrent effect of formal intervention is greatest for individuals with low self-control' (Hirtlenlenher *et al.* 2014: 144). Kennedy (2009) also argues that the risk of detection in many cases is very low and offenders are aware of this, but deterrence can be effective if attention is focused on selected offenders and groups and if messages are clearly communicated, because 'a risk that is not known cannot deter' (ibid: 27).

4.4.2 **Theoretical difficulties**

Criticism has also been levelled at the underlying principles governing utilitarianism as well as the specific problems raised by the utilitarian theory of punishment. The problem with a deterrence-based approach is that increasing severity of punishment imposes substantial economic costs, but also social costs, increasing the social exclusion of offenders. Moreover, an indiscriminate increase in levels of punishment may weaken the gap between less and more serious crimes and undermine the incentive to commit less serious crimes. A deterrence policy may itself be a high-risk policy if it imposes social costs without the benefits of crime reduction. Using the utilitarian calculus, we need to consider whether to focus attention on crimes which affect large numbers of people such as property crimes; or crimes which affect fewer people but cause more damage, such as crimes of violence; or whether to focus on crimes where risks are widely distributed or where they are concentrated. We also need to decide who to include in the calculation: just victims of crime or also those whose lives may be affected by fear of crime. So refining sentencing policy will require these calculations and the problem, as we have seen, is that we may not have the necessary information to formulate an effective policy on utilitarian criteria, regardless of the issues it raises for retributivism.

Punishing the innocent

A strong objection to this theory is that it potentially allows for punishment of the innocent if circumstances warrant it. As a majoritarian approach, utilitarianism accepts that the individual may be sacrificed for the benefit of others, in sharp contrast to the Kantian view that people should not be treated as a means to an end but rather as ends in themselves. For example, it is possible that punishing innocent third parties, such as relatives of the offender, could achieve greater deterrence than punishing the specific offender. Some regimes have done this: in Stalinist Russia the Criminal Code created the offence of being a relative of the enemy of the people, and a principle of collective family responsibility and punishment of relatives for the transgressions of individual family members is in operation now in North Korea. It was also reported in 2003 that a utility company in Vladivostok planned to confiscate the family pets of those who did not pay their electricity bills. Yet our moral intuitions tell us that the punishment of the innocent is morally wrong and unjust.

   Bagaric (2001) notes that utiliarianism lost favour because it seemed unable to confine punishment to wrongdoers and punishment of the innocent is inconsistent with the concern for individual rights. But, he argues, punishment of the innocent is no worse than many other measures we condone in extreme situations. If society is faced with desperate circumstances then it may have to sacrifice individuals for the good of the whole. In any case, retributivists have to accept that punishment of the innocent is a possibility, as any system of punishment is open to error. While the risk of error could be substantially reduced by improvements in criminal procedure, for example, by a corroboration requirement for confessions, it would not necessarily be eliminated.

Punishing the guilty: the problem of proportionality

Utilitarianism also raises problems even if punishment is confined to the guilty because it does not take sufficient account of proportionality, yet this is a fundamental principle of systems of law in France and Germany, European Union law, and the European Convention on Human Rights: the punishment should be proportionate to the crime and the remedy should be proportionate to the mischief. In the United States the Supreme Court will hold grossly disproportionate sanctions invalid under the Eighth Amendment, the constitutional prohibition on cruel and unusual punishment.

But while there is room within utilitarian theory for proportionality, it may be jettisoned when the public interest demands. Bagaric (2001) argues that proportionality is the best way of dealing with the issue of severity of punishment and sanctions should be commensurate to the offence. A disproportionate sentence undermines the criminal justice system and leads to social disorder, while proportionality improves the consistency and fairness of the sentencing process. But unlike retributivism, the proportionality principle is not absolute. However, he argues, we should retreat from proportionality only when necessary to pursue a more pressing utilitarian objective of punishment.

Ethical problems

Once proportionality is rejected in favour of utility, there may be consequences which are ethically unacceptable. Nothing is ruled out a priori on a strong utilitarian approach if it maximises happiness and public welfare. If we find that those with longer criminal histories are more likely to commit future offences, then a risk-based strategy could allow this to determine the length of sentence and extended sentences might be justified on grounds of enhanced deterrence as well as incapacitation.

For most retributivists the sentence should be based on the current offence and the risk of reoffending is irrelevant to the sentence given, as we saw in Chapter 3. Even those, such as von Hirsch, who accept that first offenders should be treated less severely than recidivists would still argue that primary emphasis should be given to the current offence and that any differential between first offenders and recidivists should be kept as low as possible. In practice most modern sentencing systems have far too wide disparities and premiums are not necessarily effective. Kazemian reviewed the available evidence and concluded that 'extended sentences for repeat offenders may, under certain circumstances, lead to crime reductions in the short term, but such policies are less likely to impact recidivism rates in the long term' (Kazemian 2010: 242).

For retributivism, as we have seen, desert is always the prime determinant of the severity of punishment for different offences. Once any minor deviation is allowed, it opens the door to larger deviations. As von Hirsch says: 'in practice, it may be quite difficult to permit only small deviations from desert parity, while holding the line at larger deviations. The operation is like inviting the hungry Doberman to share in the family picnic, but only one bite' (1986: 163).

However, Bagaric (2001) does reject additional weighting of past convictions, because it violates the principle of proportionality and effectively punishes the offender twice for the same offence; instead he favours fixed penalties. He also argues, from a utilitarian standpoint, that suspended sentences should be abolished because they involve no pain for the offender. He favours using sanctions such as the denial of work and education, even if this incurs welfare costs, as they will still be cheaper than imprisonment.

A further difficulty is that it is not clear whose interests policy-makers should be concerned with—those living now or in the future, whether short-term or long-term effects should take priority, and how conflicts between them should be resolved. This is important for penal policy in deciding whether to pursue an expansionist prison policy or to focus on the underlying causes of crime where the benefits may take longer to reap.

The concept of the individual

Difficulties also arise with utilitarianism as a theory of human behaviour. No coherent account is given of the disinterested individual, although Bentham does accept that they exist—indeed, he sees himself as one, trying to make social life better for others—but altruistic individuals are still seen as deriving pleasure from helping others. The assumption that people are governed by self-interest is clearly a crude generalisation. To dismiss altruistic individuals as pleasure-seeking does not do justice to them. Moreover, given that most criminal activities are undertaken in the context of group activities, whether gangs or subcultures or criminal networks, any intervention needs to take account of group dynamics (see Kennedy 2009).

Bentham's model seems to reduce humans to 'cheerful robots', when other motivations may supersede the pursuit of pleasure and it is hard to find a place for perfectionist aspirations within this model. His assertion that pushpin, a precursor of bingo, is equal to poetry in his *Rationale of Reward* (1825) would be challenged by perfectionists who would distinguish higher from lower pleasures, particularly when formulating public policy and funding allocations. It is also difficult to apply his felicific calculus if there is a 'subjective' element and one person's pleasure is another's pain, or to talk meaningfully of calculations in the moral sphere. However, one might defend Bentham's model of the self-interested individual governed by the quest for pleasure and avoidance of pain by saying it fits *enough* people to make policies based on it workable, even if there are some exceptional individuals who cannot be accounted for within the theory. In the case of Aristophanes' *Lysistrata*, the example given by Kennedy (2009), the eponymous heroine is motivated by altruistic wishes to end the Peloponnesian War, and yet successfully uses the threat of a ban on sex by the women of Sparta to deter the men from continuing warfare.

4.4.3 **Rights versus utility**

The role of rights in the utilitarian model is also problematic. Bentham (1843) in his discussion of the French Revolution himself dismisses rights as mischievous nonsense, and there is no room in his approach for non-legal rights. On the contrary he is extremely sceptical regarding their value in resolving difficult ethical, social, and political problems because, he argues, rights cannot be construed apart from positive law (see Schofield 2007). Even if we could identify fundamental rights, sooner or later rights conflict, and when that happens we have to weigh up conflicting interests and fall back on utility. It is this potential for rights violations which underpins the liberal critique of utilitarianism. But for liberal critics such as Dworkin (1977, 2011), rights should trump utility.

Yet utilitarianism, as Bagaric (2001) argues, is not necessarily antagonistic to rights. There is room for rights within utilitarian ethics as the recognition of rights promotes utility. An example here would be Mill's argument in *On Liberty* (1859) that the right to free speech leads to the truth and to social progress, and may therefore add to the happiness of the community. But for the utilitarians rights have no independent life of their own. Utilitarianism can also resolve clashes between rights, by considering the consequences when rights conflict, thereby providing a rational way of deciding between competing rights claims in such cases.

4.5 Reflecting on the issues

4.5.1 Alternative approaches

Utilitarianism, as we have seen, offers more scope for individualised sentencing, while retributivism favours a 'tariff' approach. But are these the only possibilities? Given the inherent problems with both retributivism and utility, several writers have tried to combine the two. For example, Brooks (2012) seeks to develop a new 'unified theory' which draws on both consequentialist and retributivist theoretical approaches, while Braithwaite and Pettit (1990) have formulated a consequentialist theory of justice which seeks to retain the future-oriented approach of utility and the use of calculations, but which treats individuals as persons rather than as means to ends and which focuses on autonomy and choice. But they are critical of proportionality, the linking of the sentence to the gravity of the offence. Braithwaite and Pettit refer to dominion rather than utility, by which they mean the individual's ability to exercise choice over how he or she lives. This would act as a restraint on sentencing because a very severe sentence would not enhance an individual's sense of control over his life. In sentencing, calculations could be made considering how much loss of dominion was caused by crime and fear of crime and how much a particular level of punishment would reduce the dominion of the person punished. The aim would be to find an optimum level which gives least loss of dominion. They also argue for a decremental strategy which reduces the levels of punishment until the point that crime starts to increase. Von Hirsch is critical of this approach and says that it would be even harder to devise a scale of punishments on this approach than on traditional utilitarianism. Moreover, on their theory preventive detention could be justified because the extended sentence would protect the dominion of potential victims. But this may open the door to the intensification of punishment if the protection of victims' dominion warrants it, especially if fear of crime is also taken into account—issues which will be discussed further in Chapters 5 and 7.

4.5.2 Discussion questions

This chapter has discussed a major theory relevant to sentencing and punishment. You may wish to consider the following questions. Guidance on answering the questions is given in the Online Resource Centre.

online
resource
centre

1. From a utilitarian standpoint, what are, or should be, the key purposes of punishment?
2. Is harsher punishment effective in reducing reoffending?
3. Consider the problems raised by utilitarian approaches to punishment.

4.5.3 Case study

To clarify the differences between the utilitarian approach considered in this chapter and the retributivist approach discussed in Chapters 2 and 3, you may wish to reflect on the following scenario. Guidance on tackling this question is given in the Online Resource Centre.

online
resource
centre

Consider the following problem:
Following lengthy deportation and extradition proceedings, John Demjanjuk was extradited from the United States to Germany in 2009 on 27,900 counts of being an accessory to murder, based on allegations of his involvement, as a camp guard, in the murder of prisoners at Sobibor Concentration Camp in Poland in 1943. He had lived in the United

States with his family since 1952 and worked as a car worker. At the time of his extradition he was aged 89 and in poor health. He had unsuccessfully challenged his extradition on the ground of being too ill to travel and had arrived in court in a wheelchair and on a stretcher. At his trial in Munich he was convicted in 2011 and sentenced to five years in prison. He was released pending an appeal against his conviction and died in a nursing home in 2012 aged 91, before his appeal could be heard.

Task:

On the facts of this case, do you think the decision to prosecute John Demjanjuk in 2009 was correct? Give reasons for your answer.

5

Risk and danger

Summary

This chapter reviews the current policy focus on the 'dangerous' offender and the aim of protecting the public from the risk posed by an offender's reoffending. It discusses developments in relation to a 'culture of control' and examines the utilitarian justifications for selective incapacitation of offenders, or groups of offenders, believed to be dangerous. The chapter examines the changes in sentencing law, focusing on particular types of penalty and order, and the provisions for control of dangerous prisoners through discretionary release procedures.

5.1 Managing criminality

5.1.1 A culture of control

In Chapter 4 we reviewed utilitarian justifications for punishment and focused on deterrence. In this chapter we focus on another utilitarian tool—incapacitation—which uses the temporary removal or, in those jurisdictions with the death penalty, the permanent removal of an offender from public life. The purpose is the management of risk by preventing an offender from reoffending, or at least by confining his offending behaviour within the walls of the prison. Such incapacitative sentences include the **indeterminate sentences** that require evidence of rehabilitation before release[1] which are increasingly used for 'dangerous' offenders.

Many would see incapacitation as a key aim of punishment at the present time, at least for certain categories of offender. For them, even if there is no prospect of reform or deterrence of offenders, at least they can be contained. If this is the only justification, prison becomes simply warehousing, a concern voiced by Rivera Beiras when he referred to the painting reproduced on the cover of the second edition of this book. That was van Gogh's *The Round of Prisoners*, in which a circle of prisoners are moving around a prison courtyard; Rivera Beiras argued that, a century later, 'this human contingent can form another "round", another circular view: such a number could go twice round the world' (2005: 167). His aim was to illuminate worldwide trends towards new punitive rationalities which have resulted in a greater use of incapacitation through imprisonment (2005: 174–5).

Recent penal policies have included provisions for 'selective incapacitation', whereby selected offenders or those convicted of particular offences can be given custodial terms

---

[1] We leave until Chapter 10 an examination of the policy aim to lower reoffending rates of convicted offenders by tailoring community punishments and post-custody licence periods to individual offenders.

which could not be justified on retributivist principles. The development of such policies is rooted in ideas about crime control, about who counts as a 'dangerous' offender, and new techniques for the management of risk. Garland (2001b) referred to these ideas collectively as a 'culture of control', a culture which is underpinned by new criminologies—new perspectives on crime and criminality—which had developed by the end of the twentieth century.

Garland places these criminologies into two categories: criminologies of 'everyday life' and criminologies of 'the other' (2001b: 182–5). While both view crime as 'a normal, routine, commonplace aspect of modern society', they have very different conceptions of 'the criminal' and of responses to criminality (2001b: 15). From the perspective of the criminology of everyday life criminals are normal and rational, and can be deterred or diverted by systematic and pragmatic techniques. These might include situational crime prevention, that is, the reduction of opportunities for crime by removing security weaknesses or coordinating transport and housing systems. Garland characterises this approach as 'amoral and technological' (2001b: 183). It does not deal in values so it 'sits easily' with policies on the one hand that would exclude certain groups of people—if that would reduce crime—or, on the other hand, that would transfer increased crime prevention resources to the most vulnerable—if they are the targets for criminality.

The criminology of the other, by contrast, focuses on values and seeks to assert absolute moral standards. The very 'normality' of crime is a catastrophe and one to be combated by the imposition of order and authority. Furthermore, from this perspective, some criminals are decidedly not 'normal' but are, rather, evil or wicked. They are, then, dangerous, different from us and, being 'other', can be dealt with in ways, such as very long or indeterminate prison sentences or community exclusion orders, which we might not otherwise endorse (2001b: 184).

Crucially, both these criminologies view the offender in ways which are very different from the 'social criminologies' dominant in the mid-twentieth century (see Garland 2001b: chapter 2). In the context of enhanced notions of risk, 'the resulting sense of insecurity has led us to embrace habits and policies that would have seemed unthinkably repressive thirty years ago' (Owen 2007: 4) and which differ from the perspectives of classical utilitarianism which underpinned the more 'welfare'-orientated approach of non-custodial sentencing at that time. Indeed, Beckett and Western (2001) argue that states with social welfare are negatively associated with incarceration. So, in the United States, states with large minority populations, particularly those with larger black populations, spend less on welfare and have higher rates of incarceration.[2]

A shift towards a more exclusionary and punitive approach to the regulation of social marginality has, then, occurred together with a view that it is pointless to expect to find the underlying causes of crime, or to search for social or political explanations of crime, if the individual is responsible for crime. However, because the new criminologies conceptualise the offender differently from previous perspectives, they justify different responses. In what is referred to as a 'post-modern penality', the individual is, it is argued, increasingly invisible. He is submerged in the actuarial, group-based approach of the so-called New Penology to which we referred in Chapter 1 and, in the new penality, a 'superordinate goal' for punishment—a specified consequence—is absent (Feeley and Simon 1992: 459). This is not to say that outcomes are unimportant, but that, within this approach, the search for, and adherence to, general justifying aims and consequences are no longer of great

---

[2] Rehabilitationism, however, has survived the challenges of the past 30 years to emerge in a new form: see Chapter 10.

importance. However, the new criminologies have refocused thinking on the particular outcome of deterrence, and also buttress the incapacitative policies which this chapter will explore.

The movement to this more 'economic' approach to punishment has been evidenced by the increased importance of a managerial discourse in the criminal justice system and also by the pervasiveness of managerial concepts and aims such as effectiveness, key performance targets, quality audit, systems management, outsourcing, and value for money (see Chapter 1).

> Managerialism—with its portable, multi-purpose techniques for accountability and evaluation and its 'can-do' private sector values—has flowed into the vacuum created when the more substantive content of the old social approach lost credibility. The crime control field—from crime prevention work and policing to the prison regimes and the practice of parole—has become saturated with technologies of audit, fiscal control, measured performance, and cost–benefit evaluation. The old language of social causation has been displaced by a new lexicon (of 'risk factors', 'incentive structures', 'supply and demand', 'stocks and flows', 'crime costing' and 'penalty pricing') that translates economic forms of calculation into the criminological field.
>
> (Garland 2001b: 188–9)

We can contextualise one particular element of the managerial discourse, that of risk management, within 'the risk society'. This is the term which some theorists coined to symbolise the apparent increasing preoccupation with risk—at the level not only of the economic but also of the personal and political—by the end of the twentieth century.

5.1.2 **Notions of risk**

In Chapters 2 and 3 on retributivism and just deserts sentencing there was little reference to risk assessments or sentencing influenced by calculations of risk to public safety. It is true that sentencers must work within statutory maxima and offence categories that Parliament has imposed in response to particular perceptions of risk and danger: the sex offender legislation is one example of this, and the increase—by s. 1 of the Criminal Justice and Courts Act 2015—to life imprisonment as the maximum penalty for a range of terrorist offences is another. Just deserts sentencing, however, should not include an assessment of risk because it looks to the past rather than the future. So those provisions which entail an assessment of the offender's potential to reoffend and to harm members of the public inevitably sit uneasily alongside the sort of sentencing examined in Chapter 3, where the focus is (only) the seriousness of the offences already committed.

The end of the twentieth century saw a focus on the 'risk society', seen as one where the management of insecurity—of potential and unknown harms—had become the dominant theme (see, for example, Beck 1992; Giddens 1990; Vail et al. 1999). As Giddens noted, 'The idea of a "risk society" might suggest a world which has become more hazardous, but this is not necessarily so. Rather it is a society increasingly preoccupied with the future (and also with safety) which generates the notion of risk' (Giddens 1999: 3). Because scientific and expert knowledge cannot ensure certain and predictable outcomes when applied to individuals, generalised prescriptions regarding risk of harm have been developed so that decisions which reduce societal anxiety can still be made. In relation to children and young people, their 'scarcity' and irreplaceability have put a much higher premium on risk management (see Farrington 2007; James and James 2008; Piper 2008). In relation to offenders, the high political and economic costs of failing to protect the public from dangerous people (see Chapter 1) have similarly imposed such a premium.

There are three implications of these trends to which we wish to draw attention. First, the attempts to manage crime and risk of crime are not confined to sentencing. Indeed, the criminal justice system itself is only one part of a government's crime reduction and risk-management strategy. We review in section 5.2.1 this 'preventive turn' in policy and the range of new coercive measures used by the state. Paradoxically, therefore, sentencing has gained a greater political importance at a time when its practical effect is diminishing. Statistics which show how marginal sentencing is in terms of the ability to punish all those who commit offences underline the importance for governments of spreading crime prevention much more widely across policy areas. Much crime is neither reported nor recorded: only about 3 per cent of crimes are proceeded with by the police or CPS, and a large proportion result in a caution.[3]

Consequently, 'a whole new infrastructure has been assembled at the local level that addresses crime and disorder in a different manner' (Garland 2001b: 16) with programmes, initiatives, and partnerships such as Safer Cities, Neighbourhood Watch, the New Deal for Communities, and Multi-Agency Public Protection Arrangements (MAPPAs).[4] These are all geared towards strengthening communities and are orientated towards a new set of objectives, 'prevention, security, harm-reduction, loss-reduction, fear-reduction', that are very different from traditional criminal justice goals (Garland 2001b: 17). What we have then is a network of community 'empowering', crime prevention partnerships which utilise managerial techniques to produce the most cost-effective ways of managing risk and of targeting resources (ibid: 19).

The second implication of the trend towards the cultural pre-eminence of a managerialist and technological, risk-management culture is that it justifies a selective response to offending. Further, its emphasis on cost-effectiveness can cut across 'justice' issues, while Hebenton and Seddon (2009) argue that 'precautionary logic' is refiguring the institutions of law and science in the management of sexual and violent offenders. The use of risk-management tools, it is argued, has reduced professional discretion to decide suitable and individualised responses.

Third, these developments led to the evolution in the 1990s in the UK of a sentencing policy which treats what was until recently a very small minority of offenders as dangerous, Garland's 'other', from which the public needs protection. Such offenders are so 'risky' that a quite different sentencing framework is legitimate for dealing with them and it is legitimised on the basis that it will prevent harm to people in the future. How important is this focus on risk and preventive sentencing? We have made frequent reference to Garland's influential book, *The Culture of Control*. He began that text with the following statement:

> We quickly grow used to the way things are . . . On both sides of the Atlantic, mandatory sentences, victims' rights, community notification laws, private policing, 'law and order' politics, and an emphatic belief that 'prison works', have become common place points in the crime control landscape . . .
>
> (Garland 2001b: 1)

Not only have we grown used to the increase in crime but we have also, he argues, accepted harsher punishments for those selected, so that 'the most prominent measures of crime

---

[3] For a discussion of the difficulties of gaining information about crime including from official statistics, see Maguire (2002).

[4] See Nash and Williams (2008: chapter 4) for a discussion of MAPPAs and also the National Offender Management Service (NOMS) in relation to serious repeat offenders.

control policy are increasingly orientated towards punitive segregation and expressive justice' (2001b: 17). What has been justified is the development of means of exclusion such as the curfew and exclusion requirements in community orders and on **early release** which stipulate times and places that are 'out of bounds', and also the range of civil orders introduced by the Sexual Offences Act 2003, including foreign travel orders, which aim to control the dangerous with the threat of a penal sanction for non-compliance. Such prevention orders are reviewed in section 5.5.1.

Other analysts have endorsed this shift in the penal culture of Western punishment in the 1990s. Pratt explains this as a move from an era of the 'civilising' of punishment with the focus on seriousness that had characterised two centuries of penal policy (1998: 506). With new cultural notions of risk, such developments are not only acceptable but also, at least in the tabloid press at the beginning of the twenty-first century, are welcomed and encouraged. This has been described as 'a new culture of intolerance' (Pratt 2000: 47).

On the other hand, some commentators contend that these developments are not as novel as they are portrayed, and even Garland makes the point that nothing in the penal system has actually been replaced. His argument is, rather, that their repositioning has been crucial in changing the penal culture. Brown similarly argues, in the context of nineteenth-century colonial history, that current more punitive policies can be 'interpreted within a framework of *recursions* within penal modernity, rather than signalling an end or fundamental transformation of the modern state' (2002: 403), while Donoghue (2010) has provided an alternative analysis of responses to anti-social behaviour.

Further, the focus on the dangerous offender is not a totally new development: 'Like the poor the dangerous have always been with us' (Freiberg 2000: 51). Nevertheless, the categories of those who are perceived as dangerous have changed over time (Dingwall 1998; Pratt 1996; see section 5.1.3). More significantly, the Criminal Justice Act (CJA) 2003 used for the first time the heading 'Dangerous Offenders' and the term 'dangerousness'. Those terms were found in commentary and reports in the past, but not in sentencing legislation until 2003. Further, the numbers of those sentenced as 'dangerous' increased significantly after the implementation of that legislation.

5.1.3 **The dangerous offender**

Risk and the designation of individuals as dangerous are not inventions of the twentieth or twenty-first centuries. Many examples of groups being designated as risks to the social order can be found in the nineteenth century (Pratt 2000: 36) and legislation was part of a mix of protective measures being taken by the state at the end of the nineteenth century against various 'evils' such as unemployment, crime, and poverty—a form of early state risk management (ibid: 38). At one level, then, 'the dangerous' are those groups which represent social dangers which are historically contingent, shaped by the result of ideas and events from a specific time and place. Such groups are not confined to the population of (convicted) offenders.

Even in relation to the offending population, what we mean by dangerous offenders is place and time contingent. As the Floud Committee, which focused in detail on dangerousness, noted: 'Dangerousness is not an objective concept. Dangers are unacceptable risks' (see Floud 1982). This transfers the quest for a definition of dangerousness to the risk discourse and rephrases the analysis into a designation of those people and crimes seen as unacceptable risks.

These two levels are linked. The development of policy has been from a concentration in the early nineteenth century on 'dangerous classes' to the current emphasis on dangerous offenders, or groups of offenders such as sex offenders (Pratt 2000: 36–8) and, more recently, those involved in terrorist activities. However, there is also a development which has focused on the individual—the pathologisation of the dangerous offender. Mason and Mercer (1999) draw on Foucault's analysis of six serious cases during the period 1799–1835 to examine the medicalisation of the offender. That development construed dangerous offenders as mentally ill and brought into question the border between sanity and insanity. This can still lead to problematic responses in regard to both the dangerous offender and those with mental health problems (see section 5.4.5 and Chapter 6, section 6.4). As Greig notes, in relation to her analysis of a high-profile Australian case, 'When the fluidity of madness is superimposed onto the notion of badness, it elicits an intuitive sense of fear among observers' (Greig 2002: 11). In 2014–15 the attacks organised by ISIS/ISIL/Daesh led to many, including the Home Secretary Theresa May, referring to the terrorists as 'murdering psychopaths'.[5]

However, most preventive sentencing measures are aimed at the offender who is mentally 'normal': there are clear and separate provisions for those who fit within the legally defined category of the mentally disordered. Yet the normal offender is affected by those social ideas which fuse mental abnormality and offending because all offenders can then be seen as in some way as irrational and a threat. Consequently, the social fear they engender can be reduced by the imposition of indefinite and disproportionate custodial sentences. So, as we saw in relation to sex offenders in Chapter 1, when perceptions of such offenders as ill have become less powerful, they have been replaced by perceptions of them as evil (Simon 1998). Both constructions of the dangerous are, then, of the 'abnormal' and legitimise the continued surveillance of offenders when they are released on licence.

5.2 Incapacitation and public protection

5.2.1 Assessing the utilitarian justification

Incapacitation as a means of crime reduction is a strong strand in current penal policy in the UK and the United States. It gathered support in the early 1980s and was a key element of the penal policy of the Reagan administration in the United States. It has also been used in the UK since the early 1990s and is reflected in the tendency towards longer sentences as well as in some non-custodial penalties. For example, the disqualification of drivers for motoring offences is a form of precautionary, incapacitative sentencing. The controls on the movements of sex offenders discussed in Chapter 1 are also intended to reduce the opportunities to reoffend. States now take a wide range of measures in the name of crime prevention and public protection (see Ashworth *et al.* 2013; Ashworth and Zedner 2014). The effect of this 'preventative turn' in crime policy with its focus on incapacitation, as Peeters argues, is 'the subordination of rehabilitative concerns to the objectives of security and public order' (Peeters 2015: 176).

Incapacitation is a utilitarian approach because its aim is to maximise happiness and to protect the interests of the majority of society by restraining and removing dangerous offenders. For persistent offenders who are not dangerous, prison removes offenders from the community for a temporary period, even if it does not succeed in deterring them. Incapacitation is not necessarily incompatible with the justification of rehabilitation, as incapacitation could be combined with programmes intended to reform the individual. So in the UK we find a strong commitment to offending behaviour programmes designed

---

[5] See, for example, http://www.telegraph.co.uk/news/uknews/terrorism-in-the-uk/11072490/Isil-killers-are-murderous-psychopaths-says-Theresa-May.html

to rehabilitate offenders, as well as acceptance of **protective sentencing**. Offenders may, therefore, be incapacitated while recognising that there is no prospect of reform.

On the utilitarian model, society should be protected for as long as possible from persistent and dangerous offenders, so the individual's liberty is sacrificed for the greater good of society. While the most effective form of incapacitation is the death penalty, imprisonment is seen as the best method in abolitionist jurisdictions. However, there is still the risk of prisoners escaping, there may be opportunities to commit a wide range of crimes in prison, and offending may be resumed upon release, so incapacitation will not necessarily guarantee long-term crime prevention. Because incapacitation is an expensive penal policy, a shift towards the use of prisons as warehouses may mean that reduced funding will be available for costly treatment programmes within the prison. There is also the problem that when offenders are incarcerated, others will move into their territory and replace them, for example in relation to drug dealing.

There is also the question of whether prison does incapacitate effectively if released prisoners display higher offending rates than those completing community sentences because of factors such as the stigmatising effects of prison, the difficulty in obtaining employment on release, the effects of prison dehumanisation on the offender, and the opportunities to learn from other offenders. As we saw in Chapters 1 and 4, there is a high level of reoffending in the UK and the relationship between imprisonment and crime levels is a complex question, not least because of the problems of isolating the effects of imprisonment from other factors. But even if we could establish that imprisoning more offenders and increasing sentence length leads to a reduction in crime, we would need to assess the economic burdens. We know that incapacitative measures, such as the 'three strikes' laws in the United States, for example, have proved to be very expensive and that the indeterminate sentence for public protection introduced by the CJA 2003 contributed to the prison overcrowding problem in England and Wales (Piper and Easton 2006/7). By the end of December 2009, 6,034 offenders had been given imprisonment for public protection (IPP) sentences (see section 5.3.4) and there were 5,828 IPP prisoners in custody in January 2010, of whom over 2,500 were detained beyond their tariff (Jacobson and Hough 2010: 9).

As Jacobson and Hough point out, these IPP prisoners also have a very low release rate, due to a range of factors, including delays in obtaining Parole Board hearings, the problem of access to offending behaviour programmes which are a crucial step towards demonstrating that they are no longer dangerous, and the increasingly risk-averse decision-making of the Parole Board. The IPP sentence was replaced by new provisions for extended sentences in the Legal Aid, Sentencing and Punishment of Offenders Act 2012, but Bettinson and Dingwall (2013) note that despite the abolition of the IPP sentence, many inmates still remain in prison and need to convince the Parole Board that their continued detention is no longer necessary to protect the public. By the end of June 2014 there were 5,119 people still serving IPP sentences in prison, of whom 71 per cent had passed their tariff expiry date (Prison Reform Trust 2014b: 24).

There would be political advantages for governments in expanding the use of imprisonment and removing offenders from society, despite the economic costs, if it were clear that doing so would lead to a substantial reduction in the crime rate. But successive research studies suggest that even a large increase in the use of custody may achieve only a small cut in the crime rate, as punishment is only one factor linked to criminality (see Tarling 1993; Spelman 2000; King, Mauer, and Young 2005). The Carter Report (Carter 2003) calculated that only a 5 per cent reduction in crime in the UK in the period from 1997 to 2003 resulted from the higher custodial rates in that period. So using incapacitation as a crime reduction strategy is therefore an extremely expensive option and may not be cost-effective if large numbers must be incarcerated to produce a small effect on crime rates.

There are a number of reasons for the relative ineffectiveness of incapacitation. First, punishment is only one factor which may influence crime rates and it may be swamped by other factors. Second, the impact of punishment on crime will be limited if only a small number of offenders come before the court and receive custodial sentences. Third, as with deterrence, it is difficult to isolate the causal effects of incapacitation and an expanding prison population on the overall crime rate. Moreover, there is an inherent tendency for incapacitation to be an expansionist policy, for if mistakes are made in predicting high-risk offenders, then the public's response may well be to demand that the range of offenders/ offences within the net is broadened. Governments may be reluctant to resist pressures for more incarceration and so be unable to abandon incapacitation as a strategy (see Chapter 1).

In light of these problems, the tendency in recent years has been to focus on the incapacitation of those particular offenders or groups of offenders who are most at risk of reoffending. From a utilitarian standpoint it is better to target resources on the most prolific offenders and reserve prison for those most likely to reoffend, which would also reduce the overall costs of imprisonment at a time when those costs have increased. So studies have been undertaken to identify the offenders most at risk of reoffending.

5.2.2 **Selective and categorial incapacitation**

We also need to distinguish different forms of incapacitation. Selective incapacitation means incapacitating particular individuals who may be at high risk of reoffending, and here a variety of factors may be identified including employment history and drug use. Categorial incapacitation focuses on incapacitating those who commit specific categories of crime, who commit offences which carry a high risk of reoffending such as burglary. Both selective and categorial incapacitation are forms of predictive sentencing.

Selective incapacitation is attractive to policy-makers and governments as it offers the possibility of reducing crime by incarcerating the most crime-prone offenders, but it may also serve to contain the size of the prison population, by allowing precious resources to be used most effectively on those offenders. So it is not surprising that it is popular with governments. To calculate the risks of reoffending various indices have been used, including data on the individual's record, employment history, or other social circumstances.

However, selective incapacitation could be seen as unethical, as it may mean that an offender is given a higher sentence than the offender deserves if he or she is deemed to be at risk of reoffending and because it denies autonomy to the individual and sacrifices the principle of proportionality for the goal of public protection. It presumes the individual will follow a particular course of action in the future and punishes that person accordingly for a choice not yet made: we do not know that the individual would have reoffended, especially if he or she is a first-time offender. For both reasons it conflicts with retributivist principles. Such policies also raise the issue of who should shoulder the risk of harm: potential future victims, or the offender who may receive a longer sentence than he or she deserves.

Moreover, we are still a long way from certainty in our predictions of future offending. Research studies are usually based on convicted offenders rather than the wider population of offenders, which includes unconvicted and potential offenders. If we overestimate the risk, there is the danger of incarcerating unnecessarily. However, the public is more concerned that the risk will be underestimated, exposing them to the release of dangerous offenders into the community. If selective incapacitation of dangerous offenders is introduced, but the policy fails to detain all dangerous offenders, then there will be an increase in public demands to broaden the categories of risk. While risk-management techniques have become more sophisticated, they may still be insufficiently precise to provide a basis for fair and just penal policies and respect for the rights of offenders. The ability to predict risk accurately may be overestimated and this may mean extended and unjustified periods of detention.

Consequently, as the focus on human rights has become more important, this may come into conflict with the emphasis on risk management (Whitty 2011). So the Strasbourg Court has used Article 3 in *Vinter and others v UK* (2013)[6] and *Hutchinson v UK* (2015) to treat whole-life sentences as inhuman and degrading, if there is no prospect of review or release if the prisoner no longer poses a risk. The Court also found a breach of Article 5(1) in *James, Wells and Lee v UK* (2012) because of the lack of opportunities for the offender to show he no longer presents a risk, for example, by successfully completing rehabilitative courses.

But is selective incapacitation inherently unfair? We know from the available research that those with a criminal history are more likely to offend in the future than those who have never committed an offence. A person subjected to a protective sentence—that is, detained on the basis that he is likely to constitute a threat to the public—is not presumptively innocent but has committed exactly the type of offence for which he is being detained, and future detention or control may be justified on utilitarian grounds. However, it is hard to justify on desert theory, as we saw in Chapter 3, as the primary focus in retributivism is on the current offence rather than past or future offences and very limited weight is given to past offences. Moreover, because the offender possesses agency and autonomy, it is possible he will not reoffend. In any case, as von Hirsch (1986) points out, a predictive index would include factors such as drug use, age, and employment, factors which would usually be irrelevant to retributivist sentencing.

Because of these problems, many prefer categorial incapacitation, in which an entire class of offenders will be incarcerated to prevent reoffending. This meets the objection of unfairness raised against selective incapacitation. It satisfies the principle of equality, in so far as it treats, for example, all burglars alike, although we still cannot know for certain that everyone in the class, or indeed any of them, would have reoffended.

However, we do know that recidivism rates vary between offences. For example, murderers have low recidivism rates and robbers higher rates, so we could in theory maximise crime prevention by giving longer sentences to those with the highest potential for reoffending. Von Hirsch (1986) does find categorial incapacitation more compatible with desert theory than selective incapacitation, provided the sentence is linked to blameworthiness and proportionality. But while it satisfies the retributivist demand for parity between offenders committing the same crime, it does not give parity with other serious crimes. Even if we operate within broad desert limits on sentencing, we are still treating offenders as a class differently, on the basis of the offence, compared to other serious offenders. It is also problematic for rank-ordering if one offence is taken out of the ordering and also does not tell us where to anchor the scale, so it does not address the issue of cardinal proportionality.

An attempt to converge past and future crimes in crime prevention strategies will undermine the principles of fairness and proportionality. Von Hirsch is sceptical regarding Morris and Miller's (1985) attempt to converge prediction and retributivism by using prediction within broad limits governed by desert, so the punishment extended by dangerousness would not go beyond that justified as a deserved punishment independent of the prediction. As he says, this still raises the question of the reliability of evidence underpinning claims of dangerousness, as well as the moral objection that it is 'unjust to give unequal

---

[6] See Mavronicola (2014).

punishments—and thereby unequal amounts of condemnation—to offenders whose conduct is equally reprehensible' (von Hirsch 1986: 141).

5.2.3 **Mass imprisonment in the United States**

An extreme example of the use of incapacitation as a penal policy is to be found in the United States, where the imprisonment rate, that is the numbers in custody as a proportion of the general population, has increased substantially since 1972 and is much higher than in European, and particularly Nordic, countries. For much of the twentieth century the imprisonment rate in the United States was around 110 per 100,000. In 1972, the rate had decreased to 93 per 100,000 of the population, but it subsequently increased substantially, to 452 per 100,000 by 1999 and 743 by 2009; it fell to 698 in 2013. Indeed, the 1990s saw a doubling of the prison population until there were over two million in prison by 2001, a shift Zimring (2001) characterises as being from 'lock them up' to 'throw away the key'. By December 2009 the prison population of the United States exceeded 2.3 million, compared to 1.2 million in 1990, but it has since declined since to just over 2.2 million, a large number of whom are black.

According to Bureau of Justice Statistics, 37 per cent of prisoners in state or federal prisons on 31 December 2013 were black (Carson 2014). The expansion of imprisonment in the United States has been marked by the presence of young black males from urban areas. One in eight of black males in their twenties is in prison. As Mauer observes, 'If current trends continue, 1 of every 3 African American males born today can expect to go to prison in his lifetime, as can 1 of every 6 Latino males, compared to 1 in 17 White males' (Mauer 2011: 88S; see also Forman 2012). Reiter (2012) also found in his research on supermax prisons in the period 1987–2007 in California that the population was disproportionately Hispanic.

The incarceration of young black males had a number of social effects, including the disenfranchisement of a section of the population, an increase in the number of single-parent families headed by women in those communities, and the alienation of those groups affected. The result has been the overlaying of penal exclusion on racial and economic exclusion, so deepening social divisions. The 1990s were also marked by increasing inequality in the United States, as the gap between the middle class and working class widened. The economic costs of mass imprisonment are also substantial.

This shift towards 'mass imprisonment' and the increase in the number of black defendants has been attributed to a combination of factors, including the rise of determinate and mandatory minimum sentences and the war on drugs, which imposed much harsher penalties for crack cocaine, for which black Americans constitute the majority of offenders, than for powder cocaine, for which white and Hispanic defendants constitute the majority of offenders. There are also stronger penalties for offences committed within school zones and as young black Americans are more likely to live in densely populated urban areas rather than suburbia, they are also more likely to commit offences within these zones. Curry and Corral-Camacho (2008) found that young minority males in their sample of drug offenders in Texas suffered a heavier penalty at the point of sentencing. The Fair Sentencing Act 2010 passed by Congress aimed to reduce this disparate impact. Prior to the Act it took 100 grams of powder cocaine to trigger the mandatory minimum prison sentence for possession with intent to distribute, compared to 1 gram of crack cocaine, but the Act reduced the disparity to 18:1. In California, however, Proposition 47 imposed identical penalties for possession of crack and powder cocaine. The Supreme Court in *Dorsey v United States* (2012) also extended the application of the Act to persons convicted before the Act was passed but sentenced afterwards.

The three strikes laws—mandatory minimum sentencing schemes to deal with repeat offenders imposing lengthy sentences for a third offence, originally adopted in nearly half of states in the US—also narrowed the gap between serious and non-serious offences, so undermining the retributivist sentencing framework. The constitutionality of the three strikes laws was upheld in *Ewing v California* (2003) where a 25-year sentence imposed for a minor theft was held not to infringe the test of gross disproportionality (see the discussion in van Zyl Smit and Ashworth 2004). Garland argues that the persistence of capital punishment is also a significant factor as 'the availability of the death penalty permits very lengthy sentences of imprisonment, even life imprisonment without parole, to appear comparatively humane, thereby contributing to the nation's extraordinary rates of imprisonment' (Garland 2010: 312).

However, these incapacitative policies have proved difficult to sustain in the context of the fiscal crisis in the United States. As the prison population expanded, this led to increased pressure on the system, resulting in severe overcrowding with some prisoners sleeping in communal areas rather than cells, as well as heavy financial burdens. This problem was acute in California, where we find a conflict between pragmatism to keep costs down and populist demands for high levels of punishment (see Barker 2009).

The courts have also become more activist in demanding improvements in prison conditions which may only be achievable through reductions in overcrowding. In *Coleman v Schwarzenegger/Plata v Schwarzenegger* (2009) the California District Court ordered the state to reduce prison overcrowding within two years, and this was upheld by the US Supreme Court in *Plata v Brown* (2011). The case focused on the implications of overcrowding for mental and physical health as the overcrowded and squalid conditions undermined the ability to provide appropriate medical care. The court ordered that by end of 2013 the population should be 137.5 per cent of capacity. By the end of 2012 it had fallen to 147 per cent of capacity. As Simon argues, the case highlighted the fact that prisoners 'are now placed *at risk* by the prison system, rather than the source *of risks* that it prevents from circulating' (Simon 2011: 253). It is also a significant turning point, he argues, in recognising the humanity of prisoners.

The impact of the *Plata/Coleman* litigation is reviewed by Schlanger, who argues that it is 'likely to succeed in prompting a politically negotiated reduction in the state prison population back to the level of 1993' (2013: 196). She notes that procedures for parole hearings were amended and many prisoners were moved from state prisons to county jails, with the counties also taking responsibility for post-release supervision in some cases. Although the burden was shifted from state to county, the increase in the county jail population was still lower than the decrease in the state prison population, not least because the counties have greater discretion. The impact of fiscal crisis on decarceration was also seen in Canada in the 1990s. As Webster and Doob (2014) show, budget cuts in Alberta, Canada led to a decline in imprisonment in the province in the period 1993–7, although as they note, while financial pressures were the catalyst for change, the form it took reflected the specific history, culture, and politico-legal structures of the province.

A further important development in California was Proposition 36, which, as we saw in Chapter 4, amended its three strikes law and allowed those convicted of life sentences for a third minor crime to petition the court for a reduced sentence if they could show they were not a risk to public safety; this resulted in the release of a large number of prisoners. The measure came into effect in November 2012 and by September 2013 1,011 prisoners had been released, with considerable financial savings. Research by the Stanford Law School Three Strikes Project and the NAACP (2013) suggests that the recidivism rate for this group was lower than the average state rate. An earlier measure to limit three strikes laws in California to new violent and serious offences had been defeated by a public vote in 2004 (Barker 2009).

As a utilitarian measure, incapacitation has to be linked to social benefits which outweigh social and economic costs, but this is difficult to demonstrate in relation to mass imprisonment. However, policy-makers and politicians may be reluctant to jettison incapacitative policies despite costs, because of the rise in populist punitiveness and public anxiety over crime, particularly dangerous offenders, and the emergence of crime and punishment as a key political issue; and this may vary between states. Since 2013, as Porter (2015) notes, a range of measures in *some* states, including statutory changes and policies, have combined to reduce the population: for example, reclassifications of certain offences from felonies to misdemeanours, statutory limits on the length of imprisonment, relaxation of laws relating to possession of marijuana, and authorisation of a wider range of non-custodial options, as well as changes to juvenile justice. Efforts are also being made to pass a bill through Congress which would reduce mandatory minimum sentences for non-violent offences. Despite these developments, the issue of racial disparity persists and, as we have seen, the United States' imprisonment rate remains much higher than that of other Western states; it is currently the second highest in the world, exceeded only by the Seychelles (International Centre for Prison Studies 2016).

5.3 Old and new ways of sentencing the 'dangerous' offender

5.3.1 The history of protective sentencing

After the implementation of the CJA 2003 the then government stated that the Act introduced for the first time 'a distinction between dangerous and non-dangerous offenders as a basis of custodial sentencing' (Home Secretary *et al.* 2006: para 1.10; see also Piper and Easton 2006/ 7). This was not a valid statement to the extent that governments had tried various ways over many years to implement an aim of incapacitating selectively those considered at the time to be dangerous. What is clear is that, while the development of protective sentencing did not begin in the twenty first century, the sentences introduced towards the end of the twentieth century and since have been more draconian in application and extent.

The early provisions for preventive detention at the beginning of the last century were aimed at persistent offenders, 'habitual' or professional criminals, seen as a danger not because of the seriousness of their offending but because of their propensity to engage in criminality as a way of life. Such behaviour not only threatened in particular the propertied classes but was evidence of a continued refusal to conform. So, for example, the Prevention of Crime Act 1908 was passed in England and Wales providing for post-sentence preventive detention of five to ten years, while the Habitual Criminals Act 1906 was passed in New Zealand and the Crimes Act in 1914 in Australia.

However, the history of sentencing 'the dangerous offender' is littered with change resulting from perceived failure or from strong opposition. In England and Wales, for example, the 1908 Act was replaced by a sentence of preventive detention for 5–14 years by the Criminal Justice Act 1948. That in turn was replaced by the extended sentence in the Criminal Justice Act 1967 (Powers of Criminal Courts Act 1973), which was a custodial sentence with a much longer period of rehabilitative probation, aimed at the persistent more serious offender who was a risk to society. That sentence was abolished in the Criminal Justice Act (CJA) 1991 (see Dingwall 1998; Scottish Executive 1999: chapter 4) and replaced by the 'longer than commensurate' sentence, which has also been repealed, and there is now again an extended sentence with a longer period on licence.

The history of the earlier provisions stands in some contrast to at least one of the later provisions—the now defunct IPP sentence introduced by the CJA 2003—in that research on the operation of the earlier provisions indicated that they were little used (Dingwall 1998: 179; Freiberg 2000; Walker 1999: 62). Explanations have been in terms of judicial adherence to retributivist principles, suspicion of expert evidence, judicial concern at encroachment on sentencing discretion, or because of more widely held ethical, constitutional, or human rights concerns. We shall see that more recently enacted sentences tailored for use with the dangerous offender have left less discretion for the courts, and the extensive use of the IPP sentence was a result of that.

What have also changed are the categories of offenders who are now perceived as the most 'dangerous' to the public. The concern with 'habitual criminals' changed into what is now a relatively long-standing legislative concern with sexual and violent offenders that has continued as the focus of the newer sentences introduced or amended by legislation in and since 1991. However, the legislation has also added drug traffickers, domestic burglars, those possessing firearms, and, most recently, those engaged in terrorist activities to the list of the dangerous.

The crucial issues for discussion relate to the new protective sentencing framework introduced by the CJA 2003, which included a separate chapter in Part 12 dedicated to 'Dangerous Offenders'. As passed, sections 225–228 provided sentences of 'life imprisonment', 'imprisonment for public protection' (with comparable forms of detention for offences committed by those under 18 years of age: see Chapter 11), and an extended sentence (for under- and over-18-year-olds). These provisions have been subject to criticism and several amendments since 2003 and there is now a somewhat different menu of options: two life sentences (ss. 224A and 225) and a rejigged extended sentence (s. 226A). It should be noted also that the persistent offender is again viewed to an extent as a social danger: in the CJA 2003, the repetition of offences may be part of the 'proof' of risk in some of the provisions, and is a mandatory aggravation in relation to all provisions (see Chapter 3, section 3.2.4).

To summarise, we shall see that the methods which governments have used to try and ensure that those deemed dangerous are 'controlled' for as long as possible, and, therefore, longer than what would be proportionate to seriousness, fall into two main groups: those imposing indeterminate or (longer) determinate sentences where the release date depends on assessment of risk, and those which impose an extension to the licence period after imprisonment and/or the imposition of incapacitating conditions on the licence period. The first group—those leading to forms of longer selective incapacitation—clearly raise rights issues and cut across judicial discretion and so have led to criticism. Where that criticism has been heeded by the government and the sentences have been withdrawn, the task has been to develop new forms of sentence which act as 'solutions' to each of these criticisms. The second group use the licence period for both control and rehabilitation and so their 'success' depends on the perceived or actual effectiveness of the supervision. We will discuss recent examples of these methods in the following sections.

5.3.2 **An additional custodial element**

The first new protective sentence in the more recent past was the 'longer than commensurate' or LTC sentence, introduced by the CJA 1991,[7] which enabled sentencers to impose longer determinate custodial sentences on those convicted of sexual or violent offences

---

[7] Later consolidated in ss. 79(2)(b) and 80(2)(b) of the Powers of Criminal Courts (Sentencing) Act (PCCSA) 2000 and repealed by the CJA 2003, Schedule 37, Part 7.

than were proportionate to seriousness. This amounted, in effect, to selective (additional) incapacitation. The range of violent and sexual offences to which these provisions related was relatively narrow, reflecting the continuing policy aim to reduce custody for most offenders while allowing for (longer) custodial sentences for a very small minority of dangerous offenders (see von Hirsch and Ashworth 1996). The sentence could be used if 'only such a sentence would be adequate to protect the public from serious harm from [the offender]' and in such cases the sentence was 'for such longer term (not exceeding that maximum) as in the opinion of the court is necessary to protect the public from serious harm from the offender'.

'Serious' harm had already been interpreted by the courts in *Birch* (1989)[8] but this new sentence left several key issues to be interpreted by the courts, notably the crucial question of the likelihood of reoffending and whether the calculation of risk could be based solely on a history of previous similar convictions (see Clarkson 1997: 287), but the most difficult issue for the sentencer was the calculation of the 'additional element' to be added to a pro-portionate sentence. Cases took a variety of views about the 'enhancement', though Clarkson (1997: 289) found an average enhancement of 73.5 per cent in cases in the period 1993 to 1997. *Chapman* (2000) stated that there was no necessary ratio between the punishment—justified on retributivist principles—and the protective parts of the sentence, but in practice the often short periods of extra incapacitation did not seem to offer the public protection which justified them (Clarkson 1997: 285; see also Walker 1999; Freiberg 2000).

The new sentence also raised an issue which was to become increasingly important—whether it was rights-compliant. *R (Giles) v Parole Board* (2004) tested the legality under Article 5(4)[9] of the European Convention on Human Rights (ECHR) of implementing the extra period of custody without an independent review once the punitive element had been served. However, the Court of Appeal and then the House of Lords stated that the whole sentence was pervaded by a punitive element and so not to be treated as having two parts. Not surprisingly, therefore, it was argued that Parliament and the Court of Appeal were at cross purposes (Dingwall 1998), that rights issues had not been given adequate appellate consideration, and that, in any case, the preventive LTC sentences were being used only sparingly by the judiciary.[10] Clearly this 'additional custodial element' approach was not effective and the CJA 2003 discontinued the LTC sentence.

5.3.3 **Mandatory (minimum) sentences**

The second set of new sentences introduced in the 1990s used a different method for selectively incapacitating repeat offenders. They specified particular minimum sentences the courts had to impose in relation to particular offences, but they were also problem-atic because they severely restricted judicial discretion and raised rights issues. (See also Chapter 2, section 2.2.5.) Until 1997, only one mandatory penalty was in existence for use by English courts—that of life imprisonment for murder. That was deemed, in *Lichniak* (2001), not to contravene either Article 3 or 5 of the ECHR[11] but the judiciary, in this and

---

[8]   In relation to s. 41 of the Mental Health Act 1983.

[9]   'Everyone who is deprived of his liberty by arrest or detention shall be entitled to take proceedings by which the lawfulness of his detention shall be decided speedily by a court and his release ordered if the deten-tion is not lawful.'

[10]   Flood-Page and Mackie (1998) found in 1995/6 that only 3 per cent of custodial sentences for violence, and 6 per cent for sexual offences, were given LTC sentences.

[11]   The judgment in *Offen No. 2* (2001) was distinguishable because that dealt with cases less serious than murder. Note however that the (English) Privy Council has jurisdiction over territories where the death pen-alty still pertains. See, for example, Bailin (2002) for rulings on death penalty cases in the Eastern Caribbean.

other jurisdictions,[12] has resisted the imposition of other mandatory provisions. Indeed, there is some intermittent pressure for repealing the mandatory sentencing for murder (see Mitchell and Roberts 2012).

The new sentences, added by ss. 2–4 of the Crime (Sentences) Act (CSA) 1997 and re-enacted in ss. 110–111 of the Powers of Criminal Courts (Sentencing) Act (PCCSA) 2000, are still in force and are mandatory in relation to specified forms of reoffending. In effect Parliament specified offending histories where it believed custody should be imposed, possibly where the court would not otherwise use custody or where a shorter term might have been imposed using a strict just deserts approach.

These particular provisions mandate a minimum sentence for a third specified offence. The court must impose a minimum sentence of seven years on the third conviction for a Class A drug trafficking offence and three years on a third domestic burglary conviction. There is a 'get-out' clause: the 'unjust to do so' provisions in ss. 110–111 which can be used to justify a departure from the rule.[13] The burden is on the defendant to show that such a sentence would be 'unjust' and so a pre-sentence report is usually required—*R v Densham* (2015)—but *R v Gallone* (2014) made clear that the fact that an offender did not receive custodial sentences for the previous drug trafficking convictions did not mean it was unjust to apply s. 110.

Ashworth argued for the relative unimportance of these provisions, given that most third-time offenders would receive seven years in relation to drug trafficking (Ashworth 2002b: 1096). However, while the number of third-time burglars sentenced under this provision was only six in 2001, it rose to 13 in 2003, 46 in 2004, and 89 in 2005 (Home Office 2007c: Table 2.6). Figures given to Parliament in September 2011 show that many third-time burglars do not get an immediate custodial sentence, although 778 did, but it is not clear from Crispin Blunt's answer whether those sentences were for three years or more (see Table 5.1).[14]

Table 5.1 Sentencing on a third burglary conviction

All offenders	2006	2007	2008	2009	2010
Absolute discharge	—	1	—	—	—
Conditional discharge	3	2	6	4	5
Fine	1	2	1	—	—
Community sentences	34	38	38	34	52
Fully suspended	23	36	51	38	37
Immediate custody	434	500	620	692	778
Other	3	14	22	21	29
All offenders	498	593	738	789	901

Source: Hansard, 7 September 2011 col 630W.

[12] See, for example, van Zyl Smit (2000) in relation to similar sentences introduced in South Africa in 1997.

[13] For examples of cases where the mandatory minimum custodial sentence was not imposed because it was 'unjust in all the circumstances' see *Hoare* (2004) and *Gibson* (2004); see also guidance on this matter in *McInerney and Keating* (2002).

[14] Available at http://www.publications.parliament.uk/pa/cm201011/cmhansrd/cm110907/text/110907 w0001.htm.

Further mandatory sentences have been introduced since 2000. Sections 287 and 292 of the CJA 2003 amended the Firearms Act 1968 and the Firearms (Northern Ireland) Order 1981, respectively, to provide for a mandatory minimum sentence of five years' imprisonment for those aged 18 or over in England and Wales (21 or over in Scotland and Northern Ireland) convicted of possessing a prohibited firearm.[15] For those aged 16–17 in England and Wales (16–20 in Scotland and Northern Ireland) the mandatory minimum is three years. Section 29 of the Violent Crime Reduction Act 2006 added a mandatory minimum five-year sentence for using someone to mind a weapon.

LASPO 2012 inserted a new s. 139AA in the Criminal Justice Act (CJA) 1988 (offence of threatening with a blade or point or offensive weapon on school premises or in a public place) to make a custodial sentence of at least six months mandatory for an offender over 18 years of age convicted of this offence unless 'unjust to do so'. The Criminal Justice and Courts Act (CJCA) 2015 also amended s. 139 of the CJA 1988—'having an article with a point or a blade in a public place'—such that a second 'relevant conviction' also leads to a minimum sentence of six months. The CJCA 2015 s. 28 similarly amended the Prevention of Crime Act 1953 s. 1—Prohibition of the carrying of offensive weapons without lawful authority or reasonable excuse—by inserting new subsections such that the conviction leads to a minimum sentence of six months if there was a previous conviction for one of the offences listed in the new s. 1ZA. Clearly the risk-based tool of mandatory sentences has been given a new lease of life.

5.3.4 New indeterminate (life) sentences

There have long been offences for which the maximum sentence is imprisonment for life. That sentence is the discretionary life sentence and will be dealt with in section 5.4.3. However, more recently there have been legislative attempts to ensure a life sentence— where there is no release until the Parole Board determines it is safe to do so—is used in a wider range of circumstances for those offenders deemed dangerous. We deal here with two which were tried and then repealed: the 'automatic life' sentences introduced in 1997 (but re-enacted as s. 109 of the Powers of Criminal Courts (Sentencing) Act 2000) and the IPP sentences—Indeterminate Sentences for Public Protection—introduced in 2003.

Automatic life sentence

The introduction of what became known as the 'automatic life sentence' heralded an apparently different approach to imposing a life sentence but it was very problematic.[16] It was a mandatory sentence of life imprisonment for a second serious violent or sexual offence: both offences had to be on the list provided. Because the provision inevitably caught people whose convictions were separated by a considerable period of time or whose offence was not of the most serious nature, the early appeals (notably *Kelly* (1999); *Offen No. 1* (2001)) focused on the interpretation of the 'exceptional circumstances' get-out provision and confirmed that this covered only circumstances that were very unusual, special, and extremely uncommon. After the implementation of the Human Rights Act 1998, Offen's further appeal, *Offen No. 2* (2001), was successful: the lack of any unacceptable risk of future harm from the offender was taken to constitute 'exceptional circumstances'.

---

[15] Firearms Act 1968, s. 51A as amended by the CJA 2003. The Firearms (Sentencing) (Transitory Provisions) Order 2007, SI 2007/1324 was introduced as a response to an appellate decision about the illegality under the Act of the sentence for those aged 16 and 17.

[16] In 2002, 44 offenders were given automatic life sentences under s. 109 (Home Office 2003g: Table 4G).

The importance of rights jurisprudence in these cases cannot be overestimated. In Matthew Offen's case, a history of psychiatric illness in childhood, and the fact that he had committed the 'amateurish' robbery in carpet slippers, that he admitted the offence to his friends immediately afterwards, and that the money was quickly recovered, had not been construed as exceptional circumstances in *Offen No. 1* (2000). Similarly in Ian Turner's case, a gap of 30 years between the commission of the two relevant offences had not amounted to exceptional circumstances but, when the Criminal Cases Review Commission brought the case back to the Appeal Court after *Offen No. 2*, the imposition of the automatic life sentence was overturned because Turner presented no risk to the public (*Turner* (2001)).[17] So *Offen* established that the justifying focus of a preventive sentence had to be on risk of future harm to the public.[18]

The automatic life sentence was repealed with effect from April 2005. However, we will see in section 5.4.2 that the new mandatory life sentence inserted in the CJA 2003 as s. 224A takes the same two strikes approach and is referred to by Thomas as a 'semi-automatic life sentence' (2013: 249).

The IPP sentence

The IPP sentence introduced by the then s. 225 of the CJA 2003 was also an indeterminate sentence, in effect a life sentence but with different provisions for release. As originally enacted, providing the dangerousness and 'serious' offence criteria were met, and if only one of the requirements for the imposition of a life sentence (whether legally available and whether the offending was sufficiently serious) could be met, the court was mandated to impose an IPP sentence.

This lack of judicial discretion led to the imposition of IPP sentences in relation to less serious trigger offences which would not have led to an indeterminate sentence before 2003. As the Carter Report noted:

> The fact that an IPP must be given, no matter how serious or otherwise the trigger offence, has led to substantial numbers of IPPs with short tariffs [minimum terms] . . . . The Review and NOMS have jointly developed proposals that will mean that the trigger offence must reach a reasonable seriousness threshold. They will allow sentencers much greater discretion about when to give an IPP; those who do merit an IPP will continue to get one.
>
> (Carter Report 2007: Annex E)

The CJIA 2008, s. 13 reintroduced more discretion by amending s. 225 of the CJA 2003 such that 'may' was substituted for 'must' in relation to the imposition of an IPP: the court was given a power rather than a duty. Further, this power could be employed only if the offender had met one of the two conditions in new subsections:

(3A)　The condition in this subsection is that, at the time when the offence was committed, the offender had been convicted of an offence specified in Schedule 15A [This was a new schedule to the CJA 2003 listing 'very serious' offences.]

(3B)　The condition in this subsection is that the notional minimum term is at least two years.

This 'seriousness' threshold in subsection 3B set at two years' minimum custodial time meant that it could be used only for those who would otherwise receive at least a four-year determinate sentence. The threshold in subsection 3A reflected the offences that Parliament had decided were most serious for this purpose. However, LASPO 2012 s. 123 abolished the IPP sentence.

---

[17] See also *Stark* (2002), *Watkins* (2002).　　[18] See *Baff* (2003) and *Wallace* (2001).

5.3.5 **Extended (determinate) sentences**

The first more recent extended sentence was introduced by s. 44 of the CJA 1991 and re-enacted as s. 85 of the PCCSA 2000. The name is somewhat misleading in that it does not extend the time in prison, simply the time on licence. It empowered the courts to make an order extending the period of release on licence in regard to sexual offences (then for sexual and violent offences) and proved more popular than the LTC sentence discussed in section 5.3.2 (Henham 2001: 707). As consolidated, s. 85 of the PCCSA 2000 allowed an extension to be added to commensurate or LTC sentences if the normal period of licence was inadequate for the purpose of rehabilitation and crime prevention.

The CJA 2003 provided a new extended sentence with similar effects. As passed, s. 227 required the courts to impose an extended sentence on an offender over 18 years if the offender was deemed 'dangerous' under s. 229, if the offence was one of those specified in Schedule 15 to the Act and it was not a 'serious' offence as defined in the Act. *Lang* (2005) gave guidance on the use of extended sentences as first enacted, emphasising that the custodial term must be a proportionate one and that the **parsimony principle** applies (at para 12).

However, after extensive criticism, s. 15 of the Criminal Justice and Immigration Act (CJIA) 2008 amended s. 227 of the CJA 2003 such that the court had a power rather than a duty to impose an extended sentence. Further, the power could be exercised only where either of two conditions was met: the immediate offence had to attract an 'appropriate custodial period' of at least four years; or the offender had on a previous occasion been convicted of one of the 23 offences listed in Schedule 15A for England and Wales, with separate lists for Scotland and Northern Ireland.

The extension period of the current extended sentence could not exceed five years for a specified violent offence or eight years for a specified sexual offence, and the whole could not exceed the maximum allowed for the offence.

LASPO 2012 s. 124 made a further change by repealing the s. 227 sentence and inserting a new extended sentence into the CJA 2003 as s. 226A, now referred to as an extended determinate sentence (EDS). This has a very similar approach: the offender must be over 18, the offence must be a specified offence listed in Schedule 15, the offender must be considered to be dangerous, the court must not be mandated to use a life sentence under s. 224A or s. 225(2), and one of the conditions A or B must be met. The conditions are as before, with condition A requiring a previous conviction for an offence in the new extensive Schedule 15B.[19] The maximum extension periods are as before but there are changes in relation to early release (see section 5.5).

5.4 The current sentencing options

5.4.1 **Protective sentencing in the CJA 2003 as amended**

In 2011 the Coalition government announced that it would introduce legislation to amend the framework of protective sentencing set up by the CJA 2003 because, inter alia, the current sentences were not sufficiently protective. It said it would achieve its objectives by:

- Abolishing IPPs, so that more dangerous offenders can be given straightforward life sentences by judges.

---

[19] Schedule 15A was repealed by LASPO 2012.

- Introducing a 'two strikes' policy so that a mandatory life sentence will be given to any-one convicted of a second serious sexual or violent crime. Making it the only time a mandatory life sentence must be given, other than for murder.
- Creating a new 'extended sentence' for criminals convicted of serious sexual or violent offences, which will mean they cannot be released from prison until they have served at least two-thirds of their sentence (by comparison to the normal halfway point) and for the most serious offenders only then if the Parole Board agrees it.
- Coupling this with long licence periods for these offenders, so that when they are released from prison they will be monitored for long periods and returned to prison if necessary.

(Ministry of Justice 2011f: 2)[20]

LASPO 2012 did indeed abolish the IPP sentence and that is to be welcomed, as it made more likely the use of determinate sentences, notwithstanding the fact that the later amendments gave back considerable discretion to the judiciary. The report on the LASPO Bill by the Human Rights Joint Committee (2011) approved of the repeal but said that there should also be legislation to deal with the many prisoners already sentenced disproportionately to an IPP sentence. This has not yet happened.

The approach of the current protective sentencing framework

The only fully mandatory sentence is the life sentence for murder. As of April 2015 there are four sentences available to the courts for (other) dangerous offenders over 18 years of age: the 'discretionary' life sentences in s. 225 and s. 224A,[21] the EDS in s. 226A, and the new 'special custodial sentence for certain offenders of particular concern' in s. 236A. We have already dealt with the extended (determinate) sentence (in section 5.3.5), and we will deal with the new s. 236A sentence in section 5.4.2 and the life sentences in section 5.4.3.

It may be helpful to summarise at this stage the general approach of the protective sentencing framework in the CJA 2003 for use with offenders convicted of offences in Schedule 15 to the Act. That Schedule provides a considerable list of 'specified' offences—a total originally of 153, including 65 specified violent offences in Part I, but others have since been added to that Part. The s. 225 life sentence and the s. 226A extended sentence can be imposed only in relation to the specified offences listed in the Schedule (the same applied to the repealed IPP sentence). All specified offences count as a 'relevant' offence for these provisions (s. 229(4)). However, there is an important subgroup of specified offences called, confusingly, 'serious offences'. These are defined as specified offences punishable by imprisonment for life or by a determinate sentence of at least ten years.

Both the s. 225 life sentence and the s. 226A extended sentences apply to persons over 18 and only where 'dangerousness'[22] is established: in other words, that 'the court considers that there is a significant risk to members of the public of serious harm occasioned by the commission by the offender of further specified offences' (s. 226A(1)(b)).[23] When the original s. 225 life and s. 227 IPP sentences were passed in 2003 they were both in effect mandatory sentences if the offender had been convicted of offences defined as 'serious offences' and the other criteria had been met. This is still the case in relation to s. 225 life sentences but not in relation to extended sentences, where s. 226A(4) states

---

[20] Originally available at http://www.justice.gov.uk/publications/bills-and-acts/bills/legal-aid-and-sentencing-bill.htm.

[21] The Sentencing Council describes these as discretionary life sentences, although of course they are both mandatory if the conditions are met.

[22] To be dealt with in section 5.4.4.   [23] There are very similar words in s. 225(1)(b).

'The court may impose an extended sentence of imprisonment on the offender'[24] if the conditions are met.

However, the new life sentence—in force since April 2015 and to be found in s. 224A—is quite different from the s. 225 and s. 226A protective sentences in the 2003 Act: there is no requirement that the offender is assessed to be a risk in the future. Nor is there risk assessment in relation to the new determinate sentence for 'certain offenders of particular concern'. We deal with this sentence in section 5.4.2.

5.4.2 **A new hybrid sentence for 'offenders of particular concern'**

This 'Special custodial sentence for certain offenders of particular concern' (SOPC) was introduced by the new s. 236A in the CJA 2003 (inserted by Schedule 1 para 2 of the Criminal Justice and Courts Act (CJCA) 2015). It is available for offenders convicted of offences listed in the new CJA 2003 Schedule 18A (predominantly terrorist offences but with some sexual and other serious offences, together with inchoate offences). 'These constitute offences deemed the most serious child sex and terrorism-related offences' (Ministry of Justice 2015f: para 18). It is, therefore, aimed at the latest danger—that of terrorist activity—as well as sexual offences. Sections 1–3 of the Criminal Justice and Courts Act 2015 ('the Act') also added further serious terrorism and terrorism-related offences to Schedule 15B of the Criminal Justice Act 2003.

The s. 236A sentence can be imposed provided the court does not impose a sentence of imprisonment for life or an extended sentence under CJA 2003 s. 226A. In other words, for offenders whose offences are on Schedule 15 and Schedule 18A there is an extra option for the courts. This sentence is a hybrid because, unlike other 'ordinary' determinate sentences, there is no automatic release. The offender must be referred to the Parole Board for consideration of release on licence, from the halfway point of the custodial term. The offender will be automatically released, if that has not already occurred, at the end of the custodial term with a mandatory one-year period on licence (Ministry of Justice 2015f: para 19): see also section 5.5.3.

5.4.3 **Discretionary life sentences**

The s. 225 and s. 224A sentences are technically discretionary life sentences but the discretionary life sentence before 2003 was simply the common law penalty.

The common law penalty

The discretionary life sentence is available where the statutory maximum (not mandatory) penalty for an offence is life imprisonment: it cannot be used unless a life sentence is legally available (*Hodgson* 1996). Until the new protective sentences, notably the life sentence in the CJA 2003 s. 225, imposed criteria for the imposition of sentences for offences to be found in Schedule 15 to the Act, the life sentence for all offences was governed only by the criteria laid down some time ago in *Hodgson* (1967). As the Bar Council noted, only the relatively few offences not on that list but which carry the life sentence as their maximum penalty, for example Class A drugs trafficking, are, presumably, subject solely to the *Hodgson* criteria (Bar Council 2006; section 3B), which required the offending to be grave, the offender to be suffering from mental instability, and the offender assessed as posing a risk to the public for some (unforeseeable) time.

---

[24] Which also applied to the previous extended sentence after 2008.

In *Wilkinson* (1983) Lord Lane CJ had noted that the discretionary life sentence should be used only in 'the most exceptional circumstances' and Smith's research, which examined 50 Appeal Court judgments over a ten-year period, found that such sentences were most commonly imposed in respect of rape convictions (23 cases) and manslaughter (12 cases) (Smith 1998). In *Chapman* (2000) the court stated that the life sentence might be used for an offence whose seriousness was proportionate to less than five years' imprisonment if the prediction was of very serious future harm. Nevertheless, *Kehoe* (2009) upheld the importance of reserving this sentence for particularly grave offences.[25] *McNee, Gunn and Russell* (2008) clarified that mental instability might not always be a requirement and that the authorities do not require, as a matter of uniform practice, medical evidence to establish good grounds for considering that the offender is likely to be a continuing danger for an indeterminate time in the future.[26]

While virtually all cases will now come within s. 225, the above jurisprudence has some relevance for judicial decision-making in relation to the approach to seriousness and the assessment of dangerousness.

CJA 2003 s. 225

If the offender is convicted of an offence listed in Schedule 15 to the CJA 2003 the 'discretionary' life sentence is now governed by the criteria in s. 225, provided that the offender has been assessed as dangerous under s. 229. The criteria are that the offence is punishable by life imprisonment and that 'the court considers that the seriousness of the offence . . . is such as to justify the imposition of a sentence of imprisonment for life' (s. 225(2)). If all those conditions are met the court 'must' impose a life sentence (ibid) or, if the offender is at least 18 but under 21, a sentence of custody for life. Nevertheless, now that the assessment of dangerousness is not constrained by presumptions (see section 5.4.4) these conditions allow the court considerable discretion in establishing both seriousness and dangerousness.

The s. 224A life sentence

LASPO 2012 s. 122 inserted a new s. 224(A) into the Criminal Justice Act 2003 and provides for a mandatory life sentence for those who have been convicted of an offence which is listed in Part 1 of the new Schedule 15B. The criteria are that the offender has previously been convicted of an offence on that list and had been given a life sentence with a minimum term of at least five years or a custodial sentence of at least ten years for that offence, that the court would otherwise be imposing a sentence of at least ten years for the current offence, and that it would not be 'unjust' to impose a life sentence under this section.

So we are back to a two strikes provision, albeit with somewhat different criteria[27] which should ensure it is used for the most dangerous offenders. However, there is still cause for concern. As a result of a reference of a sentence thought to be 'unduly lenient' the Court of Appeal considered the effect of the new sentences inserted in the CJA 2003 by LASPO 2012 (*Attorney General's Reference (No. 27 of 2013)* (2014)), including the new life sentence in s. 224(A). Commentary on the case pointed out that 'The court concluded that the effect of Sch. 15B was to increase the maximum sentences of those listed offences that did not already carry a maximum sentence of life imprisonment' and provided the following scenario to illustrate the implications:

> The effect being that, for example, where an individual committed an offence of sexual activity with a child (carrying a maximum sentence of 14 years), having received a sentence

---

[25] For further discussion of recent cases on life imprisonment see Ashworth (2010: 229–31).

[26] For further discussion of the issue of mental instability see the second edition of this book at pp. 155–6.

[27] You might at this stage wish to go back and recall the reasons why the automatic life sentence was abolished.

of 10 years' imprisonment, and then committed another offence of sexual activity with a child, with that offence effectively being 'worth' 10 years' imprisonment, the court must impose a life sentence under s.224A, notwithstanding that, on neither occasion, has the individual been found to be 'dangerous' and that neither offence carries a statutory maximum of life imprisonment.

(Sentencing News 2014: 4)

That case—*Attorney General's Reference (No. 27 of 2013)* (2014)—also set out the approach courts should take in relation to the current protective sentences:

> Courts should take the following approach, in the following order, when considering whether to impose a sentence under Pt 12 Ch.5 of the 2003 Act: (a) the court was to consider dangerousness. If the offender was not dangerous and s.224A did not apply, a determinate sentence was to be passed. If the offender was not dangerous and s.224A did apply, a life sentence had to be imposed; (b) if the offender was dangerous, the court was to consider whether the seriousness of the offence, and offences associated with it, justified a life sentence. That required consideration of the offence and associated offences, previous convictions, the level of danger to the public and whether there was a reliable estimate of the length of time the offender would remain a danger, and available alternative sentences; (c) if a life sentence was justified, a life sentence had to be passed under s.225. If s.224A also applied, that was to be recorded in open court; (d) if a life sentence was not justified, the court was to consider whether s.224A applied. If it did, a life sentence had to be imposed; (e) if s.224A did not apply, the court was to consider s.226A. Before passing an extended sentence, a determinate sentence was to be considered (see paras 22, 43 of judgment).

Attorney General's Reference (No. 27 of 2013) (2014 Para 1)

This judgment was given before the new s. 236A sentence was in force, however (see section 5.4.2).

When imposing life sentences the court must specify the part of the sentence—the minimum term—which is to be served for the purposes of punishment and deterrence. This should equate to one-half to two-thirds of what would have been the appropriate determinate sentence. It is also worth noting that, for some time, England and Wales—with over 70 offences providing a life sentence option—has had the highest lifer population out of all the 45 countries of the Council of Europe (Prison Reform Trust 2004a).

5.4.4 **Assessing dangerousness**

The assessment of dangerousness caused as many if not more difficulties than the mandatory aspect of the life, IPP, and extended sentences in their original 2003 wording. The assessment of the offender's dangerousness is crucial because—until the new ss. 224A and 236A sentences came into force—none of the protective orders were otherwise available. Section 229, headed 'the assessment of dangerousness', gives guidance in relation to the assessment of risk. It does not provide a definition and as enacted in 2003 was, in effect, a presumption which was reversed for different offenders. That presumption meant that previous offending could mandate a decision that the offender was dangerous. So, if the offender had no previous 'relevant' conviction or was under 18 years of age, the court had to take account of all information about the offence and could consider information about the offender, and any pattern of behaviour of which the offences form a part, in making a judgement about dangerousness.

For adult offenders, however, if the current conviction had been preceded by a previous conviction for a relevant, that is specified, offence then 'the court must assume there is such a risk', unless the court considered it 'unreasonable' to so conclude (s. 229(3)). The effect of this meant the IPP sentence was clearly akin to the automatic life sentence which it replaced. The 2003 provisions were drafted specifically to avoid the human rights issue to which *Offen No. 2* (2001) drew attention although, as Ashworth noted, the provisions appear to have been based 'on a policy of going as far as possible to minimize or otherwise avoid these rights' (2004: section 5(i)).

Not surprisingly the presumption of dangerousness led to appeals, the first of which was *Lang* (2005). Paragraphs 15–19 in the *Lang* judgment dealt with the assessment of dangerousness. Referring to these sections as 'labyrinthine', Rose LJ stated that '[i]n our judgement, when sections 229 and 224 are read together, unless the information about offences, pattern of behaviour and the offender . . . show a significant risk of serious harm . . . from further offences, it will usually be unreasonable to conclude that the assumption exists' (at para 15). Extensive guidance was then given on the factors to be borne in mind in assessing whether there is a significant risk, including the statement that '[i]f the foreseen specified offence is not serious there will be comparatively few cases in which a risk of serious harm will properly be regarded as serious' (at para 17). The court also made the following forceful comment: 'It cannot have been Parliament's intention, in a statute dealing with the liberty of the subject, to require the imposition of indeterminate sentences for the commission of relatively minor offences' (at para 17). It could be argued, then, that the tenor of *Lang* was towards a restrictive interpretation of the new provisions and helped to downgrade the presumption of dangerousness after convictions for two specified offences.

However, *Lang* left considerable discretion in the application of statutory criteria and the somewhat divergent judgments in the cases of *Folkes*, *McGrady*, and *Thomas* in 2006 led to the following observation:

> The source of the problem is the ill-conceived legislation which deprives courts of discretion in deciding when to use the dangerous offender sentences and when not to do so—it is unlikely in the extreme that any of the offenders in these three cases would have received a sentence of life imprisonment or a longer than commensurate sentence under the earlier legislation.
>
> (Thomas 2007: 172)

In September 2007 the SGC issued guidance which dealt with the assessment of dangerousness in Part 6. It made clear, citing *Lang*, that there are two parts to the 'serious risk' test:

- there must be a significant risk of the offender committing further specified offences (whether serious or not), and
- there must be a significant risk of serious harm to members of the public being caused by such offences.

> (Sentencing Guidelines Council 2007b: para 6.1.2)

The guideline further noted that '[t]he court is guided, but not bound, by the assessment of dangerousness in a pre-sentence report' (Sentencing Guidelines Council 2007b: para 6.1.4). Again citing *Lang*, it states, 'Usually it would be unreasonable to assume that the offender is a dangerous offender if, but for the assumption of dangerousness, the offender would not be found to be a dangerous offender' (ibid: 6.2.4).

Citing *Johnson* (2006 at para 21), the guideline specifically stated that '[t]he existence (or non-existence) of previous convictions does not determine whether an offender is a dangerous offender: an offender with no previous convictions may be a dangerous offender, whilst an offender with previous convictions may not' (ibid: para 6.4.3.1).

Given these judgments and other criticism, the CJIA 2008 s. 17 amended s. 229 of the CJA 2003 to remove the two strikes presumption of dangerousness. The relevant part of s. 229 now reads as follows:

(2) The court in making the assessment referred to in subsection (1)(b)—

(a) must take into account all such information as is available to it about the nature and circumstances of the offence,

(aa) may take into account all such information as is available to it about the nature and circumstances of any other offences of which the offender has been convicted by a court anywhere in the world,

(b) may take into account any information which is before it about any pattern of behaviour of which any of the offences mentioned in paragraph (a) or (aa) forms part, and

(c) may take into account any information about the offender which is before it.

Amendments have made clear that 'offences' includes service (armed forces) offences.

The Lord Chief Justice, in a case heard shortly after the amendments were enacted, made the following comment: 'It is worthy of immediate notice that the statutory assumption of dangerousness in section 229(3) has disappeared. No court will mourn its departure. Its judgment of dangerousness can now be made untrammeled by artificial constraints' (*Att-Gen's Reference No. 55 of 2008, R v C and other* (2008) para 6).

The removal of the presumption of risk has not reduced the difficulties in assessing risk, however. The CJA 2003 states: 'The court must obtain a pre-sentence report before deciding that the offender is a dangerous offender unless, in the circumstances of the case, the court considers that such a report is unnecessary (s 156(3) and (4))' (Sentencing Guidelines Council 2008g: 15). Although *Lang* established that the court is guided but not bound by reports (2005: 17(ii)), there is a reliance on the pre-sentence report prepared by the Probation Service, which will have used the OASys (Offender Assessment System) actuarially based tool for assessing the offender's level of risk of reoffending (see NPS 2003; Home Office 2005a; IMB 2015). Guidance states that there are three groups of factors that are relevant in the assessment of whether there is a significant risk of the offender committing further specified offences:

- the nature and circumstances of the current offence and the offender's 'offending' history . . . including whether the offending demonstrates any pattern,
- the offender's social and economic circumstances including accommodation, employability, education, associations, relationships and drug or alcohol abuse, and
- the offender's thinking, emotional state and attitude towards offending and supervision.

(Sentencing Guidelines Council 2008g: para 6.3.1)

There are no easy decisions here. The guidance makes clear that '[t]he existence (or nonexistence) of previous convictions does not determine whether an offender is a dangerous offender; an offender with no previous convictions may be a dangerous offender, whilst an offender with previous convictions may not' (ibid: para 6.3.3). Preventive sentencing will always produce moral as well as practical dilemmas when the future must be predicted for sentencing purposes.

5.4.5 **Controlling the dangerous mentally disordered offender**

In the next chapter (section 6.4) we review the policies, law and practice in relation to mentally disordered offenders generally. Here we concentrate on those who are also 'dangerous'.

However, Burney and Pearson point out that 'most mentally disordered offenders are neither seriously ill nor dangerous' (1995: 292) and evidence from the United States suggests that major mental disorder accounts for up to 3 per cent of violence only (see Bowden 1996; Peay 2002: 772–3). Indeed, research suggests that a diagnosis of schizophrenia is associated with lower rates of violence than a diagnosis of depression (see Peay 2007: 513). Nevertheless, policy in mental health as well as crime is 'permeated by perceptions and attributions of risk': mentally disordered offenders who also fall into the current constructions of 'dangerous for sentencing purposes' are then particularly likely to be perceived as 'an unquantifiable danger' (Peay 2002: 747).

For those offenders who can be categorised as 'mentally disordered' under s. 1 of the Mental Health Act (MHA) 1983, various therapeutic disposals may be considered. If the Crown Court believes that an order is necessary 'for the protection of the public from serious harm' and the offender's conviction is for an offence punishable by imprisonment, then the court can impose a hospital order (s. 40) with a restriction order under s. 41 of the MHA 1983. Section 41(1) lists the factors the court must consider in assessing dangerousness and the effect of adding a restriction order is that the offender cannot be released without the consent of the Secretary of State or a Mental Health Tribunal.[28] As Thomas points out, 'In the rare case of an offender who qualifies for an automatic life sentence under the PCCSA 2000 s 109 for a "serious" offence committed between October 1, 1997 and April 3, 2005, who would qualify for a hospital order, the court has no power to impose a hospital order and must impose a sentence of life imprisonment' (2013: 249).

A person serving a custodial sentence may be transferred to a hospital under s. 47 of the Act and a restriction direction can be added. The court which imposes a prison sentence on a mentally disordered offender may also add a direction for immediate admission to hospital, subject to restrictions (a hospital and limitation direction under s. 45A of the MHA 1983: see Peay 2015). Hospital and limitation directions were originally limited to offenders suffering from psychopathic disorder who were suitable for treatment in hospital, but were extended to all mentally disordered offenders.

The court does not have to use a hospital order even if the conditions are met and so courts may decide to imprison the dangerous offender instead. This is what happened in *R v Jenkin* (2012), where there was an appeal against sentence for grievous bodily harm with intent. The appellant had put bedclothes over his partner's head, lay on top of her, and strangled her until she was unconscious. He had then gouged out her eyes. Despite the recommendation of two psychiatrists that he be given a hospital order with restriction under MHA 1983 s. 41 he had been sentenced to life imprisonment with a specified minimum term of six years, with a hospital and limitation direction. In his commentary Thomas notes that the court, drawing attention to the fact that Jenkin had a long history of violent offending from the age of 14, concluded that 'Even if his mental disorder was cured or substantially alleviated, that risk would remain. A sentence was required which would address that residual risk' (2013: 247). Thomas concludes that one of the principles which now seem to be supported by decisions of the Court of Appeal is that where 'the offender would be considered dangerous so as to justify a sentence of life imprisonment, independently of the treatable mental illness, the proper course will be a sentence of life imprisonment, coupled with a hospital and limitation direction under the MHA 2003 s 45A' (2013: 248).

The hospital order leads to compulsory admission to a psychiatric institution or unit in a general hospital. These treatment sites are categorised in terms of degrees of security. The

---

[28] Section 40 of the Mental Health Act 2007 removed the power of the Crown Court to make restriction orders under MHA 1983, s. 41 for a limited period.

Table 5.2 Restricted patients detained in hospital by sex

England and Wales 31 December											Number of patients
Sex	1998	1999	2000	2001	2002	2003	2004	2005 (1)	2006 (1)	2007 (1)	2008 (1)
Male	2,430	2,515	2,536	2,636	2,631	2,720	2,886	2,984	3,159	3,448	3,460
Female	319	327	322	333	358	398	396	411	442	458	477
All patients	2,749	2,842	2,858	2,969	2,989	3,118	3,282	3,395	3,601	3,906	3,937

(1) Figures for 2005, 2006, 2007 and 2008 were derived from a manual matching procedure.

Source: Ministry of Justice 2010e: Table 1.

highest security hospitals, previously called special hospitals, are at Ashworth, Broadmoor, and Rampton, although patients subject to a restriction order, and others, may also be treated in regional secure units, NHS psychiatric inpatient acute units, or independent hospitals. The number of restricted patients at the end of 2006 was given as 3,601, making it the highest figure for the past decade (Ministry of Justice 2007c; for an analysis of earlier statistics, see Howard and Christophersen 2003). However, Table 5.2 (Ministry of Justice 2010e: Table 1, p. 3) gives differently calculated figures which show a continuing rising trend, while at the census point in 2013 there were 4,449 detained restricted patients (see Peay 2015: 5).

The focus on danger and security has led, it is argued, to inappropriate 'custodial' measures in secure units and hospitals. For example, the proposals of the Tilt Report (Tilt *et al.* 2000), which examined the issue of security, have been criticised by psychiatrists. 'The emphasis throughout the report on the more tangible aspects of security such as high walls and better locks, and the virtual absence of consideration of the less overt contribution of relational security, fits in with the official preoccupation with "dangerousness" in recent years' (Exworthy and Gunn 2003). Again, the tension between the focus on risk and on treatment is apparent.[29]

If, on the other hand, the use of non-punitive therapeutic disposals is to be promoted for the dangerous but mentally disordered offender, then there are clear difficulties with the current sentencing framework. Section 166 of the CJA 2003 makes clear that courts are not required to pass custodial sentences (where they would otherwise have done) on offenders who are mentally disordered. It does not say they cannot pass custodial sentences and a judge may not be able to impose a hospital order because of the lack of a suitable hospital place. The discretionary life sentence (see section 5.4.3) is also seen as an option (where available as a sentence on conviction) for the dangerous and mentally disordered offender who cannot be fitted into the criteria of the MHA 1983.

One particular group of the mentally disordered, for whom the provisions of the MHA 1983 have been seen as inadequate by legislators, are offenders suffering from a 'psychopathic disorder' as defined in the original s. 1 of the MHA 1983 but amended by the Mental Health Act (MHA) 2007. 'Appropriate medical treatment' must be available for the offender (MHA 1983, s. 37(2)(a)(i)), but that is problematic in that such disorders are generally believed to be resistant to treatment and the psychiatric report may not offer the court the reassurance it legally needs.

---

[29] See Prins (2005), an update of a text first published in 1980, which provides an interdisciplinary approach to the issues raised.

This difficulty fed into government initiatives to provide other means to deal with dangerous people with severe personality disorder, notably the DSPD (dangerous and severe personality disorder) Programme (see Department of Health/Home Office 2000; Impalox Group 2007) which became 'a prime focus for service development and legislative provision' in the decade after pilot programmes began in 2001 (see Peay 2007: 518). This was despite concerns that the programme and associated publicity could 'further demonise this group' (Peay 2007: 519; see also, Seddon 2008) and that forensic psychiatrists found no medical basis for the categorisation as DSPD (see Davies 2010). A recent summary of research studies found some favourable outcomes, but wide variations in practice (Ramsay 2011; see also Trebilcock and Weaver (2011a, 2011b).

In 2011 the Coalition government proposed to close the programmes running in hospitals but continue them in prisons, renamed as the Offender Personality Disorder Pathway (see Department of Health and NOMS Offender Personality Disorder Team 2011a and 2011b). This new Pathway has been developed and there is in place a National Evaluation of Offender Personality Disorder Pathway ('NEON') commissioned by NOMS and the NHS, who share responsibility for delivery of the Pathway projects: for an update and for more details about specific programmes see the special edition of the *Prison Service Journal* No. 218 (March 2015). These new initiatives aim to address a difficult group of prisoners who need help and from whom the public needs protection, but there are still grave concerns. As Benefield *et al.* note, 'From both a political and clinical viewpoint this is an unpopular client group with whom engagement is difficult and for whom there is as yet no definitive evidence of treatment effectiveness' (2015: 9). Further, 'dangerous' prisoners with personality disorder 'may continue to languish in prison for years to come and be punished far beyond what would be proportionate to the gravity of their crimes' (O'Loughlin 2014: 174). Consequently, O'Loughlin makes the following comment:

> This raises the question of whether the aim of the programme is really to treat personality disordered offenders with a view to eventually releasing them into the community, or whether the promise of therapy and eventual release operates in practice as a management tool that facilitates the real goal: containing troublesome prisoners.
>
> (O'Loughlin 2014: 189)

Indeed there have been proposals for persons with personality disorder to be detained indefinitely, until they are no longer a risk to the public, even if they have not committed a crime and regardless of whether there is any effective treatment. Following the Richardson Report and the White Paper of 2000, a Draft Mental Health Bill was published in June 2002. It proposed a new compulsory treatment order which would be available for those considered a risk to the public but who could not currently be sectioned under the MHA 1983, but the Draft Bill was strongly criticised by a range of professionals on the grounds, inter alia, that the proposed reforms would divert resources from other people with mental health problems, that the treatment proposed was unclear, that civil liberties might be infringed and innocent people detained compulsorily, and that such provisions would increase the stigma of mental illness. In the event, s. 32 of the MHA 2007 introduced a community treatment order (CTO) available for a person who had previously been detained in hospital, provided that—inter alia—it 'is necessary for his health or safety or for the protection of other persons that he should receive such treatment' (new s. 17A inserted in the MHA 1983).[30]

The justice of new forms of civil detention for the dangerous offender has also been considered by penologists. For example, von Hirsch (1986) acknowledges that in the case of a

---

[30] The Mental Health (Care and Treatment) (Scotland) Act 2003, Part 7 introduced new compulsory treatment orders for Scotland, in force since October 2005.

dangerous physical illness we might accept medical quarantine to protect others, but this would be very exceptional and used only if such a strategy proved to be effective in containing disease and provided that the person is not stigmatised. But incapacitation of dangerous or persistent offenders is far removed from this situation. While it might be acceptable if it were an effective strategy, it is difficult to justify if it does not work. In connection with its use in criminal justice, distinguishing between offenders who have committed the same offences is also problematic, as it shifts the focus away from the blameworthiness of the present conduct.

The courts are not required by statutory provisions to impose custody in relation to the mentally disordered and that message was reinforced by the insertion of a new subsection 1A in s. 37 of the MHA 1983. The law now states that, in the case of an offence coming under the otherwise mandatory provisions of ss. 110(2) or 111(2) of the PCCSA 2000, ss. 224A, 225(2), and 226(2) of the CJA 2003, s. 29 of the Violent Crime Reduction Act 2006, or various specified firearms offences, 'nothing in those provisions shall prevent a court from making an order . . . for the admission of the offender to a hospital'. This means that there must be other reasons why so many mentally ill offenders are imprisoned or given restriction orders (see Peay 2015).

5.5 Post-custody and other provisions

5.5.1 Prevention orders

Ashworth refers to 'the ever-lengthening list' of preventive orders and sets out 18 orders (2015: 382). Some of the preventive orders, notably the Sexual Risk Order (see Chapter 1, section 1.5.2), the Violent Offender Order, and the Serious Crime Prevention Order (SRO) (imposed under the terms of the Serious Crime Act 2007, Part 1), can be made by a court without a charge having been brought for an offence at that time. There are other ancillary orders which can be theorised as reparative or as ensuring just deserts are not undermined by profiting from an offence and these will be discussed in Chapter 7 (section 7.2), while others may be added to the punishment or be imposed by a civil court. Examples here would include anti-social behaviour orders and parenting orders (see Chapter 11, section 11.1 for their use with those under 18 years of age) as well as banning orders (Football Spectators Act 1989, s. 14A; Violent Crime Reduction Act 2006, s. 1).

All these additional and free-standing orders of an injunctive nature have contributed to the control of anti-social and nuisance behaviour as well as that deemed dangerous. As Ashworth has noted, many of these ancillary orders raise serious human rights concerns and often fudge the line between a penalty and prevention (2010: 359–60, 362). Breach of such orders is common and penalties for breach may be severe. 'Generally speaking, however, there are few procedural constraints and entitlements if criminal procedure is not applicable. In this respect, preventive measures fall into a jurisprudential black hole' (Ashworth 2015: 395; see also Ashworth and Zedner 2014: 26-62). These orders, therefore, raise serious issues but space precludes discussion of them all and we will deal with two only, those which relate to offenders deemed most dangerous.[31]

Sexual Harm Prevention Orders

As we noted in Chapter 1 (section 1.5.2), the Sexual Offences Prevention Order introduced by the Sexual Offences Act 2003 was replaced by the Sexual Harm Prevention Order

---

[31] Ashworth (2015: chapter 11) provides a very thorough discussion of ancillary orders and preventive orders and the reader is directed to that.

(SHPO) which applies to a wide range of sexual offences defined in Schedules 3 and 5 to the Act. Lasting for a minimum five years, the order can lead to the prohibition of specific activities, can include a ban on foreign travel, and makes the offender subject to the notification requirements in the 2003 Sex Offenders Act. As the Sentencing Council notes, 'The decision of the Court of Appeal in *R v Smith and others* [2011] EWCA Crim 1772 reinforces the need for the terms of a SHPO to be tailored to the exact requirements of the case.'[32] The risk the offender poses to the public must be managed by the police, probation, and prison services.

There is also a new Sexual Risk Order (SRO) introduced by a new s. 122A in the SOA 2003 to replace the Risk of Sexual Harm Order. An application for this order is usually by the police to a magistrates' court. The order can be made if it is necessary to protect the public or a particular member of the public from harm from the defendant or to protect a child or vulnerable adult from outside the UK. It is not necessary for the defendant to have been convicted but the court needs to be satisfied that the defendant has committed one act of a sexual nature.

Violent Offender Orders

The CJIA 2008 makes provision for Violent Offender Orders (Part 9) whereby magistrates' courts are empowered to make orders, on application from a Chief Officer of Police (s. 100), of at least two years' duration (s. 98). The orders impose restrictions on the offender for the purpose of protecting the public from the risk of serious violent physical or psychological harm caused by the offender committing one or more 'specified offences' (s. 98(1) and (2)). For the purpose of these orders, a specified offence is (only) one of the following (s. 98(3)):

(a) manslaughter;

(b) an offence under section 4 of the Offences against the Person Act 1861 (c. 100) (soliciting murder);

(c) an offence under section 18 of that Act (wounding with intent to cause grievous bodily harm);

(d) an offence under section 20 of that Act (malicious wounding);

(e) attempting to commit murder or conspiracy to commit murder; or

(f) a relevant service offence.

There are also specified service offences in s. 98(4) and since 2014 the Secretary of State has had the power to amend the lists of offences in subsections 98(3) and (4).

The order may be imposed on an offender aged 18 or over who has a conviction for a specified offence (as defined in s. 98(3)) and been given a prison sentence of at least 12 months. It can also be imposed on an offender found not guilty by reason of insanity, or who has been 'found to be under a disability and to have done the act charged in respect of a specified offence' and been given a hospital or supervision order (s. 99).

The CJIA 2008 also contains provisions for imposing Violent Offender Orders on offenders found guilty in countries other than England and Wales of relevant offences. The magistrates' court must decide that the offender has 'acted in such a way as to make it necessary to make a Violent Offender Order for the purpose of protecting the public from the risk of serious violent harm' (s. 101(3)). The order does not come into force until a custodial sentence or its licence period (or that of a hospital order or a supervision order) has come to an end (s. 101(4) and (5)).

---

[32] At https://www.sentencingcouncil.org.uk/explanatory-material/item/ancillary-orders/21-sexual-harm-prevention-orders/.

5.5.2 **The justifications for early release**

Early release has always been of importance to the management of prisons but it is now increasingly important for the control and rehabilitation of offenders on release.[33] Despite regular bouts of public and government criticism that prisoners are not serving the whole of the prison sentence, early release has continued: it is too important a management tool.

The earliest form of early release was the 'ticket of leave' system, awarded for good behaviour to offenders subject to transportation and so aimed at maintaining good order and discipline in prison. This is a response to the difficulty of operating suitable sanctions for what might be termed anti-social behaviour in a custodial setting. This was later replaced by forms of remission—in which time is remitted or taken off for good behaviour in prison. However, with the introduction of parole—early release on licence—came the new aim of providing an opportunity to control and/or rehabilitate offenders on their release. Custodial time is traded in for the opportunity to either reintegrate the offender more successfully back into the community or put conditions on the offender and allow the possibility of recall to prison for the purpose of public protection. The terms of the release determine whether the non-custodial period operates as a continuation of punishment in any meaningful sense in the community.

Early release from a custodial sentence before the period of custody specified has been fully served has always been viewed as problematic and is another example of the co-existence in English law, albeit uneasy, of retributivist and utilitarian principles. With a just deserts-based system of sentencing, early release, especially where discretionary, can be seen as a process which upsets all the fine-tuning of calculations of proportionality. Further, there are problems in relation to the legitimacy of the criminal justice system, given the frequently expressed view of the public that prisoners do not 'really' serve their sentences and that, therefore, the system is too lenient. In response a Conservative government in the 1990s said it wished to establish 'honesty in sentencing' (Home Office 1996a) and enacted in the Crime (Sentences) Act 1997 a new framework which included no automatic early release, but these provisions were repealed by the subsequent Labour government. Instead the provisions for custodial sentences in the CJA 2003 introduced a clear scheme of custodial penalties with specified supervision post-release.

Not all early release schemes can be justified in relation to prison discipline or benefits of supervised release, however: significant changes in early release provisions have, on two occasions, been the result of a need to reduce the prison population quickly. In 1940, when manpower was needed for the armed forces at a critical stage in the Second World War, the standard period of remission was increased from one-sixth to one-third; in 1987, at the height of a prison overcrowding crisis, the period was increased from one-third to one-half for offenders serving sentences of less than 12 months. The introduction of the Home Detention Curfew (HDC) Scheme in 1999 for earlier release of prisoners, with the use of electronic tagging, can also be seen in the same context, as can the 'end of custody licence' introduced in June 2007, which allows release up to a maximum of 18 days early for prisoners serving terms of four weeks to four years. Section 7 of CJCA 2015 now provides for mandatory electronic monitoring of offenders who are released on licence from custody (see Wasik 2015: 864).

Before the implementation of the CJA 1991 any discretionary release through the Parole Board established by the Criminal Justice Act 1967 was essentially granted to 'good' prisoners and required a prisoner to acknowledge their guilt. Release was then

---

[33] We examine aspects of early release in Chapter 10 in relation to the post-custody community supervision.

seen as another way of encouraging and rewarding good behaviour. As a consequence, while about 80 per cent of those serving sentences of less than two years received earlier release under licence, the possibly more dangerous or criminally minded had to serve their sentence until the period at which their remission began. They were therefore released directly into the community without supervision, so that, in practice, the 'worst' offenders were not controlled, supervised, or reformed on release. Further, it was seen by offenders as an unfair system and one that led to prolonged prisoner stress.

Finally, an increasingly important rights discourse meant that the discretionary elements of decision-making would come under greater criticism. Because of these problems, the government set up the Carlisle Committee, whose Report (1988) led to proposals in the 1990 White Paper (Home Office 1990a) that short sentences should no longer be subject to discretionary release but 'dangerous and uncooperative prisoners who might need the full sentence to protect the public' would continue to be subject to discretionary early release (ibid: para 6.10). The 1991 Act also made all release conditional in the sense that the offender is liable to be returned to custody on reoffending.

The scheme set up by the CJA 1991 had three principles which are still relevant: that all parts of the sentence should have some punitive meaning, that supervision post-release should be for the purpose of public protection, and that decisions on release should be based solely on an assessment of risk factors (Ashworth 2000: 255–7). Since then, new sentences for the dangerous have increased the emphasis on discretionary release, and this is particularly evident in relation to the new 'hybrid' fixed-term sentence which we deal with in section 5.5.3.

5.5.3 **Discretionary release**

Fixed-term prisoners

We summarise the law on the release of prisoners serving a 'normal' fixed-term—determinate—sentence in Chapter 10 (section 10.4.2) when we discuss supervision and rehabilitation in the community for such offenders. The law is now to be found in the CJA 2003 as amended and the general rule is now release on licence at the halfway stage. However, there are two determinate sentences which have different rules for release—the EDS and the 'special custodial sentence for certain offenders of particular concern'. We deal with them next.

Extended determinate sentence

The Criminal Justice and Courts Act (CJCA) 2015 s. 4 made changes to the release provisions of offenders on the post-2012 extended sentence—the EDS—to be found in the CJA 2003 s. 226A (for adults). Previously, where an offender received an EDS for an offence which was not on Schedule 15B, or where the offending merited a custodial term of less than ten years, he would be automatically released on licence at the two-thirds point of the custodial term. 'Now all offenders on an EDS may only be released before the end of the custodial term if the Parole Board so directs' (Ministry of Justice 2015f: para 13), unless their offence was before the coming into force of the new provision (CJA 2003 s. 246A on April 13 2015) when the previous regime applies. (See Wasik (2015: 856) for further details.)

Special custodial sentence for certain offenders of particular concern

As guidance notes, 'Section 6 and Schedule 1 to the 2015 Act amend the default determinate custodial sentence for offenders who are convicted of an offence which is listed in Schedule 18A to the 2003 Act (and were over 18 years of age when the offence was committed' (Ministry of Justice 2015d: para 16). The new sentence means that the offender's sentence comprises the appropriate custodial period together with one year under licence on release.

This is, then, a fixed-term prison sentence proportionate to seriousness, but there is no automatic release at the halfway stage: at the halfway stage the case is referred to the Parole Board. The Board can then direct release if it 'is satisfied that it is not necessary for the protection of the public that P [the prisoner] should be confined' (CJA 2003 s. 144A(4)(b)). If the Board is not so satisfied it must reconsider the case within two years (s. 224A(2)(b)) and there is no power to detain the prisoner at the end of the prison sentence unless he had previously been released and recalled (s. 224A(5)). 'The purpose of this fixed licence period is to ensure that any offenders who are not released until the end of the custodial term receive a period of supervision after release' (Ministry of Justice 2015d: para 19).

Indeterminate sentences

Indeterminate sentences have long raised issues about the use of executive, as opposed to judicial, authority to determine the release date. More recently they have raised rights issues, and several of the more recent changes in case law and statute have been the result of cases brought in relation to rights in the ECHR, particularly Articles 3, 5, 7, and 14.

The law on release from discretionary life sentences remains that established in the CSA 1997 and Practice Directions from the Lord Chief Justice. For all life sentences, the judge must now set, and explain in court, what used to be called the 'tariff' part of the sentence. In *Practice Statement (Crime, Life Sentences)* (2002), however, Lord Woolf CJ, following advice from the Sentencing Advisory Panel, mandated the use of 'minimum term' to specify the part of the custodial sentence which must be served before discretionary release can be considered. For discretionary life sentences this is normally calculated as half of the determinate sentence that would have been passed 'for punishment and deterrence', commensurate with seriousness (PCCSA 2000, s. 82A(3)). CJA 2003 s. 239 continues the role of the Parole Board in decision-making in relation to life prisoners under Chapter 2 Part 2 of the Crime (Sentences) Act (CSA) 1997.

However, Lord Carter's Review of Prisons, *Securing the Future: Proposals for the Efficient and Sustainable Use of Custody in England and Wales* (2007), stated that one of the drivers of the current increase in prisoner numbers is the 'greater awareness of risk, and greater political prominence of public protection' (2007: 5), of which one consequence is that the Parole Board rate for discretionary conditional releases had reduced from a peak of 52 per cent of 7,297 cases considered in 2004/5 to 36 per cent of 6,923 cases considered in 2006/7 (ibid: 12). The Sentencing Commission Working Group also noted that '[t]he Parole Board is more risk-averse than hitherto . . . The rate of release on parole decreased from 21.6% in 2004/05 to 14% in 2007/08 for lifer releases' (2008c: para 2.7).

Discretionary release for murderers

For life imprisonment for murder (a sentence 'fixed by law') previous practice was for the trial judge to decide on the minimum term to be recommended to the Lord Chief Justice after the trial. He in turn conferred with the Home Secretary who made the final decision. In *R (Anderson) v Secretary of State for the Home Department* (2002) the House of Lords ruled that this procedure contravened Article 6 of the ECHR and the CJA 2003 introduced provisions to rectify this. Section 269 of the CJA 2003 requires the trial judge to specify the minimum term in open court.

A *Practice Statement (Crime, Life Sentences)* (2002) gave extensive guidance on this issue, a major influence being the Practice Statement on the minimum term for juveniles convicted of murder issued after the European Court of Human Rights upheld the Article 6 claims of *Venables and Thompson* (2000) (see also Valier 2003 and Padfield 2002). The CJA

2003 s. 269 sets out the principles; Schedule 21 gives starting points (and indicative criteria) of 'whole life', 30 years, or 12 years, and the Practice Direction of May 2004 (*Practice Direction (Crime: Mandatory Life Sentences)*) gives guidance on these categories.

However, s. 27 of the CJCA 2015 amends Schedule 21 para 4 such that the murder of a police or prison officer in the course of his duty is now included in this category of exceptionally serious cases in which the court should normally start by considering a whole-life term. If the seriousness is 'particularly high' the minimum term is 30 years (para 5), for example 'a murder intended to obstruct or interfere with the course of justice'.

On 30 June 2015 there were 56 offenders serving a whole-life sentence. These include serial killers Peter Sutcliffe, Ian Brady, Dennis Nilsen, and Rosemary West.[34]

Successful applications to the European Court of Human Rights (see *Thynne, Gunnell and Wilson* (1991); *Hussain v United Kingdom* (1996)) established that all life-sentence prisoners have the right to challenge the grounds for continued detention after the minimum period has expired (Article 5(4)). A panel of the Parole Board meets at the prison where the offender is located and the prisoner is entitled to legal aid at the hearing. It is also now established that continued detention contravenes Article 5 of the ECHR if it is not justifiable on the grounds of public protection (see for example the case of *Stafford* (2002)). Article 5(1) requires a sufficient causal connection between the original offence and the risk of reoffending; Article 5(4) requires that detention after the expiry of the minimum period in custody can be justified only on the grounds of risk of reoffending associated with the original sentence.[35]

For life-sentence prisoners the licence remains in force until the offender's death and many contain specified conditions (CSA 1997, s. 31). Section 31A inserted by the CJA 2003 in regard to prisoners serving IPP sentences meant that the Parole Board can order that the licence ceases to have effect at the end of the 'qualifying period' provided the offender is no longer deemed a risk to the public. The qualifying period in this instance is ten years (of release on licence). *R v Costello* (2010) (see Update to *SGC Guideline Judgments Case Compendium* 2010) has provided detailed guidance on sentencing in relation to an offence committed on licence where the offender had been administratively recalled to prison following breach of that licence, noting the different rules regarding offences committed before or after 4 April 2005.

All these provisions have resource implications. The protective sentences potentially provide longer sentences for more offenders. The early release provisions reduce the time spent in custody for many offenders—although the new rules for the EDS and the Schedule 18A sentences will probably increase the time spent in custody—but the new provisions and conditions in licences increase the cost of community supervision.

5.6 Reflecting on the issues

5.6.1 Critique of current policy

We have already examined the criticisms of incapacitative policies from the perspective of retributivist theory (see section 5.2). Since the CJA 2003 was enacted there have been specific critiques of its provisions, notably that 'the concept of risk is becoming more and more woolly for sentencing purposes' (Carlen 2002), that there are gender

---

[34] https://www.sentencingcouncil.org.uk/about-sentencing/types-of-sentence/life-sentences/ accessed 17 November 2015.

[35] For further discussion on these issues see Amos (2004); Shute (2004b).

dimensions to risk (Hannah-Moffat and O'Malley 2007), and that incapacitation is now part of a 'smorgasbord' of sentencing aims to which the CJA 2003 returns the sentencing framework (von Hirsch and Roberts 2004). At one level these are contradictory critiques— that sentencing on risk is increasing or that it is now simply one of several approaches, including the increasingly important aim of rehabilitation.

However, public protection—whether via (longer) incapacitation or via risk manage- ment in the community on licence—is the common thread in the sentences we have reviewed in this chapter. What is also apparent is that, while the dangerousness provisions in the CJA 2003 are confined to specific sexual and violent offences, the lists in Schedule 15 and Schedule 15B (and the previous Schedule 15A) have increased in length and are now joined by Schedule 18A. Further, 'three strikes' provisions in relation to domestic burglary and drug trafficking remain and have been joined by others relating to firearms and knives, and there is now again a 'two strikes' life sentence.

All these changes suggest that the scope of the class of potential 'risky' offenders is now very wide indeed and can include legitimate provisions that pay little more than lip ser- vice to rights considerations. From a retributivist as well as a human rights perspective, potentially disproportionate sentences of the kind that have emerged from the protective provisions raise serious moral, constitutional, and practical problems (see, for example, van Zyl Smit and Ashworth 2004), but which rarely surface in public discussion and media comment. Even if we accept that a measure of (extra) detention for purposes of public protection is justifiable, the crucial question is, given our knowledge of the difficulties of accurate prediction of risk and of the limited effectiveness of extra incapacitation, 'how much inaccuracy and individual injustice can be justified in the public good?'

5.6.2 **Discussion questions**

1. Review the ethical and moral issues raised in this chapter by the practice of senten- cing for public protection.

2. Review the justifications from penal theory for a policy of selective or categorial incapacitation.

3. Read the passage below which summarises the results of a Home Office Research Study. Then answer this question: how much inaccuracy of prediction of risk can be justified on the grounds of public good?

   A study of reconviction rates years after their release from long determinate prison sen- tences among serious sex offenders who were classified as high risk by the Parole Board found the proportion reconvicted of another sexual offence during both follow-up periods was under 10 per cent, but those who were reconvicted had committed very serious offences (Hood *et al.* 2002). The figures varied according to the type of victim. None of those imprisoned for an offence against a child in their own family unit was reconvicted of a sexual or serious violent crime. Just over one-quarter of those impris- oned for a sexual offence against a child outside the family were reconvicted of another sexual offence and nearly one-third were imprisoned for a sexual or violent crime. Of those imprisoned for an offence against an adult, 1 in 13 was reconvicted of an offence against an adult and 1 in 7 was imprisoned for a sexual or violent offence within six years of release from prison. All the offenders who were reconvicted of a further sexual offence within the four-year follow-up period, and all but one followed up for six years, had been identified as high risk or dangerous by at least one member of the Parole Board. Where no member of the Parole Board panel had identified a sex offender as high risk, only one was reconvicted of a sexual offence after six years.

5.6.3 **Case study**

Read the following case scenario and then sentence Jack as suggested.

Jack and Jill lived together. Jill stopped loving Jack and left him. Jack was very angry and broke into Jill's hairdressing salon and trashed it, causing £25K worth of damage. He was arrested, pleaded guilty and was convicted at the Crown Court, under s. 9 of the Theft Act, of burglary in a non-dwelling for which the maximum penalty is ten years' imprisonment. The relevant Sentencing Council Guideline (2011b) states that the 'starting point' for the highest level of seriousness is two years with a range from 12 months to 5 years.

- First, sentence Jack under the normal retributivist framework.
- Then sentence again with the knowledge that s. 9 of the Theft Act is a 'specified offence' for the purposes of s. 224 of the Criminal Justice Act (CJA) 2003 when the intention was to cause unlawful damage in the building in question and that Jack had, some years ago, been convicted of assaulting a former girlfriend. Do those facts make any difference to your sentence? Why/why not?
- Sentence Jack on the basis that his previous conviction was for an offence on the Schedule 15B list. Does that make any difference or not?

online
resource
centre

Guidance is given in the Online Resource Centre.

You may wish to look now at the sentencing exercise at the end of Chapter 7, which also raises issues around sentencing on risk of future harm.

6

Instead of punishment?

Restorative justice, child welfare, and medical treatment

SUMMARY

This chapter looks at three very different aspects of sentencing and punishment where there are alternatives to a focus on proportional sentencing and punishment. We discuss two sets of offenders where the court does not have to sentence strictly in line with just deserts. So we focus on children and young people under 18 years of age and examine the policies developed over the past century which have taken into account the welfare of the child, such that diversion from prosecution has been justified and strict proportionality of penal response can be modified. We also focus on those offenders who are deemed to be mentally disordered and review those options available to the sentencing court which focus on treatment rather than punishment. However the chapter begins by looking at an alternative rationale and approach for responding to those who commit offences—restorative justice—and reviewing policy and practice developments. Finally, the chapter provides reflective exercises for all three (potential) alternatives to punishment.

6.1. Alternatives to a focus on punishment

6.1.1 For specified groups of offenders

We have seen in previous chapters that our sentencing framework is based largely on a retributivist justification for punishment—that we deserve punishment to the extent that we have done wrong. Punishment is therefore the aim. Utilitarian theories might justify more punishment than is strictly deserved in order to deter or to incapacitate. Conversely such theories might justify a focus on rehabilitation rather than punishment, notably via particular requirements in a community order. However, in the sentencing framework operating in England and Wales such orders are dispensed via decisions on seriousness of offending, because an offence must be serious enough to warrant the use of a community sentence. Since the 1991 Criminal Justice Act all sentences have been conceptualised as punishment.

The potential exceptions to punishment as the outcome of charge and conviction relate to two particular groups of offenders—children and young people, and those adults who have a mental disorder. We shall see in section 6.3 that the welfare of the child has been a factor in sentencing for over a century so that minors—now those under 18 years of age—can potentially be dealt with by responses which are not punishment per se. The issue to be discussed is whether in practice the welfare principle has proved strong enough to replace or reduce punishment as an outcome.

Diversion of mentally disordered offenders from prosecution has been government policy for some time. Similarly, hospital orders and other treatment outcomes for those who are classed as mentally disordered are available to the sentencing court. An issue that we will need to address in section 6.4 is why, then, there is still a larger proportion of mentally ill offenders in prison than in the general population.

6.1.2 A different approach?

This chapter will also review those elements of penal practice which are described as restorative justice (RJ). RJ is seen as a way of justifying and operationalising responses to offenders—minors and adults—which focus not on punishment but on making amends and restoring the relationship between the offender and the victim/state. Words and phrases which indicate the emergence of a new concept of 'penal' justice have been appearing in the literature of sentencing and punishment over the past four decades. Words such as making good or making amends, compensation, community, reconciliation, restoration, reintegration, and reparation have not usually been associated with punishment and have not featured in our reviews of retributivist and utilitarian justifications. These ideas around restorative justice potentially or actually constitute a third paradigm to sit alongside retributivism and utilitarianism.

Recent governments have been very enthusiastic about RJ initiatives. For example the Coalition government's response to *Breaking the Cycle* (Ministry of Justice 2010a) proposed to increase the range and availability of restorative justice approaches: 'We are proposing using restorative justice interventions at each stage of the justice system. Most responses to the consultation welcomed our emphasis on greater use of restorative justice' (Ministry of Justice 2011a: para 28). There would appear to be cross-party support for restorative justice and it is always publicly lauded but it has not yet, as we shall see, had a transformative effect on the criminal justice system, although there has been some progress. Section 6.2 will, therefore, address this apparent paradox, reviewing the roots and ideas of restorative justice, examining those aspects of the sentencing system which can be seen as restorative, and assessing the difficulties slowing the pace of progress in implementing restorative justice.

6.2 Restorative justice

You may wish to do the exercise at 6.5.1 before you read the rest of this section about restorative justice.

6.2.1 Theorising restorative justice

> Restorative justice has many routes that cannot be easily separated. It emerged as a 'movement' espoused by a relatively small but energetic group of activists, academics, non-governmental organisations and policy entrepreneurs.
>
> (McLaughlin *et al.* 2003: 2)

While all citizens potentially benefit from successful utilitarian strategies, and all may benefit from an enhanced sense of justice through retributivist sentencing, the victim and the community are largely bystanders in these accounts. In RJ, the victim and community take centre stage with the offender in responding to offending. RJ and its major focus on reparation and on victims were, by the early twenty-first century, 'receiving more concentrated attention than ever before from both criminologists and policy makers' (McEvoy *et al.* 2002: 469; see also Weitekamp and Kerner 2002). The European Forum for Victim–Offender Mediation and Restorative Justice was established in 2000,[1] the Restorative Justice Consortium (now Council) in the UK published its *General Principles for Restorative Justice* in 2002,[2] the UK government published a Consultation Paper on its restorative justice strategy in 2003 (Home Office 2003a), the Domestic Violence, Crime and Victims Act was passed in 2004, and also in 2004 the government published *Compensation and Support for Victims of Crime* (Home Office 2004a).

Since then, there has been an increased academic interest in restorative justice, evidenced by a plethora of books on restorative justice (see, for example, Aertsen *et al.* 2006; Bottoms and Roberts 2010; Braithwaite 2003; Christie 2007; Cornwell *et al.* 2013; Hall 2010; Johnstone 2011; Karstedt *et al.* 2014; Llewellyn and Philpott 2014; Miers 2004; Murphy and Harris 2007; Roche 2003; Rossner 2013; Shapland *et al.* 2008, 2011; Sherman *et al.* 2007b; Strang 2003, 2007; von Hirsch *et al.* 2005; Woolford and Ratner 2007). However, it is more difficult to find the evidence of practical changes, as Strang noted in 2007 when reviewing developments in several jurisdictions: 'While restorative justice as a justice practice attracts oodles of advocates and scholars and much commentary about its supposed unstoppable spread, there has not actually been very much extensively institutionalized in its most recent manifestation' (Strang 2007: 204).

A written answer given to Parliament the same year suggests one reason why, except in relation to children and young people, there was less activity 'on the ground': 'The [Labour] Government's strategy is to encourage, but not require, the use of adult restorative justice whilst building the evidence base to establish the impact of its use, particularly in relation to reoffending' (*Official Report*, 14 June 2007; col WA277). The Coalition government also hoped that its proposals would have implications for the reduction of reoffending (Ministry of Justice 2010a: para 79) and Sadiq Khan MP told the annual conference of the Labour Party in 2013, 'We know that victims who sit down with the offender, helped by well-trained facilitators, emerge feeling better from the experience. And done properly it reduces reoffending and, yes, saves money too. Win, win, win!'[3] More recently the Ministry of Justice published a 'Restorative Justice Action Plan for the Criminal Justice System for the Period to March 2018' which was a little cautious when it commented that 'RJ has the potential to help rehabilitate offenders and enable them to stop offending' (2014f: 3), but before the General Election of 2015 a Conservative Policy Forum presentation confidently stated that 'RJ also reduces the frequency of re-offending by 14 per cent. Some trials estimate that RJ can deliver cost savings of up to £9 for every £1 spent.'[4]

Governments have, then, been concerned to ensure there are proven cost benefits in terms of reduction of reoffending rates and restorative measures have become important in sentencing and punishment at least partly because of the coming together of a number of influences and motivations—not all consistent with each other. One important strand in the early movement was that which originated in religious communities—for example, the Mennonite sect in the United States and the Quakers in the UK—who gave priority to

[1] See http://www.euforumrj.org/.

[2] See the Restorative Justice Council website at http://www.restorativejustice.org.uk for information on the organisation and its publications.

[3] Rt Hon Sadiq Khan MP, Shadow Secretary of State for Justice, 25 September 2013; accessed at http://www.sadiqkhan.org.uk/sadiq_speech_to_labour_party_conference_2013.

[4] The presentation (see slide 7) and summary are available via http://www.readingeastconservatives.com/event/conservative-policy-forum-justice accessed 25 January 2016: see slide 7 of the attached justice_powerpoint.ppt file.

the reduction of conflict and the promotion of harmony. What was being encouraged was something to replace punishment, a form of penal intervention which does not carry the same connotations as punishment. One of the most influential early writers on restorative justice, Howard Zehr, wrote:

> We define crime as an offence against the State. We define justice as the establishment of blame and the imposition of pain under the guidance of right rules.
>
> I think it is essential to remember that this definition of crime and justice, as common-sensical as it may seem, is only one paradigm, only one possible way of looking at crime and at justice. We have been so dominated by our assumptions that we often assume it is the only way, or at least the only right way, to approach the issue.
>
> It is not. It is not the only possible model or paradigm of justice—not logically, not historically.

> (Zehr 1985: 4)

In this article Zehr used words associated with 'restorative justice' such as restitution, atonement, community, victim, accountability, victim involvement in outcome, reintegrative shaming, repairing damage, and problem-solving—words which signify concepts underpinning this different paradigm (see Table 6.1).

Restorative justice as a new paradigm not only looks for different responses to crime but locates crime in a different context altogether; not in the criminal justice system but in the whole range of social and interpersonal conflicts and disputes. (See, for example, Walgrave 2013.) Certainly, the distinction between the civil and the criminal is not universal, and disputes (including those which might otherwise be categorised as crimes) have been settled in various ways at different times and in different places. (See, for example, Roberts 1979; Sayles 1950: chapters 11 and 14; Stein 1984: chapter 5.) This wider approach to conflict management means that restorative justice proponents have encouraged the use of alternative dispute resolution (ADR) techniques and restorative justice shares values of community and individual responsibility and empowerment with the ADR movement (see Mulcahy 2000). Conversely, some sections of the 'dispute-processing industry' have incorporated and promoted restorative justice principles and techniques in their professional practice (see Kennedy 1990; Olson and Dzur 2004).

Given that restorative justice is primarily concerned with repairing damage done and restoring harmony, the role of the victim is very important in theory and practice, whether the victim be perceived as an individual or a community. Braithwaite, an influential exponent of restorative justice, notes that it has two important dimensions—process and values (Braithwaite 2003: 7–14).

In relation to process, restorative justice advocates that the victim and/or community as well as the offender should be involved in decision-making, so that techniques such as mediation become very important in this process. In relation to values this means that, in the mediation of outcome, the values of reintegration and forgiveness take precedence over notions such as punishment and retribution. For this to happen, the victim or a representative of the community must be involved in the process and also, as relevant, in the outcomes. An outcome may include an apology to the victim or it may include some form of practical reparation to the victim or to the community. The emphasis on the core values of community, opportunity, responsibility, and accountability (Le Grand 1998) in the Third Way[5] of the Labour government also resonated with restorative justice with its emphasis on

---

[5] A communitarian ideology.

Table 6.1 Paradigms of justice old and new

Old paradigm: retributive justice	New paradigm: restorative justice
1. Crime defined as violation of the state	1. Crime defined as violation of one person by another
2. Focus on establishing blame, on guilt, on past (did he/she do it?)	2. Focus on problem-solving, on liabilities and obligations, on future (what should be done?)
3. Adversarial relationships and process normative	3. Dialogue and negotiation normative
4. Imposition of pain to punish and deter/prevent	4. Restitution as a means of restoring both parties; reconciliation/restoration as goal
5. Justice defined by intent and by process: right rules	5. Justice defined as right relationships: judged by the outcome
6. Interpersonal, conflictual nature of crime obscured, repressed; conflict seen as individual vs state	6. Crime recognised as interpersonal conflict; value of conflict recognised
7. One social injury replaced by another	7. Focus on repair of social injury
8. Community on sideline, represented abstractly by state	8. Community as facilitator in restorative process
9. Encouragement of competitive, individualistic values	9. Encouragement of mutuality
10. Action directed from state to offender: – victim ignored – offender passive	10. Victim and offender roles recognised in both problem and solution: – victim rights/needs recognised – offender encouraged to take responsibility
11. Offender accountability defined as taking punishment	11. Offender accountability defined as understanding impact of action and helping decide how to make things right
12. Offence defined in purely legal terms, devoid of moral, social, economic, political dimensions	12. Offence understood in whole context—moral, social, economic, political
13. 'Debt' owed to state and society in the abstract	13. Debt/liability to victim recognised
14. Response focused on offender's past behaviour	14. Response focused on harmful consequences of offender's behaviour
15. Stigma of crime unremovable	15. Stigma of crime removable through restorative action
16. No encouragement for repentance and forgiveness	16. Possibilities for repentance and forgiveness
17. Dependence upon proxy professionals	17. Direct involvement by participant

Source: Zehr (1985).

encouraging the offender to own a sense of responsibility for what he or she has done and to be motivated, therefore, to put things right.

This does not mean that the objectives of restorative justice are in practice necessarily different from those of the traditional criminal justice system. The restorative aim of reintegrating the offender into the community entails preventing the offender from reoffending, a traditional aim of the criminal justice system. Nor is a desire to be cost-effective and to 'do justice' excluded from thinking in restorative justice. However, the concept of justice is different and the criteria for cost-effectiveness will relate not only to the narrow objectives of the criminal justice system, but may well also relate to community 'health' as well as to victim satisfaction and offender reformation.

Restorative justice can still involve denunciation, however. Censure within a restorative context can record a wrong done but is thought to be less damaging than harsh retribution. 'Reintegrative' shaming of the offender may be effective in deterring him (or her) from future criminality and allow for the offender's reintegration into society on the basis that if the offender is simply stigmatised he will be alienated and less likely to change his behaviour (Braithwaite 1989; Richards 1998).[6] So crime prevention and deterrence may be achieved in ways other than harsh punishment, as, for example through continuous reparation, and victims may want redress for harms suffered rather than punishment. Restorative justice recognises the autonomy of the offender and victim and some proponents argue that there should be a right for victims to meet offenders and a right for offenders to offer reparation (see Wright 1996).

Supporters of restorative justice have subscribed to one or other of two fundamentally different aims: that of establishing a totally new system of justice/dispute settlement to replace the traditional systems of justice, and that of establishing new techniques and principles to graft onto the old. The remainder of this chapter will examine developments in the UK to see which of these objectives is being pursued. In order to provide a historical context we first consider those earlier measures that encouraged mediation and reparation by offenders and their policy or practice aims.

6.2.2 **Earlier mediation and reparation schemes**

It was the 1980s which witnessed the development of victim–offender mediation schemes. Experimental projects were funded by the state or charitable bodies but they were 'supply-led' and were based on the idea that offending is a harm which is primarily a matter between individuals, and that the two main people, the victim and offender, should have responsibility for the outcome. These experimental schemes took from restorative justice the principle that reparation and apologising to the victim are very important, but they also took from the ADR movement the idea that the agreement should be voluntarily negotiated and imposed.

The early schemes were implemented in the UK at three different points in the criminal justice system: at the pre-prosecution stage as part of diversion of young offenders from prosecution, at the stage between conviction and sentence, and also as part of punishment itself. These three stages for restorative justice are very similar to those proposed more recently in *Breaking the Cycle* (Ministry of Justice 2010a). In the 1980s the pre-prosecution schemes were possibly of the highest profile. Davis *et al.* (1988; see also Blagg 1985; Davis 1992) found that in such schemes—usually aimed at young offenders—the reparation tended to be apologies and other symbolic offers of help. Victims sometimes felt under

---

[6] However, Braithwaite's comment is based on research on white collar offenders and so might be more likely to work for young first offenders from law-abiding regimes than with sophisticated criminals in large cities (Walker 1991: 48).

pressure to take part in these schemes of mediation, although evaluation of court-based schemes in South Yorkshire showed that participating victims found it rewarding to help young offenders change their attitudes (Smith *et al.* 1988).

Pre-sentence reparation—inserted between conviction and sentence—can be seen as reparation which gives the offender the possibility of providing himself with mitigation: a report on the outcome of victim–offender mediation is given to the court before sentencing. In the 1980s four such experimental schemes were funded by the Home Office. However, Young found that this link between mitigation and reparation appeared to be 'unpalatable to both victims and offenders' (Young 1989: 464) and he criticised the scheme for allowing the offender little choice as to whether his sentencing would be deferred, which meant victims doubted the voluntariness of the offender's involvement (Davis 1992: 140) and two-thirds of the offenders felt that even if they were genuine in their desire to mediate, the victim would still think that they were lying.

The third stage in which reparation was used in these early schemes was as part of punishment itself. Developed in North America, such schemes were referred to as victim offender reconciliation programmes (VORPs), usually entailing group meetings of victims and offenders (see Umbreit 1994 in Smith and Hillenbrand 1997: 250). They were pioneered in the UK at youth custody establishments (Liebmann 2000: 1).

Research results for these and the other schemes noted were mixed or critical. 'The current attempts to promote reparation in this country are half-baked', wrote Davis and colleagues (1988: 128), although professionals involved were in favour (Smith *et al.* 1988: 378). However, by the 1990s, the schemes were described as 'bit players' (Shapland 2003: 211; see also Stewart 1998: Table 6.1) and in the early 1990s one commentator wrote, 'It is now fair to say that, within government circles, mediation and reparation schemes constitute something of a "dead" subject' (Davis 1992: vii). Finding out why these schemes were generally seen as unsuccessful will help us evaluate current policy developments in section 6.2.4.

One possible reason is that 'restorative justice' was rarely used to describe these schemes, with many supporters of mediation and reparation viewing them simply as process tools for different end products. Proponents of a wider vision of restorative justice argued that restorative justice principles would locate such experiments differently (Marshall 1992). Perhaps more importantly, the experiments were also relatively small, time-limited under threat of withdrawal of funding, and scattered across the country. Further, the schemes were 'stand-alone' schemes (Dignan and Lowey 2000: 45) in the sense that there was no specific statutory provision authorising their development.

Yet the prediction by one critical researcher that 'the shortcomings of our criminal justice system are so profound that further attempts will be made' (Davis 1992: 1) has been fulfilled. An analysis of research findings from schemes operating in the first decade of this century concluded that 'Restorative justice has made significant progress in recent years and now plays an increasingly important role in and alongside the criminal justice systems of a number of countries in different parts of the world' (Shapland *et al.* 2011: summary). However, it went on to sound a note of caution that 'it has been difficult to gain an accurate picture of its implementation'. In the next section we review progress in relation to restorative justice with young offenders before examining current government policy more widely.

6.2.3 **Restorative justice for young offenders**

Restorative justice has been given greater priority and more resources in relation to youth justice for some time[7] because politically it is less risky and because rehabilitation of the

---

[7] Harris, for example, noted over two decades ago that 'the UK system, though not devoid of restitutive creativity, has expended much of it on juvenile work' (1992: 62).

young offender is viewed as more urgent. Restorative justice projects for young offenders have included victim–offender mediation (between the offender and the victim or a representative of the community), victim awareness programmes, reparation (symbolic in the form of an apology or as a practical piece of work), and family group conferences (FGCs: see Jackson (1999) for a discussion of practice in the 1990s). The Crime and Disorder Act (CDA) 1998 had a substantial component directed at children and young people (see Piper 1999), and the Youth Justice and Criminal Evidence Act 1999 gave statutory backing to such restorative justice processes.

Out-of-court options

Section 6.3.6 reviews the police-led out-of-court diversionary options. The original scheme, introduced by the CDA 1998, used reprimands and warnings for first- and second-time offenders, and included referral to a Youth Offending Team (YOT) on a 'final' warning. The new scheme of youth conditional cautions (YCCs) has similar provisions. YOTs were encouraged to use restorative processes in the delivery of all intervention programmes (Home Office/Youth Justice Board 2002: para 10.15) which were part of the warning scheme. Guidance now states, 'The conditions attached to the Youth Conditional Caution can be reparative, rehabilitative or punitive in nature. Punitive conditions should only be used where rehabilitative and reparative conditions are not suitable or sufficient to address the offending' (Ministry of Justice/Youth Justice Board 2013: para 3.13). Victim–offender mediation and an apology or reparation to the victim or community can be part of the conditions.

A youth restorative disposal (YRD), piloted 2008/9, 'entails a young person admitting guilt, taking responsibility for their actions and apologizing to the offended party' (Kelly and Armitage 2014/15: 6). The YOT is involved with the police in setting the conditions, which can include restorative measures to 'provide an opportunity for the offender to understand the consequences of their conduct, make reparation and avoid the criminalisation associated with a formal criminal justice outcome' (Office for Criminal Justice Reform 2010: para 4.17). Evaluation of the scheme showed the average age of the young person receiving a YRD was 13–14, 59 per cent were male (but with big variations between police forces), and shoplifting (52 per cent), assault (22 per cent), and criminal damage (19 per cent) were the main offences dealt with but, again, there were considerable differences between areas (Youth Justice Board 2011c: 3).[8] A more recent report also found 'substantial variations in practice by youth offending services making use of the YRD approach' (Kelly and Armitage 2015: 7–8).

Court orders

Reparative components have also been added to court orders for young offenders. The PCCSA 2000 (ss. 73–75)[9] provides for reparation orders and action plan orders, although the latter order is now available only for offenders whose offence was committed before 30 November 2009. If imposing a reparation order the court may order the young offender to repair any damage to the victim's property, remove any graffiti from buildings that belong to the public, or take part in 'mediation' with the victim. It usually takes 24 hours to complete a reparation order, spread over a number of days within a three-month period.[10] The reparation order can stand alone and the reparation can be directed at the community

[8] See http://yjbpublications.justice.gov.uk/en-gb/scripts/prodView.asp?idproduct=500&eP=.
[9] Originally enacted in the CDA 1998, ss. 61–64 and 69–79.
[10] For further details see http://www.direct.gov.uk/en/YoungPeople/CrimeAndJustice/Typesofsentencesyoung peoplecanget/DG_10028367.

or the victim. The Criminal Justice Act (CJA) 2003 continues the status of the reparation order as a penalty that is not a community order (see Chapter 11: section 11.3.3).

The referral order as the presumptive sentence for first-time offenders in the youth court was introduced by the Youth Justice and Criminal Evidence Act 1999. Referral is to a young offender panel where a 'programme of behaviour' is agreed (see Ball 2000: 211–22). Referral orders should lead to some reparative component and, in the 11 areas in which referral orders were piloted and researched, the most common compulsory element (in 40 per cent of all contracts) was some form of reparative activity. The most common form of reparation was community reparation (42 per cent), followed by a written apology (38 per cent), with direct reparation to the victim or payment of compensation counting for 7 per cent (Newburn *et al.* 2002: viii–ix). The introduction of the YRO and the Scaled Approach programme (see Chapter 11: sections 11.2.4 and 11.3.4) led to revised National Standards and also revised referral order guidance following the amendments made by the Criminal Justice and Immigration Act 2008 (see Youth Justice Board 2008).

Youth rehabilitation orders (YROs)—which are community orders and therefore in the second tier of orders—can also include a requirement that the young offender engage in reparation. However, in line with Recommendation No. R (99) 19 of the United Nations Congress on Crime Prevention and the Treatment of Offenders, adopted by the Committee of Ministers of the Council of Europe on Mediation in Penal Matters, the restrictions on liberty imposed by both YROs and reparation orders must be commensurate with offence seriousness (CJA 2003, s. 148(3)(b)). This contrasts with a purely utilitarian approach where a desired outcome could justify a burden heavier than that determined by seriousness.

Conferencing

Family group conferences (FGCs) and restorative conferencing were promoted in consultation documents of the Labour government: *Respect and Responsibility* (Home Office 2003b), *Every Child Matters* (DfES 2003), and *Youth Justice—The Next Steps* (Home Office 2003c). It was argued that the process of using referral orders 'draws elements from family group conferences and children's hearings in Scotland' (Ball 2000: 217).[11] They also drew inspiration from developments in other countries, notably New Zealand and Australia, where there are now statutory bases for the use of restorative conferences. In New Zealand the first scheme was set up in 1989 in response to concern about the 'cultural appropriateness' for the Maori people of the principles of family law derived from a colonial system of justice (King 1997a: 134–5). This concern about the loss of indigenous systems of justice with restorative principles was also expressed in Canada and Australia: see Tauri and Morris (2003: 45).

In the UK, however, there was no such impetus and the early schemes were ad hoc initiatives (Gelsthorpe and Morris 2002: 245; see also Dignan and Marsh 2001), although the context for their use is now as part of statutory orders and processes, directed by guidance.[12] Restorative cautioning or conferencing, developed as local initiatives by police forces in the 1990s (Hoyle *et al.* 2002: 7), and guidance urged that the meetings at which the warnings were given should if possible be organised as restorative group conferences.[13] 'A restorative approach can make final warnings more meaningful and effective . . . Research . . . shows that the use of restorative processes reduces offending . . . and can be of benefit to victims'

---

[11] For discussion re children's hearings see Young (1997).

[12] See, for example, the YJB's *Key Elements of Effective Practice: Restorative Justice, Guidance.*

[13] See, for example, Standard 7 of the YJB's *National Standards for Youth Justice* (B420), available at https://www.gov.uk/government/uploads/system/uploads/attachment_data/file/296274/national-standards-youth-justice-services.pdf.

(Home Office/Youth Justice Board 2002: para 9.22). However, the *Code of Practice for Youth Conditional Cautions* (Ministry of Justice 2013c) does not mention restorative conferences.

Restorative justice has also been seen as a way of promoting both the welfare and the rights of children and young people. Allen (1996), for example, suggests that taking part in restorative justice initiatives helps restore personal respect and encourages the taking of responsibility, avoids stigmatisation, and promotes reintegration in the community. Likewise, *No More Excuses* (Home Office 1997: 31–2) summed up restorative justice principles as the '3Rs' of restoration, reintegration, and responsibility. However, the commitment of providers to 'reintegration' has been questioned (NACRO 2003e)—a sign that it might be proving easier to incorporate individual responsibility or restoration—the making of amends—into the criminal justice system than the much wider aim of providing support and guidance to reintegrate a young person in a way that will decrease exclusion and offending.

The stated benefits of restorative approaches, in helping offenders to understand and regret the effects of their offending, are benefits, research would suggest, that can be delivered only if restorative procedures are done well (Hoyle *et al*. 2002; Holdaway *et al*. 2001: 39; see also Dignan 1999: 54).

The use of a 'script'—'doing' the techniques—is not effective without a proper understanding of the underlying principles. Wilcox *et al*. (2004) compared the reconviction rates of offenders experiencing traditional cautions with those experiencing restorative cautioning in their Thames Valley Police study but were unable to establish whether restorative cautioning made an impact on the seriousness and frequency of subsequent offending. Holdaway and Desborough, however, found that 31 per cent of their sample reoffended within a year (2004: 5).

More recent research on restorative justice within referral orders also sounded a note of caution: 'Restorative approaches are resource-hungry and should be reserved for cases where the time and resource input gives a good chance of success . . . The conclusion is that this process . . . can potentially cause more harm than good for the very few victims who are actually prepared to become involved in the process' (Newbury 2011: 263). However, evaluation of 30 funded projects including final warnings found that the majority of parents and young offenders expressed positive views about the projects, but noted that 'Despite their benefits, very few Final Warnings were restorative conferences. The overwhelming majority of warnings, 80%, were of the standard type' (Holdaway and Desborough 2004: 6–7).

Gal and Moyal, reporting on research in Australia, found that, while restorative justice was 'significantly more satisfying than court for both victims and offenders', 'conference juvenile victims were less satisfied than court juvenile victims'. Further, 'more serious harm is associated with decreased process satisfaction for all victims' (Gal and Moyal 2011: abstract). It is difficult to assess restorative justice initiatives, however, partly because of the differing conceptions of restorative justice and the different methods of delivery (Miers 2004: 30).[14] Research on Australian schemes with young offenders also draws attention to the need to research restorative justice in context, asking in particular for more detailed data on the offending histories, offence types, and offence seriousness of juveniles referred by police to restorative justice processes (Richards 2010).[15]

---

[14] Miers (2004) had evaluated seven schemes conducted for the Home Office in 1999–2000, five dealing with young offenders.

[15] See also Sherman, Strang, and Woods (2010) *Recidivism Patterns in the Canberra Reintegrative Shaming Experiments (RISE)*. Canberra, Australian National University, available via http://www.aic.gov.au/criminal_justice_system/rjustice/rise/recidivism.aspx.

6.2.4 **How important is restorative justice in current policy and practice?**

Restorative justice is still important in youth justice policy. The current chair of the Youth Justice Board (YJB), Lord McNally, said in his Foreword to an information pack about RJ for youth justice teams:

> But the beauty of the principles of restorative justice lie in the fact that they don't only apply after a crime has been committed by a young person. When used with imagination, as some youth offending teams (YOTs) are already demonstrating, it can form the foundation of early interventions with young people on the cusp of criminality, working upstream to help divert them from a criminal path.
>
> (Restorative Justice Council 2015: 3)

Lord McNally went on to say that 'The more we practise it across the country, the more embedded restorative justice becomes into the mainstream of the criminal justice system.' A similar sentiment had been expressed in *Breaking the Cycle*: 'While it is a well established concept in youth justice, restorative justice for adults is sometimes viewed as an after-thought to sentencing. We are looking at how we might change this so that in appropriate cases restorative justice is a fundamental part of the sentencing process' (Ministry of Justice 2010a: para 79) and the Paper set out three strategies to achieve that.

> Firstly, this is likely to involve using restorative approaches as a better alternative to formal criminal justice action for low level offenders . . . Secondly . . . we will explore how . . . restoration [could] be delivered as part of an out-of-court disposal, for example as a condition attached to a conditional caution. . . . Thirdly, restorative conferences carried out pre-sentence for offenders who admit guilt and who agree to participate, could be reported to the court with the victim's consent as part of pre-sentence reports. . . . In some cases, and for some offences, sentencing could be deferred pending successful completion of actions agreed.
>
> (Ministry of Justice 2010a: paras 79–81)

These strategies had been piloted some decades ago—as we saw in section 6.2.2—or had been used with young offenders (see section 6.2.3), but were presented as being relatively novel. They have now been included in legislation for England and Wales.

A new section 1ZA inserted in the Powers of Criminal Courts (Sentencing) Act 2000 by Schedule 16 Part 2 of the Crime and Courts Act 2013 is designed to make clearer that courts can use their existing powers to defer sentencing to allow for a restorative justice activity to take place—similar to the restorative justice 'as mitigation' schemes piloted in the 1980s. The Ministry of Justice has said that restorative justice will only take place where both victim and offender are willing to participate and can be delivered through a facilitated group conference or community conference, or indirectly by written correspondence, telephone, or video conference (see guidance for pre-sentence restorative justice: Ministry of Justice 2014e). The introduction of pre-sentence restorative justice is through two pathfinder projects—one in the magistrates' courts looking at processes and the other based in 10–12 specific Crown Courts focusing on outcomes.[16]

In fact the Halliday Report had proposed measures by which the court could enable the offender 'to tap into reparation and restorative justice schemes . . . at the pre-sentence

---

[16] See http://www.cps.gov.uk/legal/p_to_r/restorative_justice/. For further information see the website for the Bristol pathfinder project: http://restorativebristol.co.uk/the-pre-sentence-rj-pathfinder-programme/#.VBa6kJUtA5s.

stage' (2001: para 6.20) and the CJA 2003 s. 278 amended ss. 1 and 2 of the PCCSA 2000 to include at s. 1(1):

> The Crown Court or a magistrates' court may defer passing sentence on an offender for the purpose of enabling the court, or any other court to which it falls to deal with him, to have regard in dealing with him to—
>
> (a) his conduct after conviction (including, where appropriate, the making by him of reparation for his offence); or
>
> (b) any change in his circumstances.

There have also been developments in Northern Ireland:[17] for example, youth and family group conferencing was introduced by the Justice (Northern Ireland) Act 2002[18] and a *Protocol for Community-Based Restorative Justice Scheme* was published in 2007 (Northern Ireland Office 2007). The eighth International Conference of the European Forum for Restorative Justice (EFRJ) was held in Belfast in 2014 and the Justice Minister said that Belfast was chosen because 'Northern Ireland is internationally recognised as a significant centre for effective and innovative restorative practices in both the statutory and community sectors.'[19]

Similarly, Scotland has taken on board restorative justice conferences, family group conferences, police restorative cautioning (see Scottish Executive 2004), and also restorative justice circles (used to address the harm caused by two or more persons to an establishment, group, or community, rather than to an identifiable person).[20] Sacro runs a Restorative Justice Service which provides the Procurator Fiscal in three locations with an alternative to prosecution for those over 16 years of age.[21]

In all the jurisdictions of the UK, 'community' is now much more prominent in the rhetoric of restorative justice. Community Payback—part of a community penalty (see Chapter 10: section 10.3)—and the community impact statement are evidence of the new focus. The latter covers a specific time period and area; as a generic statement it illustrates the concerns and priorities of that community regarding crime and anti-social behaviour, and as a specific statement relates to the impact of one incident. [22] The statements are compiled by the police in the form of a witness statement and can be used to inform decisions about charging, out-of-court disposals (such as conditional cautions), and sentencing options. While this development may well have advantages it would also appear to be a response to the difficulty of implementing restorative justice in regard to particular victims or where there is no clear victim.

There is no question that all governments are loudly proclaiming their support for restorative justice initiatives and that many of these initiatives are now based in statute and receive government funding. The crucial issues concern the extent to which there is sufficient coverage of schemes such that there is not injustice by geography, and the extent to which restorative justice is put into practice in the spirit which its proponents—especially its early supporters—advocate, and within a context which does not undermine those principles.

---

[17] See Dignan and Lowey (2000) for developments at the end of the last century.

[18] See O'Mahoney (2004) and, for recent developments, http://www.fgcni.org/restorative-practice/index.php, the website of Family Group Conference (Northern Ireland).

[19] David Ford; see http://www.northernireland.gov.uk/index/media-centre/news-departments/news-doj/news-doj-120614-victims-must-be.htm?WT.mc_id=rss-news.

[20] See http://www.restorativejusticescotland.org.uk/html/restorative_justice_processes.html.

[21] See http://www.sacro.org.uk/services/criminal-justice/adult-restorative-justice.

[22] See, for further information, http://www.cps.gov.uk/legal/a_to_c/community_impact_statement_-_adult/#introduction.

Crawford asserted in 2000 that restorative justice initiatives in quantitative terms 'remain at the margins of criminal justice' in systems across Europe, North America, and Australasia (2000: 29). One of the side headings in a Working Paper on the use of restorative justice published by the Commission on English Prisons Today—'The Current State of Play: all talk and no action'—also suggested there had been insufficient progress in the first decade of the twenty-first century (Hoyle 2008: 2).

However, it is fair to say that there is now an 'industry' of training for the delivery of restorative justice. 'Restorative Solutions' was established in 2000, for example, as 'a not-for-profit Community Interest Company (CIC) committed to enabling the use of innovative restorative approaches as a practical and cost-effective intervention for reducing harm or conflict'.[23] A Restorative Justice Register of qualified restorative justice practitioners, funded by the Ministry of Justice and the Restorative Justice Council, was launched in 2011; there is now a Restorative Service Quality Mark (RSQM);[24] and there is a BTEC qualification in restorative justice.[25] Now, Wood claims: 'Over the last three decades restorative justice (RJ) has emerged from a small set of youth justice alternatives to a widely institutionalised set of justice practices.'[26]

Punishment and payback

The first chapter of *Breaking the Cycle* is entitled 'Punishment and Payback' and outlined, inter alia, the Coalition government's plans to ensure offenders 'will make greater financial reparation to the victim and the taxpayer' and also to use community sentences for 'making them pay back to society and the taxpayer'. This is another example of a greater focus on making amends to the community, either through unpaid work or through payment into the criminal justice system to benefit the taxpayer.

A conditional caution was introduced for adults by s. 22 of the CJA 2003 and the generic community order for adults allows for specified requirements which could include unpaid work[27] or restorative meetings (see Chapter 10). Section 201(2) of the CJA 2003 gives details of the 'activity requirement' which 'may consist of or include activities whose purpose is that of reparation, such as activities involving contact between offenders and persons affected by their offences'. The aggregate number of days for any activity cannot exceed 60. Similar requirements can be specified in a licence for prisoners serving the community part of a custodial sentence or for the requirements that can be specified in a suspended sentence order (s. 182). The voluntary and private sectors are also now involved in delivering these programmes (see Chapter 10).

This section has focused on new restorative ways of encouraging a just response to offending, but there are sentencing options which relate to 'making amends' which have a longer history. Confiscation and compensation have become increasingly important in sentencing but their origins are earlier, and their development was not part of an articulated restorative justice agenda. We will deal with these older forms of reparation and more recent developments which do not fit within the restorative justice paradigm in Chapter 7 (section 7.2).

---

[23] http://www.restorativesolutions.org.uk.

[24] See https://www.restorativejustice.org.uk/restorative-service-quality-mark.

[25] Advanced Award in Practitioner Training for Restorative Approaches: see http://www.cspacademy.ac.uk/BTEC-L3-RJ-Practitioner-Training.htm.

[26] W. R. Wood at http://www.crimeandjustice.org.uk/resources/can-restorative-justice-cut-prison-numbers.

[27] See *Working to Make Amends*, which is the report of an inspection of a scheme of enhanced community punishment and unpaid work under the previous sentencing options (HM Inspectorate of Probation 2006b).

6.2.5 **Tensions in policy, theory, and practice**

Restorative justice can be evaluated on two levels, the practical and the theoretical: does restorative justice 'work', and are policy and practice conceptually coherent? The two levels are linked in the sense that a focus on practice and 'effectiveness' necessitates establishing the criteria for evaluation: those depend on aims, and they in turn depend on the theoretical frame and the conceptual values that underpin practice. Morris and Maxwell rephrase the research questions into: 'are the values underpinning the particular model chosen . . . restorative?' and 'what are the consequences of adopting restorative justice processes compared with those associated with the continued existence of retributive or conventional criminal justice processes?' (2001: 267). Ashworth has also warned that the state must retain responsibility: 'If the state does delegate certain spheres of criminal justice to some form of community-based conference, the importance of insisting on the protection of basic rights for defendants is not diminished' (Ashworth 2002a: 591).

However, recent governments have focused much more narrowly on a utilitarian aim for restorative justice—does it reduce reoffending? The fourth report of Shapland and her colleagues, using data from their three schemes for adult offenders, focused on this issue and concluded (though with caveats): 'Summed over all three restorative justice schemes, those offenders who participated in restorative justice committed statistically significantly *fewer* offences (in terms of reconvictions) in the subsequent two years than offenders in the control group' (Shapland *et al.* 2008: 66). However, '[w]hen considering the restorative justice schemes summed together in terms of *severity of reconviction* there were no significant differences between the restorative justice and the control groups' (Shapland *et al.* 2008: 67, emphasis in original).

The review of research on schemes in the UK carried out almost a decade ago by Sherman, Strang, and colleagues was also generally positive, but they make significant comments: 'The most important conclusion is that *RJ works differently on different kinds of people*. It can work very well as a general policy, if a growing body of evidence on "what works for whom" can become the basis for specifying when and when not to use it', and, surprisingly perhaps, '*RJ seems to reduce crime more effectively with more, rather than less, serious crimes*' (2007b: 8; italics in the original; for further analysis see Christie 2007; Murphy and Harris 2007; Woolford and Ratner 2007). A more recent review of research results on face-to-face RJ conferences also concluded positively:

> Our synthesis . . . shows that, on average, RJCs cause a modest but highly cost-effective reduction in repeat offending, with substantial benefits for victims. A cost-effectiveness estimate for the seven United Kingdom (UK) experiments found a ratio of 8 times more benefit in costs of crimes prevented than the cost of delivering RJCs.
>
> (Strang *et al.* 2013: 6)

Miers had concluded, however, that research (Miers *et al.* 2001) offered 'no conclusive support' for the view that restorative justice is more likely to lead to mutually satisfactory outcomes than standard criminal justice responses (2004: 32). Nevertheless he noted that the mixed findings confirm a 'generally held view among both victims and offenders that such interventions are, at least at the time, "better" than the conventional alternatives' (2004: 32).

Victims have multiple roles in the criminal justice system: they are consumers on the one hand and, given the values of restorative justice, are also participants (Miers 2004: 24), but they will not automatically benefit from the initiatives promoted on their behalf. In their longer-term research Shapland *et al.* also concluded that 'overall, the findings suggest that victims and offenders participating in the three restorative justice schemes were very happy with how the schemes operated and with their experiences of restorative justice' and that, although victims had different expectations, most of their expectations were met (2007a: 46). Strang drew lessons from research on failed conferences to list the conditions which must be right if restorative practice is to be beneficial (Strang 2003; see also Tickell and Akester 2004: 24–7; Sherman et al. 2007b), while Shapland et al. noted that 'particularly if [the scheme] is set within a framework provided by criminal justice, participants need to know whether the offender has tried to complete elements of the outcome agreement and what happened at sentence (if the meeting was pre-sentence)' (Shapland et al. 2007a: 48).

There are, then, now good detailed reviews of the research on restorative justice programmes which summarise findings about different outcome measures and different models of victim–offender meetings or FGCs, which compare the results of using or not using statutory frameworks and mandatory referrals, and which focus on the influence of factors specific to particular jurisdictions and cultural contexts. All emphasise that it is not possible to generalise—and many produce findings that are not statistically significant—but there are examples of well-run projects with clear principles which achieve restorative outcomes. Within the confines of this chapter it is impossible to do justice to these reviews where the detail and the caveats are so crucial. What is clear is that 'restorative justice . . . has now become embraced by the countries of the United Nations as a preferred option for the future resolution of disputes' (Morris and Maxwell 2001: 277) and that recent and current governments in the UK fully support it.

In previous editions of this text we expressed concern that training might not be keeping up with demand for restorative justice practitioners. We referred to Tickell and Akester's comment that '[a]nger, resentment and hostility will not automatically wither away in the face of good intentions' (2004: 25) and to the example of bad practice given by Roche which entailed a 12-year-old boy agreeing in a restorative conference to the proposal of his mother and the store manager that he wear outside the shop a T-shirt announcing 'I am a thief' (2003: 1). We have already noted, however, that the issue of training and registration is now being addressed, and we welcome this.

Some commentators are not concerned with the difference between restorative justice and the traditional criminal justice system but, rather, that restorative justice has a 'correctional ethos' embedded within it (Hutchinson 2006: 450; see also Hine 2007). There is also potential gender discrimination in relation to restorative justice programmes which has so far received little attention. For example, case studies of victim–offender conferences in the *Restorative Justice* Consultation Paper (Home Office 2003a) suggest that such meetings might have a disparate impact on boys and girls (see Piper 2006: 178–9).

Thirty years ago von Hirsch wrote: 'it is unfair, once the institution of punishment is in place, to shift in an eclectic fashion between condemnatory and non-condemnatory responses' (1986: 36). This focuses us on the viability of restorative justice and victim-focused policies within a traditional criminal justice system (Shapland et al. 2007b; see also von Hirsch et al. 2003; Blad et al. 2012). Restorative justice tools and processes can be fitted more easily and effectively into some aspects of the sentencing and punishment process than into others. However, that still raises the question as to whether this can be justified as an 'add-on' to systems underpinned by retributivist or utilitarian justifications or whether the tools and processes can be used effectively to 'restore harmony' only within a system underpinned by restorative justice. We argue elsewhere that retributivist principles should continue to limit punishment and that restorative justice should remain as a useful addition (Piper and Easton 2013). However, we are aware that there are strong arguments for opposing views.

6.3 The welfare of the child

6.3.1 A different approach for children

We saw in Chapters 2 and 3 that for most offenders the sentencing decision is made on retributivist principles: justice is seen as punishing offenders in proportion to the seriousness of what they have done. It is also a justice approach in the sense that the decision-making is subject to the due process of law. For over a century in England and Wales there has been acceptance of the idea that the child and young person should be treated differently—that any responses to their criminal wrongdoing should take account of their welfare and their stage of development. However, there has rarely been a consensus on the extent to which the child's welfare—their best interests—should influence the outcome. When the child's welfare—widely interpreted—is perceived as the most important factor, the approach has been referred to as a 'welfare' model of youth justice, in contrast to the 'justice' model when principles of due process take precedence and an outcome accords with his or her 'just deserts'.

The justice approach is, then, characterised as involving 'informed and transparent decisions' in courts, and with an end product of punishment 'portrayed as rational, consistent and determinate' (Scraton and Haydon 2002: 311). The welfare approach is, instead, associated with interventionist measures of care, protection, and rehabilitation, which have drawn on knowledge from medicine and criminology since the early twentieth century. To quote Shaw, Lord Advocate in 1908, 'many high-minded men and women . . . have been working upon this subject, and of recent years one is glad to note a large development of scientific knowledge. All these facts . . . made out a case for this Bill.'[28]

The association of the welfare approach with decision-making by professionals trained in social work or the 'psy-sciences', exercising their discretion to determine what is in the child's best interests, is criticised from the justice perspective for 'leaving children to the discretionary, permissive powers of professionals' (Scraton and Haydon 2002: 311). Some proponents of children's rights would argue that 'only in a system in which children are punished for what they have done can their rights be best protected' (Asquith 2002: 276). On the other hand, the justice approach is criticised on the same ground as modern retributivism: it is unable to deliver substantive justice because it cannot take sufficient account of social mitigation (Scraton and Haydon 2002: 315).

While these models of justice and welfare are useful yardsticks, law and practice are usually more complex than the models suggest. What counts as justice also depends on changing ideas about the most important factors for promoting the welfare of the child and about changing conceptions of the child as a rights holder. Ideas about children and childhood are relevant, as are the debates charted so far on justifications for the punishment of adults. The justice approach—to a greater or lesser extent in different decades for different age groups—has incorporated a retributivist ethos of personal culpability (see Morris and Giller 1987: 247–8). The 'welfare' approach is more clearly a utilitarian approach as its justification lies in the intended outcome of improvements in the minor's development and well-being. So, in the Scottish Children's Hearings system for young offenders, established as a welfare approach, 'the anticipated consequences of the different available disposals are the overriding criteria in all decisions made on behalf of children' (Adler 1985: 77).

---

[28] Speaking in the debate on the Children Act 1908: Hansard, 1908, Vol 186, cols 1 251–2.

In practice, therefore, there has always been an uneasy integration of both justice and welfare. Sections 102–103 of the Children Act 1908 established that, to protect the child, there should be separate places of detention for the under-17s, but these were still penal establishments. Further, the long-standing duty to have regard to the child's welfare contrasts with the just deserts-based criterion of seriousness for imposing custodial and community sentences (ss. 152 and 148 of the Criminal Justice Act 2003) and may conflict with the narrower aim of preventing offending.

It has been argued that the 1960s were 'the heyday of youth justice welfarism' (Muncie and Hughes 2002: 7) but that juvenile justice had also become 'politicised' (Pitts 1988), with, broadly speaking, the Left aligned with the 'welfare' approach to juvenile justice and the Right with the 'justice' approach (Harris and Webb 1987: 24, 26). The reforms set out in White Papers for England and Wales (*The Child, the Family and the Young Offender* 1965 and *Children in Trouble* 1968) and Scotland (the Kilbrandon Report 1964) led to much stronger opposition in England and Wales (Harris and Webb 1987: 26–9). The result was that policy in England and Wales diverged from that in Scotland.

The compromise scheme introduced by the Children and Young Persons Act (CYPA) 1969 for England and Wales retained juvenile courts but lowered the age of criminal responsibility. However, several key sections were not implemented and, in effect, there occurred what was referred to as a 'back to justice' swing (Asquith 2002: 276), despite an increased role for social workers. In comparison, for Scotland, the Social Work (Scotland) Act 1968 set up a network of Children's Panels to oversee assessment, treatment, and reappraisal by social workers with outcomes such as care, supervision, and residential orders. In Northern Ireland, however, the Children and Young Persons Act (Northern Ireland) 1968 continued the mixed care and crime jurisdiction of the juvenile court as in England and Wales (see, for a critique, O'Mahoney and Deazley 2000: 56).

There are, in any case, no agreed ways to incorporate 'welfare' into practice. In France in the 1980s, for example, the juvenile court judge, the *juge des enfants*, most commonly interviewed the juvenile in the judge's office on court premises, usually with the minor's parents (Hackler and Garapon 1986: 7), and focused on the child and family functioning (King and Piper 1995: 113).

Writing in 1985, Clarke argued that it was 'ill conceived' to see juvenile justice as the site for 'justice v welfare' (Clarke 2002: 284), and developments based on restorative justice principles are also difficult to fit into those frameworks. Gelsthorpe and Morris asked whether restorative justice amounts to 'the last vestiges of welfare' (2002: 238) and Vaughan noted how the aim of prevention is justified both as a welfare measure and a retributivist focus on offending (2000: 355). More recently prevention has been justified in economic terms and in benefits to the community, not to the young offender (Ministry of Justice 2010a: para 230) and Hazell, in a comparative examination of 'system models and key principles' notes that England and Wales have been classified as 'Neocorrectionalist' (Cavadino and Dignan 2006: 2001) or 'Corporatist' (Winterdyk 2002 and 2005) (see Hazell 2008: 25–6).

Over time, therefore, the importance of the welfare principle in dealing with young offenders has fluctuated and its interpretation has varied. As a result, Fortin argues, the youth justice system can be seen as 'a strange blend of authoritarianism and liberalism . . . permeated with contradictions and tensions' (Fortin 2003: 547). Determining the extent to which there is a different approach for children is, therefore, problematic and not always helped by thinking in terms of 'welfare v justice'. A different theory—developed by Teubner (1989) and Luhman[29]—focuses on how law as a system of communication 'thinks' about the children it deals with and shows how law constructs children as victims, offenders,

---

[29] Based on the theory of autopoiesis: see King and Piper (1995: chapter 2).

or witnesses for different purposes. These constructs are not necessarily consistent with each other or with constructs from social work or medicine (King and Piper 1995: 103–12). We may be looking for a similar approach across all parts of the youth justice system which does not exist, and so we need to examine in some detail various elements of the approaches to children and young people who offend.

First, however, we need to give a context for the discussion, so we will summarise what is known about the children and young people who offend and why they do it in section 6.3.2, and in section 6.3.3 we will consider ideas about, and images of, children and young people that underpin policy.

6.3.2 **Offending by minors: who and why?**

Who?

The factors associated with offending suggest that young offenders are marginalised young people, often with a range of problems which require medical, social work, or educational responses. Those who offend might, therefore, be classed as in need of protection. Goldson argues, for example, that 'it is well established that the social circumstances of children in trouble, "young offenders", are invariably scarred by complex configurations and multiple interrelated forms of disadvantage' (Goldson 1999: 3, also 2000b; see also Barry 2005; Fortin 2009: 682–3). For example, there is earlier research evidence of the abusive background of a large proportion of 12–14-year-olds eligible for what are now detention and training orders (Crowley 1998), of those sentenced for murder and very 'grave crimes' (Boswell 1991), and of persistent young offenders (Hagell and Newburn 1994).

The vast literature on the childhood risk factors which correlate with offending by young people tells the same story (see, for example, Beinart *et al.* 2002; Farrington 2007; Youth Justice Board 2001), as does information provided for MPs about prisoners which notes the following: 'Over 25% of prisoners had been taken into care as a child compared to 2% of the population' (Berman 2011: 16). A later edition of that Note gives the following:

- 24% of prisoners had lived with foster parents or in an institution, or had been taken into care at some point when they were a child.
- 29% of prisoners had experienced emotional, physical or sexual abuse as a child. With women (53%) more likely to have experienced such abuse than men (27%).
- 41% of prisoners had observed violence at home as a child.

(Berman and Dar 2013: 18)

That document also notes that 'Over one-third of prisoners (37%) had a family member that had been found guilty of a criminal offence (non-motoring)', although recent longitudinal research using data sets from 1946 to 1981 found no significant relationship between parental imprisonment and offspring offending in the Netherlands and, in England, a relationship was found for sons only, with parental imprisonment only significantly predicting sons' offending when it happened after their seventh birthday (Besemer *et al.* 2011).

These correlations between harm done to children in childhood and their offending persist into adulthood, so it might be argued that children should not be treated as a special case, but the idea that their responsibility and culpability should be mitigated has more force in its application to children and young people. They do not have the capability and independence to rise above their circumstances and, further, propensities to offend can more easily be 'treated' when the offender is young. Deciding outcomes on retributivist—or even restorative—principles requires, then, a better understanding of the stages by which children acquire the ability to be given, and benefit from, an appropriate level of responsibility (see Weijers 2002: 139–42).

Why?

The riots in England in August 2011 led to research into the reasons why young people took part. The project commissioned by the Cabinet Office used notions of 'nudge'—factors which facilitate involvement—and 'tug'—factors which inhibit involvement. Table 6.2 summarises the factors they discovered: it emphasises the complexity of

Table 6.2 Factors affecting decision-making of young people

	Facilitators	Inhibitors
Situational	Group processes: Feeling disinhibited and swept along by the power of the group, seeing others 'get away with it', feeling anonymous	Group processes: Actively thinking toward future goals and not focusing on the 'here and now' (see also individual factors)
	Peer pressure: Friends getting involved	Peer pressure: Friends not involved
	Information: Seeing it on the TV, getting texts/Facebook/BBM messages	Information: Didn't get any messages, not watching TV
	Circumstances: Not otherwise occupied, it was nearby/easy to get to	Circumstances: More difficult to get to (further away, no buses)
	Presence of authority figure: No adult telling them not to, everybody was doing it and nobody seemed to be getting caught	Presence of authority figure: Parents, relatives or youth workers telling them not to
Individual	Previous criminal activity: Easy to get involved, 'This is what they do round here'	Previous criminal activity: Been caught once, know the risks
	Attitudes towards authority: Cynicism/anger towards politicians, authority, negative experience of the police	Attitudes towards authority: No negative experience of the police
	Prospects: Poor job prospects, low income, limited hope for the future, 'Nothing to lose'	Prospects: In work or expectations of work, aspirations – a lot to lose
Family or Community	Family attitudes: Relatives not disapproving	Family attitudes: Disapproving, 'Not brought up like that'
	Community: Attachment to a community with a culture of low-level criminality	Community: Attachment to a community with pro-social values/culture (including religious communities)
Societal	Belonging: Little sense of ownership or stake in society	Belonging: Sense of 'ownership' or stake in society
	Poverty and materialism: Desire for material goods, but no means to pay for them	

Source: Morrell *et al.* (2011: 34, Table 4.1).

motivations for offending, the interrelationship with situational factors, and the impossibility of finding easy answers as to why young people offend.[30]

Official statistics of arrests rebutted the prevalent notion, for example, that the riots were the result of gang culture: 'Overall 13 per cent of arrestees (417) were reported to be affiliated to a gang. Outside London, the majority of forces identified fewer than ten per cent of all arrestees as gang members' (Home Office 2011a: 18). Correlations between offending and particular life circumstances are certainly not the whole picture but the Home Office report included the following which bears out the links between offending and forms of deprivation:

> The findings from these analyses reveal those appearing before the courts tended to be from more deprived circumstances than the wider comparable populations in England:
>
> - Thirty-five per cent of adult defendants were claiming out-of-work benefits, compared to 12 per cent of the working age population;
>
> - Forty-two per cent of young people brought before the courts were in receipt of free school meals during their time at school, compared to 16 per cent of pupils in maintained secondary schools; and
>
> - Sixty-four per cent of those young people (for whom matched data was available) lived in one of the 20 most deprived areas in the country—only three per cent lived in one of the 20 least deprived areas.
>
> (Home Office 2011a: 20)

How many offend?

This is difficult to ascertain because there are different messages from official statistics and self-report studies about the issue of 'growing out' of crime:[31] the reduction in offending after the age of 20 may be due to engagement in less visible offending as well as reduced frequency of offending (Graham and Bowling 1995: 30). The higher visibility of offending by young people may also account for public perceptions of the danger from young criminals. Research in 2008/9 showed, for example, that 30 per cent of people perceived teenagers hanging around to be a problem in their local area (Parfrement-Hopkins and Hall 2009) and one study found that almost two-thirds of respondents (63 per cent) thought that crime had increased over the previous 12 months (Patterson and Thorpe 2006: 34). However, the MORI Youth Survey in 2008 (Youth Justice Board 2009a: 5) showed that the overall proportion of young people reporting that they had committed an offence in the previous 12 months had declined compared with previous surveys.

Further, the rate of increase of recorded crime in England and Wales slowed down in the 1980s and fell after the mid-1990s (Gelsthorpe 2002: 47; see also Scottish Executive 2002b). Data from the, then, British Crime Survey suggests that offending continued to fall until 2004/5 and remained relatively stable in 2005–8 (see NACRO 2010: 1) and a National Audit Office report asserted that there had been a 25 per cent fall between 2002/3 and 2009/10 (2010a: 11). A Statistics Bulletin from the Youth Justice Board and the Ministry of Justice in 2011 noted that '[t]here were 198,449 proven offences committed by young people aged 10–17 which resulted in a disposal in 2009/10. This is a decrease of 19% from 2008/09 and 33% from 2006/07' (Youth Justice Board 2011b: 2–3). The majority of crime committed by boys and girls is not serious offending but is property-based. 'In most categories fewer offences were committed in 2009–10 than in 2002–03, with the biggest falls in motoring offences, vehicle theft and theft and handling' (National Audit Office 2010a: 11). There has been

---

[30] See also Bowen *et al.* (2008a and b) in relation to anti-social and other problem behaviours in children.
[31] For more detail see Chapter 8, section 8.1.2 of the third edition of this text.

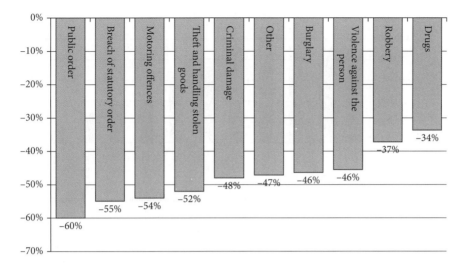

Figure 6.1 Reduction in proven offences by young people between 2010/11 and 2013/14

Source: Ministry of Justice/Youth Justice Board (2015a) *Youth Justice Statistics 2013/14 England and Wales* p. 32, Chart 4.2[32]

particular concern about young people who commit the most serious of offences, but there has been no clear upward trend as assumed (see Figure 6.1; see also Home Office 2007a: Table 2.7).

It was estimated that 11 per cent of all known offenders were between 10 and 17 years of age in 1997 (Mattinson and Mirrlees-Black 2000: 11), 12 per cent in 2005 (NACRO 2007c: 2), and 17 per cent in 2009 (National Audit Office 2010a: 11).[33] An analysis for the Home Office of police-recorded crime estimated a slightly higher figure of 23 per cent (Home Office 2012a). The 'peak' ages for offending are thought to be in the age group 15–20, with different peaks for males and females, and for different offences (Farrington 2002: 426; Graham and Bowling 1995: chapters 2 and 3; Flood-Page *et al.* 2000: 10). 'Overall, girls still appear to be involved in offending in general for a shorter period, to commit fewer offences than boys and, on the whole, to commit less serious offences' (Youth Justice Board 2009b: 19). Recent figures show that boys accounted for 83 per cent of proven offences by young people in 2013/14, slightly higher than in 2010/11. 'The proportion of proven offences committed by females was 17 per cent in 2013/14; this proportion has fluctuated between 16 and 22 per cent for the last decade' (Ministry of Justice/Youth Justice Board 2015a: 31).

In September 2011 official prison statistics showed that 4 per cent of 12–17-year-olds in custody or secure accommodation were on indeterminate sentences while 28 per cent were on determinate sentences of less than a year and 20 per cent were being held on remand (Berman 2011: 4). Overall, Youth Justice Board data in 2010 showed reduced numbers of other court-imposed orders and (the then) police reprimands and warnings (see National Audit Office (2010a: 15, Figure 4). Those trends have continued. In particular, the numbers of first-time entrants to the youth justice system have declined (see Figure 6.2).

---

[32] Available via https://www.gov.uk/government/uploads/system/uploads/attachment_data/file/399379/youth-justice-annual-stats-13-14.pdf.

[33] Based on unpublished analysis of Police National Computer data for NAO by the Ministry of Justice (November 2010): ibid fn 2.

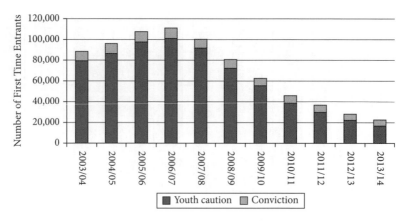

Figure 6.2 Trends in first-time entrants, 2003/4 to 2013/14

Source: Ministry of Justice/Youth Justice Board (2015a) *Youth Justice Statistics 2013/14 England and Wales* p. 25, Chart 2.2

While what we know about the incidence of offending by children and young people is contested it does not prove that offending is on the increase, either in total or in severity, despite the fact that the public continues to believe that it is. Indeed recent statistics give a very different picture:

> The overall number of young people in the YJS continued to reduce in 2013/14. Reductions have been seen in the number entering the system for the first time . . . as well as reductions in those receiving sentences in and out of court, including those receiving custodial sentences. . . . Since 2010/11, there have been 51 per cent fewer young people coming into the Youth Justice System and 40 per cent fewer young people (under 18) in custody.
>
> (Ministry of Justice/Youth Justice Board 2015a, Executive Summary: 1)

However, youth offending is still a valid cause for concern because it cannot be in the longer-term interests of young people to allow them to persist in offending without providing support and appropriate help: only a few people pursue a 'successful' career in crime.

6.3.3 Ideas about children who offend

The legislation which set up the first courts specifically for juveniles in the UK endorsed the idea that young offenders are 'children in trouble' rather than 'evil' and, in the terminology of the nineteenth century, that they could be 'saved' from a life of crime because 'kindness could nip crime in the bud' (Harris and Webb 1987: 15). Statutory provisions to set up the earlier industrial and reformatory schools[34] were also based on those ideas, although we might dispute whether treatment was kind by later standards.

By the early twentieth century, new branches of knowledge as to why children offend had led to the belief that the 'deprived', those we would now refer to as 'children in need', and the 'depraved', now children and young people who offend, are not necessarily separate categories and, though treated separately from adults, should not necessarily be treated separately from each other. That consensus of opinion did

---

[34] For a discussion of the Industrial School Acts 1857–1880 and the Youthful Offenders Act 1854, see Pinchbeck and Hewitt (1973: chapter 16).

not survive into the twenty-first century. Referring to the Children Act 1948 and the committee which made the proposals enshrined in that Act, Cretney made the following observation:

> The belief (. . . held in the Home Office well before World War II) that 'whether a young child commits an offence, goes out on the loose, or is just unruly or naughty is purely fortuitous'[35] only began to be seriously questioned in the 1970s.[36] Those responsible for the formation of policy over those years would view with disbelief the apparent consensus of the nineties on the need for a punitive approach to young delinquents. It is in this respect that the philosophy of the 1948 legislation has been most dramatically overturned: for the Curtis Committee the emphasis was not to be on what a child had done in the past but on what the child's needs were at present.
>
> (Cretney 1998: 459)

Others have also expressed concern that the youth justice system has been transformed and no longer focuses on the child's needs. According to Weijers and Duff, 'the last few decades . . . have witnessed remarkable changes in views both of juvenile offenders and of the proper role of the state' (2002: 1). Indeed, Haines and Case (2015) have argued that 'It is about time that the YJS [youth justice system] started to treat children who offend in ways that benefit their status as children.'

Our ideas and fears about children are important: how we 'visualise' children has implications for how we decide what counts as justice for them when they offend and, arguably, at the end of the twentieth century there developed a more punitive and controlling policy rhetoric underpinned by images of children which are in contrast to those that helped ensure the establishment of juvenile courts a century ago. Indeed, it is now 'youths' who offend: successive versions of the *CPS Code* transformed minors from 'juveniles' and 'young offenders' through 'youth offenders' to, simply, 'youths' (Piper 2001). How those who offend are described matters because 'penal laws and institutions . . . are framed in language and sign systems which embody specific cultural meanings' (Garland 1990: 198). At present, the cultural meanings constructed around 'youth' are often negative, conjuring up an older (male) person and, arguably, fears about 'youths hanging about' (Burney 2002: 473).

Further, how we conceptualise 'a child' (Jenks 1996: 51) and what we believe distinguishes a child from an adult (Archard 1993: 20) help determine what is appropriate treatment of children. Where there is little reference to the offending child as one who is 'in trouble' and in need of help (Vaughan 2000; Piper 2001), and if 'youth' draws on disparate ideas ranging from the 'dangerous' to the 'nearly adult', it conveys the connotation of a person who can be accorded culpability from a young age and be held to account. He or she can then be legitimately punished more harshly for persistence. In the context of parental responsibility, what has been called the 're-moralisation' agenda further legitimises a focus on discipline and responsibility: public concerns about wider social issues have led to a policy focus on the child who offends (see Koffman 2008; Piper 2008: chapter 3; Welshman 2007), and so we examine that further in Chapter 11, section 11.1.

---

[35] *Seebohm Report* (1968), para 188 (n 293 in Cretney 1998).

[36] Cretney's footnote (n 294) includes the following comment: 'The Children and Young Persons Act 1933 did make a clear distinction between prosecution and protection measures, and the anomalies to which this was thought to give rise were analysed by the Ingleby *Committee on Children and Young Persons* (1960) Cmnd. 1191, which (inter alia) recommended amendments to the "care and protection" provisions of Children and Young Persons Act 1933, s.61.'

6.3.4 **Welfare principles**

The law in the UK has long contained duties on courts—**welfare principles**—to consider the welfare of children. The 1908 Children Act, which set up the first courts specifically for juveniles in the UK, was based on the view that young offenders are 'children in trouble' and, in line with this, section 44 of the Children and Young Persons Act 1933 established that courts must 'have regard to' the welfare of the child.[37] This is an important mandatory requirement to ensure that children have been given at least a modicum of 'special' treatment when appearing in a court and, particularly, when appearing in a Youth or Crown Court. Further, under s. 10(4) and (5) of the Children Act 2004 a youth offending team (YOT) is identified as one of the authorities which is a 'relevant partner of a children's services authority in England' and therefore under a duty to cooperate with the authority in making relevant arrangements. By s. 10(2), authorities must make arrangements:

> . . . with a view to improving the well-being of children . . . so far as relating to—
>
> (a) physical and mental health and emotional well-being;
>
> (b) protection from harm and neglect;
>
> (c) education, training and recreation;
>
> (d) the contribution made by them to society;
>
> (e) social and economic well-being.

Section 11(2) of the 2004 Act also makes clear that a YOT is one of the bodies which must make arrangements for ensuring that they and any partner agencies discharge their functions 'having regard to the need to safeguard and promote the welfare of children'. So, for example, the new *Code of Practice for Youth Conditional Cautions* includes the following:

> It is the duty of key agencies who work with children and young people, including the Police and YOTs, to put in place arrangements to make sure that they take account of the need to safeguard and promote the welfare of young people . . . Agencies should ensure that a Youth conditional caution or specific conditions should not be offered if they jeopardise the welfare and safeguarding of the young person.

> (Ministry of Justice 2013c: para 3.2)

However, 'to have regard to'—in both the long-standing and the more recent duties—constitutes a weak welfare principle in comparison with the **paramountcy principle** in s. 1 of the Children Act 1989. That duty—placed on courts in the family justice system dealing with the upbringing of children—means that the child's welfare must be the determining factor in the court's decision. However, this duty does not apply to decisions about guilt or sentence in the criminal jurisdiction. The duty to 'have regard to' means that, providing consideration has been given to the interests of the child or young person, the Youth and Crown Courts can legally give precedence to other interests such as the need to protect the public and to prevent reoffending. There is, admittedly, some overlap between the family and youth justice jurisdictions. Offending may be a factor in care proceedings which are governed by the paramountcy principle, but such offending is relevant only in so far as it is evidence that the child is at risk of suffering significant harm (Children Act 1989, s. 31).

The case of *R (on the application of the Howard League for Penal Reform) v Secretary of State for the Home Department* (2002) did establish that the duties of the local authority to children in need or at risk (Children Act 1989, ss. 17 and 47) do not end at the door of a

---

[37] As did the Prosecution of Offences Act 1985 in relation to the Crown Prosecution Service (CPS).

prison service establishment (para 136 *per* Munby J). However, the paramountcy principle is not thereby incorporated into decision-making in the youth justice system or the Prison Service, while s. 37(1) of the CDA 1998 established a potentially conflicting aim by declaring the prevention of offending as the 'principal aim' of the youth justice system in England and Wales. The Criminal Justice and Immigration Act (CJIA) 2008 would have stated that '[t]he court must have regard primarily to the principal aim of the youth justice system' but that clause was dropped after opposition to such a downgrading of the welfare principle and the final version is a fudged position. Section 142A in the Criminal Justice Act 2003, inserted by s. 9(1) of the CJIA 2008, reads as follows:[38]

(2) The court must have regard to–

(a) the principal aim of the youth justice system (which is to prevent offending (or re-offending) by persons aged under 18: see section 37(1) of the Crime and Disorder Act 1998),

(b) in accordance with section 44 of the Children and Young Persons Act 1933, the welfare of the offender, and

(c) the purposes of sentencing mentioned in subsection (3).

We can see the same dual aims evident in the Justice (Northern Ireland) Act 2002. The principal aim of the youth justice system 'is to protect the public by preventing offending by children' but the relevant persons 'must also have regard to the welfare of children affected by the exercise of their functions . . . with a view to furthering their personal, social and educational development' (ss. 53(1) and (3)).

There are also relevant principles to be found in the United Nations Convention on the Rights of the Child (UNCRC) although, as we shall see in section 6.3.5, the UK was often ahead of the UNCRC.

6.3.5 **Principles from the UNCRC**

In Chapter 11 we discuss the role of rights, particularly in relation to young offenders who have been given custodial sentences. However, there are Articles in the United Nations Convention on the Rights of the Child (UNCRC) which are relevant to the discussion about the general approach taken to children who offend. In particular we will examine the issue of separate treatment, the question of diversion from prosecution, and the age of criminal responsibility.

A separate system

Article 40(3) declares that 'States Parties shall seek to promote the establishment of laws, procedures, authorities and institutions *specifically applicable* to children alleged as, accused of, or recognised as having infringed the penal law' (emphasis added). In effect this lays down the principle of separate or different treatment for children—defined in the UNCRC as those being under 18 years of age.

However, while the UNCRC was adopted by the UN as recently as 1989 and was ratified by the UK in 1991,[39] the idea and practice of having a separate system for dealing with children who offend is much older, originating with the juvenile court set up in 1908, and in the first half of the twentieth century the separateness of the juvenile court was consolidated. For example, the Children and Young Persons Act 1933 made it a requirement that there

---

[38] But not yet in force: no date appointed at 7.3.16.

[39] Although with reservations (now withdrawn) about the care of young offenders (Article 37(c)) and young refugees (Article 22). For a critical review of the UNCRC, see Fortin (2009: 36–55); also see Williams (2007).

should be an hour's interval between sittings of the adult and juvenile courts.[40] The nature of the systems for adults and minors has varied over time, as has the degree of 'separate-ness', but the distance, conceptually and spatially, from the adult criminal justice system, has been the essential attribute of the juvenile, now youth, justice system from its inception over a century ago. The commitment stemmed from our ideas about children and their development, and our fears for their 'contamination' by adult offenders.[41]

Diversion from prosecution

Article 40(3)(b) of the UNCRC states that States Parties 'Wherever appropriate and desir-able, [shall promote] measures for dealing with such children *without resorting to judicial proceedings*, providing that human rights and legal safeguards are respected' (emphasis added). In effect this endorses diversion from prosecution and court and, instead, the use of preventative or childcare measures.

Again, England and Wales pre-empted the UNCRC. The main policy tool for diverting young offenders from the criminal justice system was cautioning, first tried with young offenders after the First World War but discouraged by the Moloney Report (1927). Policy initiatives after the Second World War (see Home Office 1951) led to the establishment of juvenile liaison schemes in England and Wales by the end of the 1960s and a Home Office Circular in 1978 encouraged diversion.[42] It stated that first offenders should be cautioned for all but serious offences and that subsequent offences could also result in a caution if the offence was trivial and not committed a short time after the previous offence.[43] The first edi-tion of the *Code for Crown Prosecutors* (CPS 1988)[44] also encouraged diversion by stating that the factor of 'youth' could 'properly lead' to a caution instead of prosecution, that prosecu-tion might actually increase the likelihood of reoffending, and that 'The stigma of conviction can cause irreparable harm to the future prospects of a young adult' (CPS 1988: *Code*, para 8(iii)).[45] The government endorsed this approach (see Britton *et al.* 1988: 26) and the revised *Code* stated that 'The objective should be to divert juveniles from court wherever possible. Prosecution should always be regarded as a severe step' (CPS 1991: *Code*, paras 20–21).

Various inter-agency bodies were set up to make the 'diversion' decisions (see Rutter and Giller 1983: 20), although the source of their authority to make cautioning decisions remained with the police (see *Chief Constable of Kent and Another ex parte L* 1991). The use of cautioning vastly increased for juvenile offenders in the 1970s and 1980s (Ball 1995; Goldson 1999, 2000a; NACRO 1985: 6) and an informal option was developed—'cautioning plus'—under which a caution was accompanied by the minor's involvement in preventative programmes (see Marshall 1985).

However, at the time that the UNCRC was ratified by the UK government, diversion policy and practice began to change. The increasing influence of a managerialist discourse

---

[40] The CDA 1998, ss. 47–48 repealed this requirement and also amended Schedule 2, para 15 to the 1933 Act to allow a stipendiary magistrate (now District Judge) to sit alone in a youth court.

[41] For a historical review of juvenile justice policy in the United States see Zimring (2005).

[42] Similarly in Northern Ireland, from 1975 the police operated a specialist Juvenile Justice Liaison Scheme for 10–16-year-olds (O'Mahoney and Deazley 2000: 36–7).

[43] Subsequent circulars were issued in 1985 and 1990 (see Wilkinson and Evans 1990: 166).

[44] The *Code* gives guidance to the Crown Prosecution Service (CPS) in making a decision whether or not to prosecute any suspect above the age of criminal responsibility. It is issued by the Director of Public Prosecutions under s. 10 of the Prosecution of Offences Act 1985.

[45] The development of labelling theory (see Lemert 1967)—which proposed the idea that most children will 'grow out of' offending if they do not receive and internalise the label of 'criminal'—was influential. The White Paper *Children in Trouble* had endorsed this view (Home Office 1968: 3–4), as had the Black Committee (1979) in Northern Ireland.

(see Britton *et al.* 1988: 1; Cavadino and Dignan 2002: 292–8) led to better management being seen as an end in itself and juvenile justice could be reconceptualised as a 'delinquency management service' (Muncie 1999: 149–50; see also McLaughlin *et al.* 2001: 308). However, the decision-making was often offence-focused (King and Piper 1995: 122–5) and it was economic considerations which helped drive social work cooperation with the police (Pitts 1992a). Fears were also expressed that the 'New' Penology and actuarially based decision-making (see Chapter 1) were 'colonising' juvenile justice (Kempf-Leonard and Peterson 2000: 88).

Further, diversion became part of the policy development of 'bifurcation', whereby most young offenders are diverted from prosecution but a smaller number of serious offenders are processed through the criminal justice system and punished (Bottoms 1985). This policy means that, as with adult sentencing, the higher-profile serious cases can be seen to be treated in a 'tough justice' fashion while the rest can be diverted, either *from* the system or *to* preventive measures. Diversion might also encourage the belief that minors who are prosecuted are the 'hardened criminals' towards whom the courts can justifiably be tough.[46]

Early evidence of a sea change in thinking which 'threatened with reversal' the practice of diversion (Evans 1994: 566) was provided in 1994 by the Home Office Circular and National Standards (Home Office 1994b) and the revised *Code* for the CPS (CPS 1994). The Circular on cautioning no longer referred to young offenders as those who should normally be diverted from prosecution (Home Office 1994b: Note 3A) and it appeared to amend the policy of multiple cautioning (ibid: para 8). The CPS *Code* also indicated a tougher approach when it diluted the message about diversion: 'Young offenders can sometimes be dealt with without going to court. But Crown Prosecutors should not avoid prosecuting simply because of the defendant's age' (CPS 1994: para 6.8). By 2000 the CPS *Code* was even more direct: 'Crown Prosecutors should not avoid prosecuting simply because of the defendant's age. The seriousness of the offence or the youth's past behaviour is very important' (CPS 2000: para 6.9). Consequently, the percentage of those cautioned (out of the total of those cautioned or convicted) fell from 70 per cent in 1992 to 58 per cent in 1999 (NACRO 2001a; see also, for later statistics, Audit Commission 2004: 33–4).

We will review the policies which resulted in section 6.3.6.

The age of criminal responsibility

The Beijing Rules (see Chapter 11) state that the age of criminal responsibility should 'not be fixed at too low an age level' (rule 4.1) and the UN Committee on the Rights of the Child has issued its General Comment 10 which asserts that 'it can be concluded that a minimum age of criminal responsibility below the age of 12 years is considered by the Committee not to be internationally acceptable' (2007: para 32). However, the age of criminal responsibility is currently ten in England and Wales and, therefore, the responsibility of the youth justice system is for children and young people from the age of ten until their 18th birthday.

Debate has focused on the age at which a minor can distinguish right from wrong: as long ago as 1852/3 a Select Committee of Parliament heard conflicting evidence on the issue, with opinions setting the age of capability between 10 and 16 (see May 2002: 109). In fact the age of criminal responsibility was not raised to eight until 1933 and then ten in 1963. The CYPA 1969 had intended to raise the age from 10 to 14 but this was never implemented and was repealed in 1998.[47] However, until 1998 children aged 10–13 were

---

[46] For example, in the period 1965–77 more minors were given 'custodial' orders: see Pitts (1992a: 174).

[47] This means we have very divergent tests of competence in criminal and family law: see Keating 2007: 187 *et seq.*

presumed to be *doli incapax* so that—if the presumption was not rebutted—the age of criminal responsibility was effectively 14. The White Paper of 1997 proposed to remove the presumption on the basis that 'presuming that children of this age [10–14] generally do not know the difference between naughtiness and serious wrongdoing . . . is contrary to common sense' (Home Office 1997: para 4.4). However, the question is more complicated than this. 'Capacity to accurately gauge the consequences of actions is developing as is the ability to empathise' (Centre for Social Justice 2012: 202): adolescents—often impulsive and risk-taking—do not yet have an adequate understanding of the impact of wrongdoing.[48]

> A defendant not old enough to legally buy a hamster can be tried . . . as though the level of psychological sophistication required to look after a domesticated rodent is worthy of a longer period of development than to understand the moral responsibility inherent in the commission of a serious criminal act.
>
> (Brooks 2011)

Nevertheless, s. 34 of the CDA 1998 abolished the presumption that children aged 10–13 are not capable of being held criminally responsible. This reform was much criticised (see Ball 2004: 174–5; Bandalli 1998). England, Wales, and Northern Ireland[49] now have the lowest ages in Europe (see Howard League 2008: 6–7), with the age being set, for example, at 18 in Luxembourg and 16 in Spain and Portugal.[50]

The UN Committee on the Rights of the Child had asked the UK in 1995 to give 'serious consideration' to raising the age of criminal responsibility (Committee on the Rights of the Child 1995: para 36) but the UK's Second Report to the Committee on the Rights of the Child justified the abolition of the presumption of *doli incapax* as a means of ensuring that the courts are able to address offending behaviour by children in the 10–14 age group (UK Government 1999: 17).

Not surprisingly, in 2002 the UN Committee was more critical (Committee on the Rights of the Child 2002: para 59), and when the UK government submitted its consolidated third and fourth report to the UN Committee on the Rights of the Child in 2007 the Committee's report included a recommendation to raise the age (Committee on the Rights of the Child 2008: para 78). In 2012, following the publication of two reports, one by the Centre for Social Justice (2012) and one by the National Association for Youth Justice (Bateman 2012),[51] pressure was put on the government to raise the age of criminal responsibility. The then Minister for Criminal Justice and Police, Damian Green, believed, however, that 'it is entirely appropriate to hold children aged 10 and over to account for their actions'.[52] Lord Dholakia's Private Members' Bill introduced in 2012 to raise the age of criminal responsibility to 12 ran out of time but was reintroduced in the 2015/16 session: the second reading took place in January 2016.[53]

---

[48] See Dingwall and Hillier (2015: 53–61) for a fuller discussion of the issues.

[49] The Republic of Ireland and Scotland both raised their minimum age from 7 to 12 in 2006 and 2011 respectively.

[50] In Germany the age of criminal responsibility has been 14 since the Youth Court Act of 1923, with the equivalent of a rebuttable presumption for 14–18-year-olds: see Crofts 2002.

[51] See http://thenayj.org.uk/wp-content/files_mf/criminalisingchildrennov12.pdf.

[52] See http://www.publications.parliament.uk/pa/cm201213/cmhansrd/cm121218/debtext/121218-0001.htm#12121850000007.

[53] See http://services.parliament.uk/bills/2015-16/ageofcriminalresponsibility/stages.html for updates on progress. See also a parliamentary briefing paper by S. Lipscombe on *The Age of Criminal Responsibility in England and Wales* (18 April 2012, Standard notes SN03001).

6.3.6 **Diversion from prosecution**

We saw in section 6.3.5 that by the beginning of the twenty-first century the government appeared to be back-pedalling in relation to diversion of young offenders. Nevertheless, the economic situation meant a continuing commitment to the cheaper option of diversion and the Audit Commission's reports entitled *Misspent Youth* (1996, 1998) provided acceptable reform proposals. The 1996 report argued that custodial sentences were ineffective because 90 per cent of young males aged 14–16 sentenced to custody for up to one year were re-convicted within two years (Audit Commission: 42). However, it also provided evidence for an almost equal probability of reoffending after prosecution and after the third caution, and this was very influential (ibid: 23). Despite criticism (Jones 2001; Downes 2001/2: 9; Gelsthorpe 2002: 55), the reports were used to endorse a tougher approach (Littlechild 1997: 80). The murder of James Bulger by two ten-year-old children, Robert Thompson and Jon Venables, was, arguably, 'an exceptional tragedy conveniently exploited' to construct a 'crisis' (Scraton and Haydon 2002: 314) using the rhetoric of a **moral panic** (see Diduck 1999; Hay 1995; King 1997b; McRobbie and Thornton 2002: 69).

There were other influences (see, for example, Gelsthorpe and Morris (1999: 211)) and the result was, arguably, 'a return of unbridled "authoritarian populism" in juvenile justice' (Newburn 1996: 69). In 1997 the incoming Labour government issued a White Paper with an indicative title, *No More Excuses* (Home Office 1997), and a Preface which stated that the government aimed to 'nip offending in the bud' because 'today's young offenders can too easily become tomorrow's hardened criminals'. The Introduction argued that 'allowing young people to drift into a life of crime undermines their welfare' and the Paper proposed a new youth justice system and a statutory system of reprimands and warnings to replace cautions. This was part of the government's 'Effective Intervention in the Community' proposals (Home Office 1997: paras 5.12–5.15), with the aim of earlier intervention in the life of the young offender. It also argued for the earlier use of prosecution and appeared to undermine the premises of labelling theory and presage a less diversionary approach (see Goldson 2000a).

The original statutory system

Sections 65–66 of the CDA 1998 as passed introduced this new statutorily based pre-court system which, unlike the pre-1998 cautions, did not require the consent of the young offender. In the *Durham* (2005) case the House of Lords concluded that reprimands and warnings did not constitute punishment and that informed consent is not required of children and young people (see Koffman and Dingwall 2007 for a critique). The reprimand was, in effect, the first caution, although a young offender could be moved directly to a warning if the offence was serious. Normally, the first warning was the only warning. Guidance emphasised that seriousness of offending was a very important factor in the decision whether or not to reprimand, warn, or prosecute; that the police should use the Gravity Factor System (now Matrix) devised by ACPO (the Association of Chief Police Officers) which gives all offences a gravity score of 1–4; and that a score of 4 should always lead to a charge (Home Office/Youth Justice Board 2002: paras 4.21–4.25).

The warning[54] was accompanied by referral to a YOT for assessment with a presumption that the young offender would engage in a rehabilitation programme (CDA 1998 s. 66(2)). A matrix was provided to help YOTs decide the appropriate levels of intervention (Home Office/Youth Justice Board 2002: para 10.14; see also Giller 2000). *Youth Justice—The Next Steps* noted of reprimands and warnings: 'Young offenders who admit their offence can be

---

[54] Preferably given at a restorative conference (Home Office/Youth Justice Board 2002: 16; see also Fox *et al.* 2006).

dealt with up to twice without going to court…if the young person offends again they go straight to court' (Home Office 2003c: para 4).

The CJIA 2008 (ss. 48–50 and Schedule 9) introduced a new pre-court disposal—the youth conditional caution (YCC) for use with 10–17-year-olds who had previously been given a reprimand and/or warning and whose offence was listed in guidance. This provision was piloted from early 2010 with 16–17-year-olds. However, after amendments by LASPO 2012, in force from April 2013, new guidance about conditional cautions was issued (Ministry of Justice 2013j) and the conditional caution became part of a new pre-court scheme.

The current statutory system

The police now have the following options for diverting young offenders from prosecution (Ministry of Justice/YJB 2013: para 3.2). They can take no further action—as they have always been able to do—and they can also use an 'informal' action, now generally referred to as a community resolution. They then have the new youth caution and the youth conditional caution (YCC). If the behaviour of the child or young person is to be treated as an offence, the only other option is to prosecute. (There are also civil justice options which we will review in Chapter 11.) The government argued that the new scheme is more flexible (see Table 6.3). For example, the Guidance states that 'The LASPO Act removes the

Table 6.3 Out-of-court disposals

The diagram below provides a summary of the out-of-court disposals available following the implementation of the Legal Aid, Sentencing and Punishment of Offenders (LASPO) Act 2012 in April 2013.

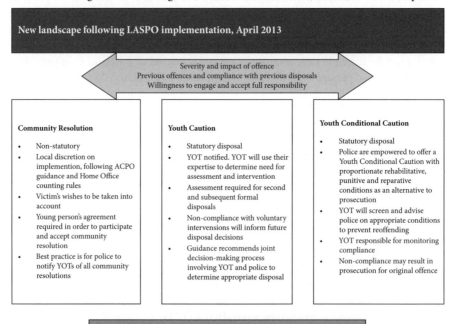

Source: Ministry of Justice/YJB (2013) *Youth Out-of-Court Disposals: Guide for Police and Youth Offending Services* p. 6 para 3.1.[55]

---

[55] Obtainable at https://www.gov.uk/government/uploads/system/uploads/attachment_data/file/438139/out-court-disposal-guide.pdf.

escalator approach to youth offending and allows offenders to be dealt with appropriately according to the offence(s) committed' (ACPO 2013: para 1.3).

Community resolutions

A community resolution is a non-statutory informal action, which can include restorative justice components, used as a response to offending by children and adults. The Youth Restorative Disposal and the Triage schemes were early examples (see Smith 2014: 112–14). Resolutions can include 'the offender being given advice about their behaviour, apologising or sending a letter of apology to the victim, or making some form of reparation such as repairing or paying for any damage done' (College of Policing, 2015; see also Ministry of Justice/YJB 2013: paras 3.7–3.9). According to the College of Policing (2015) professional practice advice on 'Possible justice outcomes following investigation':

> Community resolutions . . . are a method of dealing with an offender for a lower-level crime, in a way which is proportionate. Resolutions can be offered when the offender admits an offence and, in most cases, where the victim has agreed that they do not want more formal action taken . . . The most appropriate offences to warrant a community resolution are likely to be low-level criminal damage, low-value theft, minor assaults (without injury) and anti-social behaviour.
>
> (College of Policing, 2015)

Youth cautions

Section 135 of the Legal Aid, Sentencing and Punishment of Offenders Act 2012 was implemented in April 2013. This section repealed ss. 65–66 of the Crime and Disorder Act 1998 such that reprimands and warnings are replaced by youth cautions. For this purpose new ss. 66ZA and 66ZB are inserted after s. 66A of that Act.

Section 66ZA (1) and (2) are as follows:

(1) A constable may give a child or young person ('Y') a caution under this section (a 'youth caution') if—

    (a) the constable decides that there is sufficient evidence to charge Y with an offence,

    (b) Y admits to the constable that Y committed the offence, and

    (c) the constable does not consider that Y should be prosecuted or given a youth conditional caution in respect of the offence.

(2) A youth caution given to a person under the age of 17 must be given in the presence of an appropriate adult.

Guidance states that the key relevant factors in deciding whether to charge, caution or conditionally caution a child or young person are the following:

(a) Do they admit the offence?

(b) The seriousness of the offence,

(c) The previous offending history of the youth,

(d) Does the disposal adequately address, support and reduce the risk of reoffending?

(e) Is it in the public interest to prosecute the youth?

(f) Welfare/interest of the child/young person and;

(g) Age of the child/young person

(ACPO 2013: para 1.2).

There is no statutory restriction on the number of youth cautions that a child or young person can receive and he or she can receive a youth caution even if there are previous convictions, reprimands, warnings, youth cautions, or youth conditional cautions. However, the seriousness of the offending is still an important element in decision-making: 'The seriousness of any offence relates both to the *nature of the offence* and to the *circumstances which surround it*' (ACPO 2013: para 1.3). The Gravity Factor Matrix now states that an offence that attracts a gravity score of 2 or 3 will usually result in a youth being given a youth caution or YCC (ACPO 2013: para 15.1).

As with the previous warnings, the young person given a youth caution must be referred to a YOT.

Youth conditional cautions

The YCC was introduced by the Criminal Justice and Immigration Act ss. 48–50 and Schedule 9 which inserted new ss. 66A–H in the CDA 1998. This was further amended by LASPO 2012. A new s. 66A(6A) mandates referral to a YOT and s. 66A(1)(a) was repealed (so there is no requirement for no previous convictions). *The Code of Practice for Youth Conditional Cautions* states that YCCs 'are intended as a more robust response to offending than a Youth Caution in circumstances where public interest in the case can be met by offering a conditional caution rather than by prosecuting an offender' (Ministry of Justice 2013c: para 2.4).

A youth conditional caution can be given to a youth provided that the following five requirements (in CDA 1998 s. 66B) are met:

- The authorised person has evidence that the youth has committed an offence;
- The prosecutor is satisfied that there is sufficient evidence to charge the youth with the offence and that a youth conditional caution should be given in respect of the offence;
- The youth admits the offence to an authorised person;
- The authorised person has explained the effect of the YCC to the youth and has warned him or her that failure to comply with any of the conditions may result in a prosecution. If the youth is 16 or under this must be done in the presence of an appropriate adult;
- The youth signs a document that contains details of the offence, an admission that he committed the offence, consent to the YCC, and the conditions attached to the caution.[56]

Evaluation

We noted in section 6.3.2 that the number of first-time entrants to the YJS has declined, with a reduction of 67 per cent from 2002/3 to 2012/13 (Ministry of Justice/Youth Justice Board, 2014). Various explanations have been suggested to explain this trend: the preventative, interventionist programmes, 'creative accounting', and changes in practice generally (see, for example, Bateman 2014; Morgan 2009). Others draw attention particularly to the role of the various pre-statutory diversion schemes—those under the current umbrella term of informal resolution (Smith 2014; Kelly and Armitage 2015).

It is further argued that 'rethinking the role of "diversion" in youth justice has ramifications well beyond the youth justice "system" in so far as this is equated with the work carried out by youth offending teams' (Kelly and Armitage 2015: 2). The Centre for Social Justice research led them to identify four key shortcomings of the youth justice system, the first of which was 'The youth justice system continues to function as a backstop: sweeping up the problem cases that other services have failed, or been unable, to address' (Centre for Social Justice 2012, Executive summary: 1). So 'prevention' and intervention need to

---

[56] CPS guidance at http://www.cps.gov.uk/legal/v_to_z/youth_offenders/#a50.

start earlier than 'diversion' schemes as generally understood, and include bodies other than YOTs. This message is also given by Case and Haines, who argue for a 'Children First, Offenders Second' approach: 'The CFOS model offers a whole child, preventative and diversionary approach that normalises offending by children and promotes strengths and positive behaviour' (2015: abstract).

A Parliamentary Committee also drew attention to the need for a wider approach to prevention:

> There is a limit to what criminal justice agencies can achieve in preventing offending: young people in the criminal justice system are disproportionately likely to have high levels of welfare need and other agencies have often failed to offer them support at an early stage.
>
> (House of Commons Justice Committee 2013c)

In September 2015 the government announced a Review of the Youth Justice System (due in the summer of 2016) to 'consider the efficiency and effectiveness of the youth justice system in preventing offending, identify effective practice and make recommendations for improvement'. The Terms of Reference for the Review suggest that this wider view might be taken in that it will be able to consider:

> the actions and responsibilities of local authorities (including children's services, social services, education and housing), schools and other education providers, health services (including Children and Adolescent Mental Health Services and substance misuse services), youth offending teams, probation services, Police and Crime Commissioners (PCCs) and the police and other partners in preventing children and young people from offending.[57]

A further note of caution has been sounded: 'In this area at least, the assumption that policy represents practice...is now unsound, while the assumption that findings can be easily transferred even between local authority areas is questionable' (Kelly and Armitage, 2014/15: 14). However, the statement at the beginning of the latest national strategy for policing children and young people (National Police Chiefs' Council 2015) is to be welcomed:

> Children and young people (C&YP) account for over 12 million of the population in England, Wales and Northern Ireland. . . . C&YP are not mini-adults and a unique criminal justice system was established to respond to young people at risk. Their emotional, physical and emotional maturity is different from adults and needs to be understood—in particular, distress or trauma manifests itself differently in a young person's behaviour. Policing policies, processes and interactions with C&YP can have a significant impact on their lives, both in the short and long term.
>
> (National Police Chiefs Council 2015: 4, paras 1.1–1.20)

6.4 The treatment of mentally disordered offenders

In Chapter 5 (section 5.4.5) we briefly examined the sentencing provisions in relation to those offenders who are deemed to be both dangerous and mentally disordered.[58] In this section we discuss the measures which empower the court to order treatment instead of punishment at the sentencing stage when any offender is categorised as mentally disordered and we assess why such alternatives are so infrequently used.

---

[57] http://data.parliament.uk/DepositedPapers/Files/DEP2015-0736/2015-09-10_-_Final_TORs_for_youth_justice_review.pdf p. 1.

[58] For further discussion of these issues, see Baker (1993).

6.4.1 **The extent of the problem**

Our starting point is the fact that there are higher rates of mental health problems in the prison population than in the wider population, with a higher incidence of neuroses, psychoses, personality disorders, drug dependency, and histories of abuse (see, for example, Burney and Pearson 1995: 292–4). Research studies in the 1990s found that 37 per cent of male and 56 per cent of female sentenced prisoners had psychiatric disorders, with an incidence in the remand population of 63 per cent, and 5–10 per cent suffering from psychosis (see Peay 2002: 761, 772–5). A major study of over 1,000 prisoners, for example, found that 7 per cent of male sentenced prisoners and 14 per cent of female sentenced prisoners had a psychotic disorder (Singleton *et al.* 1998). More recently Peay, referring to work by Fazel and Baillargeon (2011) using large-scale data from Western countries to compare rates of mental illness in prison compared with the general population, drew attention to three issues:

> First, the raised levels of the most [serious] forms of mental illness; these pose stark questions about the satisfactoriness of the prior demonstration of criminal responsibility . . . Second, the most striking disparity in the figures relates to diagnoses of personality disorder (which now do come under the Mental Health Act's definition of mental disorder) and of antisocial personality disorder with respect to female offenders . . . Third, the high levels of drug misuse/dependence, which do not fall *per se* under the Mental Health Act's definition of mental disorder.
>
> (Peay 2014)

Referring to these and other studies, Peay concludes that 'even assuming that in England and Wales we are only average for psychosis in our prison population this would mean, of a population of say 75,899 *convicted* prisoners, some 2,732 people with functional psychosis are in prison. There is thus a well-documented and persistent over-representation of people with what everyone would agree to be mental illness—madness—in its most acute form' (Peay 2014). A recent report by the Prisons and Probation Ombudsman (2016) confirms that the mental health needs of prisoners are still not being met.

A report on the treatment of male prisoners with mental health problems, *Troubled Inside: Responding to the Mental Health Needs of Men in Prison* (Rickford and Edgar 2005), published by the Prison Reform Trust, reviews the treatment of such offenders and highlights the problems prisons face in managing mental health problems and the damaging effects of imprisonment on those suffering from mental illness prior to entering prison. It was highly critical of the use of prisons to warehouse those with mental health problems instead of diverting them from prison and recommended improvements in policy and practice to improve their treatment (see also Seddon 2006; Peay 2007). A review by HM Inspectorate of Prisons, *The Mental Health of Prisoners: A Thematic Review of the Care and Support of Prisoners with Mental Health Needs* (2007), also concluded that there was still too much unmet need for mental health care in prisons.

In 2009, the Department of Health published *Lord Bradley's Review of People with Mental Health Problems or Learning Disabilities in the Criminal Justice System*. The first two paragraphs of the Introduction to the Executive Summary make the following points:

1. Evidence suggests that there are now more people with mental health problems in prison than ever before. While public protection remains the priority, there is a growing consensus that prison may not always be the right environment for those with severe

mental illness. Custody can exacerbate mental ill health, heighten vulnerability and increase the risk of self-harm and suicide.

2. The policy of 'diversion' for people with mental health problems or learning disabilities has been supported by Government since as far back as 1990. But the lack of a nationally guided approach has meant that implementation has been inconsistent.

(Department of Health 2009a)

There has apparently been a particular problem in relation to offenders serving the now withdrawn IPP (imprisonment for public protection) sentence (see Chapter 5), with more than half of IPP prisoners having 'emotional well-being' problems, compared to four in ten lifers and three in ten of the general prison population (Jacobson and Hough 2010: 15–16). This research also showed a low rate of release (approximately 4 per cent) of prisoners from the IPP sentence after they had served the minimum term, and one of the reasons was that 'many of those serving IPP sentences are refused places on programmes on various grounds including limited intellectual capacity or mental illness'—and attendance at a programme was compulsory before assessment.

These statistics and research findings have fuelled demands for improvements in health care provision not only to meet the mental health care needs of prisoners, but also to divert offenders from prosecution to voluntary mental health services where appropriate, or, at the sentencing stage, to treatment under the MHA 1983 (as amended by the Mental Health Act (MHA) 2007). As the report *Snakes and Ladders: Mental Health and Criminal Justice* (O'Shea *et al.* 2003) pointed out, many people with mental health problems are caught in a cycle of crisis, crime, and mental illness, in which they are repeatedly in contact with the police and often detained in prison. The prevalence of mental health problems within the prison population also has implications for the experience of imprisonment and can add to the demands made on the Prison Service when it is already overstretched by the numbers entering prison.

Some prisoners find their health improves in prison, with a more settled routine, proper meals, and denial of access to drugs and alcohol, but those with pre-existing mental health problems may find them exacerbated by imprisonment, which could have severe consequences for their fellow prisoners as well as themselves. Until recently a prisoner with personality disorder could be transferred to a secure hospital only if his or her condition was treatable. This has now been replaced with a new 'appropriate medical treatment' test by s. 4 of the MHA 2007 (see section 6.4.3).

Lord Keith's inquiry into the murder of Zahid Mubarek by his cellmate, who suffered from a personality disorder (Keith 2006), noted that, because of insufficient appropriate resources, such prisoners could be shuttled between health care centres and the segregation unit or left with other prisoners. The Mubarek Report recommended a comprehensive review of the quality of care given to prisoners with mental health problems and the National Institute for Mental Health in England (NIMHE) was commissioned to implement a comprehensive national prison mental health programme. There has been more training in mental health awareness for officers, the commissioning of health care services was transferred to Primary Care Trusts, and the National Institute for Health and Care Excellence is currently developing guidelines on improving the mental health of people in prison.[59] In March 2015, the Coalition government stated: 'Work is currently underway with the Ministry of Justice on developing mental health care in the criminal justice system, which will ensure that prisoners receive mental health treatment equivalent to what they

---

[59] Publication is expected in November 2016.

would receive in the community and support continuity of treatment between custody and community.'[60]

The studies noted, which are evidence of the higher level of 'non-dangerous' mental illness and disorder amongst the prison population than in the population as a whole, prompt the question as to why this should be so. Possible explanations are that the mentally disordered are more inept and visible offenders, that they are repeat petty offenders, or that the 'gatekeepers' who make the decisions in the criminal justice system have stereo-typical views. For example, Cummins (2006) examines the role in this outcome of police powers and the appropriate adult at the questioning stage of police investigation. However, it may be that there is currently simply a lack of adequate mental health services to diagnose offenders early in the process.[61]

6.4.2 **A policy of diversion**

The Home Office Circular 66/1990 (*Provision for Mentally Disordered Offenders*) provided guidance on how to deal with mentally disordered offending, stating that there should not be a prosecution unless it was required by the public interest. Health service options should be used instead, with a focus on diversion of such offenders from the penal system (see Laing 1999). The Reed Report also proposed that mentally disordered offenders should, 'wherever appropriate, receive care and treatment from health and personal social services' (Department of Health and Home Office 1992: para 2.1). However, this policy has not been implemented unproblematically. As we noted in Chapter 5, there is a common perception of the mentally disordered as prone to act in dangerous and anti-social ways, with a corresponding reluctance to promote therapeutic disposals which are not under the control of the penal system.[62] From time to time such concerns are fuelled by publicity about murder cases where the defendant has been involved with mental health services.

These concerns reflect an underlying ambivalence in policy and practice, a tension between treatment and public protection aims. Further, a policy of diversion requires resources to identify and provide services and treatment for the criminal with mental health problems, but this use of scarce resources does not attract widespread public support. These often conflicting underlying principles of public protection, treatment, non-discrimination, and equal human rights (see Ashworth 2000: 342–3; Peay 2002: 748) are evident if we compare three documents published at the end of the 1990s. The Richardson Report (Department of Health 1999) gave priority to treatment over punishment for mentally disordered offenders but a Department of Health Consultation Paper (1999) was concerned with public protection and risk assessment, while the Home Office (1999a) paper on dangerous people with severe personality disorder presaged a concern with finding ways to detain such people without their having committed an offence. The subsequent White Paper on high-risk patients (Department of Health/Home Office 2000) and the draft Mental Health Bills of 2002 and 2004 (see Chapter 5, section 5.4.5) reflected, together with other developments, 'a growing desire to maintain penal control over mentally disordered offenders' (Peay 2002: 749).

---

[60] In an answer to a written question in Parliament: see http://www.parliament.uk/business/publications/written-questions-answers-statements/written-question/Commons/2015-03-10/226885/.

[61] For a systematic review of the international literature on the *Epidemiology of Mentally Disordered Offenders* see the Centre for Reviews and Dissemination (1999).

[62] See Prins (2005)—an update of a text first published in 1980—which provides a useful interdisciplinary approach to the issues.

A decade later the Bradley Report pointed out—again—that '[t]he first step to the effective management of offenders is the existence of good early identification and assessment of problems' and encouraged the greater use of the mental health requirement in a community sentence, rather than custody, for offenders with mental health problems (Department of Health 2009a: Executive Summary paras 80 and 38 respectively). The House of Commons Justice Committee welcomed Lord Bradley's preventive approach on economic grounds (2010: para 127), stating that, in relation to mentally disordered offenders, there is 'strong evidence that swift action in this area, in particular to broaden access to diversion and liaison schemes and to secure hospital treatment, could yield short, medium and long-term reductions in the prison population' (2010: para 158). The government's response to that report was positive: 'We also agree that less serious offenders can often be better dealt with in the community, and that in some cases we must do more to divert from custody those for whom a criminal sentence may not be the most appropriate response to their offending behaviour' (Ministry of Justice 2010f: 3–4).

6.4.3 **Treatment under the Mental Health Act 1983**

Statutory definitions are very important in sentencing (possibly) mentally disordered offenders: they will determine the 'label' and the options for the defendant. The legislative history of current provisions can be found in the criticisms of the Mental Health Act (MHA) 1959 by the Butler Committee and a DHSS Review in the 1970s. The legislative framework set up by the resulting MHA 1983 remains largely unchanged. Changes made by the MHA 2007, in force since 3 November 2008, amended ss. 1 and 37 of the MHA 1983 so that previous criteria and definitions no longer apply.[63]

Before the amendments made by the MHA 2007, s. 1(2) defined mental disorder as 'mental illness, arrested or incomplete development of mind, psychopathic disorder and any disorder or disability of mind' and 'psychopathic disorder' was defined as 'persistent disorder or disability of mind . . . which results in abnormally aggressive or seriously irresponsible behaviour'. There was a further categorisation into major and minor forms of mental disorder (see Peay 2002: 753) and also a 'treatability' criterion. These provisions caused difficulties.

The following are the main changes relevant to sentencing as summarised in the government's Explanatory Notes:

Definition of mental disorder: The Act changes the way the 1983 Act defines mental disorder, so that a single definition applies throughout the Act, and abolishes references to categories of disorder. These amendments complement the changes to the criteria for detention. Section 1, therefore, amends the wording of the definition of mental disorder in the 1983 Act from 'mental illness, arrested or incomplete development of mind, psychopathic disorder and any other disorder or disability of mind' to 'any disorder or disability of the mind'.

Criteria for detention: It introduces a new 'appropriate medical treatment' test which will apply to all the longer-term powers of detention. As a result, it will not be possible for patients to be compulsorily detained or their detention continued unless medical treatment which is appropriate to the patient's mental disorder and all other circumstances of the case is available to that patient. At the same time, the so-called 'treatability test' will be abolished. Because of the removal of categories of disorder by s 1, the appropriate medical treatment test applies equally to all mental disorders.

---

[63] Minor amendments have also been made by LASPO 2012 and the Criminal Justice and Courts Act 2015.

The relevant orders for the sentencing court are to be found in Part III of the MHA 1983. Section 37 allows the court to order that the offender be admitted to hospital, provided the receiving hospital agrees—s. 37(4), or be placed under the guardianship of the local social services department.[64] The conditions include that the offence of which the offender has been convicted is an imprisonable offence and the court believes an order under s. 37 is the most suitable method of dealing with the offender. Evidence from two doctors is necessary to establish that the offender is suffering from one of the forms of mental disorder and that detention for treatment in hospital is appropriate. Transfer from prison to hospital by order of the Home Secretary is possible under s. 47, and Crown Courts may impose a s. 45A order (see section 6.4.4), both on similar criteria to those in s. 37.

The effect of a hospital order is as outlined in the following information provided by the charity MIND:

> Most section 37 hospital orders are initially for six months . . . At the end of that period, you have the right to apply to the Mental Health Tribunal. Your responsible clinician (RC) has the right to discharge you at any time, as do the hospital managers, but the RC can also renew the section at the end of the first six months, again at the end of a second period of six months, and at yearly intervals thereafter. If your section is renewed, you can apply to the Mental Health Tribunal for discharge.[65]

The Mental Health Tribunal (formerly the Mental Health Review Tribunal) is now part of the First-Tier Tribunal, Health, Education and Social Care Chamber. The GOV.UK website says of its role: 'We're responsible for handling applications for the discharge of patients detained in psychiatric hospitals'[66] and 'The tribunal is independent of government and will listen to both sides of the argument before making a decision.'[67] Each tribunal must have a legal member (usually a solicitor or a barrister), a doctor (usually a psychiatrist), and a lay member (a person who is not medically or legally trained) with some mental health experience, while the detained patient, the responsible clinician, and a social worker will also attend the tribunal.[68]

If the Crown Court believes that further restrictions should be placed on release from hospital it may also make a restriction order 'where necessary for the protection of the public from serious harm' (MHA 1983, s. 41; see Chapter 5). A magistrates' court may refer a case to the Crown Court for consideration of this order. MHA 2007, s. 40 also amends s. 41 of the 1983 Act, removing the power of the Crown Court to make restriction orders for a limited period. The court cannot make such an order unless at least one of the two doctors recommending a hospital order gave evidence orally. Where a restriction order is in force the responsible clinician needs the permission of the Ministry of Justice or the Mental Health Tribunal to discharge an offender. At the end of the custodial term (now the 'release' date under s. 294 of the CJA 2003) of a prison sentence the restriction order ceases to have effect and provisions similar to those of the hospital order apply.[69]

---

[64] Guardianship orders are rarely used.

[65] See: http://www.mind.org.uk/information-support/legal-rights/mental-health-and-the-courts/ #.VhPmNctdE5s (accessed 6 October 2015).

[66] https://www.gov.uk/courts-tribunals/first-tier-tribunal-mental-health.

[67] https://www.gov.uk/mental-health-tribunal. These two websites are very scanty in their information, unlike the previous Justice website (see the third edition of this book at p. 222), but that was also not as informative as that of the former MHRT (see the second edition of this book at p. 233).

[68] See http://www.rethink.org/living-with-mental-illness/mental-health-laws/discharge-from-detention/ tribunals: a useful website produced by the Rethink Mental Illness charity.

[69] See: http://www.mind.org.uk/information-support/legal-rights/mental-health-and-the-courts/ #.VhPrp8tdE5s.

6.4.4 **Penal disposals**

The previous section briefly outlined the main possibilities for treating an offender as mentally disordered rather than as requiring punishment. There are in addition two 'mixed' orders where a penal disposal is given but it includes treatment. First, a probation or supervision order with a psychiatric treatment condition had been available since the Criminal Justice Act 1948. The PCCSA 2000, Schedules 2, 3, and 6, re-enacted the criteria and requirements in relation to community rehabilitation orders and s. 207 of the CJA 2003 provided, instead, for the imposition of a similar mental health treatment requirement in the new community order (and also in a suspended sentence order). Such a requirement under s. 207 is 'with a view to the improvement of the offender's mental condition', and the treatment can be as a resident or non-resident patient in a care home or hospital, or under the direction of a medical practitioner or psychologist. A doctor must certify that the offender's condition 'may be susceptible to treatment' but does not warrant a hospital or guardianship order.

Secondly, the Crime (Sentences) Act 1997 inserted a new s. 45A into the MHA 1983 to provide the courts with hospital and limitation directions. If the offender is suffering from a psychopathic disorder and the court, having considered a hospital order, decides to impose a custodial sentence, it can, nevertheless, direct that the offender be admitted immediately to hospital (with similar further criteria as for hospital orders). If the offender does not respond to treatment (or, possibly, recovers), he is then transferred to prison. This order is, arguably, an unjustifiable compromise between treatment and punishment. It is a clear example of the response by government and the courts to public fears that a mentally disordered offender will 'escape' punishment and control.

Such sentences do, however, provide treatment. As Peay notes, while 'some restriction orders are imposed unnecessarily . . . most disordered offenders do not receive a therapeutic "hospital order" disposal, even though their culpability may be mitigated, if not absolved, by their mental state' (2002: 755). One possible reason why those suffering from mental health problems are not treated as such at the sentencing stage is that they are not diagnosed early enough to be diverted from the penal system; another is that not all such offenders may 'fit' the MHA 1983 criteria, notably the availability of hospital care (see Genders 2003). A third explanation lies in the widespread ambivalence over the offender's culpability and just deserts, reflecting much deeper concerns regarding the origins of 'evil' in the 'normal' offender.

As a result of these conflicting imperatives and ideas, the sentencing framework allows the sentencer to choose or reject the penal options even when the MHA 1983 criteria are met. Section 166(5) of the CJA 2003 empowers the court to disregard provisions which would otherwise mandate the passing of particular sentences when the offender is mentally disordered. Section 157(1) mandates the court to obtain a medical report before passing a custodial sentence on an offender who 'is or appears to be mentally disordered', although that requirement does not apply if, 'in the circumstances of the case', the court feels that it is unnecessary. Further, before passing such a sentence the court must consider any information about the offender's mental condition and assess 'the likely effect of such a sentence on that condition and on any treatment which may be available for it' (s. 157(3)).

If the court decides that it cannot or will not use MHA 1983 options, it could choose penal disposals ranging from 'non-punitive' discharges and bind-overs, through fines, community penalties, and imprisonment. In the case of the latter, a determinate and proportionate sentence may be passed or, where available, a discretionary life sentence. Where a relatively long sentence is passed there may be time and opportunity for therapeutic treatment to be given in prison, but there can be no guarantee of this and, paradoxically, the encouragement of shorter sentences may preclude the possibility of such treatment.

This area of sentencing law and practice is complex and difficult and we have been able only to outline the possibilities and problems. What is clear is that, despite advances in diversion schemes and the standard of mental health care in prisons, our treatment of the mentally disordered offender is still a prime example of unprincipled compromise in relation to issues of sentence impact and effectiveness, as well as offender culpability. It is also an area where a propensity to label as a homogeneous category what is in practice a diverse group of people with diverse needs makes any assessment of sentence impact in individual cases very difficult. As Peay has commented, 'For many mentally disordered offenders imprisonment is not a manifest injustice, yet for some it is. And it is certainly an affront to our common notions of justice that this situation persists' (2014: 26).

6.5. Reflecting on the issues

6.5.1 Thinking about restorative justice: what 'is' reparation?

Do the following colour association test:

- *without* taking time to think in any conscious or considered way
- decide what colour you think of when focusing on the word 'reparation'.

If you completed this exercise when you first started reading this chapter you may wish to note whether your ideas have changed. If you are doing this for the first time you might wish to consider what parts of section 6.2 most influenced your response.

online resource centre

This may seem to be a rather odd way of reflecting on the issues dealt with in that section. Our intention is to help you appreciate the complexity of the concept of reparation within criminal justice and the ambiguities inherent in the different ways of encouraging or mandating the offender to make amends. In the Online Resource Centre you will find some comments on responses to this exercise.

Most of the associations suggested by the chosen colours are part of the complex mix of motivations and concepts that underpins the range of reparative and restorative options currently available in the criminal justice process. Understandings of reparation do indeed range from an account-balancing process, akin to a financial 'eye-for-an-eye' approach, to a visionary and, possibly, idealistic paradigm about social harmony and personal reintegration. Not surprisingly, questions such as 'what is reparation?' or 'what does restorative justice mean?' have no easy answer. As we have seen, it is difficult to isolate one perspective or one influence which has been the major determinant on the development of options to 'make amends' for the harm done to property, people, and relationships. For further reading on these issues see the Online Resource Centre. You might also wish to read now Chapter 7, section 7.2, which deals with older forms of reparation.

online resource centre

6.5.2 Thinking about approaches to children and young people who offend

Statement to debate:
'The benefits of the current system of youth cautions and conditional cautions outweigh the disadvantages.'

Remember that you can consult the Online Resource Centre for guidance.

online resource centre

Sentencing exercise

Ade, a student aged 20, worked on Saturdays in the local newsagents until the proprietor—Mr B—cut down on part-time staff. Because she knew about a dodgy window catch she broke into the shop one night and took several boxes of crisps and chocolate. She sold these to a local youth club for £50 (having been asked to get new supplies), saying that she had lost the till receipt. At the local magistrates' court she was found guilty of burglary. She has no previous convictions.

- Would your answer be different if Ade had worked in an electronics factory and had stolen goods worth £5,000?
- Are there options which include restorative justice that the police and CPS could have used instead of prosecution?

Decide which outcome is appropriate for Ade. You might refer to the sentencing check-list in Chapter 3 (section 3.2.1) and consider, in particular, any restorative options. The Online Resource Centre discusses possible approaches.

online
resource
centre

6.5.3 **Thinking about outcomes for the mentally disordered offender**

Statement for discussion:

'There is an established policy of diversion of mentally disordered offenders from prison and yet there is a much higher incidence of mental illness in the prison population than in the general population. The reason is that the orders in Part III of the Mental Health Act 1983 are not fit for purpose.'

Do you think this is the main reason? Why/why not?

Case study:

You might wish to look at the sentencing exercise about Zack at the end of Chapter 7: that is also relevant to this issue.

7

Impact on victims and offenders

SUMMARY

This chapter reviews, first, the increased policy focus on victims, dealing with remedies for victims of crime and more recent involvement in the sentencing process via victim impact statements. Secondly, it discusses conflicting approaches to a focus on the impact of punishment on the offender or the offender's family, covering both justifications from penology and evidence—from research and appellate cases—of practice in the courts.

7.1 An increased focus on the victim

7.1.1 **Influences on policy**

In the 1980s, Stockdale and Devlin, both Crown Court judges, quoted a Canadian writer, J. W. Mohr, noting that his comment now applied to England: 'There has been a development, even if ever so slow, to shift from principles of punishment, deterrence and rehabilitation to the principle of undoing the harm done by means such as restitution, compensation and community service' (Stockdale and Devlin 1987, citing Grosman 1980: 26). They wrote of a 'growing concern about the victim' and argued, 'Whatever doubts one may entertain about other aims of punishment, nobody doubts the justice of aiding the victim' (1987: 36–7). Similarly, as we saw in Chapter 6 (section 6.2), restorative justice—with its emphasis on the benefits for victims as well as its effects on offenders—is accepted very widely as a self-evident 'good': to argue against helping victims is akin to arguing against peace.

New measures by which a person wronged by offending behaviour could gain a remedy for loss were introduced from the 1970s and a victim focus has become very important in the legitimation of new approaches in sentencing policy. The contexts which go some way to explain this trend are the changes in governance to which we referred in Chapter 5, when rising crime rates and changing economic climates led to a view that the crime problem could not be solved but only managed (Walklate 2004: 29; see also Garland 2001b). In that transformation, not only have the public voice and interest groups become more influential, but the victim has been 'politicised' (Walklate 2004: 30–2). Consequently, the powerful idea that the state had 'stolen' the 'wrong' (that is, the offence) from the victim (Christie 1977), allowing the victim to feel excluded, powerless, neglected, and uncompensated, was, paradoxically, a politically useful one. It prompted self-evident and positive remedies: helping victims to 'cope' with the effects of crime is a welcome policy initiative to a 'less than confident State', tackling rising crime rates which appear impervious to policy initiatives (Rock 2002: 9).

By 1997 the authors of a book on victims of crime could begin by stating, 'in less than 20 years, there has been a revolution in the criminal justice system. Each criminal case involves more than the government versus the defendant. There is another party with a burning interest' (Davis *et al.* 1997: vii). The interests and feelings of victims 'are now routinely invoked in support of measures of punitive segregation' and the 'symbolic figure of the victim has taken on a life of its own', argued Garland (2001b: 11).

Yet the development of the academic study of victims—victimology—within criminology was problematic, with the early victimology being regarded as 'this dismal science' (Burney 2003: 405), the 'lunatic fringe' of criminology (Rock 2002: 3). A positivist victimology emerged in the middle of the twentieth century with the work of criminologists such as von Hentig and Mendelsohn but this early strand focused upon the responsibility of the victim for a criminal event occurring, a 'blame the victim' approach which hardly improved the plight of victims.[1] So, 'Until the late 1970s, victims were almost wholly neglected in criminology and criminal justice' (Rock 2002: 1) and Sanders argues that it was the growing interest in the effects of crime on victims—particularly victims of rape, domestic violence, and race hate crimes—and in victim involvement in the criminal justice system which reinvigorated victimology in the 1980s (Sanders 2002: 198, n 2). Consequently, the campaigns of the feminist and anti-racist movements were influential in the development of a new strand of victimology in the 1980s.

7.1.2 **What role for victims?**

'Rebalancing' the criminal justice system has been a governmental policy aim since the *Justice for All* White Paper of 2002 proposed to put victims and witnesses at the 'heart' of the criminal justice system (Home Office 2002a: para 0.22) so as to reduce crime and secure more convictions (see Jackson 2003: 311; for further discussion see Reeves and Dunn 2010; Shapland *et al.* 2011; Walklate 2011: 330). *A New Deal for Victims and Witnesses: A National Strategy to Deliver Improved Services* also stated that 'the government . . . wants to do everything it can to make sure victims and witnesses are treated with respect . . . supporting victims and witnesses is a worthwhile end in itself. It is also fundamental if justice is to be achieved' (Home Office 2003d: Foreword). Victims, then, have had a very high priority in the 'messages' that the Ministry of Justice and the Home Office have conveyed over the past decade or so. *Breaking the Cycle* was littered with references to the victim and to proposals designed to improve the outcomes for victims (Ministry of Justice 2010a: see, for example, paras 75–81), and the Conservative Party manifesto before the 2015 General Election included the following: 'Now we will strengthen victims' rights further, with a new Victims' Law that will enshrine key rights for victims, including the right to make a personal statement and have it read in court before sentencing—and before the Parole Board decides on a prisoner's release' (2015: 59).

In Scotland, too, criminal justice policy has given a high priority to victims. A *Scottish Strategy for Victims* and an accompanying *Action Plan* (Scottish Executive 2001) were published in 2001. The strategy has three 'pillars', echoing English policy objectives: provision of practical and emotional support, information to victims, and greater participation in the criminal justice system. The Scottish Executive (2002a) also explained how the Scottish criminal justice system complies with the Articles in the EU Framework Decision on the Standing of Victims in Criminal Proceedings which was implemented in 2002–6.[2] Article 2 states that '[e]ach Member State shall ensure that victims have a real and appropriate role

---

[1] See Davies *et al.* (2003: 2–5) for a review of the strengths and weaknesses of the three perspectives in victimology which developed in the second half of the twentieth century.

[2] L 082: adopted by the European Council 2001; for details, see: http://europa.eu.

in its criminal legal system' and that states 'recognise the rights and legitimate interests of victims with particular reference to criminal proceedings'.

Against this backdrop of the Council of Europe's concern to ensure minimum standards for treatment of victims across the EU, the UK's policy objectives raise several questions. Clearly a link is being made between victims and the effectiveness of witnesses,[3] but another explanation given by Jackson was that concern for victims was linked 'to the logic of Labour's philosophy that tackling crime effectively' also depends upon 'reviving the spirit of the community and empowering individuals' (Jackson 2003: 311–12). These tensions prompt the question as to whether victim involvement in the criminal justice process is being used as a means to reduce reoffending through use of restorative measures, a means to improve the victim's health and happiness, or a means to increase public confidence in the criminal justice system.[4] McEvoy and colleagues have suggested that restorative justice appeals to governments because it appears as a solution to the perceived need underpinning the proposals of the Royal Commission on Criminal Justice (1993) over two decades ago (McEvoy *et al.* 2002: 469), to 'balance' the interests of offenders, state, and victims when formulating criminal justice policy (see Ashworth 1998b: 30–40). However, the comment made some time ago still has resonance:

> This is often framed in terms of a zero-sum game: what's good for suspects and defendants (less punitiveness, more welfare) is bad for victims and vice versa. Thus increasingly authoritarian penal measures, in the UK for example over the last 10 years, are often justified by government claims to be putting victims 'at the centre' of penal policy.
>
> (Sanders 2003: 161)

Further, a review for the Ministry of Justice by the Victims' Champion of the treatment of victims and witnesses highlighted the following statement in its report: 'A great deal of positive work has been done to improve the support available for victims and witnesses but there is still a disparity between policy and reality for victims' (Payne 2009: 4). This conclusion highlights two issues: first, that the role of victims is often conflated with that of witnesses whose help is required for the sake of the system, and, secondly, that despite an increasingly public and persistent policy of support for victims, the practice is often different.

If we approach the issues historically, it is possible to see the role of victims in criminal justice policy in England and Wales changing in three stages: 1960–75—the period associated with the development of compensation; 1975–80—the period associated with the development of specific schemes to support victims; and the period from the 1980s onwards when victim support was institutionalised and a greater involvement of victims in the criminal justice process was demanded (Newburn 1995). The focus on victims in the past two decades has had two very different aspects: one could be called a victims' welfare approach, as evidenced by the Victim Support movement, while the other approach is to give victims a status to influence outcome.

Victims' Code

The needs of victims were strongly emphasised in *Criminal Justice: The Way Ahead* (Home Office 2001a) and since 2001 victims have been able to submit a personal statement to the court setting out the effects of the crime on them and their lives. A *Code of Practice for the Victims of Crime* was issued in 2006 and s. 32 of the Domestic

---

[3] For recent research on the experiences of witnesses to crime see Willoughby (2015).

[4] For recent research on public confidence in the Criminal Justice System see Jansson (2015).

Violence, Crime and Victims Act 2004 gives the victim of crime the 'right' ('is entitled') to a minimum standard of service. Further, there is now a Victims' Commissioner[5] and a new *Code of Practice for Victims of Crime* was issued in 2013 (Ministry of Justice 2013i), with a revised version in 2015. At the beginning there is a summary of 'key entitlements' which include the following:

- An enhanced service if you are a victim of serious crime, a persistently targeted victim or a vulnerable or intimidated victim;
- A needs assessment to help work out what support you need;
- Information on what to expect from the criminal justice system;
- Be referred to organisations supporting victims of crime;
- Be informed about the police investigation, such as if a suspect is arrested and charged and any bail conditions imposed;
- Make a Victim Personal Statement (VPS) to explain how the crime affected you;
- Read your VPS aloud or have it read aloud on your behalf, subject to the views of the court, if a defendant is found guilty;
- Be informed if the suspect is to be prosecuted or not or given an out of court disposal.

(Ministry of Justice 2015).

Fenwick had argued that the Charter (the original name for the *Code*) appeared to be 'a response to certain international declarations on victims' rights, including the UN Declaration of the Basic Principles of Justice for the Victims of Crime and Abuse of Power', adopted by the General Assembly of the UN in 1985 (1997: 317). The Conservative manifesto also referred to the proposed new 'Victims' Law' but it is doubtful that it is a rights-based document, notwithstanding the original subtitle, 'A statement of the rights of victims of crime'. In 1996 the subtitle was changed 'to the much less ambitious, but more accurate "A statement of service standards for victims of crime"' (Williams 1999: 387) and the latest version basically 'sets out the services to be provided to victims of criminal conduct by criminal justice organisations in England and Wales' and gives minimum standards for the services (Ministry of Justice 2013i: para 2). It would appear, then, that the *Code* can be located within a managerialist discourse where objectives are formulated and standards are set for citizens to be able to complain if necessary.[6]

Role of the National Probation Service (NPS)

The NPS has for some time had a duty to liaise with victims of serious sexual or violent offences in those cases where the offender is sentenced to more than 12 months' imprisonment, and must contact them in relation to a prisoner's release into the community. There is some evidence that the NPS finds the focus on both the victim and the offender difficult (Wargent 2002) and problematic to translate into practice (Crawford and Enterkin 2001: 708) but, nevertheless, it has built up considerable expertise in this area of work (see, for example, Home Office 2000b: Preface; Crook 2015).

However, as Crook points out, 'The community rehabilitation companies (CRCs), which are now being run by companies such as Purple Futures and Sodexo, have not been given duties towards victims (aside from a duty to participate in domestic homicide reviews), but instead must assist the NPS [to] carry out its responsibilities towards victims' (Crook 2015).

---

[5] See http://victimscommissioner.org.uk/.

[6] A Private Members Bill sponsored by Keir Starmer MP, former Director of Public Prosecutions—the Victims of Crime Etc. (Rights, Entitlements and Related Matters) Bill 2015–16—would provide additional rights and duties in relation to the *Victims' Code*.

To summarise, then, current criminal justice policy covers the following disparate elements in relation to victims of crime:

- victim support initiatives;
- facilities for, and communication/liaison with, victims during the criminal process;
- the setting of standards and expectations in the *Code of Practice for Victims of Crime*;
- victim personal statements.

This list could be seen as one that progresses from the least problematic to the most problematic aspects of victim-focused policies. The victim supportive initiatives are essentially those where victims are contacted after they have reported an offence to the police and are given counselling and any practical help which is required in order to cope with the aftermath of the offending. Secondly, facilities being provided for victims and communication with them in the course of the progress of the case may also be seen as relatively unproblematic, although not when this overlaps with the issue of support to victims in order to give evidence. That raises issues as to whether the support and possible coaching of victims is unfair to the accused and, more generally, raises the possibility of a conflict between the rights of victims and of defendants and offenders.

7.1.3 **The victim personal statement scheme (VPSS)**

Schemes, using—in the past and in other jurisdictions—victim impact statements (VIS), victim opinion statements (VOS), or, as now in England and Wales, victim personal statements (VPS), are clear evidence of a concern with the impact of crime on the victim. The statement is the means by which the court is made aware of the impact on this particular victim of the acts of the offender who is about to be sentenced. In some jurisdictions the victim has an influential say in sentencing, and might even be able to decide the penalty. In England and Wales such statements give victims a limited opportunity to present their views to the court and the government accepted that there has been 'widespread confusion about whether the personal statement is there to help courts understand the impact of a crime, to help relevant agencies assess victims' needs, or to give victims a chance to express themselves' (Ministry of Justice 2010a: 21).

The introduction of family impact statements to court in several areas in 2006—applying to offences of murder or manslaughter charged on or after 24 April 2006[7]—suggests that impact is now taken more seriously in relation to the families of victims (see Department for Constitutional Affairs 2006; Sweeting *et al.* 2008; Roberts and Manikis 2011: 7). The latest version of the guidance states that the police must offer the opportunity to make a VPS to the following people:

- any victim at the time they complete a witness statement about what has happened;
- victims of the most serious crime (including bereaved close relatives), persistently targeted victims, and vulnerable or intimidated victims, irrespective of whether or not they have given a witness statement about what happened;
- a parent or carer of a vulnerable adult or of a young victim under the age of 18 unless it is considered not to be in the best interests of the child or vulnerable adult.

(Ministry of Justice 2013h: 2)

---

[7] See *A Protocol Issued by the President of the Queen's Bench Division Setting Out the Procedure to Be Followed in the Victims' Advocate Pilot Areas*: accessed at http://www.judiciary.gov.uk/docs/victims_advocate_protocol_030506.pdf.

When such proposals were first mooted for the UK, it was argued that 'the right to submit a VIS may be high in profile but low in improving genuine respect for victims. We should hesitate and reconsider before going further in this direction' (Ashworth 1993: 509). The issues raised were the question of sentencing for unseen results of offending behaviour on the victim, the preservation of defendants' rights, and the difficulty of raising expectations in the minds of victims which cannot be met (Ashworth 1993: 505–7). Sanders *et al.* also noted that 'a firm theoretical basis for victim participation in adversarial systems has yet to be mapped out' (2001: 448).[8] It is also not clear why victims are given this role in sentencing. Edwards (2001) reviewed four possible justifications. One rationale is that the making of a VPS is therapeutic, but this is not universal in practice; nor can the VPSS ensure that the criminal justice system operates more efficiently, nor that sentencing outcomes are improved, nor that it will contribute towards establishing a more participatory and rights-based system. 'It is perhaps unrealistic though to expect sentencing procedures themselves to do too much, such as delivering real psychological benefits to victims' (Edwards 2001: 51).

In England and Wales the VPS is produced by the police in consultation with the victim/witness and can be updated at particular stages of the process. Participation is optional for victims and research found that only half (55 per cent) of all victims who recalled having been offered a VPS had completed one (Roberts and Manikis 2011: 3).

The most problematic issue, however, has been whether the VPS should include an opinion on sentence:

> Whether the victim impact statement should include the victim's opinion regarding sentence is a thorny issue, and there appears to be no consensus on this point. For example, in England and Wales and the Netherlands such a practice is generally discouraged while in the United States, most states allow presentations from victims in this regard. In South Africa the law provides no clear guidance on the issue of victims' suggestions on sentencing.

> (van der Merwe and Skelton 2015: 356)

In this jurisdiction, therefore, it is seen as problematic if a VPS unduly influenced a sentencing decision or if it were viewed as amounting to a procedural right to be involved in sentencing. For example, in its *Response to Breaking the Cycle: Effective Punishment, Rehabilitation and Sentencing of Offenders*, the Judiciary of England and Wales stated that '[t]he court can of course take the VPS into account but must not be bound by it'.[9] In a Practice Statement the Lord Chief Justice made clear that the extra information it provides to the victim about the consequences will simply be added to all the factors taken into account in sentencing; the victim's opinions about the sentence are not relevant.[10] However, there are exceptions and one such was shown in *R v Roche* (1999), 'where the court distinguished between calls for vengeance and calls for mercy—stating that a court can never become "an instrument of vengeance, nonetheless it can in appropriate circumstances, and to some degree, become an instrument of compassion"' (van der Merwe and Skelton 2015: 368; see also *R v Mills* 1998). However, van der Merwe and Skelton argue that this

---

[8] This article also reviews the arguments of Erez (1999).

[9] See http://www.judiciary.gov.uk/Resources/JCO/Documents/Consultations/judicial-response-green-paper-breaking-the-cycle.pdf.

[10] *R v Perks* (2001). However, one of the two exceptions to this is '[w]here the victim's forgiveness or unwillingness to press charges provide evidence that his or her psychological or mental suffering must be very much less than would normally be the case'. See also the SGC *Case Compendium*, section on 'Victim's Wishes', and Edwards (2002). See also *R v Roche* [1999] 2 Cr App R (S) 105.

approach has 'only led to a reduction in the custodial sentences imposed in the relevant matters, and not a replacement of the custodial sentence with a non-custodial one. This indicates that the general sentencing mode is retributive' (2015: 372).

The victim personal statement is, then, a far cry from the situation in those states where the victim's family can decide whether the death penalty should be imposed. In any case, research has shown that concerns that victims would be more punitive than the judge or the public appear to be misplaced. Dawes *et al.* note that '[w]hile a key criticism of sentencing among the public was that it did not always result in justice for the victim, some victims and witnesses actually tended to be relatively satisfied with the sentences handed down' (2011: section 2.2). They also found that, while the public associated long sentences with justice being done, victims often gave more consideration to utilitarian objectives such as changing the behaviour of the offender: 'I think that's the most important thing [to rehabilitate the offender]. I don't think we are here to revenge anybody' (Victim: quoted in Dawes *et al.* 2011: 14).

On the other hand, some victims are concerned that the VPS does not have sufficient influence on outcome: 'Of all respondents who reported having submitted a VPS, less than half (39 per cent) held the view that the statement had been fully taken into account' (Roberts and Manikis 2011: 3).

7.2 Reducing the impact on the victim

7.2.1 The policy context for compensation and confiscation

As we noted in Chapter 6, it would be wrong to think of reparation and restorative justice as totally new concepts. Within modern times, in the English legal system generally—as opposed to the criminal justice system in particular—the place of reparation has been in the civil courts. There have always been substantive laws and procedures by which civil liability can, potentially, be established and a remedy awarded to the 'victim'. Those remedies are contained within particular branches of law such as contract and tort and the remedies take the form of damages—financial restitution—or injunctions, ordered by the court or negotiated in the shadow of the law. However, the norms—the jurisprudence—and the aims of civil and criminal law have traditionally been very different. Whereas the civil law gives remedies, the criminal law aims to punish (whether for retributivist reasons or utilitarian ends) the person who commits one of those 'wrongs' which have been specifically designated as a criminal offence, an offence which is against the public good. So criminal law is activated by the state; the civil law can be activated only by an individual wronged.

In Chapter 1 (section 1.1.3) we focused on the justifications for designating certain actions as ones for which the response must or could be punitive and we contrasted that with possible social welfare, medical, or even military responses to deviant action. In a country with a traditional criminal justice system, such as the UK, if an action is specified as an offence and dealt with accordingly, the victim's remedy is to see the offender punished by the state. This may be exactly what the 'victim' wants, money not being able, in the victim's mind, to compensate for the wrong done. If that is so, it is a considerable advantage to the victim that the resources of the state are available to apprehend and punish the wrong-doer. On the other hand, this may not be what the victim wants.

Certainly, increasing evidence of the ineffectiveness and unfairness of the system of civil remedies for harm was one factor feeding into the pressure for change. The attractiveness for the wronged individual of using the civil justice system to achieve compensation or reparation decreased as evidence of the 'roulette' character of civil justice accumulated through the work of radical lawyers and socio-legal researchers in the 1960s and 1970s. To use that system the individual must successfully pass through a series of hoops: the circumstances of the wrong done must fit the legal criteria and it must be possible to pinpoint a named individual as causing the wrong; the claim against the perpetrator must be accompanied by evidence and proof which may be hard for the wronged individual to obtain; the perpetrator must be available but may be in prison, dead, or untraceable; perpetrators must have enough money to pay the damages and must not avoid attempts to make them pay; the person wronged must have the psychological or financial resources to take court action (see, for example, Genn 1988, 1999).

The focus on victims did not, of itself, challenge retributivist-based sentencing. Indeed, the focus on 'just deserts' in sentencing encouraged a focus on restitution for victims. If the punishment must be proportionate to culpability then any profit from offending must be taken into account and, in that process, returned to the victim as goods or compensation. Linked to this development was a very specific influence which stemmed from the increasingly large scale of drug trafficking in the 1980s. Because of the vast sums of money such trafficking involved, with extremely high profits for the criminal, the previously neglected issues of 'the profits of crime' became more important. Confiscation and compensation were prioritised in the Drug Trafficking Offences Act (DTOA) 1986 which specifically targeted drug-related crimes and profits and which became the forerunner of more general provisions, in particular Part VI of the Criminal Justice Act (CJA) 1993. More recently the concern with terrorist activities and the 'laundering' of money for such purposes has given a further impetus to confiscation provisions. Similar legislative developments have happened in other European jurisdictions and in the United States in relation to organised crime generally.

The consolidation of retributivist sentencing—in the 1980s in many jurisdictions, and after 1991 in the UK—was a factor that encouraged those critical of that development to look to other penal philosophies. Utilitarian theories of rehabilitation and reform were relatively unpersuasive in the 1980s, and proponents of restorative justice consequently tailored their arguments to appeal to this philosophical 'gap' (see Chapter 6, section 6.2). For example, Richards specifically reviewed the arguments made against classical justifications for punishment and argued instead for restorative justice (1998: chapter 4) whereby the victim and the offender sought 'restoration'.

Nevertheless the development of new forms of confiscation and compensation to victims 'should not be seen as being associated with a broader victims' movement' (Davies *et al.* 2003: 20): some of the developments to be discussed in the following section were changes in response to pressures within a largely retributivist framework. It is not surprising that these provisions were introduced before some of the other sentencing changes in relation to victims of offending because they could more easily fit into traditional sentencing frameworks.

7.2.2 The 'fruits of crime': restitution, forfeiture, and confiscation

Section 28 of the Theft Act 1968 gave the court the power to order the restitution, the handing back, of stolen goods (or their equivalent) to the victim. This power is now in s. 148 of the Powers of Criminal Courts (Sentencing) Act (PCCSA) 2000. The Powers of Criminal Courts Act (PCCA) 1973 originally gave the courts very limited powers of forfeiture of property connected with the offence but the amendments made by the Criminal Justice Act (CJA) 1988 extended the courts' powers to any offence, whether indictable or summary, and whether punishable or not by custody (by s. 69).

Courts also have a duty to confiscate any proceeds. The DTOA 1986 first imposed this requirement specifically in relation to the growing drug trafficking problem. As previously noted, the CJA 1988, Part VI extended it to the benefits of property obtained in relation to (that is, as a result of or in connection with the commission of) any indictable offence.[11] In 1993 the DTOA 1986 was amended, introducing detailed practical provisions to make confiscation easier for the courts to impose, and some provisions were re-enacted in the Drug Trafficking Act 1994.[12] The civil standard of proof is to be used to address the practical difficulty for the court of finding and proving what was gained in the commission of the offence. The CJA 1988 was also amended to give more compensation order situations (CJA 1993, ss. 27–28) and the Terrorism Act 2002 increased powers in relation to forfeiture orders. Cases have tested the rights compliance of these provisions, *Welch* (1995) finding that confiscation orders are to be considered as a penalty, and so retrospective implementation is in breach of Article 7 of the European Convention on Human Rights.[13]

The Proceeds of Crime Act (PCA) 2002,[14] 'designed to make the recovery of unlawfully held assets more effective' (Home Office 2002d), consolidated some existing powers and added new powers to ascertain the whereabouts of proceeds of crime.[15] It requires the Crown Court—providing the second condition is also met—to make a confiscation order against the offender in relation to any offence if (first condition) the offender was convicted, or committed for sentence, at the Crown Court (s. 6(1) and (2)) or if the prosecutor asked the magistrates' court to commit the convicted offender to the Crown Court with a view to a confiscation order being considered (s. 70). The second condition is that the prosecutor or the Director of Public Prosecutions asks the court to proceed under s. 6 or the court believes it is appropriate to do so (s. 6(3)). The court is then instructed to decide 'whether the defendant has a criminal lifestyle' (s. 6(4)(a)). If he (or she) has, the court must decide whether he has benefited from his 'general criminal conduct'; if not it must decide 'whether he has benefited from his particular criminal conduct' (s. 6(4)(b) and (c)).[16] If the court decides that the offender has benefited from either, it must decide the recoverable amount and make a confiscation order (s. 6(5)). Only if the victim is engaged in civil proceedings against the offender does this duty become a power (s. 6(6)).

The property which may be confiscated is defined as 'all property wherever situated' and includes money, all forms of real or personal property, and 'things in action and other intangible or incorporeal property' (s. 84). Confiscation orders can take precedence over fines, forfeiture, and deprivation orders (s. 13), but otherwise do not influence sentencing, so can be combined with other penalties. There are no limits on the sum to be confiscated provided it does not exceed 'the defendant's benefit from the conduct concerned' (s. 7(1)). Sections 13(5) and (6) of the PCA 2002 also impose a duty on the court to order that monies obtained from the sale of confiscated property should be used to pay part or all of a compensation order if the defendant would not otherwise have sufficient means.

---

[11] This provision also relates to a summary offence if it is joined with an indictable offence and with a high-value benefit.

[12] This Act and the provisions in the Criminal Justice Act 1988 are still in force in relation to offending before 2003.

[13] The *Welch* case has, however, been distinguished in subsequent cases. The House of Lords considered the potential impact of ECHR Article 6 and Article 1 of the First Schedule on the confiscation provisions in s. 72AA of the CJA 1988 in *Rezvi* (2002), finding them to be reasonable and proportionate responses to a public interest.

[14] Schedule 12 to the PCA 2002 repealed Part VI of the CJA 1988.

[15] The Halliday Report (2001) dealt only briefly with compensation orders: see para 6.18. For an interesting article on the tax evasion provisions see Alldridge and Mumford (2005).

[16] 'Criminal lifestyle' is defined at s. 75 and 'criminal conduct' at s. 76.

The context for the PCA 2002 is wider than sentencing alone: the concern is with the use of proceeds of crime and illegal laundering of money for terrorist and other organised international crime. Part VII of the Act (which deals with money laundering) imposes much wider—and potentially draconian—duties on the 'regulated sector', which includes practising solicitors: professional advisers must disclose information to help detect money launderers and so ultimately assist the criminal justice system and further the possibility of making confiscation orders.[17] Failure to disclose information obtained in situations not covered by the narrowly defined 'privileged circumstances' (s. 330(10)) can amount to an offence (s. 331), punishable by a maximum penalty of five years (s. 334(2)). If any person is involved in dealings in relation to 'criminal property' (see ss. 327–329) the maximum penalty is 14 years (s. 334(1)). The thinking is that 'if you find the hoard you can catch the criminal. That, put simply, is the purpose of Part VII of the Proceeds of Crime Act 2002' (Brasse 2003: 492).

The Serious Organised Crime and Police Act 2005 introduced further relevant measures. Section 97 extends the powers in Part 2 of the 2002 Act to magistrates' courts, with a limit of £10,000 on any confiscation order, although an amendment made by the Serious Crime Act 2015 empowers the Secretary of State to increase this amount. Section 98 inserted a new s. 245A in the 2002 Act such that the enforcement authority can apply to the court for freezing orders as well as recovery orders. Further, ss. 95–96 deal with international obligations in respect of forfeiture and freezing of property. In particular, the provisions respond to the Council Framework Decision 2003/577/JHA of 22 July 2003 on the execution in the European Union of orders freezing property or evidence.

Nevertheless, there will be benefits to victims where compensation results from confiscation, and where s. 72 of the PCA 2002 is used. This provision empowers a court to award compensation without a conviction in two circumstances providing there has been 'serious default' by members of specified bodies such as the police force, the Crown Prosecution Service, and the Serious Fraud Office (s. 72(9) as amended). The circumstances are that either a criminal investigation was initiated but did not result in criminal proceedings, or criminal proceedings did not result in a conviction.

Research—based on data held on the central Joint Asset Recovery Database (JARD) and on a sample of 155 confiscation order cases—found that, although the amount of criminal proceeds recovered had increased, there was 'a striking overall reduction between the value of criminal benefit initially assessed by Financial Investigators (FIs) and the amount eventually recovered—a total reduction of around 95 per cent' (Bullock *et al.* 2009: 1; see also Bullock 2010). Indeed, Fisher argues that 'It is an open secret that the restraint and confiscation regime in Pt 2 of the Proceeds of Crime Act 2002 (POCA) has failed to meet its declared objective of separating serious and organised criminals from the benefits of their crimes' and that 'In the four years between 2010 and 2013, the total value of confiscation orders amounted to £1 billion, of which only 50 per cent was collected' (Fisher 2015: 754).

The changes introduced by the Serious Crime Act (SCA) 2015 came into force in June 2015. They include provisions in ss. 1–4 to address the problems which have arisen in relation to third party interests in the defendant's assets: the provisions are designed to allow the criminal court to determine these assets before a confiscation order is made. Section 5

---

[17] An implication of the confiscation order for family lawyers is to be found in *CPS v Grimes* (2003) (see *Family Law* 2003: 635). A spouse of an offender needs to be an equitable owner or have a divorce pending; otherwise the matrimonial home could be included in the proceeds that are confiscated from the offender. See also *X v X* (2005) (re confiscation order against husband—case note in *Family Law* 2005: 543–4).

of the SCA 2015 has also substituted 'a tougher version' of the provisions in s. 11 of the Proceeds of Crime Act (PCA) 2002. Further:

> Section 7 of the SCA 2015 contains a potentially far-reaching innovation to assist in the enforcement of a confiscation order. By a new s.13A [inserted in the PCA 2002], a Crown Court may impose an order 'as it believes is appropriate for the purpose of ensuring that the confiscation order is effective'. This is to be known as a 'compliance order' and it is mandatory for a Crown Court to consider whether to impose this order at the time when the confiscation order is made (s 13A(3)).
>
> (Fisher 2015: 759)

7.2.3 **Compensation to the victim**

In *Breaking the Cycle* the government announced its intention to encourage the use of compensation orders, but such orders have been available to the courts since the 1970s and successive governments have attempted to increase their use. However, an older attempt to find a direct remedy for the victim's loss in the face of offending took two forms in relation to the development of state compensation, and we will deal with that first.

Compensation by the state

Compensation paid to the victim by the state was set up in the 1960s—earlier than the statutory scheme for criminal compensation orders. The Criminal Injuries Compensation Board (CICB), established in 1964 and now called the Criminal Injuries Compensation Authority (CICA),[18] was the first such scheme to be set up in Europe. This scheme is separate from sentencing and does not require an offender to be successfully prosecuted and sentenced, although a sentencing court will take into account any compensation paid by the CICA and vice versa so that a victim cannot be compensated twice. Not until 1988 was the scheme given a statutory basis by ss. 108–117 of the CJA 1988, with the relevant definitions in ss. 109–112 (replaced by the Criminal Injuries Compensation Act 1995).

Nevertheless, the scheme set up in 1964 was highly significant because it meant that the state had accepted responsibility for harm done to citizens through offending. The state very rarely accepts such responsibility and, as Harris noted, 'it is testimony to the political power of the victim lobby that the 1980s should have seen such unquestioning support for this position when the emphasis in other areas of social life was on self-help and personal responsibility' (1992: 60). The European Convention on the Compensation of Victims of Violent Crime was enacted in 1983 to recognise the duty of states to compensate victims if other sources were not available. Such schemes may also be seen as a symbolic act by governments to show concern for victims (see Miers 1990), but they have significant disadvantages for governments because of their high initial cost and the relative inability of governments to control take-up (Maguire and Shapland 1997: 217).

In the UK, as in some other jurisdictions where schemes are relatively long-standing, there has been a policy of restricting access to such compensation. In England and Wales and Scotland, for example, the 1964 scheme was originally a very wide-ranging scheme providing compensation to any victim—of any nationality—of violent crime. Because of the increasing cost of the scheme, the Criminal Injuries Compensation Act 1995 introduced an 'enhanced tariff' approach based on types of injury rather than individualised consideration of harm and damage. There has also been a tendency in such schemes to define the kinds of victims that are seen as deserving by states and so, for example, awards

---

[18] See https://www.gov.uk/government/organisations/criminal-injuries-compensation-authority.

may be reduced or refused if victims are not believed to be truly blameless (Maguire and Shapland 1997: 218).[19]

Compensation orders

Compensation orders imposed on individual offenders at the sentencing stage stem from the Report in 1970 of the Advisory Council on the Penal System: *Reparation by the Offender*, which led to the Criminal Justice Act 1972 (re-enacted as PCCA 1973, ss. 35–38). These provisions gave criminal courts a power and duty to consider making a compensation order at the sentencing stage in relation to a conviction or to offences taken into consideration. The power could only be exercised if the offence had caused personal injury, or loss or damage to a victim, but did not cover compensation to relatives in cases of murder. The Report of the Hodgson Committee (1984), *The Profits of Crime and Their Recovery*, resulted in a statutory power to award compensation to relatives for murder (except car death) (CJA 1988, ss. 104–105), while the Criminal Justice Act 1982 amended s. 35 of the 1973 Act so that a compensation order could be a 'stand-alone' order; in other words, it could count as the punishment. The legislation to make provision for compensation orders in Scotland was somewhat later (Criminal Justice (Scotland) Act 1980 Part IV), coming into force in 1981.

The legislation applicable to England and Wales[20] was re-enacted in the PCCSA 2000, ss. 130–134, as amended by the Criminal Justice Act (CJA) 2003, Fraud Act 2006, Legal Aid, Sentencing and Punishment of Offenders Act (LASPO) 2012, and the SCA 2015.[21] Section 130(1) gives the court discretion to impose a compensation order, but says that it must give reasons if the court does not impose an order when there is an identifiable victim (130(3)). However, LASPO 2012 inserted s. 130(2A)—'A court must consider making a compensation order in any case where this section empowers it to do so'—as the Coalition government felt the duty on the courts needed to be clearer. Whether that change will lead to more compensation actually being paid is debatable: in 2011 it was reported that about 40 per cent of the compensation was paid in the year when it was imposed and the amounts outstanding were between £120 million and £150 million.[22]

Until December 2013 the maximum award in magistrates' courts was £5,000 but this limit now applies only to offenders under 18 years of age (s. 131(1)). There is also no limit in the Crown Court and the order 'shall be of such amount as the court considers appropriate, having regard to any evidence and to any representations that are made by or on behalf of the accused or the prosecutor' (s. 1304)). A compensation order can be instead of any other disposal or punishment: PCCSA 2000, s. 130(1), except in relation to any sentencing provisions—such as those relating to murder, 'dangerous' offenders (see Chapter 5), and minimum sentences for certain offences—now listed in s. 130(2ZA). For offenders coming within those provisions the compensation order must be in addition to other penalties. However, for all other offenders the compensation order can take priority over a fine and be the sole punishment.[23]

---

[19] In Northern Ireland the compensation scheme had to be revised in the light of the particular problems presented by victims of terrorist violence: Criminal Injuries Compensation (Northern Ireland) Order 2002, SI 2002/796.

[20] See PCCSA 2000, s. 167 for the extent of the provisions of the Act.

[21] Sections 137–138 of the PCCSA 2000 deal with compensation orders to be paid by a parent or guardian where the offender is under 18 years of age.

[22] According to Helen Goodman MP, Public Bill Committee, Legal Aid, Sentencing and Punishment of Offenders Bill, Session 2010–12, Hansard col 576 15 September, available at http://www.publications.parliament.uk/pa/cm201011/cmpublic/legalaid/110915/am/110915s01.htm#11091556000107.

[23] This may be rare: see Moxon *et al.* 1992.

Compensation orders, which may be ordered for damages such as pain and suffering as well as for material loss, would seem to be an ideal response to the problem of victims' difficulties in gaining damages through the civil courts in relation to offences. However, compensation orders raise practical and theoretical difficulties. One problem has been the underuse of legislation. Moxon *et al.* (1992: 6) found that, after the 1988 CJA amendments to encourage their use, the award of compensation orders had risen to (only) 17 per cent of Crown Court cases in 1989 (as compared with 11 per cent before the Act) and to 39 per cent (from 31 per cent) of cases surveyed in magistrates' courts (1992: 10; see Newburn 1988 for earlier research). Scottish research based on data collected in the period 1989–92 found even lower use: 4.6 per cent of persons with charges proved (Hamilton and Wisniewski 1996), a figure which had risen to only 5 per cent in 2001.[24] In England and Wales there is some evidence that the introduction of the Criminal Courts Charge in April 2015—which meant convicted criminals in England and Wales had to pay up to £1,200 towards the cost of their case—may have affected the ability of courts to impose compensation orders because of the limited means of the defendant.[25]

Some sentencers may still have difficulties in assessing the amount of a compensation order and also in using an order as part of the 'punishment' repertoire (Maguire and Shapland 1997: 220). The first tier of courts is guided by *Magistrates' Court Guidelines* (now issued by the Sentencing Council and accessible online[26]). The 1997 version of the *Guidelines* incorporated examples of suitable amounts for various injuries, based on the Home Office Circular of 1993 (see Wasik *et al.* 1999), and the 2003 *Guidelines* increased the amount. Current examples of suggested starting points (from Sentencing Guidelines Council 2008h, updated 2014: 156) are: £1,200 for a fractured index finger, £1,500 for loss of a front tooth, and £1,800 for a laparotomy (stomach scar).[27]

The amount offenders can afford to pay is assessed in line with assessment for imposing fines. So, while guidance allows compensation to be paid in instalments and stresses that there can be some hardship to the offender in paying, there is still a limit to what can be paid and that limit may be less than is due to the victim. If an offender is imprisoned he may have no way of providing—for a long time—the means to pay a compensation order, a fact taken into account in *Sullivan* (2003) where the court stated that '[a] compensation order should not be made if it would subject the offender on release from prison to a financial burden he might not be able to meet without committing further crime'.

A related difficulty clearly concerned Scarman LJ when compensation orders became available: 'compensation orders were not introduced into our law to enable the convicted to buy themselves out of the penalties of crime' (*Inwood* (1974)). So, in line with this thinking, the voluntary repayment to the victim in advance of the trial is normally accepted as a mitigating factor, but the court would require evidence that the offender feels genuine remorse. There have also been instances where the offender has misled the court into believing he had the means to pay a compensation order (and so perhaps avoid a stiffer sentence) when he did not. In *Dando* (1996) the court stated that in those circumstances the offender must pay the compensation or serve an extra period in prison in default.

All these difficulties[28] arise from the uneasy mix of aims arising from the awarding of what is comparable to a civil order for damages in a sentencing court, where punishment

[24] See http://www.scotland.gov.uk/Publications/2010/01/28095318/3.

[25] See, for example, press comment at http://www.bbc.co.uk/news/uk-34085798—accessed 27 October 2015.

[26] At http://www.sentencingcouncil.org.uk/the-magistrates-court-sentencing-guidelines/.

[27] We do not know why some of these starting points are lower than the figures we gave in the third edition of this text.

[28] See Ashworth (2010: 322–7) for further discussion.

is expected. The *Magistrates Court Sentencing Guidelines* also point up the difficulty of satisfying everyone: 'Compensation should benefit, not inflict further harm on, the victim. Any financial recompense from the offender may cause distress. A victim may or may not want compensation from the offender and assumptions should not be made either way' (Sentencing Guidelines Council 2008h, updated 2014: 155). The compensation order ought to be a pragmatic compromise which satisfies judge and victim, but so far it has not always proved to be so.

7.2.4 **Victim surcharge**

A more recent development has been the establishment of a Victims' Fund in England and Wales, with money coming 'principally from imposing a surcharge on offenders and from resources released from changes to the Criminal Injuries Compensation Scheme' (Home Office 2004a: 4). The reason given for establishing the Fund was that the existing schemes did not deliver a good enough deal to victims whose offender was not convicted, so the resulting monies would be ring-fenced to fund victim support organisations and schemes. The Domestic Violence, Crime and Victims Act 2004 inserted a new s. 161A in the CJA 2003 requiring a court to impose a surcharge when dealing with an offender for one or more offences. However, as amended, if the court wishes to impose 'one or more of a compensation order, an unlawful profit order and a slavery and trafficking reparation order' and the offender has insufficient means to pay both, the court may reduce the surcharge accordingly, 'if necessary to nil' (s161A(3)).

The CJA (Surcharge) Order 2007,[29] now repealed, fixed the maximum amount of the surcharge at £15. The surcharge, which does not apply to fixed-penalty notices, came into operation on 1 April 2007 and, according to Crispin Blunt, raised £10.5 million in 2010/11, but 'This figure excludes deductions taken under the Prisoners' Earnings Act 1996[30] from which we estimate that revenue in the first 12 months, beginning in September 2011, will be up to £1 million.'[31] The surcharge is now imposed in addition to all types of sentence with a graduated maximum. For a conditional discharge it is £15, for a fine '10% of the fine value with a £20 minimum and a £120 maximum', and for a community sentence £60. For custodial sentences there is also a graduated scale: for immediate imprisonment of six months and below the surcharge maximum is £80, for a sentence of over six months to two years it is £100, and for a sentence over two years it is £120 (only in the Crown Court). For a suspended sentence of up to six months it is £80 and for six months to one year it is £100.[32]

7.3 Punishment impact on the offender

7.3.1 **Personal mitigation as a sentencing factor**

In Chapter 3 we examined the factors that could mitigate the seriousness of the offending in question and also reviewed the various categories of personal factors about the offender

---

[29] SI 2007/707.

[30] This Act, which allows deductions for the benefit of victims, did not come into force until September 2011. Previous governments had decided it would be too costly to administer but it was brought into effect by the Coalition government.

[31] In a written answer: see Hansard HC Deb, 13 October 2011, c512W 13 October 2011. For a fuller explanation of the figures see the Minister's answer to a question in Hansard HC Deb, 24 October 2011, c56W.

[32] See https://www.sentencingcouncil.org.uk/about-sentencing/types-of-sentence/other-orders-made-on-sentencing/what-is-the-victim-surcharge/.

which might be taken into account to mitigate the severity of a proportionate sentence (see Chapter 3, section 3.3.2). Such mitigation has always been highly contentious but there is now evidence that it can have a significant impact on the type and severity of punishment that the offender receives. Research indicating that it plays a crucial role in the sentencing decision has been done by Jacobson and Hough. The researchers summarise their key findings as follows:

- personal mitigation takes many forms, relating to: the offender's past; the offender's circumstances at the time of the offence; the offender's response to the offence and prosecution; and the offender's present and future

- personal mitigation plays an important part in the sentencing decision; it can be the decisive factor in choosing a community penalty in preference to imprisonment

- judges cited at least some factor of personal mitigation as relevant to sentencing in almost half of the 162 cases observed in the study

- in just under a third of the 127 cases where the judge made the role of mitigation explicit, personal mitigation was a major—usually the major—factor which pulled the sentence back from immediate custody

- in a just over a quarter of the 127 cases, mitigation including personal factors resulted in a shorter custodial sentence.

(Jacobson and Hough 2007: vii)

Jacobson and Hough had used sentencing scenarios with 40 sentencers who were asked to rank mitigating factors—whether they had a major, moderate, or minimal impact on the sentence given. The factor given most weight overall was severe clinical depression in the assault scenario. The three lowest scoring factors were in the burglary scenario: 'offender has a partner and young child', 'offender was illiterate', 'offender had been abused as a child' (Jacobson and Hough 2011: 154–5). However, the researchers also found 'marked inconsistencies' in the grading of other factors: the 'motivation to get drug treatment' factor in the burglary scenario was a major factor for 19 respondents and of minimal/no impact for seven (Jacobson and Hough 2011: 155–6).

Other research in England and Wales indicates, in particular, how important mitigation is on the 'in/out' line—in those 'cusp cases' where the seriousness of the offending lies on the community/custodial sentence boundary (Hough *et al.* 2003)—while Scottish research suggests that the criminal history of the offender is very influential in such cases (Tombs 2004), with the result that a relatively minor offence could lead to custody as a 'last resort' (Tombs and Jagger 2006).

The implication is that there needs to be a greater awareness of the importance of personal mitigation if more 'cusp cases' are to be moved down the penalty ladder. Lovegrove suggests that the public also needs more detailed information about mitigating factors in the context of real cases. His research in Victoria, Australia used actual cases and judges and the responses of the participants to sentencing decisions showed a much greater propensity to approve of mitigating factors and the application of mercy than has been found in more generalised surveys of public opinion (Lovegrove 2011).

As we saw in Chapter 3 (section 3.3.2), there is no Sentencing Council guidance on personal mitigation as such but guidelines now provide factors which could affect personal mitigation. For example, the guidance on assault offences has listed 'Factors reducing seriousness or affecting personal mitigation' at Step 2 (starting point and category range) of the seriousness assessment process (after the offence category has been determined: see Chapter 3). For the offence of common assault, for example, this includes the following: remorse; good character and/or exemplary conduct; serious medical conditions requiring urgent, intensive, or long-term treatment; mental disorder or learning disability, where not linked to the commission of the offence; sole or primary carer for dependent relatives (Sentencing Council 2011a: 25). This development is helpful although—in terms of evaluating the justification—it is a pity that the issue of (further) mitigation of seriousness and personal mitigation are placed in the same list.

In Chapter 3 (section 3.3.2) we noted that it is possible but not easy to justify taking personal mitigation into account. As Walker comments, 'Mitigation, like aggravation, is usually, though not always, based on retributive reasoning, which concludes either that the offender's culpability was not as great as the nature of the offence suggested or that . . . he will suffer more than most offenders from the normal penalty' (Walker 1999: 95). However, this leaves the crucial question as to when and how far mitigation should be applied. Should it include issues stemming from socio-economic factors, race, and gender, for example?

So far in our analysis of sentencing and punishment, we have looked only tangentially at the question of the impact of a particular punishment on an individual offender. We have reviewed research on the impact on offenders generally of deterrent and incapacitative sentencing (in Chapters 4 and 5) and we will deal with the general effect of rehabilitative penalties in Chapter 10. In Chapter 6, section 6.4 we said that the offender who has been deemed sufficiently mentally 'well' to plead or to be found guilty but is sufficiently mentally ill to come within the relevant provisions of the Mental Health Act (MHA) 1983 raises questions as to the rationale for taking mental health into account. In section 7.2.2 we also focused on the increasing use of confiscation orders so that the punishment is not negated by the offender benefiting from offending.

Considerations of space have precluded a detailed discussion of all forms of personal mitigation in this text but, in line with the themes running through this chapter, we will focus on mitigation relating to the impact of punishment on the offender. Therefore, in the next two sections we will review arguments for and against the taking account of mitigation relating to the impact of punishment on the offender and the offender's family. The approach of the courts to other personal mitigation is, however, very similar to their response in the impact cases we will discuss. In this chapter we will be focusing in some detail on the approach of the courts to physical disability, employment, old age, illness, vulnerability in prison, and family circumstances. In Chapter 10 we will focus on the issues of impact in relation to financial penalties, but this is still a selective discussion of the many aspects of justice and fairness raised by the question of sentence impact.

7.3.2 'Equalising' impact

The low priority in policy and practice for the issue of sentence impact is reflective of the fact that, while current policy focuses on the offender and what will deter or reform him most effectively, 'just deserts' is still the dominant sentencing principle and, consequently, what Shapland (1981: 55) categorised as 'future personal circumstances' present particular difficulties for retributivist theory. Not only that, this is also an issue where public opinion is a policy factor.[33] The public apparently needs to 'see' equality of treatment for similarly serious offences: an outcome that 'looks' too lenient or too severe in comparison to known cases generates a sense of injustice and undermines the legitimacy of the sentencing system. This approach to equality in sentencing appears to assume that the offender is not a variable in this calculation: the impact of the punishment is the same for all offenders, or any differential impact is irrelevant.

---

[33] For a general discussion of the importance of public opinion see Chapter 1, section 1.2.3.

Yet it is possible to argue that a retributivist approach to sentencing does not depend on an end product of a fixed amount of punishment for a particular amount of seriousness. It can also operate in terms of a proportionate amount of punishment impact where, in effect, the 'quality' of the experience is taken into account, rather than simply the quantity. This form of equal treatment means that punishments for the same offence may look different and so, while the offender and the sentencer may believe that a fairer proportionality has been achieved by a focus on impact, the process may lack legitimacy, particularly to those without knowledge of the individual offender concerned.

If it were accepted that the aim of retributivist sentencing was a just amount of impact for a particular offender, or class of offenders, then the focus of attention would shift to the selection and justification of factors in the life and health of an offender that should be allowed to influence the sentencer in determining impact. These factors could be personal or they could be structural, that is, relating to general social and economic factors. In sentencing policy (but only to a certain extent in the eyes of the public, as we will see in relation to unit fines), the financial means of the offender has been a legitimate factor to take into account—and the courts routinely do so—in the calculation of financial penalties.[34] Apart from fines, the exercise of sentencing discretion has usually focused on the impact of custodial rather than community penalties. Even here, the courts only reluctantly take into account the health and family circumstances of the offender (see section 7.4).

There are also utilitarian arguments for taking impact into account. For the utilitarian, the assessment of what Bentham referred to as 'the several circumstances influencing sensibility' (Bentham 1789: 169) and the calculation of the 'pain' of punishment are aimed at assessing the likely effectiveness of punishment. So Bentham was concerned with the issue of impact in relation to sentence outcome: 'a punishment which is the same in name will not always either really produce, or even so much as appear to others to produce, in two different persons the same degree of pain' (Bentham 1789: 169). Therefore, in determining the quantity of punishment, Bentham argues, we should take account of the 'circumstances influencing sensibility'; Bentham specifies 32 such circumstances, including health and strength, firmness of mind, strength of intellectual powers, moral biases, sympathetic biases, insanity, sex, age, rank, education, and social status (Bentham 1789: 52).

While such an extensive list could not be put into operation, more recent commentators have focused on the issue of 'sentence feasibility', the likelihood that an offender will be able to undertake the proposed sentence effectively. The utilitarian is also frugal: the amount of punishment should be the least possible and the most cost-effective for the purpose. Therefore, if an effective outcome is unlikely, this would justify reducing the use and amount of imprisonment, or not imposing particular community penalties, if it were the case that, for example, the very old or very ill were not capable of responding to rehabilitation programmes or were not in a position to reoffend. So Carlen, noting that many offenders have disadvantaged backgrounds in relation to housing, employment, and income, comments that 'their probation officers might rightly calculate that, given the tensions and frustration already existing in their homes, the clients would be unlikely to complete any [community] order involving home calls, curfews or house arrest' (1989: 22). Further, a lack of substitute carers for their children might preclude parents from being offered a community service programme, as might lack of public transport to some community schemes. Carlen also comments that 'it might be unrealistic to expect emotionally and mentally damaged recidivist clients to complete a punitive . . . order' (1989: 22).

---

[34] With the exception of fixed penalties: see Chapter 10, section 10.2.5.

There is a further issue regarding the distribution and impact of punishment which is beyond the scope of this book, a problem which Lacey has called 'the problem of uniformity of application': 'should each and every dispositionally responsible offender be detected, convicted and punished?' (1998: 404). Like cases are not treated alike if only a small proportion of offenders are detected, arrested, prosecuted, and sentenced. There is no punishment impact on the 97 per cent of offenders who do not proceed to sentence. Pettit and Braithwaite have used this as a justification for the differential treatment of offenders on conviction under their republican theory of criminal justice: 'a concern with the material differences between how we punish convicted offenders is not as well motivated as it might be if we were able to identify and indict most offenders' (1998: 330).

Given the arguments in favour of taking impact into account in order to construct an 'equal' sentence or an effective one, it is possible to isolate instances where punishment could be seen as disproportionate and so the sentencing for such punishment as unjust. In particular, 'full-time' deprivation of liberty can exacerbate or impose suffering stemming from personal circumstances or characteristics. Those who are very young, ill, old, or disabled, and those who have family members who depend on them, may suffer greater physical and psychological harm from a lack of freedom than do other inmates. In addition, those whose offending attracts the most social denunciation, notably those who sexually assault or murder children, also face a high risk of ostracism or harm from their fellow prisoners.

For all these types of offender, their vulnerability is likely to make the punishment disproportionately worse for them. As Tonry has observed:

> In subjective terms . . . two years' imprisonment in a single setting will have very different meanings to different offenders who have committed the same crime. Two years' imprisonment in a maximum security prison may be a rite of passage for a Los Angeles gang member. For an attractive, effeminate twenty-year old, it may mean the terror of repeated sexual victimization. For a forty-year-old head of household, it may mean the loss of a job and a home and a family. For an unhealthy seventy-five-year old, it may mean a death sentence.
>
> (Tonry 1996: 19)

7.3.3 Arguments against impact mitigation

Despite the arguments we have summarised in section 7.3.2, impact mitigation raises problems for both retributivism and utilitarianism. For the former, the harm caused to the victim is not lessened by the social origins or personal problems of the offender, even though we might feel compassion or sympathy for their circumstances. Reductions in such cases would seem to strike at the principles of proportionality, equality of treatment of offenders, and the presumption of human agency at the heart of retributivist theory (see Easton 2008c). If the punishment varied according to the wider social circumstances and personal problems of the offender this would bring arbitrariness back into the punishment process. While retributivists recognise the existence and effects of social inequality, the answer to the problem of inequality is deemed to lie in social welfare rather than variations in sentencing. For Hegel (1832) the answer to problems of poverty and inequality was to use social welfare to mitigate the effects of the market, rather than to retreat from the key principles of retributivist punishment.

For modern retributivists such as von Hirsch (1993), the best way to deal with this issue is through social policy combined with a limit on overall sentencing levels for all through the setting of appropriate anchoring points. Von Hirsch and Ashworth

(2005) consider the use of compassionate mitigation in Sweden and whether it could be extended to social deprivation, but conclude that it would raise both practical and political problems. The injustice of punishing someone who steals in extreme circumstances, such as the fictional Jean Valjean,[35] would be dealt with under the criminal law of necessity, but the levels of deprivation in the modern UK sentencing context are usually far removed from the levels of poverty and deprivation of the nineteenth-century France described by Victor Hugo. For those whose lives are adversely affected by their social circumstances, the solution for retributivists lies in social rather than penal policy.

For utilitarians, there would be concerns over reducing the deterrent value of penalties if sentences were reduced on the ground of deprivation. Bentham (1789) was opposed to introducing feelings into punishment, so concessions on grounds of sympathy and compassion for the accused would be difficult to justify on his theory. For Bentham, the principle of utility took precedence over principles of sympathy and antipathy which he sees as adverse to utility. Introducing feelings into punishment may lead to disproportionate punishment, both excessive and lenient.

7.4 Impact as mitigation in practice

7.4.1 The approach of the courts

In practice the defence may argue that the particular impact of the sentence on the offender or offender's family or business should be treated as a mitigating factor and sentencers, from magistrates up to the Court of Appeal, have accepted such arguments from time to time.[36] Some guidelines have also included an offender impact factor in the assessment of seriousness: for example, in the Causing Death by Driving Guideline, 'Injury to the offender may be a mitigating factor when the offender has suffered very serious injuries' and 'Where one or more of the victims was in a close personal or family relationship with the offender, this may be a mitigating factor' (Sentencing Guidelines Council 2008c: 5). Likewise, the new Theft Guideline includes 'Serious medical condition requiring urgent, intensive or long-term treatment' and 'Sole or primary carer for dependent relatives' in the list of 'Factors reducing seriousness or reflecting personal mitigation' at Step Two of the 'General Theft' section (Sentencing Council 2015a: 7).

However, as noted in Chapter 3, there is no duty on the sentencer to take impact into account, or for mitigation to have any precedence over factors relating to seriousness, and the Causing Death by Driving Guideline specifically notes that 'the degree to which the relationship influences the sentence should be linked to offender culpability in relation to the commission of the offence; mitigation for this reason is likely to have less effect where the culpability of the driver is particularly high' (Sentencing Guidelines Council 2008c: 5). Further, if impact operates as a mitigating factor it can only lead to a reduction in sentence; it cannot operate to increase a sentence to allow for greater equality of impact across the board.

Arguably, the Court of Appeal has tried 'to bring some order to an area of law which may appear as chaotic as some of the lives under review' (Piper 2007: 142). However, reported

---

[35] A character in *Les Misérables*, a novel by Victor Hugo. See also Renaud 2007.

[36] See, for example, Shapland (1981) for research on the process of, and speeches in, mitigation; Walker (1999: 100–3) on the 'exceptional circumstances' justifications for suspending a prison sentence; Jacobson and Hough for research in relation to the influence of physical illness and employment issues on sentencing in the Crown Court (2007: 36–7).

appellate cases suggest that the first concern of judges—in line with the effect of the 2008 guideline quoted—is not to downgrade a message about seriousness. So, if the court is dealing with what it considers to be serious offending, the court is anxious not to reduce the potential deterrent effects or the amount of censure by reducing a sentence. Therefore, if the circumstances of the offending are relatively less serious the courts are more likely to take into account mitigation based on impact.

If, when impact factors are taken into account, the courts explicitly justify their approach, then the reduction in sentence is generally explained as an exceptional act of mercy. For example, the following statement made by Lord Lane CJ in *Attorney General's Reference (No. 4 of 1989)* (1989) was endorsed more recently by Sir Igor Judge when declining to increase the sentence on an 81-year-old sex offender: 'Leniency is not in itself a vice. That mercy should season justice is a proposition as soundly based in law as it is in literature' (*Attorney General's Reference No. 73 of 2006* (2006)). If so, however, the courts are, arguably, mean with mercy and this approach has also led to two unhelpful outcomes: there is no clear or clearly articulated justification for taking impact mitigation into account and, in the current sentencing climate with higher levels of seriousness accorded to particular offences and factors, it is now less likely that mitigation based on impact will influence sentencing.

7.4.2 The offender: vulnerability and age

The Court of Appeal has been faced with the issue of added impact of punishment stemming from the personal vulnerability of a prisoner, whether stemming from old age, youth, or the expected 'dangers' of prison life. When being of an advanced age is allowed as mitigation, the justification is on grounds of physical infirmity and also of shorter life expectancy.

In a recent case concerning repeated child cruelty in the 1960s and 1970s, the applicant offender was 75 years old, had been in hospital since being sentenced to prison, and had recently been diagnosed with inoperable lung cancer. Picken J gave the judgment:

> These were nasty and prolonged offences which had to be marked by such sentences...Even in the light of what is now known about the applicant's life expectancy, we have concluded that immediate imprisonment in the applicant's case is appropriate. We do not regard this as an exceptional case in which it is appropriate to show mercy in such a way as to result in the imposition of a suspended prison sentence.

(*R v Taylor (William)* (2015) para 10)

However, because there had been an error in applying the maximum in place at the time of the offending, the court said that the appropriate sentences would have been 18 months to run concurrently (with a guilty plea discount) but 'We have further reduced the sentence to 12 months in the light of what is now known about the applicant's medical condition' (para 11). Clearly, for elderly prisoners the mitigation for age and ill health (see section 7.4.3) overlaps.

The overriding importance of offence gravity is also evident in a decision on the minimum term to be served by an elderly prisoner on an indeterminate sentence. *Bata* (2006) was an unsuccessful application for a reduction in his ten-year minimum term (previously notified by the Secretary of State) by an 80-year-old prisoner who had been sentenced to life for murder imposed for shooting at close range a person on his neighbouring allotment. The judge believed that the ten-year minimum already incorporated a considerable reduction for old age and illness, given the seriousness of the circumstances of the offending.

Nor is vulnerability in prison always taken into account. In *Varden* (1981) the offender—a man of 71, who had unlawful sex with a 13-year-old child with severe learning difficulties—would inevitably be spending his sentence under Rule 45 (of Prison Rules 1999, formerly R.43) in a vulnerable prisoner unit where a prisoner is segregated for his own protection. His age and likely segregation were taken into account as mitigating factors and he was given a reduced sentence, but other cases at that time held that the impact of Rule 45 was not relevant and *Parker* (1996) took that approach. The Court of Appeal said that it was not relevant to sentencing that an offender found it exceptionally hard to adjust to prison life, an approach also taken in *Nall-Cain*, where a sentence of five years imposed on Lord Brocket was upheld because 'a defendant's treatment by other inmates is not generally a factor to which this court can have proper regard' (1998 at 150, *per* Rose LJ).

The effect of the increasing number of long determinate and indeterminate sentences, together with this cautious approach to reducing the sentence of a serious offender on account of old age, has had an effect on the composition of the prison population which ought, perhaps, to be further taken into account by sentencers. Prisoners in the 'over 60 years old' category had the largest percentage increase (149 per cent) in the decade 1996–2006 ((Ministry of Justice 2007a: 96) and the numbers also rose by 164 per cent between 2002 and 2015 (Prison Reform Trust 2015a: 6). Lord Phillips, then Lord Chief Justice, warned that in 30 years' time the prisons would be full of geriatric lifers (Phillips 2007). There are now more prisoners serving life or other indeterminate sentences than in the early 1990s and older prisoners are more likely than younger prisoners to be serving longer sentences because of the type of offences committed. They may experience particular problems if they are held far from home as this will make it hard for them to maintain family ties if their visitors are also older.

Of course there are also issues around age and vulnerability in relation to younger offenders. In Chapter 6 we examined the justifications for treating children who offend differently and in Chapter 11 we examine the use of custodial penalties for children and young people, where it is acknowledged that youth is a factor to be taken into account. We have already noted that old age may be accepted as mitigation: the offender has not much time left and there is a common notion that time 'goes more quickly' the older a person is. When youth is taken into consideration it rests on the notions of reduced culpability and also loss of precious 'developmental time'. There is also research based on offenders 'doing time' which has shown that for young prisoners time passes slowly (Cope 2003).[37]

Cases would suggest that the courts consider 'youth', as with other impact mitigation, of less significance if the offending is very serious. In *Attorney General's Reference (Nos. 21 and 22 of 2004)* (2004), for example, where the offenders were aged 17 and 19, the court stated that, for such types of offending (robbery late at night on public transport as part of group), a custodial sentence must be imposed 'save in the most exceptional cases, such exceptions arising, for example, by reasons of extreme youth'. No distinction was made between the two offenders on grounds of age and no reduction was given for age. Similarly, the fact that an 18-year-old had a mental age of ten-and-a-half had little influence on the decision in a case involving a series of offences with very serious aggravating factors: '[the] youth and low intelligence of the second offender, provide no explanation and only modest mitigation' (*Attorney General's Reference (Nos. 39, 40 and 41 of 2005)* [2005] at 26, *per* Holland J). The riots in several towns in England in the summer of 2011 also led to publicity for many cases of 'tough' sentencing which appeared to take little account of (young) age (see, for example, Piper 2011).

---

[37] See also the texts by Clemmer (1940) and Toch (1976) on 'survival' techniques used by prisoners generally.

For reasons of space, we have neglected the age category of 18–20-year-old offenders in this book. They were ignored by the reforms of the Crime and Disorder Act 1998 which apply to those under 18, and '[i]mproved regimes for the under 18s have thrown into sharp relief the poor treatment of 18–20-year-olds', as revealed in reports of the Chief Inspector of Prisons (Lyon 2003: 28) and a briefing by the Prison Reform Trust (2007). An unannounced inspection in 2011 of a prison which includes a young offender institution found higher rates of victimisation and self-harm among the 18–20-year-olds (HM Chief Inspector of Prisons 2011b: 27–8), suggesting there is much room for improvement. This is an important issue and one which deserves a much higher profile than is possible within the constraints of this book. We hope that the inquiry of the House of Commons Justice Committee, which took evidence in the summer of 2015,[38] will lead to influential and positive proposals to ameliorate the impact of prison on young adult offenders.

7.4.3 Illness and disability as mitigation

There are also issues for sentencers raised by the resource difficulties faced in relation to the growing numbers of the ill and disabled in prison, partly caused by the increase in the size of the prison population and also the increase in older prisoners. A report in 2009 found that 15 per cent of prisoners reported having a disability (HM Inspectorate of Prisons 2009a); more recently the Prison Reform Trust reports that 36 per cent of prisoners are estimated to have a physical or mental disability, which compares with 19 per cent of the general population (2015a: 6).

Prisons have a duty not to discriminate against prisoners on the grounds of disability under the Equality Act 2010 (and formerly under the Disability Discrimination Act 2005), so the issue of accessibility to resources and treatment is important. Research has been undertaken on this particular group (see Crawley and Sparks 2005, 2008) and the Commission for Equality and Human Rights, which has taken over the role of the Disability Rights Commission, must enforce duties under the Equality Act 2010. A report by the Chief Inspector of Prisons found that women with disabilities were particularly critical of a range of services, including health care (HM Chief Inspector of Prisons 2008a: 28). More recently a joint inspection in relation to offenders with a learning disability found that within probation, and particularly in prisons, identification of offenders with learning disabilities remained a problem and as a result, the needs of people with learning disabilities were often missed (HM Inspectorate of Prisons/HM Inspectorate of Probation 2015).

Appellate cases reveal mixed approaches to the impact of illness and learning difficulties. The guideline judgment given in *Bernard* (1997) makes clear that a medical condition that might in the future affect life expectancy does not preclude a prison sentence (see Ashworth and Player 1998: 256–61; see also *R v Taylor (William)* [2015], which confirmed the principles in *Bernard*). Cases before and after *Bernard* suggest, however, that a high risk of (earlier) death because of prison conditions and facilities may be accepted by the court as excessive impact of punishment which merits a reduction in sentence. In *Green and Leatherbarrow* (1992), for example, Green had sickle cell anaemia and Leatherbarrow had chronic emphysema. Green's sentence had been fixed at 18 months (and would have been five years if the illness had not been taken into account). The Court of Appeal suspended 14 months of the 18-month sentence so he could be released immediately because of the risk of sudden death if there were no immediate access to suitable medical facilities.[39]

---

[38] See http://www.parliament.uk/business/committees/committees-a-z/commons-select/justice-committee/inquiries/parliament-2015/young-adult-offenders/.

[39] See Dyson and Boswell (2006) for information about the medical context for *Green*.

Leatherbarrow's 15-month sentence had not taken the illness into account; on appeal, eight months of the sentence were suspended to allow immediate release.

However, the court's approach in *Avis, Thomas, Torrington, Marques and Goldsmith* (1997) shows what is perhaps a more common stance. This case was a guideline judgment for firearms offences where, in relation to some of the appellants, old age and illness were submitted as mitigating factors, but the court argued that the aggravating factors outweighed the mitigation. It is, therefore, relatively rare for the Court of Appeal to find it appropriate to downgrade a message about seriousness by taking into account factors impacting on the prison experience. Courts might, however, refer cases to the Home Secretary for the exercise of the royal prerogative.[40]

A case involving a disabled prisoner makes clear that the courts will only apply 'mercy' when, as in equity, the claimant has clean hands. Where the court believes that the offender has 'traded' on his disability then it is unlikely any reduction in sentence will be given. Indeed, the facts might aggravate seriousness, as in *Kesler* (2005), where Ouseley J, having noted that '[h]e used to give the impression of innocent behaviour by going out with his dog to collect the drugs, and because of his disability had a stick, but it was hollowed out so that he could keep his drugs in it' (at 8), concluded as follows: '[i]t is plain that he has been using his health as a means of obtaining sympathy and of deception and he has already gained from his previous sentences such benefit as could possibly be accorded to him for those matters' (at 14).

A recent case relating to an offender with learning difficulties and a very low IQ who had been involved in a bomb hoax—*R v Perera (Rohan)* [2015]—did take these factors into account. A suspended sentence with a period of supervision was substituted for the immediate six-month custodial sentence, 25 days of which had been spent in prison. The reasoning was that the new sentence still reflected seriousness, that the offender had realised from this experience that the offending was serious, and that the supervision would be better able to ensure reintegration back into the community.

7.4.4 **Loss of employment**

Similar mixed approaches have been taken in relation to expected loss of employment resulting from conviction or imprisonment. In *Hubbard* (2002), a case concerning abuse of trust in relation to a sexual offence, the Court of Appeal upheld a two-year sentence, apparently not taking into account the devastating personal consequences for the teacher. Generally, where the offence is serious the loss of employment is not given any weight.

Where the offence is less serious and where job loss is accompanied by other mitigation (*Dockerill* (1988); *O'Hara* (2004)), it may be taken into account and research also provides 'some evidence that a defendant's steady job, or involvement in studies or vocational training, can be a mitigating factor' (Jacobson and Hough 2007: 37). In one of the cases they reviewed the 23-year-old offender was in the process of completing entry to the Marines and 'the judge stressed that the offence deserved custody but passed a community sentence—stating that a custodial sentence would prevent him "taking a course in your life that could do all of us some good"' (Jacobson and Hough 2007: 37; see also Jacobson and Hough 2011: 153 Table 8.4).

Loss of employment is also more likely to be taken into account if it impacts on third parties, whether they are family members or employees of the offender's business. For example,

---

[40] See, for example, *Moore* (1990) and *Stark* (1992), both HIV/AIDS cases.

in *Anthony James Stevenson* (2015), the appeal was upheld largely because of the fact that insufficient weight was given to the mitigation:

> The defendant was in full time employment working as a Team Leader at a local factory producing automotive components, he was the sole bread winner for the family. He had found employment within two months of his release from a custodial sentence in June 2009 and had been in full time work since that date, he married in 2011.
>
> (*R v Anthony James Stevenson* 2015: para 9)

In addition his wife was ill and had had recent operations, and so relied on Stevenson to support her and look after the children.

There is, however, an ambivalence which is reflected in public opinion. As Tonry has pointed out:

> The relevance of employment to sentencing varies with circumstances. Most people believe it is irrelevant that a wealthy securities law violator will, if imprisoned, lose his or her job . . . People have widely divergent views on whether a lower-middle-class head of household's job loss, if imprisoned, is relevant . . . From the perspective that employed defendants are often middle-class, and more likely than unemployed defendants to be white, concern about racial and class disparities may make job loss appear irrelevant.
>
> (1996: 22–3)

There is also the argument that 'although it seems reasonable to view the loss of a job as a quasi-fine, taking prospective job loss into account unintentionally discriminates against the unemployed who are unfortunate enough to have no job to lose!' (Levi 1989: 432).

Even if loss of employment is not a mitigation issue, employment status may well affect the choice of sentence. Research some time ago by Crow and Simon (1987), based on six magistrates' courts, examined unemployment rates and sentencing statistics in 1974–84, controlling for courts with above- and below-average custody rates and with un/employment categories; they found that for the unemployed the movement could be up or down the scale of penalties. Further, Crow and Simon concluded that the effect of employment status on sentence was statistically small. However, the small differences stemming from employment status could have a 'ratchet' effect in relation to sentencing on a subsequent conviction, and research in the early 1990s concluded that 'the sentencing of unemployed offenders differs considerably from the sentencing of those in employment' (Home Office 1994a: para 17).

Unemployment is another dimension of the financial circumstances of the offender which are considered in relation to the issue of compensation orders (see section 7.2.3). But the clearest impact of wealth and poverty is in relation to fines, which we will deal with in Chapter 10 (section 10.2). It is also worth noting that recent research concludes that 'Too many people end up in the prison system on remand or recall to prison because of inappropriate accommodation' (Cooper 2013: 8).

7.4.5 Impact on the offender and offender's family

The case of *Mills* (2002), also discussed in Chapter 3, does seem to allow as mitigation the particular impact, if the offender is a mother, of being allocated to a prison far from her home and children.[41] This can be theorised as causing a disproportionate impact of

---

[41] For a review of judicial thinking in the 1960s on the social consequences of conviction and the use of mitigation, see Martin and Webster (1971).

punishment because the sorrow at loss of contact with your child is greater for the main caregiver, usually the mother, and because a female prisoner is likely to be further away from home than a male prisoner and so the visits will be less frequent. The extra suffering, particularly for mothers, is now well documented (see, for example, Codd 2004, 2008; Epstein 2012). There is also a growing concern about the separation of fathers from their children, perhaps as a spin-off from the high profile given to fathers' groups campaigning for more contact with their children on separation and divorce (see Watson and Rice 2004). Epstein's research on the sentencing of mothers also found a failure in many cases to take account of the Article 8 rights of children when sentencing mothers (Epstein 2012).

The issue of prisoners' children has come to both public and academic attention in recent years (see Brooks-Gordon and Bainham 2004; Codd 2004; Salmon 2004: 18–20; Codd 2008; Scott and Codd 2010; Christian and Kennedy 2011; Barnardo's 2014; for a review of wider legal issues, see also Munro 2002). There are about 200,000 children who have a parent in custody each year in England and Wales (Barnardo's 2014: 7) but the effect on children is most acute when it is their mother, rather than their father, who is imprisoned, because, while the children of fathers in prison will usually be looked after by the other parent, this is much less likely for the children of mothers in prison. According to the Corston Report (2007), most children whose mothers were in prison were not cared for by their fathers; 12 per cent are taken into local authority care (Barnardo's 2014: 7).

Generally, however, the appellate court has taken a quite stringent approach to the question as to whether the impact on the parent, children, or other relatives is taken into account. This is exemplified by a series of cases involving women who took Class A drugs into prison for the person they were visiting (see Piper 2007: 147–8). Jeanne Batte, Sarah Witten, and Carmen Mackenzie[42] all had their sentences reduced but their family circumstances were horrendous. Batte, who was 60 and severely depressed, cared for a disabled brother of 69, had suffered the death of one child, and cared for two others who were severely ill. Witten had three children aged six, five, and three. Mackenzie had two dependants—one child and a husband with a life-threatening illness. However, relatively minor reductions were given so that the detriment to the children was only marginally reduced; the courts made clear these were exceptional cases, and in other cases, for example that of Angela Babington,[43] no reduction was given.

The judicial comment in a recent appeal case included the argument that the mitigation had been given insufficient weight. However, the comment of the judge at first instance was noted and reveals the approach of the courts in these cases: 'When sentencing, the learned judge observed it was never easy to impose a sentence which meant taking a mother away from her children but that alone could not justify a departure from such a sentence if custody was appropriate' (*R v Nadine Pirincci*: para 7). The appeal was not upheld. The courts believe that giving more weight to family impact would be problematic as it would infringe the principle of proportionality and also of equal punishment if offenders with and without families were treated differently. It might also mean that sentencers would need to judge the parenting skills of an offender to decide whether dependent children would be harmed or benefited by his or her absence, thereby introducing extrinsic factors into the sentencing process. An alternative approach might therefore be to focus on reducing the impact on third parties by giving more support to maintaining family contact during the period of imprisonment.

The never-implemented intermittent custody order (see Chapter 10, section 10.4.2), despite potential drawbacks for women, might have provided a means of imposing custody

---

[42] *Batte* (1999), *Witten* (2002), and *McKenzie* (2004).
[43] *Babington* (2005). The court distinguished *Witten* because Babington's children were older and had all been in care, and only one of her children was living with her at the time of sentence.

which does not totally disrupt care-giving relationships. When such an order was suggested in a Green Paper issued as long ago as 1984,[44] the explicit aim was to reduce the disruption of family ties and loss of employment which may result from continuous custody, and the intention in 2003 was also to 'maintain jobs, family ties or education, all of which have been shown to play a part in reducing reoffending'.[45]

We would also note that the range of protected characteristics under anti-discrimination law has broadened under the Equality Act 2010. As a consequence prisons have a duty not to discriminate against prisoners on the basis of age, disability, and other grounds, as well as a duty to promote equality and to test policies for equality impact. These issues will be discussed further in Chapter 9.

7.5 Reflecting on the issues

7.5.1 Conflating the categories

In this chapter we have reviewed the sentencing law and practice relevant to the impact of the offending and punishment on the victim and on the offender, but what is often overlooked in policy discussion is that in practice the categories of victim and offender are often not so separate. Many people are both victims and offenders.[46] Indeed, official statistics make clear that high crime areas are also areas with high rates of victimisation. Further, the criminal justice system, and particularly its custodial establishments, has its own potential to victimise the offender (see Chapters 8, 9 and 11). While we have had to focus on the victim and the offender separately, it would be helpful if both policy and practice were more aware of this overlapping of roles.

7.5.2 Discussion questions

Below is a scenario which reflects problematic issues raised by this chapter. Read the scenario and then think about the following questions:

1. How might it be possible—if at all—for the Court of Appeal to justify a decision to substitute a community order for Amy's custodial sentence?

2. What solutions to this type of situation—other than at the sentencing stage—can you suggest?

3. If Amy's offences had involved supplying drugs to local teenagers would your attitudes and responses be different? Why/why not?

4. Consider the situation of the victims. If Amy's offences had, instead, been a series of thefts from elderly neighbours do you think they would have access to adequate support and 'remedies'?

Amy is a mother with four children under ten years of age. The children's father, Ben, has been in prison for two years. Amy has several convictions for theft, all preceding the period in which she went to live with Ben and had her children. Amy got into severe financial difficulties two years ago and agreed to deliver packages of drugs, on a regular basis, to distributors. By the time she was caught she had delivered a very large quantity of a Class B

---

[44] *Intermittent Custody*, Cmnd 9281, London, HMSO.

[45] Explanatory Notes to the Criminal Justice Act 2003.

[46] For a review of research and theory about the interrelationship, and also research about the 'victimisation' of offenders on probation, see Farrall and Maltby (2003).

drug. She pleaded guilty shortly after her arrest to a charge of possession with intent to supply under the Misuse of Drugs Act 1971, s. 5(3), although she insisted that she had been led to believe the drugs were only ketamine (Class C). She received a sentence of 18 months.

Ben's family have always rejected her; her own family consists of an ill and elderly mother and a sister who has two children. No one offers to look after her children and she agrees that they be voluntarily accommodated by the local authority. A recent review by the local authority noted the children's distress in their new homes (they cannot all be accommodated in the same foster family). Amy appeals her sentence.

You might wish to consult the following publications:

Jacobson, Kirby, and Hough (2011) *Public Attitudes to the Sentencing of Drug Offences*. London, Office of the Sentencing Council.

Sentencing Council (2012a) *Drug Offences: Definitive Guideline*. London, Office of the Sentencing Council.

Sentencing Council (2015a) *Theft Offences, Definitive Guideline*. London, Sentencing Council.

7.5.3 Case study: impact on the offender

Below is a sentencing exercise which draws on the material in Chapter 5 (particularly section 5.4) and Chapter 6 (section 6.4) as well as on the themes discussed in this chapter. It brings together difficult questions relating to proportionality, dangerousness, mentally disordered offenders, and personal mitigation. Further help is available in approaching this exercise in the Online Resource Centre.

online
resource
centre

Facts of the case:

Zack is 38 years old and has suffered from mild schizophrenia for almost 20 years. Three years ago he spent a month in hospital for psychiatric treatment to establish a new medication regime. His condition has since been stable and he works as a labourer. He has always lived with his mother, who is now elderly and infirm and depends on him for her shopping, laundry, and meals.

When doing building work over a period of time in a family home Zack made friends with Yasmin, the seven-year-old daughter of the family, and persuaded her to let him take several photos of her, in particular poses, when she was undressing. He told her to keep the 'photo shoot' as their little secret but Yasmin was excited, thinking she could become a model when she grew up, so she told her parents about the photos. They contacted the police and the photos were found on the computer in Zack's house. The computer provided evidence that he had copied the photos to three friends.

Zack pleaded guilty at the magistrates' court to a charge of taking and distributing indecent photographs of a child (section 1 of the Protection of Children Act 1978). The maximum penalty for this offence on indictment is ten years and it is a specified offence listed in Schedule 15 para 99 of the CJA 2003 (and also listed in Schedule 15B which was inserted by LASPO 2012 and available for convictions on or after 3rd December 2012). The photos were referred to COPINE (Combating Paedophile Information Networks in Europe), which graded the images as being of the lowest category of obscenity. Zack has two previous convictions (for being drunk and disorderly and for theft in breach of trust) for which he received a fine and a short custodial sentence respectively.

You are Zack's solicitor. Explain to him what options are open to the magistrates' court at the sentencing hearing (including referral to the Crown Court for sentencing) and what the judge is most likely to decide.

Would your answer be any different if he was at the time of conviction still attending regular outpatient appointments at the local hospital's mental health unit?

You might wish to consult the following:

Sentencing Council (2014c) *Sexual Offences, Definitive Guideline,* London, Sentencing Council.

Sentencing Guidelines Council (2008h, updated 2014) *Magistrates Courts Sentencing Guidelines, Definitive Guideline:* online version available at http://www.sentencingcouncil.org.uk/offences/item/possession-of-indecent-photograph-of-child-indecent-photographs-of-children/.

PART B

Punishing Offenders

In Part B the focus is on the punishment of offenders. The experience of prisoners is considered and a range of dimensions of imprisonment are discussed in Chapter 8. The problems of reconciling respect for prisoners' rights with the administrative needs of the prison are discussed, as well as the extent to which the modern prison meets the aims of imprisonment. The experience of imprisonment is considered further in Chapter 9 by focusing on the experience of imprisonment for specific groups of prisoners, namely women, ethnic minorities, religious minorities, sexual minorities, prisoners with disabilities, and older prisoners. The policies designed to reduce the risk of unfair or discriminatory treatment are also reviewed.

In Chapter 10 the focus shifts to punishment and rehabilitation within the community. A range of non-custodial punishments are considered, including fines, community orders, and supervision. Recent policy trends are discussed, including the privatisation of the delivery of community penalties and the 'rehabilitation revolution'. Discussion of 'what works' in reducing reoffending is also included. The final chapter considers the range of civil and criminal orders available to the courts in dealing with children and young people who engage in anti-social or criminal activity and the role of rights in protecting them. Attention is also given in Chapter 11 to the conditions for young offenders in detention, with a focus on restraint and equality issues.

8

Justice in the modern prison

SUMMARY

In this chapter we will focus on the treatment of adult prisoners, examining a number of aspects of prison life as well as considering the aims of imprisonment. Key developments since 1990 will be considered, including the Woolf Report (Woolf and Tumim 1991), managerialism and privatisation, and the impact of the Human Rights Act (HRA) 1998, to assess whether the just treatment of prisoners has been achieved. While substantial improvements in prison regimes have been made since the early 1990s, there has also been considerable pressure on them from the expanding prison population. The problem of reconciling respect for the rights of prisoners with the administrative needs of the prison system and the deterrent function of prison will be highlighted. The potential to reduce the prison population substantially in the current political climate will also be considered. The impact of imprisonment on specific groups of prisoners will be reviewed in Chapter 9. The treatment of young offenders given a custodial order will be considered in Chapter 11.

8.1 Introduction

8.1.1 Justice behind prison doors

Throughout the book we have been exploring the notion of a just punishment with reference to a range of theoretical traditions, as well as its implications for sentencing law and policy, and for particular groups of offenders such as young people. However, justice extends beyond the prison door and we have seen the subjection of prison regimes to increasing judicial scrutiny by the domestic courts and the European Court of Human Rights. The quest for justice in imprisonment was a key theme of the Woolf Inquiry in 1991, many of whose recommendations have shaped the modern prison system. As the Woolf Report emphasised: 'The system of justice which has put a person in prison cannot end at the prison doors. It must accompany the prisoner into the prison, his cell and to all aspects of his life in prison' (Woolf and Tumim 1991: para 14.19). Lord Woolf stressed that this was not simply a matter of the formal judicial processes governing prison life or providing physical conditions which are non-degrading, but rather that 'prisoners as well as staff, must feel the system is itself fair and just' (ibid: para 14.20).

Fairness and justice are crucial because prisoners are especially vulnerable to arbitrary treatment because of their isolation and the fact that they are in prison 24 hours a day, dependent on the prison organisation for every need, and also shielded from the wider society. Given that they are 'invisible' and marginalised, protection for prisoners, whether through a system of formal rights or principles of fairness, is essential. Their rights should be infringed no more than is necessary to safeguard the security of staff, other prisoners, and the public outside the prison. Respecting rights emphasises the common heritage of prisoners and ordinary citizens and contributes to the process of **normalisation**, bringing conditions inside prison closer to those outside, contributing to a sense of justice and recognising that prisoners remain citizens during their period of incarceration. This has been stressed by prison reformers and by those responsible for the oversight of prisons, including the Chief Inspector of Prisons, as well as in the European Prison Rules which stipulate that 'Life in prison shall approximate as closely as possible the positive aspects of life in the community' (European Prison Rules 5).

The treatment of prisoners is linked to the justifications of punishment. From the standpoint of retributivist theory the offender as an autonomous individual should be treated with respect and the punishment consists purely in the deprivation of liberty. The offender should not be subjected to degrading or inhuman treatment during the period of incarceration. So this approach may give more weight to prisoners' rights and the treatment of prisoners as citizens. On utilitarian theory, the pains of imprisonment should not be imposed without positive outcomes, so the effects of imprisonment in reducing reoffending must be assessed. The positive effects could include its deterrent and incapacitative functions but also its potential rehabilitative function. Modern rehabilitationists argue that prisoners have a right to rehabilitation, the right to services and activities which enable them to address the problems which led to their offending (see Chapter 10). The state has a duty to provide them with an environment which facilitates their rehabilitation. This may also mean provision of sufficient opportunities to attend relevant courses. This is especially important if release decisions are based on risk assessments which require information based on completion of relevant offending behaviour courses.

8.1.2 **The aims of imprisonment**

The aims of imprisonment have been much debated by penologists, prison reformers, and governments. The formal and 'official' aims of the prison system in the UK have been set out in statements of purpose issued by the Prison Service and the National Offender Management Service (NOMS), are embodied in the Prison Rules, and reflect the justifications of punishment discussed in Chapters 2, 3, 4, and 5. However, there is no consensus amongst commentators on which of these aims should be given priority or the extent to which they have been realised in practice. The Woolf Report argued that prisoners should be treated with humanity and justice, by striking a balance between security, control, and justice, and that the need for justice should not be swamped by concerns with control and security (Woolf and Tumim 1991: para 1.148). Many critics argue that prisons are now merely warehouses as they struggle to cope with rising numbers of inmates. The focus on security has been strengthened, particularly over the use of drugs and mobile phones in prison. Concerns over the punitiveness of the public, as we saw in Chapter 1, have also created a climate in which penal expansion and penal austerity can flourish. However, as we shall see, this has been counterbalanced, and to some extent restrained, by the increasing emphasis on rights.

The Prison Service has described its objectives as holding prisoners securely, reducing the risk of reoffending, and providing safe and well-ordered establishments in which prisoners are treated humanely, decently, and lawfully. Its duty is to look after prisoners with humanity and to help prisoners lead law-abiding and useful lives in custody and on release. The 'decency' agenda introduced in 1999, 'caring for and treating with respect everybody in the Service's care', which has implications for suicide, accommodation, assaults, equal treatment, and participation in constructive activities, has focused attention on the prisoner's right to be treated fairly and respectfully.

In 2004 the Prison Service became part of the National Offender Management Service (NOMS), following the recommendations of the Carter Review of Correctional Services, *Managing Offenders, Reducing Crime* (Carter 2003), and in 2007 NOMS became part of the new Ministry of Justice. NOMS as an organisation is much larger than the Prison Service, and is responsible for offender management in both prison and the community. It aims to manage prison capacity while ensuring that the required standards on decency and safety are met and control in prisons is maintained.

NOMS in its Statement of Purpose says that its role is 'to commission and provide offender management services in the community and in custody ensuring best value for money from public resources. We work to protect the public and reduce reoffending by delivering the punishment and orders of the courts, and supporting rehabilitation by helping offenders to reform their lives' (NOMS 2015a: 7). It aims to treat offenders with decency and respect, taking full account of public protection when assessing risk, using resources in the most effective way, delivering value for money for the taxpayer, and incorporating equality and diversity in all its activities and providing a safe environment for prisoners. The problem of course is maintaining standards of decency in the face of expanding prison capacity and shrinking budgets.

Prison Rule (PR) 3 (formerly PR 1) states that the purpose of the training and treatment of convicted prisoners shall be to encourage and assist them to lead a good and useful life. The reference to treatment here suggests that the reports of the death of the rehabilitative ideal are somewhat exaggerated. Preventing reoffending remains a key rationale governing education and training provision in modern prison regimes. The problem has been putting PR 3 into practice in the context of rising numbers and increasing financial costs of imprisonment and in the face of public punitiveness, as we saw in Chapter 1. Moreover, the focus on treatment in the past has been used to justify indeterminate and extended sentences (see Chapter 5). Prison reformers have argued that prisoners should not be subject to treatment coercively, that they should be subject to the minimum levels of security necessary to protect the public, and that as far as possible the standards which apply to ordinary citizens in the wider society should also be applied to offenders. It is now well established that prisoners retain their rights guaranteed by the European Convention on Human Rights (ECHR) while in prison, and although these rights may be limited by the needs of the prison and the interest of the public, any infringements must be proportionate (see section 8.6). Although prison reform may be limited by potential conflicts with populist punitiveness and the **less eligibility** principle, this principle is itself being eroded by the increasing role of external standards in prison governance, drawn from international human rights instruments.

8.1.3 **Performance testing, competition, and benchmarking**

The delivery of offender management is governed by performance testing using Key Performance Indicator Targets which are set centrally and which may change over time. These have included a range of areas, including assaults, overcrowding, mandatory drug testing, matters regarding access to purposeful activities, overcrowding, and time unlocked, as well as cost per place, escapes, and pathways to reducing reoffending, which includes numbers finding employment and settled accommodation on release. However the targets, such as those on overcrowding, have been pitched too low and are unenforceable. The stress has been on quantifiable measures, such as the number of escapes, assaults, and completion of offending behaviour programmes. The impact of managerialism also means devolved budgets for criminal justice agencies. NOMS publishes annual performance ratings for each prison in England and Wales (see NOMS 2015b). Performance is assessed in relation to public protection, reducing reoffending, decency and resource management, and operational effectiveness. In addition the NOMS annual report assesses achievement in relation to business priorities (NOMS 2015a).

The managerialism governing offender management reflects a wider shift towards managerialism in the criminal justice system and public services as a whole, including the police and court services, which originated in New Right theory of the Thatcher era, was retained during the Blair and Brown Labour administrations, and was given a new lease of life by the Coalition government.

Criminal justice agencies, including NOMS, publish corporate plans, setting out priorities and performance; these are reviewed and reported annually. Performance tables are also used to assess the relative performance of individual prisons. The focus over the past 25 years has increasingly been on cost-effectiveness, limiting spending, improving efficiency, and maintaining security and safety, including controlling drug use. However, improved levels of literacy and numeracy, or basic skills, have also been included as targets. The Prison Inspectorate also carries out regular inspections, reviews key issues such as time unlocked and time in purposeful activities, and publishes thematic reviews on specific areas of concern or on particular groups of prisoners.

A new system of commissioning was introduced following the reorganisation of offender management, intended to improve the efficiency and effectiveness of service provision (see also Chapter 10, section 10.6.3). The focus has increasingly been on competition or **contestability**, in which providers of services compete for contracts, and this will be developed further in relation to rehabilitation programmes.

Changes relating to prison governance were introduced by the Offender Management Act 2007, including new provisions on powers of search and detention in contracted-out prisons (ss. 16, 17), new offences relating to prison security (ss. 21–24), and the removal of the requirement to appoint a medical officer (s. 25), a post incorporating managerial and clinical responsibilities. The change reflects the fact that clinical duties are now performed by externally contracted GPs from the NHS and managerial responsibilities are no longer part of the medical officer's role.

The Act reflected some of the proposals in *Improving Prison and Probation Services: Public Value Partnerships* (Home Office 2006b), which set out the Labour government's plans to extend contestability, partnerships with the private and voluntary sectors, and also ways of challenging underperforming prisons and Probation Boards. The Carter Review of Prisons in 2007 also envisaged further development of contestability and the need to ensure cost-effectiveness in the supply and functioning of prisons (Carter 2007).

Greater use of the private and voluntary sectors is seen as essential to the provision of rehabilitation programmes, as is made clear in the Green Paper, *Breaking the Cycle* (Ministry of Justice 2010a), and the Consultation Paper, *Transforming Rehabilitation* (Ministry of Justice 2013a), with payments linked to results.

The public sector **benchmarking** programme has been applied to prisons. It focuses on identifying the most efficient ways of working and applying them, with separate benchmarks for each type of prison and prisoner. NOMS has devised changes to the regime and staffing to apply the benchmarks, including changes to the core day, maximising opportunities for prisoners to engage in purposeful activities. Benchmarking and competition have been used to reduce costs and NOMS expect costs to be reduced by over £2,000 per place by the end of financial year 2015/16 (NOMS 2014: 7). Reductions in costs have already been achieved through closures of older prisons and cuts in the number of staff.

8.2 The prison population

8.2.1 The composition of the prison population

Information on prison life and the prison population may be obtained from official statistics, reports from the Home Office and Ministry of Justice, and reviews and reports from the Prison Inspectorate. There are relatively few qualitative studies, not least because of the problem of access to prisons and the transience of the population. The need for security and the smooth running of the prison also makes ethnographic research difficult. However, research has been undertaken by the Home Office, for the Chief Inspector of Prisons, and by campaigning groups such as the Howard League for Penal Reform, NACRO, and the Prison Reform Trust; this has focused on particular problems and particular groups of prisoners, and has highlighted the importance of humane regimes. We also have information from government-sponsored reviews, such as the Wedderburn Report and the Corston Report on Women Prisoners, as well as from the Mubarek Inquiry (see Chapter 9), the All-Party Parliamentary Group on Women in the Penal System (APGAW), the House of Commons Justice Committee (2015a), and independent researchers. An independent commission on prisons, the Commission on English Prisons Today, aimed to promote public and academic debates on imprisonment and examines the issues which have led to the rise in the prison population. It published its final report in 2009 (Commission on English Prisons Today 2009).

Although prisoners may come from a wide range of social groups and classes, a profile of the typical prisoner can be compiled from official statistics and research studies. These indicate that the typical prisoner is likely to be young, male, economically and socially deprived or socially excluded, and a persistent acquisitive offender, experiencing problems with accommodation and with finding employment—or, if in work, in an unskilled occupation—from an inner-city area, and of low educational achievement. Social exclusion is the most striking characteristic of the prison population.[1]

Prisoners are also more likely to have been in care, more likely to have been unemployed, and more likely to have been habitual truants than the general population. Many have suffered from housing problems before entering prison and also face housing problems on release. Moreover, prisoners may lose their housing as a direct result of imprisonment. A large number of prisoners are unemployed before going into prison and of course many will lose their jobs through imprisonment. This is important as homelessness and unemployment are also significant factors associated with reoffending.

A longitudinal survey, *Surveying Prisoner Crime Reduction*, considered prisoners' early life experiences, accommodation, education and employment, substance use, and mental health needs (Ministry of Justice 2010b). The survey confirmed that prisoners were less likely than the general population to have worked before entering custody and more likely to have been homeless, and had higher rates of mental health and emotional problems. Reoffending rates were also higher for those who had been excluded from school or who had prior experience of drug use.

The prison population is also still overwhelmingly male, as we can see from Figure 8.1. The proportion of female prisoners varied between 3 per cent and 4 per cent of the total prison population during most of the 1990s but by 2004 it had reached 6 per cent, and since then has fluctuated between 5 and 6 per cent. It is now 4.6 per cent. It is clear that men commit more offences than women, but also commit more offences of violence than women.

---

[1] For further discussion of social exclusion see O'Grady *et al.* (2004); Byrne (2005); Pantazis *et al.* (2006); Dorling *et al.* (2007); Dorling (2015); Silver (2015).

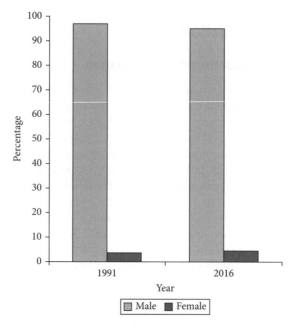

Figure 8.1 Composition of prison population by gender

The demographic structure of the prison population is also changing in relation to age. Like the population at large, the prison population is ageing and the number of elderly prisoners has increased significantly since 1995, although this may also reflect the increase in sentence length (Howse 2003). The recent growth also reflects the increase in the number serving sentences for historic sex offences. There was a 164 per cent increase in the number of sentenced prisoners aged 60 and over between 2002 and 2015 (Prison Reform Trust 2015a: 5). The number of sex offenders in the prison population increased by 33 per cent between 2010 and 2015 (Ministry of Justice 2015c). Older prisoners may also experience poorer health than younger prisoners (see Chapter 9.10.6, Department of Health 2009b, House of Commons Justice Committee 2013b).

The number of prisoners serving determinate sentences of over four years has increased in the year since the end of June 2014, to one-third of the sentenced population, while the number serving sentences of less than four years has declined (Ministry of Justice 2015c). The number of prisoners serving indeterminate sentences has declined, reflecting the decrease in the imprisonment for public protection (IPP) population.

The number of children and young people aged under 18 in custody has fallen by two-thirds in the past seven years (Youth Justice Board 2015a). The population of prisoners in the groups 15–17, 18–20, and 21–24 have continued to fall, with a reduction of nearly one-third since 2009 (Ministry of Justice 2015c).The problems young offenders face in custody will be considered in Chapter 11.

Although some prisoners have degrees before entering prison, or gain degrees while in prison, nearly half of prisoners have no formal qualifications on entering prison (Ministry of Justice 2012f). One-fifth have low levels of literary and numeracy. Many have a history of truancy, with 42 per cent having been permanently excluded or expelled from school (Prison Reform Trust 2015a). These figures are much higher than for the general population. For this reason, there is great emphasis on acquiring basic work, literacy, and numeracy skills while in custody. However, a recent survey of 343 adult learners following courses in prison found that 71 per cent had a prior qualification of some kind before entering prison (Department for Business, Innovation and Skills 2016).

It is also estimated that 20–30 per cent of prisoners have learning disabilities which will affect their ability to cope with imprisonment (see Talbot 2007, 2008; Talbot and Riley 2007; Loucks 2007; HM Inspectorate of Prisons 2009a; HM Inspectorate of Probation/HM Inspectorate of Prisons 2015, Chapter 9, section 9.10.5). Information on these disabilities will not necessarily be available to staff on arrival at prison and they may not always be identified while in prison. It is also estimated that 18 per cent of prisoners have physical disabilities.

A high number of prisoners will have been drug users before admission. The number of prisoners imprisoned for drugs offences and drugs-related crime has increased and drug use will frequently be resumed on release from prison. The rates for drug problems and mental health problems are higher within the prison population than the general population (Department of Health 2011; Dudeck *et al.* 2011). This increases the demands on prisons in dealing with problems raised by these prisoners. There may also be problems in identifying mental health problems, as the Bradley Report observed (Department of Health 2009a). A Care Not Custody Coalition was formed in 2011 by the Women's Institute with the Prison Reform Trust and now includes 34 other organisations who campaign for the diversion of individuals with mental health needs or learning disabilities from custody into treatment and care.

The Prison Inspectorate found 31 per cent of prisoners reported having an emotional well-being or mental health problem (HM Chief Inspector of Prisons (HMCIP) 2014: 40, see also Peay 2013). Moreover, mental health problems may develop for the first time inside prison. In the *Surveying Prisoner Crime Reduction* study, 17 per cent of offenders had been treated or received advice on mental health or emotional problems in the year preceding their imprisonment (Ministry of Justice 2010b). Over half of prisoners interviewed in this study had dependent children on entering custody. The impact of imprisonment on prisoners' families is wide-reaching and the problems facing prisoners' families have been charted by Codd and Epstein (Codd 2008, Epstein 2012).

A total of 26 per cent of prisoners are from minority ethnic groups, which is clearly disproportionate to the numbers in the population as a whole (Prison Reform Trust 2015a). Foreign national prisoners currently constitute 12 per cent of the prison population, compared to 14 per cent in 2008. The experiences of these groups of prisoners will be considered in Chapter 9.

8.2.2 **Prison expansion**

The prison population expanded massively during the post-war period, from 15,000 in 1945 to the current level of over 85,000. The population has steadily increased, with dramatic increases in the 1990s in both sentenced and remand prisoners.[2] In the period 1993–2008 it increased by 4 per cent per year. The most important reasons for the dramatic increase in the prison population since the early 1990s are the increases in both the custody rate—that is the percentage of persons sentenced who receive an immediate custodial sentence—and in sentence length, increased use of indeterminate sentences, and increases in the number of offenders recalled to prison following breaches of their licence conditions (see Ministry of Justice 2013b; Ministry of Justice 2015c). The prison population reached

---

[2] Prison population statistics are published annually and updated weekly by the Ministry of Justice and also recorded on the Howard League website.

a record high of over 88,000 in 2011 due to the urban riots in August 2011. But in 2012 and 2013 it fell, with a reduction in the number of remand prisoners reflecting the impact of changes in LASPO 2012, which limited the use of remand where offenders were unlikely to receive a custodial sentence, and a decline in the number of offenders under 18 going into custody (Ministry of Justice 2015c). However, from June 2013 the prison population began to rise again at about 1 per cent a year, although at a slower rate than previously. On 27 November 2015 the weekly prison population was 85,982.

The use of fines by the courts has decreased since 1999 but there has been increased use of non-court fines. However, the use of community sentences increased after 1999, but has fallen since 2013. The UK has a wide range of alternatives to custody but also, as noted in Chapter 1, a relatively high rate of imprisonment compared to other Western European states, currently reaching 148 per 100,000 of the population (International Centre for Prison Studies 2016).

There has also been an increase in the number of offenders coming before the courts and in the number of more serious offences being sentenced, although this is more evident in relation to male rather than female offenders. Other factors contributing to the expansion in the prison population include changes in sentencing law, increased public punitiveness, and the increased importance of punishment and of bringing offenders to justice in political agendas (Piper and Easton 2006/7). There has been a rise in the number of prisoners serving life sentences and other indeterminate sentences since 1999, reflecting the emphasis on risk management and public protection. Prisoners serving sentences of IPP added to the numbers, although this sentence has now been abolished and replaced by new provisions on life sentences and extended sentences (see Chapter 5, sections 5.3 and 5.4). More prisoners are also being recalled following release on licence, which is contributing to the changing demographic structure of the prison population. The amount of time served under licence and under supervision increased under the Criminal Justice Act 2003. The Parole Board has also become more risk-averse following incidents where prisoners have been released and have gone on to commit further crimes.

As we saw in Chapter 1, there has also been an increase in the number of civil orders available to and imposed by the courts, the breach of which may incur custodial penalties and add to the burgeoning prison population. There has also been an increase in the numbers serving short sentences. Some offenders are now being sent to prison when they would not have been in the early 1990s (see Hough *et al.* 2003). Although the use of community penalties since 1995 has also increased, this has not had the effect of reducing the use of custodial sentences—in fact, both have increased, while the use of fines has fallen. The prison population projections for the next five years remain high. The prison population projection for 2021, published in 2015, gives a projected figure of 89,900 (Ministry of Justice 2015g). However, this is a lower figure than anticipated in earlier projections. For example, in projections published in 2010, the highest figure for 2016 was 93,600 (Ministry of Justice 2010d), while in the 2011 projections the highest figure was 94,800 and the lowest 83,100 (Ministry of Justice 2011h). Changes to how the information is presented are currently being considered and future projections may be limited to four years.

As we saw in Chapter 1, governments are reluctant to impose penal policies, such as sentence discounts or early release, which are unpopular with the public, and seek to increase confidence in the criminal justice system in bringing offenders to justice and punishing them appropriately. So the use of reductionist measures will be limited by these pressures. Over the past 25 years successive governments have clearly been mindful of the financial burdens of high rates of incarceration, yet have continued to provide additional prison places. NOMS report a reduction in operating costs of 13 per cent per prison place and

12 per cent per prisoner from 2009/10 to 2013/14, and further reductions are anticipated in future (NOMS 2015c: 20). Net operating costs for 2014/15 were £3,762 million, which includes prisons and probation (ibid: 31). The overall cost per prison place, as noted in Chapter 1, was £36,808 in 2012/13, and the overall cost per prisoner £34,766 (NOMS 2015c: 35).

8.2.3 **The prison estate**

The increased demand for prison places has been met by an expansion of prison-building. Several new prisons opened or were commissioned in the 1970s: Long Lartin in 1972, Durham in 1978, and Channings Wood in Devon in 1982. During the 1980s and 1990s, there was a substantial building programme, with 21 new prisons opened between 1980 and 1996. A total of 20,000 new prison places were provided during the period of the Labour administration, from 1997 to 2010. A prison ship, *HMP Weare*, was also used from 1997 to 2005. Most of the new prisons constructed in the past decade have been in the private sector, although a new public sector prison, HMP Kennet, opened on Merseyside in 2007 and the new Titan prison in North Wales, HMP Berwyn, will be run by the Prison Service but with some of the services within the prison out-sourced. In July 2015 there were 105 public sector prisons, which accounted for 82 per cent of prison places (NOMS 2015a: 11), and 14 contracted-out prisons.[3] Some smaller prisons have closed, for example Ashwell and Lancaster Castle, or merged with others, while others, such as Morton Hall, have been converted to immigration removal centres. Negotiations have begun on end-ing the lease at Dartmoor Prison. Many smaller prisons have merged into clusters. For example, the Isle of Wight cluster formed in 2009 incorporated HMP Parkhurst, Albany, and Camp Hill, although Camp Hill has now been decommissioned, while HMP Humber incorporates the Wolds and Everthorpe. In November 2015 the government announced plans to build nine new modern prisons, five of which will be completed within five years. Older, less efficient prisons will be closed and sold and the land will then be made available for housing (HM Treasury 2015: 2.144). These include HMP Holloway.

The modern prison system is shaped by the legacy of the past, reflected in the prison infrastructure in the survival of Victorian prison buildings. The prison estate includes con-versions of country houses and former military camps, as well as purpose-built prisons. While some prisoners are still housed in old Victorian buildings, such as at Wandsworth, these have been refurbished and now include new modern wings. Many prisoners are housed in prisons built since the war. The current policy is to close old, inefficient facilities and replace them with more cost-effective new prisons to increase capacity and reduce running costs.

The prison estate is divided into 11 geographical areas, as well as a separate division for high-security prisons.[4] In 2015 there were 12 women's prisons. The women's prison estate includes open and closed prisons but Askham Grange and East Sutton Park, the last female open prisons, are scheduled for closure. As noted, Holloway is also expected to close in 2016. There are currently six mother and baby units in Bronzefield, Eastwood Park, Styal,

---

[3] Scotland and Northern Ireland have separate systems and space precludes a focus on their prison estates. However, information on prisons in Scotland and Northern Ireland can be obtained from the Scottish Prison Service on http://www.sps.gov.uk/ and the Northern Ireland Prison Service on https://www.dojni.gov.uk/topics/prisons.

[4] A map of the geographical distribution of prisons can be found at: http://www.justice.gov.uk/downloads/contacts/hmps/prison-finder/prisons-map.pdf, updated November 2015.

New Hall, Peterborough, and Askham Grange. The treatment of women prisoners will be considered in more detail in Chapter 9.

Local prisons, located in towns and cities, hold remand prisoners pending trial and during their trials, as well as convicted prisoners immediately after sentence, for assessment before transferring to training prisons. They may also hold convicted prisoners serving short sentences and those nearing the end of long sentences. They often experience the worst overcrowding as well as the worst conditions, and include inner-city Victorian prisons, such as Wandsworth, as well as modern prisons such as Belmarsh.

In July 2013 the government announced plans to develop 70 prisons as resettlement prisons across England and Wales. Trials were undertaken in autumn 2013 in the north-west of England and have now been extended to the rest of the prison estate in England and Wales. Prisoners serving less than 12 months will spend their sentence in these prisons, while longer-serving prisoners will spend the last three months of their sentence there. The aim is for prisoners to be located in the area where they will be released, so that they can build up links with that community and may also obtain employment or voluntary work in that area. This initiative was part of the Coalition government's *Transforming Rehabilitation* agenda (Ministry of Justice 2013a). However, while the prisons designated as resettlement prisons have now been identified, the Prison Inspectorate found that there had been little planning of how to deal with the demands of the role (HM Chief Inspector of Prisons 2014). Training prisons may be closed or open, and may be located further away from towns and cities. They include specialist prisons, for example the therapeutic prison Grendon in Buckinghamshire; there are also therapeutic communities inside HMP Gartree, Dovegate, and Send. Stevens' ethnographic research on three prisons with therapeutic communities has illustrated the potential for group psychotherapy to result in individual change, which may lead to desistance (Stevens 2013, see also Brown *et al.* 2014).

Closed training prisons have varying levels of security. Prisoners in open training prisons, such as Leyhill and Ford, clearly enjoy much greater freedom. They may work in the prison or in the local community and are allowed out on shopping visits, but the rules governing prison life will be strongly enforced to compensate for the absence of external boundaries. However, these regimes have been criticised because of prisoners absconding from Leyhill and rioting at Ford Open Prison. In January 2011, buildings at Ford were set alight by prisoners and criminal damage was inflicted, but no one was hurt. Alcohol was thought to have been a factor in the riot and prisoners suspected of taking alcohol refused to take breathalyser tests. The Prison Inspectorate had also questioned the level of staffing in the period preceding the riot.

Vulnerable prisoners, such as sex offenders, are housed in special Vulnerable Prisoners' Units (VPUs) for their own safety to protect them from assaults by other prisoners. Severely disruptive or violent prisoners may be transferred to Close Supervision Centres within the high-security prison estate. There are also Protected Witness Units for those prisoners at risk of harm from other prisoners. The modern prison system is still very expensive to run, despite concerted efforts to reduce costs, and is much more expensive than community punishment. Cost-effectiveness or value for money has become an increasingly important issue in the past 20 years as costs have risen. Prison budgets make a substantial claim on public spending which needs to be justified, especially at a time of austerity. Additional costs may also be incurred if it is necessary to use a police cell or court cell because of a lack of space.

As well as the substantial running costs, there are also the capital costs of building and maintaining prisons. Costs of maintenance and refurbishment will be sizeable in the older prisons which are not purpose built. Older buildings may also be more expensive to staff, and staffing costs constitute the principal demand on the prison budget. The location of some of these prisons also means additional costs in transporting prisoners across the country. If we include ancillary costs such as prison escort services, then the cost rises substantially. There may also be additional welfare costs for a prisoner's dependants, with the loss of the prisoner's income. As is often observed, it costs more to send an offender to prison than a student to university.

8.2.4 **The categorisation and allocation of prisoners**

Decisions on the categorisation of prisoners are distinct from and precede decisions on allocation. The procedures and criteria for both processes are set out in Prison Service Instructions (PSI 39, 40, and 41). Adult male prisoners are divided into four categories, A, B, C, and D.

Decisions on category A prisoners are made by a special Category A Committee at NOMS Headquarters. Categorisation decisions for other prisoners are a matter for the governor and are made in accordance with the National Security Framework. Prisoners should be placed in the lowest category consistent with the need for security and control. Prisons should have procedures for reviewing the categorisation of prisoners and there is a duty to give reasons for such decisions. Categorisation should take account of the current offence and sentence, previous convictions, and previous escapes, escape attempts, and absconds. Categorisation is reviewed at regular intervals and reconsidered on the basis of the risk to the public and the risk of escape. There are separate procedures for those serving life sentences and indeterminate sentences.

Category A prisoners are those who would be highly dangerous to the public, police, or the security of the state and for whom the aim must be to make escape impossible. Category B prisoners are those who do not require the highest security conditions, but for whom escape must be made very difficult. Category C prisoners are those who cannot be trusted in open conditions, but who lack the will or resources to make a determined escape attempt, while category D prisoners are those who can be reasonably trusted in open conditions and for whom open conditions are appropriate. Remand prisoners may be categorised A or are unclassified (U). Young adult male prisoners may be categorised A or as Restricted Status—used for prisoners whose escape would present a serious risk to the public and who should be held in secure accommodation—or assessed as suitable for closed or open conditions, using similar security criteria as adults. Women prisoners may be classified as category A, defined as above, or as Restricted Status, or deemed suitable for closed conditions, which covers prisoners for whom the very highest security conditions are not necessary but who present too high a risk for open conditions, or for whom open conditions are not appropriate. The fourth category is open conditions. This is used for women who present a low risk and can reasonably be trusted in open conditions, and for whom open conditions are appropriate.

Category A is further divided into three levels of escape risk: standard, high, and exceptional risk (PSI 05/2013). Standard escape risk applies to the majority of category A prisoners and means that they are not considered to have the determination and skill to overcome the security measures which apply to the custody and movement of category A prisoners. High escape risk would include, for example, members of criminal gangs with access to sufficient resources to help them escape. Prisoners are classified as exceptional escape risk when they have the skills, external resources, abilities, and determination to overcome the security measures normally used for category A prisoners, and therefore need to be contained within the most secure units available within the Prison Service. There are also special units for prisoners with dangerous and severe personality disorders within the high-security prison estate.

Regimes for category A prisoners are the most stringent, for example requiring closed visits. These prisoners are more likely to be transferred to other prisons than other categories and the courts are more reluctant to interfere with transfer decisions in such cases. If they are transferred, it may be difficult for them to complete educational or offending behaviour courses, which may also affect their chances of future reclassification. Prisoners may also be placed on the 'escape list', that is, they are deemed to be at risk of trying to escape—for example, because they have done so in the past—and will be placed on a strict security regime and required to wear special clothes.

Prisons are becoming more secure in so far as the number of escapes has declined since the early 1980s and the risk may be highest while in transit, for example on court visits. Prison categorisation was reviewed, however, when two category A prisoners escaped from Gartree in 1987 with the help of a helicopter which landed inside the grounds of the prison. Following this incident, exceptional risk categories were held in special security units for high-risk prisoners. In 2014/15 there was one escape from prison and prison escorts, compared to four the previous year (NOMS 2015a: 24).

Once sentenced, category A prisoners go to high-security prisons. These prisons will have high levels of security, including dog patrols, electronic surveillance, high walls, searching of visitors, high levels of staffing, and frequent searches of inmates as they move around the prison.[5] There are currently eight high-security prisons, namely Belmarsh, Frankland, Full Sutton, Long Lartin, Wakefield, Whitemoor, Manchester, and Woodhill. Conditions are generally better in higher security prisons for those serving longer sentences, with more educational and work opportunities, and prisoners may be able to cook their own meals. There are also special units to deal with difficult prisoners called Close Supervision Centres, where prisoners can be closely supervised and encouraged to address their disruptive behaviour. They have a structured regime through which prisoners must progress satisfactorily before leaving the unit. Conditions are harsher in so far as more time is spent locked up, visits are restricted, the furniture is made of cardboard, and prisoners sleep on concrete plinths rather than proper beds. There are also special cells for segregating difficult prisoners within high-security prisons and at local prisons.

The categorisation of prisoners was reviewed in *R (P) v Secretary of State for the Home Department* (2002). Here an elderly and ill prisoner had been placed in category A even though he would be unlikely to be able to escape, but if he did escape he would be highly dangerous to the public, or to the police, or to the security of the state. The court held that the Prison Service was entitled to have a policy to make the escape of highly dangerous prisoners virtually impossible, but should consider prisoners' cases on an individual basis, so that if the escape risk of a particular prisoner could be managed in lower security conditions, then it would be unlawful to preclude consideration of this possibility.

Category B prisoners may stay in local prisons if serving a short sentence, or go to high-security or closed training prisons. Category C prisoners go to closed training prisons with lower security and a more relaxed regime. Category D go to open training prisons, although some may be held in category C prisons. Within some C and D prisons there are also resettlement prisons to which prisoners may be transferred shortly before release, to arrange work and to increase contact with their families.

Decisions on allocation to particular prisons are made on the basis of the need for security and control, individual prisoner needs, and optimum use of available space, and these needs may sometimes conflict with each other. Individual needs would include age,

---

[5] The factors influencing the treatment of high-risk prisoners in the UK are considered by King and Resodihardjo (2010) and compared with the approach in the Netherlands and the United States.

vulnerability, any educational needs, and the prisoner's home area. Prisoners do not have a right to be allocated to any particular prison. Similar principles will apply to the allocation of young offenders although maintenance of family ties will be a key consideration, so normally young offenders are allocated to a prison as close to home as possible and when allocating women prisoners, family ties and facilitating visits from children will be significant allocation issues.

8.3 Prison conditions

Bearing in mind the objectives of imprisonment (see section 8.1.2), we will consider the conditions in modern prisons and problems which inhibit the realisation of these objectives, as well as improvements made in recent years. If we compare the prisons of the early 1990s with those of today, we find considerable progress, but also clearly room for further improvement. Prison conditions have changed since the 1990s as a result of a number of factors including the Woolf Report, the rise of the New Managerialism, the increasing focus on risk management, and the privatisation programme. The focus on risk and on transparency and measurement of prison performance has limited the autonomy and discretion of prison governors, while the increasing pressure on prison resources from the substantial increase in prison numbers has limited the scope for improving prison regimes. However, the ECHR and the HRA 1998 have had a substantial beneficial impact on prison conditions.

8.3.1 Overview

Prison conditions have improved considerably since the Woolf Report was published in 1991 and further improvements were introduced following the Human Rights Act 1998. Prison conditions are crucial to debates in penology as they have implications for the protection of human rights but also for reoffending. However, conditions still remain unsatisfactory in some prisons, particularly for those held on remand, with fewer facilities available for work and training. On the 25th anniversary of the Strangeways riot, Lord Woolf (2015)[6] noted that although progress had been made after the riots, we are now moving backwards in terms of overcrowding and conditions and a further inquiry was needed. Prisoners are still kept a long way from home in overcrowded conditions, staffing has been cut, there have been increases in suicide rates, and the prison population has doubled since the time of the riots. He was critical of the introduction of Titan prisons, with the first being at Wrexham, far from where it is actually needed in terms of centres of population but intended to provide work for the local economy. Instead he advocates clusters of small prisons so prisoners can be located near their homes.

The day-to-day life inside prison is governed by the very detailed Prison Rules 1999 issued under s. 47 of the Prison Act 1952. These rules have been regularly updated and supplemented by Prison Service Orders and Instructions. The rules include provisions on a range of issues, including work, education, access to visits, offences against discipline, and the use of constraints.

A number of performance improvement strategies have been implemented, notably the introduction of prison league tables which now rank prisons on their performance in terms of 37 indicators, in four domains: Public Protection, Reducing Reoffending, Decency and Resource Management, and Operational Effectiveness. Prisons will be awarded one

---

[6] See also Interview on *Inside Out,* BBC Northwest, broadcast 23 March 2015.

of the following four ratings: level 1, which indicates overall performance is of serious concern; level 2, overall performance is of concern; level 3, meets the majority of targets; and level 4, exceptional performance. League tables were first published in July 2003, when Holloway was awarded the lowest ranking for failing to meet performance targets or providing secure, ordered, or decent regimes; it had moved up to level 3 by 2011 (Ministry of Justice 2011b). The latest annual performance ratings for 2014/15 show three prisons at level 1—Pentonville, Nottingham, and Wormwood Scrubs, 25 at level 2, 14 at level 4, and the remainder, including Holloway, at level 3 (Ministry of Justice/NOMS 2015). The focus on contestability was also intended to drive up standards and penalise poor performance, through the competition between prisons for contracts.

Despite these improvements, it has been argued that prisoners in England experience worse conditions in terms of visitation rights, physical conditions, and relationships with staff compared, for example, with their counterparts in the Netherlands and Sweden (see Kruttschnitt and Dirkzwager 2011; Easton 2011a).

8.3.2 **Overcrowding**

Overcrowding or, as it is now termed, 'crowding', is normally measured by comparing actual numbers of inmates with Certified Normal Accommodation (CNA), that is, the uncrowded capacity calculated for each prison. Overcrowding initially declined overall during the 1990s as the supply of places expanded due to the prison building programme, although in some prisons overcrowding remained a problem, and it has increased in recent years. Overcrowding may arise not simply because of a lack of accommodation, but in part because of inflexibility of use because prisons may be too specialised to allow for the transfer of prisoners between them. Increasingly prisons have been broadening their functions as they have expanded and one reason behind the proposal for large-scale 'Titan' prisons in the Carter Review of Prisons was to allow for more flexibility in allocating accommodation, as well as cost savings (Carter 2007). However, the proposal was not implemented at the time because of the additional initial costs, but the programme has now been revived with the construction of Wrexham prison, due to open in 2017, which will be run by the Prison Service. Overcrowding is not spread evenly throughout the prison estate and it will have effects on other activities: as the Prison Inspectorate notes, 'Overcrowding is not simply an issue of prisoners being doubled-up in cells designed for one but means that the purposeful activities, rehabilitation programmes and other services and facilities are insufficient for the size of the population' (HM Chief Inspector of Prisons 2014: 8).

The rationale of the Titan prison is to concentrate facilities to achieve economies of scale and better value for money, as medical and catering services, for example, can be centralised, so it is primarily cost-driven. The building costs of larger prisons are cheaper than several smaller institutions and they are able to offer a wider range of services. However, the available research suggests that smaller-scale units are more effective in providing humane regimes rather than simply 'warehousing'. Large-scale prisons may be more cost-effective in the short term, but any disorder or disruption may be more easily managed in smaller-scale prisons. Critics have also focused on the problems of maintaining offender integration and well-being in a larger and more impersonal regime. Relations between staff and prisoners and between prisoners themselves improve in smaller-scale environments. The Chief Inspector of Prisons found a correlation between perceptions of safety, positive staff–prisoner relationships, and the smaller size of prisons (HM Chief Inspector of Prisons 2011a: 20). However, the location of prison places in or near major centres of population would be better for prisoners from those areas, instead of their being housed in a remote rural area.

With the rapid expansion of the prison population, inevitably overcrowding remains a problem for the prison system. In 2014/15 the percentage of prisoners held in accommodation units designed for fewer prisoners was 25.5 per cent, compared with 24.1 per cent the previous year (NOMS 2015a: 32). But, given the current size of the prison population, this means large numbers of prisoners are being held in cells designed for fewer prisoners.

Overcrowding will not be evenly distributed throughout the prison system, so there may still be unsatisfactory levels in specific institutions, even if the total level of overcrowding is not substantial. Overcrowding is generally worse in local prisons, which house mostly remand prisoners and those serving short sentences or awaiting transfers. Usually training prisons and young offender institutions will be protected from overcrowding at the expense of local prisons. In 2014/15 63 per cent of prisons inspected were found to be overcrowded and in over half overcrowding was worse than in previous inspections (HM Chief Inspector of Prisons 2015: 41). As in previous years, the overcrowding was worse in local prisons; Leicester had an overcrowding rate of 181 per cent, with 387 prisoners held in cells designed to accommodate 214 (ibid). In Portland some prisoners who were not employed or required for other activities spent over 22 hours in their overcrowded cells.

A statutory limit on overcrowding in the form of a new Prison Rule, under which prisons could not accommodate more prisoners than provided in its CNA except in very limited cases, was recommended by the Woolf Report, but this recommendation was not implemented (Woolf and Tumim 1991: para 1.190). The use of single cells for prisoners is also recommended by the European Prison Rules (EPR 18.5).

The effects of overcrowding are widespread. As well as worsening physical conditions, there may be more frequent transfers, so it is hard to implement proper training and provide educational programmes accessible to all prisoners, and to complete necessary assessments. Overcrowding also makes prison life more impersonal, affecting the opportunity to establish good personal relationships with staff and other prisoners, which may also have implications for the prevention of reoffending—moving prisons away from a rehabilitative to a warehousing role—and for the safety of prisoners. In severe cases, overcrowding may amount to inhuman and degrading treatment.

What is surprising is that the increase in numbers in custody in the 1980s and 1990s paralleled a policy that prison should be used as a last resort, and alternatives should be used where possible. In fact, the UK has more alternatives to custody than many other European states. But it would seem the alternatives available during that period, such as community service orders, probation, and fines, had the effect of net-widening rather than leading to a reduction in the prison population. Ultimately, of course, it is sentencers who make the decision on whether to give a custodial sentence, but they are constrained by sentencing law and procedure when looking at the individual case. In addition, magistrates and judges will have their own views, philosophies, and traditions as well as subscribing to the principles of judicial independence and autonomy (see Chapters 2 and 3).

8.3.3 Work, training, and offending behaviour programmes

Prison Rule 31(1) states that 'a convicted prisoner shall be required to do useful work for not more than 10 hours per day, and arrangements shall be made to allow prisoners to work, where possible, outside the cells and in association with one another'. Exceptions are made for those who are ill or unable to work for other reasons. Otherwise, prisoners are classified into suitability for heavy, light, or medium work. Prison Rule 31 does not stipulate a minimum time spent in work.

From the prisoner's standpoint, work can provide a relief from boredom, the opportunity to acquire skills, and a limited source of income. From the standpoint of the prison management it keeps prisoners in useful occupation and can prepare them for release. But in practice there is insufficient suitable work available for all prisoners able to benefit from it and increasing work opportunities is a key element of current penal policy. Preparing for work is important as there is a strong correlation between reoffending and unemployment, and while a correlation is not a cause, ex-offenders are more likely to reoffend if they have no legitimate source of income. The problem of providing suitable work and other purposive activities has become harder with continued expansion without corresponding increases in resources. Access to programmes varies between institutions, so may depend on where the prisoner is allocated. Although there is no formal right to work, the European Prison Rules stipulate that prisons should attempt to provide as much work of a useful nature as is possible (EPR 26.2).

In 1991 the Woolf Report recommended that work opportunities should cater for a range of abilities and that prison regimes should try to provide constructive and purposeful employment in factories and workshops for as many prisoners as possible who could usefully be deployed. The choice of work, argued Woolf, should be influenced by the need of prisoners to find work after release. A planned programme 'should bring together work, training and education in a way that provides the most constructive mix for the prisoners who are to be involved in it' (Woolf and Tumim 1991: para 14.134). The Prison Service, he argued, should give the prisoner the opportunity to serve his or her sentence in a constructive way (ibid: para 14.9) and, by making proper use of his or her time, reduce the likelihood of reoffending (ibid: para 14.10). Since the Woolf Report, there have been improvements in the provision of constructive regimes and access to basic skills education. In the late 1990s the target was 24 hours a week spent in purposeful activity, although in practice it varied between prisons and prisoners. In the mid-1990s, the average time spent out of a cell on weekdays was 11.2 hours. In 2013/14 only half of adult male prisons reviewed by the Prison Inspectorate had good or reasonably good purposeful activity outcomes and in one-quarter of prisons, outcomes were poor (HM Chief Inspector of Prisons 2014: 41). Only 17 per cent of adult male prisoners reported more than ten hours outside their cell during weekdays and only 8 per cent in local prisons. There was also variation between prisons in the quality and quantity of work available.

Adult male prisons were subject to a review in 2013/14 to develop benchmarked standard core days with a view to maximising time outside cells. While it is too early to assess the effect of these new arrangements, the Prison Inspectorate found little to suggest change in 2015. The Inspectorate expects prisoners to be unlocked for ten hours per day but in their inspection, 14 per cent of prisoners said this was not achieved. Purposeful activity outcomes were at their lowest level since information on this was first collated in 2005/6 and were good or reasonably good in only one-quarter of prisons (HM Chief Inspector of Prisons 2015: 50).

The average number of prisoners working at any one time in public sector prisons increased from 8,600 in 2010/11 to 9,900 in 2013/14 (NOMS 2015a: 27) In 2013/14 14.2 million hours were worked in public sector prisons and 1.5 million hours in private sector prisons (ibid). Although there was a 15 per cent increase in the number of prisoners working in industrial activity and a 33 per increase in the total number of hours worked between 2010/11 and 2013/14, it still amounted to a few hours per week per prisoner and the problem remains of a shortage of suitable work for prisoners (House of Commons Justice Committee 2015a: para 49). The failure to provide sufficient work for prisoners serving short sentences has been a particular problem (see National Audit Office 2010b). The menial work offered to those serving longer sentences has also been highlighted by Meek (2008).

The prisoner is entitled to be paid and, if he or she is willing to work and none is available, to receive basic pay. But rates are very low within prison compared to the labour market outside prisons, so if prisoners are able to work outside they can achieve much higher earnings. Older prisoners beyond the state retirement age receive modest retirement pay.

Remand prisoners are permitted to work but not obliged to do so, but it is usually harder for them to obtain access to work. However, most prisoners want to work to relieve the boredom and to earn money. There may be particular problems providing work for prisoners with mental health problems, older prisoners, or prisoners with learning disabilities. Prisoners are obliged to pay tax and national insurance contributions if their earnings reach the threshold and to make contributions to maintain their dependants if their earnings are sufficient. Only 9,900 adult prisoners were working in public sector prisons in 2013/14 (NOMS 2015a). The Coalition government aimed to expand the range of work available and to promote an ethos of work discipline amongst inmates (Ministry of Justice 2010a), with work supplied by either the prison or external providers or in partnership with the private sector, and sought to make it easier for private, voluntary, and community sectors to become involved in this enterprise. The Prisoners' Earnings Act, enacted in 1996 but not brought into force until September 2011, sought to facilitate reparation to victims (PSI 76/2011). Under the Act up to 40 per cent of prisoners' wages—after tax, national insurance, child support, and court-ordered payments—may be taken and given to voluntary organisations working in income support, to prisoners' dependants, to contribute to a prisoner's upkeep, or to be invested on the prisoner's behalf. Currently all levies are donated to voluntary organisations used by Victim Support. In 2014/15 £1.1 million was raised from 368 prisoners, with average earnings of £837 per month before the levy (NOMS 2015b: 52). This was obtained from the earnings of prisoners working outside on licence. A challenge to the legality of the Act brought in the High Court by two prisoners in 2012 did not succeed.

Education, physical education, and offending behaviour programmes are also important elements of constructive regimes which aim to reduce reoffending, to challenge offenders' behaviour and attitudes, and to provide value for money. For prisoners, constructive regimes can also make custody more tolerable (see Simon 1999; Gravett 2003; Trebilcock 2011). They are also important precisely because many prisoners are unemployed before beginning their sentence and, if they can obtain employment on release, they may be less likely to reoffend. Given the links between offending and social exclusion, both work and education programmes can offer a means of integrating prisoners into society. A key element of the prison regime, therefore, is the provision of basic skills.

Prisoners may be employed in prison workshops, in agriculture and horticulture, and in provision of services within the prison, as well as providing goods and services for external commercial enterprises. With the expansion of prison numbers there has been an increased demand for labour within the prison in providing cooking, cleaning, and other domestic services and most work will be within the internal labour market. But prison work has received less investment than other areas of prison life. Prison industries are expensive to run and it is difficult to find outside work.

Prisoners may be released on temporary licence (ROTL) to undertake paid or voluntary work or education and this is usually granted to those in open conditions. It is an important element of preparation for release and enables prisoners to maintain links with the community, and, for those who have served longer sentences, acclimatises them to life outside. However, following serious incidents involving prisoners released on temporary licence in 2013, access to release on temporary licence (ROTL) was restricted and the number of releases in the period July–September 2014 fell by 23 per cent from the same period the previous year (Prison Reform Trust 2015b). However, the number of absconds had fallen and the number of incidents on ROTL was low compared to the successful completion of the majority of releases. Even if prisoners are eligible for ROTL, the resources available to open prisons to conduct assessments may be insufficient (HM Chief Inspector of Prisons 2014: 52).

A great deal of work is carried out within the prison for the prison, for example, in gardens, farms, kitchens, and laundries, as well as cleaning and making furniture. Low-skilled, repetitive work will not offer the same potential for improving employment opportunities as industrial work in prison workshops. Prisoners do undertake work for the clothing industry, textile weaving, and unskilled light assembly work for outside employers and apprenticeship schemes have been set up. But opportunities for industrial training work are limited. Prison workshops may be underused because of the costs of staff supervision. However, there have been some successful collaborations with the private sector. What is needed is sufficient good-quality work, training, and education for all prisoners. The European Prison Rules stipulate that sufficient work of a useful nature or other purposeful activities should be provided to keep prisoners actively employed for a normal working day. But there is no similar provision in the Prison Rules and levels of inactivity are still higher than desirable.

The Howard League set up a very successful project, a graphic design studio at HMP Coldingley called Barbed, which paid proper levels of pay from which workers paid tax and national insurance, as well as voluntary donations to Victim Support. The project ran from 2005 to 2008 (Green 2008, 2010). The Clink Charity runs very successful restaurants staffed by prisoners at High Down, Brixton, Cardiff, and Styal. Timpsons, the retailer, also offers training to offenders in prison and work to ex-offenders on release.

However, prisoners who are serving short sentences, or prisoners serving longer sentences but subject to transfers, may not remain in the same institution long enough to benefit from interventions, for example, in drug treatment and education programmes. There is also the problem of following up the work when the prisoner is released. There has also been increased emphasis on resettlement, on assisting prisoners to find work, accommodation, or training on release from prison, which is seen as a key element in the reduction of reoffending (see Hucklesby and Hagley-Dickinson 2007). However, recent inspections suggest support for resettlement was mixed (HM Inspectorate of Prisons/HM Inspectorate of Probation/OFSTED 2014).

The provision of offending behaviour programmes is an important element of rehabilitation as it gives prisoners the opportunity to change their behaviour. While a wide range of accredited offending behaviour programmes are available, the problem in recent years has been that there are insufficient courses to meet demand. This issue is significant when completion of a rehabilitation programme is a key factor in parole decisions on whether to approve the release of a prisoner. Jacobson and Hough (2010) have highlighted the problems IPP prisoners faced in proving that they are no longer a risk to the public, as applications to the Parole Board have been delayed because of the workload of the Board and because of the problems in obtaining access to courses.

This inability to provide sufficient courses has led to a number of challenges from prisoners over this failure. In *Wells and Walker* in 2007 the High Court said this was arbitrary, unlawful, and unreasonable, while in *James* in 2007 the High Court said that if the prisoner had completed the minimum term of his sentence and he could not access the appropriate course, then he should be released. In fact his release was deferred, pending an appeal by the government to the Court of Appeal. In *Secretary of State for Justice v Walker and James* (2008) the Court of Appeal found that the Secretary of State had acted unlawfully in failing to provide appropriate access to courses to allow IPP prisoners to demonstrate to the Parole Board that their detention was no longer necessary to protect the public. There was a 'systemic' failure to put the appropriate resources in place to allow prisoners to prepare for their Parole Board assessments. The court also said that if prisoners were detained for this reason for a long time after the minimum term had been completed it *could* breach Article 5(4) of the ECHR, although it declined to uphold an order for James's release. Both parties appealed the court's decision and the House of Lords, in *Secretary of State for Justice v James (formerly Walker and another)* [2009] UKHL 11, did find that it was irrational in the public law sense to introduce the IPP sentence without adequate resources, but this did not necessarily mean that Article 5 had been infringed. For Article 5(1) to be satisfied there must be a link between the original sentence and the continued detention, which was satisfied here as the prisoner's continued detention was based on risk and that detention was still subject to regular reviews. Furthermore, while the number of courses was insufficient, there were still some courses available, so there was no breach of Article 5(4).

However, following this decision, IPP prisoners with short tariffs were given priority access to these courses. The question was considered by the Strasbourg Court in *James, Wells and Lee v UK* (2012), where the Court found that Article 5(1) had been breached because of the lack of opportunities for the offender to show he is longer a risk by successfully completing relevant rehabilitative courses. Although the IPP sentence was abolished and replaced with new determinate sentences and extended sentences in the Legal Aid, Sentencing and Punishment of Offenders Act 2012, as noted in Chapter 5, recent inspections have found that provision of programmes is variable, with shortfalls in provision for domestic violence and sex offenders (HM Chief Inspector of Prisons 2014: 50, 2015: 15). Prisoners on indeterminate sentences had passed their tariff dates while waiting for a course to become available.

8.3.4 Education

Prisoners have a right to education and training under international human rights Conventions and the European Prison Rules, which require that every prison seeks to provide prisoners with access to educational programmes which meet their needs (EPR 28.1). Prison Rule 32(1) also states that '[e]very prisoner able to profit from the educational facilities provided at a prison shall be encouraged to do so'. It also requires that educational classes shall be provided at each prison and provision made for prisoners with special needs. Prison Rule 32(2) requires that '[r]easonable facilities shall be afforded to prisoners who wish to do so to improve their education by training, by distance learning, private study and recreational classes, in their spare time'. Library facilities should be made available at every prison and should include books on criminal law and the criminal justice system, and every prisoner should be allowed to have library books (PR 33).

There has been increasing awareness of the value of prison education in recent years on the part of policy-makers and prison management, especially in view of the difficulty of finding adequate work for prisoners and the value placed on the constructive use of time, as well as the perennial problem of controlling prisoners. Clearly education, like work, is valuable in using prisoners' time effectively and preparing them for release, and qualifications may be crucial for resettlement. It also assists in rehabilitation in providing skills which may improve access to employment and prevent their exclusion (see Hawley *et al.* 2013). In a lecture to the Prisoner Learning Alliance, the new Justice Secretary Michael Gove (2015a) placed great emphasis on the need for educational support and innovation in achieving the rehabilitative goals of imprisonment. He has also indicated that prison governors will be given more autonomy and greater control over prison education and raised the possibility of prisoners earning release through the gaining of skills and educational qualifications.

But there is uneven provision of education between prisons, and within prisons the demand for classes may not match supply, and education programmes may be affected by staff shortages. The Woolf Report suggested using prisoners to teach other prisoners where appropriate and this has been implemented in some prisons. A system of peer mentoring was set up by the Prisoners' Education Trust and prisoners have been used to teach literacy skills.

The range of educational opportunities has expanded since the 1980s, with opportunities ranging from basic literacy and numeracy to Open University degrees by distance learning, as well as National Vocational Qualifications since 1994. But provision of education and training varies from establishment to establishment. Funding for university courses may come from either a student loan or the prisoner's own resources, or from relatives, charities, or third parties (see PSI 32/2012). There are possibilities for distance learning and there is a Virtual Campus resettlement tool, run by NOMS with the Skills Funding Agency and Department for Business Innovation and Skills, available to some prisoners which gives them access to training courses and allows them to apply for jobs. Obviously access to the Internet needs to be securely controlled. However, the Prison Inspectorate found the Virtual Campus was rarely fully operational (HM Chief Inspector of Prisons 2014). The provision of education in prisons and YOIs is subject to regular inspections by OFSTED and its National Director of Further Education and Skills has expressed concern over the decline in the quality of learning and skills provision in prisons (Coffey 2013).

Problems still persist in ensuring regular access to classes; classes and work activities may be disrupted by other scheduled prison activities and prisoners are not always motivated to attend. It may be hard to maintain continuity if prisoners are transferred. Some prisoners may have a negative experience of school, often being former truants or previously excluded from school, and with low levels of educational achievement. However, the prison population is a diverse group so a range of courses may be required. Classes need staff cover for security so educational provision may be vulnerable to cuts at times of staff shortages. Although prison education can play a key role as part of a constructive prison regime, in practice it may be marginalised, especially when resources are under pressure from budget cuts.

We saw earlier that the poor educational background of some prisoners means that the starting point for the acquisition of skills is in some cases very low, so remedial work is needed. A priority now in prison education is to improve the basic skills of literacy and numeracy as well as providing vocational and academic qualifications, particularly for young people, and education and training are important elements of the offender management process. Prisoners are also engaged in a variety of voluntary activities in prison, including peer support and community support schemes, as Edgar et al. have shown in their review of prisoners' activities (Edgar et al. 2011). They argue that these opportunities for active citizenship should be expanded.

However, there may be variations between prisons in terms of time spent outside cells during activity periods. For individual prisoners, it may depend on their employment status and their level on the Incentives and Earned Privileges (IEP) scheme. As the Chief Inspector of Prisons noted, 'Too many prisons lacked sufficient activity places to ensure all prisoners had good access to education or vocational training. Only 22 prisons inspected had enough activity places for the population' (HM Chief Inspector of Prisons 2014: 43). In some prisons, the lack of places meant prisoners spending more time in their cells on weekdays, while in others prisons struggled to use all the places available because of administrative problems, delayed allocation, and poorly managed waiting lists. Where places were taken up, attendance could be frustrated because of other prison activities taking precedence over classes.

New contractual arrangements for providing learning, skills, and work came into force in 2012. The quality of teaching is assessed jointly by OFSTED and the Prison Inspectorate, which found that 'The overall standard of teaching and learning was rated as good in fewer than half of the English prisons inspected' (ibid: 45). Teaching of English and maths was not prioritised in practice, with achievement rates low. However, vocational training was good. Prisoner peer mentors were also used to provide support, for example, to emerging readers. But in most prisons there were too few places available for vocational training, with many prisoners engaged in mundane work such as cleaning, and libraries were underused.

8.4 Prison unrest

8.4.1 Prison riots

The worst riots in British penal history occurred in 1990 in Strangeways in Manchester, followed by serious riots at Glen Parva, a young offenders' institution and remand centre; Cardiff and Bristol, both local prisons; Pucklechurch, a remand centre holding mostly young offenders; Dartmoor, a training prison; and elsewhere. These incidents of disorder led to damage to property, assaults, and loss of life. Following the riots in April 1990, an inquiry into the events leading up to the riots, headed by Lord Justice Woolf, was set up. It reported in 1991 (Woolf and Tumim 1991) and its findings are considered in the section 'Explaining prison riots'.

Prison riots have a long history in the UK. There were riots in the 1970s at Brixton, Hull, Gartree, and Parkhurst, and in the 1980s at Wormwood Scrubs, Albany, Haverigg, and Risley. Riots have erupted in training prisons, local and remand prisons, young offender institutions, and contracted-out prisons, and in prisons with a reputation for relaxed regimes. Since 1990 there have been incidents of disorder and riots, but not on the same scale as the earlier riots. There were incidents in Portland Young Offenders Institution in 2000 and a serious riot in Lincoln Prison in 2002, as well as riots at Hindley Prison in Wigan, which houses adults and young offenders, in 2005, and at Stoke Heath Young Offenders Institution in 2006. In June 2010 young offenders rioted at Cookham Wood when they were not allowed to watch the women's tennis quarter-final at Wimbledon, and in January 2011 prisoners at Ford Open Prison set fire to a building. Four prisoners were convicted of prison mutiny for their participation in the riot. The Independent Monitoring Board had warned of problems at the prison. Alcohol and poor relations between staff and prisoners were seen as factors in the riot but the internal report was not made public.

There was also disorder at HMP High Down in 2013, where prisoners barricaded themselves into a cell in response to a new regime at the prison. In Oakwood in 2014 there was a riot with prisoners destroying property. A letter from the then Prisons Minister, Andrew Selous, to the Shadow Justice Secretary, referred to in *The Guardian* on 28 March 2015, reported on growing unrest in the prison, with more hostage incidents, prisoners on the roof, and netting incidents and increased use of the National Tactical Response Group, the Prison Service's anti-riot squad.

The concern is that with increased overcrowding and cuts in staffing and resources, incidents of disorder may become more frequent and more violent. The number of prison officers has been reduced substantially since 2010. The Prison Inspectorate has expressed its concern over the level of violence in young offender institutions, with fights and assaults on a daily basis and inmates feeling unsafe (HM Chief Inspector of Prisons 2014: 66), and increasing violence in adult male prisons (HM Chief Inspector of Prisons 2015: 34). Safety outcomes were not good enough in over half of the male prisons inspected and in two cases worse than the previous inspection (ibid). The increase in violence has been attributed in part to a combination of lack of resources and population pressures. Conversely, if more accommodation becomes available and more staff are recruited, there should be improvements in safety. Where there are severe staff shortages, prisons may be placed on restricted regimes, with less time available for purposeful activities.

Explaining prison riots

Various explanations for the 1990 riots were advanced, for example by Woolf and Tumim (1991) and Boin and Rattray (2004). The quality of life in UK prisons in the late 1980s and early 1990s was much worse than at the present time in a number of respects. The Council of Europe's Committee for the Prevention of Torture found that conditions in Wandsworth, Brixton, and Leeds prisons in 1990 were inhuman and degrading (Council of Europe 1991). While there had been an expansion of judicial review relating to prisoners' complaints, this primarily concerned procedural problems rather than prison conditions. There were also problems of control in the 1980s and an increased focus on security because of fears of escape and in response to incidents of disorder. It was argued at the time that the policy of dispersing high-security prisoners throughout the prison system may have contributed to the problems, because it had an adverse impact on the receiving prisons, increasing the levels of security to a greater degree than was warranted for other inmates. Volatile political prisoners, disturbed prisoners, and lifers were also blamed at the time for contributing to the problems, although, again, some of the riots occurred in prisons without such prisoners. But the Woolf Report focused specifically on perceptions of unfairness and the sense of injustice.

In the 1980s there were no national operating standards for prisons. They were introduced in 1994, and prisons in England and Wales are now assessed on their performance in several areas. The UK has also adopted the European Prison Rules,[7] which apply international standards to the context of imprisonment. They set out the requirements regarding the treatment of prisoners and the management of penal institutions. These rules are not binding in law and are not legally enforceable, but are 'soft law', so they do give guidelines for best practice and recommendations for States Parties who have adopted them. However, they also allow for exceptions if circumstances dictate.

Lord Woolf in his Report on the 1990 riots argued that 'the Prison Service must set security, control and justice in prisons at the right level and it must provide the right balance between them. The stability of the prison system depends on the Prison Service doing so' (Woolf and Tumim 1991: para 1.148). By security, he meant preventing prisoners escaping; by control he meant preventing prisoners causing a disturbance; while 'justice encapsulates the obligation on the Prison Service to treat prisoners with humanity and fairness' (ibid: para 1.149). Lord Woolf concluded that the riots happened because these three elements were out of balance (ibid: para 1.150). Once control is lost, then security is also at risk and 'the ability of the Prison Service to provide conditions which accord with justice will be impaired' (ibid: para 10.41). Conversely, 'the achievement of justice will itself enhance security and control' (ibid: para 14.437).

The Woolf Report was critical of the poor physical conditions in English prisons but stressed that this was not the only or the key factor in the riots. While overcrowding may account for some of the unrest in English prisons, riots occurred in prisons where numbers were declining. The key issue was that the prisoners felt aggrieved that their complaints were not dealt with properly. Justice, as he points out, does not figure in PR 1 (now PR 3), although fair treatment is now emphasised in the current Statement of Purpose. At that time Boards of Visitors dealt with discipline and were able to impose punishments including loss of remission, but they were not seen as sufficiently independent. This led to a sense of injustice—and perceptions here are important, for if individuals see the world as unjust it will influence their actions, whether or not that perception accurately reflects reality. If prisons can achieve justice and prisoners feel that they are being treated fairly, then the problems of disorder, control, and insecurity will diminish. However, if the problem is

---

[7] The full text of the rules can be obtained from http://www.coe.int.

approached from the other standpoint by focusing on security, this is likely to increase the prisoners' sense of injustice. Improving standards of justice inside prisons means giving prisoners reasons for decisions which affect them, such as transfers and segregation, as well as a fair, independent, and expeditious grievance procedure and disciplinary procedure. Transfers against prisoners' wishes were a source of resentment, and a precipitating factor in the riots. If there is also a loss of legitimacy and a sense of unfairness, then relationships between staff and prisoners will be undermined, and in that climate it will be easier for specific incidents to trigger disorder.

Woolf argued for improvements in both physical conditions and grievance and disciplinary procedures. He also advocated housing prisoners as near to their homes as possible by building community prisons, with small self-contained units, near large cities, so that prisoners can stay in contact with their families and visiting will be less onerous for families. However, many prisoners are still now housed far from their homes. Woolf also recommended improvements in home leave and frequency of visits, extending the use of phone cards to all prisons, and removals of limits on the number of letters that prisoners could post.

Prisoners, Woolf argued, should not have to share a cell (Woolf and Tumim 1991: para 11.81), they should have proper access to sanitation (ibid: para 11.97), and the standards of hygiene in prison should be commensurate with those in the community (ibid: para 11.113). The prison system should give all prisoners the opportunity to serve their sentence in a constructive way, making proper use of the time they spend in prison.

The Woolf Report recommended introducing a national system of accredited standards governing the treatment of prisoners and also proposed improvements in the way disciplinary offences are dealt with, recommending that the Boards of Visitors should lose their adjudicative role; this was implemented in 1992. The Boards have now been renamed Independent Monitoring Boards.

The Woolf Report received support in principle from the government, in its White Paper *Custody, Care and Justice* (Home Office 1991). It was also welcomed by prison reformers. The immediate response was improved access to phones and better visiting arrangements, followed by substantial improvements in prison conditions. However, the government said at the time that it would take 25 years to implement all the recommended improvements and Lord Woolf has recently expressed concern over the current state of the prisons (Woolf 2015). Recent prison inspections also have continued to highlight problems (HM Chief Inspector of Prisons 2014, 2015).

Changing prison regimes

National operating standards were introduced in 1994, but they are not legally enforceable and were overtaken by Key Performance Indicator Targets. Changes in the disciplinary system were introduced in 1992. The Prison Rules were subsequently revised in 1999 and have been subsequently amended. So prisoners are now treated with more respect under the decency agenda. Relationships between staff and prisoners have improved compared to the time of the Strangeways riot, although these improvements may be under threat if overcrowding continues.

Each prisoner is now allocated a personal officer, although their involvement varies between prisons. Sentence planning has also been introduced, the purpose of which is to make the best use of the prisoner's time, to reduce the risk of reoffending, to prepare the prisoner for release, to coordinate the custodial and licence elements of the sentence, to inform the parole process, to act as a focal point for staff and prisoner relationships and provide opportunities to review the prisoner's progress, and to assist in targeting resources. The emphasis now is on end-to-end management of the offender throughout his time in custody and on supervision, with much closer cooperation between the Prison and Probation Services and with new service providers from the voluntary and private sector supporting short-term prisoners. The National Probation Service manages high-risk offenders while community rehabilitation companies manage low- and medium-risk offenders.

Comparing prisons with the pre-Woolf era, we find significant improvements in the complaints and disciplinary systems. An Ombudsman was appointed in 1994 as a final means of appeal against decisions in disciplinary hearings. The Prisons and Probation Ombudsman can deal with complaints on a wide range of matters, including adjudications, deaths in custody (since 2004), prison conditions, and the treatment by officers in both state and private prisons. In 2006, the remit of the Ombudsman was extended to deal with complaints from persons detained for immigration reasons.

Following an investigation of complaints the Ombudsman issues a formal report and makes recommendations; while these are not binding, they are usually accepted. However, for a complaint to be eligible the internal complaints procedure of the prison should be exhausted first and the matter must fall within the Ombudsman's remit, so using the Ombudsman is not an effective route for those serving short sentences and a large number of the complaints come from prisoners in high-security prisons. But if the prison fails to respond to the prisoner within six weeks, then the Ombudsman may receive the complaint. Since 1999, the number of complaints received has risen every year and there has also been an increase in the number of complaints deemed eligible. Cases may be resolved by mediating a settlement or upholding the complaint. Some of the complaints are deemed ineligible as they are insufficiently substantial and because it would be a waste of public money to investigate: for example, a prisoner's complaint that the provision of mince pies at a carol concert was a bribe to convert to Christianity (Prisons and Probation Ombudsman 2011: 17).

In 2014/15 the Ombudsman received 4,964 complaints, an increase of 2 per cent on the previous year, and the eligibility rate also increased (Prisons and Probation Ombudsman 2015a: 15). The Ombudsman found in favour of the complainant in 39 per cent of the cases in 2014/15 compared to 34 per cent the previous year (ibid: 10). Although the Ombudsman covers prisons, probation, and immigration referral centres, the majority of complaints concerned prisons: 92 per cent in 2014/15. Complaints were raised on a range of issues including general prison conditions, complaints about staff behaviour, and the conduct of adjudications, but the majority relate to lost property.

So, compared to the early 1990s, there are now considerably more safeguards for prisoners. For example, transfer should not be used as a system of punishment, reasons should be given, and inmates should be advised in writing of the reasons for transfer or segregation within 24 hours. Complaints should be made within seven days to the governor of the prison where the transfer decision was made. However, transfers are still used to juggle the demand for places. Decisions on transfer are reviewable, but the court is unlikely to interfere because it is open to the governor to make the decision if the governor believes the prisoner's presence affects the smooth running of the prison. Prisoners' complaints can also be made to the Independent Monitoring Boards who monitor day-to-day life in prisons and publish annual reports on individual prisons. They may also attend and observe the way serious incidents are handled, for example a death in custody or a riot.

However, the Woolf Report's recommendation for a new Prison Rule prohibiting overcrowding was rejected and his suggestion of using smaller community prisons to allow prisoners to be held nearer their homes has not been implemented. Rather, as we have seen, the trend is currently towards larger prisons, with the closures and mergers of some smaller prisons to achieve economies of scale. Although the Titan prisons proposal was initially shelved, the first is now being constructed in Wrexham, North Wales; it will be the UK's largest prison, holding 2,100 prisoners. Reports by the Prison Inspectorate on individual prisons have revealed continuing problems of poor physical conditions and poor staff relations which indicate that some of the problems still persist. The Chief Inspector has highlighted the problems facing prisons in dealing with increasing numbers of prisoners and budget cuts (HM Chief Inspector of Prisons 2015). In his latest report he noted that the outcomes in relation to safety, respect, purposeful activity, and resettlement assessed in 2014/15 'were the worst for 10 years' (ibid: 7).

There is still insufficient work provision and problems of bullying, violence, and assaults persist and may be under-reported, although reducing the number of assaults is a key goal. NOMS has reported an increase in the number of serious assaults and self-inflicted deaths and has set up a Violence Reduction Project to examine causes of violence and its prevention (NOMS 2015a: 68).

Incentives and privileges

All prisons have an IEP scheme, set up in 1995 under PR 8, in which privileges are earned by good behaviour or by reaching high standards in work or other activities. There were originally three levels: basic, standard, and enhanced. Challenging a decision to place a prisoner on a lower level may be difficult as the courts are reluctant to interfere in the way schemes are run. From the prisoners' standpoint it may be seen as an informal means of discipline without the proper safeguards of the formal disciplinary system. However, changes to the scheme were introduced in 2013 for adult male prisoners in public and private prisons, with a new 'entry' level introduced for prisoners in their first two weeks of sentence in which privileges are restricted and wearing of prison uniforms is compulsory (PSI 30/2013). Prisoners who do not engage then move to the basic level, while those who do engage move to Standard. Other changes included a longer working day, with prisoners not being allowed to watch TV at times they should be working or engaged in purposeful activity; gym access is also made dependent on engagement in rehabilitation. Prisoners have to show that they are working towards their own rehabilitation and that of others, for example by volunteering, but not all prisons offer access to volunteer schemes. The focus in the IEP scheme is on a system of incentives and privileges earned through good behaviour, rather than on prisoners' rights or legitimate expectations. Although the IEP scheme was intended to establish a national framework, the lack of standardisation has led to complaints about the variations in schemes between prisons, which present problems for prisoners who are transferred.

The changes to the IEP scheme introduced in 2013 included restrictions on receiving books and other items from relatives by post or during visits. In response to this a 'Books for Prisoners' campaign was launched and the 'book ban' was challenged in the High Court by a prisoner with a doctorate in English literature. The court ruled in December 2014 that the ban was unlawful, although the restrictions on other items remain.[8] While it was still possible for prisoners to obtain books from libraries, the availability of books varied between prisons. The court rejected the view that books should be seen as a privilege as access to books is seen as a key element of rehabilitation. Prisoners also have a right to access reading material under the European Prison Rules.

---

[8] R (on the application of Barbara Gordon-Jones v Secretary of State for Justice and the Governor of HMP Send (5 December 2014) EWHC 3997 Admin.

Security and justice

It has also been argued that justice has been subordinated to security and control. The effect of the escapes in the mid-1990s was that all prisons became more security-conscious. Following the escape from Whitemoor in 1994, the Woodcock Report published in 1994 was very critical of security procedures, and concern intensified after the escapes from Parkhurst in 1995. The Learmont Report (1995) was also critical of the standards of security, following which the then Director General of the Prison Service, Derek Lewis, was sacked. The effect of enhanced security measures meant cuts in home leave, restrictions on contact with the community, and extra time spent in cells, which added to prisoners' sense of injustice, especially as it also affected prisoners not involved in escapes or disorder. Prisoners have been handcuffed and chained during medical procedures on hospital visits (HM Chief Inspector of Prisons 2011a: 43). In 2014, a prisoner was chained to his hospital bed in Winchester as he lay dying, despite his being in a coma. This policy is now being reviewed.

Reports of the Prison Inspectorate have also expressed concern over the use of segregation and the continued detention of IPP prisoners beyond their tariff. The Prison Inspectorate found that living conditions in segregation units in older prisons were poor, particularly at Leeds, Liverpool, and Pentonville (HM Chief Inspector of Prisons 2014: 28). Segregation may also have adverse effects on prisoners' mental health, especially if they already suffer from mental health problems (see Edgar and Rickford 2009).

The modern prison regime is much more security-aware, using technological means of surveillance, such as CCTV, as well as greater staff surveillance, but escapes still occasionally occur, often while in transit. The emphasis should be on dynamic security, which means relying on good prisoner–staff relations so that problems or tensions do not escalate and prison staff are aware of developing problems and can deal with them.[9] This is more effective than relying on physical barriers or technological surveillance alone. In dealing with difficult prisoners, only the minimum amount of force necessary to prevent harm to others should be used, and for the shortest possible time.

There has also been an increasing emphasis on drugs control and policing through mandatory drug testing. The rate of drug misuse in prisons is measured by the rate of positive results from random mandatory drug testing (MDT). In 2012/13 it was 6.9 per cent, compared to 7.4 per cent in 2002 (NOMS 2015a: 32). It is estimated that over a quarter of adult and young adult males arrive at prison with drug problems, but others may start using drugs in prison. Prescription drugs may also be diverted by prisoners for recreational use and there has been evidence of the use of new synthetic drugs. Drug-testing powers in prison were increased under the Offender Rehabilitation Act 2014. Positive rates from the MDT have declined, but the tests do not detect all the prescription drugs which may be passed or sold to prisoners, or the new psychoactive substances finding their way into prison such as Spice, the collective name for a group of synthetic cannabinoids, which includes Black Mamba. Moreover, prisoners are finding new ways of smuggling drugs into prison. For example, prison officers intercepted a drone carrying drugs at HMP Bedford in March 2015.

8.4.2 Suicide and self-harm

But rioting is not the only expression of dissatisfaction or the only way prisoners deal with the pains of imprisonment. Problems with the experience of imprisonment may also

---

[9] See European Prison Rule 51.2.

be expressed through suicide and self-harm. Prison suicides are reviewed by the Prison Inspectorate and deaths in custody, which include suicides, deaths from natural causes, drug overdoses, accidents, homicides, or other causes, have been investigated by the Prisons Ombudsman since 2004. Although prison suicides may be attributed to mental health problems, isolation is a contributory factor, so any policies which increase contact with home may reduce the risk. Fazel *et al.* (2005) studied suicides of male prisoners in England and Wales between 1978 and 2003 and found that the suicide rate for males in prisons was five times higher than for males outside prison, and 18 times higher for boys aged 15–17. Being on segregation also increases the risk. Other risk factors include mental health problems and substance misuse. Several of the cases concerned offenders who had committed offences against a close relative. Precipitating factors in the period leading up to the death included breakdown of relationships, bullying or intimidation from other prisoners, and upcoming court appearances (ibid: 37). Reducing suicide was part of the 'decency' agenda and proposals have been made to address this problem (see Dear 2006).

The Prisons and Probation Ombudsman (PPO) surveyed all suicides in 2013/14 when there was a large increase in suicides in custody, with 89 self-inflicted deaths compared to 52 in the previous year—an increase of 64 per cent (PPO 2015b). Vulnerability may be increased because of segregation and lack of activity. Although there was an association between suicides and increased crowding and more time spent in cells, in one-quarter of the cases the deaths occurred amongst inmates who had over five hours a day outside their cells. The risk increased significantly in the first month of custody. The Ombudsman recommends better support on entry into prison and the use of segregation only in exceptional circumstances for those at risk of suicide. There were also a number of cases where the individuals who took their own lives were on restraining orders, preventing contact with a partner or family member because of relationship breakdown or a history of offences of violence against family members. Issues of debt and bullying relating to drug use in prison were also highlighted. Twenty-nine per cent of the prisoners were being managed under the ACCT (Assessment, Care in Custody and Teamwork) procedures for those at risk of suicide or self-harm when they died, which raises the issue of whether those procedures were being implemented properly or whether further revision is needed. The majority of suicides were white males and one-third were prisoners on remand.

A further concern is the high incidence of self-harm amongst prisoners. Vollm (2009) found that the prevalence of self-harm in the UK female prison population was high, and this confirmed the findings of earlier studies. However, there has also been an increase in the number of self-harming incidents in male prisons, with 17,474 incidents in 2013/14, compared to 16,399 in 2012/13 (HM Chief Inspector of Prisons 2015: 28).

Although there have been improvements in prison health care overall, with the transfer of responsibility for prison health care to the NHS, clearly the mental health problems of prisoners remain challenging. In 2013 NHS England took over responsibility for commissioning of services from the local primary care trusts. Health care in prisons should be provided at the same standard as health care outside on the principle of equivalence stipulated in the European Prison Rules.

8.5 Prison privatisation

8.5.1 The privatisation debate

A further significant development in the 1990s was the introduction of prison privatisation. The provisions for contracting out prisons and also escort duties were introduced in the 1991 Criminal Justice Act (ss. 80–88) and those for contracting out of parts, functions, and activities of public sector prisons in the Criminal Justice and Public Order Act 1994 (ss. 96–97). In 2015 there were 14 contracted-out prisons: Dovegate, Altcourse, Parc, Lowdham Grange, Forest Bank, Ashfield, Rye Hill, Bronzefield, Peterborough, Doncaster, Northumberland, Oakwood, Thameside, and Birmingham, which was the first public sector prison to be transferred to the private sector in October 2011. The effect of these changes means that the proportion of the prison population currently held in private prisons is higher than that in the United States.

A prison previously built and run by the Prison Service may be contracted out to a private company. New prisons may also be privately designed, constructed, managed, and financed, following which the Prison Service pays a fee for each place. Ancillary services within the prison, such as cleaning or catering, and canteens and shops have also been privatised. Competition and contestability has also been extended to rehabilitation services inside and outside prison with payment by results as part of the *Transforming Rehabilitation* agenda (Ministry of Justice 2013a). Pilots were commenced at HMP Doncaster and Peterborough and, as we noted in Chapter 1, these did show a fall in reconviction rates, based on a period of 12 months from release (Ministry of Justice 2014a). Outsourcing and public–private partnerships have also been increasingly used in policing (see White 2014).

When prison privatisation was proposed in the 1980s it was championed as a more cost-efficient way of running the prison system, as advocates argued that private companies could construct, manage, and run prisons more cheaply than the state and build them more quickly to meet the ever-increasing demand for prison places. It was thought that competition between private companies for contracts would encourage the provision of better standards at lower cost, in contrast to the monopoly position of state prisons at the time, as penalty clauses could be written into contracts to discourage breaches. It was also argued that the private prisons would be more innovative in design and management, and avoid the problems of industrial conflict, by recruiting new staff.

However, the case for privatisation was vigorously opposed.[10] It was argued that free competition could not be guaranteed as the company which wins the initial contract is likely to dominate the industry; because of its experience its costs may be lower, which will give the state an interest in renewing the contract, which may deter other companies from submitting bids. The successful company may then be able to negotiate higher prices for average standards, as happened in the US. In the UK the market is now dominated by relatively few companies, with just three companies involved at the present time: G4S, SERCO, and SODEXO. Similarly, the rehabilitation market has also been captured by a small group of companies. Twenty-one contracts were awarded to eight community rehabilitation companies in December 2014 (see Chapter 10, sections 10.4.3 and 10.6.1).

A company's obligations to its shareholders may conflict with its duty to provide the best conditions for inmates, as there will be pressures to lower costs to maximise profits. For example, if private companies reduce costs by recruiting fewer staff, paying lower wages, or reducing training, this may increase risks to staff and prisoners, as staff may be unable to manage difficult prisoners. It could also be argued that punishment should be exclusively the prerogative of the state or the integrity of the criminal justice system will be undermined. Penalty clauses may be insufficient to maintain standards if penalties are set too

---

[10] For further discussion on prison privatisation, see Matthews (1989); Schichor (1995), Jago and Thompson (2001); Prison Reform Trust (2005); Genders and Player (2007); Gaes (2008); Barak-Erez (2011); and Ludlow (2014).

low. In any case, problems may persist while the contract runs its course, which could last 25 years, or before a new contract partner is found.

Critics also argue that private companies are not necessarily cheaper providers. Comparing costs accurately may be difficult as private companies have been given low-risk and therefore low-cost prisoners and, in the early stages of privatisation, the programme was focused on remand prisoners. Similarly in probation the community rehabilitation companies have been given low- and medium-risk prisoners while the Probation Service retains high-risk prisoners. Moreover, public sector state prisons have become more cost-effective and the Prison Service has won contracts in open competition with the private sector. It has also been suggested that cost per place is actually higher in most categories of prison in the private sector than in the public sector.[11]

There are also issues regarding control and accountability, as it is arguably harder to control the private sector. There is a rigorous system of auditing public bodies and parliamentary controls over ministers, but private contractors are more removed from democratic controls. However, all private prisons have 'controllers' linking them to NOMS to ensure that companies comply with their contracts. The overall management of the private prison is in the hands of the director, an employee of the private company, but appointed by NOMS. The review and scrutiny mechanisms in the state sector, including parliamentary scrutiny, Independent Monitoring Boards, the National Audit Office, the Prison Inspectorate, and the Prisons and Probation Ombudsman, also apply to contracted-out prisons. The prisoner seeking redress for grievances will have access to the courts and to the Ombudsman. Private prisons are subject to the Prison Act and Prison Rules and the European Prison Rules and prisoners in these prisons have the same legal rights as those in public sector prisons, including the protection of the HRA 1998. Prison officers, or custody officers, receive similar training to public sector prison officers.

If control of a private prison was lost, during a riot, for example, the state would have the power to take it over. In this sense, the state is still responsible for punishment, even within a contracted-out prison; it has a responsibility to see that the service is provided properly. Nonetheless, there have been concerns over incidents of mistreatment in contracted-out prisons, including, for example, the case of Alton Manning, who was unlawfully killed through choking from an illegal neck lock while being restrained at Blakenhurst (Inquest 1998). Concerns were also raised in 2015 over the treatment of children at the Medway Secure Training Centre in Kent, run by G4S, which are being investigated.

8.5.2 **The experience of privatisation**

Research has been conducted to assess the relative strengths and weaknesses of public and private prisons in England and Wales. Public sector prisons have moved closer to the ethos of the private prison, under the influence of the New Managerialism. Indeed, defenders of privatisation argue that it is precisely the use of performance testing which has improved the standards in the public sector. Public sector prisons have also been under pressure to achieve similar efficiencies to private sector prisons through the benchmarking process. But the challenge now is how to facilitate and sustain creative innovative regimes, at a time of high numbers and limited resources and staff cuts. Private prison management was endorsed as a model for public sector financial management by the Carter Review of Prisons (Carter 2007).

James *et al.* (1997) conducted fieldwork in the Wolds and Woodhill. The Wolds was the first private prison, opening in 1992, although it returned to the public sector in 2013 and

---

[11] See Hansard, House of Commons, written answer 9 January 2007.

has now merged with HMP Everthorpe to become HMP Humber, while Woodhill was a new public sector prison which opened in 1992. James *et al.* were struck by the similarities between the two prisons in terms of their 'business like approach to management' and found that the regime at the Wolds was innovative and successful. An ethos of treating prisoners with respect prevailed which allowed for a normalisation of the prison environment. There were good staff relations, more time out of cells, better access to facilities—although because of prisoner apathy they were not always used—a high number of hours in purposeful activities, and good mechanisms for accountability.

However, the researchers also found similar innovations and achievements and good staff–prisoner relations in some new public sector prisons, including Woodhill, which opened in 1992. It aimed to provide a humane regime where as much time was spent out of cells as possible, the regime was relaxed, and prisoners wore their own clothes. With its strong focus on financial planning, careful budgeting, and devolution of budgets to units within the prison, Woodhill was similar in many ways to a private prison, although the conditions there were later criticised by the Chief Inspector of Prisons (HM Chief Inspector of Prisons 1998).

James *et al.* (1997) also examined the regimes at Blakenhurst, then a contracted-out prison, and three new public sector prisons, Belmarsh, Bullingdon, and High Down, and concluded that there was no necessary connection between innovation in regime delivery and contracted-out management status. They found that prisoners were treated with respect in both types of prison, and some public prisons had a strong value-for-money ethos with effective and high-quality senior managers. Physical conditions are usually better in newer prisons than older ones, irrespective of their public or private status.

We also find disturbances and disorder in private as well as public sector prisons. Since 1996, there have been disturbances at the Wolds, drug problems and incidents of assaults, disorder, and bullying at Doncaster, and disorder at Parc Prison, where the contractors have been fined for failing to meet minimum standards and the provision of health care has been criticised (HM Chief Inspector of Prisons 2011a: 63). There has also been overcrowding at private prisons including Doncaster, Blakenhurst, the Wolds, and Altcourse (Park 2000; HM Chief Inspector of Prisons 2007, 2011a). UKDS (now Sodexo) was fined in 1994 after losing control of Blakenhurst and the prison was later returned to the public sector. Rye Hill prison has also been criticised for failing to provide a safe regime (HM Chief Inspector of Prisons 2005). There is a higher turnover of staff in private prisons than public sector prisons, which has been attributed to the poorer working conditions and lower pay in the private sector. The National Audit Office has expressed concern over inexperienced staff working in private prisons and over the number of assaults at Dovegate, Altcourse, Ashfield, Rye Hill, and Forest Bank. By 2001 fines imposed on private prisons amounted to almost £1 million, and these related to failings including double occupancy and assaults on staff and prisoners (Jago and Thompson 2001). There is also a lower staff–prisoner ratio which may have safety implications. At Oakwood Prison, run by G4S, there was violent disorder in January 2014, and staffing levels were highlighted in a review of that incident. Although the prison's running costs were very low, there were concerns this had negative implications for the security of the regime.

A 2005 review of ten private prisons by the Prison Reform Trust found mixed results, with variations in performance. The review also raised questions regarding accountability, conflicts of interest, and profiteering from the use of private finance and the pressure for economies of scale in commercial enterprises, as well as highlighting the poorer pay and working conditions in the private sector (Prison Reform Trust 2005).

Privatisation is now deeply embedded in current penal policy; private prisons are accepted by all the main parties, and the continuing focus on contestability and the involvement of the private sector and voluntary sector has spread to other areas of the criminal justice system, principally to punishment and rehabilitation in the community (see Chapter 10). Despite Labour's hostility to prison privatisation in opposition, the Blair government persisted with the privatisation programme and commitment to contestability was extended by the Brown administration to community punishment. The Carter Review of Correctional Services (Carter 2003) and the Carter Report on Prisons (Carter 2007) advocated the expanding use of competition from private and voluntary sectors in the Prison and Probation Services to increase effectiveness and value for money. The Coalition government was strongly committed to the involvement of these sectors in rehabilitation services within and outside prison and the Conservative government has made clear its commitment to continuing with this programme. Use of the private sector in the provision of punishment and rehabilitation will remain a key element of penal policy in the next five years, although the gap between public and private prison costs has narrowed.

Ludlow (2014) has challenged the desirability of using competition as a policy mechanism to improve public services such as prisons and stresses the need for new and stronger regulatory limits to 'markets'. She conducted fieldwork on the privatisation of HMP Birmingham in 2011 and, from her data, concluded that 'competition does not work as the British Government thinks or hopes or as neo-liberalism would suggest' (Ludlow 2014: 3). The Prison Officers Association has also remained strongly opposed to privatisation, arguing that prisons should remain in the public sector as privatisation has offered no benefits and that the voluntary sector should be used only to support the work of prison officers and not as a cheap replacement. It now has many members working for private companies in prisons and immigration removal centres.

8.6 Challenging prison conditions

As well as expressing their grievances through riots, prisoners have challenged the conditions in which they are held through the courts, using private and public law. Actions have been brought in negligence, but the court will consider the context and judge by the standards appropriate to a prison. Judicial review has been more successful in providing prisoners with an avenue to challenge administrative decisions and as a means of achieving justice and, in the event of a withdrawal from the Convention, it would retain this crucial role. Decisions on disciplinary matters, categorisation, transfer and segregation, and mandatory life sentences have been subjected to judicial scrutiny as the disciplinary regime of the prison has been integrated into public law since the late 1970s. Generally, judges have felt more comfortable dealing with quasi-judicial matters, such as disciplinary hearings, rather than intervening in relation to prison conditions. The Prison Rules allow for considerable discretion, but this should not be exercised unreasonably. Before the Human Rights Act 1998, the criterion would have been the test in *Associated Provincial Picture Houses v Wednesbury Corporation* (1948), but now the courts will consider compliance with the European Convention on Human Rights where rights issues are raised, so the test will be that of proportionality (see *Daly* (2001) and *Huang* (2007)). Human rights jurisprudence has become increasingly important in prisoners' litigation (van Zyl Smit and Snacken 2009; Easton 2011a, 2013). Prisoners may also use the internal complaints procedure, make complaints to the Prisons and Probation Ombudsman, and contact their members of Parliament. Prisons are also assessed annually by the Prison Inspector using the tests of safety, respect, purposeful activity, and resettlement in assessing prison conditions.

Changes in legal aid provision were introduced by LASPO 2012 and came into force in April 2013 (see Ministry of Justice 2013g). Further restrictions, including limiting criminal legal aid for prison law matters, have been introduced since December 2013. Prisoners are expected to use the internal complaints system and the Prisons and Probation Ombudsman if necessary. However, support will continue to be available for cases involving determination of a criminal charge, for the purposes of Article 6, or concerning ongoing detention, where Article 5(4) issues are raised, where liberty is at stake, and where legal representation is a requirement under *Tarrant* (1985). A challenge to cuts in legal aid available for prison law cases brought by the Howard League and Prisoners' Advice Service was rejected by the High Court in March 2014.[12] However, the Howard League is appealing this decision.

8.6.1 **Human rights, fairness, and justice**

The protections afforded prisoners both internally and through the courts have enhanced the safety of prisoners and raised standards in prison. Procedural justice has improved substantially since the early 1990s, but there is considerable variation in prison conditions between prisons, as illustrated by the performance tables and by empirical research on prisoners' experiences, such as Meek's survey of high-security prisoners (Meek 2008).

Rights are important to prisoners because they are vulnerable and dependent, as they are unable to obtain access to key goods such as work and health care by their own efforts. Strengthening rights, fairness, and justice also provides positive benefits to the Prison Service as reducing dissatisfaction improves good order within prisons. It also creates a better climate for the rehabilitation of prisoners (Easton 2008d). Respect for rights is also a key means of ensuring the legitimacy of the prison system. The value of a human rights-based approach is that enforceable rights offer a means of maintaining and ensuring minimum standards inside prison and arguably provide greater protection than the performance testing of New Managerialism, particularly at a time of increased pressure on resources and a strong focus on public protection and risk management. At the same time, negotiating human rights has itself become a risk for prison governance (see Murphy and Whitty 2007).

A right to a minimum standard of living would potentially contribute to the improvement of prison conditions, provided that there are adequate enforcement mechanisms in place. An open grievance procedure enhances the legitimacy of the prison authority structure. There should be a right to the maximum autonomy compatible with the rights and freedoms of others and with the fact of imprisonment. The Prison Service has resisted the move towards a culture of rights, preferring to use the currency of privileges and incentives which are not legally enforceable entitlements. They can be withdrawn and used as a disciplinary measure to maintain good order and discipline within the prison. Moreover, guaranteeing legally enforceable rights is much more expensive both in terms of compliance and in defending claims made in relation to alleged breaches.

Demands for rights have met with some resistance from governments and the Prison Service because of a concern with the financial costs if it opened the floodgates to litigation, but there are disincentives for prisoners to complain, such as a fear of being seen as a troublemaker. Some prisoners may also lack the literacy skills needed to bring an action. The requirement for leave for judicial review and the continuing scope for discretion have also acted as a brake on prisoners' rights litigation. Moreover, even when prisoners have succeeded in their claims, the level of damages awarded has been relatively low. In some

---

[12] *The Queen acting on the application of the Howard League and the Prisoners' Advice Service v The Lord Chancellor* EWHC (Admin) 709 (17 March 2014) http://www.bailii.org/ew/cases/EWHC/Admin/2014/709.html.

cases, such as *Firth and others v UK* (2014), the Strasbourg Court has decided that a declaration of incompatibility has provided just satisfaction without payment of damages.

8.6.2 **Rights Conventions**

In English law, the approach of the courts has been that prisoners have the same civil rights as non-prisoners except for those taken away expressly or impliedly by imprisonment.[13] But this clearly falls far short of according prisoners special rights by virtue of the fact that they are prisoners. Because of this *lacuna*, international human rights instruments have particular significance for the prison system in the UK.

Article 5 of the Universal Declaration of Human Rights states that '[n]o one shall be subjected to torture or to cruel, inhuman or degrading treatment or punishment'. The rights in the Declaration are elaborated in rights instruments, including the International Covenant on Civil and Political Rights (ICCPR). The UK has ratified the ICCPR, which includes general provisions of relevance to punishment, such as the right to life and the right not to be detained arbitrarily. Article 10 deals specifically with the penal system:

1. All persons deprived of their liberty shall be treated with humanity and with respect for the inherent dignity of the human person.
2. (a) Accused persons shall, save in exceptional circumstances, be segregated from convicted persons and shall be subject to separate treatment appropriate to their status as unconvicted persons;
   (b) Accused juvenile persons shall be separated from adults and brought as speedily as possible for adjudication.
3. The penitentiary system shall comprise the treatment of prisoners the essential aim of which shall be their reformation and rehabilitation. Juvenile offenders shall be segregated from adults and accorded treatment appropriate to their legal status.

However, the most significant rights protection in recent years has come from the ECHR, which protects a number of rights relevant to the context of imprisonment and detention (see van Zyl Smit and Snacken 2009; Easton 2011a, 2013). Even before the HRA 1998, the ECHR influenced the English courts, although the recommendations of the European Court of Human Rights were persuasive, not binding. Many of the issues raised in the early Convention cases are also now covered by the European Prison Rules. However, in its jurisprudence, the European Court of Human Rights has tended to focus on the rights protected by the Convention rather than the standards in the European Prison Rules.

In addition, prisons are inspected periodically, and on an ad hoc basis where there are specific concerns, by the European Committee for the Prevention of Torture. Although the recommendations of the Committee are not binding, its visits to the UK and other jurisdictions have generated a jurisprudence on the psychological impact of imprisonment. Its 2009 report on the UK raised issues regarding the impact of overcrowding, the problems faced by IPP prisoners, and the treatment of young offenders (Council of Europe 2009). Its latest report arising from its visit to the UK in 2012 raised concerns regarding overcrowding at Barlinnie prison and the excessive time spent in cells, the problem of prisoners feeling unsafe at Kilmarnock, and problems in immigration removal centres (Council of Europe 2014). It recommended that prisoners with severe mental health problems should not be held in segregation units but should be transferred to appropriate inpatient facilities and that more help should be given to women

---

[13] *Raymond v Honey* (1983).

prisoners with personality disorders, that there should be enhanced safeguards in relation to discipline and segregation, and that more support should be given to foreign national prisoners.

The UK has also signed the Optional Protocol to the Convention against Torture (OPCAT), which means that the UK has to establish a National Preventive Mechanism (NPM) which makes regular and independent visits to places of detention. Instead of creating a new body, the NPM draws on the work of 18 designated existing bodies including the Prison Inspectorate, the Independent Monitoring Board, and the Care Quality Commission, with the work of the NPM coordinated by the Inspectorate of Prisons; it published its first report in 2011 (National Preventive Mechanism 2011). Its fifth report, published in December 2014, highlighted the issues of safe restraint and excessive restraint and noted the increased awareness of vulnerability in custody in relation to age, disability, and mental illness, as well as the pressures arising from increased detention and cuts in resources (National Preventive Mechanism 2014). In 2014/15 it focused on the issue of solitary confinement and isolation.

The European Convention on Human Rights has been extensively used by UK prisoners and this has had considerable impact on prisoners' lives. Prisoners retain their rights under the ECHR notwithstanding their imprisonment and restrictions on those rights need to be justified within the criteria set out in the relevant Articles of the ECHR. Convention compliance is also considered when introducing regime changes.

Legislation has also been amended in response to decisions in the European Court of Human Rights. In some cases settlements have also been reached in anticipation of the Court's decisions. However, in other cases, notably voting rights for prisoners, successive UK governments have resisted changes demanded by the Court since 2005.

The ECHR has improved the experience of punishment in a number of areas. For example, Article 2 has been used to challenge the procedures for dealing with deaths in custody, in *Edwards v UK* (2002), and in relation to the failure to prevent suicide in *Keenan v UK* (2001). An independent and expeditious review should be undertaken of any death in custody. Article 3 has been used to challenge inhuman and degrading prison conditions as well as whole-life sentences. In relation to Article 3 the Strasbourg Court has been critical of whole-life sentences where the prisoner is offered no prospect of review or release in *Vinter and others v UK* (2013) and *Hutchinson v UK* (2015).

Article 5 has been used to challenge the lawfulness of continued detention by mentally disordered offenders as well as by discretionary life and IPP prisoners (see Chapter 5). Article 6 has been used to gain access to the courts, in *Golder v UK* (1975), and to challenge the conduct of disciplinary hearings. Article 8, the right to private and family life, has been used to challenge interference with prisoners' correspondence and excessive restrictions on prison visits, and to improve contact with prisoners' families. However, restrictions on correspondence with prisoners' families may be permitted under Article 8(2). Article 8 has also been used to successfully challenge the denial of access to artificial insemination (AI) in *Dickson v UK* (2007). Following this case, the rules relating to applications for AI were modified. Article 8 was also successfully used by a prisoner in asserting the right to correspond freely with a medical specialist regarding his case, in *Szuluk v UK* (2009). Article 12 has been used to claim the right to temporary release from prison to marry in *Hamer v UK* (1979). If prisoners are refused temporary release on security grounds, they may be married inside prison. These rights also extend to same sex partners under the Marriage (Same Sex Couples) Act 2013.

Article 3 of Protocol No. 1 has been used to challenge the ban on convicted prisoners voting in *Hirst v UK* (2005). Article 10 has been used to protect prisoners' right to freedom of expression, so prisoners may communicate with the media where they are raising matters of legitimate public interest affecting prisoners or the prison system and any restrictions on their rights must be proportionate and satisfy the requirements of Article 10(2).[14] The Court has also recognised the rights of prisoners' relatives, in the case of *Dickson* (2007), which concerned the reproductive and family rights of the prisoner's wife, but also in the case of *Wainwright v UK* (2006), which related to the searching of prisoners' relatives on a prison visit.

From the standpoint of the Strasbourg Court, prisoners possess rights rather than expectations or privileges. However, the potential protection of the Convention is limited by the fact that several of the rights protected by it may be qualified, to prevent crime, in the interests of national security, and to protect the rights and freedom of others, which may be particularly appropriate to the context of imprisonment, and these qualifications have been interpreted liberally by the Court. States have in the past been accorded a wide margin of appreciation in interpreting and applying the Convention but in recent years the Strasbourg Court has become much more assertive. It has characterised the Convention as a living instrument to be interpreted in the light of present-day conditions—that is, dynamically—and stressed the need to strike a balance between the demands of the general interests of the community and the protection of individuals' fundamental rights, using the principle of proportionality. It has also become more critical of limitations on prisoners' rights and living conditions which are based on resource grounds. In many of the above contested cases, the approach of the Strasbourg Court has been more favourable than the domestic courts to the rights of the prisoner, which has brought it into conflict with both the UK government and judiciary (see Ashworth 2014).

8.6.3 **The Human Rights Act 1998**

Since the HRA 1998 came into force, reliance on Convention rights has been further enhanced. The HRA 1998 incorporated the ECHR into domestic law. Legislation must be interpreted so as to be compatible with the ECHR. If it is not possible to do so, the court should issue a declaration of incompatibility. Section 6 of the HRA 1998 makes it unlawful for public authorities to act in ways which are incompatible with the European Convention. The HRA 1998 applies to private companies if they are responsible for areas of activity which were previously in the public sector, so the Act clearly can be used against private prisons. Companies managing contracted-out prisons perform a statutory-based activity and are constrained by the same statutes and statutory instruments as public prisons, namely the Prison Act and Prison Rules. The Human Rights Act also applies to the Independent Monitoring Boards (formerly Boards of Visitors) and the Parole Board. When the HRA 1998 came into force the Prison Service took the view that its policies operating at the time were compliant with the ECHR but, since then, the application of some of these policies has been successfully challenged.

Because of the amount of time it has taken in the past for a case to be heard at Strasbourg, the ECHR was of value only to those serving longer sentences. With the HRA 1998 this problem has been substantially reduced. If a case does ultimately go to Strasbourg the procedures there have also been streamlined, with the abolition of the Commission in 1999, which came into effect in October 2000.

Before the Act, pursuing a Convention case was a burdensome and lengthy procedure. The original incident in the case of *Campbell and Fell*, for example, occurred in 1976, and the European Court's judgment was published in 1984. Those whose

---

[14] See *R v SSHD ex parte Simms and O'Brien* (2000).

Convention rights are infringed can now bring proceedings and claim remedies, including damages, in the domestic courts. A Prison Service policy may be challenged under the HRA 1998, if rights issues are raised. Prisoners should be informed of their entitlements and responsibilities on induction into prison (PSI 07/2015). *A Human Rights Information Booklet for Prisoners* has also been prepared by the Prison Reform Trust (Prison Reform Trust 2014b).

Although in the past in the domestic courts judges have been reluctant to acknowledge prisoners' rights, they have clearly responded more favourably to prisoners' rights claims since the HRA 1998 came into force, because a rights culture is now more deeply embedded in domestic law. Prisoners have increasingly used Convention rights to challenge prison regimes as well as securing procedural fairness. Indeed, prisoners' use of the Convention has been an essential element of the attack by the Conservative government and also the media on the Human Rights Act and rights culture in general. The media has also played an influential role in shaping the debate on prisoners' rights through its emphasis on critiques rather than defences of rights (see McNulty *et al.* 2014).

There have been several challenges by life-sentenced prisoners to delays in parole reviews for mandatory lifers following the European Court of Human Rights' decision in *Stafford v UK* (2002). However, the English courts have subsequently stressed in *R (Middleton) v Secretary of State for the Home Department* (2003) that the authorities should be allowed a reasonable time to take account of any changes. Following *Stafford* the arrangements for parole reviews have been amended so that all mandatory life prisoners who are near the end of their tariff will have a review which complies with Article 5(4). The review is conducted first on the papers and a recommendation is made; then either party, if unhappy with the recommendation, can request an oral hearing.

The House of Lords has also held that the Home Secretary's power to set minimum tariffs for mandatory life-sentence prisoners under s. 29 of the Crime (Sentences) Act 1997 breaches Article 6(1) of the ECHR, because the tariff should be set by an independent and impartial tribunal and not by the Home Secretary. The House of Lords therefore issued a declaration of incompatibility on this matter in *R (Anderson) v Secretary of the State for the Home Department* (2002). The courts rather than the Minister now have the responsibility of determining the punitive part of the sentence.

The Criminal Justice Act 2003 subsequently set out the principles by which judges fix minimum tariffs and requires judges to give reasons in court if they impose a term inconsistent with those principles. Successful challenges to delays in the parole process have been made by prisoners serving determinate sentences: these delays have been held to be unlawful and a breach of Article 5(4) (see *R (Johnson) v Secretary of State for the Home Department and another* [2007]). In *R v Parole Board ex parte Smith; R v Parole Board ex parte West* (2005) UKHL 1, the House of Lords said that determinate prisoners on licence should have an oral hearing to consider recall to prison in order to satisfy Article 5(4).

There have also been changes in relation to disciplinary procedures. Until 2002 the power to award additional days was vested in the governor. However, in *Ezeh and Connors v UK* (2002) the European Court of Human Rights ruled that only independent adjudicators, not prison governors, may impose additional days as punishment for disciplinary offences. Ezeh and Connors were charged separately with using threatening language and assault. They were found guilty at hearings before the governor at which they were not represented. Ezeh received 40 additional days and Connors seven additional days. The European Court of Human Rights deemed that, given the charges they faced and the extent of the penalty, Article 6 was engaged, and the refusal to allow representation did violate Article 6(3)(c).

Following that decision, the governor should decide whether a charge is so serious that it could lead to additional days if the prisoner is found guilty (PR 53A(1)). If so, the governor must refer the case to an independent adjudicator, in which case the prisoner must be offered the opportunity to seek legal representation (PR 54(3)). If the charge will not incur additional days' punishment, then the governor can conduct the adjudication (PR 54A(2)(b)). If the governor does proceed, but it becomes clear that additional days should be awarded, the governor can then refer the case to an independent adjudicator, during the hearing or after the hearing, but before imposing punishment (PR 53A(3)). The independent adjudicator can award punishments including additional days (PSI 47/2011). The most serious offences would be referred to the police by the governor and prosecuted in court.

But while more human rights cases may now be brought in the domestic courts, this does not mean that all will succeed, as many cases taken to Strasbourg in the past by prisoners failed. While cases on access to the courts and interference with privileged correspondence have met with success in Strasbourg, cases on prison conditions have been less successful. Prisoners are therefore more likely to succeed if they focus on areas such as correspondence, access to lawyers, family contact, disciplinary procedures, and treatment of life-sentence prisoners, or reviews of their detention, rather than challenging prison conditions. Even if those conditions are harsh, the nature of the prison environment means that considerable weight will be given to issues of security in both Strasbourg and the domestic courts. In *R (G) v Home Secretary* [2005] a prisoner, who had been held in a Protected Witness Unit (PWU), committed further offences after release from prison. When he was returned to prison, he was initially detained in a PWU, but was then transferred as a category A prisoner to a self-contained unit at HMP Belmarsh. A challenge to his categorisation and conditions by judicial review failed. However, in *R (Rowen) v Governor of HMP Kirkham* [2009] a judicial review challenge to a re-categorisation of a prisoner from D to C was successfully challenged and the decision quashed on grounds of irrationality and the failure to give relevant reasons for the decision.

There are also difficulties with the ECHR itself, particularly the fact that it does not include social or economic rights, reflecting the political context in which it was drafted in response to civil rights violations in Europe in the 1930s and 1940s. However, social rights are assuming more importance in international human rights law (see Búrca and de Witte 2005; Fredman 2008; King 2012; Riedel *et al.* 2014). On the positive side, however, the enactment of the HRA 1998 means that domestic courts are obliged to consider rights issues in all areas of law. The increasing pressure to improve standards from international rights jurisprudence has co-existed uneasily with the principle of less eligibility, the importance of which has been eroded (Easton 2013). The Strasbourg Court itself has become more interventionist in relation to sentencing, criminal procedure, and prison conditions, with increasing emphasis on the possibility of rehabilitation for prisoners serving whole-life terms in *Vinter v UK* (2013) and *Hutchinson v UK* (2015t).

A further conduit by means of which international standards enter into penal management is through the revised and updated European Prison Rules adopted by the Committee of Ministers of the Council of Europe in January 2006. The rules cover a wide range of areas of prison life including health care, work, recreation, and procedural fairness, including the opportunity to raise complaints. Although these do not amount to enforceable rights, they do reflect the jurisprudence of the Strasbourg Court. The revised rules take account of changes in the penal field since the 1980s, the case law and jurisprudence of the European Court of Human Rights on prison conditions, and the Reports of the European Committee for the Prevention of Torture and Inhuman or Degrading

Treatment or Punishment. The changes cover a range of issues, including health care in prison, disciplinary measures, and conditional release.

8.6.4 **Prisoners and the right to vote**

An important area where a Convention challenge has succeeded in the European Court of Human Rights is in relation to prisoner disenfranchisement. However, the Court's recommendation of changes to the law has met with considerable resistance from successive UK governments. In *Hirst v UK* in October 2005, a former prisoner argued that the provisions preventing convicted prisoners from voting in s. 3 of the Representation of the People Act 1969, as amended in 1983 and 2000, violated Article 3 of Protocol No. 1 of the ECHR, which imposes on states the obligation to hold free elections under conditions which will ensure the 'free expression of the people in the choice of the legislature'.[15] The majority of the Strasbourg Court concluded that a blanket restriction which applies regardless of individual circumstances or the gravity of the offence falls outside the margin of appreciation. The UK government had not considered fully whether such a ban was necessary. The impact of the ban excluded thousands of citizens from voting. Voting by convicted prisoners has been permitted in some other jurisdictions for many years, for example, in South Africa.

Following *Hirst* (2005) the UK government undertook a lengthy consultation process to consider whether some categories of convicted prisoner should be permitted to vote and the possible mechanisms for voting. The first Consultation Paper sought views on the general principle of restoring the vote and possible methods of doing so and whether those convicted of electoral fraud should be permitted to vote (Department for Constitutional Affairs 2006). This paper received a mixed response, although only one-quarter of respondents favoured the status quo and just under half favoured restoring the vote to all prisoners. The second Consultation Paper asked for views on the appropriate threshold for re-enfranchisement (Ministry of Justice 2009). Options considered included prisoners retaining the vote if they served less than one year, two years, or four years.

Challenges to the denial of voting rights

Since *Hirst* there have been several further challenges brought on the failure to allow prisoners to vote. Cases were brought by prisoners challenging the legality of the May 2007 elections in the domestic courts on the issue of Convention compliance but were unsuccessful, although the amount of time taken to amend the law was criticised by the courts (see *Traynor and Fisher* [2007], *Smith v Scott* [2007], and *Re Toner and Walsh* [2007]). In *R (Chester) v Secretary of State for Justice* [2009] the court made clear that it would not make a further declaration of incompatibility or pressurise the government to speed up the changes as the government was already reviewing the options.

A Draft Bill on voting rights for prisoners was considered by a Joint Committee from both Houses of Parliament in 2012/13. Written and oral evidence was taken from interested parties and the Committee considered the issues raised by the Strasbourg Court's criticism of the UK's blanket ban in *Hirst*. The Draft Bill included three possible options: disqualifying sentenced prisoners serving more than six months from voting, disqualifying sentenced prisoners serving more than four years from voting, or retaining the current blanket ban on sentenced prisoners voting. The Committee considered how to reconcile the public's

---

[15] Remand prisoners, prisoners convicted for non-payment of fines, and those imprisoned for contempt of court are permitted to vote.

opposition to change with the view of the Strasbourg Court in *Hirst* (2005) and *Scoppola* (2012) and published its report in December 2013; it concluded that 'the most persuasive argument was that those sentenced to a term of imprisonment of 12 months or less should retain the right to vote' (at para 236). In its response the government said the question remained under active consideration.[16]

However, as yet, legislation has not been introduced, despite criticism from the Committee of Ministers of the Council of Europe, which has expressed its concern over the delays. Before the May 2010 General Election it strongly advised the UK government to adopt measures to allow prisoners to vote in the forthcoming election, in anticipation of a series of applications to the Court if it failed to do so. It subsequently noted its 'profound regret' that, despite its repeated calls, the election was held in May with the blanket restriction still in place.

In December 2010 the Coalition government said that some prisoners, namely those serving shorter sentences, may be given the right to vote. The government made clear that the proposed changes were being introduced reluctantly to comply with obligations under the ECHR and to avoid making substantial compensation payments to prisoners. However, the court in the *Greens and MT* case in 2010 also made it clear that, in relation to prisoners' claims concerning denial of the right to vote, a finding of a violation constitutes just satisfaction and no damages are appropriate. However, no changes were enacted by the Coalition government and in a parliamentary debate on the issue in 2011, the granting of voting rights to prisoners was rejected by a large majority. Despite these challenges, the pressure from both the Court and the Committee of Ministers, and the recommendations of the Parliamentary Committee, the restriction remained in place for the 2015 General Election. Moreover, the fact that they had stopped prisoners having the vote was referred to as one of their key achievements in the Conservative Party's manifesto (Conservative Party 2015: 60).

The prospect of prisoners voting has caused considerable disquiet amongst MPs and sections of the media and the public, so it may be difficult even for a government committed to change to enact these reforms, given this substantial opposition. The pressure to give prisoners voting rights was also cited in the document *Protecting Human Rights in the UK*, which set out the government's plan to reduce the power of the Strasbourg's Court's judgments to an advisory role and to limit human rights to the most serious breaches (Conservative Party 2014). It said that it would negotiate with the Council of Europe regarding these changes but, if it did not succeed, would consider withdrawing from the Convention (ibid: 8). The reluctance to restore the vote reflects the government's principled opposition to re-enfranchisement as well as the practical problems of enacting change in the face of widespread parliamentary and public opposition and the current climate of hostility to human rights. So the prospect of prisoner enfranchisement has receded further.

Challenges to the ban have continued to be raised in the European Court of Human Rights and the domestic courts in the past five years. In *Greens and MT v UK* (2010) the Strasbourg Court set a date for the UK government to comply with the ruling in *Hirst*. The Court also said it would discontinue hearing these repetitive applications pending compliance by the state with the judgment. However, an extension was granted to the UK to await the outcome of the case of *Scoppola v Italy (No. 3)*, where a successful challenge to a blanket ban on prisoners' voting was referred to the Grand Chamber. The UK's Attorney General addressed the Court as a third party intervenor in that case and argued strongly that the question of prisoners' votes should be a matter for Parliament.

---

[16] http://www.parliament.uk/documents/joint-committees/Draft-Voting-Eligibility-Prisoners-Bill/Grayling-letter-to-Chair.pdf.

In *Scoppola v Italy (No. 3)* App. No. 126/05 (22 May 2012) the Strasbourg Court affirmed that states do have a margin of appreciation to decide which prisoners should be given the vote and that the issue does not necessarily have to be left to a judge, which it had previously advocated in *Frodl v Austria* in 2010. It also affirmed its earlier decision in *Hirst v UK* (2005) that a blanket ban on voting imposed on sentenced prisoners is incompatible with Article 3 of Protocol No. 1 of the European Convention. However, in *Scoppola* (2012) a ban of five years for prisoners serving three years or more was deemed compatible, though prisoners serving longer sentences could be banned for life. The fact that some prisoners were permitted to vote ensured compatibility.

In *Chester and McGeogh* (2013) the UK Supreme Court dismissed an appeal from two life-sentenced prisoners challenging their denial to vote in the UK, European, and Scottish parliamentary elections. Their Lordships declined to issue a further declaration of incompatibility or award damages and noted that in *Scoppola* a ban on prisoners serving longer sentences was considered proportionate, and under any of the proposed options the appellants would not be permitted to vote.

In *Moohan and Gillon v The Lord Advocate* [2014] CSIH 56, the prisoners challenged the ban on prisoners voting in the Scottish referendum. The court rejected their claim on the ground that the European Court of Human Rights had made no ruling on voting in a referendum, only in relation to national and local elections. In *Firth and others v UK App Nos. 47784/09 and 47806/09* (12 August 2014) the applicants complained that they had been prevented from voting in the elections for the European Parliament in 2009. The court held that there had been a violation of Article 3 of Protocol No. 1, but ruled that the finding of a violation constitutes in itself sufficient just satisfaction for any non-pecuniary damage sustained by the applicant.

This follows the Court's approach in a number of previous cases on prisoners' voting rights. Costs will be reimbursed only when it is shown that they have been reasonably and necessarily incurred, which was not the case here. A similar approach was taken in *McHugh and others v UK* (2015), where the Court reaffirmed the breach of Article 3 of Protocol No. 1 by denial of the applicants' right to vote in the European parliamentary elections in 2009, the 2010 General Election, and elections to the Scottish Parliament, the Welsh Assembly, and the Northern Ireland Assembly in 2011. The European Court of Justice has also held, in the case of *Delvigne* (2015), that a ban on a French prisoner voting was proportionate where the prisoner was a convicted murderer serving a 12-year sentence. But as the UK ban is a blanket one, we may see future challenges in relation to denial of the right to vote in European elections.

The debate on prisoner disenfranchisement

The UK government has defended prisoner disenfranchisement on the grounds that it is an appropriate punishment and will encourage civic responsibility and respect for the law, but it could also be argued that including prisoners in the electoral process will encourage civic responsibility and promote social inclusion (see Easton 2006, 2009, 2011). Defenders of prisoner disenfranchisement argue that it is a reasonable restriction and appropriate punishment for wrongdoing, and that it may promote respect for the law. It is argued that prisoners do not deserve the right to vote because of their criminal acts and also that the UK public is hostile to restoration of the vote. It is further claimed that allowing prisoners to vote may undermine the purity of the ballot box and lead to the corruption of public life if they taint the electoral process, for example by bloc voting or by electing unsuitable representatives to public office. The UK government has also stressed the fact that many other states around the world ban prisoners from voting and, compared to some other states, the UK ban is reasonable because the vote is restored as soon as prisoners return to the community. In some US states, for example, former felons may be banned for life. But all these arguments are open to challenge. While the UK position is less harsh than that of some other states, nonetheless the trend worldwide seems to be shifting towards re-enfranchisement and the right was given to convicted prisoners in the Republic of Ireland in 2006. Prisoners are also permitted to vote in many other states, including Spain and South Africa.

In *Hirst* (2005) the Strasbourg Court stressed that the blanket voting ban reduces prisoners to a state of civil death which is no longer appropriate in a modern state. Moreover, the Court said that the views of the public—while a factor to consider—should not be determinative when fundamental rights are at stake. Critics of disenfranchisement also argue that allowing prisoners to vote may promote civic responsibility by encouraging participation in the political life of the state and, by including them, a sense of citizenship may be promoted in prisoners, which may contribute to rehabilitation and reintegration (see Easton 2011a, 2012; Miller and Spillane 2012). In *Frodl* (2010) the Strasbourg Court also stressed the importance of a link between the penalty of disenfranchisement and the offence committed.

In states where voting is permitted there has been no evidence of damage to the electoral process. If postal voting is used this may be more effectively monitored inside the prison than outside. Giving prisoners the vote would give them a stronger voice, enabling them to raise issues of concern over their treatment. The area where the European Court of Human Rights is willing to accept a ban is for prisoners who have committed electoral offences.

Of course prisoners themselves may not see voting rights as a key issue compared to their concerns over the physical conditions in prison, segregation, or visiting rights, but this does not invalidate the point that enfranchisement acknowledges the prisoner remains a citizen while incarcerated. It would not be a costly measure and there are no security issues involved, as prisoners do not need to leave the prison to cast their votes.

The debate over voting rights has also highlighted the concerns over the encroachment of the Strasbourg Court on the management of the criminal justice system and social policy issues in the UK and has led to increasing calls from some politicians to repeal the HRA 1998. The Coalition government argued for reform of the Court itself, including a reduction of its workload through filtering mechanisms, maintaining freedom for states where issues have been fully considered by the domestic courts, and far greater freedom for states on matters of social policy. Questions have also been raised by some members of the judiciary over the authority and intervention of the Court.[17] A Commission to investigate the creation of a UK Bill of Rights and to consider changes to the European Court of Human Rights was established in March 2011 and published its report in December 2012 (Commission on a Bill of Rights 2012). All but two of the members of the panel, Helena Kennedy and Philippe Sands, supported a UK Bill of Rights, but one which incorporates and builds upon the UK's obligations under the European Convention. The Conservative government included repeal of the Human Rights Act in its manifesto, where it lauded its resistance to granting prisoners voting rights. However, this legislative intent to repeal the Act was not included in the Queen's Speech in May 2015 and the government announced it would conduct further research on the issue, which was interpreted by some as a recognition of the practical and political difficulties of change. Its narrow majority and opposition from some of its own backbenchers as well as other parties would make it difficult to pass such legislation.

---

[17] See, for example, *R v Horncastle and another, R v Marquis and another, R v Carter* [2009] 1 EWCA Crim 964.

8.7 **Reflecting on the issues**

If we review penal policies and particularly the use of custody in recent years, we find a tension between expansionist and reductionist penal policies, with a continuing expansion of prison numbers and commitment to prison building on the one hand, and attempts to exert controls and limits on this expansion through the use of alternatives to custody and greater controls on sentencers on the other. As governments have tried to negotiate the pressures of public opinion and anxieties over crime and security and the spiralling costs of punishment and political crises over accountability, we find conflicting trends and conflicting messages for sentencers. Moreover, when the deeper problem of the best way to deal with offending and reoffending has been addressed, there has not been a great deal of consensus on the best way forward.

We find elements of both expansionism and reductionism in penal policy over the past 15 years. The prison population has remained high, with the focus on public protection and risk management shaping penal policy. However, we can find some evidence of a continuing shift towards reductionism in other policy developments, as the costs of expansionist penal policies have been difficult to sustain. Furthermore, there has been increasing recognition that the impact of imprisonment on crime reduction is limited. In relation to some groups of offenders, principally female offenders, there have been efforts to reduce the prison population and to consider alternatives, as we shall see in Chapter 9. Proposals to reduce the size of the prison population have also been made by the House of Commons Justice Committee in its report *Cutting Crime: The Case for Justice Reinvestment*. This made suggestions to reduce the prison population including focusing resources on the prevention of criminality in high crime areas and greater use of restorative justice (House of Commons Justice Committee 2010a).

The financial imperative to cut the cost of imprisonment has also focused attention again on effective rehabilitation. Supervision in the community for prisoners leaving custody has also been expanded, including provision for those serving short sentences, which was extended by the Offender Rehabilitation Act 2014. Prison reformers and practitioners working within the criminal justice system have argued that short prison sentences are ineffective in reforming offenders and reducing crime, and have been used excessively (see Trebilcock 2010, 2011: chapter 12.4.2). However, for some prisoners the period inside prison in some cases gave them a better quality of life than was the case in the community. While the new Conservative government has been critical of the failures of the prison system, the emphasis has been on creating a modern prison estate rather than reductionism (Gove 2015a).

There have been substantial improvements in procedural justice and conditions in prisons in the past 15 years. Although the numbers in prison have continued to rise, there have been some promising developments and considerable progress. The expansion of human rights jurisprudence has had a significant effect on raising standards in prison and on recognising that prisoners remain citizens while incarcerated. Entrenched human rights provide a counterbalance to both populist punitiveness and the principle of less eligibility.

But the problems discussed in Chapter 1, of reconciling the public to prison improvements and of public punitiveness, have persisted and limited the scope for reductionist policies (see Roberts and Hough 2005a). Progressive developments, as we have seen, have co-existed uneasily with the quest for cost-effectiveness and value for money and the increasing focus on risk management and reliance on the private sector (see Murphy and Whitty 2007; Ministry of Justice 2010a). There remain variations between prisons in terms of opportunities for work and training as well as accommodation. Maintaining con-structive regimes during a period of budgetary constraints and limited resources may be difficult. But it certainly seems likely that effective use of imprisonment will remain on the political agenda.

8.7.1 **Discussion questions**

In this chapter we have examined life inside modern prisons. In revising this material you may wish to reflect on the following issues:

1. Why has the prison population expanded since 1990? How significant are changes in sentencing law and policy in this expansion?
2. What effect has this expansion had on prison conditions?
3. Does the treatment of prisoners in the UK comply with the European Convention on Human Rights?
4. What do you consider to be the best means of achieving the aims of imprisonment?

Some guidance on answering these questions is given in the Online Resource Centre.

online
resource
centre

8.7.2 **Case study**

Joe Raskolnikov is serving his first sentence of imprisonment. He is not adapting well to prison and has been disruptive, which has resulted in time spent in segregation. He has also become very depressed and suffers from both mental and physical health problems. Since coming out of segregation he has spent many hours in his cell during the working day as he has been unable to be accepted on a training course or work programme.

What can Joe do to improve his situation?

Guidance on answering this question is given in the Online Resource Centre.

9

Experiencing imprisonment

SUMMARY

In Chapter 7, we examined the issues raised in achieving justice at the point of sentencing, by considering the differential impact of the prison regime on particular groups of prisoners, and highlighted the problems which arise in taking account of differences in personal circumstances at the individual level and their implications for the issue of impact mitigation. In Chapter 8, we considered the quest for justice within the prison context. In this chapter the experience of imprisonment for specific groups, namely women, ethnic minorities, religious minorities, sexual minorities, prisoners with disabilities, and older prisoners is reviewed. Policies which aim to reduce their risk of unfair treatment will be discussed.

9.1 Equality, discrimination, and human rights

9.1.1 UK equality law

A framework of legislation designed to prevent discrimination and inequality has been in place since the 1970s but since 2005 there have been major changes in UK equality law. The Equality Act 2006 established the new Commission for Equality and Human Rights, replacing the Commission for Racial Equality, the Equal Opportunities Commission, and the Disability Rights Commission. The Act imposed on public authorities an 'equality duty', which means a duty to take positive action to eliminate unlawful discrimination on grounds of race, sex, disability, religion, sexual orientation, gender reassignment, or age. This was later followed by the Equality Act 2010, which has replaced the prior anti-discrimination law in the Race Relations Act 1976, the Equal Pay Act 1970, the Sex Discrimination Act 1975, and the Disability Discrimination Act 1995, with a single Act; harmonised the law; and imposed a duty to promote equality. The protected characteristics under the Equality Act include age, disability, gender reassignment, marriage and civil partnership, race, sex, sexual orientation, and religion or belief. This means that prison authorities have a duty not to discriminate against prisoners or staff on any of these grounds. In addition, the equality duty requires that prisons must develop policies to promote equality and test new policies for their equality impact. Prisoners may bring their individual complaints to the Commission. A disability equality duty came into force in prisons in 2006, followed by a gender equality duty in 2007. A statutory duty on prisons to promote race equality had been introduced earlier by the Race Relations (Amendment) Act 2000, which brought public services, including the Prison Service, the Probation Service, the Border Agency, and the police, within the ambit of anti-discrimination law. A focus on race equality policies has featured in prisons since the 1980s and some of the measures used to pursue equality are being extended to challenge discrimination in other areas. The gender, race, and disability equality duties were replaced by a broader equality duty under the 2010 Equality Act, so that in formulating policies public institutions must consider how different people will be affected by those activities so that services are accessible to all. The duty does not require public bodies to treat everyone the same.

Policies are formulated at the national level by NOMS but also by individual prison establishments. So the day-to-day life of the prison is governed by this framework of equality law. The duty to obtain information to avoid discrimination was imposed by s. 95 of the Criminal Justice Act 1991, which comprised a requirement to obtain relevant information to avoid discrimination on the grounds of race, sex, and other improper grounds. On the basis of this information and a number of empirical studies, we can construct a picture of the population to establish whether all offenders are treated equally, or whether some groups are treated differently, although evidence of difference may not itself indicate unjust or unfair treatment. Differential treatment may arise from indirect discrimination if an apparently neutral rule impacts unfairly on a particular group. There is a statutory duty on public authorities under the Equality Act 2010 to promote equality and this includes testing policies for their equality impact. NOMS declares that its values incorporate 'equality and diversity in all we do' (NOMS 2015a: 7). It has developed an overarching NOMS Equality Strategy which is focusing inter alia on the needs of disabled staff and prisoners. All NOMS policies are subjected to an Equality Impact Assessment, now called an Equality Analysis, which addresses any inequalities which may arise from them. The Prisons and Probations Ombudsman also receives complaints relating to equality and diversity issues (see PPO 2015a: 62).

9.1.2 European Convention and European Union law

There have also been advances in both European Union law and European Convention law. In European Union law, Article 13 EC, enacted by the Treaty of Amsterdam, introduced a general principle of non-discrimination which prohibits discrimination on sex, racial or ethnic origin, religion, disability, age, or sexual orientation and other grounds. This came into force in May 1999. A general framework for equal treatment in employment and occupation and the prohibition of discrimination in these areas was set out in Directive 2000/78 of 27 November 2008. Article 21 of the EU Charter of Fundamental Rights and Freedoms also prohibits discrimination.

Prisoners are also protected to some extent against discrimination by the European Convention on Human Rights (ECHR). As we saw in Chapter 8, with the Human Rights Act 1998 the protection of prisoners' rights under the ECHR has been strengthened and it is possible to bring a Convention challenge in the domestic courts. Cases on racism have been brought under Article 3, the right not to be subjected to degrading treatment. In *Hilton v UK* (1976), the European Commission of Human Rights said that claims of racist abuse of a prisoner by an officer could raise an Article 3 challenge of degrading treatment.[1] An action could also be brought under Article 14, which states that the enjoyment of rights under the ECHR shall be secured without discrimination on any ground such as sex, race, colour, language, religion, political or other opinion, national or social origin, association with a national minority, property, birth, or other status. However, to invoke Article 14, it is necessary to show that the discriminatory act falls within the scope of another Convention right, and that the discrimination is not justifiable. If Protocol 12 to the ECHR were to be ratified, it would be easier to bring a discrimination claim under the ECHR

---

[1] See also *East African Asians* case (1981).

without engaging the other rights, but the UK government has said that it will not ratify this Protocol. Protocol 12 states that:

1. The enjoyment of any right set forth by law shall be secured without discrimination on any ground such as sex, race, colour, language, religion, political or other opinion, national or social origin, association with a national minority, property, birth or other status.

2. No one shall be discriminated against by any public authority on any ground such as those mentioned in paragraph 1.

If a black prisoner could show he or she was treated less favourably than a white prisoner in relation to home visits, for example, the prisoner could invoke Articles 8 and 14. However, the qualifications to Article 8 might be used to take account of the security needs of the prison regime and of the public. But there would have to be reasonable and objective justification for differential treatment and the measure would have to be proportionate to its aims. A case might also be brought if it could be proved that ethnic minority offenders were sentenced disproportionately compared to white offenders. For example, in *R (Clift) v Home Secretary; R (Hindawi) and another v Home Secretary* (2007), a challenge under Article 14 and Article 5 succeeded when the House of Lords held that it was discriminatory to exclude foreign national prisoners from an early release scheme.

Women prisoners may also use Article 8 to increase access to their families and protect their right to privacy. If women prisoners are treated differently to male prisoners in relation to other Convention rights, then they could bring a case under Article 14. To prove differential treatment, the applicant has to show that she (or he) was treated less favourably than others on the basis of a personal characteristic and that the person to whom the applicant is comparing herself is in an analogous situation. In *Lockwood v UK* (1993) it was made clear that the relevant comparator would be other prisoners within the prison population, rather than an ordinary citizen in the community. For example, it could be argued that Article 8, the right to family life, is breached if women's home visits are stopped because of assumptions based on male prisoners' behaviour.

The Strasbourg Court has recognised the existence of indirect discrimination as well as direct discrimination in a line of cases, including *Abdulaziz, Cabales and Balkandali v UK* (1985) and *Thlimmenos v Greece* (2000), and has stressed the positive duty on states to investigate discrimination in *Petropoulou-Tsakiris v Greece* (2007). The Court has also upheld complaints relating to discrimination on grounds of sexual orientation, for example in *EB v France* (2008). When the HRA 1998 came into force it was thought that more cases would be brought under Articles 8 and 14, but relatively few cases have been brought under Article 14.

9.2 Women in prison

9.2.1 The female prison population

The number of women imprisoned in England and Wales increased rapidly during the 1990s, more rapidly than the number of male prisoners, although the latter also reached record levels. The number of women prisoners was 3.5 per cent of the total prison population in 1991, increasing to 4.4 per cent in 1999, then to 6.1 per cent in 2001; by the end of 2011 it was 5 per cent and by January 2016 it had fallen to 4.5 per cent. In the week ending 29 January 2016 there were 3,823 women prisoners compared to 81,692 male prisoners. Although the number of female prisoners fell in the period 2004–14, there was a substantial increase in the number of male prisoners (Ministry of Justice 2014c: 6).

Despite the dramatic percentage increase, the number of women prisoners is still relatively low compared to the number of male prisoners and relative to the number of women in the population as a whole. Women also have a lower frequency-of-offending rate than men. The majority of women offenders commit fewer and less serious crimes than men. Most offenders entering prison under sentence have committed non-violent offences. Their criminal careers are shorter and their reconviction rates have been lower than men's over the past decade (ibid: 16).

The actual numbers cited in official statistics usually represent the count on a particular day, like a snapshot, but the number of receptions in prison throughout the year may be substantially higher. There is a substantial literature explaining women's minimal presence in the crime statistics, as well as a number of explanations for their deviance, which lie outside the scope of this book.[2]

The increase in the number of women prisoners in the 1990s was attributed to several factors, including a general increase in the use of custody and an increase in average sentence length, as well as a rise in the numbers of women appearing before the courts and increasing numbers of women convicted for drugs offences, which attract longer sentences. It also reflected a general increase in punitiveness and tougher sentencing of drugs-related crime.

The chance of receiving a custodial sentence increased for both male and female offenders in the 1990s (see Hough *et al.* 2003). However, after 2012, the total prison population began to fall, including the number remanded in custody, partly in response to changes in the Legal Aid, Sentencing and Punishment of Offenders Act 2012 (LASPO) which limited the use of remand for offenders unlikely to receive a custodial sentence at trial. The number of women sentenced to custody for drug-related offences has also fallen since 2009.

In 2013 custody was the most common sentence for males convicted of indictable offences, while for women a community sentence was the most common sentence. Women were more likely to have mitigating factors, including the fact of being a prime carer, applied to their sentence, while men were more likely to have aggravating factors applied (Ministry of Justice 2014b: 14).

Theft and handling account for the highest proportion of female convictions, followed by violence against the person (principally assault occasioning actual bodily harm) and drugs offences. Shoplifting constitutes the major theft offence for men and women, but the proportion is higher for women. For those women given an immediate custodial sentence the most common offence group is violence against the person. However, fewer women than men are imprisoned for violence, and the majority of female prisoners do not present a danger to the public. Most female defendants are dealt with in the magistrates' courts and women are also more likely to commit the less serious summary offences.

The Wedderburn Report found little evidence to show that women were treated more severely than men. In fact, a lower proportion of women than men were sentenced to immediate custody for indictable offences and the average sentence length was shorter (Prison Reform Trust 2000). These patterns have persisted since the publication of that report. In the Crown Court men have a higher custody rate than women. A higher proportion of women than men in the Crown Court receive suspended sentence orders and community orders. Men are more likely than women to receive an immediate custodial sentence. Women are also more likely to receive shorter custodial sentences than men in the Crown Court. The average custodial sentence length is lower for women than men

---

[2] See, for example, the review of the literature in Howden-Windell and Clark (1999) and discussion in Silvestri and Crowther-Dowey (2008), Renzetti (2012), and Berberet (2014).

(Ministry of Justice 2014c: 12). Women also have higher Home Detention Curfew release rates than men (Ministry of Justice 2014b: 19).

Community penalties may have mixed effects if requirements are attached to those sentences which women find difficult to meet. Women may be at greater risk of breaching conditions because of the problems of meeting both the requirements of supervision and the competing demands of childcare (see Malloch and McIvor 2011). When the 2003 Act was passed, the guidance to sentencers made clear that they should take account of the offender's ability to comply with particular requirements (Sentencing Guidelines Council 2004c). A large number of receptions into custody are for breaches and this applies to women prisoners as well. According to the Corston Report, half of new receptions into Holloway prison were for breach. In some cases the breach in question may be a failure to meet an appointment, which could be because of childcare or transport problems (Corston 2007: para 5.25). The expansion of community penalties and curfews may also disadvantage women in so far as the home becomes the focus of attention of criminal justice agencies, subject to scrutiny and surveillance, which means that, as partners of male offenders, they will also be observed. Indeed, the family is often seen as a locus of criminality with the emphasis on parental responsibility for young offending (see, for example, Day Sclater and Piper 2000; Reece 2005; Hollingsworth 2007; Piper 2009; Probert *et al.* 2009).

However, under s. 10 of the Offender Rehabilitation Act 2014 there is an obligation on the Secretary of State to satisfy himself that contracts for the provision of probation services do meet the needs of female offenders. Moreover, the Act's requirement to give all offenders released from short sentences supervision in the community should also benefit women, with offenders being assessed at the beginning of their sentence, although it is too early to assess the impact of these provisions.

9.2.2 The typical woman prisoner

The experience of women as prisoners raises a number of important equality issues. The typical woman prisoner, like the typical male prisoner, is likely to have had housing problems, low educational achievement, and problems with drugs, alcohol, or mental health before entering prison. However, compared to the typical male prisoner, she is much more likely to have experienced domestic violence and sexual abuse. The Corston Report found that over one-half of women in prison reported previous domestic violence (Corston 2007: para 2.3). Two-thirds of women entering custody required drug detoxification compared to one-half of men entering prison (Corston 2007: para 2.13). Recent research suggests that 53 per cent of women in prison suffered emotional, physical, or mental abuse as a child, compared to 27 per cent of men (Prison Reform Trust 2015a: 4). Women in prison also have higher rates of mental and physical illness than women in the general population.

We noted in Chapter 8 the correlations between the risk of imprisonment and social class, housing problems, and poverty and unemployment which characterise the profile of the typical prisoner, and these correlations are stronger in relation to female imprisonment (see section 8.2.1). Women are less likely than male prisoners to have been in work before imprisonment, and more likely to be unemployed after imprisonment. Women prisoners also have more experience of being in care and there is a disproportionate number of female prisoners with mental health problems compared to male prisoners (Corston 2007). A higher proportion of women in prison had housing problems prior to imprisonment compared to male prisoners. Moreover, the loss of housing while in prison does not just pose problems for the individual, but means it may be harder for women to be reunited with their families. The Wedderburn Report argued that 'women represent the extremes of social exclusion' (Prison Reform Trust 2000: xv). Many women in prison have high levels of deprivation before conviction. In some respects women are more likely to be socially excluded because they are poverty-prone, live longer, have higher morbidity rates, and earn less than men. Social problems which existed before entering prison may also be exacerbated by prison. Women are also less likely than men to have accommodation waiting for them on release, as about one-third of women prisoners lose their homes while in prison.

However, women prisoners are not a homogeneous group; the female prison population includes black and other ethnic minority prisoners, foreign national prisoners, women living with physical and learning disabilities, women with a range of health problems, and women with literacy problems, as well as women with experience of higher education.

9.3 Life in women's prisons

9.3.1 The research base

Life in women's prisons was under-researched until relatively recently. Before the 1980s there was relatively little interest in women's prisons in penal policy and few studies were conducted, but during the 1980s interest increased, especially in relation to women with mental health problems and also regarding conditions then prevailing at Holloway prison. Research showed that women prisoners had been marginalised within the penal system, in part because of their relatively low numbers compared to men. Moreover, if they failed to 'react' to poor prison conditions in terms of violence other than against themselves, this could be seen as compliance and acceptance of their conditions, instead of a reluctance to resort to male tactics. In any event, this quiescence may have contributed to their marginalisation, so the Woolf Report (1991), for example, said very little on women's prisons.

However, since the mid-1990s women's imprisonment has been given more attention and this has facilitated the development of gender-specific penal policies. Public interest in women's imprisonment has also increased, not least because of the salacious interest of the media which has displayed in recent years a fascination with women prisoners, portraying them as either neurotic or tough and masculine. Attention has also been focused on prisoners as parents (see Umamaheswar 2013).

There is also now more information available on women's imprisonment and its impact. Several major studies of women's imprisonment have been undertaken. A review of women's imprisonment was undertaken in 1997 by the then Chief Inspector of Prisons, Sir David Ramsbotham (HM Chief Inspector of Prisons 1997), with a follow-up review in 2001 to assess progress (HM Chief Inspector of Prisons 2001) and a later report in 2010 (HM Inspectorate of Prisons 2010). Women prisoners are also given attention in the Annual Reports of the Inspectorate. The Wedderburn Report in 2000 and the Corston Report in 2007 offered further information and analysis of women's imprisonment. The All Party Parliamentary Group on Women in the Penal System also published its report in 2011 and the Prison Inspectorate also published its *Expectations for Women in Prison* in 2014 (HM Inspectorate of Prisons 2014a).

A number of issues have been raised by this research, including the excessive security used in women's prisons; the lack of consistency on privileges across the women's prison estate; the treatment of juveniles; the holding of young offenders in prison establishments; staff training; allocation procedures; the handcuffing of women during labour and on antenatal visits; reception procedures and induction programmes; the use of control and restraint techniques; access to phones and translators; visiting arrangements; and provision for women with mental health problems.

The Wedderburn Report on women's imprisonment argued that women serving short sentences for less serious offences and women with mental health problems should be diverted from custody, while sentences could be shortened for those in prison and greater use could be made of temporary release (Prison Reform Trust 2000). In addition, a major study of the physical and mental health of women prisoners, *The Health of Women in Prison*, was published in 2006 by researchers at Oxford University who interviewed 505 female remand prisoners over a period in 2004/5 (Plugge *et al.* 2006).

The Corston Report examined women with particular vulnerabilities in the criminal justice system, arguing that custody should be used only where necessary for public protection, but that there are many women in prison for non-violent offences who could be dealt with differently (Corston 2007). This research for the Review included visits to six women's prisons, three women's community centres, and a medium-secure unit. In examining 'vulnerabilities' the Report focused on issues such as domestic violence; childcare issues, including being a single parent; and personal issues, including mental illness, substance misuse, and eating disorders, as well as socio-economic factors such as poverty and unemployment (ibid: para 14).

A follow-up study was undertaken in 2009 and a report published by the All Party Parliamentary Group on Women in the Penal System (APPGW) in 2011 found that progress had been made in a number of areas, including body searching, funding for diversionary measures, and providing one-stop centres for women (see All Party Parliamentary Group on Women 2011). It highlighted the continuing challenges presented by women with alcohol and drug problems, and the experiences of domestic violence and sexual abuse and the need for funding for women's centres. The Prison Inspectorate also reviewed the treatment of black and minority ethnic women prisoners in 2009 and highlighted the particular problems they face (HM Inspectorate of Prisons 2009b).

The Prison Inspectorate's report on women prisoners in 2010 found that the majority of women's prisons were performing well, with good staff–prisoner relations, and that there had been improvements in health care, particularly mental health care, as well as in safety and the treatment of women with substance abuse problems (HM Inspectorate of Prisons 2010). However, the Report raised concerns over the use of segregation and incidents of bullying in some establishments, and noted the challenges in dealing with female prisoners with complex needs and particularly problems over the supply of primary health care and the treatment of women on remand.

In 2010/11 the Prison Inspectorate visited Holloway and Bronzefield, which had large numbers of women dependent on drugs and high levels of self-harm and mental health problems. Drake Hall was also visited and, although the performance at all three prisons was generally good, there were still concerns over health care at Bronzefield and over safety at Holloway, where some women felt unsafe when housed in dormitories. For the most part relations between staff and prisoners were good, although there were some complaints about male officers at Holloway and still too high a proportion of male officers at Bronzefield (HM Chief Inspector of Prisons 2011a). In all three establishments prisoners spent a reasonable amount of time outside their cells, but too few courses were available.

In 2014 the Prison Inspectorate published its new *Expectations* (HM Inspectorate of Prisons 2011a) in regard to women in prison, which reflected the UN 2010 Rules for the treatment of women prisoners, known as the Bangkok Rules; the document also draws from the European Prison Rules and the UN Standard Minimum Rules for Prisoners.[3] The Bangkok Rules stipulated that diversionary measures and pretrial and sentencing

---

[3] The Standard Minimum Rules were also revised in 2015 and the new Rules are referred to as the Nelson Mandela Rules.

alternatives must take account of the history of victimisation of many women offenders and their caretaking responsibilities (UNGA Res/65/229). The *Expectations* for women prisoners start from the premise that their needs are different from men's and that women are often neglected in a penal system geared to the predominantly male prison population (HM Inspectorate of Prisons 2014a). The *Expectations* cover the key areas of safety, respect, purposeful activity, resettlement, and specialist units, that is, units for women with personality disorders and therapeutic communities. They include inter alia the following: women transferring to and from prison and on reception into custody are treated with respect and must be safe at all times; the safety of women's children and other dependents on arrival at prison is assessed and safeguarded; women's needs in custody are addressed; women with complex needs are located and supported; women at risk or who have been subjected to victimisation or violence are protected in custody; where segregation is required women are segregated safely and decently for the shortest possible time; women of all nationalities and all gender identities and sexual orientations are treated equitably and according to their individual needs; women are cared for by a health service which meets their health needs while in prison; women have regular and equitable access to a range of out-of-cell activities; and women are supported to maintain contact with their families.

Using these criteria the Inspectorate found that women's prisons were performing better than men's prisons, with good relationships between staff and prisoners, good safety processes, and support for women with mental health care needs (Ministry of Justice 2014b). They were impressed by the outcomes in the women's prisons inspected in 2014 in the majority of areas inspected, including safety, respect, and resettlement: 'Women's prisons were safe, respectful and offered resettlement work, but outcomes for activity were mixed' (ibid: 67). There was also variable support for women who had been abused, victimised, or trafficked, as well as a lack of systematic identification of them. In the final report of the outgoing Chief Inspector of Prisons, Nick Hardwick, in 2015, he noted that while outcomes in prisons fell overall in 2014/15, women's prisons 'had not declined in the same way as adult men's prisons' (HM Chief Inspector of Prisons 2015: 8). He found that '(m)anagers and staff in NOMS and women's prisons responded positively to the new *Expectations* and overall outcomes in the seven women's prisons we inspected had improved' (ibid: 14).

In addition to the above sources, feminist criminologists have continued to demonstrate the gendered nature of the criminal justice system and its implications for women offenders (see, for example, Berberet 2014). Moore and Scraton, however, while acknowledging the contribution of feminist criminologists in challenging the male-oriented interpretation of the penal system, note that 'despite the recent identification of women prisoners' distinct, gendered needs, at best they remain marginal to the study and practice of imprisonment' (Moore and Scraton 2014: 1). So in their study of women prisoners in Northern Ireland they use women's own voices to further understand the experience of imprisonment.

9.3.2 The women's prison estate

The small size of the female prison population, and therefore the small size of the women's prison estate, means that women may be held far from home, making it harder to organise visits or support for their families. Although the relevant Prison Service Order, PSO 4800, stipulates that women prisoners should be held as close to home as possible, in practice women are held on average further away from home than male prisoners. The average distance from home is 60 miles but for many women the distance is much further (Prison Reform Trust 2015a: 5). This also has implications for resettlement, as it is harder to facilitate resettlement if they are accommodated far from their communities. Women's prisons may take in women from a wide range of areas so they will be dealing with a number of different local authorities.

There are large geographical areas, including the West Midlands and Wales, without women's prisons, and these problems have increased with the closure to women of Brockhill Prison at Redditch. While a new purpose-built women's prison, Bronzefield, opened in June 2004 at Ashford, Middlesex, some women's prisons have been closed—for example, the women's unit at Winchester Prison—to accommodate the increase in male prisoners, while Morton Hall became an Immigration Removal Centre and Downview was converted to a men's prison. Any cut in the women's prison estate means that women may be held even further from home; however, new places have been provided at Drake Hall, Styal, and Foston Hall to reduce the distance from home. In July 2015 there were 12 women's prisons, including two contracted-out prisons, Peterborough and Bronzefield, and two open prisons, East Sutton Park and Askham Grange. These two open prisons were scheduled for closure but this has not yet been implemented.

Because there are fewer women's prisons, the women's prison estate is also less flexible in terms of catering for different types of prisoners with particular needs. This also means it may be harder to transfer disruptive women prisoners than male prisoners, for whom more places are available. If difficult prisoners are transferred to an ordinary prison, the restrictions may mean regime changes for other prisoners and stricter control than is warranted. The changes to the prison estate in recent years mean that women of different security categories may be held together in the same prison, so that the majority of women in the prison may be held in conditions of unnecessarily stringent security (see House of Commons Justice Committee 2015a: para 43). The small size of the estate also means less flexibility for providing appropriate accommodation for prisoners or the right level of supervision. There may be places available in closed but not open prisons, and vice versa.

Women prisoners have been held in some of the worst conditions within the prison system and there has been considerable variation between prisons. When the Chief Inspector of Prisons visited Holloway in 1995 he walked out in disgust because of the squalid conditions, and in the 2003 league table Holloway was still rated the worst prison, graded at level 1. Now it is at level 3 and later reports by the Prison Inspectorate were much more positive about conditions and provisions there. Nonetheless Holloway has now been selected for closure. The 2010 Thematic Review of women in prison found that there had been improvements in most of the 14 prisons inspected, particularly in relation to safety and support for substance abuse (HM Inspectorate of Prisons 2010).

Following a review of the women's custodial estate in 2013, all women's prisons have been designated as resettlement prisons, but resettlement work is difficult if prisoners are held far from home (NOMS 2013). The Coalition government announced it would reconfigure the women's estate by opening smaller open units for women next to closed prisons. The first open unit at Styal opened in 2015. There are also plans to offer extra capacity for women from the South West, Wales, and the Midlands.

9.3.3 Women prisoners and male penal policies

Until relatively recently women's imprisonment was largely subsumed within the male prison system, so women were punished within a penal system designed for men. A major review of the experiences of women in the UK criminal justice system as victims, offenders, and workers was conducted by the Fawcett Commission and its findings were published in 2009 (Fawcett 2009). The review showed that women continued to be marginalised in a criminal justice system designed by men for men. The final report of the Commission revealed a persistent gap between strong policy development and consistent implementation. Practices and attitudes continue to discriminate against women, while women as workers are under-represented at the higher echelons of the justice system. Consequently, it is argued, the system fails to address the causes of women's offending, with too many women continuing to be imprisoned on short sentences for non-violent crime. It also fails to provide female victims of violence with support, safety, or justice. This marginalisation of women extends across the criminal justice system. Because women constitute a minority, they are at a disadvantage, as institutions will usually favour the interests of the majority for administrative convenience. This means that women may be adversely affected by policies based on the actions and experiences of male prisoners.

If women are housed within the precincts of a men's prison, it may be difficult to guarantee their security at times of disorder and also may mean that they are subject to higher levels of security than is necessary, even in normal conditions. While the regimes for men and women will be managed separately, the ethos, procedures, and systems in core areas such as security will be those of a men's prison.

The experience of the prison riots strongly influenced penal policy on enhanced security and control in the 1990s, but these were primarily male events. The focus was on accommodating women's needs within the male framework, with some minor adjustments, rather than radically rethinking the question. While the improvements in the prison regime in the immediate post-Woolf period benefited women, women also shared in the retrenchment of these benefits. Most notably they were subject to increased security after the Whitemoor and Parkhurst escapes. In this sense they were 'punished' disproportionately as the escapes, like the earlier riots, did not involve women's prisons or women prisoners. The Learmont and Woodcock Reports in the 1990s also impacted disparately on women prisoners because they resulted in greater use of shackles on outside visits and, for a period, cuts in home leave. The response to the escapes also meant more intensive controls and surveillance, including of visitors, and an increase in the numbers of women held in closed prisons, even if they met the criteria for transfer to open prisons, where there would be more access to home, their families, and outside work. Release on temporary licence has also recently been reduced for women as well as men in response to problems with a small number of male prisoners committing serious offences on release.

Yet women are less likely to escape or to riot than male prisoners. If they do escape, they are less likely to constitute a threat to the public, as they commit fewer offences of violence, and may be easier to trace, as they are likely to contact their families. Women are generally less dangerous than men, both on official statistics and self-report studies, and are less likely to abscond, yet they have been subjected to similar levels of security including full body searching. In fact, the issue during the riots was how best to protect women prisoners from male prisoners if a riot occurred at a shared site. Mandatory drug-testing policies have also been applied in men's and women's prisons even though there are fewer drugs-related incidents in women's prisons.

9.4 Women prisoners and the pains of imprisonment

Women prisoners deserve special attention because, it has been argued, they experience the pains of imprisonment more intensely than their male counterparts for a number of reasons, the principal one being that women are most likely to be the primary carers of children and therefore experience greater anxiety at separation from their children. In some cases, the women may not even know who is looking after their children. Disquiet has been expressed over the problems for women prisoners of maintaining contact with their children and over the presence of male officers in women's prisons. There is also concern over the large numbers of children who have a parent in custody. It is estimated that over 170,000 children a year are affected (Prison Reform Trust 2014b: 37). This has implications for the Article 8 rights of the child as well as a detrimental impact on the mothers (see Epstein 2012).

9.4.1 Women as carers

Women prisoners may have particular concerns about childcare and caring for elderly relatives, and anxieties about declining fertility, which will not affect men to the same extent. Women prisoners are concerned at losing contact with their children and their greatest fear is often that their children may be taken into care while they are serving their sentence. Babies are permitted to stay with their mothers for a maximum of 18 months.

Under Prison Rule 9(3) a pregnant woman can apply for transfer to a mother and baby unit (MBU). In July 2015 there were six mother and baby units, located at Askham Grange, Styal, Peterborough, New Hall, Bronzefield, and Eastwood Park, offering 54 places for mothers. Women are normally transferred to MBUs in the final stages of their pregnancy and allocations will be made on the basis of the interests of mother and child, risk assessments regarding the safety and well-being of others, and the good order of the prison. Mothers' rights to retain their babies have been strengthened by the Human Rights Act as separation may breach Article 8 of the European Convention. However, if claims are raised under Article 8, the qualifications in Article 8(2) may be used to deny access. Category A prisoners are not allowed access to these units. The Prison Inspectorate found that while mother and baby units had good facilities, they were underused (HM Chief Inspector of Prisons 2015: 15). The unit at Holloway prison was closed for this reason.

In *R (P, Q and QB) v Secretary of the State for the Home Department* (2001) the Court of Appeal, in reviewing the policy of the Prison Service to remove a child from the parent at 18 months, said that prisoners retain the right to respect for family life while in prison. In considering whether the state's grounds for interfering with the right are justified, the court will take account of the need for security in prison, the need to avoid discrimination, and whether the rule was appropriate in the individual case, and the more serious the interference, the more compelling the justification would need to be. If the policy stemmed from the welfare of the child and if, in a particular case, the effect on the child was very adverse, the court could intervene in an exceptional case. Where challenges to denial of access to an MBU have been brought, the courts have looked closely at the decision-making procedures and whether the risks in question can be managed.[4]

Trying to deal with family crises while inside prison is a major problem for women prisoners. Women usually remain responsible for family decisions and find it hard to coordinate arrangements from prison. If they are detained for a long period of time they may lose their home, which will make it harder to keep their children. While the wife of a male prisoner may struggle to keep family life going, for women, who are the main carers, prison will have a more significant impact on the structure of home life. In her study of the impact on prisoners' families, Codd (2008) describes them as living in the shadow of their partners' lives, as they are also affected adversely by imprisonment. But for women in prison the impact may be even greater.

Women are more likely than male prisoners to have dependent children and less likely than male prisoners to have a partner caring for their children. The Corston Report found that only 5 per cent of the children of women prisoners remained in their own home

---

[4] See for example *CF v Secretary of State for the Home Department* [2004].

(Corston 2007: para 2.9). Only 9 per cent were cared for by their fathers, 12 per cent were in care or with foster or adoptive parents, 25 per cent were with grandmothers, and 29 per cent were with other family members or friends. A higher proportion of children of women prisoners end up in care compared to children of male prisoners. Once in prison many prisoners lose contact with their families, because of imprisonment itself or because they are held a long way from home.

So although women may have a similar social profile to men in terms of social exclusion, this may be exacerbated by the fact of being the primary carer. As women may be allocated to prisons far from their homes, there may be problems in organising regular visits from their families as children have to be escorted. While there is a means-tested allowance for close family members to visit, this is limited and long-distance visits may be very expensive. Many prisons are located in rural areas with inadequate bus services. The costs of visits may be a problem, especially as it means time off work for the person escorting the children, given the distance from home for many prisoners. Provision for visits varies between prisons. Women may avoid having their children visit them because they think they will be distressed by the surroundings or by being searched, although visiting facilities in women's prisons are usually superior to those in men's prisons.

The pains of imprisonment may be greater because of these anxieties regarding family obligations. Anxieties about families were a major issue for women interviewed in the Oxford study of remand prisoners. Their concerns focused on their children and the plight of elderly relatives (Plugge *et al.* 2006). Longer visits which last all day would be better for women with children, as would cheap transport to the nearest railway station or arrangements for overnight accommodation. In the United States, for example, arrangements have been made in some women's prisons for children to stay with local families for the weekend to allow for longer visits. Family suites have now been opened at HMP Drake Hall and New Hall which accommodate overnight visits for women and their children. There are also full-time family engagement workers in all public sector prison. They discuss with prisoners on induction what support may be necessary to maintain family contact.

This of course is not to deny that fathers in prison may also experience distress and anxiety at separation from their families, and this is now receiving more attention, as illustrated, for example, by Ugelvik's research on fathers in Norwegian prisons (Ugelvik 2014).

9.4.2 Privacy and prison conditions

Women also may find intrusions of privacy more painful than their male counterparts, as they often have less experience of communal life; for example, women are less likely than men to participate in sports or join the armed forces. Because of this, open prisons, paradoxically, may be more stressful if it means sharing a dormitory. In addition, control in open prisons may be based more heavily on compliance with rules, rather than physical barriers, with adverse disciplinary consequences. Women may also find the physical conditions more distressing because women usually have more health awareness as the person who is most likely to take responsibility for family health. They are therefore more concerned with hygiene and may be more upset by having to eat in their cells, by the limited number of showers, and by low hygiene standards. The Corston Report found that there were still instances of slopping out because of a failure to provide 24-hour access to facilities, or queuing to use the toilet at night, which prisoners find humiliating and degrading (Corston 2007: para 3.16).

Concerns over privacy may be exacerbated by the presence of male officers. Women prisoners do not like men entering their rooms; they do not like to be observed while washing, especially if they have previously been abused, and find providing samples for drug testing, for example, quite intrusive. As large numbers of women prisoners have experienced violence from men in the past, this has made it especially difficult for them, and many women find the presence of male officers difficult to deal with. The Chief Inspector of Prisons has argued that there should be a minimum of 60 per cent female staff in women's prisons but this was not met in all prisons at the time of his 2013/14 inspection (HM Inspectorate of Prisons 2014a: 59).

In March 2015, 45 per cent of NOMS staff in the prison estate, National Probation Service, and NOMS headquarters were female (NOMS 2015a: 52). Working at women's prisons may be unpopular because it is seen as low-status work and women officers may find it difficult to transfer because of staff shortages. Further, the prevalence of male officers may generate a masculinist occupational culture. The attitudes towards female officers in men's prisons have also been examined and found to encompass a range of responses, including chivalrous, sexualised, and ambivalent attitudes (see Crewe 2006).

9.4.3 Expectations of women prisoners' behaviour

Officers' expectations of women's behaviour appear to be more demanding, in the sense that women are more likely than men to be reprimanded for petty offences such as swearing or other behaviour which is seen as unfeminine (Carlen 1998). Women prisoners have higher adjudication rates than male prisoners and higher rates for complaints. The rate of proven adjudications has been consistently higher for female than for male prisoners since 2004. In 2013 there were 126 proven adjudications per 100 of the female prison population, compared with 100 per 100 in the male population (Ministry of Justice 2014b: 12). By 2014 this had increased to 137 proven adjudications per 100 women prisoners, compared to 105 per 100 male prisoners (Ministry of Justice 2015g: 11).

Devlin (1998) argues that women are more likely to be punished for minor disciplinary matters and are subject to more intensive discipline and surveillance. Women prisoners are seen by officers as more argumentative than male prisoners and less able to accept discipline. Women may find it hard to adjust to prison for the reasons we have considered. Because women may have had greater autonomy in running their own homes, they may also find it harder to adjust to a regime which essentially infantilises them in many ways. As women's prisons are smaller, women prisoners may be subject to greater scrutiny, so disciplinary infractions are more likely to be noticed. Women with mental health problems are more likely to be charged with disciplinary offences and may react badly to being held on a segregation unit or on cellular confinement (O'Brien et al. 2001). The Prison Inspectorate found a case of a woman with acute needs held in segregation for over five years in conditions which, it argued, amounted to cruel, inhuman and degrading treatment (HM Chief Inspector of Prisons 2014: 13). While there were examples of good care of vulnerable prisoners within women's prisons, the Inspectorate noted the need for more specialist units to deal with women with complex needs and challenging behaviour (HM Chief Inspector of Prisons 2015: 70).

The disciplinary regime is used to control women's behaviour and to contain women with mental health problems. While women prisoners who are dissatisfied with their treatment have access to the same range of remedies and the complaints procedure available to male prisoners, they may be equally reluctant to complain if they think it may cause more problems for them.

9.4.4 Women prisoners' health needs

Women's health care in prison is an important issue because women prisoners have higher rates of mental health problems and prescription drug use than male prisoners (Prison

Reform Trust 2003; Social Exclusion Unit 2002, see also House of Commons Justice Committee 2015a). A survey of female prisoners found that 40 per cent had received treatment for mental health problems before entering prison and about one-half of women prisoners had some drug dependency prior to prison (Singleton *et al.* 1998; see also O'Brien *et al.* 2001).

Two-thirds of women prisoners suffer from some form of mental health problem such as depression and anxiety, and about one-half are taking prescribed psychotropic drugs. A higher proportion of women than male prisoners enter prison with mental health problems, which may be exacerbated in prison by worries about family and housing. The use of medicines increases in prison and many women take prescribed psychotropic drugs for the first time while in prison (see Prison Reform Trust 2003). In the wider society women have higher morbidity rates than men. If women prisoners do have mental health problems, this may add to the stresses of imprisonment.

But while many women prisoners have emotional and social problems, the number of disturbed and difficult prisoners with severe and untreatable problems is relatively small. While recognising their health problems, an overemphasis on women's therapeutic needs runs the risk of medicalising women's deviance, which perpetuates the perception of women as unstable.

The Oxford study found that the health status of the women who entered prison was poorer than for women in the general population and problems included both physical and mental health, which meant considerable demands were made on the health services within prison (Plugge *et al.* 2006). Women prisoners were five times more likely to have a mental health problem than women in the general population; over half had used illegal drugs before going into prison. Interestingly, the research found that the health status of some women actually improved in prison, because they did *not* have access to drugs and alcohol, but they did have regular meals, health care, and protection from abusive relationships. However, many reported becoming unfit with lack of exercise and the researchers argue that more attention should be given to support for health care in prison, especially as health issues may be linked to offending behaviour. The prisoners interviewed emphasised that they wanted more access to exercise and healthier food. The authors' recommendations include more support for prisoners who witness suicides or self-harm, more help to disabled prisoners, more support for improving physical health, for example, and better training for staff to improve delivery of health care.

Many women prisoners have drug or alcohol problems which require treatment but an unintended effect of mandatory drug testing is that some prisoners are switching from cannabis to heroin, because the latter is harder to detect. The Prison Inspectorate found that female prisoners reported the highest levels of psychological and emotional disorder and distress and were on high levels of medication when they might have benefited more from counselling (HM Inspectorate of Prisons 2007). A higher proportion of women prisoners than men reported problems with drugs and alcohol on entering prison, although inside prison drug misuse is less common and this usually involves misuse of prescription drugs rather than synthetic drugs (HM Chief Inspector of Prisons 2015).

There are also high rates of self-harm in the female prison population. In 2014 women accounted for 26 per cent of self-harm incidents yet were under 5 per cent of the prison population (ibid 15). While the rate of self-harming incidents is higher for female than male prisoners, with women seven times more likely to self-harm than male prisoners, the rates for self-harm for female prisoners have fallen in the past decade, while the rates for male prisoners had increased in 2014. Self-harm may be used as a way to deal with the stress of imprisonment or in response to poor conditions, while men may be more likely to direct violence against others or to damage property in such cases. There were also two female self-inflicted deaths (SIDs) in prison in 2014/15, although the rate for SIDs in women's prisons is lower than in men's prisons.

Given the mental health needs of some women prisoners, this raises the issue of whether prisons should be used as psychiatric hospitals and whether, given the numbers of women with mental health problems and the number of attempted suicides, it would be better to focus on the mental health needs of offenders rather than simply incarcerating them (see Prison Reform Trust 2003; Peay 2007). Women with serious mental health problems do need access to an appropriate therapeutic regime. However, therapeutic units are provided for women prisoners at HMP Send, at the Dove Centre at Styal, and at Eastwood Park, and these were praised by the Prison Inspectorate for the support given to vulnerable women prisoners (HM Chief Inspector of Prisons 2015: 69).

Although the principle of equivalence should govern prison health care, that is, standards of health care should be provided at the same level as provided by the National Health Service (NHS) in the community, there are concerns over the standards of health care in prison for prisoners with mental health problems, in terms of the services available and quality of care (see Reed and Lyne 2000). Responsibility for health care has been transferred from the Prison Service to the NHS and responsibility for funding moved from the Home Office to the Department of Health. This had a beneficial effect on health service provision, but demand for services in prisons exceeds supply because of the high rates of mental disorder, drug misuse, and self-harming of prisoners. The burden on prison medical staff and on officers and other prisoners would be reduced if more facilities were available to divert offenders with mental health problems from prison and if mental health care and drug treatment programmes within the community were improved. Policy statements including *Transforming Rehabilitation* suggest support for the principle of diversion for those with mental health problems, but clearly this needs to be backed up by sufficient resources.

The standard of care for prisoners with severe mental health problems is also dependent on facilities in the wider community. Where problems are severe and transfer to hospital is necessary, it may take several months to find a suitable hospital bed (Corston 2007: para 12). Also, it may take some time for medical staff to provide reports requested by sentencers, which may delay provision of appropriate methods of disposal for women. The failure to manage high-risk women with severe personality disorders has also been criticised by the Prison Inspectorate, particularly the use of segregation for women with mental health problems (HM Chief Inspector of Prisons 2011a: 9).

However, these health problems not only present huge demands on the prison, but also reflect wider social problems which it would be unreasonable to expect the prison system to solve. As the Corston Report concluded: 'the Prison Service cannot and should not be expected to solve social problems' (2007: para 7.24). What are needed are social policies to address these social problems, which will include greater provision for support within the community. The general health care of women in prisons has been found to be very good by the Prison Inspectorate, but there is greater difficulty in providing comprehensive mental health care in some prisons (Ministry of Justice 2014b: 72).

9.4.5 Constructive regimes for women

Until the 1970s, women's training was mainly domestic work servicing the prison, with limited opportunities for serious vocational or academic work. The focus was also on 'feminine' skills, such as taking pride in one's appearance, reflecting the view that adjusting to the gender role is part of the rehabilitation process. Although it has been criticised for this reason, courses such as hairdressing do at least offer a prospect of self-employment on release.

Domestic work also forms a large part of male prison work, of course, as the provision of cooking and cleaning services forms a substantial proportion of prison employment.

In the 1970s vocational courses were introduced, although often in subjects like home economics. The situation now is much improved, with some light industrial work for women in prison such as manufacturing clothes and furniture, printing and desktop publishing, and a wider range of educational and training courses (see Simon 1999; HM Chief Inspector of Prisons 2015). Improving the provision of work and training is crucial to strengthening women's position in the labour market when they return to the community. Many women prisoners also have lower literacy and numeracy skills than the wider population.

Given that most women are serving short sentences, they need intensive training for work. Although many jobs in prison are in housekeeping or cleaning, to meet the needs of the prison, they need work and training which give skills which will improve access to the job market. A survey of women's work and training experiences in prison and on release found that the majority of women found their prison employment was of very little value to them in finding work on release (see Hamlyn and Lewis 2000).

Because of the smaller size of women's prisons, there may be a more limited range of education and training opportunities than in men's prisons, but efforts are being made to ensure greater consistency in educational provision and greater coordination between different prison establishments. Prisoners are now being used to assist with the teaching of PE and other educational activities.

The provision of offending behaviour programmes in women's prisons should also take account of women's needs, and programmes specially designed for women offenders have now been developed and accredited. However, women offenders generally prefer and benefit from individual client-centred counselling and treatment approaches. The Corston Report (2007) also emphasised the need to give a higher priority to training in very basic life skills, such as cooking healthy meals, and organising family life for women whose lives have been chaotic. So a woman-centred approach should be applied to work, training, and education, but this means that issues such as life skills and building self-esteem, the Report argued, should be addressed as a priority and as a prerequisite for benefiting from vocational or educational courses. For those with more advanced skills, courses offering women help and advice in setting up small businesses are very useful.

The Prison Inspectorate also found a mixed picture in relation to activities, with Askham Grange offering outstanding provision and a range of work and high completion rates for courses, while in other cases provision was not sufficiently tailored to the needs of women (HM Chief Inspector of Prisons 2015: 15). For example, at Peterborough there was too much mundane work and a lack of variety during teaching sessions. However, NOMS is working with the National Institute of Continuing Education to offer a learning and skills curriculum which will provide a range of purposeful activity specifically for women. The number of accredited programme starts and completions for both female and male prisoners fell between 2009/10 and 2013/14 (Ministry of Justice 2014b: 76). However in 2014/15, the rate of accredited programme starts was higher for female prisoners than male prisoners (Ministry of Justice 2015f: 15).

9.4.6 **Black women prisoners**

Black women enmeshed in the criminal justice system negotiate the multiple hazards of class, gender, and ethnicity. They receive custodial sentences at earlier stages in their criminal careers than white women and are over-represented in prison. Explanations have focused on the impact of poor housing and social exclusion as well as the role of racism. Women from black and minority ethnic (BME) groups make up just under one-quarter of the female prison population and may face additional problems within the justice system because they are subject to racist as well as patriarchal attitudes and stereotypes. The percentage of BME prisoners in the female prison population ranges from 17 to 23 per cent depending on the age grouping (Ministry of Justice 2015f: 8).

Racism may shape the experience of imprisonment in a number of ways, in the allocation of resources and in treatment and attitudes—issues considered in the second part of this chapter. However, black and minority ethnic women have been found to be less negative about their treatment than black and minority ethnic men and, generally, relations between staff and prisoners seem to be better in women's prisons (HM Inspectorate of Prisons 2009b; HM Chief Inspector of Prisons 2015). Nonetheless, one group of female prisoners, foreign national prisoners, may experience particular problems, and a review of foreign national prisoners found that family and immigration problems were major concerns for these women (HM Inspectorate of Prisons 2006; see also section 9.7.6). Support services and advice for foreign national women prisoners is given by Hibiscus Initiatives (Hibiscus Initiatives 2014). This organisation helps women stay in contact with their families and provides support on resettlement.

The issues facing BME women prisoners were considered by the Prison Inspectorate in 2009. In *Race Relations in Prison: Responding to Adult Women from Black and Minority Ethnic Backgrounds* (HM Inspectorate of Prisons 2009b) it was noted that because black women are more likely to be single parents, they face particular problems in maintaining their households while in prison, and particular problems of drug use and social disadvantage. These women also reported problems regarding health care, felt that they were disadvantaged in their access to resources within the prison, and also reported higher rates of victimisation and lack of respect than non-minorities. The Report stressed the need to provide a specific diversity strategy for BME women prisoners as this group has tended to be overlooked in the past in race relations work. However, relations between staff and BME prisoners were better in women's prisons overall than in men's prisons, although the recent report from the Prison Inspectorate noted that BME prisoners were more negative regarding respect and victimisation.

9.5 Treating women prisoners differently

There have been some positive changes in response to the campaigns for recognition for women's particular needs and to the challenges to gender-neutral approaches (see Worrall and Gelsthorpe 2009). Section 10 of the Offender Rehabilitation Act 2014 demands that women's needs be taken account of in arrangements for supervision and rehabilitation of offenders. We have also seen the development of gender-specific policies in recent years. The need for gender-specific policies has been acknowledged by the Labour, Coalition, and Conservative governments. It is now well established that women prisoners have specific and distinct needs.

9.5.1 The introduction of gender-specific policies

As we have seen, the treatment of women prisoners has been subject to criticism on a number of grounds and the need for a *gender-specific* policy which takes account of the differing needs and circumstances of women prisoners, to achieve substantive equality rather than formal equality, has been stressed. This may entail providing different regimes for men and women, but Carlen (1998) has argued this is justified on the principle of 'ameliorative justice'. This principle 'assumes that as women (and black women in particular), because of their different social roles and relationships and other cultural difference, are likely either to suffer more pains of imprisonment than men, or to suffer in different ways, the prison authorities are justified in running different regimes for women to make up for (or ameliorate) the differential pains of imprisonment attributable to gender or ethnic difference' (ibid: 10–11). Gender testing means 'asking whether biological or ideological differences in gender identity will require proposed regime innovations to receive differential implementation in the men's and women's prisons' (ibid: 134).

A gender-specific penal policy acknowledges women as primary carers and recognises that women in prison receive far less support than male prisoners from their partners. It may also entail easing restrictions imposed on mothers in their contact with their children. Temporary release, weekend leave, and weekend visits from children, perhaps lodging with local families and visiting their parents in the day, would also assist prisoners with children. Incoming calls would enable prisoners to maintain contact with their families. The resettlement of women should also take into account the need for women to move away from their home areas to escape violent relationships. Women also need more help with drug problems, and access to gender-appropriate treatment programmes inside and outside prison. A frequent criticism of the Mandatory Drug Testing programme is that it is punitive rather than constructive and does not address the source of the problem. More attention should be given to improving access to health, education, and support on release into the community. Housing is also a major concern for women prisoners who want to be reunited with their families. Without their children it will be difficult for them to access public housing large enough to live with their children, but it will be difficult for them to regain care of their children without suitable housing.

The Wedderburn Report (Prison Reform Trust 2000) favoured replacing existing women's prisons with geographically dispersed custodial centres, and a network of supervision, rehabilitation, and support centres. It advocated a reductionist programme on the grounds that women's patterns of offending are different and because the social costs of women's imprisonment are greater than the costs of men's imprisonment.

The Corston Report (2007) also recommended replacing women's prisons with small, multifunctional, and better distributed centres and proposed a new Commission for Women who offend or are at risk of reoffending. The Report emphasised the need for a woman-centred approach which focuses on the needs of the individual women and brings together a range of services to address health, abuse, and drug and alcohol misuse in community-based centres. Although this might seem expensive, by cutting the use of imprisonment this would free up prison places. Moreover, a considerable amount of expenditure has been earmarked for prison expansion and some of this could, and should, be used for reforming the facilities available for women. There are also now more opportunities for commissioning innovative provision of community centres and community programmes to divert female offenders from custody. Those women who do need secure custody should be housed in small secure custodial units (Corston 2007: para 3.34).

One imaginative use of women's work on community schemes suggested by Corston is training women to renovate properties which could be used to provide accommodation for women on bail or on release (2007: 5.15). The existing women's prison estate could then be transferred to the male prison estate to reduce overcrowding there. The Report also argues for more attention to be given to gender issues within the sentencing guidelines. It also recommends that defendants who are primary carers of young children should be remanded in custody only after considering a probation report on the likely impact on the children (ibid: 9).

9.5.2 **Government policies on female offenders**

Successive governments in recent years have accepted that women's offending may raise different issues to men's and that women prisoners deserve separate attention, so gender-specific policies are needed. In 2000 the Labour government published its strategy for women offenders, which emphasised the importance of improving women's access to health services and support for those using drugs, focusing on women's housing, education, and employment needs, and strengthening family relationships. It also acknowledged the differential impact of imprisonment on women as primary carers and the fact that the small numbers of women prisoners may mean they are housed further from home (Home Office 2000a: 1). It also recognised the links between women's offending and social exclusion and that women offenders may be victims of abuse. It engaged in a consultation process and published its report (Home Office 2001b), following which it announced a new Women's Offending Reduction Programme (WORP) to divert women from custody. The aim was to coordinate efforts to deal with women's offending including efforts to deal with work, training, and health care, and the main focus of the programme was on community provision. Although it meant more support was given to developing new initiatives to assist women, in practice there was often insufficient funding.

The Together Women Programme was also launched in 2005 to evaluate whether a multi-agency and holistic approach to female offenders within the community could be developed to divert women from custody. Five one-stop shops were set up in women's centres in the North of England, providing support and advice on life skills, parenting, mental health services, and training and counselling as well as advice on housing and employment. The women who attended included those at risk of offending as well as those already in contact with the criminal justice system (see Roberts 2010). Hedderman *et al.* (2011) interviewed women using the centres and found a positive response in terms of the good relations with key workers and the desire to desist from offending and to deal with their drug and drink issues and mental health problems. As the authors point out, studies of what works and of desistance have mostly focused on male offenders and what works for men may not work for women. Women's centres provide a range of services and support on issues including substance abuse and domestic violence, and their scope could be expanded further to incorporate assistance with improving work and training skills.

The Labour government's strategy for women prisoners emphasised the importance of recognising their special needs and the specific factors which influence women's offending (Home Office 2000a, 2001b) and accepted many of the Corston Report's recommendations, including gender-specific standards which are intended to ensure that prison regimes are appropriate for female offenders (Ministry of Justice 2007b). It accepted that custody for women should be reserved for serious and violent offenders, that community punishment should normally be used for non-violent female offenders, and that community provision should be appropriate to women's needs. But it did not accept the recommendation that women should not be remanded in custody if they were unlikely to receive a custodial sentence at trial. It also made clear that no additional resources would be made available to implement these proposals, which will affect whether these changes are introduced and how rapidly.

The Coalition government also stressed that women offenders have different needs and more complex problems relating to their offending, including domestic violence as well as drug and alcohol problems (Ministry of Justice 2010a: para 104). It stated that it would apply lessons drawn from dealing with women offenders more widely, including the use of coordinated approaches to diverting women from custody, and the development of community provision.

In *Breaking the Cycle*, the Coalition government referred to the development of diversionary strategies for offenders with mental health problems, which may benefit women, and proposed extending some of the advances in the treatment of female offenders to the male prison estate (Ministry of Justice 2010a). But while the Coalition and Conservative governments have been strongly committed to more involvement of the voluntary sector, many of the groups currently engaged in supporting women prisoners and their families find it hard to obtain funding to support their work, and this seems unlikely to improve under the current spending cuts.

So at a policy level, there has been considerable progress on the issue of women prisoners. There have been improvements in the management of women prisoners with increasing recognition of their specific needs. Gender-specific standards for women in prison were introduced in 2008 and policies were assessed for their impact for gender equality. Accredited programmes have now been designed specifically for women. There has been improved therapeutic provision and better training for staff in mother and baby units. Provision for counselling for drug users is now in operation in all prisons and there are also intensive drug treatment programmes. Accredited programmes for women have also been developed and more research is being undertaken on 'what works' for women (see Sheehan *et al.* 2007, 2010). Young women aged 15–16 have now been removed from prison accommodation and foreign national prisoners are allocated, where possible, to hubs in specific prisons so appropriate resources can be provided for them.

But prison reformers have been disappointed at the slow pace of reform in response to the Corston Report. The problem was that the policy initiatives from the Labour government were 'too little too late', as Hedderman notes; were overtaken by changes in the criminal justice system; and were not matched by sufficient funding (Hedderman 2010: 495). The expansion of community options in the 2003 Act also had the effect of net-widening, so women were given community sentences for less serious offences and also ran the risk of a custodial sentence for breaches. Women prisoners may still be held far from home because of the small size of the estate.

The progress made since the Corston Report was reviewed by the APPGW, chaired by Baroness Corston, which reported in 2011 (APPGW 2011). It drew attention to a number of positive changes: a new gender awareness course had been provided for staff working with women in prison; a Gender Equality Scheme had been published; and a cross-department women's unit to manage the changes recommended by Corston had been created. There is also now a national service framework for female offenders and gender-specific standards are now applied to prisons. Routine full body searching of women on reception to prison is not now undertaken unless there are grounds to justify a search. But, as the APPGW Report notes, we still find a higher percentage of women than men in prison for non-violent offences.

In 2012 NOMS published its report *A Distinct Approach: A Guide to Working with Women Offenders* (NOMS 2012), offering suggestions for good practice in the criminal justice system and tips to those working with women offenders in the light of the Equality Act 2010, which focuses on performance and outcomes rather than processes and requires service providers to think about women's different needs as well as the specific needs of BME women and women with disabilities.

The general move towards a smaller number of larger establishments in the past few years is at odds with the need for small, geographically dispersed units for female prisoners. The Scottish government has accepted the need for smaller prisons for women. The independent report of the Commission on Women Offenders in 2012, chaired by Elish

Angiolini, argued for a 'radical reworking' of Scotland's criminal justice system to reduce the number of female offenders. Its recommendations included the closure of Corton Vale prison, which held over 300 prisoners (Angiolini 2012). The Scottish government responded positively to its proposals and announced in June 2015 that Corton Vale, which is due to close in 2018, will be replaced by a new prison holding only 80 offenders.

The Ministry of Justice published its Strategic Objectives for Female Offenders in 2013, which included, inter alia, ensuring provision of community options suitable for female offenders which address their specific needs, tailoring the women's custodial estate and regimes to reform and rehabilitate female offenders, meeting gender-specific standards and locating women nearer their families where possible, and using the *Transforming Rehabilitation* programme to prevent women reoffending (Ministry of Justice 2013c: 4). It also announced the creation of an Advisory Board for Female Offenders.

The House of Commons Justice Committee, in its report *Women Offenders: After the Corston Report*, reviewed progress, acknowledged that it is now well recognised that women offenders face different hurdles to men, and welcomed the commitment to move towards a holistic approach (House of Commons Justice Committee 2013a). It also noted improvements with the development of a network of community projects and stressed the importance of maintaining financial support for them. There were also concerns over how existing providers would fare in a payment-by-results system, as the smaller centres had been using performance measures, and concerns that these smaller projects would lose funding with general reductions in funding and confusion over future funding mechanisms.

However, the Committee concluded that the *Transforming Rehabilitation* reforms had been designed for male offenders. It proposed a reconfiguration of the female custodial estate as well as an increase in the use of residential alternatives to custody and the maintenance of the network of women's centres. It advocated central funding support for these centres to enable them to navigate the new commissioning arrangements. Evidence received from witnesses who gave evidence to the Committee indicated that they felt progress in implementing Corston was too slow and that there was a lack of commitment to introduce small custodial units for women. The specific strategy for women offenders was not formulated until 2013. As women are more likely to serve shorter sentences than men, they may benefit from the *Transforming Rehabilitation* proposals, but women's specific needs should be considered by providers of rehabilitative services.

In its follow-up report in 2015, the Committee noted that positive steps were being taken to deal with women offenders and stressed the need for effective provision to enable a further fall in the numbers of women in prison (House of Commons Justice Committee 2015b). It welcomed the end of strip-searching of women, the establishment of women's centres, and the acknowledgement of the need for differential treatment of women. However, it expressed concern over the funding for women's centres and the need for this to be established on a secure basis, and stressed the need to reduce the impact of recent restrictions on women's release on temporary licence. It also argued that the long-term aim should still be to deal with women offenders in small custodial units.

In its response to this report, the Conservative government set out its priorities for women offenders in July 2015 (House of Commons Justice Committee 2015b: Appendix). It does not accept that women prisoners should be held in an estate consisting primarily of small units but noted that it had opened some specialist units for women, as well as the two new units for open prisoners at Styal and Drake Hall. It acknowledged the need to ensure that restrictions on temporary release on licence did not impact unfairly on women. It was also mindful of the need to ensure that women's needs are met by probation providers under the *Transforming Rehabilitation* agenda, but stressed that it is a matter for community rehabilitation companies to decide how they want to commission services for women.

9.5.3 **Meeting the aims of women's imprisonment**

In reviewing women's imprisonment we should not lose sight of the aims of imprisonment. From the retributivist standpoint we should ask whether women's imprisonment in current conditions is proportionate and non-degrading. If imprisonment entails the loss of one's home and loss of contact with children as well as loss of liberty, it is arguably disproportionate and hard to justify on retributivist grounds. The loss of privacy, the use of male prison officers, and the indignities of imprisonment, as we have seen, may add to the humiliation and degradation of punishment beyond the actual loss of liberty demanded by retributivism.

It is also hard to justify the increased use of imprisonment on grounds of incapacitation or social protection, given the fact that the majority of women are not dangerous and serve short sentences and so could be incapacitated in the community by electronic monitoring and curfews. Whether prison does constitute a deterrent has also been open to debate, as we saw in Chapter 4.

Transferring women to smaller community-based centres, for example, would also allow more prison places to be available for men's prisons and relieve their overcrowding. It would also cut the costs of imprisonment, which are substantial, particularly when the ancillary costs of support to women's families are added to the calculation. There would also be longer-term benefits if supporting families prevented children being taken into care, which, as we have seen, strongly correlates with future offending. The impact on children is now receiving more attention. Providing more opportunities to undertake community sentences within school hours would also be helpful.

9.6 **Black and ethnic minority prisoners**

Ethnic minorities are over-represented in the prison population, relative to their proportions in the population as a whole. Ethnic monitoring of the prison population began in 1984 and since then the number of ethnic minority prisoners has steadily increased, the rate of increase being faster for black and South Asian prisoners than for white prisoners. Ethnic minorities include a wide range of groups with different issues, needs, and problems, and also include white minority groups, for example, east Europeans and Travellers. Five per cent of prisoners self-report as belonging to Romany and Traveller groups (Prison Reform Trust 2015: 5). A findings paper by the Prison Inspectorate published in 2014 found that while at some prisons support for this group was good, it was difficult for them to maintain family ties. This group was more negative about their prison experience, including feeling unsafe while in custody, were over-represented in the prison population, and received a lack of support in some prisons (HM Inspectorate of Prisons 2014c: 36).

Between 2006 and 2009 the percentage of BME prisoners in the prison population fluctuated between 26 and 27 per cent. BME prisoners constituted 25 per cent of the prison population in 2011 but this figure rose to 27 per cent by 2009 (Ministry of Justice 2011g: 30). In June 2010 just under 26 per cent of the prison population were from black and minority ethnic backgrounds (Ministry of Justice 2011c: 66), but this figure had fallen to 25 per cent in 2012 (Ministry of Justice 2013d). The average custodial sentence length for indictable offences in the period 2009–12 was higher for black and Asian offenders compared to white offenders, although this figure will reflect differences in types of offences, aggravating and mitigating factors, and the point at which the offender pleads guilty (ibid: 15). BME adults also have a higher risk of victimisation of personal crime in data provided by the Crime Survey for England and Wales.

On 31 March 2015 BME prisoners constituted 25.7 per cent of the prison population, compared to 24.3 per cent in 2004 and 27.1 per cent in 2008 (Ministry of Justice 2015f: 7). This compares with the proportion in the wider population, which was 12.4 per cent based on figures in the 2011 Census. The largest BME group of prisoners is black or black British prisoners, who comprise 12.4 per cent of the prison population. This is followed by Asian or Asian British prisoners who make up 8 per cent, mixed prisoners who account for 4.1 per cent, and Chinese or other prisoners who constitute 1.2 per cent (Ministry of Justice 2015f: 7). In all age groups, except for those over 60, BME representation is higher in the male than the female prison population.

9.7 The experience of imprisonment

9.7.1 Less favourable treatment?

While the Prison Service has no part in sentencing decisions, so cannot control the numbers entering prison, it has a duty to ensure that minority ethnic prisoners do not receive less favourable treatment on grounds of race or ethnic origins and to ensure justice inside prisons. NOMS is committed to incorporating equality and diversity in all its functions and combating unlawful discrimination has been an important element of prison governance (NOMS 2014: 4). Yet it has been argued that black and minority ethnic groups in prison have quite different experiences of prison compared to white prisoners. Research in the 1980s highlighted issues in relation to the allocation of work, training, and education, the promotion of inmates to positions of responsibility, and their treatment by officers. More recent work has focused on the experience of racial abuse and harassment and issues of safety and respect. A former Director General of the Prison Service acknowledged that the Prison Service was institutionally racist and has pockets of blatant racism (HM Prison Service 2004: Appendix 5, 15). Perceptions of discriminatory treatment have also featured in prisoners' reports of their experiences in prison (see HM Chief Inspector of Prisons 2015). These issues may also affect staff as ethnic minorities are under-represented in prison staff.

Research on racism in prisons was undertaken in the 1980s by Genders and Player (1989) and Chigwada (1989), and in the 1990s by McDermott (1990) and Fitzgerald and Marshall (1996). Since 2000 there have been investigations by NACRO (2000a, 2003f), the former Commission for Racial Equality (2003), the Prison Inspectorate (HM Inspectorate of Prisons 2005, 2006, 2009b; HM Chief Inspector of Prisons 2010b), Cheliotis and Liebling (2005), the Prison Reform Trust (2006), the Mubarek Inquiry (Keith 2006), and NOMS (2008), all of which have highlighted continuing areas of concern and made recommendations for improvement. We also now have regular reports from the Ministry of Justice detailing progress made on equality issues (Ministry of Justice 2014d, 2015f).

Racism may be direct and overt, expressed in attitudes and behaviour. Areas of discretion within the administration of the prison regime allow more opportunity for racism to be activated expressly in decisions by officers. Racism may also be indirect, in failing to take account of the social context of factors which may be relevant to offenders' behaviour in prison and overlooking the disparate effect of apparently neutral policies. It may be institutionalised in the sense that it is embedded in the culture and practices and policies of institutions and agencies. As we shall see, direct racism may be easier to challenge than more subtle and covert or institutional racism. Racism may operate at the level of individual bias and prejudice or institutionally, being built into the culture of an organisation and embedded in its policies and practices. The Macpherson Report in 1999 highlighted the problem of institutional racism within the criminal justice system and its failure to protect ethnic minorities (Macpherson 1999). Since then successive governments have taken more interest in institutional racism and there has been some progress. Racial harassment is now a criminal offence and procedures dealing with racist incidents have improved. The problems of racism within the Prison Service have also been addressed by the Prison Inspectorate, the Mubarek Report (Keith 2006), the NOMS *Race Review* (NOMS 2008), and Equalities Reports (Ministry of Justice 2014c, 2015f). Good practice in dealing with racism is now being applied to other areas of discrimination.

Statistical data on the criminal justice system suggests there are differentials in the experience of ethnic minorities at all stages of the criminal justice process, rates of stop and search and arrest, remands in custody before trial, and, importantly for our purposes, rates of imprisonment (Ministry of Justice 2013d, 2015h).[5] Data from the Crime Survey also shows a higher risk of victimisation for BME groups. Statistics would suggest that, in the criminal process, from a police stop to prosecution and bail decisions, members of ethnic minorities are likely to be over-represented as suspects and defendants. This may reflect the accumulation of past decisions which draw black suspects into the criminal justice process. The over-representation of ethnic minorities has also been attributed to a range of factors including deprivation and unemployment, which affects black people disproportionately.

There are also demographic issues. The majority of ethnic minority communities are located in urban areas where there are higher than average levels of poverty, homelessness, crime, and unemployment and this will also contribute to their higher victimisation rates. Because some ethnic minority populations are younger than the ageing white population, this will also affect the crime rate. There may also be subcultural differences within ethnic minorities in terms of how they deal with deprivation and racism. Ethnic groups are not homogeneous, but comprise diverse cultures, sources of identity, and demographic structures. Over-representation has also been attributed to racism at the level of individual decisions and differential treatment, but also to policies and practices which increase the speed with which black defendants move through the criminal justice system and move up the tariff. Some of the differentials may be due to factors such as offending patterns, while others reflect social and economic factors which increase the risk of offending and of reoffending on release. It is in the composition of the prison population in England and Wales that the disproportionate presence of ethnic minorities is most striking. We will focus here specifically on the experience of ethnic minorities in prison.

9.7.2 **Work, training, and discipline**

One of the first major studies of racism and prisons was conducted by Genders and Player (1989), who interviewed staff and prisoners and observed prison life. They found prison officers using negative racial stereotypes and expressing critical comments about race relations policies, while the majority of ethnic minority prisoners interviewed thought that there was a problem of racism in prison, even if they had not experienced problems themselves. The allocation of work is an area where discretion may be exercised by supervisors and the researchers highlighted various practices used by work supervisors to circumvent

---

[5] For further discussion of these differentials see Hood 1992; Bowling and Phillips 2002; Shute, Hood, and Seemungal 2005; Thomas 2010; Equality and Human Rights Commission 2014; Phillips and Webster (eds) 2013 and Shepherd 2015.

formal procedures and to exercise discretion, concluding that 'racial discrimination is intrinsic to the social organisation of prisons' (Genders and Player 1989: 131). For example, they found differential treatment in the allocation of work in the prison, based on racial stereotypes. White prisoners were more likely to be found in the better jobs while ethnic minorities were over-represented in the least popular jobs and more likely to be unemployed. Their research suggested a use of stereotypes, with black prisoners seen by officers as unsuitable for education and training because of a negative attitude to authority and to work.

Genders and Player (ibid) also found differences in assessment reports on those prisoners reported for disciplinary offences. They found evidence of some prison officers demonstrating high-level racist assumptions. A common assumption amongst white officers was that black prisoners were lazy, arrogant, hostile, and paranoid about racism, while Asian prisoners were seen as well-behaved and submissive. Genders and Player found that officers were more likely to take disciplinary action against black prisoners and that they saw black prisoners as harder to manage because they were hostile to authority. They concluded that racist attitudes were part of the occupational culture of officers, reflecting their isolation and the dangerousness of the occupation, which makes such occupations vulnerable to stereotyping. Other researchers at that time found similar problems. Chigwada (1989) interviewed black women in prison who believed that they were treated differently on account of their race in relation to the allocation of work and access to education, where priority was given to white women, and who thought that they were more likely to have their privileges withdrawn for minor matters. There was also an assumption amongst officers that black women needed more supervision, because they were troublemakers and harder to control, which had implications for their treatment.

McDermott (1990), in a study of five male adult prisons in the period 1985–9, found that black prisoners in her sample were more likely to be the subject of disciplinary charges and disciplined for the vaguer offences of disobeying orders or being disrespectful. They believed racism was a significant factor in these decisions. The perception of some officers was that black prisoners are anti-authority and disruptive.

Subsequent research undertaken by NACRO (2000a) found that black prisoners were the least satisfied regarding access to work, compared to Asian and white prisoners, but were happier than white prisoners regarding access to education. Black prisoners also complained that black visitors were more likely to be searched than others. A study of prisoners' perceptions of race relations in prison was also conducted by Cheliotis and Liebling (2005), using surveys of 4,860 prisoners in 49 establishments in England and Wales, and found that large proportions of the ethnic minority groups thought they were subject to unfair treatment compared to the white majority. Research by Clements at HMP Brixton also found that punishment was used disproportionately against black prisoners (Clements 2000).

Since the late 1980s, the level of awareness of the problem of racism in prison on the part of the prison management has increased, with various race relations policies being formulated (see section 11.8). The ruling in the case of *Alexander v Home Office* (1988) was circulated in all prisons and the case discussed in training. The court found that Alexander had been unlawfully discriminated against when he applied for work in the prison kitchen at Parkhurst and that he was refused work on racist grounds. The decision to allocate work was based on a report containing negative and racist comments. This was the first successful reported case brought by a prisoner under the Race Relations Act 1976.

The Race Relations (Amendment) Act 2000 imposed a statutory duty on prisons to promote race equality. The Equality Act 2010 has strengthened the equality duty and broadened the range of protected characteristics, and means that prisons must be more proactive in addressing equality issues. It is also clear in Prison Service Orders and

Instructions that allocation to accommodation, work, training, and education must be made on a non-discriminatory basis and all policies must be assessed for their equality implications (PSI 32/2011).

A major review of race relations in prison was conducted by the Prison Inspectorate in 2005 using a review of survey material from 5,500 prisoners in 18 prisons (HM Inspectorate of Prisons 2005). The survey covered all ethnic groups and used consultations with white and visible-minority staff, governors, managers and prisoners, including black, Asian, and mixed-race prisoners, women, young offenders and juveniles, and foreign national prisoners. The Review found that, instead of a shared understanding of race issues within prisons, there was a series of 'parallel worlds', with different groups of staff and prisoners having quite different views and experiences. Prisoners were asked about their direct experiences of racism. Visible-minority prisoners were more negative than white prisoners across the four key areas of safety, respect, purposeful activity, and resettlement. Most thought that racism existed, particularly in relation to differential access to the prison regime and treatment by staff, for example the way in which they were spoken to or searched, the way requests were dealt with, or how long they waited for things that they needed. However, young black prisoners were more positive than adult black prisoners. Moreover, in one area of prison life—education and training—black and Asian prisoners were more likely than white prisoners to value education.

A later report in 2008 found prisoners continuing to refer to covert racism in the form of 'favouritism' and 'subtle prejudice' (HM Chief Inspector of Prisons 2008a: 27). The NOMS *Race Review* in 2008 also reported that black prisoners reported that they felt that they were less likely to get the better quality jobs within the prison (NOMS 2008). The focus in this Review was on more subtle forms of discrimination, unconscious bias, and the exercise of discretion. Completion of offending behaviour programmes was also lower than average in 2010/11 for Asian and black prisoners (Ministry of Justice 2011g). However, the Prison Inspectorate suggested that BME prisoners were more likely to take part in training and education (HM Chief Inspector of Prisons 2010a). There are now slighter differences in start and completion rates on accredited programmes. So for 2013/14 there were 12.9 per 100 starts for white prisoners compared to 11.3 for BME prisoners, and 11.5 per 100 completions for white prisoners compared to 10.1 for BME prisoners (Ministry of Justice 2014c: 16).

A further issue is the number of prisoners with Basic Status on the IEP scheme. Mixed-ethnicity prisoners have the highest proportion on the Basic level, at 6.7 per cent. At Enhanced IEP status level, Asian and Asian British constitute the highest proportion, at 43.2 per cent, while mixed-ethnicity prisoners have the lowest, at 31.2 per cent (Ministry of Justice 2015f: 11).

9.7.3 Racial harassment

A further problem highlighted in several studies is the problem of racial harassment by both staff and other prisoners. If a prisoner wants to complain about racism, he or she can use the ordinary complaints procedure, or can complain directly to the Equality and Human Rights Commission who can advise and support complainants. In addition, the prisoner can also complain to the Ombudsman. The definition of a racist incident is 'any incident which is perceived to be racist by the victim or any other person', as used in the Macpherson Report (Macpherson 1999). However, prisoners may be reluctant to complain for fear of being seen as troublemakers or of causing trouble for themselves, or because they do not believe that their complaint will be taken seriously (see NACRO 2000a; HM Inspector of Prisons 2005; Keith 2006). A Prison Reform Trust study involving interviews with a sample of 71 prisoners found that 41 prisoners had experienced racism within the previous six months, but two-thirds had not made a complaint over the incident (Edgar 2010).

Clements' (2000) study of Brixton Prison in 2000 found evidence of racial harassment, abuse, and racist language. In other prisons, minority ethnic prisoners have been the target of racist abuse and violence and there are some indications that these incidents of harassment have been under-reported, because of concerns that they will not be taken seriously. Racist abuse in Wormwood Scrubs was the subject of a report in 1999 and the Commission for Racial Equality (CRE) has investigated racism at Brixton, Parc, and Feltham. It conducted a full investigation into racism in the Prison Service, with reference to the need to eliminate unlawful racial discrimination and to promote equality of opportunity. The CRE examined the nature and frequency of incidents of racial discrimination, the way they are investigated, and the circumstances leading to the murder of Zahid Mubarek (discussed in section 9.7.4). It examined events between mid-1991 and July 2000 in Brixton Prison, between 1998 and July 2000 in Parc Prison, and between January 1996 and November 2000 in Feltham Young Offenders Institution, in the light of reports and evidence suggesting acts of discrimination. The CRE was very critical of the Prison Service's failure to protect Mubarek and its failure to eliminate discrimination.

The CRE found the Prison Service guilty of racial discrimination at Feltham, Parc, and Brixton (Commission for Racial Equality 2003). Issues raised included the treatment of staff and prisoners; access to goods, services, and facilities; control of the use of discretion, disciplinary matters, and the Incentives and Earned Privileges Scheme; access to work; investigation of complaints; protection from victimisation; and management procedures. An Action Plan, *Implementing Race Equality: A Shared Agenda for Change*, was drawn up to address these problems (see section 9.8; HM Prison Service/ CRE 2003).[6]

A new Prison Service Order on Race Equality (PSO 2800) was issued in 2006 to further the pursuit of race equality and to implement the race equality duty; in April 2011 it was replaced by PSI 32/2011, *Ensuring Equality*, which set out the framework for dealing with equalities issues, including harassment.

The Prison Rules include disciplinary offences of racially aggravated assault and racially aggravated damage to or destruction of any part of prison or other property, and insulting behaviour. These are directed at the behaviour of prisoners rather than staff or visitors. Racially aggravated and racist offences include assault; damage or destruction of property; threatening, abusive, or insulting racist words or behaviour; and displaying any threatening, abusive, or insulting racist material. If an offence is racially aggravated, this will be reflected in increased punishment. It will be deemed to be racially aggravated if the offender expresses to the victim hostility based on the victim's membership of a racial group or is motivated by such hostility.

In addition a violence reduction strategy was introduced by the Prison Service, with all individual prisons now obliged to develop a local strategy to reduce violence and create a culture of non-violence amongst prisoners, and a new violence reduction strategy is now being developed (PS0 2750). All prisons must also have an anti-bullying strategy and procedures to deal with bullying when perpetrators have been identified, although the issue in the Mubarek case was the failure to identify the risk.

Victimisation, racism, and harassment are problems which affect ethnic minority officers as well as prisoners. Because of their numbers, they may feel isolated and may be

---

[6] The CRE has now been replaced by the Equality and Human Rights Commission, which deals with a wider range of equality issues.

more likely to suffer victimisation and harassment (McDermott 1990). A support network, RESPECT, was set up in 2001 to improve the working conditions of black and minority ethnic staff and to support staff who have been victims of racism. The Prison Reform Trust (2006) interviewed members of RESPECT in 2004–6 and found that 61 per cent of the staff interviewed believed that they had experienced racial discrimination including isolation, harassment, and verbal abuse, and had suffered this mostly from their colleagues rather than from prisoners or managers. Their respondents reported that they thought that blatant overt racism was becoming less common, but covert racism and institutional racism were more serious problems. Two-thirds of the BME staff in this survey thought that institutional racism remained a problem, particularly in relation to career development and promotion and grievance procedures, with promotion hindered by subtle discrimination. There was also a lack of confidence amongst BME staff in procedures for dealing with complaints about racism: covert racism may be harder to prove and investigators are likely to be senior white officers.

9.7.4 **Deaths in custody**

Some deaths in custody have occurred where there is evidence of a racist motive on the part of the perpetrator. Zahid Mubarek was murdered in Feltham Young Offenders Institution in March 2000. While sleeping he was clubbed into a coma by his cellmate, Robert Stewart, using part of the furniture in his cell, and he died later in hospital. Prior to the murder Stewart had written letters expressing racist views and threatened to kill his cellmate. It was clear that Stewart had a personality disorder and deeply entrenched racist beliefs and he had previously been charged with racially motivated malicious communications. The conditions in Feltham had also been criticised by the then Chief Inspector of Prisons, David Ramsbotham. In a similar incident, Shahid Aziz was murdered by his white cellmate, Peter McCann, in HMP Leeds in 2004. McCann had been classified as low risk, but the inquest was critical of the failure to pass on relevant information to the prison.

Deaths in custody have also occurred following the use of excessive physical restraints, such as the Alton Manning case referred to earlier (Chapter 8, section 8.5.1).[7] There have also been cases of deaths arising from inadequate medical treatment or failure to recognise or diagnose a medical condition. Deaths in prison and immigration centres now fall within the remit of the Prisons and Probation Ombudsman and, as we saw in Chapter 8, Article 2 claims have been successfully brought against the UK which have led to changes in the way reviews are handled. In 2012 the deaths in prison custody included 169 white, 11 black, and 7 Asian prisoners (Ministry of Justice 2013d: 107). The focus on deaths in police custody has also highlighted concerns over the use of restraints and the problems in assessing and detaining suspects with mental health problems or other vulnerabilities (see for example, Hannan *et al.* 2010; Casale 2013; Grace 2013).

The Formal Investigation of the Commission for Racial Equality into the murder of Zahid Mubarek was highly critical of failures on the part of the prison management to spot the potential risk and to protect Mubarek from Stewart, or to follow up warnings in Stewart's file, as well as failures to follow Prison Service Orders and failures by senior managers to give priority to race issues (Commission for Racial Equality 2003). These failures, it argued, if addressed could have prevented Mubarek's death. A public inquiry, chaired by Mr Justice Keith, was set up to examine the measures which needed to be taken to prevent the recurrence of such a tragedy and its report was published in 2006 (Keith 2006).

---

[7] See *R v DPP ex parte Manning* (2001).

It focused attention on the wider culture and practice of the Prison Service, just as the Macpherson Inquiry highlighted problems within the police.

The Prison Service has now developed procedures for carrying out race equality impact assessments and introduced performance targets for race equality, including staff recruitment. There are also training schemes for staff carrying out impact assessments, and a new system of consultation with prisoners, staff, and local communities on race equality issues.

The CRE, in its submission to the Mubarek Inquiry, acknowledged the efforts being made to address the problems highlighted by the death of Zahid Mubarek but found that there was still evidence of poor practice. So while the formal policies to promote race equality and challenge racism were certainly evident, they were not always being implemented (Commission for Racial Equality 2005). For example, it expressed concern about the procedures for complaints and reporting of racist incidents and noted that prisoners said they felt inhibited in making complaints because their reports were read by officers; a study by the HM Inspectorate of Prisons (2005) found this was still the case.

9.7.5 The Report of the Mubarek Inquiry

The Mubarek Report was published in June 2006 and reflected similar concerns to the CRE Report (Keith 2006). Although it focused on Feltham, where the murder occurred, many of the issues raised applied across the prison estate. The two major issues were the problems with enforced cell sharing and the failure to pass on information which might have prevented the attack. The report argued for an end to enforced cell sharing to reduce the risk of prisoner-on-prisoner attacks, with extra funds being provided from the government for this purpose. Single cells would prevent tensions escalating between prisoners as well as increasing privacy. While sharing might be desirable, for example, where there is a risk of suicide or self-harm, in most cases it should be avoided. The suitability of particular prisoners for sharing should be reviewed regularly in consultation with the prisoners' personal officers.

The other major issue in the failure to prevent the attack was the failure to pass on information about Stewart to Feltham and to circulate information, particularly about his racism, his possible involvement in a murder at another YOI, and his disruptive behaviour at other institutions. The Report recommended the importance of storing information on risk assessment on the national database for offenders in order to quickly identify prisoners who may constitute a risk to others because of their racist views or other issues. Risk assessments of prisoners should be reviewed regularly.

The emphasis in the report was on closer scrutiny and assessment of all prisoners, using **OASys**. Mr Justice Keith recommended a review of training to improve and develop interpersonal skills and a review of cell-searching policy to increase the chance of finding concealed weapons in cells, as it was clear that at Feltham full cell searches were not taking place on the unit. The report also found that the care of prisoners suffering from mental health problems at the time of Mubarek's murder was poor. It also argued for improved diversity training for officers.

Attacks on prisoners in their cells by other prisoners, it concluded, are more likely to happen in prisons which are not functioning well and the concern is that 'population pressures and understaffing can combine to undermine the decency agenda and compromise the Prison Service's ability to run prisons efficiently' (Keith 2006: para 63.7). These concerns are even more relevant now as the pressures on the population have further increased since 2006 and remain high.

By the time the report was published, many of the issues had already begun to be addressed, for example issues relating to the flow of information, and the Race Equality

Plan addressed some of the broader equality issues. The government accepted in principle that enforced cell sharing should end, although it acknowledged that it would persist for some time because of population pressures. Indeed, since 2006 the problem of cell sharing has persisted, with the prison population reaching record levels.

By 2011 NOMS had implemented 71 of the recommendations. A review of the implementation of the recommendations of the Mubarek Inquiry was undertaken by the Prison Inspectorate in 2014 which concluded that there were still significant concerns (HM Inspectorate of Prisons 2014b). While there had been some positive changes, with new systems and processes in place and better sharing of information through electronic means, the implementation of these processes was inconsistent. Risk assessment procedures in some cases were delayed or poorly implemented and too many prisoners were still sharing cells. While most establishments had a violence reduction strategy, more work to address discriminatory behaviour needed to be included in violence-reduction work (ibid: para 4.26). There had been a reduction in homicides in prison since the Cell Sharing Risk Assessment was introduced in response to the Mubarek murder, but homicides were still occurring, and enforced sharing still persists because of the pressures on the prison system. Cell sharing between convicted and unconvicted prisoners also persisted. Young adults and adults were also accommodated on the same wings in some establishments. OASys assessments were only required on prisoners serving sentences over 12 months and OASys was not being routinely used to manage or address risks to others while in custody (ibid: para 4.103). Moreover, the number of staff dealing with equality issues had been reduced. There were also specific concerns regarding the conditions in Feltham B in 2013.

9.7.6 Foreign national prisoners

As well as considering the experience of women and ethnic minority prisoners, we need to consider the position of foreign national prisoners. The percentage of foreign national prisoners in the prison population as a whole rose to 14 per cent in 2008, compared to just under 8 per cent in 2003. Since 2011 the number of foreign national prisoners has fluctuated between 12 and 13 per cent and in 2015 they constituted 12 per cent of the prison population in England and Wales (Ministry of Justice 2015b). Foreign national prisoners came from 154 states, but over half were from ten countries, namely Poland, Republic of Ireland, Romania, Jamaica, Lithuania, India, Pakistan, Nigeria, Albania and Somalia (Prison Reform Trust 2015a: 5).

Within the foreign national prison population the proportion of offenders from the white ethnic group increased by 7 per cent from 2008 to 2012, while the proportion of offenders from black ethnic groups declined by 9 per cent and that of Chinese or other by 3 per cent. The proportion of offenders from Asian and mixed groups has remained stable (Ministry of Justice 2013d: 102, 2015h: 70). They are now concentrated in foreign national prisoner hubs, so for example, they account for one-third of the population of Wormwood Scrubs.

The rise in the number of foreign national prisoners is found throughout Western Europe, where there are increasing numbers of foreign national prisoners sentenced for migration-related and drug trafficking crimes, particularly amongst the female prison population. The reasons for the increase in foreign national prisoners and its implications are considered by Banks (2011) who argues that changes in immigration policy have resulted in an increase in the numbers charged with immigration offences and fraud and forgery offences linked to attempts to enter or remain in the UK.

Convicted prisoners who have ended their sentences may be held in prison rather than immigration removal centres, while they await deportation or decisions on asylum or their immigration status, with limited access to telephones and lawyers. In March 2015 there were 374 foreign nationals being held in prison under immigration powers after completing their sentences instead of being transferred to immigration removal centres, where they would have access to the Internet, mobile phones, and legal advice (HM Chief Inspector of Prisons 2015: 45).

The policy now is to provide better services by concentrating foreign national prisoners in hubs at specific prisons, but this also makes it harder to vary security levels for this group. Foreign national prisoners can be sent to an open prison, but the decision on allocation should be based on individual risk, not simply on the fact that the person is a foreign national.

A thematic review of foreign national prisoners was undertaken by the Prison Inspectorate, focusing on prisons outside London (HM Inspectorate of Prisons 2006). At the time of their research there were approximately 10,000 foreign national prisoners—13 per cent of the prison population as a whole—drawn from 172 different countries, but with Jamaicans and Nigerians constituting the largest groups. They found that foreign national prisoners' key concerns related to family matters, particularly maintaining family links, language problems, and immigration issues. Although the staff they interviewed also recognised that these were problems they did not consider them as serious as the prisoners did, and they were unsure how to respond to the problems. Those prisoners who did not speak English experienced the greatest problems in access to resources. Language problems were a particular issue for prisoners from Vietnam, China, the Middle East, and eastern Europe, while family and immigration problems were a particular issue for women prisoners. Some prisoners may lack the language skills to obtain the necessary information from appropriate sources to address these problems or to use resources within the prison.

Foreign national prisoners experienced racism, negative stereotyping and disrespectful treatment, and resettlement problems, and had less contact with personal officers. Negative perceptions of women offenders as negligent mothers may be focused on foreign national women who have left their children behind to carry drugs. Foreign national prisoners receive fewer visits than other prisoners. Black and minority ethnic foreign national prisoners reported worse experiences than white foreign national prisoners, particularly in relation to racism and religious observance. The staff interviewed wanted more training and guidance on foreign national issues.

The review also found low awareness of available services, for example interpreters, outside agencies, or foreign national prisoner coordinators. Although Hibiscus Initiatives and the Citizens Advice Bureau gave some general information to prisoners, there was insufficient independent specialist advice on individuals' immigration problems. There was also considerable confusion and ignorance amongst staff on how to support or inform prisoners awaiting deportation and also very little contact with home countries on resettlement issues, as resettlement support tends to focus on UK resettlement. However, the review did find examples of good practice in some prisons, for example the support given by Hibiscus Initiatives, which helps prisoners in the UK and liaises with contacts overseas, but there was no coordination between the Prison Service and other agencies. Prisoners could also be given more practical support to maintain contact with their families.

While the larger minorities may be better provided for, there are problems for the smaller ethnic minorities. Foreign national prisoners are not a homogeneous group; they include a diverse range of groups. However, they may share common problems, including family problems, immigration problems, and language problems. There are particular concerns over access to translation facilities. Insufficient information in their own language and difficulty in speaking English may affect access to work and participation in programmes, which will also have implications for parole and resettlement and for accessing lawyers and the legal system, or negotiating the immigration rules and procedures.

The Prisoners' Information Handbook for male prisoners and young offenders, published jointly by the Prison Reform Trust and the Ministry of Justice, is published in 27 languages but this does not extend to minority languages within the foreign national population. Foreign nationals may be isolated by language problems; they may also have problems arranging legal representation and difficulties contacting home. When prison resources are stretched because of the increasing demands for prison places, their needs may be less likely to be addressed.

The Prison Inspectorate has found that foreign nationals were offered insufficient support, although there were some exceptions. Foreign national prisoners were more negative than British prisoners in response to a range of questions, with fewer feeling safe or respected by staff (HM Chief Inspector of Prisons 2015: 45). Many of the problems faced by women prisoners, such as separation from their families, are exacerbated for foreign national prisoners—especially for those serving long sentences, who find it difficult to provide for or keep in contact with their families and, if they do, have to deal with family problems from a distance by phone, although Skype now makes this easier (HM Inspectorate of Prisons 2006, HM Chief Inspector of Prisons 2011a).

9.8 Race relations policies in the Prison Service

As we have seen, a number of problems facing black and minority ethnic prisoners and staff have been identified. Various measures designed to address some of these issues have been introduced. The Prison Service was one of the first criminal justice bodies to collect data on ethnic minorities and the first to develop a race relations policy. It was also the first public sector organisation to impose a ban on staff affiliated with known racist groups, and operates a strict policy of intolerance and dismissal for unacceptable behaviour.

The Home Office instituted a review of prison race relations work in 1981, then issued to all establishments a Circular on Race Relations which gave advice on race relations work, emphasising the need to obtain more information on ethnic minorities and the importance of equal treatment. Governors were required to appoint Race Relations Liaison Officers (RRLOs) to provide and collect information. A *Race Relations Manual* for the Prison Service was first published in 1991 and subsequently amended. It gave more detailed guidance and policies on matters including responsibility for implementing the race relations policy, measuring progress, and training.

Research undertaken by NACRO in the late 1990s found that while there was a commitment to race equality on the part of the Director General of the Prison Service, there was still a continuing perception of unfairness among some prisoners. Prisoners and staff in public and private prisons, including young offender institutions, were interviewed and the sample also included remand and women prisoners, white and ethnic minority staff, and prisoners (NACRO 2000a). The majority of those who had received race relations training had found it useful and were in favour of ethnic monitoring, although critical of the amount of paperwork involved.

Prisoners from minority ethnic groups were less likely to assess race relations as good. The researchers found that verbal and racial abuse were still common, and there were still incidents of physical abuse from other prisoners, but few reported these incidents because they thought that there was no point, nothing would be done, and it would just cause more trouble.

The NACRO study found that although the race relations policy had a high profile in the Prison Service, it was not working so well at a day-to-day level, the policy was not fully understood, and the training was not equipping staff to deal fairly with colleagues or prisoners. Many staff were happy to leave it to the RRLOs rather than taking responsibility themselves for providing regimes which do not discriminate. A follow-up study (NACRO 2003f) found that while there had been some improvement, more progress was needed. Later research by Spencer *et al.* (2009), who interviewed officers in four prisons in 2006, found that the respondents did take race relations work seriously but felt there was too much emphasis on statistics and insufficient time for the RRLOs to undertake their work, and it was also difficult to engage the attendance of external community groups in Race Relations Management Team (RRMT) meetings.

Other measures introduced to combat racism include RESPOND (Racial Equality for Staff and Prisoners), which was launched in 1999, following the Macpherson Report, to confront racial harassment and discrimination, support ethnic minority staff, and ensure equal opportunities for ethnic minority prisoners. Targets to increase the recruitment of ethnic minorities, to review complaints procedures and improve equality training, and to monitor racist complaints and incidents and monitor the career progress of BME staff were also introduced. The CRE Report highlighted the survival of racist attitudes despite two decades of progressive legislation (CRE 2003). So while there was a commitment to racial equality in the Prison Service, it was still very hard to control discriminatory behaviour at a micro level.

An Action Plan designed by the Prison Service with the CRE identified key areas of work and relevant timescales (HM Prison Service/CRE 2003). It was designed to ensure that policies are assessed for their impact on different groups. It included inter alia revisions to the procedures for ethnic monitoring of prisoners to include a range of factors such as privilege levels, complaints, segregation, adjudication, access to activities, revisions to the Racist Incident Reporting Form, a review of complaints procedures, and clarification of the role of RRMTs. A new Prison Service Order in 2006 made a number of changes, including replacing Race Relation Liaison Officers with Race Equality Officers (REOs) and RRMTs with Race Equality Action Teams (REATs), providing more support to the REOs and establishing a framework for a more proactive approach.

The impact of the Action Plan which ended in 2008 was reviewed by the *Race Review: Implementing Race Equality in Prisons—Five Years On*, which included a survey of 900 prisoners (NOMS 2008). It reported progress had been made in a number of key areas, including training for Race Equality Action Team members. There were also improvements in monitoring, setting, and meeting race equality targets and greater involvement of outside bodies, and improvements in dealing with racist incidents and complaints. But despite these significant changes, it reported that problems still persisted. For example, black prisoners still believed that they had less access to good quality work and it was also clear that BME prisoners were more likely to be segregated for disciplinary reasons and to be subjected to disciplinary charges, areas where discretion is exercised by prison officers.

The focus has now shifted from an anti-racist strategy towards a more proactive role to promote diversity, and the pursuit of equality is now integrated into prison management and falls under the general equality duty imposed by the 2010 Equality Act, with a focus on impact assessment and outcomes.

Efforts have also been made to broaden the social composition of officers, with a higher number of ethnic minority officers. Increased recruitment of ethnic minority staff is desirable on grounds of fairness, but it may also assist in the smooth running of the prison as it legitimises the authority of prison officers and reduces tensions. BME staff comprised 5.7 per cent of NOMS staff in 2011 (Ministry of Justice 2011c: 80). The percentage of BME staff in NOMS, excluding probation, has remained at about 6 per cent for the past five years, but the proportion of BME staff in the Ministry of Justice and the Crown Prosecution Service is higher (Ministry of Justice 2013d: 115, 2015h: 93).[8]

Cheliotis and Liebling (2005) found that ethnic minority prisoners rated race relations more unfavourably than white prisoners. Perceptions of race relations correlated with other key areas of treatment including fairness, respect, humanity, relationships with staff, and safety. White prisoners had a more positive view of race relations than ethnic minority prisoners.

9.9 Challenging racism

9.9.1 Policy into practice

While there has been a shift in policy towards greater awareness of the problems facing minority ethnic prisoners at a managerial level, the difficulty remains of how to ensure that ameliorative measures are applied in practice especially in view of the substantial increases in the prison population. The Mubarek case brought the issue of race equality to the forefront of penal policy again and race equality is given a high priority at the formal policy level. The promotion of equal opportunity and non-discrimination is also beneficial to the good order of the prison as racial conflict may be a source of tension within prisons. However, it has been said that BME and white prisoners live in parallel worlds.

9.9.2 *Parallel Worlds*

A thematic study of BME prisoners by the Prison Inspectorate, *Parallel Worlds*, published in 2005, considered the views of staff and prisoners on race relations in prison and possible problems, and examined the effectiveness of monitoring and complaints procedures. It found a gap between formal policy initiatives and the experience of different groups of staff and prisoners (HM Inspectorate of Prisons 2005). Governors and white RRLOs were the most optimistic regarding race relations, thinking that the regime was operating fairly while acknowledging that more needed to be done. But ethnic minority staff were less likely to think that their prison was tackling race relations effectively, although they accepted some progress had been made. There were references to overt and subtle racism from colleagues. Ethnic minority staff also felt they had insufficient support from managers in applying for promotion. White staff, however, tended to see racism as an issue between prisoners rather than an issue for staff, and did not seem aware of the extent to which their colleagues had experienced discrimination. Some minority staff felt isolated and that they were being overlooked for promotion.

Black and minority ethnic prisoners felt they received worse treatment than white prisoners. Safety was the major concern for Asian prisoners, with between one-third and one-half saying they felt unsafe, particularly women and young adults. Asian prisoners were more likely to report bullying. Black prisoners felt safer than Asian prisoners but were more concerned than them about the lack of respect they felt in their treatment by staff. Both black and Asian prisoners were also less positive about health care and the reviewers found that providers of health care did not recognise specific needs of ethnic minority communities, for example in relation to sickle cell anaemia. BME prisoners were also under-represented at the therapeutic prison, HMP Grendon (see Sullivan 2007).

---

[8] The statistics for staff equalities for 2015 will be included in the forthcoming Ministry of Justice Diversity publication.

The outcomes of complaints of racist incidents were also examined in *Parallel Worlds*. Most related to prisoner-on-prisoner complaints. Although these investigations were undertaken properly, complaints against staff were responded to less effectively than complaints against prisoners, which undermined confidence in the complaints system. Complaints about prisoners were upheld more often than complaints against staff and the outcomes were more severe for prisoners than staff. BME prisoners were less likely than non-BME prisoners to believe that complaints would be dealt with fairly and, of course, if they feel the response will be unfair, they may be unlikely to complain at all. Furthermore, prisoners serving shorter sentences may feel it is not worth complaining.

However, in some prisons race and diversity were given a high priority. Examples of good practice included the establishment of the 'Parva against Racism' movement at Glen Parva YOI, which involved workshops, sport, and debates; the use of mediation to deal with complaints at Huntercombe; and contact with relevant outside bodies at Styal and Forest Bank.

Parallel Worlds makes depressing reading, given that it was reviewing the situation after the Mubarek and CRE Reports and showed that despite over 20 years of formal changes to reduce racism, problems still remained. A later report from the Prison Inspectorate found that 'prisoners from a black or minority ethnic background, foreign nationals, Muslim prisoners and those under the age of 21 were more likely to report having spent time in the segregation or care and separation unit in the past six months' (HM Chief Inspector of Prisons 2011a: 25). In two prisons, Norwich and Whatton, 'black and minority ethnic prisoners were disproportionately more likely to be segregated' (ibid). Investigations by the Prison Inspectorate indicate that 'young adult, foreign national, black and minority ethnic and Muslim respondents generally felt less well respected by staff' (ibid: 29).

There has been more rigorous ethnic monitoring and the investigation of racist incidents has improved. But problems clearly persist, as the Chief Inspector of Prisons has noted. There are still inequalities in relation to segregation, the use of force, and disciplinary hearings, with black and minority ethnic prisoners over-represented in some prisons inspected (ibid: 34). However, as noted earlier, the investigations of the Prison Inspectorate suggest that black women prisoners are more positive about their treatment than black male prisoners.

There were also differentials in perceptions of how prisons dealt with complaints, with foreign national prisoners, BME, Muslim, and disabled prisoners more negative than other prisoners. These prisoners were more likely to feel unsafe and to respond negatively to questions in surveys undertaken for the Prison Inspectorate. Black prisoners were particularly concerned about relations with staff, while Asian prisoners were particularly worried about safety.

Several initiatives would assist in promoting racial equality, including greater awareness and understanding on the part of staff of the impact of institutional discrimination and the differential impact of the criminal justice system on black and minority ethnic groups and greater awareness of race relations and equality policies and of the value of ethnic monitoring. Reporting of incidents should be encouraged and prisoners should be able to feel confident that they will be dealt with properly. Prisoners should also be involved in discussions on how to achieve equal access to prison facilities and how to reduce racist incidents. Prisoners are now included as diversity representatives, which is a positive step. Ethnic monitoring of adjudications is now being undertaken to examine differences in the use of disciplinary procedures. In 2013 the adjudication rate for black or black British prisoners was 118 per 100 prisoners, 163 per 100 for mixed ethnic groups, and 100 for white groups (Ministry of Justice 2014c: 12). By 2014 the rate of proven adjudications for black or black British prisoners was 126 per 100 prisoners, for mixed ethnicity prisoners it was 170 per 100 prisoners, and for white groups it was 100 per 100 prisoners (Ministry of Justice 2015f: 12).

The most recent reports from the Prison Inspectorate Report indicate that minority groups continue to report more negatively than the majority of prisoners on key outcomes: 'Prisoners from black and minority ethnic backgrounds and Muslim prisoners continued to report a worse experience than the prison population as a whole' (HM Chief Inspector of Prisons 2015: 12). They were more negative than white prisoners on many areas of prison life. However, BME prisoners were now more positive about safety than white prisoners, and in some prisons such as Elmley, 'they were more positive overall than white prisoners' (ibid: 44).

The HMIP Review of the implementation of the Mubarek Inquiry recommendations found that responses on the helpfulness of personal officers were poorer for BME prisoners (HMIP 2014b: para 4.62). But the report said that while some negative perceptions persisted, there were some changes in perceptions of different ethnic groups, for example in relation to respect, that might indicate improvement: '[h]owever, the picture is mixed and no clear overall conclusions can be drawn' (ibid, para 4.72).

The racist incident report form has been replaced by a discrimination incident report form which has improved investigation of race-related complaints. However, BME prisoners reported poorer perceptions of the complaints system than white prisoners (ibid: para 4.91). The fear of reprisals following complaints still inhibited some prisoners from making complaints. At the same time, Earle (2013) has also highlighted the resentments felt by some white prisoners in the face of the strategies used by the prison regime to combat unfair treatment of BME prisoners.

9.10 A generic approach to equality

The focus now is on a generic approach to equality and diversity which addresses a broader range of protected characteristics. The duty on prisons to meet the equality duty was set out by NOMS in its Single Equality Scheme for 2009–2012 (NOMS 2009b). The approach taken to race equality has been extended to these other areas, so annual Equalities Reports report on progress made, on equality impact assessments, and on the action taken to resolve problems as well as outcomes.

9.10.1 Focusing on diversity

The first review after the Act found that there had been improvements in data collection, with more data available on disability and sexual orientation (Ministry of Justice 2011g). All new policies were subject to equality impact assessments and were completed at both headquarters and individual prison establishments. Support groups were set up for disabled staff as well as gay, lesbian, bisexual, and transgender staff. The Prison Service Instructions on equality issues had been reviewed and revised. More guidance was given on monitoring and managing the welfare of gay prisoners. Diversity training materials were devised and introduced, as well as faith awareness courses.

More attention is now being directed towards reducing the incidence of unequal outcomes resulting from unconscious bias in the use of discretion. The focus is on setting out equality objectives, which will include collecting accurate monitoring data, identifying and reducing disparities in outcomes, achieving comprehensive screening for disabilities, and improving outcomes for women offenders.

Policies in prison now focus on diversity, which is intended to cover a wide range of protected characteristics. However, the Prison Inspectorate has found that most of the policies focus on race and ethnicity rather than the other characteristics.

The particular areas needing further work which have been highlighted in recent reports are religion, sexual orientation, age, and disability. The Prison Inspectorate has found that 'Prisoners with protected characteristics continued to report more negatively than the population as a whole' (HM Chief Inspector of Prisons 2015: 44). Monitoring to ensure equality of outcomes was often inadequate. While data on race and ethnicity was monitored by most prisons, few focused on the treatment of prisoners in relation to the other protected characteristics. While many prisons had prisoner equality representatives, few prisoners were aware of this role. Moreover, as noted by the House of Commons Justice Committee, 'A key question is whether making savings in the prison estate inevitably results in a one-size-fits-all approach to prison policy' (House of Commons Justice Committee 2015a: para 40). It stressed that 'the custodial estate needs to be designed so that it meets the different needs of different sectors of the prison population' (ibid).

9.10.2 **Religion**

As well as ethnic diversity, we find a wide range of religious beliefs held by prisoners. As well as the major religions of Christianity, Judaism, Islam, and Sikhism, prisoners may also practice Buddhism and Paganism. In 2015, 30.7 per cent reported no religious affiliation, 49.2 per cent were Christian, and 14.4 per cent were Muslim (Ministry of Justice 2015f: 8). Prisons are obliged to allow inmates to practise their religion, which means allowing them to attend services and giving them time for worship, unless there are security problems. Freedom of religion is protected by Article 9 of the ECHR and any limits on this right have to be justified under Article 9(2). Prisoners are not required to work on special religious days and should be provided with an appropriate diet as required by their religion. While the major religions are well catered for and attention to religion has improved, the Prison Inspectorate has criticised the insufficient provision for Buddhism.

The number of Muslim prisoners increased from 4,653 in 2000 to 11,248 in 2012 (HM Inspectorate of Prisons 2014c: para 4.64). By the end of March 2014 Muslim prisoners accounted for 12.4 per cent of the population, compared to 9.7 per cent in 2004. In March 2015 they constituted 14.4 per cent of the prison population (Ministry of Justice 2015f: 5). There were 12,328 Muslim prisoners in 2015 (House of Commons Justice Committee 2015a; Prison Reform Trust 2015: 5). In the 2014/15 survey by the Prison Inspectorate, 13 per cent of prisoners self-reported as Muslim, although the actual numbers varied between prisons (HM Chief Inspector of Prisons 2015: 48). They were low in some prisons, but Muslim prisoners constituted 44 per cent of the prisoners at Whitemoor. There is a high concentration of Muslim prisoners in high-security prisons. Muslim prisoners are a diverse group consisting of 41 per cent Asian, 31 per cent black, 14 per cent white, and 8 per cent mixed, and the group includes converts.

A thematic review of Muslim prisoners was undertaken by the Chief Inspector of Prisons in 2010 which involved interviews with 164 Muslim prisoners in eight prisons and with Muslim prison chaplains (HM Chief Inspector of Prisons 2010b). Research on Muslim prisoners has also been conducted by Spalek (2002) and Beckford et al. (2005). Issues have been raised over their relations with prison officers, allegations of intimidation of other prisoners and exerting pressure on prisoners to convert to Islam, and concerns that prison is now a recruiting ground for extremism. These issues were considered in the Prison Inspectorate's Review, which found that the stress on combating extremism and the media focus on Islam led to some members of staff associating all Muslim prisoners with extremism, which ran the risk of alienating prisoners and undermining efforts to combat prisoner radicalisation. The review also found little evidence of forcible conversion to Islam.

In their latest report the Inspectorate found effective responses to the risks of radicalisation (HM Chief Inspector of Prisons 2015: 48). While relations between religious groups were usually harmonious, at Whitemoor there was tension between the large Muslim population and other prisoners and staff. Some Muslim prisoners thought their beliefs were not respected and that they were discriminated against, while non-Muslim prisoners thought Muslim prisoners and staff had too much influence in the prison (ibid). However, NOMS is treating radicalisation as a priority and, as Pickering notes in his review of extremism and the offender management system in England and Wales, '[o]ffender management is and remains a critical part of the government's overall counter terrorism strategy' (Pickering 2014: 166). The type of prison regime, as Jones (2014) argues, will also have implications for the radicalisation of prisoners.

The thematic review also found that prisoners' religious needs had been met and provision was made for prayers and an appropriate diet within the prison regime. The number of Muslim prison chaplains had increased and their role had been strengthened. Asians and white Muslims reported more positive experiences of prison life than black and mixed-heritage Muslims, so race and ethnicity overlaid the religious dimension. A Muslim Prisoner Scoping study published in 2009 considered whether there should be a separate strategy for Muslim prisoners, but concluded that the emphasis should instead be on improving staff–prisoner relations generally (NOMS 2009a). The Prison Inspectorate also found that Muslim prisoners had more negative perceptions than other groups of their treatment by staff in terms of being treated with respect, and were more negative about their safety (HM Chief Inspector of Prisons 2010b). Since then faith awareness training has been improved and the Prison Inspectorate reports have been more positive on faith provision in prisons, although Muslim chaplains reported that they did not have enough time for their work (HM Inspectorate of Prisons 2014c: para 4.65). The Prison Inspectorate Report in 2015 found that Muslim prisoners 'were more negative than non-Muslim prisoners on most areas of prison life and treatment, but were more positive about respect for their religious beliefs' (HM Chief Inspector of Prisons 2015: 48).

9.10.3 Sexual orientation

The Prisons and Probation Ombudsman has also raised the problem of homophobic abuse and the lack of support for gay prisoners, who have been neglected in diversity policies. Because of the widespread homophobia inside prison, prisoners may be reluctant to complain, which makes it difficult to measure the extent of the problem. In one particular prison, the prisoner diversity representatives were clearly hostile to prisoners who were open about their sexuality. The Ombudsman was also concerned at the fact that staff stressed the need to respect cultural and religious objections to homosexuality in deciding whether it was safe for gay prisoners to reveal their sexuality inside prison. The Ombudsman noted that 'religious beliefs should be respected but this does not mean that discriminatory or antagonistic language or behaviour should be tolerated' (Prisons and Probation Ombudsman 2011: 23). This report recommended that policies on sexual orientation should be redrafted to promote a more supportive culture. The Prison Service has become more aware of its obligations not to discriminate against staff or prisoners on the grounds of sexual orientation and also has set up a network for lesbian, gay, bisexual, and transgender staff members.

The Prison Inspectorate has found the most neglected dimension of equality is sexuality (HM Chief Inspector of Prisons 2011a: 33). A visit by the Prison Inspectorate to Holloway,

Bronzefield, and Drake Hall found that all three prisons had race equality procedures but there was little on sexuality (ibid). So this was an area where more work was needed to promote equality. However, Hull and Wakefield did have support groups for gay prisoners and gay prisoner forums, and efforts were made to combat homophobia. There have also been improvements in data collection on sexual orientation, developed in consultation with Stonewall, and in the recording of complaints dealing with homophobic incidents. Gay prisoners now have the right to marry their partners whether they are inside or outside prison, as noted in Chapter 8, under the Marriage (Same Sex Couples) Act 2013 and the first marriage between gay prisoners took place in Full Sutton in March 2015.

However, the latest report of the Prison Inspectorate indicates that support for gay and bisexual prisoners is still undeveloped (HM Chief Inspector of Prisons 2015: 46). Many prisoners said that they felt unsafe in disclosing their sexuality to staff or other prisoners because of a fear of victimisation and there was little support for gay prisoners in the prisons visited.

9.10.4 Transgender prisoners

Prisons also have an equality duty to transgender prisoners under the Equality Act 2010, which means that a specific policy to deal with these prisoners is required. A Prison Service Instruction on the management of transgender prisoners has been issued. The courts also upheld the right of a pre-operative transgender prisoner to be transferred to a women's prison in *R (on the application of AB) v (1) Secretary of State for Justice (2) Governor of Manchester Prison: QBD (Admin)* 4 September 2009.

Prisoners may also begin treatment for reassignment while in custody. As noted earlier, prisoners have the same right to health care as citizens in the wider society, and this includes services for gender reassignment. Access to surgery has been a controversial issue in relation to prisoners, especially in the United States, but California recently became the first state to agree to pay for reassignment surgery (see *Quine v Beard et al.* C 14-02726 JST, 8 July 2015).

The Prison Inspectorate for England and Wales found that although the care and support for transgender prisoners varied across the prison estate, most prisons did have a written policy. In practice much will depend on the sensitivity of prison staff. The Ombudsman upheld the complaint of a male-to-female prisoner who had complained of not being allowed to wear women's clothes on the wing (PPO 2014: 45). PSI 07/2011 *The Care and Management of Transsexual Prisoners* makes it clear that allowing such prisoners to wear female clothes is not a privilege but is necessary to ensure that they can live in the gender role with which they identify. If there are concerns regarding the reaction of other prisoners, then the risk should be managed in the same way as staff would deal with other vulnerable prisoners. The experience of transgender prisoners is under-researched but Disspain and Wildgoose (2015) report on the experiences of a transgender prisoner in a therapeutic community.

The *Expectations for Women Prisoners* also refers specifically to equal treatment of transgender prisoners, so these prisoners should have access to the items needed to maintain their gender appearance and be supported by the specific groups and schemes within the prison, and those who wish to begin gender reassignment should be permitted to live permanently in their acquired gender (HM Inspectorate of Prisons 2014b: 19).

9.10.5 Prisoners with disabilities

A further area in which more work needs to be undertaken to satisfy the equality duty is in relation to prisoners with disabilities. Prison regimes must make reasonable accommodation to address their needs of disabled prisoners. A thematic review of prisoners with disabilities in 2009 found that they are also more likely to report feeling unsafe and more likely to experience victimisation compared to prisoners without disabilities (HM Inspectorate of Prisons 2009a).

Under the Equality Act 2010 there is a statutory duty on public organisations to make reasonable adjustments to services to make them accessible to all users. Guidance to prisons was given in PSI 32/2011 *Ensuring Equality* in 2011. Disabled prisoners' needs should be taken account of in allocating cells and in ensuring access to work, education and physical education. Appropriate books should be provided in the prison library. They should also not be discriminated against in relation to the Incentives and Earned Privileges Scheme, where access to a higher level is based on behaviour, which may have adverse consequences for prisoners with learning disabilities.

The Ministry of Justice estimates that 36 per cent of prisoners have a physical or intellectual disability, while 18 per cent have a physical disability (see Prison Reform Trust 2015: 6; Rack 2005; Thomson 2012). Loucks has estimated (2007) that 20 to 30 per cent of prisoners have learning disabilities which affect their ability to cope with imprisonment and they may find it difficult to adapt to the regimented nature of prison life, resulting in disruptive behaviour and segregation. They may also find it difficult to comply with community punishments. However, there are problems in identifying those with learning disabilities and in assessing, diverting, and treating these prisoners. These problems were highlighted by the Bradley Report, which recommended that further relevant research should be undertaken on this issue (Department of Health 2009a). There should also be greater coordination between agencies and continuity of care in leaving prison. These problems of identification and assessment, as Loucks (2007) points out, will be harder at times of overcrowding, when prisoners are moved around the prison estate. A review of disabled prisoners was also conducted by the Prison Inspectorate in 2009 which found that prisoners with disabilities were more negative about issues of safety and more likely to report victimisation than non-disabled prisoners (HMIP 2009a).

A Prison Reform Trust study of disabled prisoners found that provision and support were variable, and examples of good practice in some prisons were reported (Prison Reform Trust 2004b). As well as problems of access to facilities, because of the failure to incorporate the needs of prisoners with disabilities into prison design, there are problems of access to services, for example, for prisoners with visual and hearing impairments. But the problems may be even greater for prisoners with learning rather than physical disabilities. Until recently this group of prisoners was under-researched, but they are now receiving more attention. A programme, *No One Knows*, to examine and publicise the experiences of people with learning difficulties and learning disabilities who come into contact with the criminal justice system was initiated by the Prison Reform Trust, in view of the increasing numbers of such prisoners and in response to complaints of unequal access to activities and poor treatment, including examples of prisoners confined to their cells for long periods because of inadequate facilities for their needs (Loucks 2007; Talbot 2008).

The final report in the *No One Knows* series was published in 2008 and includes the results of interviews with prisoners with learning disabilities (Talbot 2008). The respondents reported problems in filling in forms and negotiating prison procedures so that they sometimes missed out on visits and had difficulty in gaining access to prison services and making themselves understood. They were also more likely than the control group to be subject to control and restraint and to be segregated, and had problems gaining access to work and to offending behaviour courses. The Report makes a number of recommendations, including awareness training and improved provision for these prisoners within prison education.

Subsequent surveys conducted by the Prison Inspectorate have found that disabled prisoners had more negative perceptions than other prisoners on issues such as safety and victimisation and respectful treatment (HM Chief Inspector of Prisons 2011a: 29). The 2015 survey also found that disabled prisoners were more negative on many aspects of prison life (HM Chief Inspector of Prisons 2015: 45). Problems of identification of their needs persisted and in many prisons disability liaison officers had been removed following the benchmarking process. Local authorities have new responsibilities for meeting the care needs of prisoners with learning disabilities under the Care Act 2014, but the Inspectorate found that in many prisons, not enough had been done to prepare for these new arrangements, which were due to come into effect in April 2015. It also found a case where a prisoner had to pay other prisoners to assist him because help to push his wheelchair was not available from the prison (HM Inspectorate of Prisons 2014a: 37).

The number of complaints from disabled prisoners is increasing and these prisoners were also more negative on the issue of how complaints were treated. However, disabled prisoners were more positive on health care than prisoners without disabilities. The emphasis in the provision for disability has been principally on the physical environment, with less focus on learning disabilities.

A key issue is the identification of disabilities, as it may be harder to identify learning than physical disabilities, as noted by the Bradley Report (Department of Health 2009a). For example, in Gartree, where 3 per cent of prisoners were identified as having a disability, 21 per cent of the respondents in the Prison Inspectorate's survey saw themselves as having a disability (HM Chief Inspector of Prisons 2011a). Disability is now being given more attention and an important advance is that all offenders undergoing learning activities are screened for learning disabilities. Greater attention is now being given to the provision for disabled prisoners in order to comply with the equality duty in the Equality Act 2010.

A joint inspection including treatment in custody conducted by the Inspectorate of Probation and the Prison Service took place in 2013/14 and results were published in 2015 (HM Inspectorate of Probation/HM Inspectorate of Prisons 2015). It noted that prisons were still failing to identify the needs of prisoners with learning disabilities, which meant opportunities to assist these offenders were lost. It found that the systems for identifying prisoners with learning disabilities in the prisons visited were poor, and in some cases where need was identified insufficient account was taken of it in anti-bullying measures, although the position in the community was slightly better.

The joint inspection found that screening tools were not used routinely during the pre-sentence stage, so there was over-reliance on disclosure by the offenders and negative findings of the inspection stemmed from the problem of identification. There were also insufficient accredited programmes for offenders with learning disabilities. Moreover, staff had received little relevant training on dealing with such offenders, although work was being done to produce a suitable offending behaviour programme for prisoners with intellectual disabilities. In two cases in the sample, existing programmes had been adapted to meet their needs. For prisoners on indeterminate sentences it was crucial to complete offending behaviour courses, but such prisoners were deemed unsuitable for group programmes and few programmes delivered one-to-one sessions. Some of the prisoners interviewed did not feel that staff understood their individual needs; they struggled with understanding prison processes because of problems with reading and writing and found it difficult to make applications or complaints. So the recommendations focus primarily on screening and on ensuring that prisoners have access to all prison procedures and that learning disabilities are considered in dealing with disciplinary or behavioural issues and in deciding the IEP level. Most prisons visited did have a policy to deal with this. However, prisoners interviewed felt that there were barriers to progressing to a higher IEP level because of problems associated with their disability.

The number of prisoners identified with learning disabilities was below the prevalence in the general population, yet the research base suggests the prevalence in the prison population is higher than that in the wider society. In some prisons the post of disability liaison officers had been removed following a review of staff posts. However, peer support schemes were running and some had mentors or buddy schemes. Prisoners with learning disabilities did have access to work, training, and education. Some information was available in Easy Read but this was not done routinely and prisoners struggled with forms, understanding the new IEP booklet, arranging visits, bringing complaints, and contacting the Independent Monitoring Board or Prisons and Probation Ombudsman. So the Report concluded that '[s]upport for prisoners with identified learning disabilities was variable' (ibid: 45). There were also particular concerns over the lack of advocacy during adjudication procedures, following the changes to legal aid in LASPO 2012. Recommendations included formulating sentence plans which take account of learning disability. The Report concluded that a screening tool should be introduced across the prison estate to identify those with learning disabilities, necessary adjustments should be made to services for those with such disabilities to comply with the Equality Act, and interventions for people with learning disabilities should be adapted to reduce the risk of reoffending. More attention is now being given to the question of offenders' communication needs which may arise from hidden differences including learning disabilities, and a toolkit is being prepared.

9.10.6 Older prisoners

The number of older prisoners has increased in recent years. At the end of December 2014 there were 3,786 prisoners over 60—an increase of 10 per cent over the previous year—some of whom were very frail and with disabilities (HM Chief Inspector of Prisons 2015: 12). Older prisoners are the fastest growing group in the prison population, with a large number of these older prisoners serving sentences for sex offences, including historic sex offences. The number of sentenced prisoners aged 60 and over increased by 164 per cent between 2002 and 2015 (Prison Reform Trust 2015: 5). There were 102 prisoners aged over 80 and five aged over 90 in March 2014 (ibid).

Older prisoners will have higher morbidity rates and make more demands on health care services within the prison, but will also face other problems, including access to employment. The ageing of the prison population may also increase the number of prisoners with disabilities. Although older prisoners are a diverse group with divergent health needs, the group does include prisoners with chronic health and social care needs. The picture emerging is mixed, with some examples of good support, but also instances of older prisoners housed in the worst accommodation and problems of restricted access to sanitation at night. A thematic review of older prisoners in 2004 made a number of recommendations to improve treatment, but not all had been met by the time of the follow-up review in 2008 (HM Chief Inspector of Prisons 2008b: 45). A Prison Reform Trust study of older prisoners also found gaps between the health care services they received in prison and the health care they would have received in the community (Prison Reform Trust 2008). Particular problems included depression, as well as higher rates of physical illness, and problems in receiving appropriate medication. They may also be held far from home, which means particular problems regarding visits from family members, who may also be older. Under the Care Act 2014 local authorities are responsible for the social care needs of prisoners and as the prison population ages, it means that prisons will effectively be providing residential care for elderly prisoners.

Older prisoners, those aged 50 or over in the 2008 Review, were more positive about most aspects of prison life than younger prisoners, although they were more likely to say that they had been victimised because of their age, disability, medication, or nature of their offence (HM Chief Inspector of Prisons 2008b: 45). However, there was inconsistency between prisons in provision for older prisoners.

An inquiry into older prisoners by the House of Commons Justice Committee recommended that the Prison Service should develop a national strategy for dealing with older prisoners, but this was rejected by the Ministry of Justice, who argued that it is not possible to generalise regarding the older prison population (House of Commons Justice Committee 2013b). In its Report the Committee found that many older prisoners with disabilities struggled in a prison system designed for fit younger men, that social care provision was variable and sparse, and that 'Older prisoners have needs that are distinct from the rest of the prison population by virtue of their severity' (ibid: 56). Some of the older prison buildings are not suitable for those with physical disabilities. Older prisoners also have different resettlement needs. As age is a protected characteristic under the Equality Act 2010, provision for older prisoners is now being given greater attention. NACRO has been working with older prisoners and has issued materials and a guidance toolkit to improve their treatment.

9.11 Reflecting on the issues

As we have seen, there is evidence of differential treatment in, and differential impact of, the criminal justice system in relation to women, ethnic minorities, and prisoners with disabilities. However, the imposition of the equality duty has had an impact on the governance of prisons and the issue of diversity is receiving more attention. At a formal level, procedures and strategies are in place to prevent discrimination on race, sex, and other grounds, but perceptions of prison life on the part of BME and disabled prisoners remain more negative than those of white prisoners and prisoners without disabilities. Progressive measures have been introduced and are having an impact on penal policy. But the success of these measures depends in part on sufficient resources, which is difficult to ensure in the context of budget cuts and expanding demand. Moreover, while progress has been made in relation to race and gender equality, there are still areas, such as homophobic behaviour, which require greater attention. The goal here should be equality of outcomes to ensure that policies and programmes do not disparately impact on particular groups of prisoners, in order to achieve justice in punishment. There are also some concerns that focusing on a broader equality duty rather than a gender equality duty will mean fewer gender-specific services will be commissioned.

9.11.1 Case study

At the end of Chapter 7 we used the following scenario to focus on the role of personal mitigation in sentencing and to ask you to consider whether better solutions to Amy's situation existed in social and welfare policies. We now wish to consider Amy's situation on the basis that her appeal was unsuccessful and she has to serve her custodial sentence. The scenario is reproduced below, followed by questions.

Amy is a mother with four children under ten years of age. The children's father, Ben, has been in prison for two years. Amy has several convictions for theft, all preceding the period in which she went to live with Ben and had her children. Amy got into severe financial difficulties two years ago and agreed to deliver packages of drugs, on a regular basis, to distributors. By the time she was caught she had delivered a very large quantity of a Class B drug. She pleaded guilty shortly after her arrest to a charge of possession with intent to supply under the Misuse of Drugs Act 1971, s. 5(3) although she insisted that she had been led to believe the drugs were only ketamine (Class C). She received a sentence of 18 months.

Ben's family have always rejected her; her own family consists of an ill and elderly mother and a sister who has two children. No one offers to look after her children and she agrees that they be voluntarily accommodated by the local authority. A recent review by the local authority noted the children's distress in their new homes (they cannot all be accommodated in the same foster family). Amy appeals against her sentence.

Questions:

1. What are the main problems that Amy will face in prison as a woman and a mother? Are these difficulties being addressed?

2. What if Ben had been released from prison eight months before Amy's conviction and Amy was six months pregnant when she began her sentence? Ben is the father but left Amy before the court case. How likely is she to be transferred to a mother and baby unit?

9.11.2 Discussion questions

In revising the issues raised in Chapter 9 you may wish to reflect on the following questions:

1. Is it fair to say that the current prison regime impacts more harshly on some groups of prisoners than others? If so, consider the ways in which equality of impact might be achieved.

2. Why were gender-specific policies introduced in prisons in England and Wales?

3. Do the experiences of ethnic minorities in prison differ from those of non-minorities?

4. Do the experiences of prisoners with disabilities in prison differ from those of prisoners without disabilities?

online
resource
centre

Guidance on dealing with these questions is given in the Online Resource Centre.

10

Punishment and rehabilitation in the community

SUMMARY

This chapter reviews the main options available to the sentencing court which do not entail immediate custody. It therefore deals with fines and community orders as well as suspended prison sentences. It discusses the tensions between imposing proportionate punishment and delivering rehabilitation programmes. It examines the policy aim of reducing reoffending through specifying in court orders requirements to control and rehabilitate the offender in the community, and discusses the theory and practice of rehabilitation that underpins these initiatives. However, because punishment and rehabilitation also take place in the community for those released from prison, this chapter examines supervision and the new 'beyond the gate' programmes for prisoners released on licence. The chapter, therefore, covers the policy trends in relation to fines, the 'rehabilitation revolution', and the privatisation of the delivery of community penalties.

10.1 Introduction

10.1.1 'Community'

This chapter deals with those two main sets of punishments which are not custodial: financial penalties—fines—and also those orders introduced in 1991 and in 2003 which are referred to as community penalties. The use of the word 'community' in the title of the chapter might, therefore, be seen as confusing. This is because, for some time, community has been a problematic word with various connotations, albeit that it is a key word in policy documents. It emerged in the 1980s and 1990s in penal policy documents such as *Punishment, Custody and the Community* (Home Office 1988a) and *Strengthening Punishment in the Community* (Home Office 1995a) and also in relation to child protection, care of the old, and those with mental health problems. It became 'one of the most promiscuous words in contemporary political usage' (Worrall 1997: 46) and 'an all-pervasive rhetoric' (Garland 2001b: 124). Enhancing and strengthening 'community' is now a taken-for-granted good, but what the word 'community' was and is meant to signify is not so easy to establish.

Some time ago Nelken said that 'communities can be the agents, *locus* or beneficiaries of crime control' (Nelken 1994: 249) and that is still a helpful starting point. It would appear that in several policy areas, the locus or site of the 'community' intervention is simply somewhere that is not an institution. So, for example, 'care in the community' means care that is not in a hospital or care home; punishment in the community means punishment imposed elsewhere than the prison setting. Interestingly, there has been an 'apparent disjuncture between the demise of community and the growth of its rhetorical appeal' (Lacey and

Zedner 1995: 301): the strength of the discourse of 'community' does not depend on there being an 'actual' community akin to the image of the ideal village.[1]

The idea of punishment *by* the community has also become increasingly important. An early policy document—*Supervision and Punishment in the Community*—devoted a chapter to 'The Voluntary and Private Sectors' (Home Office 1990b: Chapter 10), arguing for the greater involvement of the independent sector and, in particular, for partnership with the voluntary sector to 'involve the community at large much more in work with offenders' (ibid: para 10.4). More recently, policy documents such as *Punishment and Reform: Effective Community Sentences* (Ministry of Justice 2012b) and *Transforming Rehabilitation: A Revolution in the Way We Manage Offenders* (Ministry of Justice 2013a) have paved the way for the 21 'community rehabilitation companies' which became private companies delivering community programmes for offenders in February 2015. Here the 'community' appears to be the place where the providers of offender rehabilitation operate but also reflects the fact that those providers are now part of the community which provides, punishes, and rehabilitates.

Nelken also saw the community as a beneficiary and certainly community orders have been associated with reparation and restorative justice. Further, when the 'visible unpaid work initiative' was rolled out across England and Wales after 2005,[2] the idea was that the community could 'see' the 'payback' to the community by offenders. At the end of 2008, 10,000 orange vests with 'Community Payback' written on the back in purple were distributed to aid such visibility.[3] Research on Community Payback schemes suggests that 'public confidence in the CJS may be linked to the visibility of justice, and to how the CJS informs and engages with the public' (Moore *et al.* 2010: 1).

The focus on community may, then, be linked to a policy imperative of increasing the perceived legitimacy of the criminal justice system. So, it was argued, earlier local schemes such as Safer Cities and Neighbourhood Watch were encouraged to provide at least the appearance of action (Wasik *et al.* 1999: 69–83), and Daly similarly argued that 'the push towards partnership can be understood as a search for legitimacy' (2003: 123). However, for some commentators, this trend to localism, privatisation, and involvement by charitable bodies in community punishment signified an increase in social control via society's informal networks (see Brownlee 1998b: 180–2; see also Cohen 1985; Garland 1985: 239; Kemshall 2002: 41).

Yet this leaves financial penalties in an ambivalent position as regards 'the community'. They represent punishment which is not in a prison and they are imposed and can be paid locally. However, many fines, including court-imposed fines, parking fines, and fixed penalty notices (FPNs), can be paid online[4] and some fines can be taken directly from earnings or benefits. Further, the money collected does not necessarily go into local coffers: all court fines, for example, are collected and enforced by Her Majesty's Courts and Tribunals Service (HMCTS) National Compliance and Enforcement Service. It is also fair to say that fines do not generally feature in the rhetoric of community.

However, fines do not involve a move from the offender's community and, crucially, the Consultation Paper which discussed the Coalition government's 'proposals for radical

---

[1] See, for example, Hillery (1955) for a discussion of the different meanings of community in the mid-twentieth century.

[2] See Home Office Circular 66/2005 to the National Probation Service.

[3] See Bottoms (2008); see also https://www.gov.uk/community-sentences/community-payback (accessed 28 July 2015).

[4] See https://www.gov.uk/pay-court-fine-online and https://www.gov.uk/parking-tickets/paying-a-ticket (accessed 27 January 2016)

reforms to the way in which sentences served in the community operate' (Ministry of Justice 2012b: 6) dealt with both fines and community orders.

> Presently, the sentencing framework that underpins sentences in the community does not deliver what the public expect. Nor does the way in which community sentences are managed. Reoffending rates for community sentences are still too high. While enforcement of fines has increased significantly in recent years, there is scope for financial penalties to be used more flexibly in addition to or instead of other sentences.
>
> (Ministry of Justice 2012b: 6)

For this reason we decided to deal in this fourth edition with fines and community sentences in the same chapter.

10.1.2 Is prison the only 'real' punishment?

> There seems to be an assumption that custody is the only 'real' punishment.
>
> (Home Office 1990a: para 4.1)

As discussed in Chapter 1 (section 1.2), all recent governments have had to face the dilemma that custody is very expensive and in times of recession its use needs to be reduced for economic reasons, and yet—for political reasons—governments believe they need to be seen to be tough and not reduce the use of imprisonment.

Nevertheless, since the third edition of this text there have been various, often unrelated, policy developments which could be seen as contributing to a reduced reliance on custodial punishment. These include changes in relation to fines, the policy developments associated with the 'rehabilitation revolution', and the greater availability of the suspended sentence. So, for example, the removal of upper limits on fines allows a financial penalty to be perceived as more punitive and appropriate for more serious offences, while fines have been introduced as a sanction for breach of a suspended sentence rather than custody. The rehabilitation revolution and the privatisation of the greater part of the work of the National Probation Service aims to make rehabilitation—the reduction of the propensity to reoffend—more effective and, consequently, community penalties and release on licence more 'legitimate' a punishment in the eyes of the public and sentencers.

However, the use of both custodial and community sentences increased in the period 1995–2006 (Carter 2003: 3; Tarling 2006: 29–31) and the proportion of community sentences remained stable in the period 2007–2010 (Ministry of Justice 2011k: 8). Further, statistics from 2011 onwards suggest the increased use of community sentences has stalled and has recently been reversed: recent figures give a 16.7 per cent decrease in the percentage of offenders given a community sentence in the year ending September 2014 (Ministry of Justice 2015: Table Q1.2). While these figures should be set in the context of the fact that there was also a 3 per cent decrease in the number of offenders sentenced over that period, the statistics for community sentences as a proportion of all those sentenced show a reduction from 12.7 per cent to 9.3 per cent over the period 2012–2014.

It is possible that the restriction on the use of community orders such that only those convicted of imprisonable offences can be subject to such an order (CJA 2003, s. 150A) may have restricted their use. However, Table 10.1 shows that, as a proportion of all sentenced, there was no significant change in the percentage of those sentenced to either immediate or suspended custodial sentences 2013/14, but there was a 1.6 per cent increase in the use of fines that year. Currently, then, it would seem that community sentences have not yet 'taken off' as an alternative to custody. As we will see in the next section, fines have also historically not been viewed as a 'proper punishment', but there are indications of changes in their use.

Table 10.1 Offenders sentenced by principal sentence, 12 months ending September 2009 to 12 months ending September 2014

England and Wales	12 months ending						Percentage change 12 months ending September 2013 to September 2014
	September 2009	September 2010	September 2011	September 2012	September 2013	September 2014	
Total offenders sentenced(1)	1,398,752	1,373,317	1,326,966	1,243,431	1,184,982	1,149,250	−3.0%
Total persons sentenced(2)	1,390,957	1,365,372	1,319,638	1,236,820	1,178,522	1,142,918	−3.0%
Immediate custody (persons)	100,350	100,308	104,679	101,213	93,123	89,828	−3.5%
Suspended sentence (persons)	43,876	47,303	48,843	45,470	46,596	46,131	−1.0%
Community sentence (persons)	197,865	189,159	180,190	156,715	128,011	106,606	−16.7%
Fines (all offenders)	936,435	905,965	865,079	822,496	806,096	800,148	−0.7%
Other disposals (all offenders)	120,226	130,582	128,175	117,537	111,156	106,537	4.2%
Average custodial sentence length (months)(3)	13.4	13.8	14.1	14.5	15.3	15.8	0.5 months

(Continued)

Table 10.1 Continued

England and Wales	September 2009	September 2010	September 2011	12 months ending September 2012	September 2013	September 2014	Percentage change 12 months ending September 2013 to September 2014
Percentage of those sentenced							Percentage point change
Immediate custody (persons)	7.2	7.3	7.9	8.2	7.9	7.9	0.0
Suspended sentence (persons]	3.2	3.5	3.7	3.7	4.0	4.0	0.1
Community sentence (persons)	14.2	13.9	13.7	12.7	10.9	9.3	−1.5
Fines (all offenders)	67.4	66.4	65.6	66.5	68.4	70.0	1.6
Other disposals (all offenders)	8.6	9.6	9.7	9.5	9.4	9.3	−0.1

(1) The time lag between conviction and sentencing for cases committed for sentence at Crown Court can result in small differences between total offenders convicted and sentenced within reporting years.

(2) For sentences of immediate custody, suspended sentence, and community sentence, 'persons' is the same as 'offenders', as 'others' (such as companies or public bodies) cannot remise these sentences.

(3) Average custodial sentence length excludes life and indeterminate sentences. (Ministry of Justice 2015b: Table Q1.2)[5]

⁵ Accessible at https://www.gov.uk/government/uploads/system/uploads/attachment_data/file/405301/cjs-quarterly-update-september-2014.pdf.

10.2 Fines

10.2.1 Fines as punishment

Fines might appear to be the easiest and most appropriate punishment to fix proportionately, there being available a very detailed money tariff. It might, therefore, also be thought to be easy to implement the policy imperative of encouraging the use of non-custodial sentences, including fines, to reduce the use of custodial penalties. However, there are several problematic issues relating to fines. First, the issue of (in)equality of impact is more visible than in relation to other penalties: there are problematic categories of offenders in applying fines, notably the very poor (especially those dependent on state benefits), the unemployed, and the very rich. Secondly, there are issues relating to legitimacy and enforcement and, thirdly, there are financial sanctions which are not within the (direct) purview of the court system: FPNs and benefits sanctions would be examples, and these raise issues of fairness, impact, and effectiveness.

A fine is a presumptive sentence in the sense that it can be imposed without complying with a statutory seriousness hurdle as is the case with custodial and community penalties (see Chapter 3). It is, therefore, available for a wide range of offences, from the least to the more serious. A fine can also be added to other penalties (Criminal Justice Act (CJA) 2003, s. 163) and can be imposed in magistrates' and Crown Courts. There is no maximum fine in the Crown Court but the maximum for a summary or either-way offence in a magistrates' court has been £5,000 since 2002 (although higher fines are possible for certain specified offences). Fines were set at five levels by s. 37 of the Criminal Justice Act 1982 and as amended are as follows: Level 1 £200, Level 2 £500, Level 3 £1,000, Level 4 £2,500, and Level 5 £5,000.

However, the Legal Aid, Sentencing and Punishment of Offenders Act (LASPO) 2012 allows for the removal of limits on fine levels.[6] In its *Equality Impact Assessment* of this measure the Coalition government stated its belief 'that removing the upper limit represents a proportionate response so that proportionate fines can be imposed on wealthy or corporate offenders and organisations' (Ministry of Justice 2011j: 1–2). Announcing the implementation of these provisions, the then Justice Minister Jeremy Wright said in June 2014, 'Financial penalties set at the right level can be an effective way of punishing criminals and deterring them from further offending.'

Section 85 of LASPO 2012 has already removed the £5,000 maximum for Level 5 offences where that applies for an offence punishable on summary conviction.[7] Sections 86–87—in force since 28 May 2014—give the Secretary of State power to raise other fine levels and standard scale fine levels: s. 87 relates to levels 1–4 on the standard scale of fines for summary offences and s. 86 removes the £5,000 maximum for other fines in magistrates' courts.

Fines should, then, operate as a useful penalty, and in numerical terms they have done so: in 1995, 75 per cent of all those dealt with by the courts were fined (Brownlee 1998b: 137). This had dropped to 69 per cent by 2002 and 65.5 per cent by 2010 (Ministry of Justice 2011k: 7). The third edition reproduced at Figure 7.1 the statistical trends in the numbers of offenders fined 1989–2009 showing a steady downward trend for both indictable and summary offences (Ministry of Justice 2010a: Evidence Report, Figure 3.5; see also Ministry of Justice: 2011m: Table Q5.4). Figures then available also showed a 6 per cent decrease in the use of fines in the period 2010/11 (Ministry of Justice (2011n: Table Q1.2). In the Crown Court the use of financial penalties had decreased more dramatically—by 46

---

[6] In Scotland the maximum has been £1,000 since 10 December 2007.

[7] In force since 12 March 2015; see LASPO 2012 (Fines on Summary Conviction) Regulations 2015.

per cent over the period 1995–2006 (Carter 2007: 7)—and the use of fines for indictable offences generally decreased from 27 per cent in 1999 to 17 per cent in 2009, with a slight increase to 19 per cent in 2013/14 (Ministry of Justice 2015b: 15).

Recent statistics would suggest that the long-term overall decrease has not only slowed down but that—for 2013/14—fines increased by 1.6 per cent as a proportion of all those sentenced (see Table 10.1). Consequently, in 2013/14 fines were issued for 86 per cent of summary offences—dealt with almost entirely in the magistrates' courts—and 19 per cent of indictable offences (Ministry of Justice 2015b: 14–15).

Legitimacy

The long-term trend in the use of fines—possibly now changing—might be explained in relation to legitimacy and enforcement. Fines are viewed problematically as a punishment and, as we shall see in section 10.2.3, the issue of enforcement has in the past undermined confidence that punishment will be implemented. For example, Young (1989: 46) argued that fluctuations in use were due to changes in ideas about whether a fine is a suitable means of punishing an offender and, therefore, whether it is perceived as 'really' a punishment or not. It is certainly the case that one of the causes of this ambivalence over fines is that it is the designated penalty for those categories of offence which some sections of the population do not regard as 'really' criminal. Parking offences and regulatory offences such as those in relation to TV licences might come into this category. More controversially, other motoring offences such as speeding, and health and safety infractions, might also be included (see Corbett 2000; Carter 2003). Where citizens do not regard an offence as really criminal, they do not perceive the outcome as a punishment but rationalise it instead as a tax—a morally neutral nuisance which is the occasional result of choosing not to obey what are deemed as non-criminal regulations. The problem is that such thinking then influences the conceptualisation of financial penalties for 'real' crimes.[8]

Money and punishment also have very different connotations and are underpinned by very different cultural values. So there are 'shock horror' media stories about cases where even the large fine imposed has not been seen as a punishment sufficient to reflect the seriousness of the offending in question. There is a strong popular feeling that there are particular harms, notably crimes of violence and sexual offences, that are not 'compensatable' by a financial penalty, so fines have an ambivalent position as a punishment.

In relation to property offences there is the added difficulty that 'the value of the punishment must not be less in any case than what is sufficient to outweigh that of the profit of the crime' (Bentham 1789: 166). From a utilitarian perspective, the fine or other punishment, taken together with any compensation and confiscation orders, must be sufficient to make committing the crime unprofitable, otherwise there is no deterrent effect. From a retributivist perspective, as we have seen, commensurability would also be undermined by disregarding the profits of crime.

However, there is a related problem regarding the quantum of punishment, and we shall discuss that in section 10.2.2.

10.2.2 **Units of financial deprivation**

Fines punish the offender by depriving him of whatever consumables or non-working time would have been purchased with the money 'lost' through the payment of the fine. The problem with this approach is that the amount of deprivation or loss is affected by how much disposable income the individual retains, or how much impact the fine has on the

---

[8] See O'Malley (2009) for an extended discussion of issues.

person's financial circumstances. It could be theorised as the deprivation of the amount of time, 'liberty', required to earn enough to replenish personal savings.

Two approaches are possible for correlating seriousness with an amount of money:

- to have a fixed fine for each amount of seriousness (for example, by fixing a certain sum of money as the fine for each offence and with specified factors to take the amount above or below the starting point);
- to have a unit of financial deprivation correlated with each unit of seriousness (that is, the penalty is fixed at a particular percentage of the offender's financial resources for a specified level of seriousness).

The outcome in terms of an amount of money will often be very different. Let us take the scenario of a £2,000 fine. The sentencer and the public may consider that to be proportionate and justice may be perceived to have been done, but students with an income of £8,000 from part-time work lose a quarter of their income; those on £80,000 may not notice the loss. If, instead of 'visible' equality of justice, we decide to aim at equality of impact, then either the fine imposed on the student need be only £200 or, instead, £20,000 on the high earner, so that both 'suffer' an equal impact in terms of deprivation of goods that can no longer be purchased. However, the £200 fine might appear to the media as proof that the student had 'got away with it'. On the other hand, the recipient of a £20,000 fine might feel the fine is disproportionate and unjust in comparison with the student's fine.

Day fines

The approach of English sentencing law and practice until 1991 was to use a fixed amount of fine which could be reduced by the court if the offender was unable to pay. At the end of the 1980s, however, the government pursued the idea of 'day fines', which were already being used in parts of the United States and in Scandinavia. These were called day fines because what the offender earns in a day became the basis for assessments of the total fine. In England such a scheme was successfully piloted (see Gibson 1990), though referred to as 'unit fines', and was implemented across the country for magistrates' courts by means of s. 18 of the Criminal Justice Act 1991.

In the original s. 18, seriousness was designated by a number of units from 1 to 50. The fine was then determined by multiplying the number of units by an amount of money calculated on the basis of the offender's disposable income. Problems arose where the offender refused to submit details of his financial circumstances to the court for assessing this sum. The legislation provided for this by allowing the courts to take the highest figure where no information was forthcoming. The instances where this happened were highly publicised in sections of the media and brought disrepute on the system.

The original s. 18 was quickly replaced as a response to opposition.[9] At the time a lay magistrate suggested that the sense of outrage was fuelled by better-off members of society who were dismayed that '[f]ailing to comply with a traffic sign, going through a light on red or parking on a zig-zag was previously worth the price of a meal out for two; now it can cost as much as taking the family to Florida' (Block 1993: 308). A new s. 18 was inserted by s. 65 of the Criminal Justice Act 1993 and was largely re-enacted in the Powers of Criminal Courts (Sentencing) Act (PCCSA) 2000 (s. 128). This legal framework is now in ss. 162–165 of the CJA 2003.

This in effect returned the situation to what it had been before 1991, with one difference: the court could raise as well as lower the amount of the fine in taking the offender's means into account. Research would suggest that magistrates returned to imposing lower than

---

[9] See Brownlee (1998b: 146) for the role of the Magistrates' Association.

proportionate-to-impact fines on the employed (Brownlee 1998b: 147) but in 2003 it looked as if unit fines were to be reintroduced. The Carter Report proposed that fines should replace the 30 per cent of current community orders imposed on low-risk offenders (2003: 27) and that 'day fines' should be introduced, though there was no mention of the ill-fated unit fines system. The government promised to explore the issue (Home Office 2004b: Annex para 35)[10] and a study at that time of two large city-centre magistrates' courts suggested support for a new system (Moore 2003a). The Management of Offenders and Sentencing Bill 2005 did indeed propose to amend s. 164 of the CJA 2003 so that fines would be fixed by reference to daily disposable income, but the Bill fell when Parliament was prorogued for the General Election and subsequent legislation has not included such a provision.

10.2.3 **Changing thinking**

However, there have been significant changes in relation to the impact of fines. First, guidance for use by magistrates is now much more impact-focused. The introduction to the 'Approach to the Assessment of Fines' section of the *Magistrates' Courts Sentencing Guidelines* states: 'The aim is for the fine to have an equal impact on offenders with different financial circumstances; it should be a hardship but should not force the offender below a reasonable "subsistence" level' (Sentencing Guidelines Council 2008h: 148 para 2). The current approach is to place the offending in question within a band—normally one of three bands—depending on seriousness; then financial liability is fixed according to the individual's means (see Table 10.2). A band A fine is equal to half a person's disposable income, Band B equals 100 per cent of disposable income, and Band C equals 150 per cent. 'Where an offender's only source of income is state benefit . . . the relevant weekly income is deemed to be £100' (Sentencing Guidelines Council 2008h: 148). Two further bands are provided which apply where the offence has passed the threshold for a community order (Band D) or a custodial sentence (Band E) but the court decides that it need not impose such a sentence and that a financial penalty is appropriate. Band D is 250 per cent of the relevant weekly income and Band E is 400 per cent (ibid: 151).

In other words, fines in the magistrates' court are no longer fixed as a set amount which is taken up or down. This is clearly a development to be welcomed, although there remains the problem raised in relation to unit fines that the impact approach 'is best suited for defendants with regular, measurable (and legal) income flow' (Greene 1998: 269) and this clearly does not apply to all offenders. A report on day fines by the Sentencing Commission

Table 10.2 Fine bands

For the purpose of the offence guidelines, a fine is based on one of three bands (A, B, or C). The selection of the relevant fine band, and the position of the individual offence within that band, is determined by the seriousness of the offence.

	Starting point	Range
Fine Band A	50% of relevant weekly income	25–75% of relevant weekly income
Fine Band B	100% of relevant weekly income	75–125% of relevant weekly income
Fine Band C	150% of relevant weekly income	125–175% of relevant weekly income

Source: *Magistrates' Court Sentencing Guidelines* (Sentencing Guidelines Council 2008h: 148).

[10] See http://webarchive.nationalarchives.gov.uk/20130128103514/http://www.homeoffice.gov.uk/documents/reducing-crime-changing-lives?view=Binary (accessed 27 January 2016).

for Scotland (2006) which concluded that there was no 'compelling case to change the existing system governing the imposition of fines in this country' did so because, they argued, day fines could not be introduced until there was a 'simple, reliable and cost-effective method of obtaining information on offenders' income' in Scotland (ibid: Foreword by the Rt Hon Lord Macfadyen). This has also been an issue in England and Wales.

However, there will also need to be further training of those who impose the majority of fines. Research undertaken in 2006 in the magistrates' courts of England and Wales to assess the extent to which magistrates were using new structured sentencing guidance for fines found that, while all participants were using the guidance to reach a decision, many panels 'subsequently chose to change their minds' (Raine and Dunstan 2009: 29). The researchers explain that, where the guidance generated very low fines, 'the concerns were about the justice process failing to ensure "just deserts" and appropriate punishment and fears of giving the wrong message to both the offender and the wider public' (ibid: 32), while in relation to high fines for less serious offences but where the offender had the means to pay, the concern was that the outcome was based too heavily on equity and not enough on proportionality (ibid). The thinking in early cases that we noted at the beginning of this section would appear to continue.

However, another component of sentencing—the criminal courts charge[11]—undermined all attempts to calibrate fines in line with offender means for nine months in 2015. The charge was compulsory and—in a magistrates' court—ranged from £150 for pleading guilty to a summary offence to £520 for a conviction after a not guilty plea, with corresponding figures of £900 and £1,200 in the Crown Court. The Magistrates' Association was critical and the Howard League campaigned against the charge because it put people under pressure to plead guilty and took no account of ability to pay.[12] The House of Lords passed a 'motion to regret' the implementation of this regulation[13] and the Justice Select Committee asked for the charge to be abolished. The Justice Secretary, Michael Gove, decided to end the charge in December 2015: 'The basic principle behind the policy—that those who have broken the law should bear some of the costs of running the criminal courts—is right. However, as the Justice Select Committee set out in its recent report, there have been concerns raised about how this has worked in practice.'[14]

Increased fines for corporate crime

Another significant development is a focus on sentencing for serious crime by commercial firms, and the resulting guidance on fines to be imposed on companies convicted under the Corporate Manslaughter and Corporate Homicide Act 2007 has led to the setting of fines at a high level. The guideline states that for corporate manslaughter 'The appropriate fine will seldom be less than £500,000 and may be measured in millions of pounds' (Sentencing Guidelines Council 2010: para 24). It may be that this will influence thinking about the use of fines. However, while in its 2010/11 report the Health and Safety Executive reported that duty holders found guilty of health and safety offences prosecuted by them received fines totalling £18.6 million, giving average penalties on conviction of £35,938 per case (Health and Safety Executive 2011: 10), in 2013/14 the comparable figures were that fines totalled £16.7 million with an average penalty of £18,944 per offence. In the same year local authority prosecutions led to fines totalling £1.6 million, an average penalty of £8,225 per offence.[15]

---

[11] Introduced in April 2015 by the Prosecution of Offences Act 1985 (Criminal Courts Charge) Regulations 2015.

[12] See http://www.howardleague.org/criminalcharge/.

[13] Hansard HL 14 October 2015 Columns 296–310 at http://www.publications.parliament.uk/pa/ld201516/ldhansrd/text/151014-0002.htm#15101460000420.

[14] See https://www.gov.uk/government/speeches/courts.

[15] http://www.hse.gov.uk/statistics/prosecutions.htm accessed 2 June 2015.

10.2.4 **Default and enforcement**

Fines become payable as soon as imposed but guidance has established that payment can be by instalments. These should not normally be spread over more than 12 months, concern being that a long repayment period allows the poorer offender to be fined to an amount that has more impact than the same amount imposed on an offender who can afford to pay it immediately. 'It is generally recognised that the maximum weekly payment by a person in receipt of state benefit should rarely exceed £5' (Sentencing Guidelines Council 2008h: 152). *Olliver* (1989) allowed the period to be, exceptionally, 24 months, and that is the period allowed for payment of fines which are imposed in the exceptional bands D and E (ibid). The Magistrates' Courts Act 1980 ss. 79–118 provide other process options and powers for reviewing and enforcing fines.[16]

Despite these provisions, many offenders do not pay any or all of their fine. The full payment rate for fines was only 55 per cent in 2002/3 but Table 10.3, providing statistics for 2003/4 to 2010/11, shows an overall though not steady improvement in the rate of payment during that period.

More recently the Under-Secretary of State for Justice noted, 'The amount of money collected at the end of 2013/14 was £290 million. The amount of money collected reached a record high of £310 million at the end of 2014/15' (Mr Vara MP, Unpaid Fines: Written

Table 10.3 Enforcement of financial penalties 2003/4 to 2010/11 (Hansard)

Financial year	New amount owed (1) (£)	Paid (2) (£)	Payment rate (3) (%)	Payment rate excluding administrative cancellations (4) (%)
2003–04	366,653,329.16	212,785,348.05	74	—
2004–05	351,746,801.62	221,505,558.19	80	—
2005–06	368,923,934.48	233,332,326.01	83	81
2006–07	364,298,841.54	244,555,539.82	92	80
2007–08	376,569,882.06	256,117,662.65	95	82
2008–09	393,121,638.79	246,519,704.18	85	71
2009–10	406,660,591.18	259,241,082.01	86	74
2010(5)	312,719,840.11	213,916,998.74	92	80

(1) New amount owed is the sum of amounts imposed in the courts plus net transferred amounts
(2) The amount paid is monies received by the courts against any outstanding fine irrespective of age and will not necessarily be for fine amounts imposed in the same period.
(3) The payment rate is calculated by dividing the amount paid to HMCTS over a financial year by the new amount owed less the value of fines legally and net administratively cancelled for the same period.
(4) The payment rate excluding administratively cancelled is available from 2005 only. Prior to that the data are not comparable due to changes in the way the payment rate was calculated. The payment rate excluding administratively cancelled is calculated by dividing the amount paid to HMCTS over a financial year by the new amount owed less the value of fines legally cancelled for the same period.
(5) April to December only.

Source: Written Answer Hansard HC, 21 June 2011: col 174W).[17]

---

[16] For a discussion of these see Moore (2003b: 729–31).
[17] Accessed on 29 July 2015 at http://www.publications.parliament.uk/pa/cm201011/cmhansrd/cm110621/ text/110621w0002.htm#11062168000051.

question—7005 Hansard HC 14 July 2015).[18] On the other hand, the number of 'write-offs'—administrative cancellation of outstanding fines, compensation orders, and victim surcharges—has increased. In 2009/10, £47.4 million was cancelled, while £75.9 million was abandoned in 2014.[19]

There has also been a gradual increase in full payment of FPNs in England and Wales (see section 10.2.5), from 77 per cent in 1997 to 87 per cent in 2003 (Ministry of Justice 2007d: para 5.14 and Tables 5.4 and 5.5), settling at around 89 per cent in 2006–9 (Povey *et al.* 2011: Table 3d, 62).[20] Payment rates for FPNs for motoring offences were relatively stable in the period 2003–12 at nearly 90 per cent and in 2013 the fine was paid in 95 per cent of cases, with the remaining 5 per cent of cases registered in court (Home Office 2015: para 8.5).[21]

Default

Home Office research in the mid-1990s found that, despite Best Practice Guidelines issued in 1992 and 1996, there was no one standard practice—attachment of earnings or deduction from benefit, distress warrants (see Moore 2003b), reviews, warrants for arrest—by which fines were enforced (Whittacker and Mackie 1997: 5). Half of the defaulters in the sample had more than one outstanding fine, although four out of five defaulters owed less than £500 (ibid: 15). The main reasons defaulters gave for their fine arrears were that there had been a (detrimental) change in their financial circumstances since the fine was imposed and/or that they had other financial commitments and debts. Women defaulters were typically in very restricted financial circumstances, with 81 per cent having dependent children, and only 11 per cent were in employment, while 22 per cent of male defaulters were unemployed (ibid: 13–14). Moore found that in some cases it simply might not be possible for magistrates to implement the principle that a fine should have detrimental impact but not cause significant financial hardship (Moore 2003a: 23–5).

The Report of the Select Committee on Public Accounts found that, of a total of £397 million of fines imposed in 2001/2, around 59 per cent were collected, but £58 million were written off (largely because the offender could not be traced) and £90 million of fines were cancelled because of successful appeals or a significant change of circumstances (2002: para 2). There were wide variations in the collection rate and the report pointed to ineffective administration and a failure to prioritise the issue. Until the early 1990s immediate or suspended prison sentences were the main response to fine default,[22] but reliance on this sanction then decreased (see Brownlee 1998b: 148–9 for references); research found that magistrates acknowledged that fines were likely to impact disproportionately on offenders with limited means and that fines now often 'seemed like the imposition of "debt" rather than punishment' (Mackie *et al.* 2003: 28; see also Raine *et al.* 2004). Certainly the Citizens

---

[18] Accessed at http://www.parliament.uk/business/publications/written-questions-answers-statements/written-question/Commons/2015-07-14/7005/. See also the parliamentary answer given by Mr Djanogly MP in 2012 to a question about unpaid fines for details of the MCTS payment rate for financial penalties by region in the calendar years 2011, 2010, and 2009 (Hansard 23 May 2012: Column 759W).

[19] See http://www.telegraph.co.uk/news/uknews/law-and-order/10788130/Quarter-of-billion-in-court-fines-written-off.html.

[20] Hansard HC 16 April 2007, Column 9W.

[21] Payment rates for various categories of PNDs by month 2005–13 can be accessed via http://www.parliament.uk/business/publications/written-questions-answers-statements/written-question/Commons/2014-10-30/212567/.

[22] Section 82 of the Magistrates' Courts Act 1980 provides the restrictive conditions for imposing custody on fine default.

Advice Bureau has reported that their statistics showing increased demand for advice on debt issues include the category of magistrate fines and compensation orders arrears which were up by 39 per cent to 13,400 in 2014/15 (2015: 18).

The Crime (Sentences) Act 1997 extended the availability of non-custodial penalties for fine default and s. 300 of the CJA 2003 empowers magistrates to impose a 'default order' whereby the offender must comply with an unpaid work, curfew (which may include electronic monitoring), or attendance centre[23] requirement. Section 301 allows the magistrates' court to disqualify the defaulter from driving for a period of up to 12 months.

Enforcement

Over a decade ago the Labour government considered the problem of fine default to be a major reason why fines were not used more extensively. Consequently the Courts Act 2003 amended parts of previous legislation to provide a new framework for fine enforcement and a Unified Courts Agency was created in 2005, with a phased implementation of a new National Enforcement Service from April 2007.[24]

Attention has also turned to improving collection of fines. Under the Fines Collection (Amendment) Regulations 2004[25] the (then) Department for Constitutional Affairs piloted a range of new fine-collection measures including a new type of attachment of earnings order.[26] Section 41 of the Criminal Justice and Immigration Act (CJIA) 2008 amended Schedule 5, Part 3 of the Courts Act 2003, such that, on request to the Secretary of State, the staff of Her Majesty's Courts Service (HMCS) can gain access to benefit records held by the Department for Work and Pensions (DWP) for the purpose of fine enforcement.

The difficulty is that, while some offenders are in the 'won't pay' category, others 'can't pay': their non-payment is not necessarily wilful. Even research evidence that people pay fines at the last minute—when threatened with an imminent custodial order—does not prove they could have paid all along. It may also be explained by the generosity of friends who offer financial help only when that threat is likely to be implemented (Morris and Gelsthorpe 1990: 842). Where offenders have genuine difficulties in paying even small fines, for example many of the single mothers fined for non-payment of their TV licence, 'enforcement, be it deductions from benefits that are already inadequate, seizure and sale of family possessions, or especially imprisonment, that is not mitigated by positive intervention and assistance in other areas of life can only serve to reinforce existing patterns of social inequality in the criminal justice system' (Brownlee 1998b: 151).

Developments since 2003 in relation to imposition of unpaid work might be ameliorating the situation. The Courts Act 2003, s. 97 and Schedule 6, effective from 2004, made provision for people to work off the outstanding financial penalty by undertaking unpaid work. Referred to as Fine Payment Work (FPW), this was piloted in seven areas between 2004 and 2009. (See, for FPW in other jurisdictions, McIvor et al. 2013.) The court made a work order which stated the amount of the fine and, using a statutory conversion rate (£6 per hour), the hours of work to be completed. (See Rix et al. 2010 for the research report.) Section 300 of the CJA 2003, partially in force from 2005 and amended by the CJIA 2008, now empowers the court to impose such an unpaid work requirement (or a curfew, or attendance sentence order for those under 25) on a fine defaulter by means of a default order instead of issuing a warrant for commitment to prison.

---

[23] For 16–24-year-olds: inserted by CJIA 2008, s. 40.
[24] See Einat (2004) for a review of research on enforcement in other jurisdictions.
[25] Attachment of earnings: SI 2004/1407, pursuant to the Courts Act 2003, Schedule 5.
[26] See http://www.paypershop.com/news-cat/courtak.html.

10.2.5 Fixed and regulatory penalties

There are also penalties and sanctions which are imposed out of court and also outside the justice system, in that they are collected by a variety of bodies. These are usually for fixed amounts. These notices have been described as a compromise between the principle of equal impact and administrative efficiency (Ashworth 2000: 211); the level of fine does not vary according to the offender's means and the assumption is that the level is set sufficiently low for it not to cause injustice. O'Malley has critiqued this trend as depersonalising the individual and as showing a trend to the 'monetization of justice' and the development of risk-based 'technologies of governance' (O'Malley 2010: 795).

FPNs—fixed penalty notices—were first introduced in the 1950s for parking offences, and have since been extended to other motoring offences and to a wide range of other offences including, for example, environmental offences. Some of these are referred to as 'regulatory offences', often 'newer' offences regulated by bodies other than the police, which deal with issues of, for example, fair trading, consumer protection, vehicle licensing, and health and safety. Table 10.4 lists statistics collected by the Home Office in the first decade of this century but excludes those collected by other bodies, notably the Ministry of Justice and Local Authorities, and the enforcement notices issued by the Health and Safety Executive. More recently the extension of FPNs to careless driving, from August 2013 (see Easton and Piper 2013), has allowed for an immediate £50 or £100 fine to be imposed by the police, with the possibility of FPNs of £200 and £300 for specified offences.[27]

We looked briefly at the deterrent effect of such fines in Chapter 4 (section 4.4.1) in relation to regulatory offences generally, and particularly TV or road fund licence evasion. There are also PNDs (penalty notices for disorder)—one of the so-called 'on the spot' fines issued by the police—currently set at £60 or £90 depending on the offence, which were introduced by ss. 1–11 of the Criminal Justice and Police Act 2001 and implemented across England and Wales by April 2004. As Grace points out, 'Since its introduction, the remit of the PND scheme has been hugely extended; initially focused on minor incidents of adult disorder (focusing on 'false alarm' cases and alcohol-related nuisance), subsequent amendments have seen the number of penalty offences rise from ten to 29' (2014: 70). She argues that 'PNDs are now part of the mainstay of the criminal justice system' but questions whether the government's stated aims of saving police time and providing a quick, deterrent punishment have been met (2014: 71–5).

We are also concerned that official statistics suggest that the number of crimes handled directly by the police through cautions and fixed penalty fines now exceeds those dealt with by convictions in courts, although the totals may no longer be rising. In 2010 in England and Wales far greater numbers of people received PNDs for drunk and disorderly behaviour and for behaviour likely to cause harassment, alarm, or distress than were proceeded against at the magistrates' court (Grace 2014: 70). The Ministry of Justice statistics for out-of-court disposals (including PNDs) 2010/11 give a total of 448,526, which compares with 1,336,494 convictions for the same period (Ministry of Justice 2011n: Table Q1.1). However, these figures should be set in the context of lower totals for convictions and other out-of-court disposals and also of changes in police and prosecution targets 2008–10 (Ministry of Justice 2011n). Further, these statistics do not include all the other **fixed penalties** because collection of statistics on the other penalties is the responsibility of the Home Office.

---

[27] See, for more information, CPS *Road Traffic Offences: Guidance on Fixed Penalty Notices*: http://www.cps.gov.uk/legal/p_to_r/road_traffic_offences_guidance_on_fixed_penalty_notices/#fixed accessed 2 June 2015.

Table 10.4 Fixed penalty notices by offence type, 2000–2009

Numbers (thousands)

Offence group	Offence type	England and Wales									
		2000[1]	2001[1]	2002[1]	2003	2004	2005	2006	2007	2008	2009
4(pt)	Careless driving offences (excluding use of handheld mobile phone while driving)[1]	32.2	34.7	32.7	34.9	16.7	12.6	8.9	7.0	2.8	3.4
4(pt)	Use of handheld mobile phone while driving[1]	..	..	..	1.9	74.0	126.6	166.8	122.1	115.9	125.5
7, 9, 10	Licence, insurance[2] and record-keeping offences	49.5	50.3	49.6	67.6	70.0	80.3	88.7	100.8	99.7	86.1
13, 15	Vehicle test and condition offences	10.5	9.3	7.9	10.2	12.7	16.5	21.8	35.6	56.8	69.3
16	Speed limit offences	941.7	1,151.1	1,407.3	1,894.8	1,924.4	1,979.9	1,828.5	1,473.8	1,247.0	1,136.0
17–19	Neglect of traffic signs and directions and of pedestrian rights	183.4	175.1	176.9	227.0	219.6	208.6	208.5	203.8	200.1	183.0
20	Obstruction, waiting and parking offences	1,595.4	1,325.0	1,165.0	1,044.3	882.5	573.4	496.3	446.8	331.8	264.1
21, 22	Lighting and noise offences	23.0	19.9	20.7	20.1	23.2	19.4	18.9	19.0	20.4	20.9
23, 24	Other offences[3]	3.9	3.2	3.1	3.7	4.9	5.2	3.9	3.8	4.7	5.8
25(pt)	Miscellaneous motoring offences (excluding seat belt offences)	3.5	5.1	7.9	6.8	4.9	6.7	5.4	3.6	3.7	5.2
25(pt)	Seat belt offences	155.3	144.4	126.4	145.6	201.8	234.6	226.2	220.1	227.0	203.4
Total		2,998.2	2,918.0	2,997.4	3,456.7	3,434.7	3,263.9	3,073.8	2,636.6	2,310.0	2,102.7

1. Introduced as a specific offence as from 1 December 2003.
2. As from June 2003, the offence of having no insurance was added to the road traffic fixed penalty offence system.
3. Includes load offences and offences peculiar to motor cycles.

Source: Povey et al. (2011: 61, Table 3).

Other FPNs issued by the police appear to have peaked in 2003/4 (Povey *et al.* 2011: Figure 3a, see also 61–62); for example, the number of FPNs for motoring offences issued by the police (including traffic wardens) in 2009 was 2.1 million, down 9 per cent on 2008. Speed limit offences comprised 54 per cent of all FPNs issued in 2009 and, as well as fixed penalty notices, the police issued 27,000 written warnings for motoring offences and 78,000 Vehicle Defect Rectification Scheme (VDRS) notices in 2009 (Povey *et al.* 2011: 99).

These exceptions to the range of variable fines for standard criminal offences raise several issues. In relation to fixed penalties the difficulty is again the setting of the financial amount. If it is too high it may be unfair on offenders of limited means and it might also increase evasion of payment. Grace's study of PNDs found that in the force area reviewed, 51 per cent of tickets were issued to people who were unemployed, and that only 31 per cent of unemployed people paid the notice, compared with 59 per cent of people who were employed (Grace 2014: 78). If it is too low, however, it might not act as a deterrent and be treated simply as a (small) tax to be paid for the advantage gained by the illegal action (see Easton and Piper 2013).

In relation to regulatory penalties, and in relation to white collar crime generally, the issue has been whether those subject to such sentencing are treated too leniently: that the level of fines for such offenders is then unfair to other criminals treated more harshly.

Fining companies and organisations—where community or custodial sentences may not be an option—has been a particular problem for many years.[28] Croall found that few offenders were imprisoned for business regulatory offences and that fines were relatively low for offences under safety and public health legislation (1992: 111), although offences of fraud and tax evasion were given a broader range of punishments, including custody. Croall concluded that 'the broad distinction between crimes against and crimes in the course of capitalism appears to have some substance' (ibid: 112; see also Sanders 1985).

Cook came to similar conclusions in relation to the differential treatment of those defrauding the Inland Revenue by evading tax and those defrauding the Department of Social Security by claiming benefits to which they are not entitled (1989; see also Levi and Pithouse 2000). Webster has also been very critical of recent trends, pointing out that the number of financial penalties ('sanctions') imposed on benefit claimants by the Department of Work and Pensions now exceeds the number of fines imposed by the courts:

> In Great Britain in 2013, there were 1,046,398 sanctions on Jobseeker's Allowance claimants, 32,128 on Employment and Support Allowance claimants, and approximately 44,000 on lone parent recipients of Income Support. By contrast, Magistrates' and Sheriff courts [in Scotland] imposed a total of only 849,000 fines.
>
> (Webster 2015)[29]

Webster further argues that 'the "transgressions" (DWP's own word) which are punished by this system are almost exclusively very minor matters, such as missing a single interview with a Jobcentre or Work Programme contractor, or not making quite as many token job applications as the Jobcentre adviser demands' (Webster 2015). His concern that the procedure lacks safeguards echoes the issue raised by a report published in 2008: that the trend towards pre-court summary justice for a range of offences may not be being used fairly and effectively and remains outside the official inspection regime (Morgan 2008). The report warned that there is 'an accountability deficit' and called for a 'thoroughgoing' review of the use and impact of summary powers. That has not yet happened.

---

[28] See Ashworth 2010: 335–7 for further discussion.

[29] http://www.crimeandjustice.org.uk/resources/benefit-sanctions-britains-secret-penal-system (accessed 23 November 2015).

10.3 Community orders

10.3.1 Policy issues

In the third edition we said that two issues were prominent in relation to community sentences: whether supervision of offenders released from custody is adequate and whether—and how—costly and ineffective short prison sentences could be improved or replaced. The policy trend is still to encourage more use of community penalties and suspended prison sentences, by focusing on the effectiveness of rehabilitation and by making supervision more intensive and controlling, and, therefore, perceived as more punitive by sentencers and the public. More recently the government has also been concerned to improve the transition from prison to community to enhance rehabilitation.

Offenders who are not sentenced to a community penalty but are given a suspended custodial sentence—suspended sentence order(SSO)—and those who are on release from a custodial sentence are an increasingly important set of 'clients' for the Probation Service and the recently formed community rehabilitation companies. As Table 10.5 shows, in the first decade of this century over 90,000 offenders were being supervised as part of suspended or other custodial orders, compared with 120,000 on community orders. In section 10.4, therefore, we will be discussing separately in detail the question of supervision and rehabilitation of offenders serving an SSO or on release from a prison sentence.

A major issue which we will address in section 10.6 is who now delivers community punishment and supervision. With the policy focus on the 'rehabilitation revolution' and 'privatisation' of the delivery of rehabilitation programmes, there is great change occurring as we write this fourth edition. It will not be clear for some time how successful these new initiatives have been.

A further point: there are Council of Europe rules and recommendations relevant to the rest of this chapter. Recommendation CM/Rec (2010)1 defines the term 'probation' as relating to 'the implementation in the community of sanctions and measures, defined by law and imposed on an offender. It includes a range of activities and interventions, which involve supervision, guidance and assistance aiming at the social inclusion of an offender, as well as at contributing to community safety' (see Aebi et al. 2011). This broad definition masks the conflicts of aim, method, and justification which this chapter will review; it also masks the different content and use of various orders and disposals which make comparisons between countries problematic, but Table 10.6 shows the latest statistics regarding community punishments in European states.

10.3.2 The development of community penalties

At the beginning of the twentieth century there was little the sentencing court could order between prison and the forerunner of the conditional discharge—binding-over powers whose origins lie in the Justice of the Peace Act 1361—except for fines (Worrall 1997: 7). The Probation of Offenders Act 1907, the Criminal Justice Act 1948, and the Criminal Justice Act 1972 introduced probation, attendance centre orders, and community service orders, respectively, with compensation orders becoming sentences in their own right in 1988 (ibid: 8). These new disposals with a severity level above fines and below custody were usually referred to, therefore, as 'intermediate sanctions' or, sometimes, as 'alternatives to custody'. However, their use was inconsistent and there was pressure for clarification. (See Table 10.7 for relative percentages before 1991.)

Table 10.5 Offenders starting court order and pre and post release supervision by the Probation Service by sentence type and sex, (1) 2000 to 2010, England and Wales

Type of sentence	2000	2001	2002	2003	2004	2005	2006	2007	2008	2009	2010
Males and females											
All court orders	122,345	122,514	128,168	131,493	135,296	140,430	155,614	162,648	164,873	166,837	161,687
All community sentences	122,345	122,514	128,168	131,493	135,296	136,130	128,336	125,369	126,170	127,012	120,583
Community order						53,248	111,752	117,860	120,743	122,796	118,696
All pre CJA orders(2)	132162	132021	138305	142623	146372	93,925	19,530	8,625	6,248	4,864	1,842
Other sentences		...	...	...	...	5,952	33,111	44,991	46,087	47,430	48,486
Deferred sentence	...	...	...	...	...	104	384	570	585	533	584
Suspended sentence order	...	...	...	...	...	5,848	32,727	44,421	45,502	46,897	47,902
Pre and post release supervision	52,237	49,212	51,812	50,626	48,450	46,103	43,160	43,638	47,482	45,970	46,204
Males											
All court orders	102,790	102,939	107,594	111,298	114,415	119,034	132,363	138,260	139,340	140,794	136,562
All community sentences	102,790	102,919	107,594	111,298	114,415	115,204	108,595	106,022	106,392	106,846	101,302
Community order						45,832	95,111	99,573	101,552	103,074	99,598
All pre CJA orders*	111,421	111,299	116,480	121,127	124,256	78,916	16,087	7,504	5,611	4,395	1,678
Other sentences		...	...	...	...	5,206	28,752	38,930	39,499	40,497	41,683
Deferred sentence	...	...	...	...	...	81	306	460	473	423	475
Suspended sentence order	...	...	...	...	...	5,125	28,446	36,470	39,026	40,074	41,208
Pre and post release supervision	48,853	45,790	48,295	46,978	44,952	42,771	40,062	40,573	44,059	42,785	43,124
Females											
All court orders	19,555	19,575	20,574	20,195	20,881	21,396	23,251	24,388	25,333	26,043	25,125
All community sentences	19,555	19,575	20,574	20,195	20,881	20,926	19,741	19,347	19,778	20,166	19,291
Community order						7,416	16,641	18,287	19,191	19,722	19,098
All pre CJA orders	20,741	20,722	21,825	21,496	22,116	15,009	3,443	1,121	637	469	164
Other sentences		...	...	...	...	746	4,359	6,061	6,588	6,933	6,803
Deferred sentence	...	...	...	...	...	23	78	110	112	110	109
Suspended sentence order	...	...	...	...	...	723	4,281	5,951	6,476	6,823	6,694
Pre and post release supervision	3,384	3,422	3,517	3,648	3,498	3,332	3,098	3,065	3,423	3,175	3,080

(1) Each person is counted only once in the total even if they started several types of supervision in the year.

(2) For years prior to 2009, see Offender Management Caseload statistics 2008 for detailed breakdown of pre-CJA 2003 figures.

Source: Ministry of Justice (2011o: Table A 4.1).

Table 10.6 Breakdown (in percentages) of persons serving CSM or being under probation (STOCK) on 31 December 2013

Country	1.0 Total number of persons under the suspension or care of probation agencies per 100,000 population	1.1 Forms of probation/supervision before the sentence					1.2 Forms of probation/supervision after the sentence											Total %
		1.1.1 Alternatives to pre-trial detention with supervision by probation agencies (total)	1.1.2 Conditional suspension of criminal proceedings	1.1.3 Deferral (postponement of the pronouncement of a sentence)	1.1.4 Victim–offender mediation	1.1.5 Other	1.2.1 Fully suspended custodial sentence with probation	1.2.2 Partially suspended custodial sentence with probation	1.2.3 Conditional pardon or conditional discharge (with probation)	1.2.4 Community service	1.2.5 Electronic monitoring	1.2.6 Home arrest (curfew orders)	1.2.7 Semi-liberty	1.2.8 Treatment	1.2.9 Conditional release/parole with probation	1.2.10 Mixed orders	1.2.11 Other	
Albania	131.5	0.2	..	..	..	..	86.3	..	..	2.0	0.0	1.4	0.0	..	10.2	..	..	100.0
Andorra	..	..	..	..	..	..	..	..	..	..	..	..	..	..	..	..	..	0.0
Armenia	(108.0)	..	..	..	..	..	45.7	..	..	16.0	..	..	..	..	5.4	..	44.6	111.7
Austria	(154.5)	1.0	31.4	..	..	..	35.2	9.2	0.0	6.9	1.8	..	..	1.2	28.6	..	..	115.3
Azerbaijan	61.6	..	..	..	..	..	1.6	..	..	0.7	..	..	..	..	44.9	..	52.9	100.0
Belgium	353.7	6.0	..	16.4	13.1	..	33.0	..	0.0	20.8	4.4	..	0.3	..	6.1	..	..	100.0
BiH: State Level	..	..	..	..	..	..	..	..	..	..	..	..	..	..	..	..	..	0.0
BiH: Fed. BiH	..	..	..	..	..	..	..	..	..	..	..	..	..	..	..	..	..	0.0
BiH: Rep. Srpska	..	..	..	..	..	..	..	..	..	..	..	..	..	..	..	..	..	0.0
Bulgaria	(144.9)	..	2.1	..	..	34.8	0.0	..	..	34.8	0.0	0.0	0.0	0.0	3.5	97.9	9.6	182.7
Croatia	(68.2)	0.9	0.9	0.0	..	0.0	8.9	0.0	0.0	66.2	0.0	0.0	0.0	0.0	22.1	..	2.0	100.9
Cyprus	(131.4)	18.5	..	..	..	..	..	..	..	..	..	..	..	..	0.5	..	..	19.1
Czech Republic	(213.3)	3.3	0.8	..	..	28.0	31.0	..	0.2	23.3	0.0	0.7	..	1.0	17.2	..	4.6	110.2

Denmark	175.6	...	...	...	...	18.3	4.1	0.1	22.2	3.3	...	5.0	17.7	...	29.4	100.0
Estonia	485.5	0.2	...	...	...	61.5	5.9	...	21.9	0.0	...	0.0	9.4	...	1.0	100.0
Finland	46.4	...	...	...	...	...	...	...	54.8	0.6	...	...	41.1	3.5	...	100.0
France	(285.2)	...	...	0.1	...	75.4	...	...	19.6	5.4	0.9	...	3.4	0.0	5.5	112.6
Georgia	255.6	...	...	0.1	...	72.6	22.2	...	0.6	...	...	...	4.1	...	0.3	100.0
Germany	194.2	...	...	...	...	...	...	...	...	0.0	...	...	...	...	...	0.0
Greece	106.7	24.7	2.5	...	0.0	14.6	...	0.0	12.9	...	0.2	0.2	38.5	...	3.4	100.0
Hungary	385.5	...	10.8	4.3	...	16.6	...	3.5	58.0	...	...	...	6.8	...	0.0	100.0
Iceland	...	...	...	...	...	...	...	...	...	...	...	...	...	...	...	0.0
Ireland	(143.4)	...	...	...	...	15.7	12.0	25.9	35.3	...	...	...	...	0.0	12.4	101.4
Italy	55.5	...	...	...	...	15.5	...	...	13.3	...	30.7	8.8	7.9	9.7	11.7	100.0
Latvia	(858.9)	...	6.3	...	...	41.1	...	...	36.3	...	...	...	...	...	...	86.0
Liechtenstein	...	...	...	...	...	...	...	...	...	...	...	...	...	...	...	0.0
Lithuania	(279.2)	...	...	...	...	31.5	...	...	8.4	1.0	40.7	...	13.0	6.4	...	101.0
Luxembourg	(255.1)	0.9	...	0.7	...	34.3	13.1	...	33.8	0.8	1.6	...	13.9	...	0.8	100.0
Malta	(230.0)	...	...	...	...	11.5	...	...	...	...	...	...	...	3.5	0.0	15.0
Moldova	279.9	...	...	...	...	...	47.1	0.2	10.1	...	...	...	3.7	...	38.8	100.0
Monaco	105.7	...	...	...	...	95.0	...	0.0	...	...	0.0	2.5	2.5	...	...	100.0
Montenegro	...	...	...	...	...	...	...	...	...	...	...	...	...	...	...	0.0
Netherlands	256.3	7.4	5.0	...	0.0	33.0	0.0	0.0	48.3	1.0	0.6	1.0	3.5	...	0.6	100.0
Norway	37.6	0.0	0.0	0.0	0.0	28.8	0.0	0.0	47.3	7.8	0.0	...	15.0	...	0.0	100.0
Poland	(540.2)	...	1.8	...	...	80.2	...	...	...	2.3	...	0.0	18.1	...	1.7	104.0
Portugal	(247.1)	2.6	18.2	...	0.0	47.3	...	...	27.8	0.3	0.3	1.6	9.9	0.0	0.0	108.0
Romania	(93.5)	...	...	...	...	100.0	...	...	...	...	...	2.3	...	...	0.0	102.3
San Marino	(89.0)	0.0	50.0	0.0	0.0	42.9	0.0	0.0	50.0	...	3.6	0.0	3.6	0.0	0.0	150.0
Serbia	10.1	10.0	29.4	...	...	...	...	...	12.0	41.4	3.9	...	0.1	...	3.2	100.0
Slovak Republic	...	...	...	...	...	...	...	...	...	...	...	...	...	...	...	0.0
Slovenia	...	...	...	...	...	...	...	...	...	...	...	...	...	...	...	0.0

(Continued)

Table 10.6 Continued

Country	Total number of persons under the suspension or care of probation agencies per 100,000 population	1.1 Forms of probation/supervision before the sentence					1.2 Forms of probation/supervision after the sentence											Total %
		Alternatives to pre-trial detention with supervision by probation agencies (total)	Conditional suspension of criminal proceedings	Deferral (postponement of the pronouncement of a sentence)	Victim–offender mediation	Other	Fully suspended custodial sentence with probation	Partially suspended custodial sentence with probation	Conditional pardon or conditional discharge (with probation)	Community service	Electronic monitoring	Home arrest (curfew orders)	Semi-liberty	Treatment	Conditional release/parole with probation	Mixed orders	Other	
	1.0	1.1.1	1.1.2	1.1.3	1.1.4	1.1.5	1.2.1	1.2.2	1.2.3	1.2.4	1.2.5	1.2.6	1.2.7	1.2.8	1.2.9	1.2.10	1.2.11	
Spain (State Admin.)	194.8	…	…	…	0.1	…	17.4	…	…	58.0	2.3	…	8.5	1.9	11.7	0.2	…	100.0
Spain (Catalonia)	123.7	…	…	…	1.2	…	18.5	…	…	45.6	0.4	…	17.0	3.9	11.6	1.9	…	100.0
Sweden	136.8	…	…	…	…	…	…	…	…	19.9	1.8	…	…	8.9	30.7	…	38.6	100.0
Switzerland	86.9	36.0	…	…	…	…	14.2	1.9	…	16.3	2.1	…	…	8.6	20.9	…	…	100.0
Turkey	(1276.3)	19.1	…	5.7	…	…	3.0	…	14.6	1.9	…	0.1	…	50.3	0.5	…	4.9	100.0
UK: Eng./Wales	(264.2)	…	…	…	…	…	25.4	…	…	9.7	0.4	…	…	…	11.7	26.3	20.3	93.7
UK: North. Ireland	(245.2)	…	…	…	…	…	…	…	…	17.1	…	…	…	…	12.5	38.8	35.0	103.3
UK: Scotland	321.8	…	…	…	…	…	…	…	…	24.5	2.3	…	…	10.0	14.2	37.9	11.1	100.0
Mean	209.1	7.1	13.8	2.8	3.2	7.9	37.3	9.6	2.3	26.5	3.3	7.9	2.9	3.2	13.6	16.2	13.6	
Median	175.6	2.3	5.0	0.0	1.8	0.0	31.5	5.0	0.0	21.9	1.0	0.9	0.8	1.7	11.6	3.5	5.1	
Minimum	10.1	0.0	0.0	0.0	0.0	0.0	0.0	0.0	0.0	0.6	0.0	0.0	0.0	0.0	0.1	0.0	0.0	
Maximum	858.9	36.0	50.0	16.4	13.1	34.8	100.0	47.1	25.9	66.2	41.4	40.7	17.0	10.0	44.9	97.9	52.9	

Source: Aebi and Chopin (2014: Table 1.3) © Council of Europe.

See Aebi and Chopin (2014: care 5–9) for information about data and conventions used in the table.

Table 10.7 The use of non-custodial penalties as a percentage of all sentences[a]

	1978	1983	1988
Fines	Over 50%	—	Under 40%
Community Service + Probation Orders	8	14	17
Custody	14	16	17

[a] Based on sentences given for indictable offences.

Source: Figures taken from the White Paper (Home Office 1990a: para 4.2).

There were also concerns that the new sanctions lacked legitimacy in the eyes of the public, so government strategy by the end of the 1980s was to 'market' the top end of community penalties as sufficiently tough to be used instead of custody. A series of government policy papers—*Punishment, Custody and the Community* (Home Office 1988a), *Tackling Offending: An Action Plan* (Home Office 1988b), and *Supervision and Punishment in the Community* (Home Office 1990b)—asked for suggestions as to how to make probation more 'intensive', how to develop new forms of surveillance such as tracking, and how to transform probation.

Consequently, the 1990 White Paper gave a high profile to community penalties (itself a new term), arguing that prison was ineffective (Home Office 1990a: paras 2.6–2.9) and proposing that 'just deserts' should be the guiding principle even when punishment took place in the community (ibid: para 4.3). The aim was that non-custodial penalties should stand in their own right, not be seen simply as (inadequate) alternatives to custody.[30]

However, a just deserts rationale theoretically means that sentencers do not have the discretion to choose deterrence, rehabilitation, psychiatric treatment, or social work 'help' as the primary sentencing aim in relation to 'intermediate' sentences. The scheme proposed in the 1990 White Paper and incorporated in the CJA 1991 was that the court should make the initial sentencing decision on retributivist principles, and then consider other aims of sentencing when choosing the particular community penalty to impose. Depending on whether, for example, the offender was seen to need advice and training or be under a duty to make some reparation to the community, a probation order or community service order could be made (Home Office 1990a: para 4.8), with the 'amount' made proportionate to seriousness. In other words, desert determines the size of the penalty, and suitability dictates its form (Rex 1998: 383). The vexed question of ranking community punishments was not tackled in 1990/1.

Various pieces of legislation—the Criminal Justice Act 1993, the Crime (Sentences) Act 1997, the Criminal Justice and Court Services Act (CJCSA) 2000—made amendments to community sentencing, extending the possible use of such orders for fine default, introducing new names for existing orders, and introducing a range of new requirements that could be added to a community rehabilitation order. In line with the continuing focus on deprivation of liberty in the community, one of the new requirements could be a curfew condition.

The whole of the extended 1991 scheme was then re-enacted in the Powers of Criminal Courts (Sentencing) Act (PCCSA) 2000 (ss. 33–62) and had the following elements:

- 'community orders' covering a range of existing penalties which became 'sentences of the court' rather than alternatives to punishment;

---

[30] For a review of theories and projects around 'alternatives to custody' see Bottoms *et al.* (2004).

- fines as the presumptive sentence with legislative hurdles to discourage inappropriate use of community (and also custodial) penalties;

- a primary sentencing decision on the basis of seriousness as to whether to impose a community penalty, plus subsequent decisions on the type of community penalty and the commensurate 'amount' of the community penalty (PCCSA 2000, ss. 35(3)(a) and (b));

- punishment and rehabilitation as the aims of probation supervision.

Nevertheless, at the beginning of the twenty-first century there was concern that this scheme was not adequate. The Halliday Report proposed 'more flexible and effective community sentences' (Home Office 2001a: para 2.69) to provide the courts with 'a menu of options to choose from, providing elements of punishment, crime reduction and reparation, to fit both the offender and the offence' (ibid: para 2.70). The CJA 2003 did this by replacing the existing orders with a single community order, and by providing in s. 177 a range of specified requirements which courts can impose (see also section 10.3.4).

10.3.3 **The CJA 2003: seriousness and liberty**

As we saw in Part A of this book, seriousness and restrictions on liberty are important concepts in sentencing. The 1990 White Paper proposed that the new statutory rationale of just deserts would operate in community sentences as 'graduated restrictions on liberty, which are related to the seriousness of offending' (1990a: para 4.7) and the sentencing framework introduced by the CJA 1991 incorporated these ideas. The CJA 2003 largely repeated this approach (see Chapter 3), notwithstanding the emphasis on persistence and on risk. Just as with custodial sentences, a statutory hurdle was enacted for community sentences in the CJA 1991—now CJA 2003, s. 148. The court may pass a community sentence only if it is of the opinion 'that the offence, or the combination of the offence and one or more offences associated with it' is 'serious enough to warrant such a sentence'.

The CJA 2003 heralded, it was said, a more utilitarian approach to community sentences, as indicated by the title of *Making Punishments Work*, which proposed a new single community punishment order with 'ingredients' specified by the court instead of the existing community penalties (Halliday Report 2001: para 6.6). The specified elements, it proposed, would be chosen from compulsory programmes aimed at changing offending behaviour, compulsory work, restrictions and requirements such as a curfew or electronic monitoring, reparation, and supervision to support resettlement and enforce the sentence (ibid: para 6.6).

The ambiguity of rationales is again evident in that para 6.6 points out that 'the punitive weight' should determine how much should be done to reduce the risks of reoffending and make reparation. There is an echo here of a much earlier Consultation Paper where it was stated that every penalty should have three elements: deprivation of liberty, action to reduce offending, and recompense to the victim and/or public (Home Office 1988a: para 1.5). The White Paper (2001: para 2.70) endorsed the approach of the Halliday Report in relation to punitive weight and guidance on the CJA 2003 was subsequently framed in relation to three sentencing ranges (low, medium, and high), although flexibility is urged (Sentencing Guidelines Council 2004c: 8–10).

The situation is further complicated by the new CJA 2003 s. 177(2A), inserted by the Crime and Courts Act 2013 Sch.16(1) para 2, such that 'Where the court makes a community order, the court must—

(a) include in the order at least one requirement imposed for the purpose of punishment, or

(b) impose a fine for the offence in respect of which the community order is made, or

(c) comply with both of paragraphs (a) and (b).

10.3.4 **Choosing the community punishment**

The CJA 2003 simply empowered the courts to make a community order imposing on the offender 'any one or more' of the specified requirements (s. 177(1)). Sections 70–77 of LASPO 2012, together with provisions in the Offender Rehabilitation Act 2014, made various changes to these programme requirements (in force from 31 July 2015).

As summarised by the Sentencing Council, the court must now choose one or more of the following list:

- Unpaid work for up to 300 hours
- Attending appointments or participating in activities as instructed
- Undertaking a particular programme to help change offending behaviour
- Prohibition from doing particular activities
- Adherence to a curfew, so the offender is required to be in a particular place at certain times
- An exclusion requirement, so that the offender is not allowed to go to particular places
- A residence requirement so that the offender is obliged to live at a particular address
- A foreign travel prohibition requirement
- Mental health treatment with the offender's consent
- A drug rehabilitation requirement with the offender's consent
- An alcohol treatment requirement with the offender's consent
- Where offenders are under 25, they may be required to go to a centre at specific times over the course of their sentence.

> (Sentencing Council Website, November 2015 at http://www.sentencingcouncil.org.uk/
> about-sentencing/types-of-sentence/community-sentences/)

However, the Rehabilitation Activity Requirement (RAR) was introduced by the Offender Rehabilitation Act 2014, which amended the Criminal Justice Act 2003 such that the RAR replaces the Supervision and Specified Activity Requirements for all relevant sentences for offences committed on or after 1 February 2015 (the other requirements remain available to the court). The stated purpose is to give greater flexibility for providers (see section 10.6) to determine the rehabilitative interventions to be delivered to offenders. The Service Specifications produced for the delivery of the RAR by the National Offender Management Service suggest that the components will be similar to those used when supervision and/or a specified activity was ordered.[31]

Therefore, the problems of choice remain. Arguably, also, the difficulty for the courts of balancing proportionality with 'suitability' persists (Rex 1998: 384; see also Harrison 2006). Writing before the 1991 Act, Wasik and von Hirsch had considered various models for applying desert principles to the choice of non-custodial penalties. They argued that the key issue was how much substitution amongst such penalties was possible, opting for a 'partial substitution' model (1988: 561). They concluded that the punishment component, commensurate to seriousness, must take precedence, and utilitarian aims could only determine the substitution issue. Morris and Tonry, using practice in the United

---

[31] See https://www.gov.uk/government/uploads/system/uploads/attachment_data/file/310101/2014-03-28_DRAR_Specification_P1.0.pdf (accessed 23 August 2015).

States, argued for much more interchangeability of punishment (1990: 10) but when drafting what became the CJA 1991, the government appears to have taken on board the suggestions of theorists such as Wasik and von Hirsch (Rex 1998: 383; Ashworth 1992: 247).

However, there is still the difficulty of calculating the amount of deprivation of liberty which is proportionate,[32] and even if this is done satisfactorily it may mean that the amount of rehabilitation imposed is increased because of proportionality requirements rather than what is required to prevent reoffending. On the other hand, rehabilitation divorced from offence seriousness could lead to punitive levels of intervention.

A Probation Circular (Home Office 2005c) provided guidance on the implementation and use of the community order and included a table which gave detailed suggestions on hours and purposes for different levels of seriousness in relation to each main requirement (see Table 10.8). Yet, as Mair *et al.* point out, 'not only are the model combination types inadequately differentiated from each other but sentencing can also take account of several purposes' (2007: 13). In practice, however, they found that the unpaid work requirement was becoming increasingly popular and that half of the available requirements had not been used or had been used 'very rarely' (ibid: 31).[33] Their research two years later found that the average number of requirements for each order had remained stable and unpaid work had increased further in use, but that there seemed to be a slight growth in the number of single-requirement orders (Mair and Mills 2009: 46).[34] Noting that half of the requirements that are (theoretically) available were rarely used, they concluded that the community order continued to resemble the community sentences that preceded it (ibid: 46).

10.3.5 **Enforcement and compliance**

Compliance is an important area of study in the probation service . . . as Canton highlights, 'an unenforced community penalty is indistinguishable from "getting away with it"' (2011: 123) . . . Offender managers described how, 'when I first started [in 2006] it was enforcement, enforcement, enforcement but now it is compliance, compliance, compliance'.

(Phillips 2011: 9)

In a sense this is simply a change in words, but it may also signify better relationships between offenders and their 'offender managers' or be the result of changes in practice to achieve compliance targets (Phillips 2011: 9). Whatever the reason, non-compliance in regard to the requirements of a community or suspended sentence order is a factor which concerns governments and also the Probation Service, whose credibility often rests on this (see, for example, HM Inspectorate of Probation *et al.* 2007; Mair *et al.* 2007; National Audit Office 2008). For both community and suspended sentence orders, the percentage terminated for breach is decreasing: the figure for community orders dropped from 48 per cent in 2006 to 40 per cent in the second quarter of 2008, with over half of the respondents in a survey believing that enforcement 'was more effective and more robust than it had been in the past' (Mair and Mills 2009: 13, 22; see Farrall 2002 for earlier figures). However, this is still a very high figure.

---

[32] Which may account for the sentencing popularity of unpaid work requirements, because calculating punishment in hours is easier for sentencers (Rex 1998: 387–8).

[33] For further reading on community punishment, see Lewis *et al.* (2005) (focusing on issues around race) and Worrall and Hoy (2005). See also National Offender Management Service (2006a) for policy on *Working with Probation to Protect the Public and Reduce Re-offending.*

[34] Accessible at www.crimeandjustice.org.uk/sentenceshreeyearson.html.

Table 10.8 Criminal Justice Act 2003—requirements

Requirement	Level of seriousness	Length	Report	Main purpose(s)**
Unpaid work	Low	40–80 hours*	'Fast Delivery'	punishment
	Medium	80–150 hours*	'Fast Delivery'	reparation
	High	150–300 hours*	'Fast Delivery'	rehabilitation
Supervision	Low	up to 12 months	'Fast Delivery'	rehabilitation
	Medium	12–18 months	'Standard'	
	High	12–36 months	'Standard'	
Programme (Accredited)	Medium	stated number (or range) of sessions	depends on programme	rehabilitation
	High			
Drug rehabilitation Offender must consent	Low	6 months	• see footnote	rehabilitation
	Medium	6–12 months	'Standard'	
	High	12–36 months	'Standard'	
Alcohol treatment Offender must consent	Low	6 months	• see footnote	rehabilitation
	Medium	6–12 months	'Standard'	
	High	12–36 months	'Standard'	
Mental health treatment Offender must consent	Medium	up to 36 months	'Standard'	rehabilitation
	High			
Residence	Medium	up to 36 months	'Standard'	rehabilitation
	High			protection
(specified) Activity	Medium	20–30 days*	'Fast Delivery'	rehabilitation
	High	up to 60 days*		reparation
Prohibited activity	Low	up to 24/36 months for SSO/CO	'Fast Delivery'	punishment
	Medium			protection
	High			
Exclusion	Low	up to 2 months	'Fast Delivery'	punishment
	Medium	up to 6 months*		protection
	High	up to 12 months*		
Curfew typically up to 12 hours/day	Low	up to 2 months	'Fast Delivery'	punishment
	Medium	2–3 months*	'Fast Delivery'	protection
	High	4–6 months*	'Fast Delivery'	
Attendance centre	Low	12–36 hours	'Fast Delivery'	punishment

Notes:

* Length = in line with Sentencing Guidelines Council Guidelines.

Report = the minimum level of Report which should be used when proposing the Requirement (but the court may be able to make the Requirement without considering such a Report . . .).

• A 'Fast Delivery' Report may be sufficient where a current treatment plan is already available.

** Purpose = indicates NPD's interpretation of the main purpose of the Requirement. All Requirements are presumed to meet the purpose of the reduction of crime, either through rehabilitation, or by deterrence through their punitive impact.

Source: Home Office (2005c: 8).

There are two opposed schools of thought on how best to manage this. Eadie and Willis (1989), focusing on 'absenteeism', pointed to the different attitudes of community service supervisors and organisers with and without a social work qualification (ibid: 412), but a social work qualification is no longer a requirement for recruitment to either the National Probation Service (NPS) or the new community rehabilitation companies. From the first draft of the National Standards in 1988 until the present, the clear message is that that the NPS must take a tough line (see Ministry of Justice 2011i).

The CJCSA 2000, s. 53, in effect created a statutory warning that offenders would be issued with a maximum of one warning for an unacceptable failure to comply with a community sentence in any 12-month period. Previously there had been two possible warnings. Section 53 was never implemented but the law now in Schedule 8 to the CJA 2003, as amended by the Offender Rehabilitation Act 2014, takes the same approach of only one warning before a return to court. The National Offender Management Service (NOMS) has issued a new 'instruction' to cover the changes (PI 06/2014, Enforcement of Community Orders and Suspended Sentence Orders),[35] the revised procedures applying to the enforcement officers for both community orders and suspended sentences orders. If a breach is proved the court is no longer mandated to impose a custodial sentence, it being possible to impose more 'onerous' requirements in the order instead.

However, it is 'one thing to promise uncompromising discipline, but another thing to deliver it': offenders who are given community orders are often the ones who require that particular disposal in order to help them become more disciplined in terms of time management (Eadie and Willis 1989: 414; see also Mair and Mills 2009: 22–4). Early return to the courts for breach then means that their treatment cannot be successful. Financial problems, drug usage and depression are often associated with the absenteeism of offenders being supervised (Farrall 2002: 267–8). More recent research also found that 'looking at needs identified by OASys, 66% had an Education, Training and Employment (ETE) need, 46% had an alcohol use need, 42% had an accommodation need and 36% had a drug misuse need' (Wood *et al.* 2013: 3).

10.3.6 **An alternative to prison?**

The research of Mair and Mills (2009) considered the extent to which the orders have had the hoped-for impact on providing an alternative to short-term custodial sentences, as well as their impact on probation practice and the management of community-based orders. They note that '[f]or every three Community Orders started, one SSO begins' (2009: 8)—a great increase in the use of suspended (custodial) sentence orders. They also note that half of the community orders and SSOs made in the magistrates' courts were for summary offences and therefore not necessarily sufficiently serious to have led to a custodial sentence. They concluded that there was little evidence to suggest that either the community order or the SSO was acting as an alternative to custodial sentences of 12 months or less (ibid: 46).

Since then a requirement in a new s. 150A inserted into the CJA 2003 by the Criminal Justice and Immigration Act 2008 has made clearer that community orders are aimed at offences sufficiently serious to warrant custody. Now community penalties must be used only if the offence is punishable by imprisonment. Yet prison numbers have continued to rise since 2000 and currently the population remains at over 85,000.

It would appear that the more recent changes have not been sufficient to make such penalties more attractive to sentencers and the public so that they become alternatives to

---

[35] Available via http://www.justice.gov.uk/offenders/probation-instructions/pi-archive-2014.

custody rather than to fines. As Worrall noted some years ago, the lack of legitimacy of community punishment in the eyes of the public is hard to dislodge, due perhaps to the tenacious legacy of the Victorian principle of less eligibility, under which the offender's punishment must be seen as approximating to a poorer standard of life than that of the poorest respectable citizen (1997: 13).

10.4 Supervision and custodial penalties

10.4.1 The suspended sentence order

Both the community order and the suspended sentence order—or SSO—became available for adults over 18 on 4 April 2005 as a result of the implementation of s. 189 of the CJA 2003 (see detailed information for the courts in Sentencing Guidelines Council 2004c: 20–6). The original suspended custodial sentence was introduced in 1967 but lost popularity and its use was restricted by the CJA 1991. The CJA 2003 abolished this restrictive criterion—'exceptional circumstances'—and the new sentence could, therefore, be viewed 'as an attempt to revive the old-style suspended sentence by adding conditions to it', 'intended to narrow the custody/community divide' and 'to offer more robust, demanding and credible alternatives to short custodial sentences (Mair *et al.* 2008: 7). It consists of an 'operational period' (the time for which the custodial sentence is suspended) and a 'supervision period' (the time during which any requirements take effect). Until amendments[36] were made by LASPO 2012 only a custodial sentence of up to 12 months could be suspended. Section 68 now allows suspension of sentences which are between 14 days and two years.

The courts can only recommend particular requirements for post-release supervision of immediate custody sentences but the sentencing court can impose the requirements for a suspended custodial sentence. These can be one or more of the requirements listed in s. 190 of the CJA 2003, details of which can be found in ss. 199–213,[37] and are the same as those that are available for community orders (s. 177).

If the offender fails to comply with the requirements of the SSO or commits another offence during the operational period, the court is empowered to order the original custodial sentence is served. However, LASPO 2012 s. 69 inserted a new provision into paragraph 8 of Schedule 12 to the CJA 2003 to enable the court to impose a fine of up to £2,500 for breach of an SSO where it decides not to give effect to the custodial sentence.

10.4.2 Supervision in the community on release from prison

For some time it has been noted that the policy trend is that 'the boundary between custodial and community sentences is becoming more fluid', making essential more effective collaboration between the Prison and Probation Services (Raynor and Vanstone 2002: 107). To this end the Prison and Probation Services became part of NOMS in 2004 with the dual aims of punishing offenders and reducing offending: see *Reducing Crime, Changing Lives* (Home Office 2004b: para 25).

The aim is to have 'seamless' sentencing, an aim dating from the Home Office's desire for more 'flexible' sentences and the setting up of the Halliday Report (2001) to 'identify and evaluate' new frameworks 'which join up custodial and community sentences'. One

---

[36] In force since 3 December 2012.

[37] Sections 70–77 of LASPO 2012 made various changes to the programme requirements to be attached to these orders.

of the main drivers was—and still is—frustration at the ineffectiveness of short prison sentences in reducing offending: as a former Home Secretary put it, 'it is crackers to put people in jail for a short time without any measures to change them or any plan for when they come out'.[38]

Other ways of blurring the boundary of custody and community had been proposed but never implemented.[39] Intermittent custody orders—modelled on the so-called 'weekend prison' sentences available in some other jurisdictions (for example, the Netherlands)— were not implemented because of a lack of relevant resources. This is a pity as the pilots in 2004–6 showed that the level of compliance amongst offenders was 'exceptionally high' (Probation Service 2006) and that 'judges . . . were enthusiastic advocates of the disposal' in order to allow for employment and childcare responsibilities' (Penfold et al. 2006).

Early release

The current framework is simpler than that in the 1991 Act. The 1991 scheme had differ- ent frameworks for 'long-term' (four + years) and 'short-term' (under four years) prison- ers but was replaced by Chapter 6 of Part 12 of the CJA 2003 (see Gullick 2004). The law now is that fixed-term prisoners are released at the halfway stage of their sentence but that does not mean the whole scheme is wonderfully straightforward, because there are offend- ers still in prison who are subject to previous legislation or subject to the exceptions. As Padfield notes:

> English rules on early release from prison are a nightmare to understand. Not only have the rules been dramatically and regularly changed . . . but under each regime different rules apply to different 'categories' of offenders: short-term, long-term, indeterminate, determinate, and so on. In addition, there are difficulties in calculating release dates due to the complex and changing rules on consecutive sentences and the effects of pre-trial remands.
>
> (Padfield 2007: 255)

Release from prison has been automatic at the halfway stage since the implementation of the Criminal Justice Act 2003 s. 244 (but see s. 247), but release on licence did not apply to short-term prisoners. Now, except for prisoners serving a determinate sentence of less than two days, the second half of a determinate custodial sentence—for all those who are 18 years old or more at the halfway point of their sentence—is now spent on licence under the supervision of the Probation Service.[40] This first half of the sentence is the 'requisite custodial period' which has to be served and the second half is the licence period.

Previously this applied only to sentences of 52 weeks or more,[41] but the rules for the release of prisoners given sentences under two years changed on 1 February 2015 in rela- tion to all offences committed after that date. This means not only that even prisoners on short sentences are released on licence for the second half of the sentence imposed by the

---

[38] David Blunkett quoted in Ellis and Winstone 2001/2: 20. *Criminal Justice: The Way Ahead* had noted that in 1999, for sentences of less than 12 months, 47 per cent of the total discharges had no opportunity of enga- ging in rehabilitation programmes post-release (Home Office 2001a: para 2.73).

[39] LASPO 2012 s. 89 repealed custody plus and intermittent custody. The custody plus sentence, a split custody and community sentence, would have entailed custody for 2–12 weeks, plus supervision in the com- munity for six months or more (CJA 2003, ss. 183–184).

[40] The CJA 2003 s. 243A has been amended to allow release without supervision for prisoners serving a sentence of one day.

[41] The not implemented—and now repealed—arrangements for prisoners given sentences of less than 51 weeks under the Criminal Justice Act (CJA) 2003, s. 181 would have provided release under supervision.

Table 10.9 Examples of the rules before and after the changes

Sentence imposed by court	Offences committed before 1 February 2015		Offences committed on or after 1 February 2015	
	Period in custody before release	Arrangements on release	Period in custody before release	Arrangements on release
6-month sentence	3 months	3 months in community, but with no licence conditions or supervision	3 months	3 months' licence and 9 months' post-sentence supervision. Total supervision 12 months
10-month sentence	5 months	5 months in community, but with no licence conditions or supervision	5 months	5 months' licence and 7 months' post-sentence supervision. Total supervision 12 months
18-month sentence	9 months	9 months' licence	9 months	9 months' licence and 3 months' post-sentence supervision. Total supervision 12 months

Based on Sentencing Council: *Determinate Prison Sentences*, accessed at https://www.sentencingcouncil.org.uk/about-sentencing/types-of-sentence/determinate-prison-sentences/ on 28 November 2015.

court but also that they will have an additional period of post-sentence supervision. This is to ensure that all offenders with custodial sentences under two years are supervised for a period of 12 months.[42] Table 10.9 gives details of the differences this makes to post-release supervision for offences before and after that date.

In addition, most fixed-term prisoners serving sentences of between three months and four years can be considered for release on a home detention curfew (HDC) with electronic tagging, which means the offender is released up to 135 days earlier than the automatic date. As amended and in force since April 2015, s. 246 of the CJA 2003 allows this providing that the requisite custodial period is at least six weeks, that the offender has served at least four weeks of his sentence and at least one-half of the custodial period, and that the sentence imposed is less than four years.[43] Those serving less than four years might also be eligible for the end-of-custody licence scheme which could mean release 18 days early. Particular rules for extended-sentence prisoners are to be found in s. 247.

The changes have been brought about by the following pieces of legislation. The Offender Rehabilitation Act 2014 s. 1 amended section 243A of the Criminal Justice Act 2003 in relation to prison sentences of less than 12 months while s. 2 inserted s. 256AA to set up the new framework for those on sentences of less than two years. In addition, ss. 7–13 of the Criminal Justice and Courts Act (CJCA) 2015 amended various statutory provisions in relation to the detail of release, notably electronic monitoring and recall procedures,

---

[42] See, for more details, National Offender Management Service, *Sentence Calculation—Determinate Sentenced Prisoners*, PSI 03/2015 (at http://www.justice.gov.uk/downloads/offenders/psipso/psi-2015/psi-03-2015-sentence-calculation-determiante-sentenced-prisoners.pdf) and also http://www.offendersfamilieshelpline.org/index.php/sentence/#sthash.gtpGqnGQ.dpuf.

[43] The HDC is also not available for those on sentences imposed under sections 226A, 227, 228, or 236A of the CJA 2003.

while s. 14 amended s. 268 of the CJA 2003 such that the definition of 'requisite custodial period'—the period to be spent in prison—is altered in line with other changes. LASPO 2012 restricted the use of CJA 2003 s. 246 (HDC).

Since the implementation of the CJA 2003, the court has been empowered to recommend conditions which should be included in the licence (s. 238; see also Sentencing Guidelines Council 2004c: 18–19). This is not a duty and does not mean the recommendations will necessarily form part of the punishment: the Secretary of State must simply 'have regard to' the recommendations.

There are exceptions to the general rule of release at the halfway stage because in the past decade or so there has also been a focus on the supervision on release of long-term 'dangerous' prisoners to managed rehabilitation programmes in the community. We dealt with this in Chapter 5, which focused on those offenders who are deemed to be a risk. To summarise, those convicted of specified offences of sex and violence can be given several sentences, including the 'extended sentence', where the extended part of the determinate custodial sentence is served in the community (see Chapter 5, section 5.3.5). Offenders are assessed to determine their risk level, and the content of the community programme is tailored to addressing the offender's risk factors effectively. In addition, since 13 April 2015 there has been a new sentence—a 'Special custodial sentence for certain offenders of particular concern'—introduced by the new s. 236A in the CJA 2003 (inserted by Schedule 1 para 2 of the CJCA 2015) such that offenders convicted of offences listed in the new CJA 2003 Schedule 18A may end up serving the whole sentence with one year under licence on release (see Chapter 5, section 5.4.2).[44]

10.4.3 Through the gate

'Through the gate' programmes have been developed and run by voluntary organisations for some years. Writing about the St Giles Trust's Through the Gate project, launched in July 2008 and with offices in north and south London, *Community Care* commented, 'For some inmates who have completed their jail term the short walk to freedom through the prison gates can mark the start of a new sentence. One project tries to smooth the transition for those without support.'[45]

The Coalition government took over this phrase in conjunction with plans to organise 'resettlement prisons' to which prisoners were transferred some time before release and from which could be arranged continuous support from custody to community. In July 2013 the then Justice Secretary Chris Grayling announced that 70 resettlement prisons would be established, stating that 'Rehabilitation in the community must begin behind the prison walls and follow offenders out through the gates if we are to stand a chance of freeing them from a life of crime.'[46] To stress the importance of this process the Howard League for Penal Reform organised, for example, a conference in November 2014 entitled 'Through the gate: Transforming rehabilitation and the future of prisons'.

From May 2015 'through the gate' (TTG) resettlement services were rolled out nationally, with community rehabilitation companies (CRCs) delivering this service to virtually all prisoners.

---

[44] The CJA 2003 244A places a duty on the Secretary of State to refer the offender's case for consideration by the Parole Board at the halfway stage.

[45] http://www.communitycare.co.uk/2009/09/25/through-the-gate-project-helps-prisoners-on-release/ (accessed 3 November 2014).

[46] https://www.gov.uk/government/news/70-resettlement-prisons-announced-for-england-and-wales (accessed 3 November 2014).

An example

Ownership of the Kent, Surrey and Sussex (KSS) CRC transferred to the privately owned Seetec Group on 1 February 2015 to work with low- to medium-risk offenders (leaving the Probation Service to deal with high-risk offenders: see section 10.6). The website of the CRC sets out its legal obligation as follows:

> The KSS CRC Annual Service Plan sets out our approach to delivering a rehabilitation service based on our legal obligations. The plan is based around our contract requirements for service delivery as agreed with the MoJ and cited in the Amended and Restated Services Agreement.
>
> It spans a period that started with the first three months of the launch of our Through the Gate service, the Transformation phase, and continues through to the development of My Solution Information System (MySIS, the cloud-based IT platform on which the infrastructure will sit).

(https://ksscrc.co.uk/about-kss-crc, accessed 24 August 2015)

Seetec was founded in 1984 and says that it has 'become one of the UK's most experienced providers of employability services, skills training, rehabilitation support and community work placements'.[47] Their duty is to deliver rehabilitation services—including 'through the gate'—with an aim of reducing reoffending.

While the Coalition government's focus on rehabilitation was presented as a 'revolutionary' new approach, the concern with rehabilitation as a key aim of the penal system has a much longer ancestry and debates over the value of rehabilitative programmes have been a persistent feature of penological and policy debates since the increased use of imprisonment in the late eighteenth century.

10.5 Rehabilitation: old and new

10.5.1 Introduction

The aim of rehabilitation is to reduce the crime rate by reforming and rehabilitating the individual, so he is less likely to reoffend. This approach was popular in the 1950s and early 1960s, a period which is usually seen as the high point of the rehabilitative ideal. As we have seen, rehabilitation is an important element of community and SSO sentences and the licence period of custodial sentences, as well as a key factor in parole decisions. Imprisonment also offers an opportunity to reform and rehabilitate the offender, giving him skills to survive outside while also changing his attitude towards offending (see Chapter 8). Rehabilitation is utilitarian, as it is forward-looking and consequentialist: its objective is for the individual to contribute to society at the end of the period of rehabilitation and thereby add to the maximisation of happiness of society as a whole, as well as enhancing his own happiness. In Bentham's model prison, the individual was expected to undertake useful work and to learn how to contribute to society in future by developing his skills and rationality. Later, in the twentieth century, the rehabilitative ethos focused on the individualised treatment of the offender, developing the treatment appropriate to him, rather than simply reflecting the severity of the offence. On this approach proportionality is less important than rehabilitation and treatment should be provided for as long as is necessary to rehabilitate the offender, so indeterminate sentences may be favoured.

---

[47] https://ksscrc.co.uk/about-seetec (accessed 24 August 2015).

The rehabilitative ideal declined in popularity in the 1970s and 1980s, confronted by high levels of recidivism, but within the penal system there remained a commitment to it, albeit on a small scale in therapeutic programmes rather than at a macro level. The rehabilitative approach was beneficial in so far as it encouraged the development of new programmes within the Prison and the Probation Services, stimulated the search for alternatives to incarceration, and widened the range of options. At its height the rehabilitative model was seen as much more progressive than retributivism, which, as we have seen, has been (wrongly) associated with revenge and harsh punishment.

However, an attack on rehabilitation was mounted from two directions. First, it was challenged on the ground that offenders regularly reoffend despite undergoing rehabilitative programmes. Secondly, it was argued that the approach was flawed in principle because of the rights violations permitted by it. Both these criticisms will be considered.

10.5.2 Does rehabilitation 'work'?

Nothing works

A key landmark in the assault on the rehabilitative ethos was Martinson's 1974 paper 'What works?' Martinson reviewed the results of 231 research studies of a range of programmes aimed at rehabilitation in the period 1945–67, which suggested that various therapies and regimes which had been tried at that time, as well as different types of sentence, were ineffective in preventing reoffending. At best all they could do was reduce the adverse effects of imprisonment on offenders. The programmes included counselling, individual and group work, and a range of different therapeutic environments. Martinson concluded that 'with few and isolated exceptions, the rehabilitative efforts that have been reported so far have had no appreciable effect on recidivism' (1974: 25). Similar conclusions were drawn from other studies in that period, such as Brody's (1976) review of UK sentencing policies which found no evidence to suggest that a particular type of sentence was more effective than others in preventing reoffending. Martinson's conclusions were endorsed by a National Research Panel on Rehabilitative Techniques, set up in the United States in 1977, which commissioned papers on the issue and concluded that 'Lipton, Martinson, and Wilks were reasonably accurate in their appraisal of the rehabilitation literature' (Sechrest et al. 1979).

Martinson's paper was widely and mistakenly interpreted as suggesting 'nothing works', but Martinson himself was not so pessimistic (see Allen 1981). All Martinson was saying is that no one has yet proved conclusively that something works. Moreover, subsequent studies have been more promising. But the willingness to embrace a pessimistic view should also be seen in the context of the retreat from welfare in that period (see Pitts 1992b).

In the wake of Martinson's paper, the rehabilitation movement lost support, and this contributed to the loss of political will to deal with the underlying social and economic problems or to develop a socio-economic approach to crime prevention (see Allen 1981). Instead, as we saw in Chapter 1, from the mid-1980s successive UK governments have tried to fashion a more cost-effective justice system. In addition, the decline of the rehabilitative model undermined support for rehabilitation-oriented practices such as remission for good behaviour and early release mechanisms, predicated on the presumption of rehabilitation. After Martinson there were arguments—similar to those we have already encountered in our earlier discussions of deterrence and incapacitation—over the methodologies employed to prove or disprove the value of rehabilitative programmes. Opponents claimed that contrary evidence was obscured by the way the research was conducted and, given the broad timescale of Martinson's review, many of the studies cited in his paper were out of date by the mid-1970s. Large-scale studies of reoffending do not tell us enough about *which* individuals are helped by *which* programmes, and the individual who is helped may be overlooked in data on those who were not. But it would be absurd to infer from this that nothing works; rather, what evidence we now have suggests that *some* programmes are effective in reducing reoffending for *some* offenders and not others. Rehabilitative programmes are expensive so it is important to target specific programmes at those most likely to benefit.

Various approaches have been used to study the effectiveness or ineffectiveness of rehabilitation programmes, including statistical analysis, interpretive studies, and meta-analyses. Of course it is difficult when measuring reoffending to know whether offenders did reoffend but were not caught, or that they offended later, outside the period of scrutiny, or alternatively that they would not have reoffended anyway for some other reason. It is frequently observed that juvenile offenders may mature and 'grow out of crime' and that desistance may be uneven. So it is difficult for a research study to control for all these variables. It is also difficult to draw firm conclusions because, within a group of offenders going through a programme, some may not respond to any form of corrective treatment, others might have responded better to another regime than the one tried, and there may be some who do respond positively to a particular regime but are swamped by a large number of failures. Figures may also conceal whether the reoffending in question was committed before completing the programme. There is also the problem of the time lag for such studies.

Expecting a particular programme to prevent reoffending may be unrealistic because the reasons for offending and desistance from offending are so complex, and may include a range of factors including drugs and alcohol. In the early stages of desistance, as King (2013) notes, narrative and identity changes will be crucial to change. The range of reasons for reoffending and the processes involved in continuing offending and delaying desistance are also examined by Farrington and Zara (2013), who focus on why, how, and for how long an individual continues committing crimes. Desistance from offending may, as Weaver argues (2012), be seen as a process involving an interplay and relationship between external and internal or subjective factors, and this needs to be considered in devising policies intended to promote desistance. Moreover, as Rubin (2003) points out, in evaluating the rehabilitative ideal we should not assess it in terms of the complete reformation of the offender, but rather assess its value and effectiveness against alternatives, such as the incapacitation or warehousing of offenders.

What works?

A review of the available research on the effectiveness of treatment programmes on reoffending in the 1990s was undertaken by McGuire and Priestley, who found that the effect of treatment showed on average a reduction in recidivism rates of between 10 per cent and 12 per cent (McGuire and Priestley 1995: 9). This is the average figure but in some of the programmes the figures were much higher: for example, Lipsey's (1992) review of programmes for young offenders also found treatment had a positive effect in reducing reoffending in 64.5 per cent of the experiments he examined.

Many studies focus on whether the respondents reoffend and, if we find high numbers do reoffend, then the programme is deemed ineffective. Murray and Cox (1979), in their studies of delinquents in Chicago, found that those programmes with stronger supervision had the greatest effect on the rate of recidivism. Supervision appeared to be crucial whether the programme was deployed in the community or in custody. Wilson (1985) notes that various studies suggest that some types of offender are easier to change than others and further research on this is needed. Young, verbal, intelligent, and neurotic offenders seemed to be more amenable to therapy. A programme might also be deemed a partial success if it leads to offenders committing less serious offences than the one for which they were originally convicted. The successful outcome of a particular regime may also be affected by the individuals administering it, making it more difficult to assess the results than, say, drugs trials. So to say 'nothing works' is an overstatement: some things work with some offenders but not with most or not for long, and it may sometimes be difficult to identify the cases in which they do work.

Something works

Considerable research has been undertaken in recent years to establish which type of regime works best in preventing reoffending. Numerous studies have investigated the most effective practical programmes in the United States, Canada, and Europe (see McGuire 1995; see also Craig *et al.* 2013). Since the late 1990s the 'nothing works' philosophy has been replaced by the view that 'something works' and some things work for some offenders. Programmes therefore need to be carefully targeted to be cost-effective. An evaluation of the Intensive Alternatives to Custody (IAC) pilots (using community orders with an average of 3.4 requirements) showed a compliance rate of only 56 per cent but concluded that they were likely to be more cost-effective (taking account of the costs of the sentences and the costs of likely reoffending) than short custodial sentences (Hansbury 2011).[48]

Cognitive-behavioural programmes

Research suggests that cognitive-behavioural methods, rather than psychoanalytic or psychotherapeutic approaches or counselling which address deep-seated causes of crime, may be very effective in teaching new ways of thinking and behaving. These include teaching practical skills to cope with personal and social problems, using a range of methods of treatment depending on participants' abilities and levels of risk, and encouraging offenders to empathise with victims and to think about the effects of their actions. The aim is to enhance problem-solving skills so that individuals can control themselves and their environments to avoid exposing themselves to high-risk situations. A Home Office study on cognitive-behavioural programmes in England and Wales found that reconviction rates fell following the programmes (Home Office 2002a). The rates for treatment groups were up to 14 per cent lower than for control groups who did not receive treatment. Some programmes combine a variety of modes of treatment.

The emphasis, as we have seen, has been increasingly on risk assessment and management rather than on individualised approaches. Cognitive behavioural therapy (CBT) has been a favoured method within the Risk, Need, Responsivity (RNR) model which has been widely used here and in the US, Canada, and Australia in offender rehabilitation provision since 1990. It focuses on the reliable determination of the risk of reoffending, so programmes can be targeted at those with a high risk of recidivism, focusing interventions directly relating to the criminogenic needs of the individual—which might be linked for example to drug or alcohol use or anti-social personality disorder—and responsivity, that is, delivering interventions which meet the individual learning style and needs of the offender and take account of factors which affect the individual's ability to participate and benefit from those interventions (see Polaschek 2012).

There is now more optimism regarding the value of offending behaviour programmes and in this sense the rehabilitative ideal has gained ground. The available research on evidence-based crime prevention, including CBT and other interventions, in a range of contexts was reviewed by Welsh and Farrington (2006) and Sherman *et al.* (2006). Although there have been positive results, there have also been concerns that CBT is less successful in relation to women offenders, not least because women may have different learning

---

[48] See also Peck's research on reconviction among offenders eligible for Multi-Agency Public Protection arrangements suggesting lower rates than those before such arrangements (Peck 2011).

styles and different therapeutic needs. One theoretical perspective may not fit all groups, for example women or some minority ethnic groups, so a more flexible approach is needed. As we saw in Chapters 8 and 9, most of the findings on the rehabilitation of offenders have been drawn from research studies of male offenders.

Programmes for women offenders

However, more work is now being undertaken on female offenders and there is more interest in and commitment to developing gender-appropriate courses as gender-specific approaches have become embedded in penal policy in recent years. Women may benefit more from small-group therapeutic approaches, but it may be harder to 'sell' these in the prison context because of the weight given to risk-based models. 'What works' in relation to female offenders has been considered by Sheehan *et al.* (2007), Blanchette and Brown (2006), and Worrall and Gelsthorpe (2009). Roberts (2010) argues for the importance of recognising women offenders' complex needs, while Gelsthorpe (2012) notes that offender treatment programmes have been designed primarily for white, male offenders, with the knowledge base derived from those experiences applied to female offenders. Recent documents suggest the government is now more aware of the need to provide appropriate rehabilitation programmes inside and outside prison (see Ministry of Justice (2013c)). But clearly this needs to be matched by sufficient resources for those providing those programmes.

Although research is now being undertaken on the effectiveness of programmes for women offenders, as Durrance *et al.* (2010) argue, there is less research on effective practice for black and minority ethnic offenders. So in considering 'what works?', they caution, we need greater sensitivity to diversity issues and a broader conceptualisation of appropriate interventions.

Because of the success of CBT in many contexts, it may be difficult for alternative approaches to rehabilitation to be given support or credence. For example, one valuable area of rehabilitative work is provision of arts programmes. Nugent and Loucks (2011) reviewed such programmes in Cornton Vale, a women's prison in Scotland, and argue that the arts can contribute to rehabilitation but their significance has been underrated. Similarly, Parkes and Bilby (2010) also argue that artistic and spiritual activities in prison can offer a valuable contribution to rehabilitation and provide an alternative to traditional concepts of rehabilitation and treatment.

The effectiveness of short sentences

Research has also been undertaken on the effectiveness of short prison sentences because it has been questioned whether short prison sentences reform offenders or reduce crime and argued that these sentences are used excessively. A large-scale project on short sentences, surveying adult male prisoners serving sentences of up to 12 months in local prisons, was undertaken by the Howard League for Penal Reform in collaboration with the Prison Governors Association and found that many prisoners thought the prison sentence less demanding than community punishment, because they find it difficult to meet the demands made by the latter, including keeping appointments and the length of time involved in completing the sentence (see Trebilcock 2011). However, they also referred to their boredom in prison because of the lack of available activities, and particularly the fact that there were insufficient courses available.

A survey of prison governors conducted as part of this study found that 81 per cent of respondents disagreed with the statement that 'short prison sentences serve to reform or rehabilitate the offender' (Trebilcock, 2010: 2). Seventy-five per cent of respondents thought short sentences were used excessively, and 59 per cent disagreed or strongly disagreed when asked if short sentences serve to reduce crime. Reasons given for the failure of short sentences included the difficulty of changing attitudes or behaviour within a shorter space of time, or addressing mental or physical health problems or problems with drugs, alcohol, education, training, financial, housing, or family within a short sentence. The short sentences can offer little to the individual offender or to the community to which the individual returns. The approach in *Transforming Rehabilitation*, as we have seen, is to provide more support and supervision to those serving shorter prison sentences. However, prison reformers have favoured stronger community sentences as the more cost-effective option, especially at a time when cuts in resources make it harder for prisons to perform effective rehabilitation but instead see them perform a warehousing role.

For those completing longer sentences, where appropriate provision is made for therapeutic programmes, the results are more promising. Greatest improvements are made by those who complete longer periods in therapy, of at least 18 months. A number of quite promising studies have been undertaken of HMP Grendon, the therapeutic prison which opened in 1962. Marshall's study in 1997 showed lower reconviction rates for those who went to Grendon than for those who elected for Grendon but did not go, and there were similar findings by Taylor (2000) despite the fact that there are high levels of psychopathy, dangerousness, and psychological disturbances amongst the population there. The research of Wilson and McCabe (2002) considered how Grendon 'works' from the prisoners' perspectives[49] and found that treatment took time, new behaviours needed to be constantly strengthened by other prisoners and key staff members, and having a personal 'champion' on the staff was very important. Other prisoners played a key role in the therapy groups and the emphasis was on involving prisoners in community life so they experienced social inclusion rather than exclusion. The quality of life at Grendon was also significant, affecting how prisoners viewed the therapeutic process. Officers were polite, called prisoners by their first name, and treated them respectfully as human beings, which also assisted in this process of inclusion.

Genders and Player (2010) consider the problems of protecting the role of therapeutic work within prisons in the context of changes in the penal landscape in the past 20 years. Haigh (2010) explores the role of therapy within the context of a prison therapeutic community (TC) and the principles and values behind this approach, while Brown *et al.* (2014) discuss their seven-year research project on the purpose-built TC located at HMP Dovegate, which opened in 2001 and holds persistent serious offenders. They interviewed residents, ex-residents, and former residents on release and examined the role of the TC in bringing about changes in their lives. The key goal of the community was to reduce reoffending and specifically to reduce the risk of harm to others. They concluded that 'whilst it is true that some residents felt that they had made no gains or claimed to be worse off after their TC experience, the majority did positively benefit and showed some significant insights' (Brown *et al.* 2014: 241). They also stressed the need for the TC to be properly staffed, for constructive relationships between the mainstream prison and therapeutic community, and for suitable residents to be admitted. Brown *et al.* also found that personality disordered offenders benefited more from longer-term treatment, while those suffering from anti-social personality disorder were more resistant to change. More research is also needed, as Stevens notes (2013), regarding the motivation of offenders to enter therapeutic communities.

The attack on rehabilitation from the standpoint that 'nothing works' has therefore been strongly challenged in recent years, although there have been sceptical voices. For example,

---

[49] The researchers sat in on therapy groups (inmates met in small groups of up to eight people three to five times per week), interviewed inmates, sought prisoners' own views, and used prisoners' autobiographical materials.

in relation to earlier youth justice initiatives, Pitts argued that the evidence does not suggest that we have something which works, but rather the emergence of a 'something works doctrine' which serves a useful political role in legitimising government efforts to promote an alternative non-custodial sentencing tariff (Pitts 1992b). The Coalition government in its advocacy of a rehabilitation revolution has also focused attention on what works and made reducing reoffending a key goal, as well as targeting resources to groups most likely to benefit.

10.5.3 A rights critique of rehabilitation

A more compelling critique of the traditional rehabilitative model is from the rights-based perspective. It argues that the rehabilitative ideal, when applied in practice, may lead to rights violations, to injustice and unfairness, and to excessive punishment (see American Friends Services Committee 1971). It treats the offender as the passive recipient of treatment, rather than as a freely consenting subject. The decline of the rehabilitative model in the late 1970s and early 1980s can be attributed in part to the attack from civil libertarians and to their efforts to reassert due process rights in, particularly in response to indeterminate and individualised sentencing in the United States. It was the reaction to these concerns which stimulated the revival of retributivism.

The demands for justice and fairness and the importance of treating like cases alike increased the pressure for determinate sentences and specific sentences for specific crimes rather than individualised sentences, in both the UK and the United States. Rehabilitation had been strongly associated with indeterminate sentences and for allowing too much discretion to sentencers, leading to inconsistency and extended sentences. However, the attack on discretionary sentencing met with more success in the United States than the UK because attempts to curtail or limit sentencing discretion have been strongly resisted by sentencers in the UK. The revival of retributivism also occurred later in the UK, as we have seen, in the CJA 1991. Desert theory is hostile to predictive sentencing which would be acceptable on a rehabilitation model. Rehabilitative regimes may also allow the use of invasive treatments, such as drug therapies, to control behaviour.

The rehabilitative model was criticised from both left and right. From the left criticism came for failing to get to grips with the underlying social inequalities and problems which may generate crime and for treating the individual without addressing the social causes of crime. Probation practice influenced by the rehabilitative ideal was criticised on the same grounds, namely that it individualises fundamental social problems which are linked to social factors such as poverty and racism. But it also met with criticism from the right because it appeared to deny individual responsibility for crime, and also for the cost of apparently wasteful programmes. The extreme form of the rehabilitative model sees the task of the criminal justice system as curing errant individuals rather than punishing them if they are not responsible, because it would be unjust to punish if the person is not responsible because of an illness which precipitates offending.

Yet at the time of its ascendancy rehabilitation was seen as a progressive theory and anti-punitive. Moreover, its fall from popularity was followed not by a rediscovery of the social context of criminality, but rather by increased punitiveness. The decline of rehabilitation created space for incapacitation and populist punitiveness to flourish. The importance of law and order as a key political issue in turn made it difficult for rehabilitation programmes to find support and funding.

Sentencing systems with judges strongly committed to the rehabilitation model, such as in Canada and the United States in the 1980s, tended to generate longer and harsher sentences on average than retributivist justice, creating further problems of prisoners' institutionalisation. Such systems usually give substantial discretion to sentencers, and because protecting society from dangerous individuals is a priority, release of offenders will be undertaken cautiously. There may be problems in determining if and when someone has been rehabilitated. It may be hard for applicants to know what criteria are used, which will lead to frustration. From the prisoners' standpoint, indeterminate sentences are the sentences most feared. Moreover, within a therapeutic environment, the offender feels under constant observation and strong surveillance can mean the impact of imprisonment goes deeper, affecting one's sense of self, rather than being experienced as simply 'doing time'.

10.5.4 Modern rehabilitationism

In response to these criticisms, rehabilitationism has adapted. While this chapter has focused on punishment and rehabilitation in the community, modern rehabilitationists accept that prison can be used to reduce reoffending—and should be oriented towards this—but treatment should be non-coercive (Hudson 1993). So modern rehabilitationists demand something more positive than humane containment and minimum standards and modern rehabilitationism does not entail indeterminate sentencing: rehabilitative progress is not the criterion for sentence length (ibid). This raises issues regarding the right of the offender to refuse participation, but many would argue the offender generally should be obliged to take part in offending behaviour programmes. However, prisoners can now only enter therapeutic communities in prisons in England and Wales if they consent and are deemed suitable candidates for those programmes. Moreover, as we have seen, the problem for many prisoners is gaining access to courses, because there are insufficient numbers to meet demand.

Paradoxically, although the attack on the rehabilitative ideal was launched from a rights-based perspective, the revival of rehabilitation in the late 1990s was itself associated with a rights-based approach in the United States, particularly in the work of Rotman (1990). Rotman argued that the right of the state to punish and the right of the criminal not to be punished unduly are best protected by rehabilitation being offered within a determinate sentence, fixed by considerations of desert and dangerousness. The obligation of the state is to provide basic physical standards in the prison and sufficient rehabilitative facilities to ensure that the offender is not damaged by the effects of incarceration. He cites the case of *Laaman v Helgemoe*, in 1977, in which the court said that '[p]unishment for one crime, under conditions which spawn future crime and more punishment, serves no valid legislative purpose and is so totally without penological justification that it results in the gratuitous infliction of suffering in violation of the Eighth Amendment' (see Rotman 1990: 81–2). Although not explicitly referring to a right to rehabilitation, this case does so indirectly by recognising prisoners' right to dignity, and, as Ploch (2012) has argued, focusing on the right to dignity is the most promising avenue for improvements in prisoners' treatment and for developing a right to rehabilitation.

In the UK the issue has arisen in relation to whether the Secretary of State is under a duty to provide sufficient offending behaviour programmes to enable prisoners to prepare themselves for consideration for release. As we saw in Chapter 8, section 8.3.3, there are still insufficient offending behaviour courses to meet the demand, so that prisoners may be detained for longer than necessary after completing the minimum term of their sentence as the successful completion of these courses may be crucial to Parole Board decisions on release. The problems this created for IPP (imprisonment for public protection) prisoners were highlighted by Jacobson and Hough (2010).

The provision of constructive regimes is a key element in the prisoner's rehabilitation. Several first instance cases found that the issue was not justiciable, but in *R (Cawser) v Secretary of State for the Home Department* (2003), the Court of Appeal thought it would be irrational to have a policy of making release dependent on the completion of such courses without making reasonable provision for those courses.

Subsequently, further Convention challenges were brought by IPP prisoners who argued that the failure to provide sufficient courses constitutes a breach of Article 5 of the Convention, when they are detained beyond the minimum term because of this failure. In *Secretary of State for Justice v Walker and James* (2008), the Court of Appeal found a potential breach of Article 5(4) in the failure to grant IPP prisoners access to these courses, which would allow them to show to the Board their suitability for release. However, the House of Lords in *Secretary of State for Justice v James (formerly Walker and another)* [2009] UKHL 11, while critical of the inadequate resources available, did not find a breach of Article 5(1), as the prisoners' continued detention was still subject to regular reviews and was based on continuing risk; neither was Article 5(4) breached as some courses were offered. Following this case, IPP prisoners on shorter tariffs were given priority. The Strasbourg Court in *James, Wells and Lee v UK* (2012) did find a breach of Article 5(1) because of the lack of opportunities for the offender to show he is no longer a risk by successfully completing relevant rehabilitative courses. The IPP sentence was abolished by LASPO 2012 and replaced by new sentences (see Chapter 5, section 5.4).

Rotman (1990) distinguished the rights-based model of rehabilitation from the earlier penitentiary model, which seeks to reform through contemplation and submission to the regime, and from the therapeutic and social learning models. As we have seen, the latter are problematic because it is questionable whether the individual does engage in such contemplation, or whether such regimes are effective or rather coercive. Modern rehabilitationism emphasises justice rather than treatment, so the offender's due process rights are respected and he is protected from coercive treatment. It treats the individual as possessing rights and as capable of making choices but also as having a positive right to appropriate treatment to prevent reoffending. The emphasis is on non-coercive training and treatment and on reintegrating the offender within the community. So treatment programmes may be part of restorative justice, while also respecting the human rights of both offender and victim (see Chapter 6).

At the same time, efforts have been made to 'rehabilitate' the rehabilitative ideal in the face of the extensive criticisms made during the 1970s and 1980s. Rubin (2003) rejects the association of rehabilitation with coercion, pointing out that it is absurd to dismiss this approach on the basis of its abuse by some regimes and institutions. In any event, historically rehabilitation can also be associated with progressive policies which, at the time, provided an alternative to more repressive penal practices. Moreover, within the modern American prison context, he argues, it provides the most humane way of structuring prison life: 'the rehabilitative ideal, together with the insistence on regularized, bureaucratic governance, remains the principal source of decent and humane correctional practices' (ibid: 82). He also rejects the inevitable association of rehabilitation with the use of indeterminate sentences, pointing out that such sentences can also be found in contexts where no efforts are made to rehabilitate but are used purely to incapacitate offenders. Rehabilitation, he argues, could also impose more restraint on prison expansion, or what he describes as the 'incarcerative frenzy' in the United States, than rival theories of punishment.

Modern approaches to rehabilitation therefore focus on offenders changing themselves and on active citizenship and the emphasis is on social inclusion (see Priestley and Vanstone 2010). Brayford *et al.* (2010) argue for a more open and holistic approach to intervention which considers the context of the offending and the local community and victims. What is needed, they argue, are desistance-based rehabilitative and reintegrative practices which engage with the life of the offender and treat the offender as an agent with the capacity for change, instead of the currently prevailing 'top down' model and the heavily centralised and politically driven provision of services, which is primarily focused on risk. Their preferred path is creative practice which considers the personal, social and emotional context of the offender's life:

> The context for creative practice is therefore as equally concerned with social justice and social inclusion as it is with the accountability and reform of the individual offender. It affords responsibility and social agency to offenders and other socially excluded people, offering them real opportunities to change while holding them personally accountable for the impact they have on others.
>
> (Brayford *et al.* 2010: 266)

Focusing on desistance, by taking a holistic approach and using offender-focused interventions and developing the social capital of offenders, may provide an alternative to current reliance on risk-based and cognitive-behavioural approaches. A broader approach is also recommended by Ward and Maruna (2007), who argue for a Good Lives Model, which incorporates offenders' views of what helps them refrain from offending and offers a more active view of change. These ideas are explored further by Laws and Ward (2010) in relation to the rehabilitation of sex offenders.

We have seen in recent years much more research on desistance and Weaver examines its implications for the management of high-risk offenders. She stresses the importance of developing the ties which matter to individuals, to enhance their abilities to sustain positive roles and relationships and 'support them to build networks and contexts in which shifts in identities can be embedded, nurtured and sustained' (Weaver 2014: 12). We need to consider 'how processes and practices are co-constructed in relationships between practitioners, offenders and those significant others that matter to them' (ibid 18). Weaver emphasises that high-risk offenders are not a homogeneous group and their routes to desistance are individualised.

10.5.5 **The 'resurgence' of rehabilitation**

Although we find numerous references to the decline of rehabilitation in commentaries on penal policy, nonetheless the commitment to rehabilitation remains an element of UK penal policy. It survived the negative reaction to Martinson's paper, in specific programmes for offenders within prison and in work with young offenders and with specific groups such as sex offenders and, as Zimring and Hawkins (1995) have observed, rehabilitation generated far more discussion than incapacitation in penological research in the 1980s. It also remained a rationale of the work at Grendon and Dovegate and now underpins offending behaviour programmes in contemporary prisons (see Chapter 8). Resettlement has also been given greater priority inside prison. Robinson (2008) challenges the view that rehabilitation as a penal strategy is moribund or irrelevant and considers the way it has adapted to the modern penal context of England and Wales. It was also a key element of the Corston Report (2007) on vulnerable women offenders and the Bradley Report on the needs of those with mental health problems or disabilities within the criminal justice system (Department of Health 2009a).

Rehabilitation was emphasised in the Halliday Report. It was also a feature of the White Paper *Criminal Justice: The Way Ahead* (Home Office 2001a), which stressed the importance of looking at what works for which type of offender and improving the funding for Prison Service offending behaviour programmes as well as practical skills courses and more drug programmes, given the strong link between unemployment, homelessness, and reoffending.

Rehabilitation is clearly back on the political agenda. In *Breaking the Cycle* (Ministry of Justice 2010a) the need for rehabilitation is strongly emphasised, with the promise of a rehabilitation revolution and payment by results for service providers who achieve this goal, as well as practical support for drug and alcohol abuse and mental health provision, and on making prisons more effective in preparing offenders for release and resettlement. The implications of this were considered by Ledger (2010).

While the strong concern with rehabilitation clearly is crucial to those working in probation, it coexists alongside the obligation to manage risk and the challenges faced by the loss of the Probation Service's contributions in the management of low- and medium-risk offenders under the *Transforming Rehabilitation* agenda. In the Prison Service too we find offending behaviour programmes which are concerned with rehabilitation and which have achieved some success.

Because of the developments in penal policy considered in Chapter 1, including the focus on managerialism, risk management, cost-effectiveness, and increasing centralised control, however, the scope for alternative rehabilitative interventions has been limited. Moreover, the greater emphasis on the voluntary sector has not been matched by sufficient funding for many of these groups, for example, in relation to implementing the recommendations of the Corston Report.

10.6 Delivering rehabilitation

10.6.1 The changes in 2015

Despite dealing with more offenders than the prison service, at lower cost and with reconviction rates that are lower than those associated with prisons, the Probation Service has been ignored, misrepresented, taken for granted and marginalized, and probation staff have been sneered at as 'do-gooders'. The service as a whole is currently under serious threat as a result of budget cuts, organizational restructuring, changes in training, and increasingly punitive policies.

(Mair and Burke 2011)

This is how the authors describe the focus of their book entitled *Redemption, Rehabilitation and Risk Management* (Mair and Burke 2011). There is no question that the Probation Service (now NPS) has undergone several reincarnations in its history—most imposed by developments outside its control—which, it is argued, have led to the 'systematic fragmentation and demoralisation of a probation service' (Howard League for Penal Reform 2010a: 1). 'Instead of being allowed to engage with vulnerable men and women in the community, the probation service and its functions have been warped by NOMS' framework of mechanistic targets' (ibid: 1). At the same time Ledger wrote an article entitled 'Rehabilitation Revolution: Will Probation Pay the Price?' (Ledger 2010). Since these comments were made in 2010/11, probation *has* paid the price and change has been even more draconian. Until very recently, there would have been no question that the National Probation Service would be responsible for delivering all punishment, supervision, and rehabilitation in the community. That is not so now.

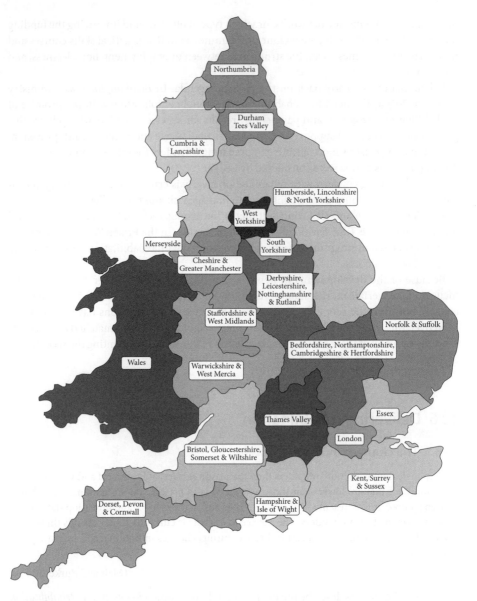

Figure 10.1 Geographic areas of the 21 community rehabilitation companies

Source: National Offender Management Service 2015: accessed at https://www.gov.uk/government/uploads/system/uploads/attachment_data/file/315721/CRC-area-map.pdf

The changes mandated by the *Transforming Rehabilitation* agenda have replaced the previous 35 individual Probation Trusts with a single National Probation Service, responsible for the management of high-risk offenders (only), and 21 community rehabilitation companies (CRCs) responsible for the management of low- to medium-risk offenders in 21 areas across England and Wales (see Figure 10.1). These areas are now referred to as Contract Package Areas (CPAs).

The successful bidders in the competition for CRC contracts began to deliver programmes from 1 February 2015. The winners were often a consortium formed for the purpose of applying and they can now also subcontract the work to other public, private or voluntary sector bodies.

Case example

The government announced the 'preferred bidders' for the various areas and, for the Derbyshire, Leicestershire, Nottinghamshire, and Rutland (DLNR) CRC, the composition of the preferred bidder was as follows:

> The Reducing Reoffending Partnership (RRP—an Equity Joint Venture) [which] brings together the experience, capabilities and values of three leading mission driven organisations which are:
>
> - Ingeus UK, a private organisation;[50]
> - St Giles Trust, a Charity; and
> - Crime Reduction Initiatives (CRI), a Charity.[51]

This company was awarded the contract and is now the DLNR Community Rehabilitation Company Ltd, whose vision is 'to become a centre of excellence in protecting the public through the successful rehabilitation of offenders'.[52] The company has considerable powers. For example, under 'Work with Prisons', it states in its brochure:

> Our staff assist with sentence planning and ensure that release from prison is governed by strict conditions. These conditions can stipulate where the offender should live, whom they may or may not see, and compulsory attendance on programmes such as anger management. If an offender breaks these conditions they can be sent back to prison.

So how has this situation come about? While for most of the history of the (then) Probation Service the current privatisation could not have been envisaged, the latest episode in its history is not without seeds of change over the past 30 years. We will, therefore, briefly summarise that history.[53]

10.6.2 **The rise and fall of the Probation Service?**

The practice ethos of what became the Probation Service by the Probation of Offenders Act 1907—originally the Police Court Mission—was, from the 1870s to the 1920s, that of 'pleading' for the offender in court and acting as a friend—to 'advise assist and befriend'—when released to the service for supervision (Raynor and Vanstone 2002: 12–16). The development of the positivist school of criminology in the last quarter of the nineteenth century provided a theory of crime causation which focused on environmental factors and which, therefore, validated a treatment approach to dealing with offenders (see Brownlee 1998b: chapter 3; Cavadino and Dignan 2002: 49–50) which became very important from the 1930s onward until the 1970s, when the casework approach was challenged (Raynor and Vanstone 2002: 41–4).

During the 1970s the very basis of probation—the possibility of rehabilitation—was also challenged by the emergence of a 'nothing works' orthodoxy, and by the end of the 1970s the Probation Service was in crisis, split over ideals and aims. Different schools of thought emerged which were still present in debate in the twenty-first century (see, for example, Mantle and Moore 2004). The radical strand believed the problem was structural (see Worrall 1997: 70), the personalist strand that there should be concentration on practical

---

[50] Ingeus is not a CJS organisation but a private company providing employment and training services. It was a provider of the Department of Work and Pensions Work Programme. See http://www.ingeus.co.uk/about.

[51] See https://www.gov.uk/government/uploads/system/uploads/attachment_data/file/368266/table-of-preferred-bidders.pdf.

[52] See http://dlnrcrc.co.uk/wp-content/uploads/2014/07/DLNR-LF-018_The-DLNR-CRC-Ltd-About-Us.pdf (accessed 24 August 2015).

[53] Readers who want more detail are referred to previous editions of this text.

help (see Bottoms and McWilliams (1979); Celnick and McWilliams 1991: 166; Harris (1980); Raynor and Vanstone 2002: 44–5), and the managerial strand focused on the management of groups of offenders in cost-effective ways. This latter strand was to become very influential.

The clearest evidence of its increasing importance was the publication of the 'Statement of National Standards and Objectives for the Probation Service' (SNOP) by the Home Office in 1984. McLaughlin and Muncie (1994) argued that the key to this shift lay in the managerialist aims of having quantifiable outcomes for probation practice. These National Standards prescribed a series of objectives in which the functions of the Probation Service were redefined: to divert high-risk offenders away from prison, to reduce the incidence of crime, and to deploy resources in the most cost-effective fashion. The managerialist focus also underpinned the development of the use of commercial and voluntary providers of Probation Service projects.

The rebranding, in the CJA 1991, of probation and other community penalties as first and foremost punishments which involved control and loss of liberty also prompted a rethink. Until 1948 probation had been used instead of a conviction, and until 1991 instead of a sentence, and so probation officers had conceptualised their work as an alternative to punishment.[54]

Arguably, in the 1990s probation officers consequently turned into penal managers or correctional officers in the community. Also, despite opposition (see Aldridge and Eadie 1997: 111), the requirement of a social work qualification for probation officers was removed (Home Office 1995b). The ethos of probation was changing rapidly even before the end of the twentieth century.

Despite these concerns, as noted in section 10.5.5, there were signs of hope for the Probation Service in new approaches to rehabilitation (see, for example, Burnett and Roberts 2004; Harper and Chitty 2005)[55] and the focus on actuarial methods. The Service had also been reorganised into a national body—the National Probation Service (NPS) for England and Wales set up by the CJCSA 2000. That Act also affirmed the wide remit of the new NPS: the extensive tasks of the Service were set out in s. 1 and its aims in s. 2 (both were repealed seven years later). Section 41 of the PCCSA 2000 re-enacted[56] the aim of probation (rehabilitation) orders as that of securing the offender's rehabilitation, or protecting the public from harm from the offender, or preventing the committing by the offender of further offences.

The CJCSA 2000 also changed the regional structure of the Service into 42 local areas, each coterminous with the local Police Service area on the basis that this would enable more efficient collaboration (Home Office 1998a). The revised National Standards (Home Office et al. 2000) could also be seen 'part of a wider development that devolves to the Probation Officer increasing responsibility for punishment beyond the walls of the prison' (Sparrow et al. 2002: 33). 2001 saw the publication of the mission statement for the new National Probation Service, *A New Choreography* (Wallis 2001).[57]

10.6.3 The move towards privatisation

However, the overwhelming threat to the Probation Service came from the increasing privatisation of its work, and that began in the 1990s with a greater use of probation–private

---

[54] Many argued strongly for this to continue. See, for example, Stopard (1990); Singer (1991); McWilliams and Pease (1990).

[55] In particular, the use of cognitive behaviourism from psychology: see Home Office (2003d).

[56] Section 41(1) was largely a re-enactment of the revised s. 2 of the 1973 Act.

[57] Though Nellis asked, very aptly in relation to a policy statement so strangely entitled, whether the NPS was indeed 'dancing to a new tune' (2002: 369).

partnerships. Ring-fenced probation budgets—with money that could only be spent on partnership projects—meant that, with no increased resources, some forms of community penalties and rehabilitative projects could be provided only by projects part-funded and perhaps wholly run by voluntary or commercial agencies. The development necessitated the probation officer becoming a manager and fundholder with a key role in partnerships. This led Drakeford (1993) to ask 'who will do the work?', raising issues that are still very pertinent: statutory responsibilities being carried out by voluntary or commercial bodies, the potential downgrading of professional skills, the potential incompatibility of aims,[58] and accountability (see the discussion in Chapter 8 in relation to prison privatisation). As we have noted, the trend towards 'outsourcing' has now been taken much further.

Contestability and payment by results

Provisions in the Offender Management Act (OMA) 2007 brought to the fore issues around accountability and responsibility that, arguably, should have received earlier attention (Faulkner 2005). The Consultation Paper which preceded the OMA 2007, *A Five-Year Strategy for Protecting the Public and Reducing Re-offending*, had argued that 'we need to make sure that the way our system is designed helps us bring in the best possible people and organisations to support every offender' (Home Office 2005b: 8) and proposed a system of commissioning. The Paper reasoned that if those who buy services for offenders are separated out from the providers of those services, 'there is no incentive to deliver services that do not work' (ibid).[59]

Part 1 of the OMA 2007 replaced local probation boards with probation trusts—which have now themselves been replaced—but s. 1(1) is still current law (as slightly amended) and defines 'probation purposes' as:

(a) courts to be given assistance in determining the appropriate sentences to pass, and making other decisions, in respect of persons charged with or convicted of offences;

(b) the giving of assistance to persons determining whether conditional cautions should be given and which conditions to attach to conditional cautions;

(c) the supervision and rehabilitation of persons charged with or convicted of offences;

(d) the giving of assistance to persons remanded on bail;

(e) the supervision and rehabilitation of persons to whom conditional cautions are given;

(f) the giving of information to victims of persons charged with or convicted of offences.

Section 2 gave the Secretary of State the duty to ensure there was sufficient provision for probation purposes to be delivered and s. 3(2) gave the Secretary of State the power to 'make contractual or other arrangements with any other person for the making of the probation provision'.

The first NOMS 'Commissioning Framework' was also published in 2007 (National Offender Management Service 2007). The Foreword to this document includes the following statement:

As we move to a needs based commissioning system, commissioners will make judgements about what type of service is needed to manage offenders effectively and to reduce reoffending. These judgements need to be based on the best available evidence about what

[58] See, for example, Smith *et al.* (1993: 33–4); see also Bretherton (1991) for the difficulties of putting partnership into practice in relation to one particular project.

[59] See also National Offender Management Service (2006b) regarding *Public Value Partnerships*.

is working and what isn't, what the priorities for improvement are, where and with whom resources should be invested.

(National Offender Management Service 2007: 1)

A 'contestability prospectus'—a five-year strategy—aimed at the public, voluntary, and private sector suppliers and specifying the type, length, and value of contracts available had already been published (National Offender Management Service 2006b) and received criticism as containing 'a whole range of unproven assertions' (NAPO 2006: 2). Concerns were also raised more generally about the overall impact on the NPS and the impact of penal populism on government policy (see McKnight 2009). After the changes in 2007, Oldfield and Grimshaw wrote that 'our overall impression has been that a period of stability, reflection and objective analysis would be beneficial for the probation service. We are doubtful that this is likely to be the case' (2008: 5). Their doubts were well founded and the process of change continued.

Breaking the Cycle (Ministry of Justice 2010a) proposed the development of Integrated Offender Management using local agencies, including police, probation, prisons, local authorities, and voluntary partners, while it was argued that providers of rehabilitation programmes should be given more freedom to introduce innovative programmes and, significantly, should be paid by results (except in relation to high-risk offenders). How to measure rehabilitation is of course problematic. Further, research on the voluntary sector's involvement in delivering projects had stressed the potential problems for that sector caused by increased commissioning and contestability: 'The importance of retaining the values underpinning voluntary organisations, its ethical core, will be vital in helping the sector tackle new processes and partnerships without becoming assimilated and subservient' (Silvestri 2009: 6).

10.6.4 Community rehabilitation companies

In 10.6.1 we summarised the current organisation structure for the delivery of rehabilitation services. The majority of probation services have now been out-sourced by competitive tendering to CRCs, with a residual public Probation Service managing high-risk cases. The changes were preceded by Consultation Documents, notably *Punishment and Reform: Effective Community Sentences*, Ministry of Justice (2012b); *Punishment and Reform: Effective Probation Services* (Ministry of Justice 2012a); and *Transforming Rehabilitation: A Revolution in the Way We Manage Offenders* (Ministry of Justice 2013a).

There is no question that one driver of change was the economic situation in the past decade, and in particular the 'austerity agenda' of the Coalition government. In England and Wales this has led, as Garside points out, to the reorganisation of criminal justice institutions along market lines, with somewhat different approaches in Wales and Northern Ireland (Garside 2014). Nevertheless, it is difficult to resist the conclusion that political ideology has determined the response in England and Wales and that 'the specific policies adopted, the preferred criminal justice structures and arrangements, are down to choices and agendas that are essentially political in nature' (Garside 2014). As Hall has commented, 'The programme might be called "Transforming Rehabilitation" but it is really about transforming the public sector' (2015).

In this context the government has put great importance on the involvement of the voluntary sector in the implementation of the reforms. For example, in 2013 the Ministry of Justice awarded the Association of Chief Executives of Voluntary Organisations (ACEVO) a £150,000 grant—part of the £500,000 voluntary sector capability-building grant—to deliver a series of skills and information workshops to support voluntary sector organisations to deliver services as part of the Rehabilitation Programme. ACEVO planned to deliver the workshops in partnership with the National Council for Voluntary Organisations (NCVO), Rocket Science, TPP Law, and Candour Collaborations.[60]

However, there has been criticism that in practice the voluntary providers are not as involved as they anticipated. *Third Sector*, a publication and website for voluntary and not-for-profit companies, noted that 16 voluntary organisations were named in the successful partnerships for prime contracts and about 75 per cent of the 300 subcontractors included in the winning bids were not-for-profits, but that by June 2015 'one large charity in a prime partnership has withdrawn and many smaller voluntary organisations that expected to be involved have not yet been given any work' (Third Sector 2015). Similarly, a survey conducted by NCVO showed that organisations felt that 'The pace of change has been slower than many in the voluntary sector anticipated, leaving organisations in a state of limbo, waiting to see how or if they will be involved in service delivery, making strategic planning and staff retention difficult.'[61]

The shift away from existing professionals towards a broader range of providers raised concerns over their expertise and experience as well as concerns over safety, and met with opposition from those working in the Probation Service. However, the changes have sometimes been justified on the basis of the inadequacy of the NPS. This argument has been contested: Hall notes that the National Audit Office (2014) in its *Landscape Review* of probation concluded: 'In general the probation sector has been performing effectively' (Hall 2015: 327). Moreover, given the wide range of factors which affect offending, it is difficult to see why improving competition per se will provide a panacea for existing problems. There is, of course, mileage in the argument that some probation officers have not been working in the most cost-effective way—that they have not been sufficiently 'offence-focused' in their work, with elements of the old 'befriending' and case work ethos still persisting. However, Guilfoyle, a probation officer, uses a real-life case study to question whether profit should always come first (Guilfoyle 2015).

10.7 Reflecting on the issues

10.7.1 Justice in community punishment

The theme running through this book is 'the quest for justice'—what counts as justice in sentencing and punishment and how that can be achieved—but in the context of the delivery of punishment and supervision/rehabilitation in the community there are no easy answers. Some years ago a chief probation officer argued that putting into practice the restorative concepts of penance, making amends, and the involvement of the community and victim are essential aspects of 'just' practice (Harding 2000), but Duff argued that was not feasible, given the 'client' base (2003a: 192–4). Young offenders are most likely to come from particular neighbourhoods and schools with particular factors—such as unemployment, debt, and disability—in their background (Lacey 2002: 29–30; see also Mair and May 1997) and so combating social exclusion may be more important.

A further concern is that the sought-after 'flexibility' in community sentencing has 'the potential for arbitrariness and discrimination' in deciding how much 'treatment' offenders need in the community; 'flexibility' might be the opposite of justice (Raynor and Vanstone 2002: 106). Resource constraints may affect the provision of community

---

[60] Email from partners@mojconnect.justice.gov.uk. Ministry of Justice: 5 July 2013.
[61] Posted on the NCVO website, 24 August 2015, by Nick Davies.

penalties differentially and there is evidence of race discrimination (Denny 1992), male/female variations in the use of requirements, and a wide variation between probation areas with regard to the number and type of requirements used in orders (Mair *et al.* 2007: 31; see also McIvor 1998 and Bowen *et al.* 2002 for similar research results). It remains to be seen whether the wide discretion of the new consortia delivering rehabilitation programmes leads to innovative, productive programmes which punish through restriction of the offender's time (only)—and provide effective reductions in criminality—or whether the result is a chaotic situation where there is injustice by geography.

A recent article argues that probation—as historically conceptualised—'matters because of its role in creating a humane justice system':

> At probation's core is a value base which unites the profession and has been sustained through political change. The politically driven restructuring of probation through 'Transforming Rehabilitation' did not build on probation's achievements, nor was it evidence led. International examples show the negative impact of privatisation if values are secondary to profit.
>
> (Hall 2015: 321)

Arguably, a stronger human rights culture is needed in relation to community punishment (Hudson 2001). Nevertheless, Brownlee's comment that community punishment is 'less dehumanising' than custody and drives 'fewer of those who endure it to self-harm and suicide' (Brownlee 1998b: 180) is still very pertinent.

10.7.2 **Rehabilitation or better risk management?**

The nature of rehabilitation as practised in the last two decades is unclear. It could be delivering a 'soft' version of discipline and rehabilitation by instilling values and helping the offender to establish a 'normal' lifestyle—the 'normalising' element of the modern penal-welfare complex which Garland set out (1985: 238ff). On the other hand, it could be an example of postmodern penality—the risk management machine—focusing on an actuarially based management of risk (see Robinson 2002: 5).

These models are further complicated by the fact that the victim now has an enhanced role (see Chapter 7). Successive revisions to National Standards have shown an increased emphasis on the rights and experiences of victims within supervision programmes and yet the focus of offence-focused work is the offender. This leaves the NPS with an ambiguous role[62] and role conflicts.

However, there have been attempts to analyse risk management and rehabilitation in practice to determine whether they are in fact radically different (Robinson 1999; see also FitzGibbon 2007; Hutchinson 2006). It could be argued, however, that the conflation of risk management with rehabilitation conceptualises modern rehabilitationism in a very narrow way. An example given of the practical integration of risk management and rehabilitation is the evolution of 'third-generation assessment instruments'. A level of service inventory, for example, measures both the likelihood of reconviction and information about the personal characteristics and the offender's social life which increase his chances of reconviction (see Robinson 1999: 429). An inspection report also suggested an individualised risk-based approach: 'A key to effective supervision is therefore to approach each case individually and tailor supervision to its particular needs' (HM Inspectorate of Probation 1997: 252–3). Yet, in her empirical research, Robinson concluded that normalisation—dependent on personal

---

[62] See, for further earlier comment, May (1990) and Sheppard (1990).

interactions between the probation officer and the offender—'is no longer at the heart of probation practice' (2002: 5).

The managers of what has sometimes been called 'correctional policy'[63] in the community have been robust in their criticism of the 'pockets of antediluvian officers' who oppose change (Hopley 2002: 298), but that approach ignores intense debates about the values inherent in probation work[64] and in the newer bodies delivering value-for-money preventive programmes. Whether the 'rehabilitation revolution' will release sufficient resources and be regulated by sufficiently broad targets—rather than a narrow payment by (immediate) results—to make a significant difference is yet to be seen.

10.7.3 **Discussion questions**

The following questions raise important issues. There is further reading, and also guidance on thinking about these issues, in the Online Resource Centre.

online
resource
centre

1. How does modern rehabilitationism differ from earlier forms of rehabilitation?

2. What did the Coalition government mean by a 'Rehabilitation Revolution'? What constraints are there on the translation of this aim into practice?

10.7.4 **Dangerous dogs case study**

Read the following scenario and then sentence Amos.

> Amos owns two dogs which he usually takes to nearby wasteland for exercise. One day when on holiday he took them to a park where a notice said that dogs were not permitted. However he let the dogs, who were not muzzled, off the lead and one dog ran up to a child and bit her before running back to Amos. Amos did not wait or apologise but left with his dogs. A passer-by took a video of the incident and posted it on YouTube. This eventually led to the police arresting Amos who was charged with the aggravated offence of being in charge of a dog 'dangerously out of control in any place in England or Wales (whether or not a public place) where a person is injured' under s. 3(1) of the Dangerous Dogs Act 1991 (as amended 13 May 2014). Amos pleaded guilty at the earliest opportunity.
>
> The young girl's injuries were serious, necessitating an operation and leaving a scar. The court accepted that Amos was remorseful and that his dogs had not attacked anyone before. Amos is now a single parent looking after a five-year-old daughter with the help of his sister, who lives near him. He has some minor and mostly not very recent convictions, including one for possession of cannabis and one for driving while uninsured. At the time of the offence Amos was on bail in relation to a careless driving charge which was later dropped.

Note:

The maximum penalty for this aggravated offence is now five years (new s. 1(4A)(b) of the Dangerous Dogs Act 1991 Act inserted by s. 106 of the Anti-social Behaviour, Crime and Policing Act 2014). The 2012 Definitive Guideline had been revised because it was written when the maximum was two years and then the offence range was discharge–18 months' custody. The Draft Guideline in the 2015 Consultation Paper suggested an offence range of discharge–four years' custody and the new Guideline confirms that range (Sentencing Council 2016: 9).

For this exercise you should, therefore, use the revised Guideline which is effective from 1 July 2016.

---

[63] See, for an example of the use of this phrase, Home Office (1999b) *The Correctional Policy Framework.*

[64] See, for example, a series of articles in the *Howard Journal* in 1995 (James 1995; Nellis 1995; Masters 1997; Spencer 1995).

You may wish to read again relevant sections of Chapter 3 to remind yourself of the sentencing framework and the approach to sentencing issues raised by this case scenario. You may also wish to read sections 7.3.1 and 7.4.5 in Chapter 7 about personal mitigation.

Reading:

Ares, E. and Coe, S. (2013) *Dangerous Dogs*, Standard Note SN/SC/4348, House of Commons Library, available at: http://www.parliament.uk/briefing-papers/SN04348.

Sentencing Council (2012b) *Dangerous Dog Offences, Definitive Guideline*, pp. 9–13 (but sentence range is no longer applicable).

Sentencing Council (2015d) *Dangerous Dog Offences Guideline Consultation*. London, Sentencing Council (see p. 71 for the relevant offence).

Sentencing Council (2016) *Dangerous Dog Offences, Definitive Guideline*. London, Sentencing Council (ss pp. 9–14 for the relevant offence).

Dangerous Dogs Act 1991 s. 4—destruction and disqualification orders (in force since 22 September 2015).

Guidance on doing this sentencing exercise is given in the Online Resource Centre.

11

Court orders for young offenders

SUMMARY

This chapter considers the range of civil and criminal orders available to the courts in responding to anti-social or criminal behaviour by children and young people. It also discusses selected aspects of conditions in secure accommodation and reviews the role and achievements of using rights in responding to problematic issues.

11.1 Using the civil justice system

11.1.1 The policy contexts

In Chapter 6, section 6.3 we reviewed the options open to the police to divert young offenders from a criminal prosecution. So we discussed community resolutions, cautions, and youth conditional cautions. In this chapter we discuss the options available if these youth justice responses are deemed to be inappropriate or insufficient. We will first review those civil options which the police and other bodies can use to respond to unacceptable behaviour by children and young people, before examining the options open to the criminal court at the sentencing stage.

As we saw in Chapter 6, section 6.3, in the past decade there have been changes in diversionary policies and practices such that fewer children and young people are prosecuted and sentenced and more are the subject of community resolutions. This is at least to an extent the result of governments wishing to reduce the cost of court processing and detention. However, there is a wider picture in relation to dealing with young offenders, and we need to review that now. It helps to explain the parallel developments which focused on producing new responses which are, on the face, outside the youth justice system, although we will see that there are overlaps.

The family and re-moralisation

One trigger for these policy developments was a growing concern about the role of the family. The family has long been viewed by sociologists as a site for forms of 'gentle' social control (see, for example, Foucault 1977; Donzelot 1980; Rose 1987, 1990), but concern developed as to whether the family could still act as 'a place of socialisation of the young' (Junger-Tas 1994: 18). In particular, an influential body of opinion explained the perceived increased lawlessness of the young as being the result of their not having been taught right from wrong, and so the family needed to be 're-moralised'. Consequently, previous Labour governments developed policies to support and 'encourage' parents. *Building on Progress: Families* stated that the family is a 'fundamental building block of society' (PMSU 2007: 10) but the clear message of policy documents was that parents were being made more accountable (see Reece 2005). A review of mechanisms introduced to encourage parental responsibility in the youth justice context focuses on a 'matrix of powers' to 'instil' parental responsibility: the liability of parents in relation to fines and parental compensation orders, the power of the courts to bind parents over,[1] the introduction and increasing scope of parenting orders, and sanctions for non-compliance (Hollingsworth 2007; see also Koffman 2008).

More recently, the Coalition government expressed similar sentiments after the riots in the summer of 2011: 'Tragically, we . . . saw people who were just drawn into it, who passed the broken shop window and popped in and nicked a telly. That is a sign of moral collapse, of failing to recognise the difference between right and wrong.'[2] This is not a new concern: it would appear that research on young offenders 'habitually produces results that point to the adverse effects of certain features of family life' (Day Sclater and Piper 2000: 138 and references therein). Not surprisingly, then, the 'parenting theme' has always been dominant in policy debates about criminality. Debate focuses on the correlation between offending and family disruption, and includes a particular concern that boys are not receiving discipline and support from (non-residential) fathers. Research which found, for example, that boys not living with their mothers were most likely to become persistent offenders would suggest the situation is more complex (Haas *et al.* 2004).

So none of this proves that there is a decline in moral authority or parental discipline, but these attitudes feed into a belief 'that the process of change and modernity has gone too far' (Pearson 2002: 45–6) and legitimate provisions to make parents responsible for their children's behaviour. The focus on the family to ensure the young are adequately socialised has another implication if it is believed that the task of moralisation cannot safely be left to the family alone. 'The only norm enforcing system that remains in force and has the pretension to fill the void is the criminal and juvenile justice system' (Junger-Tas 2002: 40). From this perspective, an increase in the scope of, and sanctions available to, the youth justice system is both necessary and legitimate. Further, it has legitimised the range of civil orders to control both parents and children, which focus on anti-social behaviour rather than offending but are increasingly being seen as part of the repertoire of youth justice. It also legitimised an extension of these controlling measures as part of what was called the 'Respect' campaign.

Anti-social behaviour

In the 1990s the Audit Commission had flagged up the difficulties for the police in dealing with what they referred to as 'juvenile nuisance', the subject of 10–20 per cent of calls to the police (1996: 13; see also Straw 1996: 1). A new term—anti-social behaviour—became very influential and legitimised the introduction of new statutory responses to the behaviour of children and young people, notably new civil orders—anti-social behaviour orders (ASBOs) for children of ten years old and above (see Cracknell 2000; see also Burney 2002: 473; Campbell 2002), child safety orders for children under ten years old (see Hayes and Williams 1999; Piper 1999), and parenting orders. Their introduction by the Crime and Disorder Act (CDA) 1998 led Muncie to conclude that 'now it is not so much neglect and delinquency that are conflated, but misbehaviour and crime' (1999: 170).

Respect and Responsibility—Taking a Stand against Anti-social Behaviour proposed further civil penalties on the basis that anti-social behaviour 'creates an atmosphere in which more serious crime takes hold' (Home Office 2003b). The Labour government established

---

[1] CJA 1991, ss. 57–58 and Criminal Justice and Public Order Act 1994 Schedule 9 para 50.

[2] 'Rioters need tough love, says David Cameron', BBC News, 2 September 2011, accessed 28 November 2015 at http://www.bbc.co.uk/news/uk-politics-14760686.

a Respect Unit, originally based in the Home Office, and in *Youth Matters* referred to young people 'who do not respect the opportunities they are given, by committing crimes or behaving anti-socially' (DfES 2005: 1). A new Respect Action Plan was issued in 2006 (Respect Task Force 2006: 30; see also Home Office 2006c), while *Tools and Powers to Tackle Anti-social Behaviour* (Respect Task Force 2007) summarised the results of research.[3]

What these developments illustrate is that non-criminal deviance, anti-social behaviour, began to be dealt with in ways which blur the boundaries of the criminal and civil systems and law. This has been viewed as an indicator of a trend noted in other jurisdictions towards the use of 'criminalisation' as a state response where structural factors such as poverty and educational disadvantage ought rather to be addressed (Boyle and Lipman 2002; see also the discussion at the end of section 6.3 in Chapter 6). It could also be seen as 'a tendency to criminalise children unnecessarily and at younger ages, and a corresponding tendency to treat them as adults too soon' (Monaghan *et al.* 2003: 6).

11.1.2 **Civil orders**

The civil orders and similar contracts and agreements constituted new tools but they have an ambivalent role: the orders are an alternative court-based method of responding to anti-social and criminal behaviour through the civil justice system and they are also seen as a method of delaying the 'criminalisation' of children. In practice these developments have, arguably, drawn more children and young people within the ambit of state surveillance and, as we shall see, may hasten entry into the criminal justice system.

Further, there are other concerns because of the context for these initiatives. Cleland and Tisdall have noted that the traditional 'triangle of relationships between the state, parents and children' should be replaced with a square, because of a fourth 'side' which is now very important—the community—but, they go on to argue, the values represented by that fourth element encourage punitive treatment of children engaging in anti-social behaviour (Cleland and Tisdall 2005: 413). There are also rights issues raised by these developments. We will look in some detail at the early orders because research on their operation reveals the drawbacks of such options and raises concerns in regard to the orders replacing the ASBO.

The first new orders

ASBOs and child safety orders were introduced in 1998. The common criterion is that the child or adult has acted 'in a manner that caused or was likely to cause harassment, alarm or distress to one or more persons not of the same household as himself'[4] (CDA 1998, ss. 1(1) (a) and 12(3)(c)). The ASBO had to last for not less than two years, while the maximum period for a child safety order is now 12 months. ASBOs were awarded by magistrates in their civil jurisdiction or, after the implementation of the provisions in the Police Reform Act 2002 (and the Criminal Procedure (Scotland) Act 1995), could be imposed by the criminal courts against individuals convicted of a criminal offence. These orders are sometimes referred to as CRASBOs. The number of such orders came to exceed the number imposed as a result of 'stand-alone' applications under s. 1 of the CDA 1998. Child safety orders, however, are a little-used family jurisdiction supervision order.

The Anti-social Behaviour Act (ASBA) 2003 widened the scope and use of ASBOs (s. 85), increased the range of the 'relevant authorities' who could apply for an ASBO

---

[3] For critique, see McDonald 2006, especially 196–8.
[4] Still 'not of the same household as himself' for child safety orders.

(ss. 85–86), and introduced a presumption that a parenting order is made with an ASBO (s. 85, amending the CDA 1998, s. 9). As a result of amendments made by the CJA 2003 and the Criminal Justice and Immigration Act (CJIA) 2008 a new s. 1AA in the CDA 1998 added the presumption that an ISO (individual support order) would be made alongside an ASBO for the under 18s 'in the interests of preventing any repetition of the kind of behaviour which led to the making of the anti-social behaviour order'. The ASBA 2003 also provided the police with controversial new powers to disperse groups in 'designated areas' and to return home an under-16-year-old (ss. 30–36: repealed October 2014), although *R (W) v Commissioner of Police of the Metropolis and another* (2005) held that s. 30(6) did not give the police the power to use reasonable force to return a child home (see Hollingsworth 2006).

The government had originally expressed its unwillingness to use ASBOs with juveniles, explaining that they were aimed at adults, but then stated that they would be used only for those over 12, before reducing the lower age to ten (see Burney 2005: 97–8). The result was that, by the end of 2004, 52 per cent of orders had been given to 10–17-year-olds and research done for the Youth Justice Board (2006a) found that a disproportionate number of the sample—22 per cent—were from black and minority ethnic groups. It is local authorities and the police who apply for ASBOs but some commentators pointed to the role of the judiciary in their (then) increasing use: Bateman accused magistrates of giving insufficient attention to the legal requirement to impose an order only if it is 'necessary', assuming—wrongly—that alternatives have been tried already (Bateman 2007: 313–20; see also Donoghue 2007: 428). Further, in the *McCann* (2003) case in relation to Article 6 of the European Convention on Human Rights (ECHR)—the right to a fair trial and the issue of the standard of proof—the Court of Appeal decided, albeit not unanimously, that 'these restrictions are imposed for preventative reasons not punishment' (*per* Lord Hope).

ASBOs could include various constraining requirements, but Youth Justice Board research found 'Young people and their parents/carers reported that being prohibited from associating with friends in familiar local territories resulted in a serious—and in some cases counter-productive—restriction of normal daily activities' and that the majority of breach cases concerned this type of prohibition (Youth Justice Board 2006a: 8; see for critique Hollingsworth 2012b: section 2). Certainly, ASBOs were ineffective if the number of breaches of prohibitions is an indicator: the Audit Office found that over half of those in their sample group—46 per cent of whom were under 18—breached their order, and a third did so on two or more occasions (Home Office 2006c: paras 5b and 5h of the Executive Summary). Breaches provided the sentencing courts with a growing body of work and the Sentencing Advisory Panel (SAP) issued advice on the sentencing of young offenders for breach (2007: para 78ff). However, the use of ASBOs has declined since 2005: see Figure 11.1.

A further issue raised by the practice of ASBOs is the issue of the 'naming and shaming' of those given orders, which may be seen as an element of what Cobb describes as the incremental reduction in anonymity rights for minors over the past decade (Cobb 2007: 360–1). Yet *Stanley v Metropolitan Police* (2004) did not declare the publicity practices to be in breach of Article 8(1) of the ECHR (see Burney 2005: 96–7; see also Taylor 2006), although the practice of 'aggressive publication of ASBOs' was criticised by a Commissioner for Human Rights (Gil-Robles 2005: 37). The Judicial Studies Board justified the procedure because 'Unless the nuisance is extremely localised, enforcement of the order will normally depend upon the general public being aware of the order and of the identity of the person against whom it is made' (undated: section 3.6). The Children and Young Person's Act 1933, s. 39, as amended by the Youth Justice and Criminal Evidence Act 1999, gives the court a discretion to forbid identification in any civil or criminal proceedings, but the courts have justified overriding the child's anonymity: 'these deterrents are

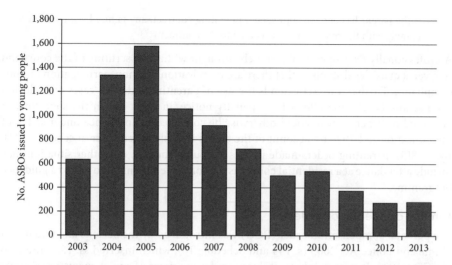

Figure 11.1 Trends in Anti-Social Behaviour Orders for young people, 2003 to 2013

Source: Ministry of Justice/Youth Justice Board (2015a) *Youth Justice Statistics 2013/14 England and Wales* p. 21, Chart 1.3

proper objectives for the court to seek' because the effect is beneficial in reducing the young person's offending (*Winchester Crown Court* 2000: para 13 *per* Brown LJ).

Parenting orders

Parenting orders have been available since 2000 and are triggered if the child or young person is subject to a range of orders and injunctions,[5] is convicted of a criminal offence, or fails to comply with a school attendance order.[6] They were introduced by the CDA 1998 (ss. 8–11) and can last up to 12 months. Particular requirements can be added if the court considers it to be desirable to prevent further anti-social behaviour or offending. Parents must also attend, for a concurrent period not exceeding three months and not more than once a week, parenting classes or counselling as determined by the responsible officer. However, in *R (M) v Inner London Crown Court* (2003) the court concluded that a parenting order did not breach either Articles 6 or 8 of the ECHR because it deemed a parenting order not to be disproportionate, given the pressing social need to address the problems created by juvenile crime and the early research on such orders.[7]

The ASBA 2003 widened the scope of parenting orders and included detailed provisions in relation to parenting contracts (ss. 19 and 25). The latter were developed as voluntary agreements between **youth offending teams** and parents of children referred to them, but s. 27 of the Act (as amended) mandates the court, when deciding whether to make a parenting order under s. 26,

to take into account (amongst other things)—

(a) any refusal by the parent to enter into a parenting contract under section 25, 25A or 25B in respect of the child or young person, or

---

[5] Including a child safety order, an anti-social behaviour order, and a Sex Offender Order (now Sexual Offences Prevention Order).

[6] Under the Education Act 1996, ss. 443–444: CDA 1998, s. 8(1)(d).

[7] In fact the order was quashed in this case because the magistrates' decision to impose the order in relation to a neighbour dispute was seen as irrational: see [2003] Fam Law 477–8.

(b) if the parent has entered into such a parenting contract, any failure by the parent to comply with the requirements specified in the contract.

A professionally developed tool is thereby brought within the scrutiny of the court and so given a quasi-legal status in that there are ramifications for non-participation or non-compliance. Further, the Act extends the use of parenting orders in cases of exclusion from school (s. 20) and allows for a penalty notice, in effect an 'on the spot' fine, to be served on a parent who could otherwise be convicted of an offence under s. 444 of the Education Act 1996 on account of the child's irregular attendance at school (s. 23). By s. 18(3), parenting orders made in these circumstances or any other situation may include attendance at a residential course as part of the requirement to attend a guidance programme.

Parental compensation orders

The parental compensation order (PCO) was introduced by the Serious and Organised Crime and Police Act 2005 (s. 144 and Schedule 10), which inserted ss. 13A–13E into the CDA 1998. It relates only to children under ten years of age. A magistrates' court may make a PCO on application from a local authority when it is satisfied that the child (who must be under ten) has taken, or caused loss of or damage to, property in the course of committing an act which, 'if he had been aged 10 or over, would have constituted an offence; or acting in a manner that caused or was likely to cause harassment, alarm or distress to one or more persons not of the same household as himself; and that it would be desirable to make the order in the interests of preventing a repetition of the behaviour in question'. However, the Act has only been in force since 2006 in ten pilot areas.

Criminal behaviour orders and injunctions

The legislation relating to ASBOs was repealed in March 2015. The replacements were proposed in the White Paper, *Putting Victims First—More Effective Responses to Antisocial Behaviour* (Home Office 2012b): a new Criminal Behaviour Order (CBO) which would ban an individual from particular activities or places; a civil Crime Prevention Injunction (CPI) which would give agencies an immediate power to protect victims and communities; and simpler powers to close premises that are a magnet for trouble and tougher action over 'nightmare neighbours'. Repeated breaches of the new injunctions could result in those aged between 14 and 17 being ordered into custody.

The Anti-social Behaviour, Crime and Policing Bill introduced the following year included the proposed changes and received Royal Assent in 2014. The power to grant the new injunction 'to prevent nuisance and annoyance' is in s. 1 of the Anti-social Behaviour, Crime and Policing Act 2014[8] and 'replaces a range of current tools including the anti-social behaviour order ('ASBO') on application, the anti-social behaviour injunction ('ASBI'), the drinking banning order on application, intervention orders and individual support orders' (Explanatory Notes to the Bill). Section 1 reads as follows:

(1) A court may grant an injunction under this section against a person aged 10 or over ('the respondent') if two conditions are met.

(2) The first condition is that the court is satisfied, on the balance of probabilities, that the respondent has engaged or threatens to engage in anti-social behaviour.

---

[8] In force from 23 March 2015.

(3) The second condition is that the court considers it just and convenient to grant the injunction for the purpose of preventing the respondent from engaging in anti-social behaviour.

(4) An injunction under this section may for the purpose of preventing the respondent from engaging in anti-social behaviour—

    (a) prohibit the respondent from doing anything described in the injunction;

    (b) require the respondent to do anything described in the injunction.

A breach of the injunction allows a Youth Court to impose a supervision order or a detention order (Schedule 2 para 1).

The CBO is in s. 22 of the Act and has been in force since October 2014. Under s. 25(2) it is an order which

for the purpose of preventing the offender from engaging in such behaviour—

(a) prohibits the offender from doing anything described in the order;

(b) requires the offender to do anything described in the order.

The two conditions which must be met are:

s22(3) The first condition is that the court is satisfied, beyond reasonable doubt, that the offender has engaged in behaviour that caused or was likely to cause harassment, alarm or distress to any person.

    (4) The second condition is that the court considers that making the order will help in preventing the offender from engaging in such behaviour.

The court may make a CBO against the offender only on the application of the prosecution and only in addition to a sentence or conditional discharge. Further, 'The prosecution must find out the views of the local youth offending team before applying for a criminal behaviour order to be made if the offender will be under the age of 18 when the application is made' (s. 22(8)).

Issues of concern

In this section we have reviewed a diverse range of orders which affect parents, and indeed the whole family, of children who engage in criminal and anti-social behaviour. Some of them would appear to be disproportionate to the behaviour which triggers them and would appear to punish family members who might have little influence on the actions of other family members. They evidence a grey area in policy and they may not achieve their aims. Rather, they may create further problems for parents and their children. We hope that the new orders are used more sparingly and appropriately.

11.2 Sentencing options

11.2.1 The youth justice system

In Chapter 6, section 6.3 we covered the welfare and Convention principles which have influenced policy development and we noted the role of youth offending teams (YOTs). The youth justice system as a statutory body was not created, however, until the CDA 1998, and it might be helpful to review that system now as it is relevant to court-imposed orders as well as pre-court processes.

The CDA 1998 set up a national and local administrative framework for the youth justice system in England and Wales. Section 38 imposed duties on each local authority, police authority, probation committee, and health authority to provide—or cooperate in providing—youth justice services. It also required that each local authority (LA) area set up inter-agency YOTs (s. 39). The Act also set up a national Youth Justice Board (YJB) for England and Wales to monitor the youth justice system and to advise the Secretary of State (s. 41) and introduced for the first time in legislation in the UK an aim for the new youth justice system—to prevent offending.

The YOT is now one of the seven partners of the children's services authority listed in s. 10(4) of the Children Act 2004. All of these partners 'must co-operate with the authority in the making of arrangements' as specified, 'with a view to improving the well-being of children' in relation to the five outcomes for children which are also specified in s. 10.

Figure 11.2 gives an indication not only of the different ways in which young offenders are dealt with but also the numbers for each route in 2013/14.

11.2.2 **The range and use of orders**

Strictly speaking it is inaccurate to speak of 'sentencing options': juveniles are not 'sentenced' after 'conviction'. Instead, since the implementation of the Children and Young Persons' Act 1933, the youth court 'makes an order upon a finding of guilt' (s. 59) in relation to those minors who have been successfully prosecuted. If the minor is prosecuted the case is normally heard in the youth court, formerly the juvenile court, the name having been changed when the upper age was raised from 17 and non-criminal cases were moved to the newly created Family Proceedings Court.[9]

However, on a first appearance at a youth court a minor is normally given a referral order which entails referral to a multi-disciplinary Youth Offender Panel (YOP). This Panel, which includes lay members, agrees a contract of activities with the young offender (ss. 18, 21–27) and might be seen as an attempt to include a more welfare-orientated decision-making process. On subsequent appearances at court the full range of disposals is available to the magistrates, from those available in the 'first tier' of penalties—discharges, fines, compensation orders, reparation orders—through youth rehabilitation orders[10] to a detention and training order (DTO) or other custodial orders. In England and Wales, community and custodial orders for minors, as for adults, are subject to the same statutory seriousness hurdles that we discussed in Chapter 3. Further criteria will be discussed in this chapter.

The situation in Northern Ireland is very similar, although different legislation and terminology apply to many aspects of youth justice. In 1999, Northern Ireland also changed the name of the juvenile court to the youth court (Criminal Justice (Children) Order 1998, Article 27) and s. 63 of the Justice (Northern Ireland) Act 2002 raised the upper limit from 17 to 18 years old. Sections 57–61 of the 2002 Act provide youth courts with powers to refer offenders to a 'youth conference' where an agreed plan is negotiated, somewhat similar to the referral order in England and Wales. Scotland, as we noted in Chapter 8, has a different history since the 1960s and, as Muncie points out, the more recently devolved governments of the UK have taken the opportunity to rethink youth justice policies so that Wales has, he contends, more progressive policies with an ethos of 'children first' (Muncie 2011: 42).

---

[9] Criminal Justice Act 1991, s. 68 and Schedule 8, Children (Allocation of Proceedings) Order 1991, SI 1991/1677.

[10] In force since April 2009.

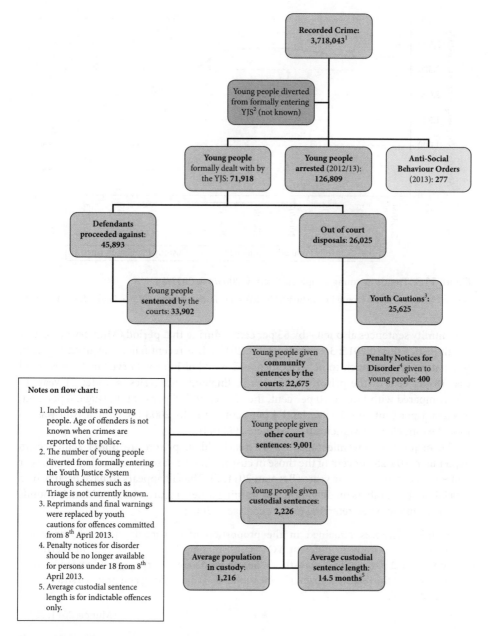

Figure 11.2 Flows through the youth justice system, 2013/14

Source: Ministry of Justice/Youth Justice Board (2015a) *Youth Justice Statistics 2013/14 England and Wales* p. 14

Use of orders

When we wrote the second edition of this book in 2008, the number of boys and girls in prison (minors on remand or sentenced) in England and Wales was double the number in 1993. However, as we noted in Chapter 6, the past decade has seen a fall in the numbers of young people given a custodial sentence: see Figure 11.3. Indeed by 2014/15 the average population (under 18) in custody had fallen by 62 per cent since 2004/5 (Ministry of Justice/Youth Justice Board 2016: 46), and the number of young people sentenced to

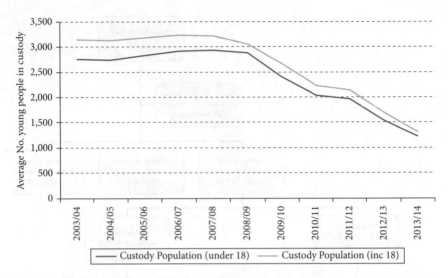

Figure 11.3 Trends in young people in custody, 2003/4 to 2013/14

Source: Ministry of Justice/Youth Justice Board (2015a) *Youth Justice Statistics 2013/14 England and Wales* p. 11

community sentences also fell—by 63 per cent—during that period (Ministry of Justice/ Youth Justice Board 2016: 36; see also Allen 2011). This recent fall in the juvenile prison population is very much to be welcomed: a Council of Europe Survey in 1996 showed that 18 per cent of the prison population in England and Wales is under 21 years of age, compared with France 10 per cent, the Netherlands 8 per cent, Portugal 6 per cent, Sweden 4 per cent, and Switzerland 4 per cent,[11] and by 2008 the comparison was no more favourable (see Muncie 2011; Muncie 2008: 116).

The majority of juveniles aged 15–17 years old in prison are under sentence: in September 2011 28 per cent of the those in custody had been sentenced to less than a year and 9 per cent to over four years (Berman 2011: 7). The fall appears to have been driven by a fall in the numbers on detention and training order (Figure 11.4) but Muncie sounds a note of caution when referring to the decrease in 2009:

> Notable differences remained in the proportion of convicted under 18-year-olds sentenced to custody in different YOT areas, ranging from 20 per cent in Merthyr Tydfil . . . to 2 per cent in Newcastle . . . Such a 'postcode lottery' suggests a need . . . to learn more of the relative impact of professional decision making and practice strategies at a local level.
>
> (Muncie 2011: 52)

11.2.3 Sentencing guideline

At the end of 2009 the Sentencing Guidelines Council (SGC) published a definitive guideline on sentencing young offenders in the context of the introduction of the youth rehabilitation order. It had been preceded by a consultation guideline to which the Commons Justice Select Committee had responded, stating that the guidance 'fills a critical gap', and that the evidence they had received suggested a varied understanding

---

[11] See House of Commons Home Affairs Select Committee Session 1997–8, Minutes of Evidence, Annex A, 5 May 1998.

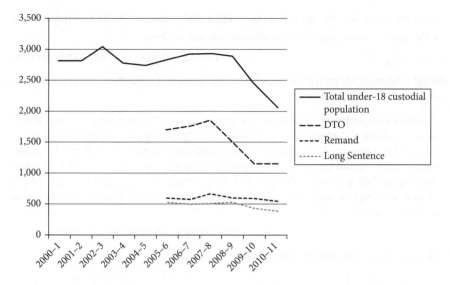

Figure 11.4 Total under-18s in custody 2000/1 to 2010/11 against DTO, remand, and long sentences 2005/6 to 2010/11

Source: Allen (2011: figure 1) Prison Reform Trust

amongst sentencers of the concept that custody should only ever be 'a sentence of last resort for young people'.[12]

The guideline included the important statement that 'Even within the category of "youth", the response to an offence is likely to be very different depending on whether the offender is at the lower end of the age bracket, in the middle or towards the top end; in many instances, the maturity of the offender will be at least as important as the chronological age' (Sentencing Guidelines Council 2009b: para 2.2). It also drew attention to the requirement to 'have regard to' the welfare of the young offender (see Chapter 6, section 6.3.4) and spelt out in some detail, and highlighted in red, what this entailed:

In having regard to the 'welfare' of the young person, a court should ensure that it is alert to:

- the high incidence of mental health problems amongst young people in the criminal justice system;
- the high incidence of those with learning difficulties or learning disabilities amongst young people in the criminal justice system;
- the effect that speech and language difficulties might have on the ability of the young person (or any adult with them) to communicate with the court, to understand the sanction imposed or to fulfil the obligations resulting from that sanction;
- the extent to which young people anticipate that they will be discriminated against by those in authority and the effect that it has on the way that they conduct themselves during court proceedings;
- the vulnerability of young people to self harm, particularly within a custodial environment;

---

[12] See House of Commons Justice Committee (2009: 3), available at http://www.publications.parliament.uk/pa/cm200809/cmselect/cmjust/497/497.pdf.

- the extent to which changes taking place during adolescence can lead to experimentation;
- the effect on young people of experiences of loss or of abuse.

(Sentencing Guidelines Council 2009b: para 2.9)

The guideline also addressed the question of the amount of impact on the sentence that the age of the offender should have:

[T]here is an expectation that, generally, a young person will be dealt with less severely than an adult offender, although this distinction diminishes as the offender approaches age 18 (subject to an assessment of maturity and criminal sophistication). In part, this is because young people are unlikely to have the same experience and capacity as an adult to realise the effect of their actions on other people or to appreciate the pain and distress caused and because a young person is likely to be less able to resist temptation, especially where peer pressure is exerted.

(Sentencing Guidelines Council 2009b: para 3.1)

Such clear statements are to be welcomed.

11.2.4 Assessment and information

A new assessment framework is in the process of being rolled out, but YOTs have for some time used the assessment tool Asset[13] at various stages to determine what form and quantity of intervention is required to reduce the risk that the child reoffends. The focus on risk and the use of numerical scales produce a score to determine outcome and were developed as part of a trend towards 'actuarial justice' (see Chapter 1, section 1.3.1). For example, at the end of part 1 of the 'Core profile' the assessor had to rate on a score of 0–4 the extent to which the young person's living arrangements are associated with the likelihood of further offending. For a child 'in need'[14] who also offends, the end product—even with the inclusion in the assessment checklists of 'dynamic' factors, such as physical or mental health and empathy with victims—might, it is argued, be an intervention which is inappropriate to the child's needs or disproportionate to the offending (Hudson 2003: 49–50).

Children's Services use the 'common assessment framework' so Asset is a separate tool from that used in relation to local authority child protection duties; see *Working Together to Safeguard Children* (HM Government 2015). However, the YOT can refer a young offender to Children's Services if the Asset assessment reveals behaviour attributable to harm within the family. It may be that members of YOTs focus on the risk of offending at the expense of an understanding of children's needs (see, for example, Calder 2003: 29), which is of some concern in relation to 'looked-after' children,[15] who have been in local authority care, whose offending rate is much higher than the offending rate of other children: 'Over a quarter of young men and over half of young women [in Young Offender Institutions] said they had spent some time in local authority care' (Summerfield 2011: 7).

However, an Audit Commission report (2004) concluded that Asset was usually completed to an acceptable standard and 'is a major step forward in providing a comprehensive risk and needs assessment' (Audit Commission 2004: 73). Wilson and Hinks found

---

[13] The version published in April 2014 was accessed at https://www.gov.uk/government/publications/asset-documents.

[14] This is a term used in s. 17 of the Children Act 1989 to refer to children whose health or development requires or will require the provision of services by the local authority.

[15] 'Looked-after children' are children voluntarily accommodated by, or in the care of, the local authority (under ss. 20 and 31 respectively of the Children Act 1989).

that Asset was a good predictor of proven reoffending within a one-year period and that factors which were 'highly statistically significant predictors' included 'substance use' and 'motivation to change' (2011: ii–iii). A recent Youth Justice Board report based on visits to 20 YOTs found that 'To a greater or lesser degree, the YOTs that we visited were becoming more closely integrated with other local authority services. YOT managers often managed other youth or family services as well as youth offending' (Youth Justice Board 2015b: para 1.4). Indeed, 'There were concerns that the specialist risk-based services delivered by YOTs to a complex and high risk group of children and young people could be diluted' (ibid: para 1.7).

Further, AssetPlus has now been published and is due to replace Asset in a phased introduction from late 2015. The guidance claims that 'AssetPlus has been designed to provide a holistic end-to-end assessment and intervention plan, allowing one record to follow a child or young person throughout their time in the youth justice system' (Youth Justice Board 2014a: Overview).[16] It is based on research and will give more weight to the professional judgement of practitioners.

For minors, as for adults, the court has required a pre-sentence report (PSR) since the Criminal Justice Act (CJA) 1991. Earlier guidance made clear that the assessment of the young offender had to be based on an Asset assessment (Youth Justice Board 2010: 49); recent guidance refers to AssetPlus (Youth Justice Board 2014b). Pre-AssetPlus guidance also noted that '[w]here a YRO is recommended, not only should the appropriate requirement(s) be identified but, in addition, the level of intervention and supervision envisaged under the Scaled Approach should be made clear' (Youth Justice Board 2010: 50). The new guidance also says the scaled approach must be used (Youth Justice Board 2014b: para 2.15).

The 'scaled approach', for use with young offenders on reparation and youth rehabilitation orders, as well as undergoing post-custody supervision, is seen as an important risk-based assessment tool which aims to target resources more economically:

> The Scaled Approach will use quality assessment to determine the likelihood of reoffending and risk of serious harm to others. This, alongside professional judgement, will help establish which intervention level a young person needs: standard, enhanced, or intensive. The intervention level determines the minimum statutory contact a young person will have with the YOT or other assigned professionals.
>
> (Youth Justice Board: *The Scaled Approach*, undated leaflet: 2)

Arguably, 'youth justice practitioners and courts are thus … encouraged to allow risk to supplant considerations of "just deserts" in practice' (Bateman 2011: 173).

Earlier research suggested that there is a correlation between the quality of PSRs and levels of custodial sentencing with, for example, more than 40 per cent of PSRs being assessed as unsatisfactory or poor in high-custody areas (NACRO 2000b: 2–3). While the proportion of reports recommending custody or giving no clear proposal varied, it was as high as 32 per cent in one high-custody area (ibid: 3). There is also a suggestion of racial discrimination in operation via PSRs. A review by HM Inspectorate of Probation (2000) of adult defendants found that, while 60 per cent of reports on white defendants were satisfactory, the equivalent for African or African-Caribbean defendants was 49 per cent. The quality and the type of information before the sentencing court are, then, very important.

---

[16] Accessed at https://www.gov.uk/government/publications/assetplus-assessment-and-planning-in-the-youth-justice-system/assetplus-assessment-and-planning-in-the-youth-justice-system.

11.3 Non-custodial orders

11.3.1 Introduction

In our review of protective sentencing in Chapter 5 we noted the importance of risk assessment (of reoffending and of harm to others) in decision-making, in Chapter 6 we reviewed the development of restorative approaches, and in Chapter 10 we focused on rehabilitation as an aim in community supervision and the 'what works' approach to choice of prevention programmes to be used. Minors are not exempt from any of these trends and concerns.

In section 11.2.2 we noted that fines and other financial orders fall into the 'first tier' of penalties but that on a first conviction at a youth court a referral order must be considered, so we will deal with that in section 11.3.2 before reviewing other 'first tier' orders in section 11.3.3. We deal, therefore, with fines and the reparation order, but also cover fixed penalties, which are pre-court but have court-based sanctions for non-payment. Finally, in 11.3.4 we consider youth rehabilitation orders (YROs)—the only 'community' order for those under 18 years of age.

11.3.2 Referral orders

This order was introduced by the Youth Justice and Criminal Evidence Act 1999, re-enacted in Part III ss. 16–28 of the Powers of Criminal Courts (Sentencing) Act (PCCSA) 2000, and since amended. It has a somewhat ambivalent status in that it is a criminal order, imposed by a youth court, yet diverts the offender from the court to a YOP to agree a programme of preventive or restorative activities rather than to impose punishment. It is a compromise which has its roots in the 1960s (see Chapter 6, section 6.3.1) and the use of referral orders could be said to have established something similar to the approach envisaged then and implemented in Scotland in Children's Hearings.

The referral order can be for 3–12 months and amounts to a new form of diversion—that of diversion from any other order that could have been imposed by the court. The YOP to which the young offender is referred includes lay members and the young offender is expected to help negotiate and agree a contract of activities—individualised preventive measures—to address his or her offending. These may require the young offender to engage in a form of restorative justice under which meetings are organised, with the attendance where possible of the victim and significant others in the life of the young offender (see Chapter 6, section 6.2.3). Failure to agree or comply can mean referral back to the youth court. If the contract is successfully 'signed off' the conviction is regarded as spent.

As originally passed, this provision for offenders under 18, who pleaded guilty to all offences charged and who had no previous convictions or bind-overs, mandated a referral order, with the following exceptions.[17] If the court considered the offence to be very serious, a custodial penalty could be imposed; if the court considered the offence to be sufficiently minor, an absolute discharge could be given; and if the Mental Health Act 2003 provisions are applicable, a hospital order can be made (PCCSA 2000 s16). The intent was to remove the discretion of the youth court to 'punish' young offenders on a first prosecution,

---

[17] PCCSA 2000, ss. 16 and 19. The only other exception allowed by these provisions is if the Mental Health Act 1983 is applicable and a hospital order is made.

provided they pleaded guilty. Discretion to use the referral order or not remained where the young offender pleaded guilty to only some of the charges.

However, the referral conditions have been amended in response to several pressures. First, there was evidence of a rise in the number of apparently tactical 'guilty' pleas and in the number of absolute discharges by youth courts, possibly because of concern by magistrates that the resources of the YOP were being 'unnecessarily' expended (NACRO 2003b; see also Greenhow 2003: 267). Further, while some magistrates appeared to view referral as too heavy-handed, others were critical of the loss of their discretion to impose more punitive orders (Ball 2000).

As a result of these criticisms the compulsory referral conditions now have the add¯ itional condition that the offence being dealt with must be an imprisonable one (s. 17(1)), while the court has discretion to impose the order on the same conditions (in addition to the existing conditions) if the offence is not imprisonable (s. 17(1A) of the PCCSA 2000).[18] The Criminal Justice and Immigration Act (CJIA) 2008 amended s. 17(1A) and (2) so that the court could make a referral order if the offender had been dealt with by a court on one previous occasion and, exceptionally, even if he had been referred to a YOP.[19] It also enabled the court to extend the term of a referral order for up to three months on the recommendation of the YOP (s. 27B).

The Legal Aid, Sentencing and Punishment of Offenders Act (LASPO) 2012 amended s. 16(1)(c) such that courts can also impose a conditional discharge rather than a referral order, and repealed s. 17(2A)–(2C) so that the discretionary conditions are now simply that the compulsory conditions are not met and the offender has pleaded guilty to at least one offence before the court. The Criminal Justice and Courts Act 2015 ss. 43–45 made further amendments to the PCCSA 2000 such that if a young offender is referred back to the court because of failure to complete the terms of the contract, as well as revoking the order the court can impose a fine up to £2,500 or extend the referral order. The court can also extend the period of compliance of the referral order on a subsequent conviction (rather than imposing another penalty). Revised guidance has been issued for the courts, YOPs, and YOTs (Ministry of Justice/ Youth Justice Board 2015b).

When first implemented the scheme was criticised for assuming a young offender had sufficient maturity to engage in negotiating a package of activities or to understand fully the implications of breaking the terms of the 'contract' (see Wonnacott 1999). Using words such as 'contract' for the outcome of this process was criticised as 'an abuse of contractual language' which hides 'too much executive discretion in respect of the contents of the order' (Ashworth 2000: 332–3).

However, early Home Office research found that some of the concerns had not materialised, with positive comments being made by parents and young offenders (Newburn *et al.* 2002). Further, the profile of the volunteer members of the YOPs may be more akin to that of the general population in age and ethnicity than to that of the lay magistracy (see Audit Commission 2004: 24).[20] There would seem to be some optimism that referral orders are effective in reducing offending rates and diverting from more penal options: as Fortin notes, a former chair of the Youth Justice Board, Rod Morgan, referred to them as the 'jewel in the crown' of the youth justice system (Fortin 2009: 727).

---

[18] Referral Orders (Amendment of Referral Conditions) Regulations SI 2003/1605.

[19] Section 35; see also ss. 36–37.

[20] This may be partly the result of a lower minimum age (18) for panel members as opposed to the 27-year-old minimum for the magistracy.

11.3.3 **First tier orders**

Financial penalties

The young offender can be given a fine or compensation order, as can an adult (see Chapter 10, section 10.2). The Sentencing Council website states that 'as with adults, the fine should reflect the offence committed and the offender's ability to pay. For offenders under 16, paying the fine is the responsibility of a parent/guardian and it will be their ability to pay that is taken into account when setting the level of the fine.'[21] If the magistrates' court has the power to exceed a fine of £1,000 for an adult it cannot do so for an offender under 18, or exceed £250 for one under 14 (PCCSA 2000, s. 135). The court can make a parent or guardian liable not only for the fines, but also the victim surcharge, or compensation order of any young offender under 18 (s. 137(1) and (1A)). Parents can also be ordered to pay fines for breach of a youth rehabilitation order or reparation order and for breach of requirements of a supervision under a detention and training order (s. 137(2)).

Reparation order

The reparation order—although carried out in the community—is not technically a community order. It was introduced by ss. 67–68 of the CDA 1998, re-enacted in ss. 73–75 of the Powers of Criminal Courts (Sentencing) Act 2000, and so continues as an order separate from the YRO. The distinction is of significance because, since the CJA 1991, there has been a statutory hurdle for the imposition of a community penalty on minors and adults—that the offence is 'serious enough to warrant such a sentence' (see Chapter 3). The reparation order can be imposed in relation to less serious offending. The order is available only for those under 18 years of age and cannot be added to a custodial or community sentence. It can involve reparation to the individual victim, if that is what the victim wants, or to the community, but the young offender cannot be required to work more than 24 hours in total over a maximum period of three months.

Fixed penalties

Young offenders can also be given pre-court financial penalties—fixed penalty notices (FPNs)—and, until 2013, could be given penalty notices for disorder (PNDs). Technically, therefore, FPNs do not fit into this chapter on court orders, but non-payment can result in a prosecution and so we mention them here.

  Many FPNs are for environmental offences—for example, dropping litter—and are governed by DEFRA guidance. However, local areas can set their own policies for enforcement. For example, one County Council issues the FPN at Step 3 and then in its final stage (Step 4) for the 10–15-year-old offender states: 'Non-payment of the fixed penalty notice and failure to complete the Litter Pick session will still result in the person's case being put forward for consideration for prosecution' (Cornwall Council 2013: 5). For 16–17-year-olds Step 1 offers them the choice of an FPN or involvement in a restorative justice scheme—for example, litter picking—and notifies the YOT (ibid: 7). FPNs can also be used for traffic offences.

  Until recently young people of 16 or 17 years of age who had committed offences such as theft or being drunk and disorderly could receive a PND. Often referred to as 'on the spot fines', they were introduced under the Criminal Justice and Police Act 2000, piloted in four police force areas in England and Wales from August 2002, and rolled out to all 43 police forces in England and Wales by April 2004. (For the last batch

---

[21] Accessed at https://www.sentencingcouncil.org.uk/about-sentencing/young-people-and-sentencing/types-of-sentences-for-young-people/.

of statistics see Ministry of Justice/Youth Justice Board 2015a: 21–22). However, PNDs have not been available for those under 18 since April 2013.

11.3.4 **Youth rehabilitation orders**

When we wrote the second edition of this book there was a range of separate community-based orders available to the courts, a new community order for those under 16, and various provisions which had not been implemented or repealed. *Youth Justice—Next Steps* proposed to replace all nine non-custodial sentences for 'juveniles' with one sentence, a broader Action Plan Order (Home Office 2003c: paras 7 and 17; see also DfES 2004: para 4.21). The sentencing situation is now much simpler. What has replaced all the previous community orders is a similar order, for all minors and with a different name—the youth rehabilitation order (YRO) introduced by Part 1 of the CJIA 2008. It is available for all convicted offenders under 18 and involves the court adding any of the 15 requirements specified in s. 1 (see also Schedule 1). So, for example, the youth rehabilitation order can have a supervision requirement.

YROs can also include a mental health or drug treatment requirement or a local authority residence requirement, but also curfew, exclusion, electronic monitoring, and prohibited activity requirements. These latter options all have their origins in orders introduced since 1998 and are evidence of the more restrictive nature of some requirements and orders. For example, curfew orders, introduced by the CDA 1998, were extended to children under 16 years of age by s. 48 of the Criminal Justice and Police Act 2001 until repealed in 2010. Another example is s. 1 of the Anti-social Behaviour, Crime and Policing Act 2014, introducing the new injunction in relation to anti-social behaviour, which gives the court the following power:

> s1(4) An injunction under this section may for the purpose of preventing the respondent from engaging in anti-social behaviour—
>
> (a) prohibit the respondent from doing anything described in the injunction;
>
> (b) require the respondent to do anything described in the injunction.

There are rights issues here, given the use of civil orders where the proceedings are not subject to the same safeguards as orders imposed in criminal proceedings.

Intensive supervision and surveillance programmes (ISSPs)

The CJIA 2008 Schedule 1 para 3(5) now states that 'A youth rehabilitation order which imposes an extended activity requirement (and other requirements in accordance with sub-paragraph (4)) is referred to in this Part of this Act as *"a youth rehabilitation order with intensive supervision and surveillance"."* However, the ISSP was introduced by the Youth Justice Board in 2001, aimed at 15–17-year-old offenders who had been charged or warned at least four times in the previous 12 months and so were at high risk of (further) imprisonment (see Leigh 2001/2). The ISSP—which can also be a condition of post-release supervision in the second half of a detention and training order (see section 11.4.1) and as part of bail conditions—uses a combination of electronic and other forms of tracking, with staff sent to deal with non-compliance as soon as possible. In addition there can be compulsory educational or other activities, such as reparation or offending behaviour programmes. This requirement makes sense in the context of the strong link between educational attainment and offending (see Moore 2004; Waters 2007). The ISSP must last at least six months (CJIA 2008, Schedule 1, para 32).

The ISSP is used in England and Wales. Research on the first 41 pilot schemes concluded that 'The frequency of offending in the ISSP sample went down by 40% over one year and by 39% over two years. The seriousness of any further offending went down by 13% in both one and two years after ISSP' (Gray *et al.* 2005: 9). Offenders who were 'persistent and serious' experienced a significant reduction in offending frequency and 'in terms of reduced offence frequency and gravity, young women performed significantly better than young men on ISSP' (Gray *et al.* 2005: 9). An earlier study had found that reconviction rates were unaffected but that there was a 30–50 per cent reduction in the volume of crime committed by ISSP participants surveyed (Little *et al.* 2004).

Scotland has a similar scheme—the Scottish Intensive Monitoring and Supervision (ISMS) programme—and a review of research on both schemes concluded that they 'appear to reduce the frequency, severity and risk of offending in young people, although probably no more than other levels of supervision' and that one of the key factors is 'flexibility in the intervention to allow the needs of different types of young people to be met' (IRISS 2010).

Section 88 of the ASBA 2003 made available the fostering requirement: a child or young person can be required to live with a local authority foster parent for a period up to 12 months as part of the, then, supervision order. Section 1(3) of the CJIA 2008 now provides the power for a YRO with fostering. However, these 'extended activity' YROs can be used only if all the relevant criteria for a custodial sentence (see section 11.4) are met. In considering the use of ISSP and intensive fostering, the 'scaled approach' (see section 11.2) will be used during and after assessment of the young offender. Given that the scaled approach—using Asset's future risk-based scores—to determining levels of intervention can undermine proportionality and the young offender's rights (Bateman 2011), it is to be hoped the new more flexible AssetPlus assessment framework can avoid these problems.

The Youth Justice Reinvestment Custody Pathfinder Initiative, which began in 2011 in pilot areas, provided extra funding to YOTs in return for their pledging to cut the use of custody over two years. It was, then, an example of the increasingly used 'payment by results' (PbR) approach by commissioning bodies. Failure to reduce custody levels by the agreed amount would incur a penalty. Research on the first year identified key lessons and was unable to predict whether areas would meet their targets (Wong *et al.* 2013), and two sites did indeed withdraw at the end of year one. A later 'final process evaluation' report found that the sites (one in the north of England consisting of a consortium of five authorities; the other a consortium of four London boroughs) had exceeded their targets (Wong *et al.* 2015). A report by the Revolving Doors Agency, while generally praising this initiative, warns that 'there is currently a significant danger that existing PbR schemes are simply recreating and reinforcing silos as they continue to be developed in isolation by individual commissioners and government departments' (2015: 11).

11.4 Detention

11.4.1 The range, use, and site of custodial sentences

The passing of the Children's Act, 1908, which practically forbids imprisonment before 16 years of age, marks the last stage in that slow and tedious journey which had to be undertaken by many devoted men and women who were conscious of the grave evils resulting from imprisonment, before it was generally realized that it was not by throwing children and young persons automatically and indiscriminately into gaol, that the grave problem of juvenile delinquency was going to be solved.

(Sir Evelyn Ruggles-Brise K.C.B., Chairman of the Prison Commission, in *The English Prison System*, Macmillan, 1921: 101)

We draw attention to this quotation in the context of a recent decreased use of imprisonment for children and young people, but in the following sections we review the range of orders available to the court to allow them to impose custody, a range which has over the years increased. We also cover those provisions which allow longer or indeterminate sentences which, as Bateman notes, are in contrast to 'many jurisdictions [that] have established an upper limit to child imprisonment: three years in Uganda, Brazil, Bolivia and Peru, four years in Switzerland, and 10 years for most Eastern European counties' (Bateman 2015: 41).

Children and young people can be sentenced to determinate and indeterminate custodial sentences. The main determinate sentence is the detention and training order—the DTO. A longer determinate sentence can be imposed for 'grave crimes'—those serious offences which are defined in statute for the purpose of PCCSA 2000 s. 91. However, there are also determinate sentences which have an extended supervision period post-release. This used to be called the extended sentence for public protection but was rejigged to form the extended determinate sentence. The indeterminate sentences—those with no prescribed amount of time (although a minimum period is specified by the sentencing judge)—are imposed because the offence is murder (PCCSA 2000 s. 90), and because the conditions for a sentence of detention for life under CJA 2003 s. 226 are fulfilled, the young offender being deemed to be 'dangerous'. Previously the indeterminate sentence for public protection (DPP sentence) was also available.

In the 12 months ending in September 2014 the following figures are recorded for the numbers of sentenced juveniles:

Sections 90–92 PCC(S) Act 2000	242
Detention and Training Order	1,680 (i.e. 87% of the total)
Extended sentence for public protection	0
Indeterminate sentence for public protection	0
Extended determinate sentence	16
Total sentenced to immediate custody	**1938**

(Extracted from Table Q5.6 of Ministry of Justice (2015b) *Criminal Justice Statistics, Quarterly Update to September 2014, England and Wales*)

In Table 11.1 below there are some comparable figures for 2010/11 which again show the overall decrease in numbers, but with a breakdown of some of the categories.

Table 11.1 Type of custodial sentence received

Type of sentence	N	% of cases
Detention and Training Order	2,577	78%
DTO recall	384	12%
Section 91 sentence	250	8%
Section 91 recall	30	1%
Detention for public protection	17	1%
Extended sentence	16	<1%
Recall of extended sentence	2	<1%
Mandatory life sentence	7	<1%
Total	3,283	100%

Source: Jacobson *et al.* (2011: Table 2.1).

Overall the average length of time spent in custody increased by eight days to 85 days in 2012/13 (Ministry of Justice/Youth Justice Board 2014: 4), with a further increase to 90 days in 2013/14 but remaining largely unchanged at 89 days in 2014/15 (Ministry of Justice/Youth Justice Board 2016: 50). For longer sentences the large increase from an average of 302 to 409 days in the previous two years has not continued and was at 323 days in 2014/15 (ibid: 50); for DTOs there was a decrease from 115 to 109 days in 2013/14 (Ministry of Justice/Youth Justice Board 2015a: 45) and to 108 in 2014/15 (Ministry of Justice/Youth Justice Board 2016: 50). These averages are still too high but the recent trend is encouraging.

In 2014/15, 96 per cent of the children and young people (under 18) held in the custodial estate were male, 96 per cent were aged 15–17 years, and 60 per cent were from a white ethnic background, while those from a black ethnic background accounted for 21 per cent of young people in custody (Ministry of Justice/Youth Justice Board 2016: 48).

Where served

When a child or young person under 18 is sentenced to custody, the decision as to where he or she should be placed has been made since 2000 by the Youth Justice Board for England and Wales (YJB). The young offender can be allocated to a secure training centre (STC), a local authority secure children's home (SCH) or an under-18 young offender institution (YOI—for young males only). Theoretically this choice gives more flexibility to address the needs of the young offender. The presumption is that 15–17-year-old boys will be placed in YOIs, whether open or closed institutions, while 12–14-year-olds (and 10–11-year-olds under other provisions) will be accommodated outside the Prison Service. All female YOIs were decommissioned in July and August 2013, therefore any 17- and 18-year-old females that remain in the youth secure estate will be held in STCs or SCHs. In 2013/14, most (69 per cent) children and young people (under 18) held in custody were in YOIs, 21 per cent were in STCs, and the remaining 10 per cent were in SCHs (Ministry of Justice/Youth Justice Board 2016: 49).

Vulnerability and gender may allow for different placements but in practice, discretionary placement outside the Prison Service is difficult because the majority of the secure juvenile estate is still to be found in Prison Service establishments (for criticism, see NACRO 2001b: 6). There are of course cost implications: the average cost of incarceration per young offender across different sectors in 2012/13 was £60,000 for placement in a YOI, £178,000 in a secure training centre, and £212,000 in a local authority secure children's home.[22] The cost of the YOI had risen to £72,000 in 2013/14.[23] The fact that it is cheaper to allocate to the Prison Service is of concern during a time of 'austerity' budgets.

11.4.2 **Determinate sentences**

Detention and training order (DTO)

The criteria for the imposition of a DTO, which is an option if the offence is one for which an adult could be imprisoned, are to be found in s. 100 of the PCCSA 2000. Section 298 of the CJA 2003, if ever implemented, will amend the PCCSA 2000, s. 101(2), so that six months would be the maximum term magistrates could impose on a young offender for a summary offence if the maximum for an adult is 51 weeks. Section 101(4) allows

---

[22] https://www.gov.uk/government/uploads/system/uploads/attachment_data/file/273405/tyc-impact-assessment.pdf at p. 7.

[23] https://www.gov.uk/government/uploads/system/uploads/attachment_data/file/367551/cost-per-place-and-prisoner-2013-14-summary.pdf Table 1.

a maximum of 24 months for the detention and training order for other offences, providing it does not exceed the maximum allowed for that offence for an offender over 21 years.

The CJA 1991 repealed the relevant sections of the Criminal Justice Act 1982 so that minors and adults are now subject to the same statutory criteria for the imposition of community and custodial penalties (CJA 2001, ss. 148 and 152). However the research by Glover and Hibbert found that 35 per cent of their sample of 12–14-year-olds on a DTO did not appear to meet the custody thresholds (2009: 4; see also NACRO 2011). Section 143(2) of the CJA 2003 also applies to minors, such that more weight is now given to previous offences in calculating seriousness.

The DTO is now, in law, available to all those over ten years old (although there are currently no designated institutions for 10- and 11-year-olds under this order). The earlier 'normal' custodial sentence (in the CJA 1991) was detention in a youth offender institution for those aged 15–17 (only) but the Criminal Justice and Public Order Act (CJPOA) 1994, ss. 1–4, lowered the age at which a child could be detained by introducing secure training orders (STOs) for 12–14-year-olds. This possibility was continued in the CDA 1998, which combined the two forms of detention into 'detention and training orders' (s. 73), lowered the minimum age to ten, and raised the maximum length to two years. These draconian changes were referred to as a 'legislative clampdown on children and young people' (Scraton and Haydon 2002: 314). But the provisions in s. 73 were re-enacted in the PCCSA 2000.

The CDA 1998 enacted or re-enacted the criteria for imposing custody on the lower age groups—now in the PCCSA 2000 s. 100(2): for those under 15 the child must be a 'persistent' offender, defined in *R v TTG* (2003) as having more than two previous convictions; in addition, for those under 12 the order must be necessary to protect the public. In 2003 the government proposed to remove the 'persistence' condition for 12–14-year-olds on the ground that it had 'proved complex in practice' (Home Office 2003c: para 21) but this has not been done. Indeed, the criteria need to be more stringent: this condition is now less restrictive than the criteria for the previous STO (see Glover and Hibbert 2009: 5).

Half the length of the order is served in an institution; the remainder is spent on supervision in the community, with breaches leading to further detention. PCCSA 200 s. 102(4) as amended allows for release one to two months earlier than the halfway stage, possibly with an electronic monitoring requirement.[24]

Longer sentences for 'grave' crimes

For particular offences, longer sentences than the 24-month maximum available to the youth court can be imposed. For murder and for certain serious offences (for example, where the adult maximum penalty would be 14 years' imprisonment), the Crown Court has powers to make orders for detention at Her Majesty's pleasure or detention for a specific period (PCCSA 2000, ss. 90 and 91), and also an order for detention for life for specified serious offences (CJA 2003, s. 226). Such cases will be transferred to the Crown Court which has greater sentencing powers. The PCCSA 2000, ss. 90–91, largely re-enacted legislation first passed in the Children and Young Persons Act 1933, s. 53 to provide longer periods of detention to cater for what was anticipated as the exceptional circumstance of a minor committing murder (s. 53(1), now PCCSA 2000, s. 90) or a grave crime (s. 53(2), now PCCSA 2000, s. 91). Both sets of provisions now apply to all minors above the age of criminal responsibility. The murder provision had always so applied but the minimum age for the grave crimes provision was 14, until s. 16 of the CJPOA 1994 lowered it to ten. There

---

[24] For guidance issued by the Youth Justice Board in 2000 and 2002 see NACRO (2003a).

are, however, some offences which trigger s. 91 only for 14–17-year-olds, notably causing death by dangerous driving.

Until the Criminal Justice Act 1961, only murder, attempted murder, manslaughter, and wounding with intent to do grievous bodily harm could trigger the orders for detention at Her Majesty's pleasure (s. 90) or for a specified period (s. 91). In 1961 the definition of grave crimes was extended to those where the offence carried a maximum penalty of 14 years for an adult. Since then legislation has inadvertently extended the scope of the grave—now serious—crimes provision by the addition of offences with a 14-year maximum. The CJA 2003 and the Sexual Offences Act 2003 introduced further relevant maxima and the scope of s. 91 was extended by the addition of specific offences for which the provision applies, for example, in relation to indecent assault since the CJPOA 1994 (see PCCSA 2000, s. 91(1) and (2)).

The use of the grave/serious crimes provision greatly increased over the years, particularly during the period 1993–7. Compared with only six sentences made under s. 53(2) (or, later, s. 91) in 1970, 65 were made in 1980, and 607 in 1999 (NACRO 2001b). The generally upward trend until the past decade is probably explained by the changes in the law together with, arguably, the increased punitiveness on the part of youth court magistrates.

A problem—in the eyes of magistrates in youth courts—had been the restrictive nature of the criteria for imposing DTOs on offenders under 16 years of age. Their 'solution' was to decline jurisdiction so that the Crown Court could impose detention under s. 91(3) 'if the court is of the opinion that none of the other methods in which the case may legally be dealt with is suitable'. *Mills and related appeals* (1998) had held, contrary to previous practice, that if the maximum period for a detention and training order is deemed insufficient in relation to seriousness, the court can impose a s. 91 sentence just above that maximum.

R v Manchester City Youth Court (2002) saw a change in thinking, and in *R (on the application of W) v Thetford Youth Court* (2002) the Divisional Court made clear that justices could not decline jurisdiction when they had no power to impose a custodial sentence simply because they felt custody was warranted. In the *Thetford* case the young offender was an 11-year-old and the circumstances of his offending could not meet the statutory criteria for a detention and training order. The Divisional Court stated that Parliament's intention to restrict the use of custody in relation to those under 14 should be upheld. In *C v Balham Youth Court* (2003) the court similarly confirmed this reasoning in relation to a 14-year-old, stating that cases which came within the s. 91 provision should not be transferred to the Crown Court unless a sentence of more than two years was envisaged.

These cases have clearly had some influence. There has been a decline in the use of s. 91 since then, the total for 2010 being 250 (see Table 11.1 and Figure 11.5) and a total of 242 young offenders sentenced in relation to ss. 90–91 in 2013/14.[25]

Mandatory minimum sentences

In addition there is a new set of provisions in the CJA 2003 (ss. 289–293) which import into the grave/serious crimes provision another means by which this longer sentence can be imposed on 16- and 17-year-olds at the Crown Court. This is similar to the requirement that the offender is over 16 in relation to the mandatory minimum sentences for a third drug trafficking or domestic burglary offence (PCCSA 2000, ss. 110 and 111. The CJA 2003, s. 287 provides for minimum sentences for listed firearm-related offences if the offence is

---

[25] See Table Q5.6 of Ministry of Justice (2015b) *Criminal Justice Statistics, Quarterly Update to September 2014, England and Wales.*

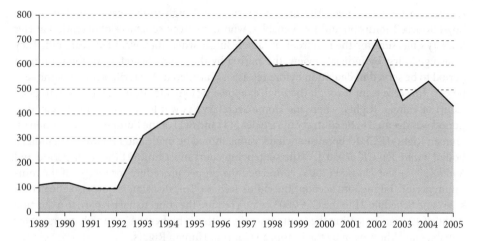

Figure 11.5 Sentences under s. 91 (1980–2005)

Source: NACRO (2007d: 3)

committed when the offender is 16 years old or over.[26] While the prescribed minimum for adults is five years, for an offender under 18 in England and Wales, or under 21 in Scotland, the minimum is three years. If the conditions are met—unless 'exceptional circumstances' apply—the courts must impose on the minor a sentence of detention 'of at least that term' (new s. 91(5)). This provision automatically takes the offences beyond the sentencing powers of the youth court and so within the s. 91 arrangements, but would appear to override the requirement in s. 91(3) that the courts must be 'of the opinion that none of the other methods in which the case may legally be dealt with is suitable'.

Extended sentences

The CJA 2003 introduced new protective sentences for both adult and juvenile 'dangerous' offenders (see Chapter 5, section 5.4) so that after April 2005 until December 2012, when the revised extended sentence came into force, the courts could use the 'old' extended sentence of detention. Both new and old versions constitute a determinate prison sentence with an extended period of supervision on release. The original 2003 version was more draconian before amendments made by the CJIA 2008. The current law is that, for the under-18s, the courts have a discretion to use this sentence if the offence is one of the specified offences listed in Schedule 15 to the CJA 2003, if the offender is deemed to be a risk to the public, and if the court considers the proportionate sentence for this offence would be at least four years (s. 226B). The custodial period must be at least 12 months and the extension period cannot exceed, for adults and minors, five years for violent offences or eight years for sexual offences. Since February 2015 the extension period must be at least a year (s. 226B(5A)).

11.4.3 **Indeterminate sentences**

For murder

The penalty for murder is mandatory—in effect a life sentence—and this has raised issues of rights in relation to the length of time spent in detention for murder before discretionary

---

[26] However, the CJA 2003, s. 291 gives the Secretary of State the necessary powers to increase to 18 the minimum age for the new firearms provisions.

release can be considered. The most important and high-profile case was that of two boys, Robert Thompson and Jon Venables, who were given sentences of detention at Her Majesty's pleasure for their murder of James Bulger when they were ten years old. They challenged, first by judicial review, the raising by the Home Secretary of the minimum period to be served in detention before release is considered (the tariff element of the sentence). This case went through the English appeal system and ultimately to the European Court of Human Rights, where the Home Secretary's power to set a minimum detention period was deemed to be contrary to Articles 5(4) and 6(1) of the European Convention on Human Rights (ECHR) because such decisions should be made and reviewed by a judicial body (*V and T v UK* (2000)).[27] The sentencing court must now set the tariff period and *Smith* (2005) and *Dudson* (2005) concerned the proper procedure for review of the minimum period, taking into account the child's welfare. This decision is now also affected by s. 269 and Schedule 21 to the CJA 2003, which require the court to have regard to a 'starting point' of 12 years in setting the tariff for a minor. This is higher than the eight years set for Venables and Thompson by the European Court of Human Rights.

There has been no noticeable trend in the number of murders by 10–17-year-olds for whom a sentence under s. 90 must be imposed, with total annual figures varying from 10 to 25 cases in 1989–99 (NACRO 2001b) to seven in 2010 (Jacobson *et al.* 2011: 14), with figures peaking around 26 from time to time in between (NACRO 2007d: 2).

For 'dangerous' young offenders

As previously noted, the CJA 2003 introduced provisions for 'dangerous' offenders, including those under 18. As passed there were two options under s. 226—detention for life and detention for public protection (DPP). The latter new sentence was deeply problematic and was amended but has now been repealed by the Legal Aid, Sentencing and Punishment of Offenders Act 2012. Detention for life—as before—can now be imposed if the conviction of the young offender is for a 'serious' specified offence and the court believes that there is 'a significant risk to members of the public' that the young offender will cause them serious harm 'by the commission by him of further specified offences'. For this part of the Act a 'specified offence' is one of the many sexual or violent offences listed in Schedule 15 to the Act, while a 'serious offence' is a subcategory of specified offences for which the maximum penalty for an adult would be life or ten years. If the young offender would otherwise have been eligible for a sentence of detention for life under the PCCSA 2000, s. 91 and the offence seriousness justifies it, the court must impose that sentence. This then is not a new sentence but one with an extra set of criteria within the CJA 2003.

Assessing whether the young person is 'dangerous' as required before these new sentences can be imposed (CJA 2003, s. 229) is, as NACRO's first *Youth Crime Briefing* on the dangerousness provisions pointed out, crucial for the young person, and yet assessment of risk is difficult and prone to inaccuracy. The Asset assessment tool, it contends, is 'something of a compromise between clinical and actuarial approaches to assessment' but 'does not provide any easy answers' (NACRO 2005: 4; see also NACRO 2006). The AssetPlus tool has yet to be assessed in practice.

Some of the specified offences for the purposes of these provisions would not otherwise permit a sentence of long-term detention (NACRO 2004: 7). They require the youth court to consider, when deciding on jurisdiction, whether the criteria are likely to be made out and, if so, to commit the young person for trial at the Crown Court. It may

---

[27] For a detailed discussion of the tariff (minimum term) element and this mandatory sentence more generally, see McDiarmid (2000).

also commit to the Crown Court for sentence, having received more information in the course of the trial.

11.4.4 **Conditions in detention**

The Howard League's participation project, U R Boss, worked with 15–17-year-old boys in YOIs to produce *Life Inside 2010,* a report covering their day-to-day experiences. The project notes that the issue which aroused most passion in nearly all the children was in relation to the food (Howard League for Penal Reform 2010b). The report notes that bags of fruit were in such high demand that children were bullied into buying them and handing them over. 'We were also told how fruit has become currency in one YOI because it is in such short supply' (ibid: 2). This may seem trivial but, given the tedium of life for many young prisoners, meal times are disproportionately important, as is the question of a healthy diet for all children and young people.

As already noted, Prison Service establishments—rather than units run by social services—have been increasingly used for young offenders yet, as with adult prisoners, many young offenders have a history of social exclusion, including unemployment—in relation to those over 16 years of age—and also exclusion from school (see Chapter 6, section 6.3.2). In particular, young offenders are much more likely to have mental health problems than other young people: in 2009 a report said that 43 per cent of children in contact with the youth justice system have emotional or mental health needs (Healthcare Commission 2009; see also Walker and Beckett 2003: 98; Lader *et al.* 2000; Lyon *et al.* 2000; Summerfield 2011: 17) and one in eight has experienced the death of a parent or sibling. The Justice Committee of the House of Commons gave the following list about children and young people in custody:

- 40% have previously been homeless.
- Two out of five girls and one out of four girls have reported suffering violence at home and one in three girls and one in 20 boys report having been sexually abused.
- 39% have been on the child protection register or have experienced neglect or abuse. (para 81)
- A third of children in YOIs had a problem with drugs when they first arrived.
- 18% of 13–18 year olds in custody had depression, 10% anxiety, 9% post-traumatic stress and 5% psychotic symptoms.

(House of Commons Justice Committee 2013c: para 81)

How these vulnerable children are looked after is, therefore, important.

Restraint

Conditions in YOIs have been subject to severe criticism, particularly the use of certain forms of restraint and the neglect of issues leading to the suicide or murder of young offenders in Prison Service establishments. Indeed, Goldson (2006), examining these criticisms in the context of the current United Nations concern about violence against children, concludes that what occurs is 'tantamount to institutional child abuse'.

Clearly there will be an issue of disorder and indiscipline in YOIs: young offenders were involved in prison riots and disturbances in 1990 at Glen Parva and Pucklechurch, for example, and that disorder may stem, at least in part, from frustration with poor conditions (Woolf and Tumim 1991). Inspections of youth offender institutions have, however, provided numerous examples over many years of poor practice in keeping good order. For example, Group 4's privately run Medway Secure Training Centre for 12–14-year-old persistent offenders was severely criticised after an inspection in 1999 for its use of restraints and dangerous neck locks, for using unqualified staff who lacked experience of working with children, and for the absence of procedures for dealing with bullying.[28] Sixteen years later YOTs refused to send young people to the G4S Rainsbrook Secure Training Centre following an Ofsted inspection report which revealed gross misconduct by staff at the facility.[29] The list of actions which the report said should be taken 'immediately' included the following:

- The centre should ensure that all staff working with young people adhere to high standards of behaviour and fully comply with clear professional expectations and codes of conduct

- Ensure that nurses are present at all restraints as soon as practicably possible once response has been called

- ensure anti-ligature knives are fit for use and available at all times

- force should only be used as a last resort. All incidents involving force should be reviewed to learn lessons and continuously improve practice.

                                                                      (Ofsted 2015: 4–5)

Problems in relation to restraint, therefore, have a long history, but tragic events in 2004 provided a public impetus to reform. Gareth Myatt died after losing consciousness while being restrained by staff at the Rainsbrook Secure Centre, and four months later Adam Rickwood was found hanging in his cell after he had been restrained by staff at Hassockfield STC. As a result the YJB published a draft Code of Practice in 2005 'for managing the behaviour of the troubled and troublesome young people that are cared for in secure accommodation', with a final version issued in 2006 (Youth Justice Board 2006b). In response to pressure, the government also set up a review of restraint in juvenile secure settings in 2007. However, the situation proved resistant to radical change. For example, the then Chief Inspector of Prisons, Anne Owers, recommended the closure of Oakhill STC, a privately run centre, because of the 'staggering levels of use of force by staff' (see HM Inspectorate of Prisons 2008).

In 2008 the Justice Minister David Hanson announced that the report of the review would be delayed to allow time for the National Children's Bureau to collect evidence on the use of restraint in secure children's homes (Children's Rights Alliance 2008: 2). When the report was eventually published it recommended that the Prison Service should provide staff with safe restraint techniques, designed specifically for young people and which do not rely on pain compliance (Smallridge and Williamson 2008: para 8.33). For example, the government should forbid use of the 'nose control' technique, its continued use being inconsistent with the earlier removal of the identical 'nose distraction' technique, and batons should not be routinely deployed (ibid: paras 8.7 and 8.39).

In its response to the review (Ministry of Justice/DCSF, 2008), the government accepted or partially accepted most recommendations, notably that the government should permanently remove nose distraction and the double basket hold from the techniques currently used in secure training centres, but, in relation to YOIs, the response was that it was 'looking to replace the nose control technique with a safer alternative within the next six months'. However, the 'exceptional circumstances' exception has been criticised and complaints about treatment have continued. A report by the Children's Commissioner noted

---

[28] The STC received a better report in 2003 (Social Services Inspectorate 2004), though problems persisted.
[29] See Centre for Crime and Justice Studies, 11 June 2015 at http://www.crimeandjustice.org.uk/news/youth-offending-teams-boycott-g4s-secure-training-centre.

that the Ministry of Justice had published in 2010 a manual on safe methods of restraining young people in secure training centres, but summarised criticism of slow progress as suggesting 'distance between internationally agreed standards for the use of restraint and practice in England' (Office of the Children's Commissioner 2011: 7–9). Having asked young offenders for their views and experiences, the report recommended that:

1. young people with experience of the youth justice system are actively involved and engaged in reviewing and evaluating policy and practice (UNCRC, article 12);
2. the deliberate use of pain to enforce order and control is prohibited;
3. internationally agreed standards, as set out by the United Nations (including UNCRC, article 37) and European Council are used as a benchmark for how and when restraint is used on children and young people;
4. these standards are applied consistently between institutions; and
5. best practice is used across the secure estate.

(Office of the Children's Commissioner, 2011: 22–3)

A report by the Howard League also criticised continuing methods of restraint and noted the increase in the average proportion of young people in custody who were restrained to 12 per cent in 2009/10, with more girls than boys restrained (Howard League 2011: 2). Quoting examples of injuries suffered by 15-year-old boys, they stated that '[w]here restraints are necessary and appropriate, there are very clear authorised methods. If restraints are carried out properly these kinds of injuries should never occur. Their presence suggests that the children have been assaulted rather than restrained' (2011: 4).

In 2012 the government issued a new set of guidelines on restraint called *Minimising and Managing Physical Restraint* (MMPR), to be used in STCs and YOIs (Ministry of Justice 2012d): 'MMPR allows for pain compliant restraints to be used on children and young people, including, mandibular angle technique (MAT), wrist flexion and thumb flexion. The mandibular angle technique, for example, involves a member of staff approaching from behind and applying pressure at a point below the ear' (Howard League 2012: 4). The guidelines were updated in 2015, largely in relation to procedures and monitoring.[30] Nevertheless, there are clearly still infractions: in January 2016 police began investigating allegations of abuse by G4S staff at Medway STC.[31]

Recent YJB statistics have shown that the numbers of restrictive physical interventions (RPIs) have decreased but that the number of RPIs per 100 young people has not:

The number of RPIs per 100 young people increased by 60 per cent from the year ending March 2010 (17.6 RPIs per 100 young people to 28.2 in the year ending March 2015) and remains consistent compared with the year ending March 2014 with a decrease of less than 1 per cent.

(Ministry of Justice/Youth Justice Board 2016: 54)

Willow has commented as follows:

Child prisoners are exposed to practices that would invite state intervention were they to happen in the community. A parent who locked a child in a tiny room for more than 20 hours a day would, at the very least, be sent on a compulsory course to correct his or her

---

[30] See https://www.gov.uk/government/uploads/system/uploads/attachment_data/file/456672/minimising-managing-physical-restraint.pdf.

[31] See, for example, http://prisonwatchuk.com/2016/01/13/g4s-staff-sacked-over-allegations-of-abuse-of-young-offenders/.

abusive behaviour. Yet such mistreatment is routinely perpetrated by a punitive state that abandons child protection norms when it comes to young offenders.

> (Carolyne Willow: Prison a Treacherous Place for a Child at http://thejusticegap.com/
> 2015/06/prison-a-treacherous-place-for-a-child/)

Gooch (2015) also argues that 'thus far, the treatment of child prisoners has not given appropriate recognition to the status of the child prisoner as a child and independent rights holder with the effect that physical restraint has been used inappropriately, routinely and, in the worst cases, unlawfully, exposing children to harm' (Gooch 2015: abstract).

> The Government appears to have given only scant regard to the possibility that the use of pain compliance techniques is in breach of international human rights law (see written answer to Baroness Stern's question, Hansard, 9 Nov 2011: Column WA71). The MoJ has stipulated that such techniques are only permitted if there is an immediate risk of serious physical harm . . . However, this does not meet the State's obligations under international human rights law, which does not envisage the deliberate infliction of pain for any purposes.

> (Gooch 2015: 15)

Safeguarding and vulnerability

Safeguarding young people in detention has a wider remit than that of restraint techniques. A report by HM Inspectorate of Prisons (2004) found that over one-third of those 15–18-year-olds surveyed had felt unsafe at some time while in custody (including all the 15-year-old girls), a quarter said they had not received any visitors, and only 30 per cent of boys said it had been easy for their parents to visit. More than a decade ago the Youth Justice Board had indicated that there needed to be 'a greater emphasis on safeguarding arrangements to protect children from suicide, self-harm, bullying and harm from staff and other adults' (see NACRO 2003d: 1). Unfortunately recent statistics about 'behaviour management' of young people in custody are not encouraging: 'The number of assaults per 100 young people increased from 10.1 in both 2010/11 and 2012/13 to 14.6 in 2013/14' and 'The number of self harm incidents per 100 young people increased from 4.1 in 2010/11 and 5.2 in 2012/13 to 6.6 in 2013/14' (Ministry of Justice/Youth Justice Board 2015a: 5). Sadly the latest available figures show a further increase to 7.7 incidents per 100 young people: a 17 per cent increase (Ministry of Justice/Youth Justice Board 2016: 55).

The propensity to suicide is higher amongst prisoners, including minors, than amongst the population outside: 25 boys aged 15–17 hanged themselves while in custody in the period 1990–2003 and the Prisons and Probation Ombudsman was subsequently given the responsibility for investigating all deaths in custody. When Liam McManus, a 15-year-old boy serving a six-week sentence for breach of a supervision order, was found hanged in his cell in 2007 at Lancaster Farms Young Offenders' Institution, the tally of juveniles to die in custody since 1990 reached 30.[32] The spring of 2011 then saw the deaths of five teenagers in five different institutions across England in five weeks. A report published in 2014 and entitled 'Deaths of Children in Custody: Action Taken, Lessons Learnt' states: 'Sixteen boys have died in custody since the YJB took responsibility for placements and commissioning in the secure estate in April 2000. With the exception of Gareth Myatt, all of the boys' deaths are thought to have been self-inflicted' (Youth Justice Board 2014c: 4). This report lists actions taken under each heading: it is to be hoped they are having a significant impact.

---

[32] Reported in *The Guardian*, 30 November 2007 on p. 15.

Goldson has criticised the lack of a wider enquiry:

> On one level, state agencies acknowledge the harmful and violent rhythms of penal regimes . . . But . . . The tightly circumscribed nature of acknowledgement is such that, despite the deaths of children in custody, not a single independent public inquiry has been initiated. Indeed, the UK government and relevant state agencies have steadfastly resisted authoritative calls for a transparent, comprehensive and truly independent inquiry into child deaths in penal custody in England and Wales.
>
> (Goldson 2014)

11.4.5 Equality issues

Girls in prison

While the majority of young detainees are boys and their conditions are a source of concern, there are also problems specific to girls. In October 2015 there were only 32 girls in custody[33]—evidence of a considerable reduction over the last decade—and the Youth Justice Board stopped commissioning places in YOIs for girls in 2013. However, little has been researched or written on gender differences in juvenile justice since the 1970s and 1980s until recently (see Piper 2006, 2009).

Girls in Prison (Ofsted 2004) and a report by the Howard League for Penal Reform (2004), *Advice, Understanding and Underwear*, provided evidence of what amounts to discriminatory treatment of girls in custodial establishments, stemming from the much smaller numbers of young female detainees and from their different needs. The comments by the girls on the community part of their sentence—which they felt was too risky for them—and on the standard of resettlement support were also negative (Ofsted Report 2004; see also Douglas and Plugge 2007).

A report by the Children's Commissioner also found gender differences in offender responses to physical restraint:

> The use of restraint generated strong emotional responses from most of the participants, but the way girls experienced restraint varied dramatically from the boys. Many of the girls felt that the procedure impacted on them negatively in terms of their mental health and well being, and they disliked it intensely. Boys in contrast reported feelings of anger, indifference or they accepted that it was a necessary element of the custodial regime.
>
> (Office of the Children's Commissioner 2011: 21)

An inquiry in 2012 made the following 'key points':

> There is a lack of awareness among magistrates and other professionals of the specific needs of girls ...

> Magistrates are confusing welfare needs with high risk of reoffending and increasing the severity of the sentence or 'up-tariffing' girls . . .

> There is a lack of gender-specific provision for girls once sentenced

> The needs of girls are overlooked due to the small number of girls in the penal system

> Contrary to the United Nations Convention on the Rights of the Child, custody is not invariably being used as a last resort for girls.
>
> (All Party Parliamentary Group on Women in the Penal System 2012: 1)

---

[33] Week ending 16 October 2015: http://www.howardleague.org/weekly-prison-watch/.

There is still pressure for changes to be made. 'An Agenda for the New Government' sets out the parameters for better practice:

> Based on the specific needs and vulnerabilities of girls and young women, practice with this group needs to be shaped by three related gender-sensitive dimensions:
>
> 1. **Vulnerabilities** resulting from experiences of trauma and abuse should be addressed
>
> 2. **Relationships** are a critical focus, including abuse in past relationships, developing trust with professionals now, and promoting positive future relationships
>
> 3. **Empowerment** to make positive choices will counterbalance vulnerabilities and experiences of subordination.
>
> (Ryan *et al.* 2015: 6)

Young black and minority ethnic prisoners

Between April 2005 and April 2006 the numbers of 'white' children and young people in the secure estate dropped from 1945 to 589, whereas the corresponding numbers for 'black' children and young people went from 304 to 215.[34] There are, therefore, issues of racial discrimination for young offenders as for adults (see Chapter 9), with black children over-represented in custodial establishments.[35] During 2014/15, 40 per cent of prisoners aged under 18 were from black, Asian, mixed race or 'other' ethnicity backgrounds (Ministry of Justice/Youth Justice Board 2016: 48). Clearly this raises questions as to the fairness of pre-court processes.

However, there are indications that young black and ethnic minority prisoners may not be treated appropriately in custody. Wilson's ethnographic research on a small group of 16–17-year-old young black men in a YOI found that, for this group at least, 'the Govs [the staff] were universally perceived to be able to "get away with more" than the police in the community' with regard to racist behaviour (Wilson 2003: 422–3).

Education

In 2013, Chris Grayling, then Secretary of State for Justice, said that young offenders in custody are ten times more likely than the population as a whole to have learning disabilities (23–32 per cent versus 2–4 per cent): 'Around half of 15 to 17 year olds entering custody had the literacy or numeracy levels you would expect of children in the last years of primary school.'[36] Yet these problems are often neglected, notwithstanding the potential for imprisonment to exacerbate them. For example, 'The number of GCSE passes attained by young people in prison has dropped by nearly a half. There were 119 GCSE passes in public sector YOIs in 2010–11, compared to 232 in 2009–10' (Howard League 2013: 5).

According to the Consultation Paper 'Transforming Youth Custody: Putting education at the heart of detention', the Coalition government intended to put 'high quality education at the centre of youth custody'. The context however was the much criticised proposal for secure colleges. Nevertheless, the Paper asked respondents to consider issues of 'tailoring education to young people in custody' (Ministry of Justice 2013e). The government's response to the Consultation focused mostly (eight out of the ten pages on education) on provision within the proposed secure colleges (Ministry of Justice 2014d). The provision for establishing secure colleges is in the Criminal Justice and Courts Act 2015 ss. 38–40 but Michael Gove, as the (then) Justice Secretary of the Conservative government, announced

---

[34] Ministry of Justice: Youth Custody Report August 2015 Chart 7 accessed at https://www.gov.uk/government/statistics/youth-custody-data.

[35] Black Britons represent around 2.8 per cent of the general population.

[36] https://www.gov.uk/government/speeches/crime-in-context-speech.

in July 2015 that the building of the first large college would not go ahead. That has been welcomed, given that, as Sara Campion MP pointed out in debate, 'I also find the fact that there was no commitment for qualified teachers extremely worrying, and it confirms to me that the college is just a holding borstal, rather than an educational establishment as it is described.'[37]

There are also problems with the management of the transition from custody to community (see Hollingsworth 2012a). A report by Ofsted (2010) drew attention to the variable standards of support when children and young people move into and out of custody. The report highlights how poor initial assessment of learning needs and insufficient preparation for independent living leaves children and young people ill-equipped for outside life. The government response to the *Transforming Youth Justice* paper states that 'In advance of a young person's release from custody, it is vital that a place in education, training or employment is secured and begins on their first day back in the community' (Ministry of Justice 2014d: para 40), but it is too soon to assess the success of this aim.

11.5 The role of rights for young offenders

11.5.1 Cases

The policy of the Howard League in recent years, particularly since the implementation of the Human Rights Act 1998, has been to use the courts to challenge government policies on the treatment of young offenders (Crook 2003). We have already referred to the case which successfully challenged the interpretation in Prison Service Order (PSO) 4950 of the duty of the local authority to children in need in a custodial establishment in that area (see Chapter 6, section 6.3.4). A further case, that of *R (on the application of BP) v Secretary of State for the Home Department* (2003), concerned a 17-year-old who had been in what amounted to solitary confinement for over 23 hours a day during two periods of five and four days and who claimed breaches of Articles 3 and 8 of the ECHR. The court ruled that the rules of the institution had been breached and that insufficient regard had been had to the young man's known vulnerability, but did not expressly forbid the use of segregation.

Another Howard League case—*R (K) v Manchester City Council* (2006)—in relation to assessing whether a child in custody would be 'in need' on release led to a judgment against the argument that the YOT was the 'agency best suited to meeting the needs of K . . . The defendant authority is required itself to carry out an assessment. It is not entitled to delegate that function.'

The case of *R (C) and Secretary of State* (2008) considered the use of restraint on children in secure training centres. The court made it clear that restraint for good order and discipline engages Article 3 of the ECHR, and that it would be for the Secretary of State to justify the necessity of force. The scenarios put to the court by the private company running the STC consisted of examples where restraint was considered necessary to ensure discipline and a safe custodial environment. These scenarios were not accepted by the court as sufficient to justify the use of force for good order and discipline. In the case of *R (M) v The Chief Magistrate* (2010), the legal team working at the Howard League successfully argued that due process of law and good practice in any disciplinary proceeding or appeals mean that the person concerned should know what is the case against them. The child, known as M, had been awarded extra days by an independent adjudicator. He had

---

[37] See: http://www.sarahchampionmp.com/wp-content/uploads/2014/06/Giant-childrens-prison-should-not-go-ahead-says-Sarah.pdf.

had no legal advice and was not legally represented. The judgment highlights the need for a proactive approach to legal representation for young people facing adjudications and, as a consequence, the Prison Service will have to consider possible changes. In this case the judge, Collins J, made the following significant comment: 'The welfare of the child is an important and indeed fundamental consideration in determining how a child who has committed offences should be dealt with . . . a young person's welfare is something that has to be properly taken into account and, indeed, that is clear from section 37 of the 1998 Act' (at para 7).

In *R (on the application of MA) v Independent Adjudicator* 2013 the Howard League represented all the young men, aged 17, and the High Court adjudged the privately run Ashfield children's prison to have unlawfully punished seven boys after they were involved in a protest over conditions on their wing: they were kept in isolation and five were subjected to an informal 'shadow segregation' regime, deemed unlawful because it lacked any of the safeguards applicable to formal segregation procedures. The case also upheld that their right to a fair trial had been violated by the failure to provide essential documents in advance of hearings before the Independent Adjudicator.

11.5.2 Conventions

Rights-based jurisprudence can, then, be used successfully to improve the lives of young offenders. Not only are there rights applying to all age groups—notably, for the UK, the Human Rights Act 1998 and the jurisprudence of the ECHR, to which we have referred elsewhere—but there are several conventions applying exclusively to minors. The United Nations Convention on the Rights of the Child (CRC) is the best known and the most influential statement of principle on children's rights generally, but there are associated conventions which focus on juvenile justice: the Beijing Rules 1985 (the UN Standard Minimum Rules for the Protection of Juvenile Liberty), the Riyadh Guidelines 1990 (UN Guidelines for the Prevention of Juvenile Delinquency), and the Tokyo Rules 1990 (UN Standard Minimum Rules for Non-Custodial Measures). The CRC also published a General Comment (No. 10, 2007) on 'Children's rights in juvenile justice'.

Yet the use of rights as a tool for improving the lives of children, whether as offenders or not, can produce problems. Their employment can produce different approaches to children's welfare and their utility is sometimes questioned.[38] A recent research-based article has argued that 'the treatment of child prisoners has not given appropriate recognition to the status of the child prisoner as a child and independent rights holder with the effect that physical restraint has been used inappropriately, routinely and, in the worst cases, unlawfully, exposing children to harm' (Gooch 2015: 1).

Article 40(2)(b) of the CRC enjoins governments to ensure in particular that '[e]very child alleged or accused of having infringed the penal law has at least the following guarantees' which include being presumed innocent until proven guilty, having access to information and legal advice, and being dealt with 'without delay by a competent, independent and impartial authority', with access to review of a penal decision, as well as having his or her privacy respected. We have already noted that Article 40 also promotes separate and different treatment and it would appear that the youth court is sufficiently separate to comply with this (Fortin 2003: 563). The CRC does not give any direct remedy for infringements, however. Those jurisdictions which have ratified the CRC are deemed to have promised to

---

[38] For a useful review of the different theoretical perspectives and of the sources of international rights, see Fortin (2009: Part One and also pp. 714–28 in relation to issues raised in this chapter). For a theoretical critique of reliance on rights to achieve improvements for children, see King (1997a).

amend and operate the laws of the country to bring them in line with the CRC. The (only) sanction is the international and national censure when the Committee on the Rights of the Child publicly reports on the extent of a government's compliance with the CRC's principles. The UK government has suffered criticism in response to its first two Reports to the Committee, particularly, as we noted in Chapter 6, in regard to the age of criminal responsibility.

For individuals and for pressure groups supporting young offenders, the ECHR may provide a surer remedy. Since October 2002 children, as people, have been able to complain directly to the domestic court that their rights under the ECHR are being infringed. Several Articles, notably Article 3 (no inhuman or degrading treatment), Article 6 (the right to a fair trial), and Article 7 (no punishment without law), are of potential utility for children as well as for adult defendants and offenders. The courts have ruled that the lack of legal representation for minors in Children's Hearings in Scotland, though civil proceedings, has infringed the child's rights under Article 6 (*S v Principal Reporter and the Lord Advocate* (2001)). Failing to warn a young person that an admission of guilt regarding a sexual assault—as part of the process of giving a reprimand or warning—will result in their being placed on the sex offenders' register has also been acknowledged as a breach of Article 6.[39] However, Hollingsworth (2007; see also 2012b) argues, in the light of recent jurisprudence, that there is a lack of judicial consistency in relation to children's rights under the ECHR.

The procedures adopted by the youth courts are generally compliant with the ECHR and magistrates. However, the Crown Court, to which minors are transferred in relation to more serious crimes is more problematic. The high-profile trial of Venables and Thompson, aged 11, brought this issue to public attention. The formal setting, the relentless publicity, their relative isolation, and the length of the proceedings were at odds with the requirement under the CRC Article 40(1) that they be treated 'in a manner consistent with the promotion of the child's sense of dignity and worth', and the requirement of the Beijing Rules that the proceedings 'be conducted in an atmosphere of understanding' where the juvenile can properly participate (r 14.2). More importantly, it was argued to the European Court that it infringed Articles 3 and 6 of the ECHR. While the claim under Article 3 was rejected, an infringement of Article 6—the right to a fair trial—was upheld because they had been unable to participate fully in a trial pitched at the level of understanding of adult participants.

This case (*V and T v United Kingdom* (2000)) did not prohibit the use of the Crown Court for minors, although it led to a direction by the Lord Chief Justice (*Practice Note (trial of children and young people)* 2000) requiring a variety of practical changes to make the courtroom and process more conducive to the participation of minors. The result is, in relation to the Crown Court, that 'children are still required to sit in a dock, stared at by a jury, and cross-examined by barristers' (Fortin 2003: 565).

Of perhaps most importance, given the problems we have reviewed in the previous section, is the extensive use of detention for young offenders by the courts in England and Wales. Article 37 of the CRC states that it should be 'a measure of last resort' and the Committee on the Rights of the Child has criticised the UK for the earlier ages at which detention is now used, as well as the greater numbers being detained, the longer sentences available, and the unacceptable conditions in YOIs (Committee on the Rights of the Child 2002: paras 59–62).

---

[39] *R (U) v Comr of Metropolitan Police; R (U) v Chief Constable of Durham Constabulary* (2002): see Fortin (2003: 562–3).

11.5.3 **The utility of rights**

As Scraton and Haydon (2002) have argued, it is too easy for the government to hide a lack of attention to the rights of minors behind a rhetoric of rights. In reference to the UK's Second Report to the Committee on the Rights of the Child (UK Government 1999), they make the following comment: 'Using a discourse of "rights" and "responsibilities", the punitive potential of the [1998] Act is reconstructed as enabling, supportive welfare intervention.' In an ironic interpretation of Article 3, the report states: 'It is in the interests of children and young people themselves to recognise and accept responsibility, and to receive assistance in tackling criminal behaviour' (Scraton and Haydon 2002: 321).

The 'clarification' of Articles 37 and 40 of the UN CRC in the General Comment on rights in juvenile justice (Committee on the Rights of the Child 2007) has been helpful. It points out, for example, that Article 3 should be heeded in relation to young offenders: the best interests of the child should be a 'primary consideration' but we saw in Chapter 6 that even the weak welfare test in s. 44 of the 1933 Children and Young Persons Act is being downgraded in importance. However, as Kilkelly and Lundy (2006) argue, the CRC can be used as an 'auditing' tool to assess the extent of compliance or non-compliance within policy and practice.

Ferguson (2013) and Hollingsworth (2014) also point to a 'theory gap' in relation to the rights of young offenders. Hollingsworth, for example, argues for 'a particular category of childhood rights, "foundational rights", that support the conditions that make it possible for the child to live a *de facto* fully autonomous life at the point when she acquires *de jure* autonomy' and so asks for an approach 'allowing us to demand special treatment for children without diminishing their claims to rights *qua* offender' (Hollingsworth 2014: 9, 12). Weijers earlier made a similar point: there is the problem that in dealing with minors the criminal justice system 'will always have to take account of the dilemma that, while they are developing towards responsibility, they are presumed to be dependent and not yet fully responsible' (Weijers 2002: 139).

Unfortunately, conditions and suicides in youth prisons do not lead to a national 'scandal' in the same way that some other child deaths do: Victoria Climbié was portrayed as a victim, Gareth Myatt was not (see Drakeford and Butler 2007). The pressures on politicians to 'talk tough', to respond to perceived public opinion, and not to challenge negative images of young people make it very difficult to successfully implement either the welfare or the rights of young offenders.

11.6 **Reflecting on the issues**

11.6.1 **What is justice for juveniles?**

Part A of this book examined sentencing principles and policies, mainly with reference to adult offenders, but, of course, much of the discussion in previous chapters is also relevant to those under 18 years of age. Rights are as relevant for young offenders as for adults and determination of their sentence and punishment should also be governed by the proportionality principle. Chapter 6, when focusing on restorative justice, referred mainly to schemes for young offenders (section 6.2.3) because the youth justice system is where restorative policies are currently most important. Further, while the justifications for the punishment of minors have often been located within different theoretical frameworks, retributivism and utilitarianism have underpinned those frameworks. The developments in out-of-court processing which we reviewed in Chapter 6 (section 6.3) have also legitimised the lack of any substantial change to youth courts: they continue to be used basically like adult sentencing courts. Indeed, arguably, the raising of the upper age limit of the youth court and the changes made by legislation in and since 1998 have further aligned the adult and youth courts.

However, 'The "new" never replaces the old. In the twenty-first century discourse of protection, restoration, punishment, responsibility, rehabilitation, welfare, retribution, diversion, human rights and so on exist alongside each other in some perpetually uneasy and contradictory manner' (Muncie 2004: 249; see also Muncie 2006; Cobb 2007: 369). Many of the provisions enshrined in legislation passed in 1994–2003 were developed in the 1980s, often as ad hoc local initiatives, using powers and resources available to the Police and Probation Services and Social Work Departments. *No More Excuses* (Home Office 1997) also echoed a much earlier document in its use of the courts to order preventive programmes: in 1927 an official report had concluded that the practice of cautioning to divert from court was 'objectionable' because it was 'usurping the functions of the tribunal' (Moloney Report 1927: 22) and the court was perceived as the site for assessment (see Pratt 1986: 214–19). The Ingleby Report had also argued that trivial offences are 'often only a symptom of an underlying condition requiring early and specialised treatment that was revealed only when the child came before the court' (1960: 51). On the other hand, the current practice trend to use more diversionary community resolutions, and the greater flexibility in using cautions and conditional cautions, has echoes of much earlier examples of diversion from criminal processes.

In Chapter 6, section 6.3.1 we reviewed policy reasons for supporting diversion in the 1970s and 1980s and there is clearly continuity between those factors and the policy imperatives in the early twenty-first century, notably the need to legitimise the system by reducing offending and by locating initiatives within—or in proximity to—the legal process. There are further continuities in the policy desire to reduce expenditure by diversion from custody and also to reduce recidivism through pre-court interventions.

Whether the repackaging of 'old' products incorporates lessons from the past is debatable (see Downes 2001/2: 8). There is the related concern that there is little acknowledgement of the disadvantages of pre-court processing. Cautioning was not without its critics in the 1970s and 1980s, particularly in relation to the issue of whether there was 'injustice by geography'; whether discriminatory decision-making was taking place, which research suggested there might be (Ditchfield 1976; Farrington and Bennet 1981; Landau 1981); or whether there was 'net widening' (Pratt 1986: 212). Similar criticisms have developed more recently: see, for example, Field (2007); Hine (2007); and Koffman and Dingwall (2007).

We cannot assume, however, that the effective lowering of the age of criminal responsibility in England and Wales by abolishing the presumption of *doli incapax* equates to a more punitive policy. There are jurisdictions with a low age of criminal responsibility but with infrequent use of criminal processes for children, as, for example, in Scotland, where the age was still eight until 2011 (when s. 52 of the Criminal Justice and Licensing (Scotland) Act 2010 raised the age to 12). Conversely, a youth justice policy which aims to make young people more accountable does not necessarily require a lower age: the Canadian Youth Criminal Justice Act 1999 left the age of criminal responsibility at 12 (Junger-Tas 2002: 33). What matters is how the possibility of prosecution is used.

There is, in any case, a difficulty in trying to assess current trends in current youth justice policy and practice (see Pitts 2015). The policies of the Labour government had been critiqued and were being rethought by 2010 (see for example, Carrabine 2010; Home Office *et al.* 2008; Silvestri 2011; Solomon and Garside 2008). The Coalition government issued *Breaking the Cycle*, which stated that '[i]ntervening early in the lives of children at risk and their families, before behaviour becomes entrenched, can present our best chance to break the cycle of crime' (Ministry of Justice 2010a: para 230)[40] and accepted the need for 'a local, joined up approach to address the multiple disadvantages that many young offenders have and the chaotic lifestyles that many lead' (ibid: para 232). However, 'The Conservative Government's policy in relation to children who break the law has shown considerable continuity with the approach of the Coalition administration which it replaced' (Bateman 2015: 2–3) and it is not clear how it will develop over the next five years.

In 2011 Muncie argued that 'youth justice throughout the United Kingdom now appears ever more hybrid and contradictory' (Muncie 2011: 51) and it is as difficult to summarise past trends as it is to predict future trends. There have been encouraging developments in relation to preventive and restorative justice projects and a greater understanding on the part of some of our judiciary about both the rights and welfare of young offenders. Yet there is still a very worrying propensity on the part of the press and the government to talk tough, with resulting sentencing and penal policy which is disproportionate or unlikely to be effective. It is a pity that this more 'audible' strand of youth justice policy is punitive and underpinned by images of minors which focus on near-adult and 'dangerous' aspects because it obscures the fact that there are positive approaches in juvenile justice and developments in other areas of government policy which take into account what is known about the multiple causality of offending and which aim to respond to social deprivation and need. Their lower priority precludes a wider debate about young offenders.

So what *is* justice for 10–17-year-olds? Developments in children's services around 'safeguarding' and the links now being made across youth justice, child protection, and children's services are, we hope, allowing more focus on the welfare of young offenders. However, we would argue that rights—as well as a greater focus on welfare—could be more important in resolving at least some of the conditions and processes identified as unacceptable.

11.6.2 **Case study**

The following case study covers material in Chapter 6 as well as this chapter. There is guidance in the Online Resource Centre to help you advise these two young people.

**online
resource
centre**

Bart aged 13, and his cousin Lisa aged 17, were arrested in a video warehouse which they had entered by prising open a small window. They were taken to the local police station where, in the presence of a solicitor and an appropriate adult, Bart confessed to burglary. Bart had been given a caution the previous year.

You are the solicitor:

1. Explain to Bart what decision the police are likely to make about him.
2. Explain to Bart what would happen if the police decided to give him a youth conditional caution.

Then:

Lisa was found to have stolen and hidden a quantity of videos before the arrival of the police. Lisa who had been given a youth caution for an offence a year previously, was prosecuted for the offence of burglary of commercial premises (Theft Act 1968, s. 9) for which the maximum penalty is ten years. She decided to plead guilty.

3. Explain to Lisa what options are open to the youth court and which option they are most likely to choose.

---

[40] See, for a discussion of early intervention, Piper (2008).

4. Explain to Lisa whether the options would be different if she had committed burglary of a residential property (for which the maximum penalty is 14 years).

Consider this alternative scenario:

Assume that Bart and Lisa confess to having jointly committed the offence of having possession of a Class B drug with intent to supply (Misuse of Drugs Act 1971, s. 5(3)—for which the maximum penalty is 14 years' imprisonment). The youth court decides that a custodial sentence is the only appropriate sentence for both of them.

5. Explain to Bart and Lisa how and where might such a sentence be imposed and on what criteria. (Bart is still 13 and Lisa is still 17.)

11.6.3 Discussion questions

1. 'Rights have proved to have limited value in improving conditions within the secure estate for children and young people.' Do you agree?

2. To what extent do you think that civil orders to address anti-social behaviour are problematic when imposed on those under 18 years of age?

Bibliography

ABEL, R. (1982) *The Politics of Informal Justice*. New York, Academic Press.

ACPO (2013) *Youth Offender Case Disposal Gravity Factor Matrix*, ACPO. Available at http://cps.gov.uk/legal/assets/uploads/files/Gravity%20Matrix%20May09.pdf.

ADLER, R. (1985) *Taking Juvenile Justice Seriously*. Edinburgh, Scottish Academic Press.

ADVISORY COUNCIL ON THE PENAL SYSTEM (1977) *The Length of Prison Sentences*, Interim Report. London, HMSO.

ADVISORY COUNCIL ON THE PENAL SYSTEM (1978) *The Review of Maximum Sentences*, Final Report. London, HMSO.

AEBI, M. AND CHOPIN, J. (2014) *Council of Europe Annual Penal Statistics—SPACE II Survey Persons Serving Non-Custodial Sanctions and Measures in 2013*, PC-CP (2014) 12, Council of Europe.

AEBI, M., DELGRANDE, N. AND MARGUET, Y. (2011) *Annual Penal Statistics, SPACE II 2009, Survey on Non-Custodial Sanctions and Measures in the Council of Europe Member Countries*, PC-CP (2011) 4, Council of Europe.

AERTSEN, I., DAEMS, T., AND ROBERT, L. (eds) (2006) *Institutionalizing Restorative Justice*. Cullompton, Willan.

ALDRIDGE, M. AND EADIE, T. (1997) 'Manufacturing an Issue: The Case of Probation Officer Training' *Critical Social Policy* Vol 17(1), 111–24.

ALL PARTY PARLIAMENTARY GROUP ON WOMEN IN THE PENAL SYSTEM (2011) *Women in the Penal System, Second Report on Women with Particular Vulnerabilities in the Criminal Justice System*. London, Howard League.

ALL PARTY PARLIAMENTARY GROUP ON WOMEN IN THE PENAL SYSTEM (2012) *Inquiry on Girls: From Courts to Custody*. London: Howard League for Penal Reform.

ALLDRIDGE, P. AND MUMFORD, A. (2005) 'Tax Evasion and the Proceeds of Crime Act 2002' *Legal Studies* Vol 25(3), 353–73.

ALLEN, F. (1981) *The Decline of the Rehabilitative Ideal*. New Haven, Yale University Press.

ALLEN, R. (1996) *Children and Crime*. London, Institute for Public Policy Research.

ALLEN, R. (2011) *Last Resort? Exploring the Reduction in Child Imprisonment 2008–11*. London, Prison Reform Trust.

ALLEN, R. (2014) *Justice Reinvestment: Empty Slogan or Sustainable Future for Penal Policy?*, London, Transform Justice.

ALLEN, R. AND STERN, V. (eds) (2007) *Justice Reinvestment: A New Approach to Crime and Justice*. London, ICPS.

ALTHUSSER, L. (1971) *Lenin and Philosophy*. London, New Left Books.

ALZNAUER, M. (2015) *Hegel's Theory of Responsibility*. Cambridge, Cambridge University Press.

AMADI, J. (2008) *Piloting Penalty Notices for Disorder on 10- to 15-year-olds: Results from a One Year Pilot*, Ministry of Justice Research Series 19/08. London, Ministry of Justice.

AMERICAN FRIENDS SERVICES COMMITTEE (1971) *Struggle for Justice: A Report on Crime and Punishment in America*. New York, Hill and Wang.

AMOS, M. (2004) 'R v Secretary of State for the Home Department ex parte Anderson— Ending the Home Secretary's Sentencing Role' *Modern Law Review* Vol 67(1), 108–23.

ANDENAES, J. (1974) *Punishment and Deterrence*. Ann Arbor, University of Michigan Press.

ANGIOLINI, E. (2012) *Commission on Women Offenders, Final Report*. Edinburgh, Commission on Women Offenders.

ARCHARD, D. (1993) *Children, Rights and Childhood*. London, Routledge.

ARES, E. AND COE, S. (2013) *Dangerous Dogs*, Standard Note SN/SC/4348, House of Commons Library. Available at: http://www.parliament.uk/briefing-papers/SN04348.

ASHWORTH, A. (1983) *Sentencing and Penal Policy*. London, Weidenfeld and Nicolson.

ASHWORTH, A. (1984) 'Techniques of Guidance on Sentencing' *Criminal Law Review*, 519–30.

ASHWORTH, A. (1987) 'Disentangling Disparity' in C. Pennington and S. Lloyd-Bostock (eds) *The Psychology of Sentencing*. Oxford, Oxford Centre for Socio-legal Studies, Wolfson College, Oxford University, 24–7.

ASHWORTH, A. (1992) 'Non-Custodial Sentences' *Criminal Law Review*, 242–51.

ASHWORTH, A. (1993) 'Victim Impact Statements and Sentencing' *Criminal Law Review*, 498–509.

ASHWORTH, A. (1998a) 'Structuring Sentencing Discretion' and 'Four Techniques for Reducing Sentencing Disparity' in A. von Hirsch and A. Ashworth (eds) *Principled Sentencing: Readings on Theory and Practice* (2nd edn). Oxford, Hart Publishing, 212–19, 227–39.

ASHWORTH, A. (1998b) *The Criminal Process* (2nd edn). Oxford, Clarendon Press.

ASHWORTH, A. (2000) *Sentencing and Criminal Justice* (3rd edn). London, Butterworths.

ASHWORTH, A. (2002a) 'Responsibilities, Rights and Restorative Justice' *British Journal of Criminology* Vol 42, 578–95.

ASHWORTH, A. (2002b) 'Sentencing' in M. Maguire *et al.* (eds) *The Oxford Handbook of Criminology* (3rd edn). Oxford, Oxford University Press, 1076–112.

ASHWORTH, A. (2003) 'New Sentencing Proposals for England and Wales' *Sentencing Observer* No. 2, 9.

ASHWORTH, A. (2004) 'Criminal Justice Act 2003: Part 2: Criminal Justice Reform—Principle, Human Rights and Public Protection' *Criminal Law Review*, 516–32.

ASHWORTH, A. (2005) *Sentencing and Criminal Justice* (4th edn). Cambridge, Cambridge University Press.

ASHWORTH, A. (2008) 'English Sentencing Guidelines in their Public and Political Context' in A. Freiberg and K. Gelb (eds) *Penal Populism, Sentencing Councils and Sentencing Policy*. Cullompton, Willan Publishing, 112–25.

ASHWORTH, A. (2010) *Sentencing and Criminal Justice* (4th edn). Cambridge, Cambridge University Press.

ASHWORTH, A. (2011) 'Re-evaluating the Justifications for Aggravation and Mitigation at Sentencing' in J. Roberts (ed) *Mitigation and Aggravation at Sentencing*. Cambridge, Cambridge University Press, 21–39.

ASHWORTH, A. (2013) 'The Struggle for Supremacy in Sentencing' in A. Ashworth and J. Roberts (eds) *Sentencing Guidelines: Exploring the English Model*. Oxford, Oxford University Press, 15–30.

ASHWORTH, A. (2014) 'A Decade of Human Rights in Criminal Justice' *Criminal Law Review*, 325–37.

ASHWORTH, A. (2015) *Sentencing and Criminal Justice* (6th edn). Cambridge, Cambridge University Press.

ASHWORTH, A. AND PLAYER, E. (1998) 'Sentencing, Equal Treatment and the Impact of Sanctions' in A. Ashworth and M. Wasik (eds) *Fundamentals of Sentencing Theory*. Oxford, Clarendon Press.

ASHWORTH, A. AND PLAYER, E. (2005) 'The Criminal Justice Act 2003: The Sentencing Provisions' *Modern Law Review* Vol 68(5), 822–38.

ASHWORTH, A. AND ROBERTS, J. (2013) 'The Origin and Nature of the Sentencing Guidelines in England and Wales' in A. Ashworth and J. Roberts (eds) *Sentencing Guidelines: Exploring the English Model*. Oxford, Oxford University Press, 1–14.

ASHWORTH, A. AND VON HIRSCH, A. (1997) 'Recognising Elephants: The Problem of the Custody Threshold' *Criminal Law Review*, 187–200.

ASHWORTH, A. AND ZEDNER, L. (2014) *Preventive Justice*. Oxford, Oxford University Press.

ASHWORTH, A., ZEDNER, L., AND TOMLIN, P. (eds) (2013) *Prevention and the Limits of Criminal Law*. Oxford, Oxford University Press.

ASNAUER, M. (2015) *Hegel's Theory of Responsibility*. Cambridge, Cambridge University Press.

ASP, P. (2010) 'Previous Convictions and Proportionate Punishment under Swedish Law' in J. V. Roberts and A. von Hirsch (eds) *Previous Convictions at Sentencing, Theoretical and Applied Perspectives*. Oxford, Hart, 207–26.

ASQUITH, S. (2002) 'Justice, Retribution and Children' in J. Muncie, G. Hughes, and E. McLaughlin (eds) *Youth Justice, Critical Readings*. London, Sage, 275–83.

AUDIT COMMISSION (1996) *Misspent Youth: Young People and Crime*. London, Audit Commission.

AUDIT COMMISSION (1998) *Misspent Youth, 98: The Challenge for Youth Justice*. London, Audit Commission.

AUDIT COMMISSION (2004) *Youth Justice 2004*. London, Audit Commission.

AULD, LORD JUSTICE (2001) *Review of the Criminal Courts of England and Wales*. London, The Stationery Office.

BADAWI, R. (2015) *1,000 Lashes: Because I Say What I Think*. Vancouver, Greystone Books.

BAGARIC, M. (2001) *Punishment and Sentencing: A Rational Approach*. London, Cavendish.

BAILEY, W. C. (1980) 'Deterrence and the Celerity of the Death Penalty: A Neglected Question in Deterrence Research' *Social Forces* Vol 58, 1308–33.

BAILEY, W. C. AND PETERSON, R. D. (1997) 'Murder, Capital Punishment and Deterrence: A Review of the Literature' in H. Bedau (ed) *The Death Penalty in America: Current Controversies*. New York, Oxford University Press, 135–61.

BAILIN, A. (2002) 'The Inhumanity of Mandatory Sentences' *Criminal Law Review*, 641–5.

BAKER, E. (1993) 'Dangerousness, Rights and Criminal Justice' *Modern Law Review* Vol 56, 528–47.

BAKER, E. AND CLARKSON, C. M. V. (2002) 'Making Punishments Work? An Evaluation of the Halliday Report on Sentencing in England and Wales' *Criminal Law Review*, 81–97.

BAKER, K. (2010) 'More Harm Than Good? The Language of Public Protection' *Howard Journal* Vol 49(1), 42–53.

BAKER, K., JONES, S., MERRINGTON, S., AND ROBERTS, C. (2005) *Further Development of Asset*. London, Youth Justice Board.

BALL, C. (1995) 'Youth Justice and the Youth Court—The End of a Separate System?' *Child and Family Law Quarterly* Vol 7(4), 196–208.

BALL, C. (2000) 'The Youth Justice and Criminal Evidence Act 1999 Part I: A Significant Move towards Restorative Justice or a Recipe for Unintended Consequences?' *Criminal Law Review*, 211–22.

BALL, C. (2004) 'Youth Justice? Half a Century of Responses to Youth Offending' *Criminal Law Review*, 167–80.

BANDALLI, S. (1998) 'Abolition of the Presumption of *Doli Incapax* and the Criminalisation of Children' *Howard Journal* Vol 37(2), 114–23.

BANKS, J. (2011) 'Foreign National Prisoners in the UK, Explanations and Implications' *Howard Journal* Vol 50(2), 184–98.

BAR COUNCIL (2006) *Guide to Sentences for Serious Crimes*. Available at http://www.criminalbar.com/210/redirect/SentencingNov06.pdf.

BARAK-EREZ, D. (2011) 'The Private Prison Controversy and the Privatization Continuum' *The Law & Ethics of Human Rights* Vol 5(1), Article 4. Available at http://www.bepress.com/lehr/vol5/iss1/art4.

BARCLAY, G. AND MHLANGA, B. (2000) *Ethnic Differences in Decisions on Young Defendants Dealt With by the Crown Prosecution Service*, Home Office Section 95 Findings 1. London, Home Office.

BARKER, V. (2009) *The Politics of Imprisonment: How the Democratic Process Shapes the Way America Punishes Offenders*. New York, Oxford University Press.

BARNARDO's (2014) *On the Outside: Identifying and Supporting Children with a Parent in Prison*. London, Barnardo's.

BARRY, M. (2005) *Youth Policy and Social Inclusion*. London, Routledge.

BATEMAN, T. (2007) 'Ignoring Necessity: The Court's Decision to Impose an ASBO on a Child' *Child and Family Law Quarterly* Vol 19(3), 304–21.

BATEMAN, T. (2011) 'Punishing Poverty: The "Scaled Approach" and Youth Justice Practice' *Howard Journal of Criminal Justice* Vol 50(2), 171–83.

BATEMAN, T. (2012) *Criminalising Children for No Good Purpose: The Age of Criminal Responsibility in England and Wales*, National Association for Youth Justice. Available at http://thenayj.org.uk/wp-content/files_mf/criminalisingchildrennov12.pdf.

BATEMAN, T. (2014) 'Where Has All the Youth Crime Gone? Youth Justice in an Age of Austerity' *Children and Society* Vol 28(5), 416–24.

BATEMAN. T. (2015) *The State of Youth Justice 2015: An Overview of Trends and Developments*, NAYJ Briefing. National Association for Youth Justice.

BECCARIA, C. (1767) *On Crimes and Punishments and Other Writings*, ed. R. Bellemy (1995). Cambridge, Cambridge University Press.

BECK, U. (1992) *Risk Society: Towards a New Modernity*. London, Sage.

BECKETT, K. AND WESTERN, B. (2001) 'Governing Social Marginality: Welfare, Incarceration and the Transformation of State Policy' in D. Garland (ed) *Mass Imprisonment*. London, Sage, 35–50.

BECKFORD, J. A., JOLY, D., AND KHOSROKHAVAR, F. (2005) *Muslims in Prison: Challenge and Change in Britain and France*. London, Palgrave.

BEDAU, H. (1997) 'Prison Homicides, Recidivist Murder and Life Imprisonment' in H. Bedau (ed) *The Death Penalty in America: Current Controversies*. New York, Oxford University Press, 176–82.

BEINART, S., ANDERSON, B., LEE, S., AND UTTING, D. (2002) *Youth at Risk? A National Survey of Risk Factors and Problem Behaviour among Young People in England, Scotland and Wales*. London, Communities that Care.

BENEFIELD, N., JOSEPH, N., SKETT, S., BRIDGLAND, S., D'CRUZ, L., GOODE, I., AND TURNER, K. (2015) 'The Offender Personality Disorder Strategy Jointly Delivered by NOMS and NHS England' *Prison Service Journal* 218: 4–9.

BENTHAM, J. (1789) *Introduction to the Principles of Morals and Legislation*, ed J. L. Burns and H. L. A. Hart (1996). Oxford, Clarendon.

BENTHAM, J. (1825) 'The Rationale of Reward' in J. Bowring (ed) (1843) *The Works of Jeremy Bentham*. Edinburgh, William Tait, 189–266.

BENTHAM, J. (1830) *The Rationale of Punishment*, ed J. McHugh (2009). Amherst, New York, Prometheus Books.

BENTHAM, J. (1843) 'Anarchical Fallacies' in J. Bowring (ed) *The Works of Jeremy Bentham*. Edinburgh, William Tait, 489–536.

BENTON, D. (2007) 'The Impact of Diet on Anti-Social, Violent and Criminal Behaviour' *Neuroscience & Biobehavioral Reviews* Vol 31(5), 752–74.

BERBERET, R. (2014) *Women, Crime and Criminal Justice*. London, Routledge.

BERMAN, G. (2011) *Prison Population Statistics*, SN/SG/4334. London, House of Commons Library.

BERMAN, G. AND DAR, A. (2013) *Prison Population Statistics*, Standard Note SN/SG/4334. London, House of Commons Library.

BESEMER, S., VAN DER GEEST, V., MURRAY, J., BIJLEVELD, C., AND FARRINGTON, D. (2011) 'The Relationship Between Parental Imprisonment and Offspring Offending in England and the Netherlands' *British Journal of Criminology* Vol 51, 413–37.

BETTINSON, V. AND DINGWALL, G. (2013) 'Challenging the Ongoing Injustice of Imprisonment for Public Protection: *James, Wells and Lee* v *The United Kingdom*' *Modern Law Review* Vol 76(6), 1094–1105.

BEYLEVELD, D. (1980) *A Bibliography on General Deterrence*. Farnborough, Saxon House.

BIANCHI, H. (1986) 'Abolitionism, Assensus and Sanctuary' in H. Bianchi and R. van Swaaningen (eds) *Abolitionism, Towards a Non Repressive Approach to Crime*. Amsterdam, Free Press, 113–26.

BLACK COMMITTEE (1979) *Report of the Children and Young Persons' Review Group*. Belfast, HMSO.

BLAD, J., CORNWELL, D., AND WRIGHT, M. (eds) (2012) *Civilising Criminal Justice*. Winchester, Waterside Press.

BLAGG, H. (1985) 'Reparation and Justice for Juveniles' *British Journal of Criminology* Vol 25(7), 267–79.

BLANCHETTE, K. AND BROWN, S. L. (2006) *The Assessment and Treatment of Women Offenders: An Integrative Perspective*. Chichester, John Wiley.

BLOCK, B. (1993) 'A Fine Mess' *Justice of the Peace*, 16 May, 308.

BLUMSTEIN, A., COHEN, J., AND NAGIN, D. (1978) (eds) *Deterrence and Incapacitation*. Washington DC, National Academy of Sciences.

BOHM, R. (2008) 'Karl Marx and the Death Penalty' *Critical Criminology* Vol 16(4), 285–91.

BOIN, A. AND RATTRAY, W. A. (2004) 'Understanding Prison Riots: Towards a Threshold Theory' *Punishment and Society* Vol 6(1), 47–66.

BONGER, W. (1916) *Criminality and Economic Conditions*. Boston, Little, Brown.

BOONE, M. AND MOERINGS, M. (eds) (2007) *Dutch Prisons*. The Hague, BJu Legal Publishers.

BOSWELL, G. (1991) *Section 53 Offenders: An Exploration of Experience and Needs*. London, The Prince's Trust.

BOTTOMS, A. (1985) 'Justice for Juveniles 75 years on' in D. Hoath (ed) *75 Years of Law at Sheffield 1909–84*. Sheffield, University Printing Unit.

BOTTOMS, A. (1995) 'The Philosophy and Politics of Sentencing' in C. M. V. Clarkson and R. Morgan (eds) *The Politics of Sentencing Reform*. Oxford, Clarendon, 17–49.

BOTTOMS, A. (2002) 'On the Decriminalisation of English Juvenile Courts' in J. Muncie, G. Hughes, and E. McLaughlin (eds) *Youth Justice, Critical Readings*. London, Sage, 216–27.

BOTTOMS, A. (2008) 'The Community Dimension of Community Penalties' *Howard Journal* Vol 47(2), 146–69.

BOTTOMS, A. AND MCWILLIAMS, W. (1979) 'A Non-Treatment Paradigm for Probation Practice' *British Journal of Social Work* Vol 9(2), 159–202.

BOTTOMS, A. AND ROBERTS, J. (eds) (2010) *Hearing the Victim: Adversarial Justice, Crime Victims and the State*. Cullompton, Willan.

BOTTOMS, A., REX, S., AND ROBINSON, G. (eds) (2004) *Alternatives to Prison: Options for an Insecure Society*. Cullompton, Willan.

BOWCOTT, O. (2011) 'Appeal Court Criticises Judge's Approach to Riot Sentencing' *The Guardian* 27 September.

BOWDEN, P. (1996) 'Violence and Mental Disorder' in N. Walker (ed) *Dangerous People*. London, Blackstone, 13–27.

BOWEN, E., BROWN, L., AND GILCHRIST, E. (2002) 'Evaluating Probation-Based Offender Programmes for Domestic Violence Perpetrators: A Pro-feminist Approach' *Howard Journal* Vol 41(3), 221–36.

BOWEN, E., EL KOMY., M., AND HERON, J. (2008a) *Anti-social and Other Problem Behaviours among Young Children, Patterns and Associated Child Characteristics*, Findings 282. London, Home Office.

BOWEN, E., EL KOMY, M., AND STEER, C. (2008b) *Characteristics Associated with Resilience in Children at High Risk of Involvement in Anti-social and Other Problem Behaviour*, Findings 283. London, Home Office.

BOWLES, R., FAURE, M., AND GAROUPA, N. (2008) 'The Scope of Criminal Law and Criminal Sanctions: An Economic View and Policy Implications' *Journal of Law and Society* Vol 25(3), 389–416.

BOWLING, B. AND PHILLIPS, C. (2002) *Racism, Crime and Justice*. London, Longman.

BOWLING, B., PHILLIPS, C. AND SHEPTYCKI, J. (2014) '"Race", Political Economy and the Coercive State' in T. Newburn and J. Peay (eds) *Policing, Politics, Culture and Control*. Oxford, Hart, 43–68.

BOYD, C. M. J. (2009) 'Can a Marxist Believe in Human Rights?' *Critique* Vol 37(4), 579–600.

BOYLE, M. H. AND LIPMAN, E. (2002) 'Do Places Matter? Socioeconomic Disadvantage and Behavioral Problems of Children in Canada' *Journal of Consulting and Clinical Psychology* Vol 70(2), 378–89.

BRAITHWAITE, J. (1989) *Crime, Shame and Reintegration*. Cambridge, Cambridge University Press.

BRAITHWAITE, J. (2000) *Regulation, Crime, Freedom*. Aldershot, Ashgate.

BRAITHWAITE, J. (2002) *Restorative Justice and Responsive Regulation*. Oxford, Oxford University Press.

BRAITHWAITE, J. (2003) 'Principles of Restorative Justice' in A. von Hirsch, J. Roberts, A. Bottoms, K. Roach, and M. Schiff (eds) *Restorative Justice and Criminal Justice, Competing or Reconcilable Paradigms?* Oxford, Hart Publishing, 1–20.

BRAITHWAITE, J. AND PETTIT, P. (1990) *Not Just Deserts: A Republican Theory of Criminal Justice*. Oxford, Clarendon Press.

BRASSE, G. (2003) 'Money Laundering—Who's Been Taken to the Cleaners?' *Family Law* Vol 33, 492–6.

BRAYFORD, J., COWE, F., AND DEERING J. (eds) (2010) *What Else Works? Creative Work with Offenders*. Cullompton, Willan.

BRETHERTON, H. (1991) 'Partnership in Practice' *Probation Journal* Vol 38(3), 132–5.

BRITTON, B., HOPE, B., LOCKE, T., AND WAINMAN, L. (1988) *Policy and Information in Juvenile Justice Systems*. London, NACRO/Save the Children Fund.

BRODY, S. (1976) *The Effectiveness of Sentencing*, Home Office Research Study No. 35. London, HMSO.

BROOKS, L. (2011) 'An Ugly Totem for the Abject Failure of Our Criminal Justice System' *The Guardian*, 18 March.

BROOKS, T. (2012) *Punishment*. London, Routledge.

BROOKS-GORDON, B. AND BAINHAM, A. (2004) 'Prisoners' Families and the Regulation of Contact' *Journal of Social Welfare and Family Law* Vol 26, 263.

BROWN, G. (2013) 'Sentence Discounting in England and Scotland—Some Observations on the Use of Comparative Authority in Sentence Appeals' *Criminal Law Review* 8, 674–7.

BROWN, J., MILLER, S. NORTHEY, S., AND O'NEILL, D. (2014) *What Works in Therapeutic Prisons: Evaluating Psychological Change in Dovegate Therapeutic Community*. London, Palgrave Macmillan.

BROWN, M. (2002) 'The Politics of Penal Excess and the Echo of Colonial Penality' *Punishment and Society* Vol 4(4), 403–23.

BROWNLEE, I. (1998a) 'New Labour—New Penology? Punitive Rhetoric and the Limits of Managerialism in Criminal Justice Policy' *Journal of Law and Society* Vol 25(3), 313–35.

BROWNLEE, I. (1998b) *Community Punishment*. London, Longman.

BRUNTON-SMITH, I. AND HOPKINS, K. (2013) *The Factors Associated with Proven Re-offending following Release from Prison: Findings from Waves 1 to 3 of SPCR.* London, Ministry of Justice Analytic Series.

BULLOCK, K. (2010) 'Enforcing Financial Penalties—The Case of Confiscation Orders' *Howard Journal* Vol 49(4), 328–39.

BULLOCK, K., MANN, D., STREET, R., AND COXON, C. (2009) *Examining Attrition in Confiscating the Proceeds of Crime,* Home Office Research Report No. 17. London, Home Office.

BÚRCA, G. AND DE WITTE, B. (2005) (eds) *Social Rights in Europe.* Oxford, Oxford University Press.

BURNETT, R. AND ROBERTS, G. (eds) (2004) *What Works in Probation and Youth Justice: Developing Evidence-Based Practice.* Cullompton, Willan.

BURNEY, E. (1985) 'All Things to All Men: Justifying Custody under the 1982 Act' *Criminal Law Review,* 284–93.

BURNEY, E. (2002) 'Talking Tough, Acting Coy: What Happened to the Anti-Social Behaviour Order?' *Howard Journal* Vol 41(5), 469–84.

BURNEY, E. (2003) Book review. *Howard Journal* Vol 42(4), 405–6.

BURNEY, E. (2005) *Making People Behave: Anti-social Behaviour, Politics and Policy.* Cullompton, Willan.

BURNEY, E. AND PEARSON, G. (1995) 'Mentally Disordered Offenders: Finding a Focus for Diversion' *Howard Journal* Vol 34, 291–313.

BURTON, M. (2006) 'Judicial Monitoring of Compliance: Introducing "Problem Solving" Approaches into Domestic Violence Courts in England and Wales' *International Journal of Law, Policy and Family* Vol 20(3), 366–78.

BYRNE, D. (2005) *Social Exclusion* (2nd edn). London, Sage.

CADDLE, D. AND CRISP, D. (1997) *Imprisoned Women and Mothers,* Home Office Research Study No. 162. London, Home Office.

CALDER, M. (2003) 'The Assessment Framework: A Critique and Reformulation' in C. Calder and S. Hackett (eds) *Assessment in Child Care: Using and Developing Frameworks for Practice.* Lyme Regis, Russell House Publishing, 3–60.

CAMPBELL, S. (2002) *A Review of Anti-Social Behaviour Orders,* Home Office Research Study No. 236. London, Home Office.

CAMPBELL, T. (1983) *The Left and Rights: A Conceptual Analysis of the Idea of Socialist Rights.* London, Routledge & Kegan Paul.

CAMPBELL, T. (2010) *Justice* (3rd edn). Basingstoke, Palgrave Macmillan.

CANTON, R. (2011) *Probation: Working with Offenders.* Abingdon, Routledge.

CARLEN, P. (1989) 'Crime, Inequality and Sentencing' in P. Carlen and D. Cook (eds) *Paying for Crime.* Milton Keynes, Open University Press, 8–28.

CARLEN, P. (1998) *Sledgehammer: Women's Imprisonment at the Millennium.* London, Macmillan.

CARLEN, P. (ed) (2002) *Women and Punishment: The Struggle for Justice.* Cullompton, Willan.

CARLISLE, LORD (1988) *The Parole System in England and Wales,* Report of the Review Committee. London, HMSO.

CARRABINE, E. (2010) 'Youth Justice in the United Kingdom' *Essex Human Rights Review* Vol 7(1), 12–24. Available at http.ehrr.org.

CARSON, E. A. (2014) *Prisoners in 2013.* Washington DC, US Department of Justice.

CARTER, LORD (2007) *Securing the Future: Proposals for the Efficient and Sustainable Use of Custody in England and Wales.* London, Ministry of Justice.

CARTER, P. (2003) *Managing Offenders, Reducing Crime: A New Approach* (The Carter Report). London, The Stationery Office.

CASALE, S. (2013) *Report of the Independent External Review of the IPCC Investigation into the Death of Sean Rigg.* London, IPCC.

CASE, S. P. AND HAINES, K. R. (2015) 'Children First, Offenders Second: The Centrality of Engagement in Positive Promotion' *Howard Journal* Vol 54(2), 157–75.

CAVADINO, M. AND DIGNAN, J. (2002) *The Penal System* (3rd edn). London, Sage.

CAVADINO, M. AND DIGNAN, J. (2013) *The Penal System* (5th edn). London, Sage.

CAVADINO, M. AND DIGNAN, J. (2006) *Penal Systems: A Comparative Approach*. London, Sage.

CAVADINO, M. AND WILES, P. (1994) 'Seriousness of Offences: The Perceptions of Practitioners' *Criminal Law Review*, 489–98.

CELNICK A. AND MCWILLIAMS, W. (1991) 'Helping, Treating and Doing Good' *Probation Journal* Vol 39, 164–70.

CENTRE FOR REVIEWS AND DISSEMINATION (1999) *Systematic Review of the International Literature on the Epidemiology of Mentally Disordered Offenders*, CRD Report 15. York, York University.

CENTRE FOR SOCIAL JUSTICE (2012) *Rules of Engagement: Changing the Heart of Youth Justice*. London, Centre for Social Justice.

CHAPLIN, R., FLATLEY, J., AND SMITH, K. (2011) *Crime in England and Wales 2010/11 Findings from the British Crime Survey and Police Recorded Crime*, Home Office Statistical Bulletin 10/11. London, Home Office.

CHELIOTIS, L. K. AND LIEBLING, A. (2005) 'Race Matters in British Prisons: Towards a Research Agenda' *British Journal of Criminology* Vol 46, 286–317.

CHIGWADA, R. (1989) 'The Criminalisation and Imprisonment of Black Women' *Probation Journal* Vol 37, 100–5.

CHIGWADA-BAILEY, R. (2003) *Black Women's Experience of Criminal Justice: A Discourse on Disadvantage* (2nd edn). Winchester, Waterside.

CHILDREN'S RIGHTS ALLIANCE (2008) *Children's Rights Bulletin for Children and Young People* Issue 27 May. London, CRAE.

CHILDRIGHT (2005) 'Which Youth Matters? Comments on the Government Green Paper' *Agenda*. Colchester, Children's Legal Centre, University of Essex.

CHRISTIAN, J. AND KENNEDY, L. W. (2011) 'Secondary Narratives in the Aftermath of Crime: Defining Family Members' Relationships with Prisoners' *Punishment and Society* Vol 13(4), 379–402.

CHRISTIE, N. (1977) 'Conflicts as Property' *British Journal of Criminology* Vol 17(1), 1–15, reprinted in E. McLaughlin, R. Ferguson, G. Hughes, and L. Westmarland (2003) *Restorative Justice, Critical Issues*. Milton Keynes, Open University Press and London, Sage. Chapter 1.

CHRISTIE, N. (1982) *Limits to Pain*. Oxford, Martin Robertson.

CHRISTIE, N. (2007) 'Restorative Justice: Answers to Deficits in Modernity' in D. Downes, P. Rock, C. Chinkin, and C. Gearty (eds) *Crime, Social Control and Human Rights*. Cullompton, Willan, 368–78.

CHRISTIE, N. (2010) 'Victim Movements at a Crossroad' *Punishment and Society* Vol 12(2), 115–22.

CITIZENS' ADVICE BUREAU (2015) *Advice trends: Quarterly client statistics of the Citizens Advice service in England and Wales, 2014/15 Quarter 4*. London, Citizens Advice.

CLARKE, J. (2002) 'Whose Justice? The Politics of Juvenile Control' in J. Muncie, G. Hughes, and E. McLaughlin (eds) (2002) *Youth Justice, Critical Readings*. London, Sage, 284–95.

CLARKE, K. (2010) *Speech for the Judges*, Mansion House, 13 July 2010. London, Ministry of Justice.

CLARKE, K. (2011) Comment, *The Guardian online* 5 September 2011.

CLARKSON, C. (1997) 'Beyond Just Deserts: Sentencing Violent and Sexual Offenders' *Howard Journal* Vol 36(3), 284–92.

CLEAR, T. (2007) *Imprisoning Communities*. New York, Oxford University Press.

CLELAND, A. AND TISDALL, K. (2005) 'The Challenge of Anti-social Behaviour: New Relationships between the State, Children and Parents' *International Journal of Law, Policy and the Family* Vol 19(3), 395–420.

CLEMENTS, J. (2000) *Assessment of Race Relations at HMP Brixton*. London, Prison Service.

CLEMMER, D. (1940) *The Prison Community*. New York, Holt, Rhinehart, and Winston.

COBB, N. (2007) 'Governance through Publicity: Anti-Social Behaviour Orders, Young People, and the Problematization of the Right to Anonymity' *Journal of Law and Society* Vol 34(3), 342–73.

CODD, H. (2004) 'Prisoners' Families: Issues in Law and Policy' *Amicus Curiae* Vol 55, 2.

CODD, H. (2008) *In the Shadow of Prison, Families, Imprisonment and Criminal Justice*. Cullompton, Willan.

COFFEY, M. (2013) Speech, HMP Wormwood Scrubs, 10 October 2013.

COHEN, J. (1978) 'The Incapacitative Effect of Imprisonment' in A. Blumstein, J. Cohen, and D. Nagin *et al.* (eds) *Deterrence and Incapacitation: Estimating the Effects on Crime Rates*. Washington, National Academy of Sciences, 187–243.

COHEN, S. (1985) *Visions of Social Control*. Cambridge, Polity Press.

COLEMAN, R. AND MCCAHILL, M. (2010) *Surveillance and Crime*. London, Sage.

COLLEGE OF POLICING (2015) *Possible Justice Outcomes following Investigation*. Available at https://www.app.college.police.uk/app-content/prosecution-and-case-management/justice-outcomes/ accessed 6 October 2015.

COMMISSION FOR RACIAL EQUALITY (2003) *A Formal Investigation by the CRE into HM Prison Service, England and Wales, Part I, The Murder of Zahid Mubarek; Part II, Racial Equality in Prisons*. London, CRE.

COMMISSION FOR RACIAL EQUALITY (2005) *Submission to the Zahid Mubarek Inquiry*. London, CRE.

COMMISSION ON A BILL OF RIGHTS (2012) *A UK Bill of Rights? The Choice Before Us*. London, Ministry of Justice.

COMMISSION ON ENGLISH PRISONS TODAY (2009) *Do Better Do Less: The Report of the Commission on English Prisons Today*. London, Howard League.

COMMITTEE OF PUBLIC ACCOUNTS (2002) *Collection of Fines and Other Financial Penalties in the Criminal Justice System*, HC999, Sixty-eighth Report of Session 2001–02, London: The Stationery Office.

COMMITTEE ON THE RIGHTS OF THE CHILD (1995) *Concluding Observations of the Committee on the Rights of the Child: United Kingdom of Great Britain and Northern Ireland*. CRC/C/15/Add 34. Geneva, Centre for Human Rights.

COMMITTEE ON THE RIGHTS OF THE CHILD (2002) *Concluding Observations of the Committee on the Rights of the Child: United Kingdom of Great Britain and Northern Ireland*. CRC/C/15/Add 188. Geneva, Centre for Human Rights.

COMMITTEE ON THE RIGHTS OF THE CHILD (2007) *Children's Rights in Juvenile Justice*. CRC/C/GC/10. Geneva, Centre for Human Rights.

COMMITTEE ON THE RIGHTS OF THE CHILD (2008) *Consideration of Reports Submitted by States Parties Under Article 44 of the Convention, Concluding Observations, United Kingdom of Great Britain and Northern Ireland*. CRC/C/GBR/CO/4. Geneva, Centre for Human Rights.

CONSERVATIVE PARTY (2014) *Protecting Human Rights in the UK: The Conservatives' Proposals on Changing Britain's Human Rights Laws*. London, The Conservative Party.

CONSERVATIVE PARTY (2015) *The Conservative Party Manifesto 2015*. London, The Conservative Party.

COOK, D. (1989) 'Fiddling Tax and Benefits' in P. Carlen and D. Cook (eds) *Paying for Crime*. Milton Keynes, Open University Press, 109–27.

COOPER, V. (2013) *No Fixed Abode: The Implications for Homeless People in the Criminal Justice System*. London, Howard League. Available at https://d19ylpo4aovc7m.cloudfront.net/fileadmin/howard_league/user/pdf/Publications/No_fixed_abode_report.pdf.

COPE, N. (2003) 'It's No Time or High Time: Young Offenders' Experience of Time and Drug Use in Prison' *Howard Journal* Vol 42(2), 158–75.

CORBETT, C. (2000) 'The Social Construction of Speeding as Not "Real Crime"' *Crime Prevention and Community Safety* Vol 2(4), 33–46.

CORBETT, C. AND CARAMLAU, I. (2006) 'Gender Differences in Responses to Speed Cameras: Typology Findings and Implications for Road Safety' *Criminology and Criminal Justice* 4, 411–33.

CORNWALL COUNCIL (2013) *Juvenile Enforcement Procedure, Environmental Crime Offences, Juveniles 10–17 Years of Age*. Cornwall Council.

CORNWELL, D., BLAD, J., AND WRIGHT, M. (eds) (2013) *Civilising Criminal Justice*. Hook, Waterside Press.

CORSTON, J. (2007) *The Corston Report: A Report by Baroness Jean Corston of a Review of Women with Particular Vulnerabilities in the Criminal Justice System*. London, Home Office.

COUNCIL OF EUROPE (1987) European Prison Rules, adopted 12 February 1987. Strasbourg, Council of Europe.

COUNCIL OF EUROPE (1991) *Report to the United Kingdom Government on the Visit to the United Kingdom Carried Out by the European Committee for the Prevention of Torture and Inhuman or Degrading Treatment or Punishment from 29 June 1990 to 10 August 1990*. Strasbourg, Council of Europe.

COUNCIL OF EUROPE (2009) *Report to the United Kingdom Government on the Visit to the United Kingdom Carried Out by the European Committee for the Prevention of Torture and Inhuman or Degrading Treatment or Punishment (CPT) from 18 November to 1 December 2008*, CPT/Inf (91) 30. Strasbourg, Council of Europe.

COUNCIL OF EUROPE (2014) *Report to the Government of the United Kingdom on a Visit to the UK Carried Out by the European Committee for the Prevention of Torture from 17–28 September 2012, CPT/Inf* (2014) 11. Strasbourg, Council of Europe.

COUNCIL OF EUROPE, PARLIAMENTARY ASSEMBLY (2011) *The Death Penalty in Council of Europe Member and Observer States: A Violation of Human Rights*, Doc 12456. Strasbourg, Council of Europe.

CPS (1988) *Annual Report 1987–8*. London, HMSO.

CPS (1991) *Annual Report 1990–91*. London, HMSO.

CPS (1994) *The Code for Crown Prosecutors* (3rd edn). London, Director of Public Prosecutions.

CPS (2000) *The Code for Crown Prosecutors* (4th edn). London, Director of Public Prosecutions.

CRACKNELL, S. (2000) 'Anti-Social Behaviour Orders' *Journal of Social Welfare and Family Law* Vol 22(1), 108–15.

CRAIG, L., GANNON, T., AND DIXON, L. (2013) *What Works in Offender Rehabilitation: An Evidence Based Approach to Assessment and Treatment*. Chichester, John Wiley.

CRAWFORD, A. (1997) *The Local Governance of Crime*. Oxford, Oxford University Press.

CRAWFORD, A. (2000) 'Justice de Proximité— The Growth of "Houses of Justice" and Victim/Offender Mediation in France: A Very UnFrench Legal Response?' *Social & Legal Studies* Vol 9(1), 29–53.

CRAWFORD, A. (2003) 'Contractual Governance of Deviant Behaviour' *Journal of Law and Society* Vol 30(4), 479–505.

CRAWFORD, A. (2009) 'Governing Through Anti-Social Behaviour, Regulatory Challenges to Criminal Justice' *British Journal of Criminology* Vol 49, 810–31.

CRAWFORD, A. AND ENTERKIN, J. (2001) 'Victim Contact Work in the Probation Service: Paradigm Shift or Pandora's Box?' *British Journal of Criminology* Vol 41, 705–25.

CRAWLEY, E. AND SPARKS, R. (2005) 'Hidden Injuries: Researching the Experience of Older Men in English Prisons' *Howard Journal* Vol 44(4), 345–6.

CRAWLEY, E. AND SPARKS, R. (2008) *Age of Imprisonment*. Cullompton, Willan.

CRETNEY, S. (1998) 'The State as a Parent, the Children Act 1948 in Retrospect' *Law Quarterly Review* Vol 114, 419–59.

CREWE, B. (2006) 'Male Prisoners, Orientation towards Female Officers in an English Prison' *Punishment and Society* Vol 8(4), 395–421.

CREWE, B. (2013) *The Prisoner Society: Power, Adaptation and Social Life in an English Prison*. Oxford, Oxford University Press.

CROALL, H. (1992) *White Collar Crime*. Milton Keynes, Open University Press.

CROFTS, T. (2002) *The Criminal Responsibility of Children and Young Persons: A Comparison of English and German Law*. Aldershot, Ashgate.

CROOK, F. (2003) 'Children in Prison: Advocating for the Human Rights of Young Offenders' *Criminal Justice Matters* 54, 24–5.

CROOK, F. (2015) 'Comment: Who Will Look after Victims Now Grayling Has Privatised Probation?' Politics.co.uk. Available at http://www.politics.co.uk/comment-analysis/2015/04/24/comment-who-will-look-after-victims-now-grayling-has-privati.

CROSS, R. (AND ASHWORTH, A.) (1981) *The English Sentencing System*. London, Butterworths.

CROSSMAN, G. (2007) *Overlooked: Surveillance and Personal Privacy in Modern Britain*. London, Liberty.

CROW, I. AND SIMON, F. (1987) *Unemployment and Magistrates' Courts*. London, NACRO.

CROWLEY, A. (1998) *A Criminal Waste: A Study of Child Offenders Eligible for Secure Training Centres*. London, The Children's Society.

CUMMINS, I. (2006) 'A Path Not Taken? Mentally Disordered Offenders and the Criminal Justice System' *Journal of Social Welfare and Family Law* Vol 28 (3–4), 267–81.

CUNLIFFE, J. AND SHEPHERD, A. (2007) *Re-offending of Adults: Results from the 2004 Cohort*. London, Home Office.

CUPPLEDITCH, L. AND EVANS, W. (2005) *Re-offending of Adults: Results from the 2002 Cohort*. Home Office Statistical Bulletin. London, Home Office.

CURRY, T. R. AND CORRAL-CAMACHO, G. (2008) 'Sentencing Young Minority Males for Drug Offenses, Testing for Conditional Effects between Race/Ethnicity, Gender and Age during the US War on Drugs' *Punishment and Society* Vol 10(3), 253–76.

DA SILVA, N., COWELL, P., CHINEGWUNDOH, V., MASON, T., MARESH, J., AND WILLIAMSON, K. (2007) *Prison Population Projections 2007–2014, England and Wales*. London, Ministry of Justice.

DALY, M. (2003) 'Governance and Social Policy' *Journal of Social Policy* Vol 32(1), 113–28.

DARBYSHIRE, P. (2011) *Sitting in Judgment: The Working Lives of Judges*. Oxford, Hart.

DAVIES, A. (2010) 'Dangerous Offenders Scheme to be Axed?' *Channel 4 News*, 15 February. Available at http://www.channel4.com/news/dangerous-offenders-scheme-to-be-axed

DAVIES, P., FRANCIS, P., AND JUPP, V. (2003) *Victimisation, Theory, Research and Practice*. Basingstoke, Palgrave Macmillan.

DAVIS, A. Y. (2003) *Are Prisons Obsolete?* New York, Seven Sisters Press.

DAVIS, G. (1992) *Making Amends: Mediation and Reparation in Criminal Justice*. London, Routledge.

DAVIS, G., BOUCHERAT, J., AND WATSON, D. (1988) 'Reparation in the Service of Diversion: The Subordination of a Good Idea' *Howard Journal* Vol 27(2), 127–33.

DAVIS, K. C. (1969) *Discretionary Justice: A Preliminary Inquiry*. Baton Rouge, Louisiana State University Press.

DAVIS, M., TAKAL, J-P., AND TYRER, J. (2004) 'Sentencing Burglars and Explaining the Differences between Jurisdictions' *British Journal of Criminology* Vol 44, 741–58.

Davis, R., Lurigio, A., and Skogan, W. (eds) (1997) *Victims of Crime* (2nd edn). Thousand Oaks, CA, Sage.

Dawes, W., Harvey, P., McIntosh, B., Nunney, F., and Phillips, A. (2011) *Attitudes to Guilty Plea Sentence Reductions*, Sentencing Council Research Series 02/11. London, Sentencing Council.

Day Sclater, S. and Piper, C. (1999) 'The Family Law Act 1996 in Context' in S. Day Sclater and C. Piper (eds) *Undercurrents of Divorce*. Ashgate, Aldershot, 3–29.

Day Sclater, S. and Piper, C. (2000) 'Re-moralising the Family? Family Policy, Family Law and Youth Justice' *Child and Family Law Quarterly* Vol 12(2), 135–51.

DCSF (Department for Children, Schools and Families) (2007) *The Children's Plan: Building Brighter Futures* Cm 7280. London, The Stationery Office.

De Cou, K. (2002) 'A Gender-Wise Prison: Opportunities for, and Limits to, Reform' in P. Carlen (ed) *Women and Punishment: The Struggle for Justice*, Cullompton, Willan, 97–109.

De Giorgi, A. (2010) 'Immigration Control, PostFordism and Less Eligibility: A Materialist Critique of the Criminalization of Immigration across Europe' *Punishment and Society* Vol 12(2), 147–67.

De Giorgi, A. (2012) 'Punishment and Political Economy' in J. Simon and R. Sparks (eds) *Handbook of Punishment and Society*. London, Sage, 40–59.

De Koster, W., van der Waal, J., Achterberg, P., and Houtman, D. (2008) 'The Rise of the Penal State, New-Liberalization or New Political Culture?' *British Journal of Criminology* Vol 48(6), 720–34.

Dear, G. E. (2006) *Preventing Suicide and Other Self-Harm in Prison*. London, Palgrave.

Death Penalty Information Center (2015) *The Innocence List*. Available at http://www.deathpenaltyinfo.org/innocence-list-those-freed-death-row accessed 28 March 2015.

Deering, J. (2011) *Probation Practice and the New Penology*. Aldershot, Ashgate.

Demker, A., Towns, A., Duus-Otterström, G., and Sebring, J. (2008) 'Fear and Punishment in Sweden: Exploring Penal Attitudes' *Punishment and Society* Vol 10(3), 319–32.

Denny, D. (1992) *Racism and Anti-Racism in Probation*. London, Routledge.

Denver, M., Best, J., and Haas, K. C. (2008) 'Methods of Execution as Institutional Fads' *Punishment and Society* Vol 10(3), 227–52.

Department for Business, Innovation and Skills (2016) *Prior Qualifications of Adult OLASS Learners,* Research Paper No. 260. London, Department for Business, Innovation and Skills.

Department for Constitutional Affairs (2006) *Your Choice to Have a Voice in Court*. London, Office for Criminal Justice Reform.

Department for Transport (2013) *Government Response to Consultation on the Treatment of Careless Driving Penalties and Other Motoring Fixed Penalties*. London, DfT.

Department of Health (1999) *Review of the Mental Health Act 1983*. London, Department of Health.

Department of Health (2000) *Framework for the Assessment of Children in Need and their Families*. London, HMSO.

Department of Health (2009a) *The Bradley Report: Lord Bradley's Review of People with Mental Health Problems or Learning Disabilities in the Criminal Justice System*. London, Department of Health.

Department of Health (2009b) *A Resource Pack for Working with Older Prisoners*. London, Department of Health/NACRO.

Department of Health (2011) *No Health Without Mental Health*. London, Department of Health.

Department of Health and NOMS Offender Personality Disorder Team (2011a) *Consultation on the Offender Personality Disorder Pathway Implementation Plan*. London, Department of Health.

DEPARTMENT OF HEALTH AND NOMS OFFENDER PERSONALITY DISORDER TEAM (2011b) *Response to the Offender Personality Disorder Consultation.* London, Department of Health.

DEPARTMENT OF HEALTH/HOME OFFICE (1992) *Review of Mental Health and Social Services for Mentally Disordered Offenders and Others Requiring Similar Services* Vol 1: Final Summary Report, Cm 2088. London, HMSO.

DEPARTMENT OF HEALTH/HOME OFFICE (2000) *Reforming the Mental Health Act: Part II High Risk Patients* Cm 5016-II. London, The Stationery Office.

DEVLIN, A. (1998) *Invisible Women.* Winchester, Waterside Press.

DfES (Department for Education and Skills) (2003) *Every Child Matters* Cm 5860. London, The Stationery Office.

DfES (Department for Education and Skills) (2004) *Every Child Matters: Next Steps.* London, The Stationery Office.

DfES (Department for Education and Skills) (2005) *Youth Matters* Cm 6629. London, The Stationery Office.

DfES (Department for Education and Skills) (2007) *Every Parent Matters.* London, DfES.

DICEY, A. V. (1885) *Introduction to the Study of the Law of the Constitution.* London, Macmillan.

DIDUCK, A. (1999) 'Justice and Childhood: Reflections on Refashioned Boundaries' in M. King (ed) *Moral Agendas for Children's Welfare.* London, Routledge, 120–37.

DIGNAN, J. (1999) 'The Crime and Disorder Act and the Prospects for Restorative Justice' *Criminal Law Review,* 48–60.

DIGNAN, J. AND LOWEY, K. (2000) *Restorative Justice Options for Northern Ireland: A Comparative Review.* Belfast, Criminal Justice Review Group.

DIGNAN, J. AND MARSH, P. (2001) 'Restorative Justice and Family Group Conferences in England: Current State and Future Prospects' in A. Morris and G. Maxwell (eds) *Restorative Justice for Juveniles:*

Conferencing, Mediation and Circles. Oxford, Hart Publishing, 85–101.

DINGWALL, G. (1998) 'Selective Incapacitation after the Criminal Justice Act 1991: A Proportional Response to Protecting the Public?' *Howard Journal* Vol 37(2), 177–87.

DINGWALL, G. (2008) 'Deserting Desert? Locating the Present Role of Retributivism in the Sentencing of Adult Offenders' *Howard Journal* Vol 47(4), 400–10.

DINGWALL, G. AND HILLIER, T. (2015) *Blamestorming, Blamemongers and Scapegoats.* Bristol, Policy Press.

DISSPAIN, S. AND WILDGOOSE, E. (2015) 'Exploration of a Transfemale Prisoner's Experience of a Prison Therapeutic Community' *Prison Service Journal* Vol 219, 9–18.

DITCHFIELD, J. (1976) *Police Cautioning in England and Wales,* Home Office Research Study No. 37. London, HMSO.

DOBSON, G. (2010) 'New Labour's Prison Legacy' *Probation Journal* Vol 57(3), 322–8.

DOMANICK, J. (2004) *Cruel Justice: Three Strikes and the Politics of Crime in America's Golden State.* Berkeley, University of California Press.

DONOGHUE, J. (2007) 'The Judiciary as a Primary Definer on Anti-Social Behaviour Orders' *Howard Journal* Vol 46(4), 417–30.

DONOGHUE, J. (2010) *Anti-Social Behaviour Orders: A Culture of Control?* London, Macmillan.

DONOHUE, J. J. AND WOLFERS, J. (2006) 'Uses and Abuses of Empirical Evidence in the Death Penalty Debate' *Stanford Law Review* Vol 58, 791–846.

DONZELOT, J. (1980) *The Policing of Families.* London, Hutchinson.

DORLING, D. (2015) *Injustice: Why Social Inequality Still Persists* (5th edn). Bristol, Policy Press.

DORLING, D., RIGBY, J., WHEELER, B., BALLAS, D., THOMAS, B., FAHMY, E., GORDON, D., AND LUPTON, R. (2007) *Poverty, Wealth and Place in Britain, 1968 to 2005.* Bristol, Policy Press.

Douglas, N. and Plugge, E. (2007) 'The Health of Young Women in Custody: Emerging Concerns and a Case for Advocacy' *Childright* CR 238, 14–17.

Downes, D. (2001/2) 'Four Years Hard: New Labour and Crime Control' *Criminal Justice Matters* Vol 46, 8–9.

Drakeford, M. (1993) 'But Who Will Do the Work?' *Critical Social Policy* Vol 3(2), 64–76.

Drakeford, M. and Butler, I. (2007) 'Everyday Tragedies: Justice, Scandal and Young People in Contemporary Britain' *Howard Journal* Vol 46(3), 219–35.

Dudeck, M., Drenkhahn, K., Spitzer, C., Barnow, S., Kopp, D., Kuwert, P., Freyberger, H., and Dünkel, F. (2011) 'Traumatization and Mental Distress in Long-Term Prisoners in Europe' *Punishment and Society* Vol 13(4), 403–23.

Duff, A. (2002) 'Punishing the Young' in I. Weijers and A. Duff (eds) *Punishing Juveniles: Principle and Critique*. Oxford, Hart Publishing, 115–34.

Duff, A. (2003a) 'Probation, Punishment and Restorative Justice: Should Altruism Be Engaged in Punishment?' *Howard Journal* Vol 42(2), 181–97.

Duff, R. A. (2003b) *Punishment, Communication and Community*. Oxford, Oxford University Press.

Dunbar, I. and Langton, A. (1998) *Tough Justice, Sentencing and Penal Policies in the 1990s*. London, Blackstone Press.

Dupont, C. and Zakkour, P. (2003) *Trends in Environmental Sentencing in England and Wales*. London, Department for Environment, Food and Rural Affairs.

Durrance, P., Dixon, L., and Singh Bhui, H. (2010) 'Creative Working with Minority Ethnic Offenders' in J. Brayford, F. Cowe, and J. Deering (eds) *What Else Works? Creative Work with Offenders*. Cullompton, Willan, 138–54.

Dworkin, R. (1977) *Taking Rights Seriously*. London, Duckworth.

Dworkin, R. (1986) *A Matter of Principle*. Oxford, Oxford University Press.

Dworkin, R. (2011) *Justice for Hedgehogs*. Cambridge, MA, Harvard University Press.

Dyson, S. and Boswell, G. (2006) 'Sickle Cell Anaemia and Deaths in Custody in the UK and USA' *Howard Journal* Vol 45(1), 14–28.

Eadie, T. and Willis, A. (1989) 'National Standards for Discipline and Breach Proceedings in Community Service: An Exercise in Penal Rhetoric?' *Criminal Law Review*, 412–19.

Earle, J., Nadin, R., and Jacobson, J. (2014) *Brighter Futures: Working Together to Reduce Women's Offending*. London, Prison Reform Trust.

Earle, R. (2013) 'Inside White – Racism, Social Relations and Ethnicity in an English Prison' in C. Phillips and C. Webster (eds) *New Directions in Race, Ethnicity and Crime*. London, Routledge, 160–77.

Easton, S. (2006) 'Electing the Electorate: The Problem of Prisoner Disenfranchisement' *Modern Law Review* Vol 69(3), 443–52.

Easton, S. (ed) (2008a) *Marx and Law*. Aldershot, Ashgate.

Easton, S. (2008b) 'Marx's Legacy' in S. Easton (ed) *Marx and Law*. Aldershot, Ashgate, xi–xxix.

Easton, S. (2008c) 'Dangerous Waters: Taking Account of Impact in Sentencing' *Criminal Law Review* 2, 105–20.

Easton, S. (2008d) 'Constructing Citizenship, Making Room for Prisoners' Rights' *Journal of Social Welfare and Family Law* Vol 30(2), 127–46.

Easton, S. (2009) 'The Prisoner's Right to Vote and Civic Responsibility: Reaffirming the Social Contract' *Probation Journal* Vol 56(3), 224–37.

Easton, S. (2011a) *Prisoners' Rights, Principles and Practice*. London, Routledge.

Easton, S. (2011b) 'Possession of Extreme Pornography, Sword or Shield?' *Journal of Criminal Law* 75, 391–413.

Easton, S. (2012) 'Should Prisoners Be Allowed to Vote?' *Criminal Justice Matters* December, 43.

EASTON, S. (2013) 'Protecting Prisoners: The Impact of International Human Rights Law on the Treatment of Prisoners in the UK' *The Prison Journal* Vol 93(4), 475–492.

EASTON, S. (forthcoming) *The Politics of the Prison and the Prisoner*. London, Routledge.

EASTON, S. AND PIPER, C. (2013) 'Fixed Penalties for Careless Driving: The Delusion of Deterrence?' *Contemporary Issues in Law* (2013, published 2015) Vol 13(3), 175–92.

EDGAR, K. (2010) *A Fair Response: Developing Responses to Racist Incidents that Earn the Confidence of Black and Minority Ethnic Prisoners*. London, Prison Reform Trust.

EDGAR, K. AND RICKFORD, D. (2009) 'Neglecting the Mental Health of Prisoners' *International Journal of Prisoner Health* Vol 5(3), 166–70.

EDGAR, K., JACOBSON, J., AND BIGGAR, K. (2011) *Time Well Spent: A Practical Guide to Active Citizenship and Volunteering in Prison*. London, Prison Reform Trust.

EDWARDS, I. (2001) 'Victim Participation in Sentencing: The Problems of Incoherence' *Howard Journal* Vol 40(1), 39–54.

EDWARDS, I. (2002) 'The Place of Victims' Preferences in the Sentencing of "their" Offenders' *Criminal Law Review*, 689–702.

EDWARDS, I. (2006) 'Restorative Justice, Sentencing and the Court of Appeal' *Criminal Law Review*, 110–23.

EHRLICH, I. (1975) 'The Deterrent Effects of Capital Punishment: A Question of Life or Death' *American Economic Review* Vol 65, 397–417.

EINAT, T. (2004) 'Criminal Fine Enforcement in Israel' *Punishment and Society* Vol 6(2), 175–94.

ELLIS, T. AND WINSTONE, J. (2001/2) 'Halliday, Sentencers and the National Probation Service' *Criminal Justice Matters* No. 46 Winter, 20.

ENGELS, F. (1843) 'Outline of a Critique of Political Economy' in *Marx and Engels: Collected Works* Vol 3. London, Lawrence & Wishart (1975), 418–43.

EPSTEIN, R. (2012) 'Mothers in Prison: The Sentencing of Mothers and the Rights of the Child'. *Coventry Law Journal* 1–33 December Special Issue: Research Report. Available at http://www.makejusticework. org.uk/wp-content/uploads/Mothers-in-Prison-by-Rona-Epstein.pdf.

EQUALITY AND HUMAN RIGHTS COMMISSION (2014) *Stop and Think Again: Towards Race Equality in Police PACE Stop and Search*. London, EHRC.

EREZ, E. (1999) 'Who's Afraid of the Big Bad Victim? Victim Impact Statements as Victim Empowerment and Enhancement of Justice' *Criminal Law Review*, 545–56.

ETZIONI, A. (1993) *The Spirit of Community: Rights, Responsibilities and the Communitarian Agenda*. New York, Crown Publishers.

ETZIONI, A. (2003) *The Monochrome Society*. Princeton, Princeton University Press.

ETZIONI, A. (2014) *The New Normal: Finding a Balance between Individual Rights and the Common Good*. New Brunswick, Transaction.

EVANS, R. (1994) 'Cautioning: Counting the Cost of Retrenchment' *Criminal Law Review*, 566–75.

EXWORTHY, T. AND GUNN, J. (2003) 'Taking Another Tilt at High Secure Hospitals' *British Journal of Psychiatry* Vol 182, 469–71.

FAIRLIE, M. (2013) '*Miranda* and its (More Rights-Protective) International Counterparts' *UC Davis Journal of International Law and Policy* Vol 20, 1–45.

FARRALL, S. (2002) 'Long Term Absences from Probation: Officers' and Probationers' Accounts' *Howard Journal* Vol 41(3), 263–78.

FARRALL, S. AND MALTBY, S. (2003) 'The Victimisation of Probationers' *Howard Journal* Vol 42, 32–54.

FARRALL, S., BOTTOMS, A., AND SHAPLAND, J. (2010) 'Social Structures and Desistance from Crime' *European Journal of Criminology* Vol 7(6), 546–70.

FARRINGTON, D. (1997) 'Human Development and Criminal Careers' in M. Maguire *et al.* (eds) *The Oxford Handbook of Criminology* (2nd edn). Oxford, Oxford University Press, 361–408.

FARRINGTON, D. (2002) 'Understanding and Preventing Crime' in J. Muncie, G. Hughes, and E. McLaughlin (eds) *Youth Justice, Critical Readings*. London, Sage, 425–30.

FARRINGTON, D. (2007) 'Childhood Risk Factors and Risk-Focused Prevention' in M. Maguire, R. Morgan, and R. Reiner (eds) *The Oxford Handbook of Criminology* (4th edn). Oxford, Oxford University Press, 602–40.

FARRINGTON, D. AND BENNETT, T. (1981) 'Police Cautioning of Juveniles in London' *British Journal of Criminology* Vol 21(1), 123–35.

FARRINGTON, D. AND ZARA, G. (2013) *Criminal Recidivism: Explanation, Prediction and Prevention*. London, Routledge.

FARRINGTON, D., DITCHFIELD, J., HOWARD, P., AND JOLLIFFE, D. (2002) *Two Intensive Regimes for Young Offenders: A Follow-Up Evaluation*, RDSD Findings 163. London, Home Office.

FAULKNER, D. (2005) 'Relationships, Accountability and Responsibility in the National Offender Management Service' *Public Money and Management* Vol 25(5), 299.

FAWCETT COMMISSION ON WOMEN AND THE CRIMINAL JUSTICE SYSTEM (2009) *Engendering Justice, From Policy to Practice: Final Report on Women and the Criminal Justice System*. London, Fawcett Society.

FAZEL, S. AND BAILLARGEON, J. (2011) 'The Health of Prisoners' *Lancet* 377, 956–65.

FAZEL, S., BENNING, R., AND DANESH, J. (2005) 'Suicides in Male Prisoners in England and Wales, 1978–2003' *Lancet* Vol 366(9493), 1301–2.

FEELEY, M. AND SIMON, J. (1992) 'The New Penology: Notes on the Emerging Strategy of Corrections and its Implications' *Criminology* Vol 30(4), 449–74.

FEINBERG, J. (1994) 'The Expressive Function of Punishment' in A. Duff and D. Garland (eds) *A Reader on Punishment*. Oxford, Oxford University Press, 71–91.

FELDMAN, M. (1992) 'Social Limits to Discretion' in Hawkins, K. (ed) *The Uses of Discretion*. Oxford, Clarendon, 164–83.

FEMALE PRISONERS' WELFARE PROJECT/ HIBISCUS (2010) *Annual Report* 2009/10. London, FPWP.

FENWICK, H. (1997) 'Procedural "Rights" of Victims of Crime: Public or Private Ordering of the Criminal Justice Process?' *Modern Law Review* Vol 60(3), 317–33.

FERGUSON, L. (2013) 'Not Merely Rights for Children but Children's Rights: The Theory Gap and the Assumption of the Importance of Children's Rights' *International Journal of Children's Rights* Vol 21, 177–208.

FIELD, S. (2007) 'Practice Cultures and the "New" Youth Justice in (England and) Wales' *British Journal of Criminology* Vol 47, 311–30.

FIONDA, J. (1999) 'New Labour, Old Hat: Youth Justice and the Crime and Disorder Act' *Criminal Law Review*, 36–47.

FISH, M. J. (2008) 'An Eye for an Eye, Proportionality as a Moral Principle of Punishment' *Oxford Journal of Legal Studies* Vol 28(1), 57–71.

FISHER, J. (2015) 'Part 1 of the Serious Crime Act 2015: Strengthening the Restraint and Confiscation Regime' *Criminal Law Review* 754.

FITZGERALD, M. AND MARSHALL, P. (1996) 'Ethnic Minorities in British Prisons: Some Research Implications' in R. Matthews and P. Francis (eds) *Prisons 2000: An International Perspective on the Current State and Future of Imprisonment*. London, Macmillan, 139–62.

FITZGIBBON, D. (2007) 'Risk Analysis and the New Practitioner' *Punishment and Society* Vol 9(1), 87–97.

FLAHERTY, P. (2006/7) 'Sentencing the Recidivist: Reconciling Harsher Treatment for Repeat Offenders with Modern Retributivist Theory' *Contemporary Issues in Law* Vol 8(4), 319–36.

FLETCHER, G. (1982) 'The Recidivist Premium' *Criminal Justice Ethics* Vol 1(2), 54–9.

FLOOD-PAGE, C. AND MACKIE, A. (1998) *Sentencing Practice: An Examination of Decisions in Magistrates' Courts and the Crown Court in the mid-1990s*, Home Office Research Study No. 180. London: Home Office.

FLOOD-PAGE, C. *et al.* (2000) *Youth Crime: Findings from the 1998/99 Youth Lifestyles Survey*, Home Office Research Study No. 209. London, Home Office.

FLOUD, J. (1982) 'Dangerousness and Criminal Justice' *British Journal of Criminology* Vol 22(3), 213–28.

FORLIN, G. (2015) 'Case Comment "Many Rivers to Cross"—Sentencing for Environmental Crimes' *Archbold Review* No. 8, 4.

FORMAN, J. (2012) 'Racial Critiques of Mass Incarceration: Beyond the New Jim Crow' *New York University Law Review* Vol 87, 101–46.

FORTIN, J. (2003) *Children's Rights and the Developing Law* (2nd edn). London, Lexis Nexis.

FORTIN, J. (2009) *Children's Rights and the Developing Law* (3rd edn). Cambridge, Cambridge University Press.

FOUCAULT, M. (1977) *Discipline and Punish: The Birth of the Prison*. London, Allen Lane.

FOX, C. AND ALBERTSON, A. (2010) 'Could Economics Solve the Prison Crisis?' *Probation Journal* Vol 57(3), 263–80.

FOX, D., DHAMI, M., AND MANTLE, G. (2006) 'Restorative Final Warnings: Policy and Practice' *Howard Journal* Vol 45(2), 129–40.

FREDMAN, S. (2008) *Human Rights Transformed, Positive Rights and Positive Duties*. Oxford, Oxford University Press.

FREIBERG, A. (2000) 'Guerillas in our Midst? Judicial Responses to Governing the Dangerous' in M. Brown and J. Pratt (eds) *Dangerous Offenders*. London, Routledge, 51–69.

FROST, N. A. (2008) 'The Mismeasure of Punishment: Alternative Measures of Punitiveness and their Substantial Consequences' *Punishment and Society* Vol 10(3), 277–300.

GAES, G. (2008) 'Cost, Performance Studies Look at Prison Privatization' *National Institute of Justice Journal*, Issue No. 259, 32–6.

GAL, T. AND MOYAL, S. (2011) 'Juvenile Victims in Restorative Justice: Findings from the Reintegrative Shaming Experiments' *British Journal of Criminology* Vol 51, 1014–34.

GARCIA HERNANDEZ, C. C. (2014) 'Immigration Detention as Punishment' *UCLA Law Review* Vol 61(5), 1346.

GARLAND, D. (1985) *Punishment and Welfare: A History of Penal Strategies*. Aldershot, Gower.

GARLAND, D. (1990) *Punishment and Modern Society: A Study in Social Theory*. Oxford, Clarendon Press.

GARLAND, D. (1991) 'Sociological Perspectives on Punishment' in N. Morris and M. Tonry (eds) *Crime and Justice* Vol 14. Chicago, University of Chicago Press, 115–65.

GARLAND, D. (ed) (2001a) *Mass Imprisonment*. London, Sage.

GARLAND, D. (2001b) *The Culture of Control*. Oxford, Oxford University Press.

GARLAND, D. (2010) *Peculiar Institution: America's Death Penalty in an Age of Abolition*. Oxford, Oxford University Press.

GARSIDE, R. (2014) *Criminal Justice in the United Kingdom since 2010*, Centre for Crime and Justice Studies October 2014 ebulletin website 31 October 2014. Available at http://www.crimeandjustice.org.uk/resources/criminal-justice-united-kingdom-2010.

GELB, K. (2008) *More Myths and Misconceptions*. State of Victoria, Sentencing Advisory Council.

GELB, K. (2010) *Gender Differences in Sentencing Outcome*. Melbourne, Sentencing Advisory Panel.

GELSTHORPE, L. (2002) 'Recent Changes in Youth Justice Policy in England and Wales' in I. Weijers and A. Duff (eds) *Punishing Juveniles: Principle and Critique*. Oxford, Hart Publishing, 45–66.

GELSTHORPE, L. (2012) 'Providing for Women Offenders: The Risks of Adopting a Payment by Results Approach' *Probation Journal* Vol 59(4), 374–90.

GELSTHORPE, L. AND MORRIS, A. (1999) 'Much Ado About Nothing—A Critical Comment on Key Provisions Relating to Children in the Crime and Disorder Act 1998' *Child and Family Law Quarterly* Vol 11(3), 209–21.

GELSTHORPE, L. AND MORRIS, A. (2002) 'Restorative Youth Justice: The Last Vestiges of Welfare?' in J. Muncie, G. Hughes, and E. McLaughlin (eds) *Youth Justice: Critical Readings*. London/ Milton Keynes, Sage/Open University Press, 238–54.

GELSTHORPE, L. AND PADFIELD, N. (eds) (2003) *Exercising Discretion: Decision-Making in the Criminal Justice System and Beyond*. Cullompton, Willan.

GENDERS, E. (2003) 'Privatisation and Innovation—Rhetoric and Reality: The Development of a Therapeutic Community Prison' *Howard Journal* Vol 42(2), 137–57.

GENDERS, E. AND PLAYER, E. (1989) *Race Relations in Prison*. Oxford, Clarendon Press.

GENDERS, E. AND PLAYER, E. (2007) 'The Commercial Context of Criminal Justice: Prison Privatisation and the Perversion of Purpose' *Criminal Law Review*, 513–29.

GENDERS, E. AND PLAYER, E. (2010) 'Therapy in Prison, Revisiting Grendon 20 Years On' *Howard Journal* Vol 49, 431–50.

GENN, H. (1988) *Hard Bargaining: Out of Court Settlement in Personal Injury Actions*. Oxford, Clarendon Press.

GENN, H. (1999) *Paths to Justice: What People Do and Think about Going to Law*. Oxford, Hart Publishing.

GESCH, C. B., HAMMOND, S. M., HAMPSON, S. E., EVES, A. AND CHOWDER, M. J. (2002) 'Influence of Supplementary Vitamins, Minerals and Essential Fatty Acids on the Antisocial Behaviour of Adult Prisoners: Randomised, Placebo-Controlled Trial' *British Journal of Psychiatry* Vol 181, 22–8.

GIBSON, B. (1990) *Unit Fines*. Winchester, Waterside Press.

GIDDENS, A. (1990) *The Consequences of Modernity*. Cambridge, Polity Press.

GIDDENS, A. (1998) *The Third Way*. Cambridge, Polity Press.

GIDDENS, A. (1999) 'Risk and Responsibility' *Modern Law Review* Vol 62(1), 1–10.

GIDDENS, A. (2000) *The Third Way and its Critics*. Cambridge, Polity Press.

GIES, L. (2014) *Mediating Human Rights: Media, Culture and Human Rights Law*. London, Routledge.

GILL, M. AND SPRIGGS, A. (2005) *Assessing the Impact of CCTV*, Home Office Research Study No. 292. London, Home Office.

GILLER, H. (2000) *Final Warning Interventions*. London, Youth Justice Board.

GIL-ROBLES, A. (2005) *Report by the Commissioner for Human Rights on his Visit to the UK*. Strasbourg, Council of Europe.

GLENN, A. L. AND RAINE, A. (2014) 'Neurocriminology: Implications for the Punishment, Prediction and Prevention of Criminal Behaviour' *Nature Reviews: Neuroscience* 15, 54–63.

GLOVER, J. AND HIBBERT, P. (2009) *Locking Up or Giving Up? Why Custody Thresholds for Teenagers Aged 12, 13 and 14 Need to Be Raised*. Ilford, Barnardo's.

GOLDSON, B. (1999) 'Youth (In)Justice: Contemporary Developments in Policy and Practice' in B. Goldson (ed) *Youth Justice: Contemporary Policy and Practice*. Aldershot, Ashgate, 1–27.

GOLDSON, B. (2000a) 'Wither Diversion? Interventionism and the New Youth Justice' in B. Goldson (ed) *The New Youth Justice*. Lyme Regis, Russell House Publishing, 35–7.

GOLDSON, B. (2000b) 'Children "in Need" or "Young Offenders"? Hardening Ideology, Organisational Change and New Challenges for Social Work with Children in Trouble' *Child and Family Social Work* No. 5, 255–65.

GOLDSON, B. (2006) 'Damage, Harm and Death in Child Prisons in England and Wales: Questions of Abuse and Accountability' *Howard Journal* Vol 45(5), 449–67.

GOLDSON, B. (2014) 'We Must Do More to Protect Children in Prison' *Crime and Justice Studies* 9 May. Available at http://www.crimeandjustice.org.uk/resources/we-must-do-more-protect-children-prison.

GOOCH, K. (2015) 'Who Needs Restraining? Re-examining the Use of Physical Restraint in an English Young Offender Institution' *Journal of Social Welfare and Family Law* Vol 37(1), 3–20.

GOVE, M. (2015a) 'The Treasure in the Heart of Man:—Making Prisons Work', Speech to Prisoner Learning Alliance, 17 July. London, Ministry of Justice.

GOVE, M. (2015b) Speech, Howard League Annual General Meeting, London, 5 November 2015.

GRACE, K. (2013) *Deaths During or Following Police Contact: Statistics for England and Wales 2012/13*, IPCC Research Series Paper 26. London, IPCC.

GRACE, S. (2014) 'Swift, Simple, Effective Justice? Identifying the Aims of Penalty Notices for Disorder and Whether These Have Been Realised in Practice' *Howard Journal of Criminal Justice* Vol 53(1), 69–84.

GRAHAM, J. AND BOWLING, B. (1995) *Young People and Crime*, Home Office Research Study No. 145. London, Home Office.

GRAVETT, S. (2003) *Coping with Prison*. London, Sage.

GRAY, E., TAYLOR, E., ROBERTS, C., MERRINGTON, S., FERNANDEZ, R., AND MOORE, R. (2005) *Intensive Supervision and Surveillance Programme: The Final Report*. London, Youth Justice Board.

GRAY, P. (2007) 'Youth Justice, Social Exclusion and the Demise of Social Justice' *Howard Journal* Vol 46(4), 401–16.

GREEN, P. (2008) *Prison Work and Social Enterprise: The Story of Barbed*. London, Howard League.

GREEN, P. (2010) *Barbed: What Happened Next? Follow Up Story of Employees of a Prison Social Enterprise*. London, Howard League.

GREENE, J. (1998) 'The Unit Fine: Monetary Sanctions Apportioned to Income' in A. von Hirsch and A. Ashworth (eds) *Principled Sentencing, Readings on Theory and Policy*. Oxford, Hart Publishing, 268–71.

GREENFIELD, V. A. AND PAOLI, L. (2013) 'A Framework to Assess the Harms of Crimes' *British Journal of Criminology* Vol 53, 864–85.

GREENHOW, J. (2003) 'Referral Orders: Problems in Practice' *Criminal Law Review*, 266–8.

GREER, S. (2010) 'Anti-Terrorist Laws and the United Kingdom's "Suspect Muslim Community": A Reply to Pantazis and Pemberton' *British Journal of Criminology* Vol 50, 1171–90.

GREIG, D. (2002) *Neither Bad nor Mad: The Competing Discourses of Psychiatry, Law and Politics*. London, Jessica Kingsley.

GRIMSHAW, R., MILLS, H., SILVESTRI, A., AND SILBERHORN-ARMANTRADING, F. (2010a) *Prison and Probation Expenditure, 1999–2009*. London, Centre for Crime and Justice Studies.

GRIMSHAW, R., MILLS, H., SILVESTRI, A., AND SILBERHORN-ARMANTRADING, F. (2010b) *Magistrates' Courts and Crown Court Expenditure, 1999–2009*. London, Centre for Crime and Justice Studies.

GROSMAN, B. (ed) (1980) *New Directions in Sentencing*. Toronto, Butterworths.

GROSS, S. R., O'BRIEN, B., HU, C., AND KENNEDY, E. H. (2015) 'Rate of False Conviction of Criminal Defendants Sentenced to Death' *Proceedings of the Academy of Sciences of the United States of America* Vol 111(2), 7230–5.

GUILFOYLE, M. (2015) *A Changing Service*, Centre for Crime and Justice Studies eBulletin February 2015. Available at http://www.crimeandjustice.org.uk/resources/mike-guilfoyle-changing-service.

GULLICK, M. (2004) 'Sentencing and Early Release of Fixed Term Prisoners' *Criminal Law Review*, 653–62.

HAAS, H., FARRINGTON, D., KILLIAS, M., AND SATTAR, G. (2004) 'The Impact of Different Configurations on Delinquency' *British Journal of Criminology* Vol 44, 520–32.

HACKLER, J. AND GARAPON, A. (1986) *Stealing Conflicts in Juvenile Justice: Contrasting France and Canada*, Discussion Paper 8, Centre for Criminological Research, Edmonton, Alberta, University of Alberta.

HADFIELD, P. (2006) *Bar Wars*. Oxford, Oxford University Press.

HAGELL, A. AND NEWBURN, T. (1994) *Persistent Young Offenders*. London, Policy Studies Institute.

HAIGH, R. (2010) 'Grendon's Contribution to Therapeutic Communities and Personality Disorder' *Howard Journal* Vol 49(5), 503–12.

HAINES, K. AND CASE, S. (2015) 'An Alternative Model of Positive Youth Justice' Centre for Crime and Justice Studies 23 January at http://www.crimeandjustice.org.uk/resources/alternative-model-positive-youth-justice.

HALL, M. (2010) *Victims and Policy-Making: A Comparative Perspective*. Cullompton, Willan.

HALL, S. (2015) 'Why Probation Matters' *Howard Journal of Criminal Justice* Vol 54(4), 321–35.

HALLIDAY REPORT (2001) *Making Punishments Work: Review of the Sentencing Framework for England and Wales*. London, Home Office.

HAMILTON, J. AND WISNIEWSKI, M. (1996) *The Use of the Compensation Order in Scotland*, Crime and Criminal Justice Research Findings No. 14. Edinburgh, The Scottish Office.

HAMLYN, B. AND LEWIS, D. (2000) *Women Prisoners: A Survey of their Work and Training Experiences in Custody and on Release*, Home Office Research Study No. 208. London, Home Office.

HANEY, L. A. (2010) *Offending Women: Power, Punishment and the Regulation of Desire*. Berkeley, University of California Press.

HANMER, J., GRIFFITHS, S., AND JERWOOD, D. (1999) *Arresting Evidence, Domestic Violence and Repeat Victimisation*, Police Research Series, Paper 104. London, Home Office Policing and Reducing Crime Unit, Research and Statistics Directorate.

HANNAH-MOFFAT, K. (2002) 'Creating Choices: Reflecting on Choices' in P. Carlen (ed) *Women in Punishment: The Struggle for Justice*. Cullompton, Willan, 199–219.

HANNAH-MOFFAT, K. AND O'MALLEY, P. (eds) (2007) *Gendered Risks*. London, Routledge-Cavendish.

HANNAN, M., HEARNSDEN, I., GRACE, K., AND BUCKE, T. (2010) *Deaths in or Following Police Custody: An Examination of the Cases 1998/9—2008/9*, IPCC Research Series Paper 17. London, IPCC.

HANSBURY, S. (ed) (2011) *Evaluation of the Intensive Alternatives to Custody Pilots*, Research Summary 3/11. London, Ministry of Justice.

HANSEN, B. (2014) *Punishment and Deterrence: Evidence from Drunk Driving*, Cambridge, MA, National Bureau of Economic Research, Working Paper No. 20245.

HARDING, J. (2000) 'A Community Justice Dimension to Effective Probation Practice' *Howard Journal* Vol 39(2), 132–49.

HARPER, G. AND CHITTY, C. (eds) (2005) *The Impact of Corrections on Re-offending: A Review of 'What Works'* (3rd edn), Home Office Research Study No. 291. London, HORDSD.

HARRIS, R. (1980) 'A Changing Service—The Case for Separating Care and Control in Probation Practice' *British Journal of Social Work* Vol 10(3), 163–84.

HARRIS, R. (1992) *Crime, Criminal Justice and the Probation Service*. London, Routledge.

HARRIS, R. AND WEBB, D. (1987) *Welfare, Power and Juvenile Justice*. London, Tavistock.

HARRISON, K. (2006) 'Community Punishment or Community Rehabilitation: Which Is the Highest in the Sentencing Tariff?' *Howard Journal* Vol 45(2), 141–58.

HARRISON, K. (2011) *Dangerousness, Risk and the Governance of Serious Violent and Sexual Offenders*. London, Routledge.

HART, H. L. A. (1968) *Punishment and Responsibility: Essays in the Philosophy of Law*. Oxford, Oxford University Press.

HARVEY, C. W. (1984) 'Hegel's Theory of Punishment Reconsidered' *Dialogos* Vol 43, 71–80.

HARWIN, J. AND RYAN, M. (2007) 'The Role of the Court in Cases Concerning Parental Substance Misuse and Children at Risk of Harm' *Journal of Social Welfare and Family Law* Vol 29(3 and 4), 277–92.

HARWIN, J., RYAN, R., TUNNARD, J., POKHREL, S., ALROUH, B., MATIAS, C., AND MOMENIAN-SCHNEID, S. (2011) *The Family Drug & Alcohol Court (FDAC) Evaluation Project Final Report*. Brunel University, Uxbridge.

HAWKINS, K. (2002) *Law as Last Resort*. Oxford, Oxford University Press.

HAWKINS, K. (ed) (1992) *The Uses of Discretion*. Oxford, Clarendon.

HAWLEY, J., MURPHY, I., AND SOURO-OTERO, M. (2013) *Prisoners' Education and Training in Europe*. London, GHK Consulting.

HAY, C. (1995) 'Mobilisation through Interpellation—James Bulger, Juvenile Crime and the Construction of a Moral Panic' *Social and Legal Studies* Vol 4(2), 197–223.

HAY, D., LINEBAUGH, P., AND THOMPSON, E. P. (1975) *Albion's Fatal Tree*. London, Allen Lane.

HAYES, M. AND WILLIAMS, C. (1999) '"Offending" Behaviour and Children under 10' *Family Law* Vol 29, 317–20.

HAZELL, N. (2008) *Cross-National Comparison of Youth Justice*. London, YJB.

HEALTH AND SAFETY EXECUTIVE (2011) *Statistics 2010/11*, London, HSE.

HEALTHCARE COMMISSION (2009) *Actions Speak Louder: A Second Review of Healthcare in the Community for Young People who Offend*. London, Commission for Healthcare Audit and Inspection and HM Inspectorate of Probation.

HEBENTON, B. AND SEDDON, T. (2009) 'From Dangerousness to Precaution: Managing Sexual and Violent Offenders in an Insecure and Uncertain Age' *British Journal of Criminology* Vol 49, 343–62.

HEDDERMAN, C. (1990) *The Effect of Defendants' Demeanour on Sentencing in the Magistrates' Courts*. Home Office Research and Development Research Bulletin No. 29, 32–6.

HEDDERMAN, C. (2010) 'Government Policy on Women Offenders, Labour's Legacy and the Coalition's Challenge' *Punishment and Society* Vol 12(4), 485–500.

HEDDERMAN, C. AND GELSTHORPE, L. (1997) *Understanding the Sentencing of Women*, Home Office Research Study No. 170. London, HMSO.

HEDDERMAN, C., GUNBY, C., AND SHELTON, N. (2011) 'What Women Want: The Importance of Qualitative Approaches in Evaluating Work with Women Offenders' *Criminology and Criminal Justice* Vol 11(1), 3–19.

HEGEL, G. W. (1832) *Hegel's Philosophy of Right*, trans. T. M. Knox, 1952. Oxford, Clarendon Press.

HEIDENSOHN, F. (ed) (2006) *Gender and Justice: New Concepts and Approaches*. Cullompton, Willan.

HENHAM, R. (1995) 'Sentencing Policy and the Role of the Court of Appeal' *Howard Journal* Vol 34(3), 218–27.

HENHAM, R. (1997) 'Anglo-American Approaches to Cumulative Sentencing and the Implications for UK Sentencing Policy' *Howard Journal* Vol 36(3), 263–83.

HENHAM, R. (1999) 'Bargain Justice or Justice Denied? Sentence Discounts and the Criminal Process' *Modern Law Review* Vol 62(4), 515–38.

HENHAM, R. (2001) 'Sentencing Dangerous Offenders: Policy and Practice in the Crown Court' *Criminal Law Review*, 693–711.

HENHAM, R. (2012) *Sentencing and the Legitimacy of Criminal Justice*. London, Routledge.

HETHERINGTON, A. (1996) 'The Legitimacy of Capital Punishment in Hegel's *Philosophy of Right*' *Owl of Minerva* Vol 27, 167–74.

HEYMAN, S. J. (1996) 'The Legitimacy of Capital Punishment in Hegel's *Philosophy of Right*: A Comment' *Owl of Minerva* Vol 27, 175–80.

HIBISCUS INITIATIVES (2014) *Annual Report 2013-2014*, London, Hibiscus.

HILLERY, G. (1955) 'Definitions of Community: Areas of Agreement' *Rural Sociology* Vol 20(2), 111–23.

HINCHMAN, L. P. (1991) 'On Reconciling Happiness and Autonomy: An Interpretation of Hegel's Moral Philosophy' *Owl of Minerva* Vol 23, 29–48.

HINE, J. (2007) 'Young People's Perspectives on Final Warnings' *Web JCLI* Vol 2. Available at http://www.bailii.org/uk/other/journals/WebJCLI/2007/issue2/hine2.html.

HIRTLENLENHER, H., PAUWELS, L., AND MEŠKO, G. (2014) 'Is the Effect of Perceived Deterrence on Juvenile Offending Contingent on the Level of Self-Control? Results from Three Countries' *British Journal of Criminology* Vol 54(1), 128–50.

HM CHIEF INSPECTOR OF PRISONS (1997) *Women in Prison: A Thematic Review*. London, Home Office.

HM CHIEF INSPECTOR OF PRISONS (1998) *Report on an Unannounced Short Inspection of HMP Woodhill 14–16 July 1998*. London, HMCIP.

HM CHIEF INSPECTOR OF PRISONS (2001) *Follow Up to Women in Prison: A Thematic Review*. London, Home Office.

HM CHIEF INSPECTOR OF PRISONS (2005) *Report on an Unannounced Inspection of HMP Rye Hill, 11–15 April 2005*. London, HMIP.

HM CHIEF INSPECTOR OF PRISONS (2007) *Annual Report England and Wales 2005–06*. London, Stationery Office.

HM CHIEF INSPECTOR OF PRISONS (2008a) *Annual Report England and Wales 2006–07*. London, The Stationery Office.

HM CHIEF INSPECTOR OF PRISONS (2008b) *Older Prisoners in England and Wales: A Follow-Up to the 2004 Thematic Review by HM Chief Inspector of Prisons*. London, HMIP.

HM CHIEF INSPECTOR OF PRISONS (2010a) *Annual Report 2008–09*. London, HMIP.

HM CHIEF INSPECTOR OF PRISONS (2010b) *Muslim Prisoners' Experiences: A Thematic Review*. London, HMIP.

HM CHIEF INSPECTOR OF PRISONS (2011a) *Annual Report 2010–11*. London, HMIP.

HM CHIEF INSPECTOR OF PRISONS (2011b) *Report on a Full Unannounced Inspection of HMP & YOI Parc, 15–24 September 2010*. London, HMIP.

HM CHIEF INSPECTOR OF PRISONS (2014) *Annual Report 2013–14*. London, HMIP.

HM CHIEF INSPECTOR OF PRISONS (2015) *Annual Report 2014–15*. London, HMIP.

HM GOVERNMENT (2005) *Statutory Guidance on Inter-agency Co-operation to Improve the Wellbeing of Children: Children's Trusts*. London, DfES.

HM GOVERNMENT (2015) *Working Together to Safeguard Children: A Guide to Inter-agency Working to Safeguard and Promote the Welfare of Children*. London, Department for Education.

HM INSPECTORATE OF PRISONS (2004) *Juveniles in Custody*. London, HMIP.

HM INSPECTORATE OF PRISONS (2005) *Parallel Worlds: A Thematic Review of Race Relations in Prison*. London, HMIP.

HM INSPECTORATE OF PRISONS (2006) *Foreign National Prisoners: A Thematic Review*. London, HMIP.

HM INSPECTORATE OF PRISONS (2007) *The Mental Health of Prisoners: A Thematic Review of the Care and Support of Prisoners with Mental Health Needs.* London, HMIP.

HM INSPECTORATE OF PRISONS (2008) *Report on an Announced Inspection of the Management, Care and Control of Young People at Oakhill Secure Training Centre.* London, HMIP.

HM INSPECTORATE OF PRISONS (2009a) *Disabled Prisoners: A Short Thematic Review on the Care and Support of Prisoners with a Disability.* London, HMIP.

HM INSPECTORATE OF PRISONS (2009b) *Race Relations in Prison: Responding to Adult Women from Black and Minority Ethnic Backgrounds.* London, HMIP.

HM INSPECTORATE OF PRISONS (2010) *Women in Prison: A Short Thematic Review.* London, HMIP.

HM INSPECTORATE OF PRISONS (2014a) *Expectations: Criteria for Assessing the Treatment of and Conditions for Women in Prison.* London, Ministry of Justice.

HM INSPECTORATE OF PRISONS (2014b) *Report of a Review of the Implementation of the Zahid Mubarek Inquiry Recommendations, A Thematic Review by HM Inspectorate of Prisons.* London, HMIP.

HM INSPECTORATE OF PRISONS (2014c) *People in Prison: Gypsies, Romanies and Travellers — A Findings Paper.* London, HMIP. Available at http://www.justiceinspectorates.gov.uk/prisons/wpcontent/uploads/sites/4/2014/04/gypsies-romany-travellers-findings.pdf.

HM INSPECTORATE OF PRISONS, HM INSPECTORATE OF PROBATION, AND OFSTED (2014) *Resettlement Provision for Adult Offenders: Accommodation and Education, Training and Employment.* London, HM Inspectorate of Prisons.

HM INSPECTORATE OF PROBATION (1997) 'Risk Management Guidance' in *Management and Assessment of Risk in the Probation Service.* London, Home Office.

HM INSPECTORATE OF PROBATION (2000) *Towards Race Equality: A Thematic Inspection.* London, HMSO.

HM INSPECTORATE OF PROBATION (2006a) *An Independent Review of a Serious Further Offence Case: Anthony Rice.* London, Home Office.

HM INSPECTORATE OF PROBATION (2006b) *Working to Make Amends.* London, HMIP.

HM INSPECTORATE OF PROBATION, HM INSPECTORATE OF COURTS ADMINISTRATION, HM INSPECTORATE OF CONSTABULARY (2007) *A Summary of Findings on the Enforcement of Community Penalties from Three Joint Area Inspections,* Thematic Inspections Report. London, Home Office.

HM INSPECTORATE OF PROBATION /HM INSPECTORATE OF PRISONS (2015) *A Joint Inspection of the Treatment of Offenders with Learning Disabilities within the Criminal Justice System: Phase Two in Custody and the Community.* London, HM Inspectorate of Prisons.

HM PRISON SERVICE (2004) *Annual Report 2003–2004.* London, HM Prison Service.

HM PRISON SERVICE (2007) *Business Plan 2006–2007.* London, NOMS.

HM PRISON SERVICE/CRE (2003) *Implementing Race Equality in Prisons: A Shared Agenda for Change.* London, HM Prison Service.

HM TREASURY (2015) *Spending Review and Autumn Statement 2015,* Cm 9162. London, HM Treasury.

HOBBES, T. (1651) *Leviathan,* ed. J. Plamenatz (1962). Glasgow, Collins.

HODGSON COMMITTEE (1984) *The Profits of Crime and their Recovery.* Aldershot, Gower.

HOLDAWAY, S. AND DESBOROUGH, S. (2004) *The National Evaluation of the Youth Justice Board's Final Warning Projects.* London: YJB.

HOLDAWAY, S., DAVIDSON, N., DIGNAN, J., HAMMERSLEY, R., HINE, J., AND MARSH, P. (2001) *New Strategies to Address Youth*

Offending—The National Evaluation of the Pilot Youth Offending Teams, RDS Occasional Paper 69. London, Home Office.

HOLLINGSWORTH, K. (2006) 'R (W) v Commissioner of Police for the Metropolis and Another—Interpreting Child Curfews: A Question of Rights?' *Child and Family Law Quarterly* Vol 18(2), 253–68.

HOLLINGSWORTH, K. (2007) 'Responsibility and Rights: Children and their Parents in the Youth Justice System' *International Journal of Law, Policy and the Family* Vol 21(2), 190–219.

HOLLINGSWORTH, K. (2012a) 'Securing Parity, Achieving Responsibility: The Legal Support for Children Leaving Custody' *Legal Studies* Vol 33(1), 22–45.

HOLLINGSWORTH, K. (2012b) 'Youth Justice Reform in the "Big Society"' *Journal of Social Welfare and Family Law*, Vol 34(2), 245–59.

HOLLINGSWORTH, K. (2014) 'Re-imagining Justice for Children: A New Rights-Based Approach to Youth Justice' *Howard League What is Justice? Working Papers. 10/2014*. London, Howard League.

HOLMGREN, M. (2012) *Forgiveness and Retribution: Responding to Wrongdoing*. Cambridge, Cambridge University Press.

HOME OFFICE (1951) *Sixth Report on the Work of the Children's Department*. London, HMSO.

HOME OFFICE (1968) *Children in Trouble*, Cmnd 3601. London, HMSO.

HOME OFFICE (1984) *Statement of National Standards and Objectives for the Probation Service*. London, Home Office.

HOME OFFICE (1988a) *Punishment, Custody and the Community* Consultation Paper, Cm 424. London: HMSO.

HOME OFFICE (1988b) *Tackling Offending: An Action Plan*. London, HMSO.

HOME OFFICE (1990a) *Crime, Justice and Protecting the Public: The Government's Proposals for Legislation*, Cm 965. London, HMSO.

HOME OFFICE (1990b) *Supervision and Punishment in the Community*, Cm 966. London, HMSO.

HOME OFFICE (1990c) *Partnership in Dealing with Offenders in the Community*, London, HMSO.

HOME OFFICE (1990d) *Provision for Mentally Disordered Offenders*. Circular 66/1990. London, HMSO.

HOME OFFICE (1991) *Custody, Care and Justice: The Way Ahead for the Prison Service in England and Wales*, Cm 1647. London, HMSO.

HOME OFFICE (1994a) *Monitoring of the Criminal Justice Acts 1991 and 1993—Results from a Special Data Collection Exercise*, Home Office Statistical Bulletin Issue 20/94. London, Home Office.

HOME OFFICE (1994b) *Revised Standards: The Cautioning of Offenders*. London, Home Office.

HOME OFFICE (1995a) *Strengthening Punishment in the Community*, Cmnd 2780. London, HMSO.

HOME OFFICE (1995b) *New Arrangements for the Recruitment and Qualifying Training of Probation Officers*. London, Home Office.

HOME OFFICE (1996a) *Protecting the Public: The Government's Strategy on Crime in England and Wales*, Cm 3190. London, HMSO.

HOME OFFICE (1996b) *The Prison Population in 1995*, Home Office Statistical Bulletin Issue 14/96. London, Home Office.

HOME OFFICE (1997) *No More Excuses: A New Approach to Tackling Youth Crime in England and Wales*, Cm 3809. London, The Stationery Office.

HOME OFFICE (1998a) *Joining Forces to Protect the Public: Prisons—Probation*. London, Home Office.

HOME OFFICE (1998b) *Bind Overs: A Power for the 21st Century*, Cm 3908. London, Home Office.

HOME OFFICE (1999a) *Managing Dangerous People with Severe Personality Disorder*.

Proposals for Policy Development. London, Home Office.

HOME OFFICE (1999b) *The Correctional Policy Framework*. London, Home Office.

HOME OFFICE (2000a) *The Government's Strategy for Women Offenders*. London, Home Office.

HOME OFFICE (2000b) *The Victim Perspective: Ensuring the Victim Matters*. Thematic Inspection Report, HM Inspectorate of Probation. London, Home Office.

HOME OFFICE (2001a) *Criminal Justice: The Way Ahead*. Cm 5074. London, HMSO.

HOME OFFICE (2001b) *The Government's Strategy for Women Offenders: Consultation Report*. London, Home Office.

HOME OFFICE (2001c) *Victim Personal Statements*, Circular 35/2001. London, Justice and Victims' Unit, Home Office.

HOME OFFICE (2002a) *An Evaluation of Cognitive Behavioural Treatment for Prisoners*. London, Home Office.

HOME OFFICE (2002b) 'Falconer—Clear and Effective Sentencing Policy', Press Release: 257/2002. London, Home Office.

HOME OFFICE (2002c) *Justice for All*, Cm 5563. London, The Stationery Office.

HOME OFFICE (2002d) *Press Release 274/ 2002*. London, Home Office.

HOME OFFICE (2003a) *Restorative Justice: The Government's Strategy*, Consultation Paper. London, Home Office.

HOME OFFICE (2003b) *Respect and Responsibility—Taking a Stand against Anti-Social Behaviour*, Cm 5778. London, Stationery Office.

HOME OFFICE (2003c) *Youth Justice—The Next Steps*. London, Home Office.

HOME OFFICE (2003d) *A New Deal for Victims and Witnesses*. London, Home Office.

HOME OFFICE (2003e) *Valuing the Victim— An Inspection into National Victim Contact Arrangements*, Thematic Inspection Report,

HM Inspectorate of Probation. London, Home Office.

HOME OFFICE (2003f) *Prison Statistics: England and Wales 2002*, Cm 5996. London, The Stationery Office.

HOME OFFICE (2003g) *Criminal Statistics, England and Wales 2002*, Cm 6054. London, The Stationery Office.

HOME OFFICE (2004a) *Compensation and Support for Victims of Crime*, Consultation Paper. London, Home Office.

HOME OFFICE (2004b) *Reducing Crime, Changing Lives*. London, The Stationery Office.

HOME OFFICE (2005a) *OASys Implementation and its Development*, Probation Circular 14/2005. London, Home Office.

HOME OFFICE (2005b) *A Five Year Strategy for Protecting the Public and Reducing Re-offending*, Cm 6717. London, The Stationery Office.

HOME OFFICE (2005c) *Probation Circular 25/2005: Criminal Justice Act 2003: Implementation on 4 April*. London, Home Office. Available at http://webarchive. nationalarchives.gov.uk/20101216070244/ http://www.probation.homeoffice.gov.uk/ files/pdf/PC25%202005.pdf.

HOME OFFICE (2006a) *Rebalancing the Criminal Justice System in Favour of the Law-Abiding Majority: Reducing Reoffending and Protecting the Public*. London, Home Office.

HOME OFFICE (2006b) *Improving Prison and Probation Services: Public Value Partnerships*. London, Home Office.

HOME OFFICE (2006c) *Tackling Anti-Social Behaviour*, National Audit Office 'Value for Money' Report by the Comptroller and Auditor General, HC 99 2006–7. London, The Stationery Office.

HOME OFFICE (2007a) *Cutting Crime: A New Partnership*. London, Home Office.

HOME OFFICE (2007b) *Bringing Offenders to Justice: Criminal Justice Penalties and Sentencing*. London, Home Office.

HOME OFFICE (2007c) *Sentencing Statistics 2005 England and Wales,* Home Office Statistical Bulletin 03/07. London, Home Office.

HOME OFFICE (2007d) *Guidance on the Use of Acceptable Behaviour Contracts and Agreements.* London, Home Office.

HOME OFFICE (2008) *Working Together to Protect the Public: The Home Office Strategy 2008–11.* London, Home Office.

HOME OFFICE (2010) *Prolific and Other Priority Offenders, Results from the 2009 cohort for England and Wales.* Available at https://www.gov.uk/ government/uploads/system/uploads/ attachment_data/file/115712/misc0310. pdf.

HOME OFFICE (2011a) *An Overview of Recorded Crimes and Arrests Resulting from Disorder Events in August 2011.* London, Home Office.

HOME OFFICE (2011b) *More Effective Responses to Anti-Social Behaviour.* London, Home Office.

HOME OFFICE (2012a) *An Estimate of Youth Crime in England and Wales: Police Recorded Crime Committed by Young People in 2009/10,* Home Office Report 64. London, Home Office.

HOME OFFICE (2012b) *Putting Victims First—More Effective Responses to Antisocial Behaviour.* Cm 8367. London, TSO.

HOME OFFICE (2013) *Surveillance Camera Code of Practice.* London, TSO.

HOME OFFICE (2015) *Police Powers and Procedures England and Wales Year Ending 31 March 2014.* London, Home Office.

HOME OFFICE, DEPARTMENT OF HEALTH, AND WELSH OFFICE (2000) *National Standards for the Supervision of Offenders in the Community.* London, The Stationery Office.

HOME OFFICE, MINISTRY OF JUSTICE, CABINET OFFICE, DEPARTMENT FOR CHILDREN, SCHOOLS AND FAMILIES (2008) *Youth Crime Action Plan 2008.* London, HM Government.

HOME OFFICE/YOUTH JUSTICE BOARD (2002) *Final Warning Scheme: Guidance to the Police and Youth Offending Teams.* London, Home Office.

HOME SECRETARY, LORD CHANCELLOR AND ATTORNEY GENERAL (2006) *Making Sentencing Clearer: A Consultation and Report of a Review.* London, Home Office.

HOOD, R. (1962) *Sentencing in Magistrates' Courts.* London, Tavistock.

HOOD, R. (1992) *Race and Sentencing.* Oxford, Clarendon Press.

HOOD, R. AND HOYLE, C. (2008) *The Death Penalty: A Worldwide Perspective* (4th edn). Oxford, Clarendon.

HOOD, R. AND HOYLE, C. (2015) *The Death Penalty: A Worldwide Perspective* (5th edn). Oxford, Oxford University Press.

HOOD, R., SHUTE, S., FEILZER, M., AND WILCOX, M. (2002) *Reconviction Rates of Serious Sex Offenders and Assessments of their Risk,* HORS 164. London, Home Office.

HOPLEY, K. (2002) 'National Standards: Defining Service' in D. Ward, J. Scott, and M. Lacey (eds) *Probation: Working for Justice* (2nd edn). Oxford, Oxford University Press, Chapter 18.

HOUGH, M. AND JACOBSON, J. (2008) *Creating a Sentencing Commission for England and Wales: An Opportunity to Address the Prison Crisis.* London, Prison Reform Trust.

HOUGH, M. AND ROBERTS, J. (1998) *Attitudes to Punishment: Findings from the British Crime Survey,* Home Office Research Study No. 179. London, HMSO.

HOUGH, M. AND ROBERTS, J. (2005) 'Sentencing Young Offenders: Public Opinion in England and Wales' *Criminal Justice* Vol 5(3), 12–32.

HOUGH, M., FARRALL, S., AND MCNEIL, F. (2013) *Intelligent Justice: Balancing the Effects of Community Sentencing and Custody.* London, Howard League.

HOUGH, M., JACOBSON, J., AND MILLIE, A. (2003) *The Decision to Imprison: Sentencing and the Prison Population.* London, Prison Reform Trust.

HOUGH, M., ROBERTS, J. V., JACOBSON, J., MOON, N., AND STEEL, N. (2009) *Public Attitudes to the Principles of Sentencing*, Sentencing Advisory Panel Report No. 6. London, Sentencing Advisory Panel.

HOUSE OF COMMONS JUSTICE COMMITTEE (2009) *Draft Sentencing Guideline: Overarching Principles—Sentencing Youths*, Tenth Report of Session 2008–9, HC 497. London, The Stationery Office.

HOUSE OF COMMONS JUSTICE COMMITTEE (2010) *Cutting Crime, the Case for Justice Reinvestment*, First Report of Session 2009–10 Vol 1, HC 94–1. London, The Stationery Office.

HOUSE OF COMMONS JUSTICE COMMITTEE (2011) *Revised Sentencing Guideline: Assault, Justice*, First Report of Session 2010–11, HC 637. London, TSO.

HOUSE OF COMMONS JUSTICE COMMITTEE (2013a) *Women Offenders: After the Corston Report*, Second Report of Session 2013–14. London, TSO.

HOUSE OF COMMONS JUSTICE COMMITTEE (2013b) *Older prisoners: Fifth Report of Session 2013–14*. London, House of Commons.

HOUSE OF COMMONS JUSTICE COMMITTEE (2013c) *Youth Justice, 7th report of session 2012–13*, HC 339, Vol 1. London: TSO. Available at http://www.publications. parliament.uk/pa/cm201213/cmselect/ cmjust/339/33902.htm.

HOUSE OF COMMONS JUSTICE COMMITTEE (2015a) *Prisons: Planning and Policies, Ninth Report of Session 2014–15*. London, TSO.

HOUSE OF COMMONS JUSTICE COMMITTEE (2015b) *Women Offenders: Follow-Up*, HC 849. London, TSO.

HOWARD, D. AND CHRISTOPHERSEN, O. (2003) *Statistics of Mentally Disordered Offenders 2002*. RDS 14/03. London, Home Office.

HOWARD LEAGUE (2008) *Punishing Children: A Survey of Criminal Responsibility and Approaches Across Europe*. London, Howard League.

HOWARD LEAGUE (2012) 'News', *ECAN Bulletin* Issue 16. London, Howard League.

HOWARD LEAGUE (2013) 'Drop in GCSE Passes of Young People in Custody', *ECAN Bulletin* Issue 19. London, Howard League.

HOWARD LEAGUE FOR PENAL REFORM (2000) *A Chance to Break the Cycle: Women and the Drug Treatment and Testing Order*, Briefing Paper. London, Howard League for Penal Reform.

HOWARD LEAGUE FOR PENAL REFORM (2004) *Advice, Understanding and Underwear: Working with Girls in Prison*. London, Howard League for Penal Reform.

HOWARD LEAGUE FOR PENAL REFORM (2007) *Children in Prison: An Independent Submission to the United Nations Committee on the Rights of the Child*. London, Howard League for Penal Reform.

HOWARD LEAGUE FOR PENAL REFORM (2010a) *Submission to the Justice Affairs Select Committee Inquiry on the Role of the Probation Service*, 16 September. London, Howard League.

HOWARD LEAGUE FOR PENAL REFORM (2010b) *Life Inside 2010: A Unique Insight into the Day to Day Experiences of 15–17 Year Old Males in Prison*. London, Howard League.

HOWARD LEAGUE FOR PENAL REFORM (2011) *Twisted: The Use of Force on Children in Custody*. London, Howard League.

HOWDEN-WINDELL, J. AND CLARK, D. (1999) *Criminogenic Needs of Female Offenders: A Literature Review, Report to Women's Policy Group*. London, Home Office.

HOWSE, K. (2003) *Growing Old in Prison—A Scoping Study of Older Prisoners*. London, Prison Reform Trust.

HOYLE, C. (2008) *Restorative Justice Working Group Discussion Paper*. London, Commission on English Prisons Today.

HOYLE, C., YOUNG, R., AND HILL, R. (2002) *Proceed with Caution: An Evaluation of the Thames Valley Police Initiative in Restorative Cautioning*. York, Joseph Rowntree Foundation.

HUCKLESBY, A. AND HAGLEY-DICKINSON, L. (eds) (2007) *Prisoner Resettlement: Current Policy and Practice*. Cullompton, Willan.

HUDSON, B. (1993) *Penal Policy and Social Justice*. London, Macmillan.

HUDSON, B. (1998) 'Mitigation for Socially Deprived Offenders' in A. von Hirsch and A. Ashworth (eds) *Principled Sentencing: Readings on Theory and Policy*. Oxford, Hart, 205–8.

HUDSON, B. (2001) 'Human Rights, Public Safety and the Probation Service: Defending Justice in the Risk Society' *Howard Journal* Vol 40(2), 103–13.

HUDSON, B. (2001/2) 'The Halliday Report: Opening or Closing the Revolving Door?' *Criminal Justice Matters* No. 46, 7–8.

HUDSON, B. (2003) *Justice in the Risk Society*. London, Sage.

HULSMAN, L. (1991) 'Alternatives to Criminal Justice, Decriminalization and Depenalization' in Z. Lazocik, M. Platek, and I. Rzeplinska (eds) *Abolitionism in History, On Another Way of Thinking*. Warsaw, Institute of Social Prevention and Resocialization, 47–62.

HUMAN RIGHTS JOINT COMMITTEE (2011) *Twenty-Second Report, Legislative Scrutiny, Legal Aid, Sentencing and Punishment of Offenders Bill*. London, Houses of Parliament.

HUTCHINSON, S. (2006) 'Countering Catastrophic Criminology' *Punishment and Society* Vol 8(4), 443–67.

HUTTON, N. (2005) 'Beyond Popular Punitiveness?' *Punishment and Society* Vol 73(3), 243–58.

IEVINS, A. AND CREWE, B. (2015) '"Nobody's better than you, nobody's worse than you": Moral Community among Prisoners Convicted of Sexual Offences' *Punishment and Society* Vol 17(4), 482–501.

IMB (INDEPENDENT MONITORING BOARDS) (2015) *Oasys in Prisons: Monitoring Fairness and Respect for People in Custody*, Report of the OASYS Investigation Group. Available at http://www.imb.org.uk/wp-content/uploads/2015/07/IMB-Offender-Assessment-Group-Report.pdf.

IMPALOX GROUP (2007) *Evaluation of the Assessment Procedure at Two Pilot Sites in the DSPD Programme*. London, Home Office.

INGLEBY REPORT (1960) *Report of the Committee on Children and Young Persons* Cmnd 1190. London, HMSO.

INQUEST (1998) *Report on the Death in Prison Custody of Alton Manning*. London, Inquest.

INTERNATIONAL CENTRE FOR PRISON STUDIES (2011) *World Prison Brief*. Colchester, University of Essex.

INTERNATIONAL CENTRE FOR PRISON STUDIES (2015) *World Prison Brief*. Colchester, University of Essex.

INTERNATIONAL CENTRE FOR PRISON STUDIES (2016) *World Prison Brief*. Colchester, University of Essex.

IRISS (THE INSTITUTE FOR RESEARCH AND INNOVATION IN SOCIAL SERVICES) (2010) *Intensive Supervision, Surveillance and Monitoring of Young People*, IRISS Insights, No. 9. Glasgow, IRISS.

JACKSON, E. (2007) 'Prisoners, their Partners and the Right to Family Life' *Child and Family Law Quarterly* Vol 19(2), 239–46.

JACKSON, J. (2003) 'Justice for All: Putting Victims at the Heart of Criminal Justice' *Journal of Law and Society* Vol 30(2), 309–26.

JACKSON, J., BRADFORD, B., HOUGH, M., MYHILL, A., QUINTON, P. AND TYLER, T. R. (2012) 'Why Do People Comply with the Law?: Legitimacy and the Influence of Legal Institutions' *British Journal of Criminology* Vol 52, 1051–71.

JACKSON, S. (1999) 'Family Group Conferences and Youth Justice' in B. Goldson (ed) *Youth Justice: Contemporary Policy and Practice*. Aldershot, Ashgate.

JACOBSON, J. AND HOUGH, M. (2007) *Mitigation: The Role of Personal Factors in Sentencing*. London, Prison Reform Trust.

JACOBSON, J. AND HOUGH, M. (2010) *Unjust Deserts: Imprisonment for Public Protection*. London, Prison Reform Trust.

JACOBSON, J. AND HOUGH, M. (2011) 'Personal Mitigation: An Empirical Analysis in England and Wales' in J. Roberts (ed) *Mitigation and Aggravation at Sentencing*. Cambridge, Cambridge University Press, 146–67.

JACOBSON, J., BHARDWA, B., GYATENG, T., HUNTER, G., AND HOUGH, M. (2011) *Punishing Disadvantage: A Profile of Children in Custody*. London, Prison Reform Trust.

JACOBSON, J., KIRBY, A., AND HOUGH, M. (2011), *Public Attitudes to the Sentencing of Drug Offences*, Sentencing Council Research Series 01/11. London, Office of the Sentencing Council.

JAGO, R. AND THOMPSON, E. (2001) 'Private Prison Contractors' in M. Leech and D. Cheney (eds) *The Prisons Handbook*. Winchester, Waterside Press, 253–6.

JAMES, A. (1995) 'Probation Values for the 1990s—and Beyond?' *Howard Journal* Vol 34(4), 326–43.

JAMES, A. AND JAMES, A. L. (2008) 'Changing Childhood in England: Reconstructing Discourse of "Risk" and "Protection" in Children's Best Interests' in A. James and A. L. James (eds) *European Childhoods: Culture, Politics and Participation*. Basingstoke, Palgrave Macmillan.

JAMES, A. L., BOTTOMLEY, A. K., LIEBLING, A., AND CLARE, E. (1997) *Privatizing Prisons: Rhetoric and Reality*. London, Sage.

JANSSON, K. (2015) *Public Confidence in the Criminal Justice System—Findings from the Crime Survey for England and Wales (2013/14), Analytical Summary 2015*. London, Ministry of Justice.

JEFFREY, C. R. (1965) 'Criminal Behaviour and Learning Theory' *Journal of Criminal Law, Criminology and Police Science* Vol 56, 294–300.

JENKS, C. (1996) *Childhood*. London, Routledge.

JOBARD, F. (2009) 'Rioting as a Political Tool: The 2005 Riots in France' *Howard Journal of Criminal Justice* Vol 48(3), 235–44.

JOHNSON, D. (2009) 'Anger about Crime and Support for Punitive Criminal Justice Policies' *Punishment and Society* Vol 11(1), 51–66.

JOHNSTONE, G. (ed) (2011) *Restorative Justice* (2nd edn). London, Routledge.

JONES, A. AND SINGER, L. (2007) *Statistics on Race and the Criminal Justice System—2006*. London, Ministry of Justice.

JONES, C. R. (2014) 'Are Prisons Really Schools for Terrorism? Challenging the Rhetoric on Prison Radicalization' *Punishment and Society* Vol 16(1), 74–103.

JONES, D. (2001) ' "Misjudged Youth": A Critique of the Audit Commission's Reports on Youth Justice' *British Journal of Criminology* Vol 41, 362–80.

JUDICIAL STUDIES BOARD (undated) Reporting Restrictions: Magistrates' Courts. Available at http://www.jsboard.co.uk/publications/rrmc/index.htm accessed 12 September 2007.

JUNGER-TAS, J. (1994) 'The Changing Family and its Relationship with Delinquent Behaviour' in C. Henricson (ed) *Crime and the Family*, Family Policy Studies Centre Occasional Paper 20. London, Family Policy Studies Centre, 18–25.

JUNGER-TAS, J. (2002) 'The Juvenile System: Past and Present Trends in Western Society' in I. Weijers and A. Duff (eds) *Punishing Juveniles, Principle and Critique*. Oxford, Hart, 23–44.

JUSTICE (1998) *Victims in Criminal Justice*, Report of the JUSTICE Committee on the Role of the Victim in Criminal Justice. London, JUSTICE.

JUSTICE COMMITTEE (2009) *Sentencing Guidelines and Parliament: Building a Bridge*, Sixth Report of the House of Commons Justice Committee Session 2008–9. Available at http://www.publications.parliament.uk/pa/cm200809/cmselect/cmjust/715/71502.htm.

KANT, I. (1796–7) *The Metaphysics of Morals*, trans. Mary Gregor (1991). Cambridge, Cambridge University Press.

KARSTEDT, S., LOADER, L., AND STRANG, H. (eds) (2014) *Emotions, Crime and Justice.* Oxford, Hart.

KAZEMIAN, L. (2010) 'Assessing the Impact of a Recidivist Sentencing Premium' in J. V. Roberts and A. von Hirsch (eds) *Previous Convictions at Sentencing, Theoretical and Applied Perspectives.* Oxford, Hart Publishing, 227–50.

KAZEMIAN, L., FARRINGTON, D. P., AND LeBLANC, M. (2009) 'Can We Make Accurate Predictions about Patterns of De-escalation in Offending Behaviour?' *Journal of Youth and Adolescence* Vol 38, 384–400.

KEATING, H. (2007) 'The "Responsibility" of Children in Criminal Law' *Child and Family Law Quarterly* Vol 19(2), 183–203.

KEITH, B. (2006) *Report of the Zahid Mubarek Inquiry*, HC 1082. London, The Stationery Office.

KELLY, D. P. AND EREZ, E. (1997) 'Victim Participation in the Criminal Justice System' in R. C. Davis, A. J. Lurigio and W. G. Skogan (eds) *Victims of Crime* (2nd edn). Thousand Oaks, Sage, 211–30.

KELLY, L. AND ARMITAGE, V. (2015) 'Diverse Diversions: Youth Justice Reform, Localized Practices, and a 'New Interventionist Diversion'? *Youth Justice* Vol 15(2), 117–33.

KEMPF-LEONARD, K. AND PETERSON, E. (2000) 'Expanding the Realms of the New Penology' *Punishment and Society* Vol 2(1), 66–97.

KEMSHALL, H. (2002) 'Effective Practice in Probation: An Example of "Advanced Liberal" Responsibilisation?' *Howard Journal* Vol 31(1), 41–58.

KEMSHALL, H. AND WOOD, J. (2010) *Child Sex Offender Review (CSOR) Public Disclosure Pilots, A Process Evaluation* (2nd edn), Home Office Research Report No. 32. London, Home Office.

KENNEDY, D. M. (2009) *Deterrence and Crime Prevention: Reconsidering the Prospect of Sanction.* London, Routledge.

KENNEDY, L. (1990) *On the Borders of Crime, Conflict Management and Criminology.* New York, Longmans.

KERSHAW, C., GOODMAN, J., AND WHITE, S. (1999) *Reconvictions of Offenders Sentenced or Discharged from Prison in 1995 in England and Wales*, Home Office Statistical Bulletin 19/99. London, Home Office.

KILBRANDON, LORD (1964) *Children and Young Persons, Scotland.* Edinburgh, Scottish Home and Health Department.

KILKELLY, U. AND LUNDY, L. (2006) 'Children's Rights in Action in Using the UN Convention on the Rights of the Child as an Auditing Tool' *Child and Family Law Quarterly* Vol 18(3), 331–50.

KING, A. AND MARUNA, S. (2009) 'Is a Conservative Just a Liberal Who Has Been Mugged? Exploring the Origins of Punitive Views' *Punishment and Society* Vol 11(2), 147–69.

KING, J. (2012) *Judging Social Rights.* Cambridge, Cambridge University Press.

KING, M. (1997a) *A Better World for Children? Explorations in Morality and Authority.* London, Routledge.

KING, M. (1997b) 'The James Bulger Trial: Good or Bad for Guilty or Innocent Children?' in M. King, *A Better World for Children.* London, Routledge, 109–32.

KING, M. AND PIPER, C. (1995) *How the Law Thinks about Children* (2nd edn). Aldershot, Arena.

KING, R. AND RESODIHARDJO, S. (2010) 'To Max or not to Max. Dealing with High Risk Prisoners in the Netherlands and England and Wales' *Punishment and Society* Vol 12(1), 65–84.

KING, R. S., MAUER, M., AND YOUNG, M. C. (2005) *Incarceration and Crime, A Complex Relationship.* Washington DC, The Sentencing Project.

KING, S. (2013) 'Early Desistance Narratives: A Qualitative Analysis of Probationers' Transitions towards Desistance' *Punishment and Society* Vol 15, 147–65.

KNIGHT, C. AND STEMPLOWSKA, Z. (eds) (2014) *Responsibility and Distributive Justice.* Oxford, Oxford University Press.

KOFFMAN, L. (2006) 'The Rise and Fall of Proportionality: The Failure of the Criminal Justice Act 1991' *Criminal Law Review,* 281–99.

KOFFMAN, L. (2008) 'Holding Parents to Account: Tough on Children, Tough on the Causes of Children?' *Journal of Law and Society* Vol 35(1), 113–30.

KOFFMAN, L. AND DINGWALL, G. (2007) 'The Diversion of Young Offenders: A Proportionate Response?' *Web JCL* 2, ISSN 1360–1326.

KRAMER, M. (2011) *The Ethics of Capital Punishment: A Philosophical Investigation of Evil and its Consequences.* Oxford, Oxford University Press.

KRUTTSCHNITT, C. AND DIRKZWAGER (2011) 'Are There Still Contrasts in Tolerance? Imprisonment in the Netherlands and England 20 Years Later' *Punishment and Society* Vol 13(3), 283–306.

LABOUR PARTY (1964) *Crime: A Challenge to Us All.* London, Labour Party.

LACEY, M. (2002) 'Justice, Humanity and Mercy' in D. Ward, J. Scott, and M. Lacey *Probation, Working for Justice* (2nd edn). Oxford, Oxford University Press, 25–38.

LACEY, N. (1988) *State Punishment.* London, Routledge.

LACEY, N. (1998) 'Punishment and Community' in A. von Hirsch and A. Ashworth (eds) *Principled Sentencing: Readings on Theory and Policy.* Oxford, Hart, 394–408.

LACEY, N. (2003) 'Penal Theory and Penal Practice: A Communitarian Approach' in S. McConville (ed) *The Use of Punishment.* Cullompton, Willan, 175–98.

LACEY, N. (2008) *The Prisoner's Dilemma: Political Economy and Punishment in Contemporary Democracies.* Cambridge, Cambridge University Press.

LACEY, N. AND PICKARD, H. (2015) 'The Chimera of Proportionality: Institutionalising Limits on Punishment in Contemporary Social and Political Systems' *Modern Law Review* Vol 78(2), 216–40.

LACEY, N. AND ZEDNER, L. (1995) 'Discourses of Community in Criminal Justice' *Journal of Law and Society* Vol 22(3), 301–25.

LADER, D., SINGLETON, N., AND MELTZER, H. (2000) *Psychiatric Morbidity among Young Offenders in England and Wales,* Report by the ONS (Office for National Statistics) for the Department of Health. London, ONS.

LAING, J. (1999) 'Diversion of Mentally Disordered Offenders: Victim and Offender Perspectives' *Criminal Law Review,* 805–19.

LANDAU, S. (1981) 'Juveniles and the Police—Who Is Charged Immediately and Who Is Referred to the Juvenile Bureau?' *British Journal of Criminology* Vol 21(1), 27.

LAWS, R. AND WARD, T. (2010) *Desistance from Sex Offending: Alternatives to Throwing Away the Keys.* London, Routledge.

LE GRAND, J. (1998) 'The Third Way Begins with CORA' *New Statesman* 6 March.

LEA, J. AND YOUNG, J. (1984) *What Is to Be Done about Law and Order?* Harmondsworth, Penguin.

LEARMONT, J. (1995) *Review of Prison Service Security in England and Wales and the Escape from Parkhurst Prison on Tuesday 3rd January 1995,* Cm 3020. London, HMSO.

LEDGER, J. (2010) 'Rehabilitation Revolution: Will Probation Pay the Price?' *Probation Journal* Vol 57(4), 415–22.

LEIGH, A. (2001/2) 'Keeping on the Right Track' *Safer Society* Winter, 25–6.

LEMERT, E. (1967) *Human Deviance, Social Problems and Social Control.* Englewood Cliffs, Prentice Hall.

LEVI, M. (1989) 'Suite Justice: Sentencing for Fraud' *Criminal Law Review,* 420–34.

LEVI, M. AND PITHOUSE, A. (2000) *White Collar Crime and its Victims.* Oxford, Clarendon.

LEWIS, S., RAYNOR, P., SMITH, D., AND WARDACK, A. (eds) (2005) *Race and Probation*. Cullompton, Willan.

LIBERTY (2006) *Renewing the Prevention of Terrorism Act 2005: Submission to the Joint Committee on Human Rights*. London, Liberty.

LIBERTY (2007) *Briefing on the Criminal Justice and Immigration Bill*. London, Liberty.

LIEBMANN, M. (2000) 'A Survey of RJ in Custodial Settings' *RJ* Issue 3, 1.

LIPPKE, R. L. (2007) *Rethinking Imprisonment*. Oxford, Oxford University Press.

LIPSEY, M. W. (1992) 'The Effect of Treatment on Juvenile Delinquents: Results from Meta-analysis' in F. Losel, T. Bliesener, and D. Bender (eds) *Psychology and Law: International Perspectives*. Berlin, de Gruyter, 131–43.

LITTLE, M., KOGAN, J., BULLOCK, R., AND VAN DER LAAN, P. (2004) 'An Experiment in Multi-Systemic Responses to Persistent Young Offenders Known to Children's Services' *British Journal of Criminology* Vol 44, 225–40.

LITTLECHILD, B. (1997) 'Young Offenders, Punitive Policy and the Rights of Children' *Critical Social Policy* Vol 17(3), 73–91.

LLEWELLYN, J. AND PHILPOTT, D. (eds) (2014) *Restorative Justice, Reconciliation and Peace-Building*. Oxford, Oxford University Press.

LOUCKS, N. (2007) *No One Knows: The Prevalence and Associated Needs of Offenders with Learning Difficulties and Learning Disabilities*. London, PRT.

LOVEGROVE, A. (2011) 'Putting the Offender Back into Sentencing: An Empirical Study of the Public's Understanding of Personal Mitigation' *Criminology and Criminal Justice* Vol 11(1), 37–57.

LUDLOW, A. (2014) *Privatising Prisons*. Oxford, Hart.

LYON, D. (ed) (2006) *Theorizing Surveillance: The Panopticon and Beyond*. Cullompton, Willan.

LYON, J. (2003) 'The Cost of a Broken Promise' *Criminal Justice Matters* Vol 54, 28–9.

LYON, J., DENNISON, C., AND WILSON, A. (2000) *Tell Them so They Listen: Messages from Young People in Custody*, Home Office Research Study No. 201. London, HMSO.

MACDONALD, S. AND TELFORD, M. (2007) 'The Use of ASBOs against Young People in England and Wales: Lessons from Scotland' *Legal Studies* Vol 27(4), 604–29.

MACKENZIE, S., BANNISTER, J., FLINT, J., PARR, S., MILLIE, A., AND FLEETWOOD, J. (2010) *The Drivers of Perceptions of Anti-Social Behaviour*, Research Report 34. London, Home Office.

MACKIE, A., RAINE, J. W., BURROWS, J., HOPKINS, M., AND DUNSTAN, E. (2003) *Clearing the Debts: The Enforcement of Financial Penalties in Magistrates' Courts*, Home Office Online Report 09/03. London, Home Office.

MACPHERSON, W. (1999) *The Stephen Lawrence Inquiry, Report of an Inquiry by Sir William Macpherson of Cluny, Advised by Tom Cook, The Right Revd Dr John Sentamu and Dr Richard Stone*, Cm 4262-1. London, Home Office.

MAGISTRATES' ASSOCIATION (1997, 2003) *Magistrates' Court Guidelines*. London, The Magistrates' Association.

MAGUIRE, M. (2002) 'Crime Statistics' in M. Maguire, R. Morgan, and R. Reiner (eds) *The Oxford Handbook of Criminology* (3rd edn). Oxford, Oxford University Press, 322–75.

MAGUIRE, M. AND SHAPLAND, J. (1997) 'Provision for Victims in an International Context' in R. Davis, A. Lurigio, and W. Skogan (eds) *Victims of Crime* (2nd edn). Thousand Oaks, Sage, 211–28.

MAIR, G. (1997) 'Community Penalties and Probation' in M. Maguire, R. Morgan, and R. Reiner (eds) *The Oxford Handbook of Criminology* (2nd edn). Oxford, Clarendon Press, 1195–232.

MAIR, G. AND BURKE, L. (2011) *Redemption Rehabilitation and Risk Management*. London, Routledge.

MAIR, G. AND MAY, C. (1997) *Offenders on Probation*, HORS 167. London, Home Office.

MAIR, G. AND MILLINGS, M. (2011) *Doing Justice Locally, The North Liverpool Community Justice Centre*. London, Centre for Crime and Justice Studies.

MAIR, G. AND MILLS, H. (2009) *Three Years On: The Community Order and Suspended Sentence Order—The Views and Experiences of Probation Officers and Offenders*. London, Centre for Crime and Justice Studies.

MAIR, G., CROSS, N., AND TAYLOR, S. (2007) *The Use and Impact of the Community Order and the Suspended Sentence Order*. London, Centre for Criminal Justice Studies.

MAIR, G., CROSS, N. AND TAYLOR, S. (2008) *The Community Order and the Suspended Sentence Order: The Views and Attitudes of Sentencers*. London, Centre for Crime and Justice Studies.

MALLOCH, M. AND McIVOR, G. (2011) 'Women and Community Sentences' *Criminology and Criminal Justice* Vol 11(4), 325–44.

MANTLE, G. AND MOORE, S. (2004) 'On Probation: Pickled and Nothing to Say' *Howard Journal* Vol 43(3), 299–316.

MARKEL, D. (2005) 'State Be Not Proud, A Retributivist Defence of the Commutation of Death Row and the Abolition of the Death Penalty' *Harvard Civil Rights—Civil Liberties Law Review* Vol 40, 407–80.

MARQUART, J. W., EKLAND-OLSEN, S., AND SORENSEN, J. R. (1989) 'A National Study of *Furman*-Commuted Inmates: Assessing the Threat to Society from Capital Offenders' *Loyola of Los Angeles Law Review* Vol 23(1), November 5–28.

MARSH, I., MELVILLE, G., MORGAN, K., AND NORRIS, G. (2006) 'Explaining the Criminal Behaviour of Ethnic Minorities' in I. Marsh (ed) *Theories of Crime*. London, Routledge, 162–83.

MARSHALL, P. (1997) *A Reconviction Study of HMP Grendon Therapeutic Community*. London, Home Office.

MARSHALL, T. (1985) *Alternatives to Criminal Courts*. Aldershot, Gower.

MARSHALL, T. (1992) Seminar, 21 January, Law Department, Brunel University.

MARSHALL, T. H. (1950) *Citizenship and Social Rights*. Cambridge, Cambridge University Press.

MARTIN, J. AND WEBSTER, D. (1971) *The Social Consequences of Conviction*. London, Heinemann.

MARTINSON, R. (1974) 'What Works? Questions and Answers about Prison Reform' *The Public Interest* (Spring), 22–54.

MARX, K. (1853) 'Capital Punishment' first published in *New York Daily Tribune*, February 17 and 18, reprinted in *Marx and Engels: Collected Works* Vol 11. London, Lawrence and Wishart (1979), 495–501.

MARX, K. AND ENGELS, F. (1845) 'The Holy Family' in *Marx and Engels: Collected Works* Vol 4 (1975), London, Lawrence and Wishart (1975), 5–211.

MASLEN, H. (2015) *Remorse, Penal Theory and Sentencing*. Oxford, Hart.

MASON, T. AND MERCER, D. (1999) *A Sociology of the Mentally Disordered Offender*. London, Longman.

MASON, T., DE SILVA, N., SHARMA, N., BROWN, D., AND HARPER, G. (2007) *Local Variation in Sentencing in England and Wales*. London, Ministry of Justice.

MASTERS, G. (1997) 'Values for Probation, Society and Beyond' *Howard Journal* Vol 36(3), 237–47.

MATHEWS, J. (2010) 'The Management of Sex Offenders in the Community' *Probation Journal* Vol 57(4), 423–4.

MATHIESEN, T. (2006) *Prison on Trial* (3rd edn). Winchester, Waterside Press.

MATHIESEN, T. (2013) *Towards a Surveillant Society: The rise of Surveillance Systems in Europe*. Hook, Waterside Press.

MATTHEWS, R. (1988) *Informal Justice*. London, Sage.

MATTHEWS, R. (ed) (1989) *Privatising Criminal Justice*. London, Sage.

MATTINSON, J. AND MIRRLEES-BLACK, C. (2000) *Attitudes to Crime and Criminal Justice: Findings from the 1998 British Crime Survey*, Home Office Research Study No. 200. London, Home Office.

MAUER, M. (2001) 'The Causes and Consequences of Prison Growth in the United States' in D. Garland (ed) *Mass Imprisonment*. London, Sage, 4–14.

MAUER, M. (2011) 'Addressing Racial Disparities in Incarceration' *Prison Journal Supplement* Vol 91(3), 87S–101S.

MAVRONICOLA, N. (2014) 'Inhuman and Degrading Punishment, Dignity, and the Limits of Retribution' *Modern Law Review* Vol 77(2), 292–307.

MAY, M. (2002) 'Innocence and Experience: The Evolution of the Concept of Juvenile Delinquency in the Mid-Nineteenth Century' in J. Muncie, G. Hughes, and E. McLaughlin (eds) (2002) *Youth Justice, Critical Readings*. London, Sage, 98–114.

MAY, T. (1990) *Probation: Politics, Policy and Practice*. Milton Keynes, Open University Press.

MAY, T., GYATENG, T., AND HOUGH, M. (2010) *Differential Treatment in the Youth Justice System*, EHRC Report 50. London, ICPR.

McBRIDE, W. L. (1975) 'The Concept of Justice in Marx, Engels and Others' *Ethics* Vol 85, 204–18.

McDERMOTT, K. (1990), 'We Have No Problem: The Experience of Racism in Prison' *New Community* Vol 16(2), 213–28.

McDIARMID, C. (2000) 'Children Who Murder: What Is Her Majesty's Pleasure?' *Criminal Law Review*, 547–63.

McDONALD, I. (2006) 'The "Respect Action Plan": Something New or More of the Same?' *Journal of Social Welfare and Family Law* Vol 28(2), 191–200.

McEVOY, K., MIKA, H., AND HUDSON, B. (2002) 'Practice, Performance and Prospects for Restorative Justice' *British Journal of Criminology* Vol 42, 469–75.

McGUIRE, J. (ed) (1995) *What Works? Reducing Reoffending*. Chichester, John Wiley.

McGUIRE, J. AND PRIESTLEY, P. (1995) 'Reviewing "What Works": Past, Present and Future' in J. McGuire (ed) *What Works? Reducing Reoffending*. Chichester, John Wiley, 3–34.

McIVOR, G. (1998) 'Jobs for the Boys? Gender Differences in Referral to Community Service' *Howard Journal* Vol 37(3), 280–90.

McIVOR, G., PIRNAT, C., AND GRAFL, C. (2013) 'Unpaid Work as an Alternative to Imprisonment for Fine Default in Austria and Scotland' *European Journal of Probation* Vol 5(2), 3–28. Available at http://www.ejprob.ro/uploads_ro/794/Unpaid_work_as_an_alternative_to_imprisonment_for_fine_default_in_Austria_and_Scotland.pdf.

McKEEVER, G. (2004) 'Social Security as a Criminal Sanction' *Journal of Social and Welfare Law* Vol 26(1), 1–16.

McKNIGHT, J. (2009) 'Speaking Up for Probation' *Howard Journal* Vol 48, 327–43.

McLAUGHLIN, E. AND MUNCIE, J. (1994) 'Managing the Criminal Justice System' in J. Clarke, A. Cochrane, E. McLaughlin (eds) *Managing Social Policy*. London, Sage, 115–40.

McLAUGHLIN, E., FERGUSON, R., HUGHES, G., AND WESTMARLAND, L. (2003) *Restorative Justice, Critical Issues*. Milton Keynes, Open University Press and London, Sage.

McLAUGHLIN, E., MUNCIE, J., AND HUGHES, G. (2001) 'The Permanent Revolution: New Labour, New Public Management and the Modernization of Criminal Justice' *Criminal Justice* Vol 1(3), 301–18.

McNULTY, D., WATSON, N., AND PHILO, G. (2014) 'Human Rights and Prisoners' Rights: The British Press and the Shaping of Public Debate' *Howard Journal of Criminal Justice* Vol 53(4), 360–76.

McROBBIE, A. AND THORNTON, S. (2002) 'Rethinking "Moral Panic" for Multi-mediated Social Worlds' in J. Muncie, G. Hughes, and E. McLaughlin (eds) *Youth Justice: Critical Readings*. London, Sage, 68–79.

McWILLIAMS, W. AND PEASE, K. (1990) 'Probation Practice and an End to Punishment' *Howard Journal* Vol 29(1), 14–24.

MEEK, R. (2008) *High Security Prisons, Prisoner Perspectives*. London, Howard League.

MIAO, M. (2013) 'The Politics of China's Death Penalty Reform in the context of global abolitionism' *British Journal of Criminology* Vol 53(5), 500–19.

MIERS, D. (1990) *Compensation for Criminal Injuries*. London, Butterworths.

MIERS, D. (2004) 'Situating and Researching Restorative Justice in Great Britain' *Punishment and Society* Vol 6(1), 23–46.

MIERS, D., MAGUIRE, M., GOLDIE, S., SHARPE, K., HALE, C., NETTON, K., DOOLIN, S., UGLOW, S., ENTERKIN, J., AND NEWBURN, T. (2001) *An Exploratory Evaluation of Restorative Justice Schemes*. Crime Reduction Research Series Paper 9. London, Home Office.

MILL, J. S. (1859) *On Liberty and Other Essays*, ed J. Gray (2008). Oxford, Oxford University Press.

MILL, J. S. (1861) *Utilitarianism*. Oxford, Oxford University Press, 1998.

MILLER, B. L. AND SPILLANE, J. (2012) 'Civil Death: An Examination of Ex-felon Disenfranchisement and Reintegration' *Punishment and Society* Vol 14(4), 402–28.

MILLS, M. (2009) 'Cruel and Unusual, *State v Mata*, the Electric Chair and the Nebraska Supreme Court's Rejection of a Subjective Intent Requirement in Death Penalty Jurisprudence' *Nebraska Law Review* Vol 88, 235–260.

MINISTRY OF JUSTICE (2007a) *Offender Management Caseload Statistics 2006*. London, Ministry of Justice.

MINISTRY OF JUSTICE (2007b) *The Government's Response to the Report by Baroness Corston of a Review of Women with Particular Vulnerabilities in the Criminal Justice System*, Cm 7261. London, The Stationery Office.

MINISTRY OF JUSTICE (2007c) *Statistics of Mentally Disordered Offenders 2006, England and Wales*, Statistical Bulletin. London, Ministry of Justice.

MINISTRY OF JUSTICE (2007d) *Sentencing Statistics 2006 England and Wales*, Statistical Bulletin. London, Ministry of Justice.

MINISTRY OF JUSTICE (2009) *Voting Rights of Convicted Prisoners Detained within the United Kingdom, Second Stage Consultation*. London, Ministry of Justice.

MINISTRY OF JUSTICE (2010a) *Breaking the Cycle, Effective Punishment, Rehabilitation and Sentencing of Offenders*. London, Ministry of Justice.

MINISTRY OF JUSTICE (2010b) *Compendium of Reoffending Statistics and Analysis, Ministry of Justice Statistics Bulletin*. London, Ministry of Justice.

MINISTRY OF JUSTICE (2010c) *Statistics on Women and the Criminal Justice System*. London, Ministry of Justice.

MINISTRY OF JUSTICE (2010d) *Prison Population Projections 2010–2016*, Ministry of Justice Statistics Bulletin. London, Ministry of Justice.

MINISTRY OF JUSTICE (2010e) *Statistics of Mentally Disordered Offenders 2008 England and Wales*. London, Ministry of Justice.

MINISTRY OF JUSTICE (2010f) *Multi Agency Public Protection Arrangements Annual Report 2009/10*. London, Ministry of Justice Statistics Bulletin.

MINISTRY OF JUSTICE (2011a) *Breaking the Cycle, Government Response*, Cm 8070. London, Ministry of Justice.

MINISTRY OF JUSTICE (2011b) *Prison Annual Performance Ratings*. London, Ministry of Justice/NOMS.

MINISTRY OF JUSTICE (2011c) *Statistics on Race and the Criminal Justice System*. London, Ministry of Justice.

MINISTRY OF JUSTICE (2011d) *National Offender Management Service Annual Report 2009/10 Management Information Addendum*. London, Ministry of Justice.

MINISTRY OF JUSTICE (2011e) *Competition Strategy for Offender Services*. London, Ministry of Justice.

MINISTRY OF JUSTICE (2011f) *IPP Factsheet*. London, Ministry of Justice.

MINISTRY OF JUSTICE (2011g) *Equalities Annual Report 2010–2011*. London, Ministry of Justice.

MINISTRY OF JUSTICE (2011h) *Prison Population Projections 2011–2017 England and Wales*. London, Ministry of Justice.

MINISTRY OF JUSTICE (2011i) *National Standards for the Management of Offenders*. London, Ministry of Justice.

MINISTRY OF JUSTICE (2011j) *Increasing the Magistrates' Court Fine Limit—Equality Impact Assessment*. Tabled at Commons Report Stage, Legal Aid Sentencing and Punishment of Offenders Bill.

MINISTRY OF JUSTICE (2011k) *Criminal Justice Statistics Quarterly Update to December 2010*, Ministry of Justice Statistics Bulletin. London, Ministry of Justice.

MINISTRY OF JUSTICE (2011m) *Criminal Justice Statistics Quarterly Update to March 2011*, Ministry of Justice Statistics Bulletin. London, Ministry of Justice.

MINISTRY OF JUSTICE (2011n) *Criminal Justice Statistics, England and Wales— 12 Months Ending June 2011*. London, Ministry of Justice.

MINISTRY OF JUSTICE (2011o) *Offender Management Caseload Statistics 2010*, London Ministry of Justice.

MINISTRY OF JUSTICE (2012a) *Punishment and Reform: Effective Probation Services*, Cm 8333. London, Ministry of Justice.

MINISTRY OF JUSTICE (2012b) *Punishment and Reform: Effective Community Sentences*, Cm 8334. London, Ministry of Justice.

MINISTRY OF JUSTICE (2012c) *Swift and Sure Justice: The Government's Plans for Reform of the Criminal Justice System*, Cm 8388. London, Ministry of Justice. Available at https://www.gov.uk/government/uploads/system/uploads/ attachment_data/file/162284/swift-and-sure-justice.pdf.pdf.

MINISTRY OF JUSTICE (2012d) *Minimising and Managing Physical Restraint*. London, Ministry of Justice.

MINISTRY OF JUSTICE (2012e) *Use of Restraint Policy Framework for the Under-18 Secure Estate*. London, Ministry of Justice.

MINISTRY OF JUSTICE (2012f) *The Pre-custody Employment, Training and Education Status of Newly-sentenced Prisoners*. London, Ministry of Justice.

MINISTRY OF JUSTICE (2013a) *Transforming Rehabilitation: A Revolution in the Way We Manage Offenders*, Consultation Paper Cm 8517, CP1/2013. London, TSO.

MINISTRY OF JUSTICE (2013b) *Story of the Prison Population 1993–2012 England and Wales*. London, Ministry of Justice. Available at https://www.gov.uk/ government/uploads/system/uploads/ attachment_data/file/163144/story-prison-population.pdf.pdf.

MINISTRY OF JUSTICE (2013c) *Strategic Objectives for Female Offenders*. London, Ministry of Justice.

MINISTRY OF JUSTICE (2013d) *Statistics on Race and the Criminal Justice System 2012*. London, Ministry of Justice.

MINISTRY OF JUSTICE (2013e) *Transforming Youth Custody: Putting Education at the Heart of Detention*, Consultation Paper CP4/2013, CM 8564. London, TSO.

MINISTRY OF JUSTICE (2013f) *Strategic Objectives for Female Offenders*. London, Ministry of Justice.

MINISTRY OF JUSTICE (2013g) *Transforming Legal Aid: Delivering a More Credible and Efficient System*, Consultation Paper CP14/2013. London, Ministry of Justice.

MINISTRY OF JUSTICE (2013h) *Making a Victim Personal Statement*. London, Ministry of Justice. Available at https://www.gov.uk/government/publications/ victim-personal-statement.

MINISTRY OF JUSTICE (2013i) *Code of Practice for Victims of Crime*. London, TSO.

MINISTRY OF JUSTICE (2013j) *Code of Practice for Youth Conditional Cautions, Crime & Disorder Act 1998 (as amended by the Criminal Justice & Immigration Act 2008 and the Legal Aid, Sentencing and Punishment of Offenders Act 2012)*. London, Ministry of Justice.

MINISTRY OF JUSTICE (2014a) *Peterborough Social Impact Bond, HMP Doncaster Payment by Results Pilots, Final Re-Conviction Results for Cohort 1*, Ministry of Justice Statistics Bulletin. London, Ministry of Justice.

MINISTRY OF JUSTICE (2014b) *Statistics on Women and the Criminal Justice System 2012*. London, Ministry of Justice.

MINISTRY OF JUSTICE (2014c) *National Offender Management Service Offender Equalities Annual Report 2013/14*. London, Ministry of Justice.

MINISTRY OF JUSTICE (2014d) *Transforming Youth Custody: Government Response to the Consultation*, Cm 8792. London, TSO.

MINISTRY OF JUSTICE (2014e) *Pre-sentence Restorative Justice (RJ)*. London, Ministry of Justice.

MINISTRY OF JUSTICE (2014f) *Restorative Justice Action Plan for the Criminal Justice System for the Period to March 2018*. London, Ministry of Justice.

MINISTRY OF JUSTICE (2015a) *Proven Re-offending Statistics Quarterly Bulletin January to December 2013, England and Wales*. London, Ministry of Justice.

MINISTRY OF JUSTICE (2015b) *Criminal Justice Statistics Quarterly Update to September 2014 England and Wales*. London, Ministry of Justice.

MINISTRY OF JUSTICE (2015c) *Offender Management Statistics Bulletin, England and Wales, Quarterly January to March 2015*. London, Ministry of Justice.

MINISTRY OF JUSTICE (2015d) *Criminal Justice and Courts Act 2015 Circular 2015/01*. Criminal Law and Policy Unit, London, Ministry of Justice. Available at https://www.gov.uk/government/uploads/system/uploads/attachment_data/file/428204/cjc-act-circular.pdf.

MINISTRY OF JUSTICE (2015e) *Multi-Agency Public Protection Arrangements Annual Report 2014/15, Ministry of Justice Statistics Bulletin*. London, Ministry of Justice.

MINISTRY OF JUSTICE (2015f) *National Offender Management Service Offender Equalities Report 2014/15*. London, Ministry of Justice.

MINISTRY OF JUSTICE (2015g) *Prison Population Projections 2015–2021 England and Wales*. London, Ministry of Justice.

MINISTRY OF JUSTICE (2015h) *Statistics on Race and the Criminal Justice System 2014*. London, Ministry of Justice.

MINISTRY OF JUSTICE (2015i) *Code of Practice for Victims of Crime*. London, TSO.

MINISTRY OF JUSTICE/DCSF (2008) *The Government's Response to the Report by Peter Smallridge and Andrew Williamson of a Review of the Use of Restraint in Juvenile Secure Settings*, Cm 7501. London, The Stationery Office.

MINISTRY OF JUSTICE/NOMS (2013) *NOMS: Offender Equalities Annual Report 2012/13*. London, Ministry of Justice.

MINISTRY OF JUSTICE/NOMS (2015) *National Offender Management Service: Prison Annual Performance Ratings 2014–2015*. London, Ministry of Justice.

MINISTRY OF JUSTICE/YOUTH JUSTICE BOARD (2013) *Youth Out-of-Court Disposals, Guide for Police and Youth Offending Services*. London, Ministry of Justice.

MINISTRY OF JUSTICE/YOUTH JUSTICE BOARD (2014) *Youth Justice Statistics 2012/13 England and Wales*. London, Ministry of Justice.

MINISTRY OF JUSTICE/YOUTH JUSTICE BOARD (2015a) *Youth Justice Statistics 2013/14 England and Wales*. London, Ministry of Justice.

MINISTRY OF JUSTICE/YOUTH JUSTICE BOARD (2015b) *Referral Orders and Youth Offender Panels: Guidance for the Courts,*

Youth Offending Teams and Youth Offender Panels. London, Ministry of Justice.

MINISTRY OF JUSTICE/YOUTH JUSTICE BOARD (2016) *Youth Justice Statistics 2014/15 England and Wales*. London, Ministry of Justice.

MIRRLEES-BLACK, C. (2001) *Confidence in the Criminal Justice System: Findings from the 2000 British Crime Survey*, Home Office Research Findings No. 137. London, Home Office.

MITCHELL, B. AND MACKAY, R. D. (2011) 'Investigating Involuntary Manslaughter: An Empirical Study of 127 Cases' *Oxford Journal of Legal Studies* Vol 31(1), 165–91.

MITCHELL, B. AND ROBERTS, J. V. (2010) *Public Opinion and Sentencing for Murder. An Empirical Investigation of Public Knowledge and Attitudes in England and Wales*. Available at http://www.nuffieldfoundation.org.

MITCHELL, B. AND ROBERTS, J. V. (2012) 'Sentencing for Murder, Exploring Public Knowledge and Public Opinion in England and Wales' *British Journal of Criminology* Vol 52(1), 141–58.

MOLONEY REPORT (1927) *Report of the Departmental Committee on the Treatment of Offenders*, Cmnd 2381. London, HMSO.

MONAGHAN, G., MOORE, S., AND HIBBERT, P. (2003) *Children in Trouble: Time for Change*. Barkingside, Barnardo's.

MOORE, L. AND SCRATON, P. (2014) *The Incarceration of Women: Punishing Bodies, Breaking Spirits*. London, Palgrave.

MOORE, L., PHILLIPS, A., AND KOSTADINTCHEVA, K. (2010) *Community Payback and Local Criminal Justice Engagement Initiatives, Public Perceptions and Awareness*, Research Summary 3/10. Ministry of Justice, London.

MOORE, R. (2003a) 'The Use of Financial Penalties and the Amounts Imposed: The Need for a New Approach' *Criminal Law Review*, 13–27.

MOORE, R. (2003b) 'Executing Warrants against Fine Defaulters: The Continuing Search for Effectiveness and Efficiency' *Criminal Law Review*, 595–606.

MOORE, R. (2004) 'Intensive Supervision and Surveillance Programmes for Young Offenders: The Evidence Base so Far' in R. Burnett and C. Roberts (eds) *What Works in Probation and Youth Justice: Developing Evidence-Based Practice*. Cullompton, Willan, 159–79.

MOORE, S. E. H. (2014) *Crime and the Media*. London, Palgrave Macmillan.

MORGAN, R. (2000) *The Judiciary in the Magistrates' Courts*, Home Office RDS Occasional Paper No. 66. London, Home Office.

MORGAN, R. (2008) *Summary Justice, Fast—but Fair?* London, Centre for Crime and Justice Studies, Kings College.

MORGAN, R. (2009) 'True Scale of Juvenile Offending Masked with "Creative Maths"' *Telegraph*, 9 January 2009. Available at http://www.telegraph.co.uk/news/uknews/law-and-order/4176689/True-scale-of-juvenileoffending-masked-with-creative-maths.html.

MORRELL, G., SCOTT, S., MCNEISH, D., AND WEBSTER, S. (2011) *The August Riots in England: Understanding the Involvement of Young People*. London, National Centre for Social Research.

MORRIS, A. AND GELSTHORPE, L. (1990) 'Not Paying for Crime: Issues in Fine Enforcement' *Criminal Law Review*, 839–51.

MORRIS, A. AND GILLER, H. (1987) *Understanding Juvenile Justice*. Beckenham, Croom Helm.

MORRIS, A. AND MAXWELL, G. (2001) 'Implementing Restorative Justice: What Works?' in A. Morris and G. Maxwell (eds) *Restorative Justice for Juveniles: Conferencing, Mediation and Circles*. Oxford, Hart, 267–81.

MORRIS, N. (1974) *The Future of Imprisonment*. Chicago, University of Chicago Press.

MORRIS, N. AND MILLER, M. (1985) 'Predictions of Dangerousness' in M. Tonry and N. Morris (eds) *Crime and Justice: An Annual Review of Research* Vol 6. Chicago, University of Chicago Press, 1–50.

MORRIS, N. AND TONRY, M. (1990) *Between Prison and Probation*. Oxford, Oxford University Press.

MOSTER, A., WNUK, D. W., AND JEGLIC, E. J. (2008) 'Cognitive Behavioural Therapy Interventions with Sex Offenders' *Journal of Correctional Health Care* Vol 14(2), 109–21.

MOXON, D., CORKERY, J. M., AND HEDDERMAN, C. (1992) *Some Developments in the Use of Compensation Orders in Magistrates' Courts since 1988*, Home Office Research Study 126. London, HMSO.

MULCAHY, L. (2000) 'The Devil and the Deep Blue Sea? A Critique of the Ability of Community Mediation to Suppress and Facilitate Participation in Civil Life' *Journal of Law and Society* Vol 27(1), 133–50.

MUNCIE, J. (1999) 'Institutionalised Intolerance: Youth Justice and the 1998 Crime and Disorder Act' *Critical Social Policy* Vol 19(2), 147–75.

MUNCIE, J. (2000) 'Pragmatic Realism? Searching for Criminology in the New Youth Justice' in B. Goldson (ed) *The New Youth Justice*. Lyme Regis, Russell House Publishing, 14–34.

MUNCIE, J. (2004) *Youth and Crime: A Critical Introduction* (2nd edn). London, Sage.

MUNCIE, J. (2006) 'Repenalisation and Rights: Explorations in Comparative Youth Criminology' *Howard Journal* Vol 45(1), 42–70.

MUNCIE, J. (2008) 'The Punitive Turn in Juvenile Justice, Cultures of Control and Rights Compliance in Western Europe and the USA' *Youth Justice, An International Journal* Vol 8, 107–21.

MUNCIE, J. (2011) 'Illusions of Difference, Comparative Youth Justice in the Devolved United Kingdom' *British Journal of Criminology* Vol 51, 40–57.

MUNCIE, J. AND HUGHES, E. (2002) 'Modes of Youth Governance: Political Rationalities, Criminalization and Resistance' in J. Muncie, G. Hughes, and E. McLaughlin (eds) *Youth Justice: Critical Readings*. London, Sage, 1–18.

MUNRO, V. (2002) 'The Emerging Rights of Imprisoned Mothers and their Children' *Child and Family Law Quarterly* Vol 14, 303.

MURPHY, J. G. (1973) 'Marxism and Retribution' *Philosophy and Public Affairs* Vol 2, 217–43.

MURPHY, K. AND HARRIS, N. (2007) 'Shaming, Shame and Recidivism' *British Journal of Criminology* Vol 47(6), 900–17.

MURPHY, T. AND WHITTY, N. (2007) 'Risk and Human Rights in UK Prison Governance' *British Journal of Criminology* Vol 47(5), 798–816.

MURRAY, C. AND COX, L. (1979) *Beyond Probation: Juvenile Corrections and the Chronic Delinquent*. Beverly Hills, CA, Sage.

NACRO (1985) *Juvenile Crime*, Juvenile Crime Briefing. London, NACRO.

NACRO (1986) *Cautioning and Diversion of Juvenile Offenders*, Juvenile Crime Briefing. London, NACRO.

NACRO (1989) *Diverting Juvenile Offenders from Prosecution*, Juvenile Crime Policy Paper 2. London, NACRO.

NACRO (1993) *Supplementary Guidance on Cautioning*, NACRO Briefing, December. London, NACRO.

NACRO (2000a) *Race & Prisons*. London, NACRO.

NACRO (2000b) *Pre-Sentence Reports and Custodial Sentencing*, NACRO Briefing, December. London, NACRO.

NACRO (2000c) *Some Facts about Young Offenders*, NACRO Briefing. London, NACRO.

NACRO (2001/2) 'Children Who Commit Grave Crimes' *Safer Society* Winter, 8–9.

NACRO (2001a) *Public Opinion and Youth Justice*, Youth Crime Briefing. 12/01. London.

NACRO (2001b) *The Grave Crimes Provision*, Youth Justice Briefing. London, NACRO.

NACRO (2003a) *Detention and Training Order Early Release—The Revised Guidance and Use of Electronic Monitoring*, Youth Crime Briefing, March. London, NACRO.

NACRO (2003b) *Youth Crime, Section Update, September 2003*. London, NACRO.

NACRO (2003c) *Looked After Children Who Offend: The Quality Protects Programme and YOTS*, Youth Crime Briefing. London, NACRO.

NACRO (2003d) *Youth Crime, Section Update, December*. London, NACRO.

NACRO (2003e) *Family Group Conferencing and Youth Justice*, Youth Crime Briefing. London, NACRO.

NACRO (2003f) *Race and Prisons: Where Are We Now?* London, NACRO.

NACRO (2004) *New Legislation—Impact on Sentencing*, Youth Crime Briefing. London, NACRO.

NACRO (2005) *Dangerousness and the Criminal Justice Act 2003*, Youth Crime Briefing, June. London, NACRO.

NACRO (2006) *Managing Risk in the Community in the Youth Justice System*, Youth Crime Briefing, September. London, NACRO.

NACRO (2007a) *Further Developments in Measures Related to Anti-Social Behaviour*, Youth Crime Briefing, March. London, NACRO.

NACRO (2007b) *The Detention and Training Order*, Youth Crime Briefing, June. London, NACRO.

NACRO (2007c) *Some Facts about Children and Young People Who Offend—2005*, Youth Crime Briefing. London, NACRO.

NACRO (2007d) *'Grave Crimes' Mode of Trial and Long Term Detention*, Youth Crime Briefing. London, NACRO.

NACRO (2008) *Some Facts about Children and Young People Who Offend—2006*, Youth Crime Briefing. London, NACRO.

NACRO (2010) *Some Facts about Children and Young People Who Offend—2008*, Youth Crime Briefing. London, NACRO.

NACRO (2011) *Reducing the Number of Children and Young People in Custody*. London, NACRO.

NAGIN, D. S. AND PEPPER, J. V. (eds) (2012) *Deterrence and the Death Penalty*. Washington DC, National Academic Press.

NAPO (2006) *News*, Issue 182, 15 September.

NASH, M. AND WILLIAMS, A. (2008) *The Anatomy of Serious Further Offending*. Oxford, Oxford University Press.

NATIONAL AUDIT OFFICE (2008) *National Probation Service: The Supervision of Community Orders in England and Wales*. London, The Stationery Office.

NATIONAL AUDIT OFFICE (2010a) *The Youth Justice System in England and Wales: Reducing Offending by Young People*, Report by the Comptroller and Auditor General, HC 663 Session 2010–2011. London, The Stationery Office.

NATIONAL AUDIT OFFICE (2010b) *Managing Offenders on Short Custodial Sentences*. London, The Stationery Office.

NATIONAL AUDIT OFFICE (2014) *Probation: Landscape Review* (HC1100). Available at http://www.nao.org.uk/wp-content/uploads/2014/03/Probation-landscape-review.pdf.

NATIONAL OFFENDER MANAGEMENT SERVICE (NOMS) (2006a) *Working with Probation to Protect the Public and Reduce Re-offending*. London, Home Office.

NATIONAL OFFENDER MANAGEMENT SERVICE (NOMS) (2006b) *Improving Prison and Probation Services: Public Value Partnerships*. London, Home Office.

NATIONAL OFFENDER MANAGEMENT SERVICE (NOMS) (2007) *Commissioning Framework, National Commissioning Plan 2007–8*. London, Home Office.

NATIONAL OFFENDER MANAGEMENT SERVICE (NOMS) (2008) *Race Review Implementing Race Equality in Prisons—Five Years On*. London, Ministry of Justice.

NATIONAL OFFENDER MANAGEMENT SERVICE (NOMS) (2009a) *Muslim Prisoners Scoping Study*. London, NOMS.

NATIONAL OFFENDER MANAGEMENT SERVICE (NOMS 2009b) *Promoting Equality in Prisons and Probation: The National Offender Management Service Single Equality Scheme 2009–2012*. London, NOMS.

NATIONAL OFFENDER MANAGEMENT SERVICE (NOMS) (2011) *Annual Report and Accounts 2010–2011*. London, The Stationery Office, HC 1345.

NATIONAL POLICE CHIEFS COUNCIL (2015) *National Strategy for the Policing of Children & Young People*. National Police Chiefs' Council.

NATIONAL PREVENTIVE MECHANISM (NPM) (2011) *Monitoring Places of Detention, First Annual Report of the United Kingdom's National Preventive Mechanism, 1 April 2009–31 March 2010*, Cm 8010. London, The Stationery Office.

NATIONAL PREVENTIVE MECHANISM (2014) *Monitoring Places of Detention: Fifth Annual Report of the United Kingdom's National Preventive Mechanism 1 April 2013–31 March 2014*, Cm 8964. London, HMSO.

NATIONAL PROBATION SERVICE (NPS) (2003) *OASys: The New Offender Assessment System: Important Information for Sentencers*, Briefing note Issue 3. London, National Probation Service.

NELKEN, D. (1994) 'Community Involvement in Crime Control' in N. Lacey (ed) *A Reader in Criminal Justice*. Oxford, Oxford University Press, 247–77.

NELLIS, M. (1995) 'Probation Values for the 1990s' *Howard Journal* Vol 34, 19–44.

NELLIS, M. (2002) 'Probation Partnership and Civil Society' in D. Ward, J. Scott, and M. Lacey (eds) *Probation, Working for Justice* (2nd edn). Oxford, Oxford University Press, 356–74.

NEUMANN P. (2010) *Prisons and Terrorism: Radicalisation and De-radicalisation in 15 Countries*. London, ICSR.

NEUMANN, P. AND ROGERS, B. (2008) *Recruitment and Mobilisation for the Islamic Militant Movement in Europe*. London, Kings College, ICSR.

NEWBURN, T. (1988) *The Use and Enforcement of Compensation Orders in Magistrates Courts*, Home Office Research Study No. 102. London, HMSO.

NEWBURN, T. (1995) *Crime and Criminal Justice Policy*. London, Longmans.

NEWBURN, T. (1996) 'Back to the Future? Youth Crime, Youth Justice and the Rediscovery of "Authoritarian Populism"' in J. Pilcher and S. Wagg (eds) *Thatcher's Children: Politics, Childhood and Society in the 1980s and 1990s*. London, Falmer Press, 61–76.

NEWBURN, T., CRAWFORD, A., EARLE, R., GOLDIE, S., HALE, C., HALLAM, A., MASTERS, G., NETTEN, A., SAUNDERS, R., SHARPE, K., AND UGLOW, S. (2002) *The Introduction of Referral Orders into the Youth Justice System: Final Report*. Home Office Research Study No. 242. London, Home Office.

NEWBURY, A. (2011) ' "I would have been able to hear what they think": Tensions in Achieving Restorative Outcomes in the English Youth Justice System' *Youth Justice* Vol 11(3), 250–65.

Nicholson, P. (1982) 'Hegel on Crime' *History of Political Thought* Vol 3, 103–21.

NOMS (2012) *A Distinct Approach: A Guide to Working with Women Offenders*, London, NOMS Women and Equalities Group.

NOMS (2013) *Women's Custodial Estate Review*, London, NOMS.

NOMS (2014) *Annual Report and Accounts 2013–2014*, London, Stationery Office.

NOMS (2015a) *Annual Report and Accounts 2014–2015*, London, Stationery Office.

NOMS (2015b) *National Offender Management Service Annual Report and Accounts 2014/15: Management Information Addendum*. London, Ministry of Justice

NOMS (2015c) *Business Plan 2014–2015*. London, Stationery Office.

Norrie, A. (1998) 'The Limits of Legal Ideology' in A. von Hirsch and A. Ashworth (eds) *Principled Sentencing: Readings on Theory and Policy*. Oxford, Hart, 369–80.

Northern Ireland Office (2007) *A Protocol for Community-Based Restorative Justice Schemes*. Belfast, Northern Ireland Office.

Nozick, R. (1974) *Anarchy, State and Utopia*, Oxford: Blackwell.

Nugent, B. and Loucks, N. (2011) 'The Arts and Prisoners: Experiences of Creative Rehabilitation' *Howard Journal* Vol 50, 356–370.

O'Brien, M., Mortimer, L., Singleton, N., and Meltzer, H. (2001) *Psychiatric Morbidity among Women Prisoners in England and Wales*. London, Office for National Statistics.

Office for Criminal Justice Reform (2009) *Engaging Communities in Criminal Justice*. London, Ministry of Justice.

Office for Criminal Justice Reform (2010) *Initial Findings from a Review of the Use of Out-of-Court Disposals*. London, Ministry of Justice.

Office for National Statistics (2015) *Crime in England and Wales, Year Ending September 2014*. London, ONS.

Office for National Statistics (2016) *Crime in England and Wales: Year Ending September 2015*, London, ONS.

Office of Juvenile Justice and Delinquency Prevention (2009) *Characteristics of Juvenile Suicide in Confinement*. Washington, US Department of Justice.

Office of Juvenile Justice and Delinquency Prevention (2010) *Youth's Needs and Services, Findings from the Survey of Youth in Residential Placement*. Washington, US Department of Justice.

Office of the Children's Commissioner (with User Voice) (2011) *Young People's Views on Restraint in the Secure Estate*. London, Office of the Children's Commissioner.

Ofsted (Office of Standards in Education in consultation with HM Chief Inspector of Prisons) (2004) *Girls in Prison: The Education and Training of Under-18s Serving Detention and Training Orders*. London, HM Inspectorate of Prisons.

Ofsted (2010) *Transition through Detention and Custody: Arrangements for Learning and Skills for Young People in Custodial or Secure Settings*. London, Ofsted.

Ofsted (2015) *Inspection of Rainsbrook Secure Training Centre: February 2015*. London, TSO.

O'Grady, A., Pleasance, P., Balmer, N. J., Buck, A., and Genn, H. (2004) 'Disability, Social Exclusion and the Consequential Experience of Justiciable Problems' *Disability and Society* Vol 19(3), 259–72.

Oldfield, M. and Grimshaw, R. (2008) *Probation Resources, Staffing and Workloads 2001–2008*. London, Centre for Crime and Justice Studies, King's College, in association with NAPO.

O'Loughlin, A. (2014) 'Offender Personality Disorder Pathway: Expansion in the Face of Failure?' *Howard Journal of Criminal Justice* Vol 53(2), 173–92.

Olson, S. and Dzur, W. (2004) 'Revising Informal Justice: Restorative Justice and Democratic Professionalism' *Law and Society Review* Vol 38(1), 139–76.

O'Mahoney, D. (2004) 'Restorative Justice and Youth Conferencing—Transforming Youth Justice in Northern Ireland'. Paper presented at the SLSA Annual Conference April, Glasgow University.

O'Mahoney, D. and Deazley, R. (2000) *Juvenile Crime and Justice*, Review of Criminal Justice in Northern Ireland, Research Report 17. Belfast, Northern Ireland Office.

O'Malley, P. (2000) 'Risk Societies and the Government of Crime' in M. Brown and J. Pratt (eds) *Dangerous Offenders*. London and New York, Routledge, 17–33.

O'Malley, P. (2009) *The Currency of Justice, Fines and Damages in Consumer Societies.* Abingdon, Routledge.

O'Malley, P. (2010) 'Simulated Justice, Risk, Money and Telemetric Policing' *British Journal of Criminology* Vol 50(5), 795–807.

Orton, S. and Vennard, J. (1988) 'Minor Offences and the Fixed Penalty: A Survey in England and Wales' in N. Walker and M. Hough (eds) *Public Attitudes to Sentencing.* Aldershot, Gower, 160–77.

Osborne, S. (ed) (2009) *The New Public Governance?* London, Routledge.

O'Shea, N., Moran, I., and Bergin, S. (2003) *Snakes and Ladders: Mental Health and Criminal Justice.* London, Revolving Doors Agency.

Owen, T. (2007) 'Culture of Crime Control: Through a Post-Foucauldian Lens' *Internet Journal of Criminology.* Available at http://www.internetjournalofcriminology.com.

Padfield, N. (2002) 'Tariffs in Murder Cases' *Criminal Law Review,* 192–204.

Padfield, N. (2007) 'Distinguishing the Unlawful from the Unjustifiable in the Rules on Early Release from Prison' *Cambridge Law Journal* Vol 66(2), 255–8.

Padfield, N. (2013) 'Exploring the Success of Sentencing Guidelines' in Ashworth, A. and Roberts, J. (eds) *Sentencing Guidelines, Exploring the English Model.* Oxford, Oxford University Press, 31–51.

Pantazis, C. and Pemberton, S. (2009) 'From the "Old" to the "New" Suspect Community: Examining the Impacts of Recent UK Counter-Terrorist Legislation' *British Journal of Criminology* Vol 49(5), 646–66.

Pantazis, C. and Pemberton, S. (2011) 'Restating the Case for the "Suspect" Community: A Reply to Greer' *British Journal of Criminology* Vol 51(6), 1054–62.

Pantazis, C., Gordon, D., and Levitas, R. (2006) *Poverty and Social Exclusion: The Millennium Survey.* Bristol, Policy Press.

Parfrement-Hopkins, J. and Hall, P. (2009) 'Perceptions of Anti-Social Behaviour' in Moon, D. and Walker, A. (eds) *Perceptions of Crime and Anti-social Behaviour, Findings from the 2008/09 British Crime Survey Supplementary Volume 1 to Crime in England and Wales 2008/09, 17/09.* London, Home Office.

Park, I. (2000) *Review of Comparative Costs and Performance of Privately and Publicly Operated Prisons 1998–9,* Home Office Statistical Bulletin, 6/00. London, Home Office.

Parker, M. (2006) (ed) *Dynamic Security: The Democratic Therapeutic Community in Prison.* London, Jessica Kingsley.

Parkes, R. and Bilby, C. (2010) 'The Courage to Create: The Role of Artistic and Spiritual Activities in Prisons' *Howard Journal* Vol 49, 97–110.

Patterson, A. and Thorpe, K. (2006) 'Public Perceptions' in A. Walker, C. Kershaw, and S. Nicholas (eds) *Crime in England and Wales 2005/2006,* Home Office Statistical Bulletin 12/06. London, Home Office.

Payne, S. (2009) *Redefining Justice: Addressing the Individual Needs of Victims and Witnesses.* Available at http://www.justice.gov.uk/publications/docs/sara-payne-redefining-justice.pdf.

Pearson, G. (2002) 'Youth Crime and Moral Decline: Permissiveness and Tradition' in J. Muncie, G. Hughes, and E. McLaughlin (eds) *Youth Justice, Critical Readings.* London, Sage, 45–9.

Peay, J. (2002) 'Mentally Disordered Offenders, Mental Health and Crime' in M. Maguire, R. Morgan, and R. Reiner (eds) *The Oxford Handbook of Criminology* (3rd edn). Oxford, Oxford University Press, 746–91.

Peay, J. (2007) 'Mentally Disordered Offenders, Mental Health and Crime' in M. Maguire, R. Morgan, and R. Reiner (eds) *The Oxford Handbook of Criminology* (4th edn). Oxford, Oxford University Press, 496–527.

PEAY, J. (2013) 'Mental Disorder and Imprisonment: Understanding an Intractable Problem?' in A. Dockley and I. Loader (eds) *The Penal Landscape: The Howard League Guide to Criminal Justice in England and Wales*. London, Routledge, 133–49.

PEAY, J. (2014) 'Imprisoning the Mentally Disordered: A Manifest Injustice?' *LSE Law, Society and Economy Working Papers 7/2014*.

PEAY, J. (2015) 'Sentencing Mentally Disordered Offenders: Conflicting Objectives, Perilous Decisions and Cognitive Insights'. *LSE Legal Studies Working Paper 1/2015*.

PECK, M. (2011) *Patterns of Reconviction Among Offenders Eligible for Multi-Agency Public Protection Arrangements*, Ministry of Justice Research Series 6/1. London, Ministry of Justice.

PEETERS, R. (2015) 'The Price of Prevention: The Preventative Turn in Crime Policy and its Consequences for the Role of the State' *Punishment and Society* Vol 17(2), 163–83.

PENFOLD, C., HUNTER, G., AND HOUGH, M. (2006) *The Intermittent Custody Pilot: A Descriptive Study*, Home Office Findings No. 280. London, Home Office.

PETERSON, R. AND BAILEY, W. (2003) 'Is the Death Penalty an Effective Deterrent for Murder? An Examination of Social Science Research' in J. Acker, R. Bohm, and C. Lanier (eds) *America's Experiment with Capital Punishment*. Durham, Carolina Academic Press, 251–82.

PETTIT, P. WITH BRAITHWAITE, J. (1998) 'Republicanism in Sentencing: Recognition, Recompense and Reassurance' in A. von Hirsch and A. Ashworth (eds) *Principled Sentencing: Readings on Theory and Policy*. Oxford, Hart, 317–30.

PHILLIPS, C. AND WEBSTER, C. (eds) (2013) *New Directions in Race, Ethnicity and Crime*. London, Routledge 160–77.

PHILLIPS, J. (2011) 'The Exercise of Discretion in the Probation Service and Bottoms' Model of Compliance' in *ECAN Bulletin* 11 (Oct.) 9–12. London, Howard League for Penal Reform.

PHILLIPS, LORD (2007) 'Issues in Criminal Justice—Murder' Speech, University of Birmingham, March 8. Available at http://webarchive.nationalarchives.gov.uk/20131202164909/http://judiciary.gov.uk/Resources/JCO/Documents/Speeches/lcj08032007.pdf.

PICHÉ, J. (2009) 'Penal Abolitionism: A Different Kind of Reform' *Criminal Justice Matters* Vol 77(1), 30–1.

PICKERING, R. (2014) 'Terrorism, Extremism, Radicalization and the Offender Management System in England and Wales', in A. Silke (ed) *Prisons, Terrorism and Extremism: Critical Issues in Management, Radicalisation and Reform*. London, Routledge, 160–8.

PINCHBECK, I. AND HEWITT, M. (1973) *Children in English Society: From the 18th Century to the Children Act 1948* Vol 2. London, Routledge & Kegan Paul.

PIPER, C. (1999) 'The Crime and Disorder Act—Child or Community Safety?' *Modern Law Review* Vol 62, 397–408.

PIPER, C. (2001) 'Who Are These Youths? Language in the Service of Policy' *Youth Justice* Vol 1(2), 30–9.

PIPER, C. (2006) 'Feminist Perspectives on Youth Justice' in A. Diduck and K. O'Donovan, *Feminist Perspectives on Family Law*. London, Routledge Cavendish.

PIPER, C. (2007) 'Should Impact Constitute Mitigation? Structured Discretion versus Mercy' *Criminal Law Review*, 141–55.

PIPER, C. (2008) *Investing in Children: Policy, Law and Practice in Context*. Cullompton, Willan.

PIPER, C. (2009) 'Rights and Responsibility: Girls and Boys Who Behave Badly' in J. Wallbank, S. Choudhry, and J. Herring (eds) *Rights, Gender and Family Law*. London, Routledge, 70–92.

PIPER, C. (2011) 'The English Riots and Tough Sentencing'. Available at http://blog.oup.com/2011/09/tough-sentencing.

PIPER, C. AND EASTON, S. (2006/7) 'What's Sentencing Got to Do with It?'

Contemporary Issues in Law Special Issue: Current Issues in Sentencing Policy Vol 8(4), 356–76.

PIPER, C. AND EASTON, S. (2013) 'Seriousness: Limiting a Disproportionate Construction?' in D. Cornwell, J. Blad, and M. Wright (eds) *Civilising Criminal Justice*. Hook, Waterside Press.

PITTS, J. (1988) *The Politics of Juvenile Justice*. London, Sage.

PITTS, J. (1992a) 'Juvenile Justice Policy in England and Wales' in J. Coleman and C. Warren-Adamson (eds) *Youth Policy in the 1990s*. London, Routledge, 172–88.

PITTS, J. (1992b) 'The End of an Era' *Howard Journal* Vol 31(2), 133–49.

PITTS, J. (2015) 'Youth Crime and Youth Justice: 2015–2020' *Youth and Policy* Vol 114, 31–42.

PLAYER, E. (2005) 'The Reduction of Women's Imprisonment in England and Wales' *Punishment and Society* Vol 7(4), 419–39.

PLOCH, A. (2012) 'Why Dignity Matters: Dignity and the Right (or Not) to Rehabilitation from International and National Perspectives' *NYU Journal of International Law and Politics* Vol 44, 889–949.

PLOTNIKOFF, J. AND WOOLFSON, R. (2005) *Review of the Effectiveness of Specialist Courts in Other Jurisdictions*, DCA Research Series 3/05. London, Department for Constitutional Affairs.

PLUGGE, E., DOUGLAS, N., AND FITZPATRICK, R. (2006) *The Health of Women in Prison*. Oxford, Department of Public Health, University of Oxford.

PMSU (PRIME MINISTER'S STRATEGY UNIT) (2007) *Building on Progress: Families*. London, Cabinet Office.

POLASCHEK, D. L. L. (2012) 'An appraisal of the Risk–Need–Responsivity (RNR) Model of Offender Rehabilitation and its Application in Correctional Treatment' *Legal and Criminological Psychology* Vol 17(1), 1–17.

PORTER, N. D. (2015) *The State of Sentencing 2014: Developments in Policy and Practice*. Washington DC, The Sentencing Project.

POTEAT, S. (2002) 'The Women at Risk Programme' in P. Carlen (ed) *Women and Punishment: The Struggle for Justice*. Cullompton, Willan, 125–37.

POVEY, D. (ED), MULCHANDANI, R., HAND, T., AND PANESAR, L. K. (2011) *Police Powers and Procedures 2009–10* (2nd edn), Home Office Statistical Bulletin 7/11. London, Home Office.

PRATT, J. (1986) 'Diversion from the Juvenile Court' *British Journal of Criminology* Vol 26(3), 212–33.

PRATT, J. (1996) 'Governing the Dangerous: An Historical Overview of Dangerous Offender Legislation' *Social and Legal Studies* Vol 5(1), 21–36.

PRATT, J. (1998) 'Towards the "Decivilizing" of Punishment?' *Social and Legal Studies* Vol 7(4), 487–515.

PRATT, J. (2000) 'Dangerousness and Modern Society' in M. Brown and J. Pratt (eds) *Dangerous Offenders*. London, Routledge, 35–48.

PRATT, J. AND ERIKSSON, A. (2013) *Contrasts in Punishment: An Explanation of Anglophone Excess and Nordic Exceptionalism*. London, Routledge.

PRIESTLEY, P. AND VANSTONE, M. (eds) (2010) *Offenders or Citizens: Readings in Rehabilitation*. Cullompton, Willan.

PRINS, H. (2005) *Offenders, Deviants and Patients*. London, Routledge.

PRISON REFORM TRUST (2000) *Justice for Women: The Need for Reform*. London, Prison Reform Trust.

PRISON REFORM TRUST (2003) *Troubled Inside: Responding to the Mental Health Needs of Women in Prison*. London, Prison Reform Trust.

PRISON REFORM TRUST (2004a) *Briefing Paper*. London, Prison Reform Trust.

PRISON REFORM TRUST (2004b) *Disabled Prisoners*. London, Prison Reform Trust.

PRISON REFORM TRUST (2005) *Private Punishment: Who Profits?* London, Prison Reform Trust.

PRISON REFORM TRUST (2006) *Experiences of Minority Ethnic Employees in Prisons*. London, Prison Reform Trust.

PRISON REFORM TRUST (2007) *Bromley Briefings Prison Factfile*, December. London, Prison Reform Trust.

PRISON REFORM TRUST (2008) *Doing Time: The Experiences and Needs of Older People in Prison*. London, Prison Reform Trust.

PRISON REFORM TRUST (2010) *Bromley Briefings Prison Factfile*, December. London, Prison Reform Trust.

PRISON REFORM TRUST (2011a) *Bromley Briefings Prison Factfile*. London, Prison Reform Trust.

PRISON REFORM TRUST (2011b) Prison Reform Trust submission to the Ministry of Justice, *Breaking the Cycle, Effective Punishment, Rehabilitation and Sentencing of Offenders*. London, Prison Reform Trust.

PRISON REFORM TRUST (2014a) *A Human Rights Information Booklet for Prisoners*. London, PRT.

PRISON REFORM TRUST (2014b) *Bromley Briefings: Prison Factfile, Autumn*. London, PRT.

PRISON REFORM TRUST (2015a) *Bromley Briefings: Prison Factfile, Summer*. London, PRT.

PRISON REFORM TRUST (2015b) *Inside Out: Release on Temporary Licence and its Role in Promoting Effective Resettlement and Rehabilitation*. London, PRT.

PRISONS AND PROBATION OMBUDSMAN (2014) *Annual Report 2013–2014*. London, PPO.

PRISONS AND PROBATION OMBUDSMAN (2015a) *Annual Report 2014–15*. London PPO.

PRISONS AND PROBATION OMBUDSMAN (2015b) *Learning from PPO Investigations: Self-Inflicted Deaths of Prisoners—2013/14*. London, PPO.

PRISONS AND PROBATION OMBUDSMAN (2016) *Learning from PPO Investigations: Prisoner Mental Health*. London, Prisons and Probation Ombudsman.

PRISONS AND PROBATION OMBUDSMAN FOR ENGLAND AND WALES (2011) *Annual Report 2010–2011*, CM 8105. London, Office of the PPO.

PROBATION SERVICE (2006) *Intermittent Custody: Withdrawal of Authority to Supervise Offenders*. National Probation Service Bulletin Issue 41, 084/06.

PROBERT, R., GILMORE, S., AND HERRING, J. (eds) (2009) *Responsible Parents and Parental Responsibility*. Oxford, Hart Publishing.

RACK, J. (2005) *The Incidence of Hidden Disabilities in the Prison Population*. Egham, The Dyslexia Institute.

RAINE, A. (2013) *The Anatomy of Violence: The Biological Roots of Crime*. New York, Pantheon.

RAINE, J. AND DUNSTAN, E. (2009) 'How Well Do Sentencing Guidelines Work? Equity, Proportionality and Consistency in the Determination of Fine Levels in the Magistrates' Courts of England and Wales' *Howard Journal* Vol 48(1), 13–36.

RAINE, J., DUNSTAN, E. AND MACKIE, A. (2004) 'Financial Penalties: Who Pays, Who Doesn't and Why Not?' *Howard Journal* Vol 43(5), 518–38.

RAMSAY, M. (2011) *The Early Years of the DSPD (Dangerous and Severe Personality Disorder) Programme: Results of Two Process Studies*, Research Summary 4/11. Ministry of Justice, London.

RAWLS, J. (1971) *A Theory of Justice*. Cambridge, MA, Harvard University Press.

RAYNOR, P. AND VANSTONE, M. (2002) *Understanding Community Penalties, Probation Policy and Social Change*. Buckingham, Open University Press.

REECE, H. (2005) 'From Parental Responsibility to Parenting Responsibly' *Current Legal Issues* Vol 8, 459–83.

REED, J. L. AND LYNE, M. (2000) 'In-patient Care of Mentally Ill Prisoners: Results of a Year's Programme of Semi-structured Inspections' *British Medical Journal* Vol 320, 1031–4.

REEVES, C. (2013) '"The Others": Sex Offenders' Social Identities in Probation

Approved Premises' *Howard Journal of Criminal Justice* Vol 52(4), 383–98.

REEVES, H. AND DUNN, P. (2010) 'The Status of Crime Victims and Witnesses in the 21st Century' in A Bottoms and J Roberts (eds) *Hearing the Victim: Adversarial Justice, Crime Victims and the State.* Cullompton, Willan Publishing, 46–71.

REITER, K. A. (2012) 'Parole, Snitch, or Die: California's Supermax prisons and Prisoners 1997–2007' *Punishment and Society* Vol 14(5), 530–63.

RENAUD, G. (2007) *Les Misérables on Sentencing: Valjean, Fantine, Javert and the Bishop Debate the Principles.* Melbourne, Sandstone Press.

RENZETTI, C. M. (2012) *Feminist Criminology.* London, Routledge.

RESPECT TASK FORCE (2006) *Respect Action Plan.* London, Home Office.

RESPECT TASK FORCE (2007) *Tools and Powers to Tackle Anti-Social Behaviour.* London, Home Office.

RESTORATIVE JUSTICE COUNCIL (2015) *Restorative Justice in Youth Offending Teams: Information Pack.* London, Restorative Justice Council.

REVOLVING DOORS AGENCY (2015) *Adding Value? Reflections on Payment by Results for People with Multiple and Complex Needs.* London, Revolving Doors Agency.

REX, S. (1998) 'Applying Desert Principles to Community Sentences: Lessons from Two Criminal Justice Acts' *Criminal Law Review,* 381–91.

REYNOLDS, F. (1985) 'Magistrates' Justifications for Making Custodial Orders on Juvenile Offenders' *Criminal Law Review,* 294–8.

RHODE, D. (1989) *Gender and Justice.* Cambridge, MA, Harvard University Press.

RICHARDS, K. (2010) 'Police-Referred Restorative Justice for Juveniles in Australia' *Trends & Issues in Crime and Criminal Justice* No. 398. Canberra: Australian Institute of Criminology.

RICHARDS, M. (1998) *Censure without Sanctions.* Winchester, Waterside Press.

RICKFORD, D. AND EDGAR, K. (2005) *Troubled Inside: Responding to the Mental Health Needs of Men in Prison.* London, Prison Reform Trust/King's Fund.

RIEDEL, E., GIACCA, G., AND GOLAY, C. (eds) (2014) *Economic, Social and Cultural Rights in International Law: Contemporary Issues and Challenges.* Oxford, Oxford University Press.

RINGLAND, C. AND FITZGERALD, J. (2010) *Factors which Influence the Sentencing of Domestic Violence Offenders,* Crime and Justice Statistics Issue Paper No. 48, NSW Bureau of Crime, Statistics and Research.

RIVERA BEIRAS, I. (2005) 'State Form, Labour Market and Penal System: The New Punitive Rationality in Context' *Punishment and Society* Vol 7(2), 167–82.

RIX, A., SKIDMORE, K., MAGUIRE, M., AND PIERPOINT, H. (2010) *Fine Payment Work Process Study,* Research Summary 8/10. London, Ministry of Justice.

ROBERTS, J. (2002) 'Alchemy in Sentencing: An Analysis of Sentencing Reform Proposals in England and Wales' *Punishment and Society* Vol 4(4), 425–42.

ROBERTS, J. (2008a) 'Aggravating and Mitigating Factors at Sentencing, Towards Greater Consistency of Application' *Criminal Law Review,* 264–76.

ROBERTS, J. (2008b) *Punishing Persistent Offenders,* Oxford, Oxford University Press.

ROBERTS, J. (2010) 'Women Offenders: More Troubled than Troublesome?' in J. Brayford, F. Cowe and J. Deering (eds) *What Else Works? Creative Work with Offenders.* Cullompton, Willan, 91–116.

ROBERTS, J. (2011a) 'Sentencing Guidelines and Judicial Discretion: Evolution of the Duty of Courts to Comply in England and Wales' *British Journal of Criminology* Vol 51(6), 997–1013.

ROBERTS, J. (2011b) 'Punishing More or Less: Exploring Aggravation and Mitigation at Sentencing' in J. Roberts (ed) *Mitigation and Aggravation at Sentencing.* Cambridge, Cambridge University Press, 1–20.

ROBERTS, J. (ed) (2011c) *Mitigation and Aggravation at Sentencing*. Cambridge, Cambridge University Press.

ROBERTS, J. (2013) 'Complying with Sentencing Guidelines: Latest Findings from the Crown Court Sentencing Survey' in A. Ashworth and J. Roberts (eds) *Sentencing Guidelines, Exploring the English Model*. Oxford, Oxford University Press, 104–21.

ROBERTS, J. AND HOUGH, M. (2005a) 'The State of the Prisons: Exploring Public Knowledge and Opinion' *Howard Journal* Vol 44(3), 286–306.

ROBERTS, J. AND HOUGH, M. (2005b) *Understanding Public Attitudes to Criminal Justice*. Milton Keynes, Open University Press.

ROBERTS, J. AND HOUGH, M. (2013) 'Sentencing Riot-Related Offending: Where Do the Public Stand?' *British Journal of Criminology* Vol 53(2), 234–56.

ROBERTS, J. AND MANIKIS, M. (2011) *Victim Personal Statements: A Review of Empirical Research*, Report for the Commissioner for Victims and Witnesses in England and Wales. London, Ministry of Justice.

ROBERTS, J. AND PINA-SÁNCHEZ, J. (2014) 'Previous Convictions at Sentencing: Exploring Empirical Trends in the Crown Court' *Criminal Law Review* 575.

ROBERTS, J., HOUGH, M., JACOBSON, J., BREDEE, A., AND MOON, N. (2008) 'Public Attitudes to Sentencing Offences Involving Death by Driving' *Criminal Law Review* 7, 525–38.

ROBERTS, J., HOUGH, M., JACOBSON, J., AND MOON, N. (2009) 'Public Attitudes to Sentencing Purposes and Sentencing Factors: An Empirical Analysis' *Criminal Law Review* 11, 771–82.

ROBERTS, S. (1979) *Order and Dispute*. Harmondsworth, Penguin.

ROBINSON, G. (1999) 'Risk Management and Rehabilitation in the Probation Service: Collision and Collusion' *Howard Journal* Vol 38(4), 421–33.

ROBINSON, G. (2002) 'Exploring Risk Management in Probation Practice' *Punishment and Society* Vol 4(1), 5–25.

ROBINSON, G. (2008) 'Late-Modern Rehabilitation: The Evolution of a Penal Strategy' *Punishment and Society* Vol 10(4), 429–46.

ROBINSON, P. (2008) 'Competing Conceptions of Modern Desert: Vengeful, Deontological, and Empirical' *Cambridge Law Journal* Vol 67(1), 145–75.

ROBINSON, P. AND DARLEY, J. M. (2004) 'Does Criminal Law Deter? A Behavioural Science Investigation' *Oxford Journal of Legal Studies* Vol 23(2), 173–206.

ROCHE, D. (2003) *Accountability in Restorative Justice*. Oxford, Oxford University Press.

ROCK, P. (2002) 'On Becoming a Victim' in C. Hoyle and R. Young (eds) *New Visions of Crime Victims*. Oxford, Hart, 1–11.

ROSE, N. (1987) 'Beyond the Public/Private Division: Law, Power and the Family' *Journal of Law and Society* Vol 14, 61–76.

ROSE, N. (1990) *Governing the Soul: The Shaping of the Private Self*. London, Routledge.

ROSS, H. L. (1973) 'Deterrence Regained: The Cheshire Constabulary's Breathalyzer Blitz' *Journal of Legal Studies* Vol 2, 1–78.

ROSS, H. L. (1992) *Confronting Drunk Driving*. New Haven, CT, Yale University Press.

ROSS, J., RICHARDS, S., NEWBOLD, G., LENZA, M., AND GRIGSBY, R. (2011) 'Convict Criminology' in W. S. DeKeseredy and M. Dragiewicz (eds) *Routledge Handbook of Critical Criminology*. London, Routledge, 160–71.

ROSS, R. AND HILBORN, J. (2007) *Rehabilitating Rehabilitation: Neurocriminology for Treatment of Antisocial Behaviour*. Ottawa, Cognitive Centre of Canada.

ROSSI, P., WAITE, E., BOSE, C. E., AND BERK, R. E. (1974) 'The Seriousness of Crime: Normative Structure and Individual

Differences' *American Sociological Review* Vol 39, 224–37.

ROSSNER, M. (2013) *Just Emotions: Rituals of Restorative Justice*. Oxford, Clarendon Press.

ROTMAN, E. (1990) *Beyond Punishment: A New View of the Rehabilitation of Offenders*. Connecticut, Greenwood Press.

ROUSSEAU, J.-J. (1743) *The Social Contract*, ed M. Cranston (1968). Harmondsworth, Penguin.

ROYAL COMMISSION ON CAPITAL PUNISHMENT (1953) *Report*, Cmnd 8932. London, HMSO.

ROYAL COMMISSION ON CRIMINAL JUSTICE (1993) *Report* (Chair: Lord Runciman), Cm 2263. London, HMSO.

ROYAL COMMISSION ON CRIMINAL PROCEDURE (1981) *Report*, Cm 8092. London, HMSO.

RUBIN, A. (2011) 'Punitive Penal Preferences and Support for Welfare: Applying the Governance of Social Marginality Thesis on the Individual Level' *Punishment and Society* Vol 13(2), 198–229.

RUBIN, E. (2003) 'Just Say No to Retribution' *Buffalo Criminal Law Review* Vol 7(1), 17–83.

RUGGIERO, V. (2010) *Penal Abolitionism*. Oxford, Oxford University Press.

RUSCHE, G. AND KIRCHHEIMER, O. (1939) *Punishment and Social Structure*. New York, Russell and Russell.

RUTTER, M. AND GILLER, H. (1983) *Juvenile Delinquency: Trends and Perspectives*. Harmondsworth, Penguin.

RYAN, S., HYDE, S., AND WILKINSON, S. (2015) 'Re-settlement of Girls and Young Women: An Agenda for the New Government', Paper presented at the Criminal Justice Alliance Conference 10 March 2015.

RYBERG, J (2005) 'Retributivism and Multiple Offending' *Res Publica* Vol 11(3), 213–33.

SALMON, S. (2004) 'Children with a Prisoner in the Family' *Childright* Vol 203, 18–20.

SALTER, M. AND TWIST, S. (2007) 'The Micro-Sovereignty of Discretion in Legal Decision-Making: Carl Schmitt's Critique of Liberal Principles of Legality' *Web Journal of Current Legal Issues* Vol 3, 1–20. Available at http://www.bailii.org/uk/other/journals/WebJCLI/2007/issue3/salter3.html#_Toc170785162.

SANDERS, A. (1985) 'Class Bias in Prosecutions' *Howard Journal* Vol 24(3), 176–99.

SANDERS, A. (2001) *Community Justice: Modernising the Magistracy in England and Wales*. London, IPPR.

SANDERS, A. (2002) 'Victim Participation in an Exclusionary Criminal Justice System' in C. Hoyle and R. Young (eds) *New Visions of Crime Victims*. Oxford, Hart.

SANDERS, A. (2003) Book Review, *Modern Law Review* Vol 66(1), 160–7.

SANDERS, A. AND LOVEDAY, B. (2001/2) Editorial, CJM No. 46 Winter. London, Centre for Crime and Justice Studies, Kings College.

SANDERS, A., HOYLE, C., MORGAN, R., AND CAPE, E. (2001) 'Victim Impact Statements: Don't Work, Can't Work' *Criminal Law Review*, 447–58.

SANDERS, A., YOUNG, R., AND BURTON, M. (2010) *Criminal Justice* (4th edn). Oxford, Oxford University Press.

SARAT, A. (1976) 'Public Opinion, the Death Penalty and the Eighth Amendment' *Wisconsin Law Review* Vol 17, 171–206.

SARAT, A. (2014) *Gruesome Spectacles: Botched Executions and America's Death Penalty*. Stanford, Stanford University Press.

SARMA, B.J. (2015) 'How *Hall v Florida* transforms the Supreme Court's Eighth Amendment Evolving Standards of Decency Analysis' *UCLA Law Review Discourse* Vol 62, 186–201.

SATZ, D. AND REICH, R. (eds) (2009) *Toward a Humanist Justice: The Political Philosophy of Susan Moller Okin*. Oxford, Oxford University Press.

SAYLES, G. (1950) *The Medieval Foundations of England* (2nd edn). London, Methuen.

SCHICHOR, D. (1995) *Punishment for Profit: Private Prisons, Public Concerns*. Thousand Oaks, CA, Sage.

SCHLANGER, M. (2013) '*Plata v Brown* and Realignment: Jails, Prisons, Courts and Policies', *Harvard Civil Rights—Civil Liberties Law Review* Vol 48(1), 165–215.

SCHOFIELD, P. (2007) 'Jeremy Bentham: The French Revolution and Political Radicalization' in F. Rosen (ed) *Jeremy Bentham*. Aldershot, Ashgate, 535–8.

SCOTT, D. AND CODD, H. (2010) *Controversial Issues in Prisons*. Maidenhead, McGraw Hill/Open University Press.

SCOTTISH EXECUTIVE (1999) *A Review of the Research Literature on Serious Violent and Sexual Offenders*. Edinburgh, Scottish Executive.

SCOTTISH EXECUTIVE (2001) *Scottish Strategy for Victims*. Edinburgh, Scottish Executive.

SCOTTISH EXECUTIVE (2002a) *Victims in the Scottish Criminal Justice System. The EU Framework Decision on the Standing of Victims in Criminal Procedure*. Edinburgh, Scottish Executive.

SCOTTISH EXECUTIVE (2002b) *Youth Justice in Scotland: A Progress Report for All Those Working for Young People*. Edinburgh, Scottish Executive.

SCOTTISH EXECUTIVE (2004) *Police Restorative Warnings in Scotland: Guidance for the Police*. Available at http://www.gov.scot/Publications/2004/06/19497/38781.

SCRATON, P. AND HAYDON, D. (2002) 'Challenging the Criminalization of Children and Young People' in J. Muncie, G. Hughes, and E. McLaughlin (eds) *Youth Justice: Critical Readings*. London, Sage, 311–28.

SECHREST, L. B., WHITE, S. O., AND BROWN, E. D. (1979) *The Rehabilitation of Criminal Offenders*. Washington DC, National Academy of Sciences.

SEDDON, T. (2006) *Punishment and Madness*. London, Routledge.

SEDDON, T. (2008) 'Dangerous Liaisons, Personality Disorder and the Politics of Risk' *Punishment and Society* Vol 10(3), 301–17.

SENSEN, O. (ed) (2015) *Kant on Moral Autonomy*. Cambridge, Cambridge University Press.

SENTENCING ADVISORY PANEL (2000) *Advice to the Court of Appeal—4. Racially Aggravated Offences*. London, Home Office.

SENTENCING ADVISORY PANEL (2002) *Minimum Terms in Murder Cases: The Panel's Advice to the Court of Appeal*. London, Home Office.

SENTENCING ADVISORY PANEL (2003) *Driving Offences—Causing Death by Driving: The Panel's Advice to the Sentencing Guidelines Council*. London, SAP.

SENTENCING ADVISORY PANEL (2007) *Consultation Paper on Breach of an Anti-Social Behaviour Order*. London, SAP.

SENTENCING COMMISSION WORKING GROUP (2008a) *A Structured Sentencing Framework and Sentencing Commission: A Consultation*. London, Sentencing Commission Working Group.

SENTENCING COMMISSION WORKING GROUP (2008b) *A Summary of Responses to the Sentencing Commission Working Group's Consultation Paper*. London, Sentencing Commission Working Group.

SENTENCING COMMISSION WORKING GROUP (2008c) *Sentencing Guidelines in England and Wales: An Evolutionary Approach*, The Gage Report. London, Sentencing Commission Working Group.

SENTENCING COUNCIL (2010) *Breaking the Cycle: Effective Punishment, Rehabilitation and Sentencing of Offenders, Response from the Sentencing Council*. London, Sentencing Council.

SENTENCING COUNCIL (2011a) *Assault: Definitive Guideline*. London, Sentencing Council.

SENTENCING COUNCIL (2011b) *Burglary Offences: Definitive Guideline*. London, Sentencing Council.

SENTENCING COUNCIL (2011c) *Consultation Stage Resource Assessment: Guidelines on Totality, TICs and Allocation.* London, Sentencing Council.

SENTENCING COUNCIL (2011d) *Crown Court Sentencing Survey, October 2010 to March 2011 Results.* London, Sentencing Council.

SENTENCING COUNCIL (2012a) *Drug Offences: Definitive Guideline.* London, Office of the Sentencing Council.

SENTENCING COUNCIL (2012b) *Dangerous Dog Offences, Definitive Guideline.* London, Sentencing Council.

SENTENCING COUNCIL (2012c) *Offences Taken into Consideration and Totality: Definitive Guideline.* London, Sentencing Council.

SENTENCING COUNCIL (2014a) *Fraud, Bribery and Money Laundering Offences: Definitive Guideline.* London, Sentencing Council.

SENTENCING COUNCIL (2014b) *Environmental Offences, Definitive Guideline.* London, Sentencing Council.

SENTENCING COUNCIL (2014c) *Sexual Offences, Definitive Guideline.* London, Sentencing Council.

SENTENCING COUNCIL (2014d) *Crown Court Sentencing Survey Annual Publication January to December 2013 England and Wales.* London, Sentencing Council.

SENTENCING COUNCIL (2015a) *Theft Offences, Definitive Guideline.* London, Sentencing Council.

SENTENCING COUNCIL (2015b) *Health and Safety Offences, Corporate Manslaughter and Food Safety and Hygiene Offences, Definitive Guideline.* London, Sentencing Council.

SENTENCING COUNCIL (2015c) *Crown Court Sentencing Survey, Annual Publication January to December 2014 England and Wales.* London, Sentencing Council.

SENTENCING COUNCIL (2015d) *Dangerous Dog Offences: Consultation.* London, Sentencing Council.

SENTENCING COUNCIL (2016) *Dangerous Dog Offences, Definitive Guideline. London,* Sentencing Council.

SENTENCING GUIDELINES COUNCIL (2004a) *Overarching Principles: Seriousness.* London, SGC.

SENTENCING GUIDELINES COUNCIL (2004b) *Reduction in Sentence for a Guilty Plea.* London, SGC.

SENTENCING GUIDELINES COUNCIL (2004c) *New Sentences: Criminal Justice Act 2003.* London, SGC.

SENTENCING GUIDELINES COUNCIL (2005) *Guideline Judgments Case Compendium.* London, SGC.

SENTENCING GUIDELINES COUNCIL (2006) *Overarching Principles: Domestic Violence.* London, SGC.

SENTENCING GUIDELINES COUNCIL (2007a) *Definitive Guideline on the Reduction in Sentence for a Guilty Plea.* London, SGC.

SENTENCING GUIDELINES COUNCIL (2007b) *Dangerous Offenders: Guide for Sentencers and Practitioners.* London, SGC.

SENTENCING GUIDELINES COUNCIL (2007c) *Sexual Offences Act 2003: Definitive Guideline.* London, SGC.

SENTENCING GUIDELINES COUNCIL (2008a) *Assault and Other Offences against the Person. Definitive Guideline.* London, SGC.

SENTENCING GUIDELINES COUNCIL (2008b) *Overarching Principles: Assaults on Children and Cruelty to a Child.* London, SGC.

SENTENCING GUIDELINES COUNCIL (2008c) *Causing Death by Driving: Consultation Guideline.* London, SGC.

SENTENCING GUIDELINES COUNCIL (2008d) *Theft and Burglary in a Building Other than a Dwelling: Definitive Guideline.* London, SGC.

SENTENCING GUIDELINES COUNCIL (2008e) *Causing Death by Driving: Definitive Guideline.* London, SGC.

SENTENCING GUIDELINES COUNCIL (2008f) *Overarching Principles, Assaults on Children and Cruelty to a Child: Definitive Guideline,* London, SGC.

SENTENCING GUIDELINES COUNCIL (2008g) *Dangerousness: Guide for Sentencers and Practitioners* (Supplement to the Compendium). London, SGC.

SENTENCING GUIDELINES COUNCIL (2008h) *Magistrates' Court Sentencing Guidelines: Definitive Guideline.* London, SGC.

SENTENCING GUIDELINES COUNCIL (2009a) *Sentencing for Fraud: Statutory Offences.* London, SGC.

SENTENCING GUIDELINES COUNCIL (2009b) *Overarching Principles: Sentencing Youths, Definitive Guideline.* London, SGC.

SENTENCING GUIDELINES COUNCIL (2010) *Corporate Manslaughter & Health and Safety Offences Causing Death, Definitive Guideline,* SGC.

SENTENCING NEWS (2014) 'Case Comment: Guidance on Sentencing Dangerous Offenders post-LASPOA', 1(Nov.), 4, Westlaw. Available at https://login.westlaw. co.uk/maf/wluk/app/document?src=doc& linktype=ref&context=59&crumb-action= replace&docguid=ICEE3F180867811E4BD D699A1896A4037.

SHAPLAND, J. (1981) *Between Conviction and Sentence: The Process of Mitigation.* London, Routledge & Kegan Paul.

SHAPLAND, J. (2003) 'Restorative Justice and Criminal Justice: Just Reponses to Crime?' in A. von Hirsch, J. Roberts, A. Bottoms, K. Roach, and M. Schiff (eds) *Restorative Justice and Criminal Justice: Competing or Reconcilable Paradigms?* Oxford, Hart, 195–218.

SHAPLAND, J. (2011) 'Personal Mitigation and Assumptions about Offending and Desistance' in J. Roberts (ed) *Mitigation and Aggravation at Sentencing.* Cambridge, Cambridge University Press, 60–80.

SHAPLAND, J. AND BOTTOMS, A. (2011) 'Reflections on Social Values, Offending and Desistance among Young Adult Recidivists' *Punishment and Society* Vol 13(3), 256–82.

SHAPLAND, J., ATKINSON, A., ATKINSON, H., CHAPMAN, B., DIGNAN, J., HOWES, M., JOHNSTONE, J., ROBINSON, G., AND SCORSBY, A. (2007a) *Restorative*

Justice: The Views of Victims and Offenders—The Third Report from the Evaluation of Three Schemes. Ministry of Justice Research Series 3/07. London, Ministry of Justice.

SHAPLAND, J., ATKINSON, A., ATKINSON, H., COLLEDGE, E., DIGNAN, J., HOWES, M., JOHNSTONE, J., ROBINSON, G., AND SCORSBY, A. (2007b) 'Situating Restorative Justice within Criminal Justice' *Theoretical Criminology* Vol 10(4), 505–32.

SHAPLAND, J., ATKINSON, A., ATKINSON, H., DIGNAN, J., EDWARDS, L., HIBBERT, J., HOWES, M., JOHNSTONE, J., ROBINSON, G., AND SORSBY, A. (2008) *Does Restorative Justice Affect Reconviction? The Fourth Report from the Evaluation of Three Schemes,* Ministry of Justice Research Series 10/8. London, Ministry of Justice.

SHAPLAND, J., ROBINSON, G., AND SORESBY, A. (2011) *Restorative Justice in Practice.* London, Willan/Routledge.

SHEEHAN, R., MCIVOR, G., AND TROTTER, G. (eds) (2007) *What Works with Women Offenders.* Cullompton, Willan.

SHEEHAN, R., MCIVOR, G., AND TROTTER, C. (eds) (2010) *Working with Women Offenders in the Community.* London, Routledge.

SHEPHERD, B. (2015) Improving Outcomes for Young Black and/or Muslim Men in the CJS' *Probation Journal* Vol 62(2), 181–3.

SHEPPARD, G. (1990) 'Management: Short of Ideals?' *Probation Journal* Vol 37(4), 176–9.

SHERMAN, L. W. AND BERK, R. A. (1983) 'The Specific Deterrent Effects of Arrest for Domestic Assault: Preliminary Findings', Unpublished Paper, Police Foundation, Washington.

SHERMAN, L. W. AND STRANG, H., WITH BARNES, G., BENNETT, S., ANGEL, C. M., NEWBURY-BIRCH, D., WOODS, D. J., AND GILL, C. E. (2007b) *Restorative Justice: The Evidence.* London, Smith Institute.

SHERMAN, L. W., FARRINGTON, D. P., LEYTON MACKENZIE, D., AND WELSH, B. C. (eds)

(2006) *Evidence-Based Crime Prevention.* London, Routledge.

SHERMAN, L. W., STRANG, H., NEWBURY-BIRCH, D., AND BENNETT, S. (2007a) *Key Indicators of Effective Practice in Restorative Justice (KEEP).* London, Youth Justice Board.

SHERMAN, L. W., STRANG, H., AND WOODS, D. (2010) *Recidivism Patterns in the Canberra Reintegrative Shaming Experiments (RISE).* Canberra. Available at http://www.aic.gov.au/criminal_justice_system/rjustice/rise/recidivism.aspx.

SHUTE, S. (2004a) 'The Sexual Offences Act 2003 (4) New Civil Preventative Orders: Sexual Offences Prevention Orders; Foreign Travel Orders; Risk of Sexual Harm Orders' *Criminal Law Review,* 417–40.

SHUTE, S. (2004b) 'Punishing Murderers: Release Procedures and the "Tariff", 1953–2004' *Criminal Law Review,* 873–95.

SHUTE, S., HOOD, R., AND SEEMUNGAL, F. (2005) *A Fair Hearing? Ethnic Minorities in the Criminal Courts.* Cullompton, Willan.

SILVER, H. (2015) *Social Exclusion.* Oxford, Polity Press.

SILVESTRI, A. (2009) *Partners or Prisoners?* London, Centre for Crime and Justice Studies.

SILVESTRI, A. (ed) (2011) *Lessons for the Coalition, an End of Term Report on New Labour and Criminal Justice.* London, Centre for Crime and Justice Studies.

SILVESTRI, M. AND CROWTHER-DOWEY, C. (2008) *Gender and Crime.* London, Sage.

SIMON, F. (1999) *Prisoners' Work and Vocational Training.* London, Routledge.

SIMON, J. (1995) 'The Boot Camp and the Limits of Modern Penality' *Social Justice* Vol 22(2), 25–48.

SIMON, J. (1998) 'Managing the Monstrous: Sex Offenders and the New Penology' *Psychology, Public Policy and the Law* Vol 4(1), 1–16.

SIMON, J. (2007) *Governing Through Crime: How the War on Crime Transformed American Democracy and Created a Culture of Fear.* New York, Oxford University Press.

SIMON, J. (2011) 'Mass Incarceration on Trial' *Punishment and Society* Vol 13(3), 251–5.

SIMON, J. AND FEELEY, M. (2003) 'The Form and Limits of the New Penology' in T. Blomberg and S. Cohen (eds) *Punishment and Social Control.* New York, Aldine de Gruyter, 75–116.

SIMONS, K.W. (2012) 'Is Strict Criminal Liability in the Grading of Offences Consistent with Retributive Desert?' *Oxford Journal of Legal Studies* Vol 32(3), 445–466.

SINGER, L. (1991) 'A Non-Punitive Paradigm of Probation Practice: Some Sobering Thoughts' *British Journal of Social Work* Vol 21, 611–26.

SINGH BHUI, H. (ed) (2009) *Race and Criminal Justice.* London, Sage.

SINGLETON, N., MELTZER, H., GATWARD, R., COID, J., AND DEASY, D. (1998) *Psychiatric Morbidity among Prisoners.* London, HMSO.

SMALLRIDGE, P. AND WILLIAMSON, A. (2008) *Independent Review of Restraint in Juvenile Secure Settings.* London, Ministry of Justice/Department for Children, Schools and Families.

SMART, J. J. C. AND WILLIAMS, B. (1973) *Utilitarianism: For and Against.* Cambridge, Cambridge University Press.

SMITH, A. (1998) 'Psychiatric Evidence and Discretionary Life Sentences' *Journal of Forensic Psychiatry* Vol 9(1), 17–38.

SMITH, B. AND HILLENBRAND, S. (1997) 'Making Victims Whole Again' in R. Davis, A. Lurigio, and W. Skogan (eds) (1997) *Victims of Crime* (2nd edn). Thousand Oaks, CA, Sage, 245–56.

SMITH, D. (2010) *Public Confidence in the Criminal Justice System: Findings from the British Crime Survey 2002/03 to 2007/08.* London, Ministry of Justice.

SMITH, D., BLAGG, H., AND DERRICOURT, N. (1988) 'Mediation in South Yorkshire' *British Journal of Criminology* Vol 28(3), 378–95.

SMITH, D., PALER, I., AND MITCHELL, P. (1993) 'Partnerships between the Independent Sector and the Probation Service' *Howard Journal* Vol 32(1), 25–39.

SMITH, R. (2014) 'Re-inventing Diversion' *Youth Justice* Vol 14(2), 109–21.

SOCIAL EXCLUSION UNIT (2002) *Reducing Re-Offending by Ex-Prisoners*. London, Social Exclusion Unit.

SOCIAL SERVICES INSPECTORATE (2004) *Inspection of Medway Secure Training Centre, Kent*. London, Department of Health.

SOLANKI, A. AND UTTING, D. (2009) *Fine Art or Science Sentencers? Deciding between Community Penalties and Custody*. London: Youth Justice Board.

SOLOMON, E. AND GARSIDE, R. (2008) *Ten Years of Labour's Youth Justice Reforms, an Independent Audit*. London, Centre for Crime and Justice, Kings College.

SPALEK, B. (ed) (2002) *Islam, Crime and Criminal Justice*. Cullompton, Willan.

SPALEK, B. (ed) (2008) *Ethnicity and Crime: A Reader*. Milton Keynes, Open University Press.

SPARKS, C. AND TAYLOR, M. (2001/2) *Challenging Times*, CJM No. 46, Winter, 6–7. London, Centre for Crime and Justice Studies, Kings College.

SPARROW, P., BROOKS, G., AND WEBB, D. (2002) 'National Standards for the Probation Service: Managing Post-Fordist Penality' *Howard Journal* Vol 41(1), 27–40.

SPELMAN, W. (2000) 'The Limited Importance of Prison Expansion' in A. Blumstein and J. Wallman (eds) *The Crime Drop in America*. Cambridge, Cambridge University Press, 97–129.

SPENCER, J. (1995) 'A Response to Mike Nellis: Probation Values for the 1990s' *Howard Journal* Vol 34(4), 344–9.

SPENCER, J., HASLEWOOD-POCSIK, I., AND SMITH, E. (2009) '"Trying to get it right": What Prison Staff Say About Implementing Race Relations Policy' *Criminology and Criminal Justice* Vol 9(2), 187–206.

SQUIRES, P. AND LEA, J. (ed) (2012) *Criminalisation and Advanced Marginality: Critically Exploring the Work of Loic Wacquant*. London, Policy Press.

STANFORD LAW SCHOOL THREE STRIKES PROJECT AND NAACP LEGAL DEFENSE AND EDUCATION FUND (2013) *Progress Report Three Strikes Reform: Proposition 36*. Stanford, California, Stanford Law School Three Strikes Project and NAACP Legal Defense and Education Fund.

STANTON, J. M. (1969) 'Murderers on Parole' *Crime and Delinquency* Vol 15, 149–55.

STEEN, S. AND BANDY, R. (2007) 'When the Policy Becomes the Problem: Criminal Justice in the New Millennium' *Punishment and Society* Vol 9(1), 5–26.

STEIN, P. (1984) *Legal Institutions: The Development of Dispute Settlement*. London, Butterworths.

STEVENS, A. (2013) 'Prisoners' Motivation for Therapeutic Community Treatment: In Search of a "Different" Approach to Offender Rehabilitation' *Probation Journal* Vol 66(2), 152–67.

STEVENS, A. (2014) *Offender Rehabilitation and Therapeutic Communities*. London, Routledge.

STEWART, S. (1998) *Conflict Resolution: A Foundation Guide*. Winchester, Waterside Press.

STOCKDALE, E. AND DEVLIN, K. (1987) *Sentencing* (1st edn). London, Waterlow Publishers.

STOPARD, P. (1990) 'Punishment and Probation: The Rhetoric and Reality of the White Paper' *Probation Journal* Vol 3(3), 123–6.

STRANG, H. (2003) *Repair or Revenge*. Oxford, Oxford University Press.

STRANG, H. (2007) 'Institutionalizing Restorative Justice' *British Journal of Criminology* Vol 47(4), 704–6.

STRANG, H., SHERMAN, L., MAYO-WILSON, E., WOODS, D. AND ARIEL, B. (2013) 'Using Face-to-Face Meetings of Offenders and Victims: Effects on Offender Recidivism and Victim Satisfaction. A Systematic Review', *Campbell Systematic Reviews*

Vol 9(12). Available at http://www.crim.cam.ac.uk/people/academic_research/heather_strang/rj_strang_review.pdf.

STRAW, J. (1996) *Tackling Disorder, Insecurity and Crime*. London, Labour Party.

SULLIVAN, E. (2007) 'Straight from the Horse's Mouth' *Prison Service Journal* September Vol 173, 9–14.

SUMMERFIELD, A. (2011) *Children and Young People in Custody 2010–11: An Analysis of the Experiences of 15–18-year-olds in Prison*, HM Inspectorate of Prisons/Youth Justice Board. London, The Stationery Office.

SWEETING, A., OWEN, R. AND TURLEY, C. (2008) *Evaluation of the Victims' Advocate Scheme Pilots*. London, Ministry of Justice.

TAKET, A., CRISP, B., NEVILL, A., LAMARO, G., GRAHAM, M., AND BARTER-GODFREY, S. (2009) *Theorising Social Exclusion*. London, Routledge.

TALBOT, J. (2007) *No One Knows: Identifying and Supporting Prisoners with Learning Difficulties and Learning Disabilities: The Views of Prison Staff*. London, Prison Reform Trust.

TALBOT, J. (2008) *No One Knows, Report and Final Recommendations: Prisoners' Voices, The Experience of the Criminal Justice System by Prisoners with Learning Disabilities and Difficulties*. London, The Prisoner Reform Trust.

TALBOT, J. AND RILEY, C. (2007) 'No One Knows: Offenders with Learning Difficulties and Learning Disabilities' *British Journal of Learning Disabilities* Vol 35(3), 154–61.

TARLING, R. (1979) *The 'Incapacitation' Effects of Imprisonment*, Home Office Research Bulletin No. 7, 6–8. London, Home Office.

TARLING, R. (1993) *Analysing Offending: Data, Models and Interpretations*. London, HMSO.

TARLING, R. (2006) 'Sentencing Practice in Magistrates' Courts Revisited' *Howard Journal* Vol 45(1), 29–41.

TAURI, J. AND MORRIS, A. (2003) 'Reforming Justice: The Potential of Maori Processes'

in E. McLaughlin, R. Ferguson, G. Hughes, and L. Westmarland (eds) *Restorative Justice, Critical Issues*. Milton Keynes, Open University Press and London, Sage, 44–53.

TAYLOR, R. (2000) *A Seven Year Reconviction Study of HMP Grendon Therapeutic Community*. London, Home Office.

TAYLOR, R. (2006) 'Re S (A Child) (Identification: Restrictions on Publication) and A Local Authority v W: Children's Privacy and Press Freedom in Criminal Cases' *Child and Family Law Quarterly* Vol 18(2), 269–86.

TEUBNER, G. (1989) 'How the Law Thinks: Towards a Constructive Epistemology of Law' *Law and Society Review* Vol 23(5), 727–56.

THE SENTENCING COMMISSION FOR SCOTLAND (2006) *The Basis on Which Fines Are Determined*. Available at http://www.scotland.gov.uk/Resource/Doc/925/0116782.pdf.

THIRD SECTOR (2015) *Transforming Rehabilitation: Will the sector be properly involved?* Posted 30 June at http://www.thirdsector.co.uk/transforming-rehabilitation-will-sector-properly-involved/policy-and-politics/article/1352244.

THOMAS, C. (2010) *Are Juries Fair?* Ministry of Justice Research Series 1/10. London, Ministry of Justice.

THOMAS, D. (1995) 'Sentencing Reform in England and Wales' in C. Clarkson and R. Morgan (eds) *The Politics of Sentencing Reform*. Oxford, Clarendon Press.

THOMAS, D. (2002) 'The Sentencing Process' in M. McConville and G. Wilson (eds) *The Handbook of the Criminal Process*. Oxford, Oxford University Press, 473–86.

THOMAS, D. (2007) 'Case Commentary: *Thomas* [2006] EWCA Crim 2036' *Criminal Law Review*, 171–2.

THOMAS, D. (2013) Case Comment: *R v Jenkin: Sentencing—Mentally Disordered Offender—Choice between Hospital Order and Life Imprisonment*, Court of Appeal (Criminal Division) [2012] EWCA Crim 2557, *Criminal Law Review* 3, 246–250.

THOMPSON, E. P. (1977) *Whigs and Hunters: The Origin of the Black Act.* Harmondsworth, Penguin.

THOMSON, K. (2012) 'Disability amongst Prisoners' *Probation Journal* Vol 59(3), 282.

THORBURN, M. (2012) 'Proportionate Sentencing and the Rule of Law' in L. Zedner and J. Roberts (eds) (2012) *Principles and Values in Criminal Law and Criminal Justice: Essays in Honour of Andrew Ashworth*. Oxford, Oxford University Press, 269–84.

TICKELL, S. AND AKESTER, K. (2004) *Restorative Justice: The Way Ahead.* London, JUSTICE.

TILT, R., PERRY, B., MARTIN, C., *et al.* (2000) *Report of the Review of Security at the High Security Hospitals.* London, Department of Health.

TIMMERMANN, J. (ed) (2013) *Kant's 'Groundwork of the Metaphysics of Morals': A Critical Guide.* Cambridge, Cambridge University Press.

TITMUSS, R. (1968) *Commitment to Welfare.* London, Allen and Unwin.

TOCH, H. (ed) (1976) *Living in Prison: The Ecology of Survival.* Maryland, American Psychological Association.

TOMBS, J. (2004) *A Unique Punishment: Sentencing and the Prison Population in Scotland.* Edinburgh, Scottish Consortium on Crime and Criminal Justice.

TOMBS, J. AND JAGGER, E. (2006) 'Denying Responsibility: Sentencers' Accounts of their Decision to Imprison' *British Journal of Criminology* Vol 46, 803.

TOMBS, S. AND WHYTE, D. (2013) 'The Myths and Realities of Deterrence in Workplace Safety Regulation' *British Journal of Criminology* Vol 53, 746–63.

TONRY, M. (1993) 'Proportionality, Interchangeability and Intermediate Punishments' in R. Dobash, A. Duff, and D. Marshall (eds) *Penal Theory and Penal Practice*. Manchester, Manchester University Press.

TONRY, M. (1996) *Sentencing Matters.* Oxford and New York, Oxford University Press.

TONRY, M. (2009) 'Explanations of American Punishment Policies, A National History' *Punishment and Society* Vol 11(3), 377–94.

TONRY, M. (2010) 'The Costly Consequences of Populist Posturing, ASBOs, Victims, "Rebalancing", and Diminution in Support for Civil Liberties' *Punishment and Society* Vol 12(4), 387–413.

TRAVIS, A. (2011) 'Teenage Deaths in Prison Cause Mounting Concern' *The Guardian* 4 May.

TREBILCOCK, J. (2010) *The Reality of Short Term Prison Sentences: Early Findings from Research with the Prison Governors' Association.* London, Howard League.

TREBILCOCK, J. (2011) *No Winners—The Reality of Short Term Prison Sentences.* London, Howard League.

TREBILCOCK, J. AND WEAVER, T. (2011a) *Multi-Method Evaluation of the Management, Organisation and Staffing (MEMOS) in High Security Services for People with Dangerous and Severe Personality Disorder (DSPD).* London, Ministry of Justice.

TREBILCOCK, J. AND WEAVER, T. (2011b) *Study of the Legal Status of Dangerous and Severe Personality Disorder (DSPD) Patients and Prisoners, and the Impact of DSPD Status on Parole Board and Mental Health Review Tribunal Decision-Making.* London, Ministry of Justice.

UGELVIK, T. (2014) 'Paternal Pains of Imprisonment: Incarcerated Fathers, Ethnic Minority Masculinity and Resistance Narratives' *Punishment and Society* Vol 16(2), 152–68.

UGELVIC, T. AND DULLUM, J. (2011) (eds) *Penal Exceptionalism: Nordic Prison Policy and Practice.* London, Routledge.

UK GOVERNMENT (1999) *Second Periodic Report to the United Nations Committee on Rights of the Child* (CRC/C/83/Add.3).

UMAMAHESWAR, J. (2013) 'Gendered Representations of Parents behind Bars:

An Analysis of Newspaper Reports' *Punishment and Society* Vol 15(3), 274–303.

UMBREIT, M. (1994) *Victim Meets Offender: The Impact of Restorative Justice and Mediation.* Monsey, NY, Criminal Justice Press.

UNNEVER, J. (2010) 'Global Support for the Death Penalty' *Punishment and Society* Vol 12(4), 463–84.

US DEPARTMENT OF JUSTICE, OFFICE OF JUSTICE PROGRAMS, NATIONAL INSTITUTE OF JUSTICE (2008) *Prisoner Radicalization, Assessing the Threat in U.S. Correctional Institutions.* Washington DC.

VAIL, J., WHEELOCK, J., AND HILL, M. (eds) (1999) *Insecure Times.* London and New York, Routledge.

VALIER, C. (2003) 'Minimum Terms of Imprisonment in Murder, Just Deserts and the Sentencing Guidelines' *Criminal Law Review,* 326–35.

VAN DEN HAAG, E. (1981) 'Punishment as a Device for Controlling the Crime Rate' *Rutgers Law Journal* Vol 33, 706–20.

VAN DEN HAAG, E. (1985) 'The Death Penalty Once More' *University of California Davis Law Review* Vol 18, Summer, 957–72.

VAN DER MERWE, A. AND SKELTON, A. (2015) 'Victims' Mitigating Views in Sentencing Decisions: A Comparative Analysis' *Oxford Journal of Legal Studies* Vol 35, 355–372.

VAN MARLE, F. AND MARUNA, S. (2010) '"Ontological Insecurity" and "Terror Management": Linking Two Free-Floating Anxieties' *Punishment and Society* Vol 12(1), 7–26.

VAN ZYL SMIT, D. (2000) 'Mandatory Sentences—A Conundrum for the New South Africa?' *Punishment and Society* Vol 2(2), 197–212.

VAN ZYL SMIT, D. AND ASHWORTH, A. (2004) 'Disproportionate Sentences and Human Rights Violations' *Modern Law Review* Vol 67(4), 541–60.

VAN ZYL SMIT, D. AND SNACKEN, S. (2009) *Principles of European Prison Law and Policy, Penology and Human Rights.* Oxford, Oxford University Press.

VANDEVIVER, C., VAN DAELE, S. AND VANDER BEKEN, T. (2015) 'What Makes Long Crime Trips Worth Undertaking? Balancing Costs and Benefits in Burglars' Journey to Crime' *British Journal of Criminology,* Vol 55(2), 399–420.

VAUGHAN, B. (2000) 'The Government of Youth: Disorder *and* Dependence?' *Social and Legal Studies* Vol 9(3), 347–66.

VOLLM, B. A. (2009) 'Self-Harm among UK Female Prisoners: A Cross-Sectional Study' *Journal of Forensic Psychiatry and Psychology* Vol 20(4), 741–51.

VON HIRSCH, A. (1976) *Doing Justice: The Choice of Punishments.* New York, Hill and Wang.

VON HIRSCH, A. (1986) *Past or Future Crimes: Deservedness and Dangerousness in the Sentencing of Criminals.* Manchester, Manchester University Press.

VON HIRSCH, A. (1993) *Censure and Sanctions.* Oxford, Clarendon.

VON HIRSCH, A. (1998) 'Selective Incapacitation: Some Doubts' in A. von Hirsch and A. Ashworth (eds) *Principled Sentencing: Readings on Theory and Practice.* Oxford, Hart, 121–6.

VON HIRSCH, A. (1999) *Criminal Deterrence and Sentence Severity.* Oxford, Hart.

VON HIRSCH, A. (2011) 'Foreword' in Roberts, J. (ed) *Mitigation and Aggravation at Sentencing.* Cambridge, Cambridge University Press.

VON HIRSCH, A. AND ASHWORTH, A. (1996) 'Protective Sentencing under Section 2(2)(b): The Criteria for Dangerousness' *Criminal Law Review,* 175–83.

VON HIRSCH, A. AND ASHWORTH, A. (eds) (1998) *Principled Sentencing: Readings on Theory and Practice* (2nd edn). Oxford, Hart.

VON HIRSCH, A. AND ASHWORTH, A. (2005) *Proportionate Sentencing: Exploring the Principles.* Oxford, Oxford University Press.

VON HIRSCH, A. AND ROBERTS, J. (1997) 'Racial Disparity in Sentencing: Reflections on the Hood Study' *Howard Journal* Vol 36(3), 227–36.

von HIRSCH, A. AND ROBERTS, J. (2004) 'Legislating Sentencing Principles: The Provisions of the Criminal Justice Act 2003 Relating to Sentencing Purposes and the Role of Previous Convictions' *Criminal Law Review*, 639–52.

von HIRSCH, A., ASHWORTH, A., AND SHEARING, C. (2005) 'Restorative Justice: A "Making Amends" Model?' in A. von Hirsch and A. Ashworth, *Proportionate Sentencing*. Oxford, Oxford University Press, 110–30.

von HIRSCH, A., BOTTOMS, A. E., BURNEY, E., AND WIKSTROM, P.-O. (1999) *Criminal Deterrence and Sentence Severity*. Oxford, Hart.

von HIRSCH, A., ROBERTS, J., BOTTOMS, A., ROACH, K., AND SCHIFF, M. (eds) (2003) *Restorative Justice and Criminal Justice: Competing or Reconcilable Paradigms?* Oxford, Hart.

WACKS, R. (2013) *Privacy and Media Freedom*. Oxford, Oxford University Press.

WACQUANT, L. (2001a) *Prisons of Poverty*. Minneapolis, University of Minnesota Press.

WACQUANT, L. (2001b) 'Deadly Symbiosis: When Ghetto and Prison Meet and Mesh' *Punishment and Society* Vol 3(1), 95–133.

WACQUANT, L. (2007) *Urban Outcasts: A Comparative Study of Advanced Marginality*. Cambridge, Polity Press.

WACQUANT, L. (2008a) 'Ghettos and Anti-Ghettos: An Anatomy of the New Urban Poverty' *Thesis Eleven* Vol 94, 113–18.

WACQUANT, L. (2008b) *Urban Outcasts*. Cambridge, Polity Press.

WACQUANT, L. (2009) *Prisons of Poverty*. Minneapolis, University of Minnesota Press.

WACQUANT, L. (2012) 'The Prison as an Outlaw Institution' *Howard Journal of Criminal Justice* Vol 51(1), 1–15.

WAHIDIN, A. (2004) *Older Women in the Criminal Justice System*. London, Jessica Kingsley.

WAITON, S. (2008) *The Politics of Antisocial Behaviour: Amoral Panics*. London, Routledge.

WALGRAVE, L. (2013) 'From Civilising Punishment to Civilising Criminal Justice: From Punishment to Restoration' in D. Cornwell, J. Blad, and M. Wright (eds) *Civilising Criminal Justice*. Hook, Waterside Press, 347–77.

WALKER, K. (2011) 'Equality before the Law: Race and Social Factors as Sources of Mitigation in Sentencing' in J. Roberts (ed) *Mitigation and Aggravation at Sentencing*. Cambridge, Cambridge University Press, 124–45.

WALKER, N. (1985) *Sentencing: Theory, Law and Practice*. Oxford, Oxford University Press.

WALKER, N. (1991) *Why Punish?* Oxford, Oxford University Press.

WALKER, N. (1999) *Aggravation, Mitigation and Mercy in English Criminal Justice*, Oxford, Blackstone.

WALKER, S. AND BECKETT, C. (2003) *Social Work Assessment and Intervention*. Lyme Regis, Russell House.

WALKLATE, S. (2004) 'Justice for All in the 21st Century: The Political Context of the Policy Focus on Victims' in E. Cape (ed) *Reconcilable Rights?* London, Legal Action Group, 27–36.

WALKLATE, S. (2011) 'Review' *New Criminal Law Review* Vol 14(2), 330.

WALLIS, E. (2001) *A New Choreography— An Integrated Strategy for the National Probation Service for England and Wales Strategic Framework 2001–2004*. London, Home Office.

WALSH, C. (2011) 'Youth Justice and Neuroscience, A Dual-Use Dilemma' *British Journal of Criminology* Vol 51(1), 21–39.

WALTER, L. (2010) *Seatbelt and Mobile Phone Usage Surveys: England and Scotland 2009*. London, TRL.

WALTON, A. S. (1983) 'Hegel, Utilitarianism and the Common Good' *Ethics* Vol 93, 753–71.

WARD, T. AND MARUNA, S. (2007)
Rehabilitation, Beyond the Risk Paradigm.
London, Routledge.

WARGENT, M. (2002) 'The New Governance
of Probation' *Howard Journal* Vol 41(2),
182–200.

WARNER, K. AND DAVIS, J. (2012) 'Using
Jurors to Explore Public Attitudes to
Sentencing' *British Journal of Criminology*
Vol 52(1), 93–112.

WASIK, M. (1983) 'Excuses at the Sentencing
Stage' *Criminal Law Review*, 450–65.

WASIK, M. (2001) 'The Vital Importance of
Certain Previous Convictions' *Criminal
Law Review*, 363–73.

WASIK, M. (2015) 'Sentencing and Early
Release Provisions in the Criminal Justice
and Courts Act 2015' *Criminal Law Review*,
855–65.

WASIK, M. AND TURNER, A. (1992)
'Sentencing Guidelines for the Magistrates
Courts' *Criminal Law Review*, 345–56.

WASIK, M. AND VON HIRSCH, A. (1988)
'Non-Custodial Penalties and the Principles
of Desert' *Criminal Law Review*, 555–71.

WASIK, M. AND VON HIRSCH, A. (1994)
'Section 29 Revisited: Previous Convictions
in Sentencing' *Criminal Law Review*,
409–18.

WASIK, M., GIBBONS, T., AND REDMAYNE, M.
(1999) *Criminal Justice, Text and Materials.*
London, Longman.

WATERS, I. (2007) 'The Policing of Young
Offenders' *British Journal of Criminology*
Vol 47(4), 635–54.

WATSON, S. AND RICE, S. (with prisoners
at HMP Wolds) (2004) *Daddy's Working
Away.* London, Care for the Family.

WEATHERBURN, D. AND MOFFATT, S. (2011)
'The Specific Deterrent Effect of Higher
Fines on Drink-Driving Offenders' *British
Journal of Criminology* Vol 5(5), 789–803.

WEAVER, B. (2012) 'The Relational Context
of Desistance: Some Implications and
Opportunities for Social Policy' *Social
Policy and Administration* Vol 46(4),
395–412.

WEAVER, B. (2014) 'Control or Change?
Developing Dialogues between Desistance
Research and Public Protection Practices'
Probation Journal Vol 61(1), 8–26.

WEBER, L., FISHWICK, E., AND MARMO, M.
(2014) *Crime, Justice and Human Rights.*
London, Palgrave Macmillan.

WEBSTER, C. M. AND DOOB, A. N. (2014)
'Penal Reform "Canadian Style": Fiscal
Responsibility and Decarceration'
Punishment and Society Vol 16, 3–31.

WEBSTER, D. (2015) *Benefit Sanctions:
Britain's Secret Penal System.* Centre for
Crime and Justice Studies. London, Centre
for Crime and Justice Studies. Available
at http://www.crimeandjustice.org.uk/
resources/benefit-sanctions-britains-
secret-penal-system.

WEIJERS, I. (2002) 'The Moral Dialogue:
A Pedagogical Perspective on Juvenile
Justice' in I. Weijers and A. Duff (eds)
Punishing Juveniles: Principles and Critique.
Oxford, Hart, 135–54.

WEIJERS, I. AND DUFF, A. (2002)
'Introduction: Themes in Juvenile Justice'
in I. Weijers and A. Duff (eds) *Punishing
Juveniles: Principles and Critique.* Oxford,
Hart, 1–21.

WEITEKAMP, E. AND KERNER, H.-J. (eds)
(2002) *Restorative Justice: Theoretical
Foundations.* Cullompton, Willan.

WELSH, B. C. AND FARRINGTON, D. P. (2002)
*Crime Prevention Effects of Closed Circuit
Television: A Systematic Review,* Home
Office Research Study No. 252. London,
Home Office.

WELSH, B. C. AND FARRINGTON, D. P. (eds)
(2006) *Preventing Crime: What Works for
Children, Offenders, Victims and Places.*
New York, Springer.

WELSHMAN, J. (2007) *From Transmitted
Deprivation to Social Exclusion:
Policy, Poverty and Parenting.* Bristol,
Policy Press.

WHITE, A. (2014) 'Post-Crisis Policing and
Public–Private Partnerships' *British Journal
of Criminology* Vol 54(6), 1002–22.

WHITTACKER, C. AND MACKIE, A. (1997) *Enforcing Financial Penalties*, Home Office Research Study No. 165. London, Home Office.

WHITTY, N. (2011) 'Human Rights as Risk, UK Prisons and the Management of Right and Risks' *Punishment and Society* Vol 13(2), 123–48.

WILCOX, A., YOUNG, R., AND HOYLE, C. (2004) *An Evaluation of the Impact of Restorative Cautioning: Findings from a Reconviction Study*, Home Office Findings 255. London, Home Office.

WILKINSON, C. AND EVANS, R. (1990) 'Police Cautioning of Juveniles—The Impact of Circular 14/1985' *Criminal Law Review*, 165–76.

WILLIAMS, B. (1999) 'The Victims Charter: Citizens as Consumers of the Criminal Justice Service' *Howard Journal* Vol 38(4), 384–96.

WILLIAMS, J. (2007) 'Incorporating Children's Rights: The Divergence in Law and Policy' *Legal Studies* Vol 27(2), 261–87.

WILLOUGHBY, M. (2015) *Witnessing Crime—Findings from the Crime Survey for England and Wales 2013/14, Analytical Summary 2015*. London, Ministry of Justice.

WILLOW, C. (2015) *Children behind Bars: Why the Abuse of Child Imprisonment Must End*. Bristol, Policy Press.

WILLS, J. L. AND MASTROFSKI, S. D. (2012) 'Compstat and the New Penology: A Paradigm Shift in Policing?' *British Journal of Criminology* Vol 51(1), 73–92.

WILSON, D. (2003) ' "Keeping Quiet" or "Going Nuts": Some Emerging Strategies Used by Young Black People in Custody at a Time of Childhood Being Re-constructed' *Howard Journal* Vol 42(5), 411–25.

WILSON, D. AND MCCABE, S. (2002) 'How HMP Grendon Works in the Words of Those Undergoing Therapy' *Howard Journal* Vol 41(3), 279–91.

WILSON, E. AND HINKS, S. (2011) *Assessing the Predictive Validity of the Asset Youth Risk Assessment Tool Using the Juvenile Cohort Study* (JCS), Ministry of Justice Research Series 10/11. London, Ministry of Justice.

WILSON, J. Q. (1985) *Thinking about Crime* (2nd edn). New York, Vintage Books.

WINDZIO, M. (2006) 'Is There a Deterrent Effect of Pains of Imprisonment? The Impact of "Social Costs" of First Incarceration on the Hazard Rate of Recidivism' *Punishment and Society* Vol 8(3), 341–64.

WINTERDYK, J. A. (2002) *Juvenile Justice Systems, International Perspectives*. Toronto, Canadian Scholars Press.

WINTERDYK, J. A. (2005) 'Juvenile Justice in the International Era' in P. Reichel (ed) *Handbook of Transnational Crime and Justice*. Thousand Oaks: Sage, 457–70.

WOLPIN, K. I. (1978) 'An Economic Analysis of Crime and Punishment in England and Wales, 1894–1967' *Journal of Political Economy* Vol 86, 815–40.

WONG, K., ELLINGWORTH, D., AND MEADOWS, L. (2015) *Youth Justice Reinvestment Custody Pathfinder: Final Process Evaluation Report*, Ministry of Justice Analytical Series. London, Ministry of Justice.

WONG, K., MEADOWS, L., WARBURTON, F., WEBB, S., ELLINGWORTH, D., AND BATEMAN, T. (2013) *Youth Justice Reinvestment Custody Pathfinder: Findings and Delivery Lessons from the First Year of Implementation*, Ministry of Justice Analytical Series. London, Ministry of Justice.

WONNACOTT, C. (1999) 'The Counterfeit Contract—Reform, Pretence and Muddled Principles in the New Referral Order' *Child and Family Law Quarterly* 271.

WOOD, A. (1972) 'The Marxian Critique of Justice' *Philosophy and Public Affairs* Vol 1(3), 244–82.

WOOD, A. (2004) *Karl Marx* (2nd edn). London, Routledge.

WOOD, J. AND KEMSHALL, H. (2007) *The Operation and Experience of Multi-Agency*

Public Protection Arrangements, Home Office Findings 285. London, Home Office.

WOOD, M., CATTELL, J., HALES, G., LORD, C., KENNY, T., AND CAPES, T. (2013) *Re-offending by Offenders on Community Orders: Preliminary Findings from the Offender Management Community Cohort Study*, Analytical Summary 2013. London, Ministry of Justice.

WOOD, W. (2015) *Can Restorative Justice Cut Prison Numbers?* Centre for Crime and Justice Studies, posted 23 February 2015 at http://www.crimeandjustice.org.uk/resources/can-restorative-justice-cut-prison-numbers.

WOODCOCK, J. (1994) *The Escape from Whitemoor Prison on Friday 9th September 1994, the Woodcock Enquiry*, Cm 2741. London, HMSO.

WOOLF, H. AND TUMIM, S. (1991) *Prison Disturbances April 1990*. Report of an Inquiry, Cm 1456. London, HMSO.

WOOLF, LORD (2003) Speech, Perrie Lecture Awards, 6 June.

WOOLF, LORD (2015) *Strangeways 25 Years On: Achieving Fairness and Justice in Prison*, Lecture, The Inner Temple, April 2015.

WOOLFORD, A. AND RATNER, R. S. (2007) *Informal Reckonings: Conflict Resolution in Mediation, Restorative Justice and Reparations*. London, Routledge-Cavendish.

WORRALL, A. (1990) *Offending Women: Female Law-Breakers and the Criminal Justice System*. London, Routledge.

WORRALL, A. (1997) *Punishment in the Community*. London, Addison Wesley Longman.

WORRALL, A. AND GELSTHORPE, L. (2009) 'What Works with Women Offenders, the Past 30 Years' *Probation Journal* Vol 56(4), 329–45.

WORRALL, A. AND HOY, C. (2005) *Punishment in the Community* (2nd edn). Cullompton, Willan.

WRIGHT, M. (1996) *Justice for Victims and Offenders* (2nd edn). Winchester, Waterside Press.

YOUNG, J. (1999) *The Exclusive Society*. London, Sage.

YOUNG, J. (2002) 'Crime and Social Exclusion' in M. Maguire, R. Morgan, and R. Reiner (eds) *The Oxford Handbook of Criminology* (3rd edn). Oxford, Oxford University Press, 457–90.

YOUNG, P. (1989) 'Punishment, Money and a Sense of Justice' in P. Carlen and D. Cook (eds) *Paying for Crime*. Milton Keynes, Open University Press, 46–65.

YOUNG, P. (1997) *Crime and Criminal Justice in Scotland*. Edinburgh, Stationery Office.

YOUNG, W. AND KING, A. (2013) 'The Origins and Evolution of Sentencing Guidelines, A Comparison of England and Wales and New Zealand' in A. Ashworth and J. Roberts (eds) *Sentencing Guidelines, Exploring the English Model*. Oxford, Oxford University Press, 202–17.

YOUTH JUSTICE BOARD (2001) *Youth at Risk? A National Survey of Risk Factors, Protective Factors and Problem Behaviour among Young People in England, Scotland and Wales*, London, YJB.

YOUTH JUSTICE BOARD (2004a) *MORI Youth Survey*. London, YJB.

YOUTH JUSTICE BOARD (2004b) *Restorative Justice in the Juvenile Secure Estate*. London, YJB.

YOUTH JUSTICE BOARD (2006a) *Anti-Social Behaviour Orders (Summary)*. London, YJB.

YOUTH JUSTICE BOARD (2006b) *Managing Children and Young People's Behaviour in the Secure Estate: A Code of Practice*. London, YJB.

YOUTH JUSTICE BOARD (2006c) *Dangerousness and the New Sentences for Public Protection: Guidance for Youth Offending Teams*. London, YJB.

YOUTH JUSTICE BOARD (2006d) Common Assessment Framework, Draft Guidance for Youth Offending Teams. London, YJB.

YOUTH JUSTICE BOARD (2008) *Referral Order Action Plan 2009–10*. London, YJB.

YOUTH JUSTICE BOARD (2009a) *Youth Survey 2008: Young people in mainstream education*. London, YJB.

YOUTH JUSTICE BOARD (2009b) *Girls and Offending—Patterns, Perceptions and Interventions*. London, YJB.

YOUTH JUSTICE BOARD (2010) *National Standards for Youth Justice Services, B420*. London, YJB.

YOUTH JUSTICE BOARD (2011a) *Monthly Data and Analysis Custody Report—April 2011*. London, YJB.

YOUTH JUSTICE BOARD (2011b) *Youth Justice Statistics 2009/10 England and Wales Statistics Bulletin*. London, Ministry of Justice.

YOUTH JUSTICE BOARD (2011c) *Youth Restorative Disposal Process Evaluation*. London, Ministry of Justice.

YOUTH JUSTICE BOARD (2011d) *Monthly Youth Custody Report October 2011*. London, YJB.

YOUTH JUSTICE BOARD (2014a) *Guidance: AssetPlus: Assessment and Planning in the Youth Justice System*. London, YJB.

YOUTH JUSTICE BOARD (2014b) *Guidance: Use Reports: Section 5 Case Management Guidance*. London, YJB.

YOUTH JUSTICE BOARD (2014c) *Deaths of Children in Custody: Action Taken, Lessons Learnt*. London, YJB.

YOUTH JUSTICE BOARD (2015a) *Monthly Youth Custody Report—March 2015*. London, Ministry of Justice.

YOUTH JUSTICE BOARD (2015b) *Youth Offending Teams: Making the Difference for Children and Young People, Victims and Communities, Final Report*. London, YJB.

ZEDNER, L. (2003) 'The Concept of Security: An Agenda for Comparative Analysis' *Legal Studies* Vol 23(1), 151–76.

ZEHR, H. (1985) 'Retributive Justice, Restorative Justice' *New Perspectives in Crime and Justice* Vol 4. Akron, OH, MCC Office of Crime and Justice.

ZIMRING, F. (2001) 'Imprisonment Rates and the New Politics of Criminal Punishment' in D. Garland (ed) *Mass Imprisonment*. London, Sage, 145–9.

ZIMRING, F. (2005) *American Juvenile Justice*. New York, Oxford University Press.

ZIMRING, F. AND HAWKINS, G. (1986) *Capital Punishment and the American Agenda*. New York, Cambridge University Press.

ZIMRING, F. AND HAWKINS, G. (1995) *Incapacitation: Penal Confinement and the Restraint of Crime*. New York, Oxford University Press.

Index